Dead End

DEAD END

Suburban Sprawl and the
Rebirth of American Urbanism

BENJAMIN ROSS

OXFORD
UNIVERSITY PRESS

OXFORD
UNIVERSITY PRESS

Oxford University Press is a department of the University of Oxford.
It furthers the University's objective of excellence in research, scholarship,
and education by publishing worldwide.

Oxford   New York
Auckland   Cape Town   Dar es Salaam   Hong Kong   Karachi
Kuala Lumpur   Madrid   Melbourne   Mexico City   Nairobi
New Delhi   Shanghai   Taipei   Toronto

With offices in
Argentina   Austria   Brazil   Chile   Czech Republic   France   Greece
Guatemala   Hungary   Italy   Japan   Poland   Portugal   Singapore
South Korea   Switzerland   Thailand   Turkey   Ukraine   Vietnam

Oxford is a registered trademark of Oxford University Press
in the UK and certain other countries.

Published in the United States of America by
Oxford University Press
198 Madison Avenue, New York, NY 10016

Library of Congress Cataloging-in-Publication Data
Ross, Benjamin.
Dead end : suburban sprawl and the rebirth of American urbanism / Benjamin Ross.
pages cm
Summary: "A witty, readable, and highly original tour through the history of America's suburbs and
cities to uncover the human impulses that keep sprawl spreading"— Provided by publisher.
ISBN 978–0–19–936014–7 (hardback)
1. Suburbs—United States.   2. Cities and towns—United States—Growth.
3. Urbanization—United States.   4. Traffic flow—United States.
5. Land use—United States—Planning.   I. Title.
HT352.U6R67 2014
307.740973—dc23
2013044046

9 8 7 6 5 4 3 2 1
Printed in the United States of America
on acid-free paper

Contents

17. On Track toward Livable Cities 199

Introduction
Escape from the Suburbs

The place where I grew up might have been a museum of suburbia.

Albertson Downs was five blocks of Cape Cod houses built by Levitt and Sons just after the Second World War. The subdivision rose on small lots near the Long Island Railroad, 17 miles from Times Square, as the Levitts were perfecting their techniques of suburban development. A few years later and a few miles to the east, they would burst onto the national stage with Levittown, the vast expanse of tract housing that pioneered assembly-line construction.

Historic highways were close at hand. A thousand feet to the south, on the other side of a horse farm, sat a strip of broken asphalt. What we knew as the Old Motor Parkway was a remnant of the world's first limited-access roadway. A mile to the east was the southward jog of the Northern State Parkway. The parkway's creator, the master highway-builder Robert Moses, had here suffered a rare defeat. In 1929, after an epic battle, the heirs of the previous century's robber barons compelled him to divert his road around their great estates.

On a street full of children, we played ball in the roadway. We fed the horses sugar cubes through the pasture fence. Fathers walked to the train station each morning and went into New York. Mothers stayed home and kept house. By the station stood a supermarket and a drugstore, their doors next to the sidewalk and parking off to the side.

By the time we reached high school, our world was changing. The horse farm made way for houses; the supermarket and drugstore closed; mothers went to work. A civic association, never much more than the organizer of July Fourth fireworks, was defunct. Life in the suburbs seemed boring and oppressive. We waited eagerly for the weekend and the opportunity to escape to what everyone called "the city."

What was it that we sought to flee? What was the city that we yearned for? These worlds were not defined by municipal boundaries; they were kinds of places, almost different states of mind.

What we fled is sprawl. The term, coined years earlier by specialists, came into wider use as I grew up in the 1950s. Sprawl is suburbs spread helter-skelter across the land, inhabited in isolated pods. Houses are in one place, factories and offices in another, stores in a third. Stringing them together are wide highways where no one walks. For the simplest errand, there is no choice but to get in a car.

The city of our desire was no abstraction. It was where grandparents lived and where fathers worked. It had neighborhoods with corner stores, bustling shopping districts, skyscraper downtowns. It was full of people and of life. Its streets were not barren suburban highways. They were natural, connected, and truly human.

For my parents' and grandparents' generations, leaving the city was an escape from crowded streets and sooty air. Half a century has passed, and the suburban oasis they moved out to has proved a mirage.

They left the city to escape congestion and found traffic jams. They fled factory smoke, only to breathe auto fumes. They sought peace and quiet; they got nerve-wracking commutes.

Cities had been feared for their infectious diseases. Now suburbs are in need of medical attention. Automobile crashes cause carnage on the road; lack of movement on foot brings obesity and diabetes.

Suburbs were where children could be raised in safety and ease. Away from the dangers of city streets, they would have room to play and freedom to roam. Instead, we have play dates and "helicopter parents," children robbed of spontaneity and parents hovering constantly above them. Street play is proscribed; in places, even sidewalk games are against the law.

After a century, the outward migration is running up against physical limitations. The automobile, a necessity of suburban travel, runs on oil that is ever more expensive to extract. The time, cost, and bother of long-distance commuting surpasses the limits of toleration. And with the wasteful use of energy on cars, houses, and lawns comes the disaster of global warming.

Even before I was born, experts saw that suburban growth was on a path that could not be sustained. As new subdivisions spread across the land, the first warnings reached the public. Just after my tenth birthday in 1959, the *New York Times* raised the alarm in front-page articles. "Cars Choking Cities as 'Urban Sprawl' Takes Over," one headline warned.

It took longer to understand why we, like young suburbanites elsewhere, yearned so strongly for the city. In 1961 Jane Jacobs published her classic *The Death and Life of Great American Cities* and demolished the theories that justified the suburb. Jacobs denied that people and things need to be sorted out, with each kind given a place of its own. She celebrated the vitality and diversity of urban neighborhoods.

Within a decade, the city Jacobs loved reasserted itself. The destruction of neighborhoods by urban renewal ground nearly to a halt, bogged down in heavy opposition. A massive freeway revolt confronted the powerful highway lobby. Across the country, it rubbed interstate highways off maps, and subways were built instead. The profession of land-use planning was in turmoil, searching for new ideas to replace old and discredited concepts.

As the seventies began, the forces gathered against sprawl grew even stronger. A rising environmental movement smashed cars, saved trees, and became a political power. On the suburban fringe, a wave of protest against development toppled local power structures. Towns, counties, and even states enacted laws for growth control. Sprawl, it seemed, was being tamed.

Jane Jacobs was not the only self-educated woman to challenge the orthodoxies of the 1950s. Rachel Carson's *Silent Spring*, published a few months after *Death and Life*, revealed the hazards imposed on nature and human life by spraying with synthetic pesticides. The chemical and agrobusiness interests Carson challenged were as potent as the highway lobby, yet the environmental movement achieved fundamental change. DDT was banned; rivers no longer smell; the air is easier to breathe.

The movement Jacobs helped inspire won victories too. The destruction of cities by redlining, urban renewal, and expressway building was largely checked. Urban life has regained appeal, and cities that declined for decades grow again.

Yet lively, stable, and economically diverse neighborhoods remain hard to find. Decay and gentrification keep nibbling away at what escaped the wrecking balls of the mid-twentieth century. Builders hasten to transform old factory districts into city neighborhoods. But with their wide streets, condos, and chain stores, the new urban quarters still seem less appealing than places built a century and more ago.

Meanwhile, ugly suburbs still spread outward, consuming rural land and carrying the failings of their predecessors to new extremes. Cheap townhouses, tony high-rise apartments, and pretentious McMansions scatter across the landscape, entangled in an ever-expanding web of highways and parking lots.

The house I grew up in is no more, torn down a few years ago to build something bigger. My classmates have moved on, some still in suburbs and others seeking urban places. And today's suburban children are denied the pleasures of our generation. They see their friends when parents arrange it; they rarely walk to school. If a lively city is nearby—sometimes there's just a clump of office buildings—it's hard to reach without a car.

These suburbs have their advocates. Sprawl, they contend, is how people choose to live. The automobile creates a freedom to move about that is unprecedented in human history. City dwellers, crammed into apartments, dream of escaping to a spacious home of their own.

These arguments are not frivolous, but they never appealed to me. I went to school in Cambridge, Massachusetts, where I walked to stores, to restaurants, and across the river to Fenway Park. When I graduated I worked in Cambridge and commuted by bicycle. A new job in the suburbs gave me no choice but to drive, but my two feet and the Boston subway still carried me after five o'clock.

I moved to Washington, DC in 1981. Three years later the Metro arrived where I had settled, outside the city in Montgomery County, Maryland. From the first day on, I took the train to work, but there were few other reasons to ride it. Lively streets were still scarce in Washington. Two more decades would have to pass before a quilt of walkable neighborhoods emerged, one flowing into another as in Boston and New York.

My walk to the subway took me down a street with no sidewalk. When I asked to have one built, county bureaucrats sent me on a paper chase. I discovered a tiny sidewalk-building budget and an ever-growing mountain of requests. The waiting list was ideal fodder for an organizer—I had plenty of experience from my years in Cambridge—and soon the county council, flooded with letters of complaint, raised the budget to a reasonable level.

In 1996 I was asked to be president of the Action Committee for Transit, founded ten years earlier to promote a light rail line. The group's field of action already took in the whole range of transit issues, and it soon widened to include development around the stations. I came to grapple directly with the forces of sprawl, and I saw how hard it is to overcome them.

I puzzled over questions with import far beyond my own suburb. Why is our nation still addicted to sprawl, so long after experts raised the alert? What is the compulsion that keeps us building what so many revile? Why are urban streets, so much in demand, so rarely supplied? Why do attempts at cure so often worsen the disease? How can we break free of our addiction, and create the cities we desire?

This book is a quest for answers to these riddles. The inquiry must start with a search for the roots of sprawl, roots buried deep in history.

1

The Strange Birth of Suburbia

"The mutant spawn of a socialist commune." Of all the imprecations that a blanket of McMansions on a once-wooded hillside might provoke, this is surely among the least likely to escape beholders' lips. Yet it is what the aggrieved onlookers see.

The American suburb has a most peculiar parentage. The neighborhood of crescent streets and cul-de-sacs was born from a nineteenth-century experiment in social engineering. What now are hallmarks of conformity—enforced exclusion of commerce, rules for setbacks and lot sizes, the meddlesome homeowner association—were created by the dissidents of another era, abolitionists, sexual pioneers, seekers of spiritual enlightenment.

A century and more has passed, and these long-forgotten origins still shape the landscape of subdivision and strip mall. An inherited system of belief limits the use of private land and makes owners yield to neighbors' preferences. From this doctrine of collectivism comes today's suburban scheme of governance, with its zoning codes, deed covenants, and preservation rules. Landowners are told how big to build a house, where to dry their wash, and even what color to paint the door.

This terrain is rife with pettiness and paradox. A Michigan woman is threatened with jail for growing vegetables in her yard. A rabbi in Chicago strives to make his synagogue's environs Vietnamese. A California city specifies which breeds of goats its citizens may keep. In Maryland, barbecues are banned from "public use space" because they would encourage the public to use the space.

Such everyday oddities betray a profound confusion of beliefs and rules, the legacy of suburbia's tangled past. Ardent defenders of property rights insist on telling neighbors how to use their land. Trailer parks and parking lots are hailed as landmark architecture. Zoning proscribes what historic preservation requires. New neighborhoods may not resemble the most admired old ones.

Ideas and history are what make sprawl, as much as brick, shingle, and asphalt. Our ideological inheritance is at the root of what makes change so slow. It insists that what exists is the natural and immutable order of things, and without breaking free of it we can barely even imagine other ways to live. Even when we seek something different, all we know how to ask for is more of the same.

Our story begins in the second quarter of the nineteenth century. Cities then were small and crowded, their size limited to the distance one could walk. As the industrial revolution advanced, machines and people flooded in. Workers toiled long hours in the "satanic mills" and went home to horrific slums. A wave of ferment followed. Why, it was asked, did progress bear such bitter fruit? And how could things be bettered?

The answer, for many, was to leave the old cities and build towns of a new kind, organized on collective principles. In Europe, where these ideas first arose, the good land was already taken and the theories stayed mostly on paper. The United States, with its empty western territories and its openness to new thinking, had room for reformers to put their plans into practice. Over the course of the quarter-century, well over a hundred utopian colonies sprang up, sprinkled from the Atlantic coast to the frontier.

These settlements drew inspiration from a French thinker, Charles Fourier, who laid out detailed plans for ideal communities he called phalansteries. Albert Brisbane, a young American studying in Europe, came across Fourier's writings and brought them home. Brisbane did not lack for erudition—in Berlin, he learned philosophy from Hegel—and he managed to attract the interest of leading American thinkers.

The phalanstery aimed for spiritual enlightenment along with social harmony. Workplace and residence were housed together in a single structure, divided into sections serving body, soul, and intellect. Private property did not disappear; investors financed the community and shared its revenue with workers in a fixed ratio. Capital's share was divided in proportion to the money each put in. Wages were inverse to the enjoyment of the work, and heavy manual labor paid best.[1]

These agricultural communes were launched with much enthusiasm but scant calculation, and they found it hard going. Abstract theory was not easy to translate into practice, and intellectuals made mediocre farmers. Most settlements foundered within months, and even those that managed to sustain themselves rarely prospered.

A few did survive for years. The best remembered is Brook Farm, founded outside Boston in 1840 by the circle of New England intellectuals that included Ralph Waldo Emerson, Nathaniel Hawthorne, and Henry David Thoreau. Seeking transcendence more than sustenance—its residents "dove into the infinite, soared into the illimitable, and never paid cash," a clear-eyed teenaged onlooker would later recall—Brook Farm in 1844 adopted an eclectic version of Fourierism.[2]

By the time Brook Farm expired in 1846, the flaws in Fourier's economic blueprint were obvious, and his remaining followers pursued their ideals by other means. Watered-down utopias sprang up outside New York, featuring individually owned houses and outside employment. These colonies pursued different strands of utopian thought, but they moved in geographic parallel— on a heading toward today's suburbia.

One group narrowed its vision to economic reform. An "Industrial Home Association," aiming to protect its members against the power of capital and land monopoly, settled Mount Vernon north of New York. By now the new railroads had made commuting possible, at least for those who could afford the fares. By 1852, three hundred houses were going up on quarter-acre lots around a train station.[3]

Elsewhere the intellectual ferment continued. Horace Greeley, radical publisher of the *New York Tribune*, was among investors in the Long Island community of Modern Times. The residents—abolitionists, feminists, and transcendentalists—lived with no laws or jails and rejected the institution of marriage. The settlement was soon a magnet for cranks and eccentrics, and it became notorious for its unconventional ideas. Things calmed down during the Civil War, and the town, wishing to escape its reputation, changed its name to Brentwood.[4]

Some Fourierists still soldiered on. Albert Brisbane remained active in the city, writing a column in the *Tribune* and organizing. He came to grief in 1855 when the police—egged on by Greeley's upstart rivals at the *New York Times*—raided a meeting of an alleged Free Love Society and briefly jailed the organizers.

One orthodox colony remained: the North American Phalanx in Red Bank, New Jersey. Even it was riven by internal disagreements, and in 1853 there was a split. The minority, less attached to communalism, attracted new adherents whose striving for spiritual and artistic elevation overshadowed the egalitarian aspects of their philosophy. Under the leadership of a wealthy New York merchant, Marcus Spring, they undertook to build their own colony on the nearby coast.

Spring was an intellectual as well as a businessman. He and his wife had accompanied the transcendentalist Margaret Fuller on her trip to Europe a few years earlier. To design the new community—known to history as the Raritan Bay Union—he engaged a leading architect of the day, Alexander Jackson Davis. For himself Spring built a fine private house alongside the imposing communal structure, and other wealthy members could erect individual homes as well. Davis took advantage of this assignment to exchange visits with a young architect of his acquaintance who lived across the bay in Staten Island, Frederick Olmsted.[5]

From Raritan Bay Union sprang the settlement that laid down a pattern for the suburbia to come. There Davis had designed a three-sectioned house for New York merchant Llewellyn Haskell. The two men joined together again to create a new community in South Orange, New Jersey, an hour by train and ferry from New York. Davis was enamored of the beauty of Orange Mountain, and the land, unsuitable for agriculture, was cheap. An architect of genius, he took full advantage of the situation—the property, which Haskell dubbed Llewellyn Park, possessed extraordinary views across Newark all the way to the harbor and city of New York.

Llewellyn Park was built for the upper middle class rather than the wealthy. To limit maintenance expense, formal gardens were omitted and the forest growth largely retained. Davis laid out curving streets, then a novelty, to follow the terrain. Homes were set back from the street, within the woods, on lots of an acre or larger. Departing from the prevailing custom—developers of the time subdivided land into lots but did not build—Davis designed the first residences himself in a consistent style, Gothic revival, which stood on the architectural avant-garde of the moment. The park-like naturalism of the design, although it drew on precedents from London and Manchester, was an innovation in its openness and its adaptation to the landscape.

Haskell and Davis were attempting only a partial retreat from Fourierist communalism. The imposing common edifices that had reached an apogee at Raritan Bay Union shrank into a few rustic buildings and a planned but never built Lyceum. A large park occupied a rugged and picturesque portion of the land, maintained by a self-governing association that all property owners were required to join. Covenants attached to each deed made mandatory the setbacks and minimum lot sizes, banned commercial activities, and required payment of assessments to the association.[6]

Llewellyn Park retained a tone of social and political innovation. The son of antislavery leader William Lloyd Garrison was among the first residents. Another early purchaser was Theodore Tilton, editor of a widely read abolitionist magazine. Tilton, in 1871, would write of the Paris Commune that "the central idea of communism is the same that George Washington spent seven years in killing his fellow-countrymen to achieve—the same which Alexander Hamilton wrote into a constitution which survives to this day."[7]

Along with radical politics came sexual experimentation, more discreet than at Modern Times but hardly invisible. As a newspaper recounted a May Day celebration, the high point of the community's life:

> In the center of the green, the May Pole was erected. It was a tall tulip tree, stripped of the bark, and the top of it was clasped by a garland of flowers and ribands, as in the old heathen days, when Priapus was a god, and all the people did him reverence...

Just how the celebrants honored the Greek god of the phallus can only be guessed today, but what they thought of Victorian morality is beyond doubt.[8]

The institutional structure that undergirded Llewellyn Park's physical layout—a structure replicated countless times in the ensuing 160 years—stood only a short step removed from its socialist forerunners. In an experiment in communal living, it was only natural to exclude profit-making commerce and establish a governing body. With separately owned structures taking the place of a single edifice, setback and lot size covenants were essential to the achievement of a common vision; these rules were far less onerous than the regulations of a phalanstery.

Still, the direction such a colony was headed in could be sensed. For two critics on the left, writing in 1848, "abolition of the distinction between town and country" ranked first among the useful concepts to be found in Fourier's writings. But his followers, they observed, had been "compelled to appeal to the feelings and purses of the bourgeois."

The pamphlet where these remarks appeared, under the title of *The Communist Manifesto*, has rarely been accused of excessive timidity. Yet in this matter Karl Marx and Friedrich Engels were, if anything, too mild in their judgment. A partial retreat is the most difficult of maneuvers, and at Llewellyn

Park the retreat from socialism turned into a rout. This offspring of the pha-lanstery soon developed an appeal that was quite exclusively bourgeois. By the end of the 1880s Llewellyn Park was a bastion of suburban wealth. It boasted Thomas Edison as a resident and was emulated by a growing number of purely capitalist real estate operators.

The modern suburb, far removed from these origins, still conserves their ideological heritage. Each Llewellyn Park property owner, Theodore Tilton wrote in 1864, "possesses the whole park in common, so that the fortunate purchaser of two or three acres becomes a virtual owner of the whole five hun-dred."[9] Here in germ is the belief of today's suburban homeowner that prop-erty rights include a veto over building on neighbors' land—an understanding shared by even the most ardent defenders of private property.

Historians of architecture see Alexander Jackson Davis' invention of the lay-out of the modern suburb as the key to Llewellyn Park's longevity—it remains little changed today—and its long-lasting influence. But what enabled this style of land use to persist and multiply was an equally innovative institutional structure. A trait that played no small role in the failure of Fourierist social-ism—the imposition of a predesigned structure highly resistant to change—endowed capitalist suburbs with market appeal and resilience.

A single man, Frederick Olmsted, was largely responsible for perpetuat-ing the organizational and architectural heritage of Llewellyn Park. Olmsted gained fame through his design of New York's Central Park, an assignment he and Calvert Vaux won in an 1858 competition. The architectural firm the two men established is best remembered for its parks, civic jewels of New York, Boston, and other cities, but real estate promoters engaged it too for the design of park-like suburbs.

The first of these assignments was Riverside, built after the Civil War on 1600 acres of prairie outside Chicago. Here the layout took another step toward the modern suburb. Divided into 2250 lots of about a half-acre each, the community was centered around a small commercial district at the rail-road station. Houses were set back at least 30 feet from the winding roads and surrounded by trees and well-kept gardens. Olmsted's design adorned the community with numerous parks; however, these were slow to appear, and it soon emerged that the developers were of dubious character. They went bank-rupt in the Panic of 1873, but Riverside filled out and remains a prosperous enclave today.[10]

In the two decades that followed, Olmsted and Vaux designed fifteen more railroad suburbs. All followed the architectural and institutional model of

Llewellyn Park and Riverside. Houses were set back on curved streets, commerce was excluded from residential districts, and the entire edifice rested on a structure of legal covenants that the Olmsted firm soon systematized. Most of these subdivisions endure to this day as wealthy neighborhoods of single-family homes, among them such prestigious suburbs as Chestnut Hill in Massachusetts, Druid Hills near Atlanta, and Tarrytown Park, New York.[11]

Only the affluent could afford to live in communities that met these high standards. For Olmsted, whose crowning achievements were parks open to the entire population, this was a matter of regret. His intent in employing legal covenants was to ensure the fulfillment of his artistic vision and then protect it from unwanted commercial intrusions that, he recognized, the very success of his creations would attract. As years went by and neighborhoods matured, the covenants and homeowner associations proved effective indeed in accomplishing their purpose—so effective that they attracted imitators who cared little for Olmsted's artistic and social ideals.

As Llewellyn Park and its progeny grew into havens for the wealthy, it could be seen that the covenants excluded more than unwanted architectural intrusions. They excluded people—people whose incomes fell short of what became the community standard. By the 1880s, subdividers began to make this explicit, setting a minimum cost for the houses that went up on the lots they sold. After a few more years, developers of large tracts would carefully apportion their land into zones of differing status, with a sliding scale of prescribed construction costs.

Toward the end of the 1880s, a new wave of railroad suburbs arrived. In organization and layout they followed the pattern of Llewellyn Park, but they were planned and marketed on a frankly elitist basis. "Park" might still be the name, but a members-only country club and its golf course took the place of public open space. At Short Hills in New Jersey and the Chicago suburb of Kenilworth, developers screened prospective purchasers by judging their social graces in a personal interview. The subdivisions of this era include such renowned bastions of privilege as Bronxville and Tuxedo Park in New York's Westchester County.[12]

The pattern set by upscale railway suburbs would later become the suburban norm, but in the years after the Civil War these enclaves constituted only a tiny part of urban expansion. What enabled cities to spread far beyond their historic limit, the distance of a reasonable walk to work, was the new technology of the street railway. Even when pulled by horses, streetcars could carry commuters into former countryside. In the 1890s electric power expanded their range. The fare, usually a nickel on electric lines, was low enough that clerks and artisans could commute, and urban growth became a movement of the masses.

Streetcars quickly became big business. Real estate speculation often promised bigger profits than the transit line itself, so operators would buy up farms and extend the tracks beyond the limits of existing settlement. The land was sold to subdividers, a mix of large and small promoters, who sold off the lots and left construction to the purchaser. There were a multitude of small-scale builders and contractors, and future residents erected many houses themselves.

The communities built around streetcar lines have come to be known as streetcar suburbs. Today most of them are thought of as urban neighborhoods. Some older cities like Boston and San Francisco are, outside their downtowns, made up almost entirely of streetcar suburbs.

The streets that carried the tracks are, naturally enough, the main axes of streetcar suburbs. Along them commercial activity is strung out in a thin line. Side streets are straight, parallel, and closely spaced, with long blocks, an arrangement that offered rapid access to the streetcar and maximized the number of saleable lots. There are regional variations in the type of structure—small single-family bungalows predominate in Chicago and the Midwest, Baltimore and Philadelphia have brick row houses, wooden two-, three-, and even six-family houses are common in New England—but subdividers everywhere created small lots to squeeze in more homes and make them affordable.[13]

While all classes had lived in proximity in the old walking cities, residents of the new streetcar suburbs soon found themselves sorted by income level. One cause of this separation was transportation. Sam Bass Warner's classic study of Boston, *Streetcar Suburbs,* shows how the more affluent segment of the city's middle class, with steady downtown jobs, moved to outer suburbs where streetcars ran only toward the city center. Artisans, salesmen, and factory workers were confined to inner suburbs, where development was more advanced and the population was dense enough to justify crosstown transit. The desire of homebuyers to live near people like themselves reinforced this social sorting, as did the natural conservatism of small builders. The builders could be sure that houses would find buyers if they resembled what had already been sold on the same block.[14]

The streetcars, like the suburbs, assumed the social status of their occupants. In Henry James' 1886 novel *The Bostonians,* the well-born, socially conscious Olive Chancellor considers how to move about her city:

She would have taken the public conveyance (in her heart she loathed it) to the South End. Boston was full of poor girls who had to walk about at night and to squeeze into horse-cars in which every sense was displeased; why should she hold herself superior to these?

Social prestige attached, as we will see again and again, to the mere presence of an upscale clientele, quite apart from the intrinsic merit of what they purchased. Olive, accompanying a visiting cousin to hear a speech on women's rights, thought it best to hire a carriage. That vehicle, it turned out, offered little more comfort than the horse-car; she found herself "bouncing and bumping over the rail-way tracks very little less, after all, than if their wheels had been fitted to them."[15]

A more affluent ridership could make streetcars—especially the electrically powered kind—attractive even to the wealthy residents of restricted railroad suburbs. By 1910 a Portland, Oregon real estate promoter would advertise that "the fact that the Broadway car line, for its entire course, runs through a restricted residence district insures a desirable class of fellow passengers." When Senator Francis Newlands set out in 1891 to create the expensive Chevy Chase neighborhood outside Washington, DC, he made sure there was access by both streetcar and railroad. The streetcars, running straight up Connecticut Avenue through affluent Cleveland Park, were soon full of passengers; the railroad followed a less direct route and never carried anything but freight.[16]

By the end of the 1880s, older streetcar suburbs were changing as the city grew past them, and the evolution began to trouble both subdividers and homeowners. One had sold, and the other had bought, a cut-rate version of the rural ideal of Olmsted and Vaux, and part of the package was the reflected social glory of expensive railroad enclaves. Even the architectural ornaments on streetcar suburb houses were usually knockoffs of recent fashion among the more affluent. But in crowded neighborhoods close to the city, social pretensions rested on precarious foundations. As a district evolved, it became more than just a bedroom suburb for downtown. There came new land uses, and new residents, of lower social status. The remaining vacant lots grew too expensive for peers of the first wave of buyers, who were outbid by builders of crowded rental housing for workers and the lower middle class.[17]

Olmsted had identified the problem two decades earlier. A growing population attracted "butchers and bakers and tinkers and dramsellers and the followers of other bustling callings," who could easily find places for their businesses along streets laid out in a grid. The new residents who accompanied these enterprises might fill small lots with "ill-proportioned, vile-colored, shabby-genteel dwelling houses." Olmsted had architectural remedies for this problem in curving streets and large lots, but few streetcar-line subdividers had the means to implement them. It was the legal device he had long championed—the restrictive covenant—that offered hope of a quick and easy cure. Real estate promoters, who wanted mostly to hold off deterioration of the neighborhood just long enough to sell all the lots, found covenants especially attractive.[18]

Homebuyers initially resisted limits on their right to use property as they saw fit. For new landowners, an important appeal of the suburbs was the chance to escape subordination to a landlord. Moreover, the effect of restrictions was to prevent changes in land use that would raise property values. The buyer of a restricted lot was trading money for social status. As time passed, upwardly mobile city dwellers came to find this an attractive exchange. By the end of the 1890s, covenants were in wide use, sometimes even in less expensive neighborhoods.[19]

A breakthrough in the use of covenants came with the upscale Baltimore community of Roland Park. George Kessler, a well-regarded planner of parks and boulevards who had assisted Olmsted in the design of Central Park, laid out the first phase of this development in 1891. He banned business establishments outside of a designated commercial center, set back houses 30 to 40 feet from the street, and specified a minimum price of house construction. The second phase of development was designed in 1898 by the Olmsted firm itself. Olmsted's sons, who now ran the firm, promoted the separation of social classes without their father's hesitations. They added more restrictions, including a developer veto over the design of each house.[20]

Roland Park was a commercial success, and it attracted imitators across the country. The most prominent of these was Jesse Clyde Nichols, whose real estate business began in 1905 with a ten-acre plot next to the Kansas City Country Club. Within three years, Nichols and his backers gained control of more than one thousand acres and arranged for streetcars to reach their property. They laid out the new development, dubbed the Country Club District, with wide curving streets. Stringent covenants, including minimum house prices graded by neighborhood, enabled Nichols to boast of "1000 acres restricted." After he made direct contact with the developers of Roland Park in 1912, he copied their system of architectural review and established homeowner associations to enforce these and other rules.

Nichols, a careful follower of land-use trends, is credited with many innovations in suburban development. He devised covenants that were effectively

Sign advertising J. C. Nichols' Country Club District.
(Courtesy of the State Historical Society of Missouri, J. C. Nichols Company scrapbooks.)

immortal, overcoming long-standing legal doctrines that limited the lifetime of restrictions on real estate. He was also among the earliest designers of residential suburbs for the automobile. His subdivisions intentionally discouraged walking so that buyers would feel insulated from the city. Blocks were enlarged and sidewalks shrunk; by 1921 pedestrians were rare enough in the more affluent sections that sidewalks could be eliminated there entirely. And in 1923 he opened a regional shopping center, the best known of all his firsts. Earlier planned suburbs had neighborhood stores at railroad stations and streetcar lines; Country Club Plaza was conceived on a grand scale to draw shoppers by car from the entire metropolis. Located at a highway junction and surrounded by parking lots, it was the prototype of the modern shopping mall.[21]

Nichols' leadership in trade associations gave the Country Club District immense influence. With deep insight into social and economic trends joined to an intellectual bent uncommon among real estate promoters, he laid out his ideas in well-publicized talks at public meetings as well as closed sessions among developers. Nichols first attended the National Conference on City Planning in 1912 and was soon elected to its General Committee. He also served on the City Planning Committee of the National Association of Real Estate Boards, which in 1919 initiated annual meetings of "Developers of High-Class Residential Property." Within a few years the Country Club District was inspiring other expensive suburbs, such as Houston's River Oaks, designed from the start for access exclusively by automobile.[22]

The developers understood what their buyers sought—the defining characteristic of their market segment was "high class" rather than high price. The property they offered was, to be sure, conveniently placed and attractive to the eye, but these were secondary attributes, chosen to elevate social status as much as for their intrinsic worth. A planner of Palos Verdes Estates, a famous subdivision laid out near Los Angeles by Frederick Olmsted Jr. in the 1920s, explained it this way:

> The type of protective restrictions and the high class scheme of layout which we have provided tends to guide and automatically regulate the class of citizens who are settling here. The restrictions prohibit occupation of land by Negroes or Asiatics. The minimum cost of house restrictions tends to group the people of more or less like income together as far as it is reasonable and advisable to do so.[23]

The rules set down by these developers include many of today's suburban norms, sometimes taken so much for granted that the original purpose is hard to discern. Here Thorstein Veblen's classic analysis of status-seeking, *The Theory of the Leisure Class*, offers guidance. The core of Veblen's theory is that the visible display of unproductive expenditure—what he called conspicuous waste or conspicuous consumption—elevates social standing whereas routine useful labor degrades it.

Conspicuous waste is easy to observe in the suburbs. Houses must be set back from the street. Covenants (and later zoning ordinances) require large front lawns, space that gets far less use than the backyard. Chickens provide food and are often proscribed; pets serve no productive function and are allowed. The dog in particular is a suburban favorite; Veblen explained that it is an especially honorable beast:

> The dog has advantages in the way of uselessness as well as in special gifts of temperament.... He is the filthiest of the domestic animals in his person, and the nastiest in his habits. For this he makes up in a servile fawning attitude towards his master, and a readiness to inflict damage and discomfort on all else.[24]

Wealth and habits of consumption were not, of course, the only attributes of a desirable neighbor in early-twentieth-century America. Race was an unavoidable issue in a country resegregating after the Civil War and Reconstruction. Developers of expensive real estate were rarely willing to sell property to blacks, but for a long time they hesitated to include racial restrictions in their deed covenants. They did not want to risk invalidating the entire structure, under legal doctrines that allowed covenants to limit the use of property but not its sale. Only in the early 1900s, when covenants gained easier acceptance in the courts, did racial clauses become commonplace. Blacks were by far the most severely affected, but they were not alone in their exclusion—Jews were a frequent target, covenants drafted on the West Coast often kept Asians out, and sometimes even Italians, Greeks, and Slavs were proscribed.[25]

Along with these covenant-controlled developments, the years after the First World War brought yet another burst of speculation in unregulated building lots. As in the previous generation, transportation controlled urban form, but now the automobile had arrived to rival the streetcar. This new means of transport freed subdividers from earlier constraints, and the layout of their new suburbs showed the effect.

Henry Ford's introduction of the Model T in 1908 made the car an option for the masses, and by 1920 there was one auto for every thirteen Americans. The rapidly expanding automobile industry, its national clout complemented by the local influence of car dealers, gas station owners, and road builders, joined with real estate interests to lobby for better roads. By the early 1920s well-paved highways were fanning out from the cities. Traffic engineers, already seeking to separate automobiles from pedestrians, were developing the concepts that matured into today's interstates.

The first highway built for cars, Long Island's Motor Parkway of 1908, was a private enterprise intended for racing and "pleasure driving" by wealthy estate owners. But road-building quickly became a public undertaking. Road Acts of 1916 and 1921 began the policy of federal aid to state highway builders. State gasoline taxes, first enacted in Oregon in 1919 and in effect ten years later in all forty-eight states, yielded a steady flow of funds. City dwellers, whose local taxes maintained the streets that drivers used, paid indirectly through the gas tax for the spread of suburbs. Streetcars, meanwhile, remained in private hands, wasting away as subsidized competition sapped their revenues and rapacious owners starved them of investment.

Houses no longer had to cluster along streetcar lines and could spread across the countryside. Real estate promoters were quick to take advantage of the opportunity, selling land to buyers with meager financial resources. Vast expanses of mostly empty lots soon surrounded Los Angeles and Detroit, the fastest-growing cities. Here and there someone built a house, but most of the new owners could barely afford a shack.[26]

The twin forces of rising incomes and easy mortgage credit set off a suburban land bubble in the early 1920s. Speculation was, as usual, accompanied by fraud. One Florida developer was Charles Ponzi of Boston, remembered today as perpetrator of a pyramid investment scheme, who sold property "near Jacksonville" that was actually 65 miles away. (Ponzi, for all his other faults, appreciated the value of urban density—he cut his land up into twenty-three lots per acre.) The boom in Los Angeles peaked in 1923, but in Florida the mania progressed until 1926. Demand began to falter in the spring, and then two autumn hurricanes delivered the coup de grace. The flow of money through Miami banks in 1928 was one-seventh of what it had been three years earlier.[27]

Since the last years of the nineteenth century, covenants had been widely used to exclude undesirable people, buildings, and activities from new subdivisions. But these private contracts worked only imperfectly and incompletely. Older neighborhoods still lacked their protection. In principle, landowners could establish restrictions at any time, but in practice covenants had to be imposed in advance by the subdivider because a large group of homeowners could never agree on the details of the rules. And even when in place, covenants were hard to enforce. Individuals had little incentive to undertake expensive legal action against violators, and homeowner associations sucked up time and money that were hard to come by in less affluent neighborhoods. Homeowners and real estate developers desired more comprehensive and more effective controls. This was something only the power of government could achieve.[28]

The call for action was not unanimous. What covenants and zoning offered homebuyers was permanence—assurance that in future years they would be surrounded by people and buildings of the same quality as when they moved in. Stopping change was not in everyone's interest. The subdividers of large tracts, who maximized the value of the initial sale with promises of permanence, benefited most. They spearheaded the push for government regulation as they had for deed covenants. Small-scale speculators, who dealt in property already subdivided and hoped to profit from new and denser uses, led the opposition.

Los Angeles took a first step toward the systematic separation of land uses in 1908. The Los Angeles Realty Board, dominated by developers of upscale restricted neighborhoods, urged zoning on the city with the support of affluent homeowners. A pair of ordinances created seven industrial districts and defined nearly all of the city's remaining territory as residential districts. There businesses were allowed only when the City Council granted an exception. Other cities soon followed this example. In 1913 Wisconsin, Minnesota, and

New York authorized cities, when property owners so requested, to establish districts where nonresidential uses were banned. The Illinois legislature passed a similar law that died when the governor, on being advised that it was unconstitutional, used his veto.[29]

Early zoning laws often proscribed unwanted races along with unwanted land uses. In 1910 a Baltimore ordinance kept blacks from any block where more than half the residents were white. Birmingham, Atlanta, Richmond, St. Louis, and other municipalities soon enacted racial zoning as well. Blacks could of course sleep in white neighborhoods when they were household help living on their employers' property—and the Atlanta ordinance also permitted black homeowners to house white servants. This bow to constitutional doctrine showed how hollow was the promise of "separate but equal." A black man who presumed, in that time and place, to hire whites as domestic help would be lucky to see another sunrise.

Such maneuvers were too transparent even for the conservative judges of the day. In a 1917 case that gave the National Association for the Advancement of Colored People its first legal victory, a unanimous Supreme Court struck down racial zoning. Louisville's zoning ordinance, the court held, violated the white landowner's constitutional right to sell property to blacks. Racial segregation would have to rely on private contracts.[30]

Zoning codes could no longer divide races, but they could still separate uses, and soon the nation's largest city had one. The skyscrapers that would dominate New York's skyline had just appeared, and many feared these giant buildings would shut off light and air and congest traffic. Meanwhile, the spread of garment manufacturers into the upscale shopping district on Fifth Avenue was annoying retailers. Their customers were now forced to mix on sidewalks with immigrant workers. "Gentlemen, you are like cattle in a pasture, and the needle trades workers are the flies that follow you from one pasture to another," storeowners were told at a private luncheon. Such rhetoric lacked mass appeal, so the merchants promoted zoning with other arguments. Their well-funded publicity campaign warned of a grab bag of evils from truck traffic to overcrowding to high rents.

The city's major real estate and commercial interests joined retailers and municipal reformers to seek the separation of land uses, and action came quickly. In 1914 the city gained authority to impose zoning, and two years later a detailed ordinance was in place. Its underlying principle, as the framers conceded, was to freeze in place the existing land use. This entailed not a full spatial separation along the lines of upscale suburbs but a pattern similar to streetcar suburbs—midblock parcels were restricted to residential use, with commerce allowed on the avenues that carried through traffic. The code also placed limits on tall buildings, imposing gradual setbacks of higher stories to allow light and air to enter. From this rule came the terraced skyscrapers that have long defined New York's skyline.[31]

New York's adoption of a zoning code triggered a frenzy of activity in cities large and small. The landowning public clamored for separation of land uses, and developers of restricted communities joined in the call for government control. Machine politicians joined municipal reformers in the embrace of zoning—it was easy to see that variances, exceptions, and rezonings would open up a cornucopia of patronage and graft.[32] By 1920 zoning ordinances were in place in 904 cities, including 82 of the 93 municipalities with populations over 100,000. Given further encouragement by a model ordinance issued by Secretary of Commerce Herbert Hoover in 1924, a wave of regulation rolled on through the decade.[33]

The zoning movement quickly advanced beyond the isolation of residential uses to the exclusion of apartment houses from residential areas. The middle and upper classes did not like apartments. The most varied objections were raised. They were ugly; they gave off noise and smoke. They were simply not the way Americans should live. But most of all, zoners objected to the people who lived in apartments. The flavor of the tenement seemed to attach to even the most luxurious buildings. Residents were prone to disease and immorality. Tenants were "a class of nomads," said Harvard University president Charles Eliot, "that have no stable footing in the town."[34]

Many cities were already manipulating their fire and building codes to keep apartments out; with zoning they could reach the same end more directly. Berkeley, California, was the first to take this path. Its zoning ordinance, adopted in 1917, enforced a rigid separation of uses that went far beyond contemporaries. At a time when other cities were merely separating residential uses from commercial and industrial ones, Berkeley established a multitude of zones—twenty-seven in all. One-family, two-family, and apartment houses each had their own assigned districts, and homes were kept out of industrial areas as industry was from residential areas. Almost immediately, the exclusion of multifamily residences from single-family districts became a standard zoning rule.[35]

But zoning, despite all its advantages, was not a complete replacement for the older restrictive covenants. For one thing, racial zoning had been ruled out by the Supreme Court. Not only did new subdivisions continue to include racial covenants in their deeds, but also homeowners in existing neighborhoods added them. Less affluent homeowners sought to raise their status by imitating "high-class" suburbs. In the racist atmosphere of the early 1920s, with a revived Ku Klux Klan flourishing in both the North and the South, it was not hard for neighbors to come to consensus on racial exclusion.[36]

Control over the appearance of buildings was another reason for private agreements. The legal doctrines justifying zoning did not, until later modified, allow restrictions that were based on aesthetics. Upscale subdivisions like Roland Park and the Country Club District needed covenants to impose architectural review of house designs. And even for purposes that zoning could accomplish, private restrictions might be piled on top. Deed covenants offered a permanence that zoning, subject to the vagaries of the political process, could not ensure.[37]

Just one large American city, Houston, has never passed a zoning law. While restrictive covenants once covered almost every acre of the city, most became inoperative because only wealthier neighborhoods could afford to enforce them. Beginning in the 1920s, the developers of River Oaks led the city's business elite in repeated efforts to enact a zoning ordinance. But smaller property owners, black and white, wanted no limits on their chances to profit from changes in land use, and successive referendums went down to defeat.

In the end, though, landowners are constrained in Houston much as they are elsewhere. Minimum lot sizes were enacted in 1940, effectively banning construction of row houses in middle- and lower-income neighborhoods. Setbacks from the property line were required for buildings of all kinds, and stringent minimum parking requirements followed a few years later. After yet another failure at the polls, the pro-zoning forces turned to the state legislature in 1965. The city was empowered to enforce private deed restrictions, and a simple majority of the property owners in a subdivision can put in place new covenants that are enforceable against dissenters. This, for all practical purposes, is zoning, minus only the ability of the population as a whole to override the exclusionary wishes of a single neighborhood.[38]

By now, restrictive covenants and zoning had created a new form of land tenure. A landowner's property rights no longer end at the lot line but extend beyond it to the entire neighborhood. When Theodore Tilton wrote in 1864 that "the fortunate purchaser of two or three acres becomes a virtual owner of the whole five hundred," he was describing a single community of fifty-odd residences. Six decades later, the doctrine of common ownership was second nature to suburban Americans.

The regime of covenants and zoning obliterated a basic principle of nineteenth-century real estate law: that owners of land could build as they liked absent special circumstances. Free trade in land, which had earlier displaced feudal landholding in Europe, now gave way to the new suburban land tenure. The collectivist spirit of the new system was a sharp departure from the individualism of American legal and economic thinking. Sacred doctrines of freedom of contract and freedom of movement were set aside; people and buildings would henceforth be separated according to fine gradations of social status.

New systems of government arose to oversee the intertwined property rights of suburbia. Homeowner associations allowed only landowners to vote, reverting to a constitutional arrangement obsolete since the days of Andrew Jackson.[39] With zoning, the new property regime gained the support of law enforcement and tax revenue.[40] Owners of nearby homes enjoy a right that, even when much weaker in form, often amounts in practice to a veto over new construction. This right attaches to property and not citizenship; "public" input into decisions comes (sometimes de jure and almost always de facto) from landowners rather than the entire population.[41]

The path from the invention of suburban land tenure to its general acceptance was anything but straight. The sentiments that brought wide acceptance were almost polar opposites to those that had given it birth. Dissidence gave way to conformism. Manual labor, once rewarded, was disdained. Deed covenants devised by abolitionists now enforced racial segregation.

Did suburban land tenure arise by mere happenstance, engendered by the odd conjuncture of an unlikely collection of people and ideas? Or was its emergence the inevitable consequence of suburban growth?[42] The new doctrine reflected a reality of real estate—the enjoyment of one's land depends greatly on what one's neighbor builds—and it was propelled forward by powerful social and economic forces. Yet it could be propelled because it was already there, embodied in wood, brick, pavement, and grass. For the practical men and women who sold lots and built houses, Llewellyn Park and Roland Park were compelling examples that no abstract theory could have matched.

What would have happened had not the socialistic impulse of lapsed Fourierists first put the modern suburb into concrete form and the artistic genius of Frederick Olmsted kept it alive in the public eye? To such questions, history can offer no sure answer.

2

Planners and Embalmers

The system of landholding based on restrictive covenants and zoning would have momentous consequences for the future growth of American cities. Yet no grand plan had conceived it. Stepwise changes, each justified on narrow grounds, had accumulated into a dimly understood whole. Only in retrospect could it be seen how far the new order departed from received economic doctrines and accepted legal precedents. The creators of suburban land tenure had never articulated any underlying rationale, but without a clearly stated justification for the rejection of past jurisprudence, the entire structure stood on shaky legal foundations.

A new doctrine was needed to underpin the altered governance of land use. Such a doctrine must necessarily begin by explaining for what purpose the established rights of property owners had been curtailed. But those who undertook this task came immediately up against an obstacle: honesty was not an option. In a country founded on the rejection of aristocracy, the maintenance of status distinctions was not a proper purpose of government. Americans in their private lives might obsess over social rank, but as an explicit object of public policy the entire subject was out of bounds. Other motivations must stand in for status.

One early favorite was appearance. Wealthy suburbs were indeed attractive, and their history lent support to this line of thought. The first devisers of residence-only covenants, men like Alexander Jackson Davis and Frederick Olmsted Sr., were unquestionably devoted to artistic goals. And the order that zoning imposes on neighborhoods surely contributes to aesthetic harmony.

But intrusive government regulation could not be justified on artistic grounds alone. Beauty is, after all, a matter of taste. And art is the fruit of individual creation, rarely improved by bureaucratic supervision. Americans are a people disinclined to let officials tell us what to do, unless compelled by depression or war. Almost nowhere would government intrusion be less welcome than in the appearance of one's house.

A more promising candidate was property values. Here there was no need to be shy. If status is America's dirty secret, money-making is its pride. Zoning's partisans were quick to take this tack.

They were so quick, in fact, that they neglected to sort out whether zoning would make real estate prices go up or down. Harland Bartholomew, whose consulting firm wrote zoning ordinances for dozens of cities, claimed that zoning was needed to keep property prices up. Prices rose in restricted suburbs, he argued, and fell in those that allowed "promiscuous" mixed-use development. This had a certain plausibility; the most expensive suburbs were indeed highly restricted.[1]

But zoning had its main effect not in elite enclaves but in streetcar suburbs where the masses lived. Here zoning brought *lower* property values. Sam Bass Warner's later research into Boston suburbs shows that the introduction of mixed uses increased the price of land. Zoning proponents understood this and saw it as an advantage. They argued that holding property prices down improves neighborhoods by filling them with single-family houses. When apartment buildings are allowed, speculators buy up land and keep it empty in the hope of selling to a developer later.[2]

Advocates could list other benefits. Factory smoke and odors were kept out of residential neighborhoods. Large buildings brought traffic congestion. Most of all, though, and coming closest to the truth, owners of single-family homes were protected from change. "The protection of the homes of the people is probably the primary purpose of use districting," wrote Robert Whitten, who helped write the New York zoning law and then drafted Atlanta's separate-but-equal rules and ordinances for Dallas, Providence, and other cities and suburbs.[3]

These arguments, and others like them, were used to good political effect. But they did not add up to an overarching theory of land-use regulation. For that, control proponents turned to an economic doctrine in wide fashion in the 1920s: the idea that the destructive anarchy of the market must be tamed through planning. This was a widely held belief, from the extremes of Vladimir Lenin and Benito Mussolini to the sober center of Herbert Hoover. Hoover, the dominant American political figure of the decade, controlled domestic policy-making as secretary of commerce even before he became president. The planners, in his conservative vision, were not government bureaucrats but industry assembled into trade associations. Government's role was to encourage the organization and modernization of the private sector. Housing was a segment of the economy particularly in need of such transformation.

Comprehensive city planning was not a new idea; it was a prominent item on the agenda of Progressive-Era municipal reformers. Cities, without question, were plagued with poverty, pollution, and overcrowding. Planning was the solution. Calculate the city's needs, measure its physical and human resources, and bring destructive chaos under control by scientifically matching resources to needs.

Advocates had been writing earnest reports since the first years of the century, and in 1909 they organized on a national scale. A National Conference on City Planning and the Problems of Congestion was held in Washington. Practical experience was not lacking among the attendees; such men as Frederick Olmsted Jr. and George Kessler were succcessful designers of parks, boulevards, and upscale suburbs. But the ambition to map out entire cities had as yet produced only paper studies that lacked the force of law.[4]

The conference met annually, its attendance and influence growing as theorists and consultants were joined by the entrepreneurs who built expensive suburbs. Edward Bouton, the creator of Roland Park, attended the first year, and developers and real estate agents arrived in numbers in 1912. As the developers saw it, the private sector was already doing what the planning movement wanted for the entire community. High on their agenda was zoning. It would give their projects protection beyond the limits of the land that could be assembled under a single ownership.[5]

From the beginning, the city planners had observed the spread of land-use restrictions with great interest. The congestion that the title of their first gathering warned against was an excess not of automobiles but of people, and zoning promised to outlaw excessive human density. Beyond that, the zoning movement had a natural appeal to planning enthusiasts. Many of them were veterans of the Progressive-Era municipal reform movement and its fight against urban machine politics. The animus of reformers often extended beyond the political machines to the immigrants whose votes they relied on. Zoning, with its exclusionary thrust, could protect the Anglo-Saxon middle class against new arrivals.[6]

More important, perhaps, land-use regulation offered a means to advance planning from report-writing into reality. A central thrust of progressivism was the substitution of rational principles for politics; the planners were in a position to supply those principles. The planners thus endorsed the idea of zoning with enthusiasm, and they added an appeal for delineation of the zones on a basis that was scientific rather than political.[7]

Rushing to jump on the zoning bandwagon, planners sometimes placed expediency ahead of rigor. Many had first encountered urban problems as supporters of Henry George's single tax movement in the 1880s, and some still held to his theories. The premise of the single tax was that urban problems are caused by too little development. George recommended taxing only land, and not structures, to create incentives for more building. For not a few of his followers, one of the single tax's benefits was that covering the ground with single-family houses would keep apartments out. Zoning undoubtedly did serve the aim of excluding apartments, but its basic thrust of limiting development went directly against George's theories. Nonetheless, there were many single taxers among the leading zoning advocates, and they gave no sign of seeing any inconsistency. What mattered, their actions said, was having a plan.[8]

Cities that adopted zoning were slow at first to take up the planners' offers of help. They might well hire a planning consultant to write the ordinance— two dozen firms, Harland Bartholomew's being the biggest, offered their services. But of the cities that had zoning ordinances in the late twenties, fewer than one in five had a written plan. And even where there was a plan, there was little desire for the more systematic kind of planning that the profession's leaders advocated.[9]

Still, zoners had a compelling reason to adopt the agenda of the planning enthusiasts—to ensure that the rules were constitutional. Judges of the day were deeply hostile to restraints on the rights of private property. The Supreme Court had even thrown out a New York statute that said bakers could not work more than ten hours a day. Zoning laws limited owners' ability to use their land, and they would be struck down if they merely protected private parties like the Fifth Avenue merchants. They could be justified only as a means of protecting the general welfare—something that could be demonstrated by deriving them from a comprehensive city plan.

At the 1914 national planning conference, a Cincinnati attorney named Alfred Bettman laid out the legal logic. For zoning to pass muster, he said, "It is…necessary to show that the particular residential-district ordinance or statute under discussion has behind it a motive other than an aesthetic motive, has a motive related to safety or comfort or order or health." Before adopting a zoning ordinance, he advised, cities should undertake "some scientific study of the city's plan, so that the residential-district ordinance may bear a relation to the plan of the city, and the plan should be devised with a view to the health or the comfort or the safety of the people of the city."[10]

Here was a mandate that could loosen the pursestrings of stingy city fathers. The way was open for planning to grow from a cause into a remunerated profession.

Bettman had good reason to warn that zoning laws stood on fragile constitutional footing. Jurists were far from unanimous in their opinion of the matter. By 1925 the highest courts of nine states had upheld zoning. But the temper of the judiciary was hostile to government interference in the economy. The Supreme Court, dominated by a bloc of highly conservative justices, regularly struck down social legislation.

The high court spoke in a case from Euclid, Ohio. In 1922, this Cleveland suburb enacted a code that placed most of its territory in residential zones. One affected landowner was the Ambler Realty Company, which ten years earlier had purchased a sixty-eight-acre tract in anticipation of industrial development. On half of Ambler's land, only one- and two-family homes were allowed.

Ambler, joined by other aggrieved property owners, filed suit in federal district court. Their attorney was Newton Baker, former mayor of Cleveland and secretary of war in the Woodrow Wilson administration. Baker argued that Ambler had the right to develop its land for industrial purposes. Judge Dale Westenhaver, his former law partner, agreed, and the ordinance was ruled unconstitutional as a taking of property without compensation.

The city appealed to the Supreme Court. After hearing arguments from both sides, the closely divided justices called for a rehearing. At this point Alfred Bettman filed a crucial "friend of the court" brief, offering the arguments laid out in his 1914 speech. Zoning was an exercise of the police power, government's inherent right to suppress public nuisances and keep order. Bettman's reasoning won the day, and in November 1926 a 6-to-3 decision upheld zoning.

The case moved quickly beyond the specifics of Ambler's property; from the beginning, the principle of zoning was at stake. And the main principle was the exclusion of people, the people who lived in apartment houses. "In the last analysis," Judge Westenhaver wrote perceptively in his opinion, "the result to be accomplished is to classify the population and to segregate them according to their income or situation in life." The Supreme

Court saw the issue similarly. The village's power to keep out factories was not really in doubt, it observed: "The serious question in the case arises over the provisions of the ordinance excluding from residential districts apartment houses, business houses, retail stores and shops, and other like establishments."

The court's answer to this question left no doubt about whether it was permissible to segregate the population "according to their income or situation in life." Looking at apartments very much from the single-family owner's point of view, it wrote that

> ...the development of detached house sections is greatly retarded by the coming of apartment houses, which has sometimes resulted in destroying the entire section for private house purposes; that in such sections very often the apartment house is a mere parasite, constructed in order to take advantage of the open spaces and attractive surroundings created by the residential character of the district. Moreover, the coming of one apartment house is followed by others, interfering by their height and bulk with the free circulation of air and monopolizing the rays of the sun which otherwise would fall upon the smaller homes, and bringing, as their necessary accompaniments, the disturbing noises incident to increased traffic and business, and the occupation, by means of moving and parked automobiles, of larger portions of the streets, thus detracting from their safety and depriving children of the privilege of quiet and open spaces for play, enjoyed by those in more favored localities—until, finally, the residential character of the neighborhood and its desirability as a place of detached residences are utterly destroyed. Under these circumstances, apartment houses, which in a different environment would be not only entirely unobjectionable but highly desirable, come very near to being nuisances.[11]

The Supreme Court decision put new wind in planners' sails. Zoning was constitutional unless it was arbitrary and unreasonable, and in finding that the Euclid ordinance passed that test the court stressed how the subject had "received much attention at the hands of commissions and experts." The message was reinforced two years later by the case of *Nectow v. Cambridge*, in which the court overturned a zoning decision because no benefit to the city as a whole had been shown. Towns seeking to zone their land would be well advised, if they wanted their rules to stand up, to put the experts to work and produce paperwork that would pass muster in court.

Hoover's Commerce Department reinforced the push from the Supreme Court. In 1924 it issued a model state enabling act for zoning, whose drafters included many planning enthusiasts. The act provided that zoning maps "shall be made in accordance with a comprehensive plan." What that plan might entail was spelled out four years later, when the committee issued a model act for city planning. Many states adopted these texts without change.

The 1928 model act situated zoning as one element of a "master plan" that encompassed parks, streets, public buildings, and utilities. The plan would be drawn up by a commission conceived, in the high style of municipal reform, as a nonpolitical body of experts resistant to the pressures of venal politicians. The plan might extend into unincorporated areas beyond a city line, and there was even a hopeful bow to regional planning. So far the act fulfilled all the hopes of the planning movement.

But the enabling act was not the product of planners alone. Key provisions were worked out in advance through negotiations between the American City Planning Institute and the National Association of Real Estate Boards. The realtors, chastened after the mid-1920s collapse of the real estate bubble, wanted to control the supply of new lots. They sought to block competition from cut-rate subdividers, who did indeed often leave behind messes that others would have to clean up. Where realtors' interests were at stake, the final document fell short of planning enthusiasts' hopes. The realtors were not troubled by the nonpolitical planning commission; the "experts," they foresaw, might be found among their own ranks. But they killed a requirement that developers set aside land for parks. And, most important, cities could adopt land-use restrictions immediately, without waiting for the comprehensive plan.

The people who staffed the new planning bureaucracies had much useful work to do. Although they might, in practice, have little influence on the zoning of the areas already built up, subdivision control empowered them to shape the rapidly growing new suburbs. Without question, unplanned suburbs had evils in need of correction: uncontrolled rainwater runoff, badly built streets, groundwater polluted for lack of sewers. Still, as a historian of planning has recognized, the overall effect was to "encourage cities to portray in long-range plans the conditions of the present rather than the changes required." New subdivisions would avoid past mistakes, but the rigid zoning structure prevented future adjustment if their design was later found lacking. Planners might dream of molding the city of the future. They found themselves embalming the city of the present.[12]

Planners did look to the future; subdivision controls required it even if zoning did not. When they did, transportation was at the center of their concerns. And the transportation they privileged was the automobile.

Automobiles, as writers recognized, had a cachet other transportation lacked. The hero of F. Scott Fitzgerald's *The Great Gatsby* wooed Daisy Buchanan in a yellow Rolls Royce. Sinclair Lewis, in his 1922 bestseller *Babbitt*, veered from fiction into sociology:

> In the city of Zenith, in the barbarous twentieth century, a family's motor indicated its social rank as precisely as the grades of the peerage determined the rank of an English family.

For the title character, Lewis tells us, driving was a sacred recreation, second only to (of course) golf. "His motor car was poetry and tragedy, love and heroism."[13]

On suburban roads drivers found little in their way, but on busy city streets others were there first with long-established rights. Children played in the roadway; pushcarts and newsstands lined curbs. Pedestrians were accustomed to crossing the pavement at their own convenience. Streetcars unloaded their passengers in the middle of the road. Collisions with cars exacted a rapidly rising toll of deaths, and in the early 1920s a broad popular movement for safer streets arose with the aim of taming auto traffic.

Motorists and carmakers fought back, and the traffic tamers went down swiftly to defeat. From the beginning, cars were able to chase competitors off the street with their sheer mass. Then the auto manufacturers' lobby, with Herbert Hoover doing its bidding, rewrote the rules of the road. Those on foot became subordinate to cars, responsible for avoiding collisions with them. "Safety" campaigns belittled pedestrians who resisted the new order as jaywalkers, a new word coined from *jay*, which meant a country bumpkin, and shamed them into compliance by public ridicule. The ownership of space was here at issue more than safety. Motorists were free to plant their feet on the pavement to leave a parked car—but a pedestrian who stood on the same spot was an interloper on the roadway.[14]

Planners, in this conflict, were enthusiastic allies of the auto interests. For many among them, the prestige of the automobile was reason enough to prefer it to walking and mass transit. But there were other motivations too, motivations that were easier to speak out loud. To decentralize the cities, as most saw it, was a positive good; cars allowed suburbs to spread, while rail lines, especially underground or elevated ones, would only bring more people downtown. For Edward Bassett, the preeminent zoning expert of the time, the greatest danger of unregulated growth was the congestion caused by new subway lines.

New suburban roads, moreover, could be laid out in a logical pattern, while the tangle of existing trolley lines resisted planners' science. And automobile manufacturers were not shy in lobbying for better roads, while streetcar operators often saw transit improvements as threats to existing monopolies.

The creators of the new regulated city thus tended to the automobile just as they tended to the single-family home. Planners dreamed of highway networks fanning out across the countryside, of overpasses, of double-decked streets, of superhighways. Elevated railways, detested for their noise and pollution, were torn down, and in their place rose elevated highways, even noisier and dirtier once they filled with traffic.

The planners tended most to what was known as pleasure driving. Pleasure driving, the least productive use of a vehicle, had special prestige, just as the dog was most honorable of domestic animals. A particular favorite was the parkway, a road surrounded by parks and nature. Its allure was so great that Thomas MacDonald, the master highway builder who long headed the Bureau of Public Roads, was moved in 1924 to issue an unneeded caution. Fearing an angry public reaction against the desecration of "pleasure parkways," he urged against their conversion to utilitarian arteries.[15]

The planning profession, driven by its scientific pretensions and encouraged by automotive lobbies, outsourced the design of roads to specialists. As Harland Bartholomew later put it, the design of highways was "a scientific process or an engineering matter, just as the design of sewer and drainage systems." Traffic engineers could determine the proper width of streets in much the same way that sanitary engineers calculated the diameter of sewer pipes.[16]

As they assembled their recipes for regulated subdivision, planners began with a well-stocked intellectual cupboard. It was furnished from two principal sources: the Garden City of turn-of-the-century England; and the American City Beautiful. But the practical planners of the new generation applied these doctrines selectively at best, and not rarely in ways that undid their intent.

The City Beautiful movement aimed to bring the beauty of classical architecture to the central cores of American cities, creating a republican version of the grandeur of European capitals. Its principal figures were Charles McKim (who had grown up in Llewellyn Park), Frederick Olmsted Jr., and Daniel Burnham. "Make no little plans," said Burnham, "they have no magic to stir men's blood," and their ideas played out on a vast scale. First the Chicago

World's Fair of 1893, and then a comprehensive plan for the city of Washington in 1902, won widespread praise and imitation.[17]

The classicism of the City Beautiful was still in vogue in the 1920s among architects and builders of public buildings, but the new city planning profession had moved on. Zoning rules, the Supreme Court had ruled, must contribute demonstrably to "public health, safety, morals, or general welfare." Planners had the job of making these demonstrations. They were now technocrats, collecting facts and using them to calculate the future course of the metropolis.

Attention thus turned from old downtowns to new subdivisions. Parks remained a central concern; they served definable functions of fresh air and recreation. But otherwise planners lowered their sights. Instead of designing grand boulevards, they engineered the movement of traffic. Landmarks gave way to separated uses. What stirred suburban blood, after all, was keeping big things out.[18]

A second source of inspiration was the Garden City of Ebenezer Howard. An English social reformer, Howard imagined slums and crowded cities replaced by new towns set among farms and fields. Self-sufficient communities of thirty thousand residents would feature a mix of industry, commerce, and homes, kept efficient and sustainable by common ownership of land. In 1903 his followers undertook to build a first example, Letchworth, north of London. They entrusted the design of Letchworth to the architect Raymond Unwin. He had made a name as advocate and designer of better working-class housing, and in 1909 he published a book titled *Town Planning in Practice*.

The Garden City, in origin more functional than artistic, remained in fashion among American planners in the twenties. But in their version, many of the precepts laid down by Howard and Unwin were abandoned. No clear boundary was set between town and country; city planning boards had neither the power to create permanent agricultural belts nor the desire to do so. The egalitarianism that was a main feature of the Garden City was gone; municipal planners created few homes for workers. Where the main point of Howard's concept had been to replace oversized cities with self-contained communities of manageable size, the Americans found themselves endlessly expanding those cities through the addition of new suburbs. On this last subject Unwin himself had experienced a change of heart when charged during the war with creating new housing for workers. On a visit to the United States, he found himself admiring J. C. Nichols' Country Club District.[19]

Street layout was a topic to which Unwin gave much thought. He rejected the practice, then widespread, of laying out straight streets in a rectangular grid. Instead, he tried to focus residential life on courtyards and narrow

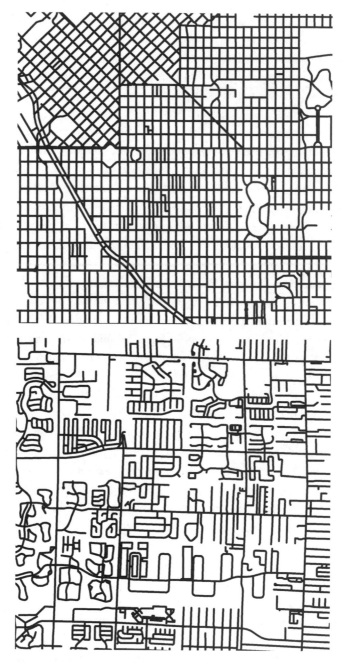

Grid and superblock street layouts. Examples from Denver, Colorado (above), and Palm Beach County, Florida (below).

dead-end streets. The American planners took up some of these ideas with enthusiasm. They replaced the street grid with a hierarchy of roads. Through traffic was removed from residential streets and channeled onto arterials. The favored road layout was the "superblock," bounded by wide highways and lacking internal connections.

But similar concepts were applied toward very different ends. Unwin, when he accepted the suburb, had concluded that traffic congestion is unavoidable. His purpose, in pushing cars out of neighborhoods onto arterials, was to relocate the congestion. Americans sought instead to move automobiles ever faster on ever-bigger roads. Unwin narrowed residential streets and placed footpaths where automobile traffic was shut off. American superblocks repelled pedestrians, their wide internal streets often lacking sidewalks altogether.[20]

It did not take long for practices to gel into a doctrine, taught in the universities that were beginning to grant degrees in planning and practiced in the bureaucracies of cities large and small. Among its chief tenets were separation of land uses, low density, and the fastest possible movement of automobiles. It loved parks, abhorred grid streets, and tried not to think about people who couldn't afford to buy a house.[21]

The human congestion of the founding years of their profession had abated—New York's Lower East Side lost more than half its population between 1910 and 1930—but planners still sought to empty out cities. Their new orthodoxy owed less to earlier theorists than to high-end suburban developers, the first clients of the leading figures in the field.[22]

Regardless of scientific pretension, status remained the lodestar of land-use regulation. A town might allow a supermarket yet judge the same land unsuitable for a discount store. Motels were banned where hotels and country inns were welcome.[23]

This point was driven home by a craze miniature golf in the early 1930s. Golf courses were a permitted use in residential zones, modeled as they were after Jesse Nichols' Country Club District. Owners of unbuilt house lots, put out of work after the crash, spied a loophole in the law and opened putt-putt operations on land not otherwise usable to earn a living. A loud outcry soon ensued. Planners, in their wisdom, determined that the miniature sport was not the noble game of golf at all. It was a commercial recreation unfit to coexist with homes.[24]

Planners had set out in a burst of optimism and idealism, in search of a better and more beautiful city. They had, they would admit, made compromises along the way. They recognized that narrow interests of real estate developers and suburban exclusionists might often outweigh the broader public interest. But their work, they insisted, still served its original mission. And public opinion agreed. Planning, as a profession and as a theory, retained an aura of idealism from its progressive birth.

Even critics of the planning orthodoxy accepted many of its premises. What faults were recognized were chalked up to the insufficient application of the planners' concepts, not to any error in the ideas themselves. Lewis Mumford, in 1927, came before the city planners' annual conference to denounce "the domination of purely financial values." But Mumford shared the hostility to dense cities that united planners and suburban developers. Crowded skyscrapers and packed subways were the problem; the solution was "countryside and city developed together."[25]

What made this theory so attractive to progressive thinkers? One source of its appeal was American culture's idealization of the open land. America was the refuge of "huddled masses yearning to breathe free." A ban on huddling in apartment houses fulfilled the promise of the lamp beside the golden door. It bore no animus against the poor and tempest-tossed.

Critics of the decade's business-dominated politics felt an inchoate but deeply rooted distrust of the metropolis. For municipal reformers, from whose ranks the first planners derived, loathing of political corruption easily spilled over into a dislike of the immigrant-filled cities that bred Tammany Hall and its ilk. Other progressives might not share that bias, but for reasons of their own they were no enthusiasts of urban life.

Rural populism, no longer an organized movement, was still an influence. In 1920 it was only twelve years since its champion William Jennings Bryan had been the Democratic Party's candidate for president. Bryan did not merely voice the economic interests of rural farmers; he celebrated their way of life. "Burn down your cities and leave our farms, and your cities will spring up again as if by magic. But destroy our farms and the grass will grow in the streets of every city in the country," he declaimed in the famous "cross of gold" speech that won his first presidential nomination.

The urban Left as well had an inherited suspicion of city living. The oppressive working and living conditions of the early industrial revolution had led a young Karl Marx to endorse the "abolition of the distinction between town and country." These urban ills were still far from fully cured, and any scheme for getting rid of tenements could win a hearing. Marx had not idealized the countryside—he spoke of "the idiocy of rural life"—but his followers' ears were open to promises, made by new towns and old suburbs alike, that the advantages of town and country would be combined.

Still, it was not the substance of planning that excited 1920s progressives most. It was the new land-use rules' rejection of the ruling doctrine of laissez-faire. Government, in one sphere at least, was actively interfering in economic life and was even purporting to direct it.

The Supreme Court's approval of zoning came as a rare breath of fresh air from judges willing to strike down even the mildest reform legislation—even more so because the opinion was written by Justice George Sutherland. That deeply conservative jurist had led the court in holding that a minimum wage for women in the District of Columbia was an unconstitutional interference with the right of contract. By affirming the permissibility of government interference with property rights, *Euclid v. Ambler* set a welcome precedent that might bring a future reversal of judicial fortunes.

More broadly, the wide vistas of the city planners' ambitions encouraged—one might even say seduced—believers in economic planning. The profession claimed a steadily expanding scope, encompassing new topics and new territory. Practitioners were soon called "planners," without any limiting modifier. Indeed, it was hard to see how one could with any specificity direct the growth of a city, unless one also directed to some degree its economy. The model planning law of 1928 fed these hopes in an optional section on regional planning, with vague but enticing hints of regional government and statewide planning.

A contradiction lay at the heart of the planners' agenda. One plans for the future because it may be different from the present. But the aim of zoning, which they administered and justified, was to embalm the present.

A lapse of time must necessarily pass before the consequences of that embalming would emerge. Events conspired to prolong the interval. When the planning apparatus came into full flower with the 1928 model planning act, the real estate bubble of the 1920s had already burst. Depression and war followed; private-sector construction did not fully resume until 1946. The problems that turned up in the twenties could be blamed very plausibly on the haphazard and unscientific drafting of early zoning ordinances. Whatever the question, planners could answer with new rules and tighter controls. Only in the 1950s, with the maturing of zoned subdivisions, could the fruit of their work be tasted. By then the compromises that accompanied the birth of the profession were long forgotten.

As official doctrine had it, the planners were scientific optimizers, the Master Plan was their grand design, and zoning was a tool they employed to bring that design to fruition. But the reality was otherwise. Land-use restrictions were an end in themselves, and the primal urge that caused them to multiply was status-seeking. Planning was pasted over the midsection of the zoning code, a fig leaf hiding its unmentionable reproductive organs.

3
Government-Sponsored Sprawl

As the newly professionalized city planning agencies settled into a routine at the end of the 1920s, the unequal balance of power between planners and real estate developers was about to shift. The depression shut down privately financed building, and the New Deal soon stepped into the breach. Now the bureaucrats in federal agencies, and in the local governments they financed, were the ones with the money. Where planners had once evangelized builders, the builders now needed to convince planners. To that end they employed, along with instruments of suasion, the potent tools of lobbying and political pressure.

Reversal of roles brought only a partial reversal of policy. Public housing, once barely discussable in polite company, was now a major goal of government. But planning theories devised in a more conservative era dictated the design of government-sponsored housing and how it was inserted into the surrounding landscape. And real estate lobbyists, fearful of government-sponsored competition, kept the new housing projects under constant criticism and succeeded in denying their benefits to all but the certifiably poor.

Meanwhile, builders and reformers reached a modus vivendi over homes for the middle class. Government support for private construction mushroomed, untroubled by controversy, while political battles raged over public housing. Federal intervention thus accelerated the trends of the preceding

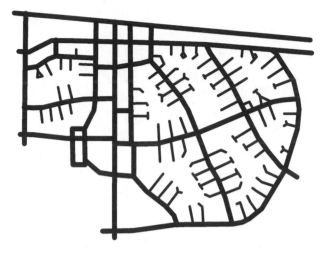

Street map of Radburn.

half-century. It made the automobile-dependent lifestyle, earlier a mark of exclusivity, accessible to clerks and factory workers. Home ownership became far more widespread, but the housing market remained segregated by income and race.

New York's City Housing Corporation, set up before the crash to take the profit motive out of housing, showed the way for later New Deal programs. Its work was made possible by a state law that offered tax advantages in exchange for a limitation on investors' returns. A gallery of reform luminaries graced its board of directors, among them Eleanor Roosevelt, the Ethical Culture leader Felix Adler, and assorted philanthropists and settlement-house directors. Building began with a financially successful and innovatively designed row house project in Queens. This was followed in 1929 by the new town of Radburn, near Paterson, New Jersey, which pointed the way to the car-centered suburbia of the future.

Radburn consciously imitated the Garden City, but in the hands of American planners Ebenezer Howard's concept mutated into a somewhat denser approximation of an upscale suburb. Individual ownership replaced common property, under a private government whose authority rested on deed covenants. Roads, laid out in an irregular pattern, divided the community into superblocks a quarter-mile across. Single-family homes were set on cul-de-sacs within the superblocks. Children had playgrounds, and pedestrians came off the streets too. Footpaths, set behind the houses in commonly owned parkland, crossed the roadways through tunnels.[1]

Aiming to integrate pedestrians and motorists, Radburn wound up pioneering the future of automotive sprawl. Its winding roads and dead ends discouraged through car traffic as intended, but they also made it all but impossible to get anywhere by walking along the street. Radburn compensated with its footpaths, but for-profit imitators found it easier to forget altogether about those on foot. The layout of superblocks and cul-de-sacs would come to shape the car-centric American suburb.

The crash of 1929 brought building to a near halt, and it put existing homeowners at risk too. The house-building boom of the 1920s had been financed with short-term loans, the only form of credit then available. When the balloon mortgages came due, banks were loath to lend. Delinquent mortgages added more fuel to the fire of financial crisis.

With both banks and borrowers in need of relief, one of the first undertakings of the New Deal was the Home Owners Loan Corporation. President Franklin Roosevelt proposed a law to establish the HOLC in April 1933, just a month after taking office, and he signed it two months later. Within two years it had issued more than a million loans. It refinanced one-tenth of all the nonfarm houses in the United States with long-term, fixed rate mortgages at low interest rates.

The HOLC was a stopgap, but its influence lingered for decades. It perfected and popularized the long-term mortgage. These self-amortizing loans freed borrowers from the overhanging threat of a balloon payment that required them to return to the credit market. Home ownership became more affordable and more stable, laying a foundation for the suburban boom after the Second World War.

Equally important was the HOLC's pioneering effort to create a uniform system of appraisal. Systematic procedures were needed to manage the vast number of loans the agency issued. Even after the HOLC expired, its system of valuing real estate endured, the basis for a large-scale inflow of private capital that made it easier to finance homes.

The HOLC appraisal methods did vast damage. Recognizing that the value of a house depends on its surroundings, the agency established four categories of neighborhoods. Its ratings reflected the housing market's established pecking order of social status. Newly built subdivisions automatically scored higher than older ones, and traditional urban layouts, such as houses built close to the street, were downgraded. Old streetcar suburbs lacked access to funds that flowed into newer developments built for the automobile.

Appraisers judged a neighborhood's ethnic character along with its buildings. A place with even an "infiltration of Jews" was ineligible for the highest rating, and African American districts were grouped with areas of prevalent poor maintenance or vandalism and given the lowest grade. Color-coded maps displayed the results of this evaluation, with the lowest category shown in red. For years afterward these maps were used by private banks for lending decisions, giving rise to the term *redlining*.[2]

The HOLC was effective at rescuing homeowners and stabilizing banks, but it did little to encourage new construction. Unemployment was the central problem of the depression, and many of the lost jobs were in the building industry. The Roosevelt administration, moreover, was under political pressure to do something about private-sector jobs in addition to its government employment programs. The result in June 1934 was the creation of the Federal Housing Administration.

The new agency had a mission of reviving house construction by insuring mortgage loans made by private banks. Where commercial banks had previously demanded 50% down payments, the FHA required only 20%, and that figure was soon reduced to 10%. Three-year balloon mortgages gave way to loans that amortized over twenty or even twenty-five years. Not only were the terms more generous, but government guarantees also brought interest rates down by two or three points. These incentives worked; housing starts jumped from 93,000 in 1933 to 332,000 in 1937 and 619,000 in 1941.

The FHA began life with the enthusiastic support of developers, and it did not disappoint them. Staffed largely with executives from real estate and financial businesses, its policies closely tracked the agenda of the large-scale suburban developers. Its guidelines and controls retained the HOLC appraisal system—it is unclear whether the same maps were used—and went far beyond it to shape the design of new housing and new communities. The ostensible purpose of the guidelines was to ensure that only economically viable loans were issued, but in practice their scope was much broader. The FHA imposed the style of subdivision pioneered by the "high-class" developers as a national norm. This was a major item on the agenda of the real estate developers, because the willingness of local politicians to grant exceptions undercut their efforts to enforce such controls through zoning.

"If a neighborhood is to retain stability," the FHA's underwriting manual said, "it is necessary that properties shall continue to be occupied by the same social and racial classes." The agency denied insurance to new housing

Wall built at the behest of the Federal Housing Administration to separate black and white neighborhoods in Detroit.
(Courtesy of Library of Congress, Farm Security Administration collection.)

in towns that lacked zoning or passed ordinances that allowed the density of existing neighborhoods to increase. As a further bulwark against change, it recommended—and often insisted on—restrictive covenants covering race, house design, and maintenance. In one section of Detroit, it refused to insure houses because blacks and whites were living too close together and only relented when the developer built a concrete wall to separate the races.

While the agency by law was to finance both apartments and single-family houses, its policies had a strong suburban bias. Neighborhoods that were crowded or contained older buildings were disfavored. Lending commitments, even for apartment buildings, were concentrated in the periphery of metropolitan areas; the recommended setting for rental development was "what amounts to a privately owned and privately controlled park area." Loans for new one-family houses carried much more favorable terms than those for multifamily buildings or rehabilitation of existing homes.

FHA design standards specified minimums for lot sizes, front and side setbacks, and the width of the house. Some traditional home styles, such as Baltimore's sixteen-foot row houses, were entirely ineligible. Front yards were to be lawns, with a limited presence of trees and shrubs. Grid street plans were strongly discouraged in favor of superblocks penetrated by cul-de-sacs and curving streets. Field staff, a historian of the building industry reports, adhered to these rules "with messianic fervor."

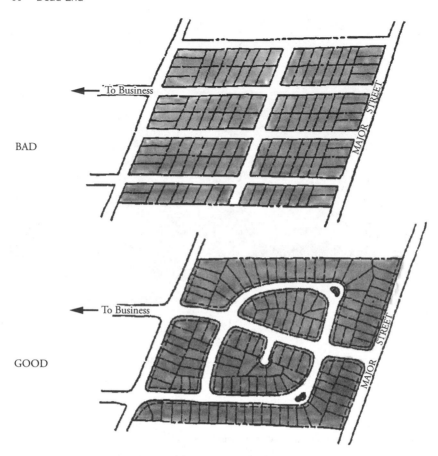

Good and bad street layouts according to the Federal Housing Administration.
(From Planning Profitable Neighborhoods, 1938.)

Developers who laid out entire communities and built the houses were privileged with commitments to approve loans before the houses were built. The FHA did not make construction loans, but its promise of mortgages made private financing much easier to get. The stated purpose of the preference for large-scale operations was to reduce construction costs through mass production and raise standards. Another reason for this policy, surely, was the dominant role of the big builders in the trade associations that influenced the agency's actions.

FHA guidelines were presented as mere recommendations, different in nature from the New Deal regulations that businessmen found so oppressive. In reality they were nearly mandatory; financing was all but unobtainable for builders who failed to conform. New development was frozen in the status-driven and automobile-centered pattern laid down by developers, zoners, and planners of the preceding decades. What we now know as sprawl was here.[3]

The New Deal concerned itself too with housing for the less affluent, a problem swept under the rug in the 1920s. Government, free from the ideological inhibitions of previous generations, built inexpensive dwellings. There was even an innovative effort to build new towns along the Garden City model of Ebenezer Howard and Raymond Unwin; three communities were created before congressional conservatives killed the program.[4]

The public housing program began in 1934 and was continued by the Housing Acts of 1937 and 1949. On one level, it was a success. Within four years 130,000 new apartments sprang up, and by 1962 more than two million people were living in a half-million public housing units. Housing projects filled a real need; as late as 1950 New York had one hundred thousand apartments without private toilets and nearly a quarter-million homes without central heating. Long waiting lists for vacant units demonstrated that tenants found the projects far superior to available alternatives.

Still, as the waiting lists demonstrated, the supply of public housing fell far short of the demand. This was largely the result of limited funding, a problem that the more politically popular FHA did not face. The United States built less publicly owned housing than other industrial countries. And public housing had defects—most, but not all of them, the result of compromises made to pass the legislation—that led to the decay and eventual destruction of much of what did get built.

For one thing, income limits restricted public housing to the poor. The most stable residents were often forced to leave as their conditions improved. These limits were imposed at the insistence of the private real estate industry, fearful of government-sponsored competition even as FHA subsidies were essential to its own prosperity. The program was further handcuffed with intermittent bans on building on vacant land. A slum housing unit had to be destroyed for every new apartment built. And, because public housing was exempt from property taxes, local officials had reason to put it where taxes would be least—on low-value land in undesirable areas.

Fears that public housing would bring minorities into homogeneous neighborhoods added to the long-standing dislike of apartment buildings, stirring up opposition among homeowners. Local governments held a veto over the placement of projects, and public housing easily became a political football. In New York City, where renters had the power of numbers, giant public and cooperative apartment complexes rose on empty land in the outer boroughs. But in Detroit, a city of single-family homes, the powerful auto workers union was abandoned by its members on the housing issue. A conservative Republican running on an anti-public housing platform overwhelmed the labor-backed candidate for mayor in 1949, and the city built no more projects outside the worst sections of the central city.

Republicans, when they regained the presidency in 1953, did not end public housing as some of their supporters would have liked, but the Dwight D. Eisenhower administration was careful to avoid any disturbance of the racial status quo. Public housing was kept out of suburbs and concentrated near downtown. The projects brought more low-income residents to old neighborhoods that were already filling with the poor as a consequence of redlining and zoning. These former streetcar suburbs became the decaying inner city.

On top of the injuries imposed by economic and racial segregation came self-inflicted wounds, the consequence of planning doctrines. Housing authorities ripped up street grids, placing apartment towers in superblocks devoid of commerce. Theories born in affluent suburbs, when applied in the conditions of poverty, quickly showed their defects. Crime flourished, sending many projects into decline. In the 1960s new rules let welfare recipients into housing first intended for the working poor, and the downward spiral accelerated.[5]

The end of the Second World War brought boom years to the American economy. Consumers had savings to spend, accumulated during a wartime of long work hours, union wages, and shortages of consumer goods. In no sector of the economy was there more pent-up demand than for housing. Returning GIs, newly married and with children on the way, crammed into tiny apartments or doubled up. The federal government responded as it had to the unemployment of the thirties—with more suburbanization. In 1944, even before the war ended, congress established a Veterans Administration mortgage program modeled on the FHA.

Construction flourished. Single-family housing starts in 1946 were 50% higher than in 1941, and in the next four years they nearly doubled again. Shifts in industry structure accompanied the growth. Subdividers were now builders as well, selling completed houses instead of leaving construction to the lot buyer. Large firms emerged, building cheaply with techniques of mass production borrowed from factories.

New Deal reforms had created a far broader housing market. Unions raised wages and stabilized employment, while the FHA and VA offered mortgages to workers with income but no wealth. Builders, with a strong push from the FHA, responded with neighborhoods that were priced for economy but designed as stripped-down versions of the previous generation's upscale suburbs. House lots were bigger than in streetcar suburbs. Subdivisions were cut into superblocks, with interior streets that curved and dead-ended. Sidewalks, if built at all, led uselessly to unwalkable arterials. The highways, given little thought, were soon lined with ugly commercial strips. New housing was nearly unreachable without a car.

The largest and best known of the new suburbs was Levittown, named for the family that built it. Its 17,400 houses, set on former potato farms 25 miles east of New York City, offered cut-rate entry to the middle class. They bore the trappings of higher status inside and out, but the Levitts did not build for the long term. Buyers got brand-name washing machines but no sewers, and rules requiring owners to mow their lawns were enforced only so long as new dwellings were on sale nearby.

The structures went up on an assembly line, with twenty-seven crews marching down a street to carry out successive tasks. Four-room Cape Cods were priced at $7990 and ranches at $9500, underselling competitors by a wide margin. Across the country, large-scale builders were soon imitating Levittown's widely publicized success.[6]

By many means, government policy in the postwar years reinforced the automobile orientation of the new suburbs. Construction of new subway lines had slowed after the First World War, and the depression halted it almost completely. The New Deal's vast public works programs poured federal money into highways; streetcars, owned by private monopolies that reformers detested, were ineligible for aid. The only major rail projects to win support were subways in Chicago and on New York's Sixth Avenue.

Streetcars had been losing customers since the twenties, and they lost speed as they got stuck behind cars. Where they mixed with car traffic, drivers wanted them and their passengers off the road; where they didn't, the powerful automobile lobby coveted their right of way. Faced with tax-supported competition from the roads, street railways were no longer able to make a profit. By the end of sixties streetcar tracks were largely gone. Buses, bumpy and usually infrequent, filled the gap, patronized for the most part by those unable to drive by reason of age, poverty, or infirmity.[7]

As rail transit decayed, the country invested massively in new roads. In the postwar years, there was no federal transit funding at all, and local budgets had similar priorities. Los Angeles built its famous network of freeways;

expressways cut through New York; and other cities imitated them. Suburban arterials grew wider and straighter, and many states followed the prewar examples of Pennsylvania and Connecticut by connecting their major cities with toll-financed limited access highways.

But this was only the beginning. President Eisenhower in 1954 brought together highway proponents, previously divided over whether to pay for new roads with tolls, a gas tax, or general revenues. Francis du Pont, whose family had owned the controlling interest in General Motors, was put in charge of the Bureau of Public Roads, and Gen. Lucius Clay, a GM board member, headed a study of highway needs. In 1956, Clay's committee recommended a vast network of toll-free superhighways financed by increasing the federal gasoline tax. Congress agreed and launched construction of a 41,000-mile system with 90% of the cost paid by the federal government.

The new roads were called the interstate highway system, but they served local commuting as much as long-distance travel. The damage done to cities was twofold. By subsidizing long-distance commuting, expressways accelerated the stampede to the suburbs and sucked life out of urban neighborhoods. Beltways around cities, justified as bypasses to divert through traffic past congested downtowns, rapidly became crowded rush-hour routes. Meanwhile, the new highways devastated neighborhoods, tearing down what lay directly in their path and spreading a pall of noise, soot, and fumes over what remained standing.

If one man was the face of the expressway era, it was Robert Moses. A master builder with an almost countless collection of official titles, he remade New York City. He was an advocate for road-building on the national stage and a consultant who devised elaborate highway networks for other cities. He built parks, highways, and housing projects, going from big to bigger, rolling over almost anyone and anything that got in his way.

Moses' career epitomized the trajectory of urban reform in the midtwentieth century. After starting as a municipal reformer and enemy of political patronage, he grew close to Governor Al Smith and was put in charge of a new Long Island State Park Commission. He pushed aggressively forward to create a chain of parks centered at Jones Beach, opened to New York's masses by new parkways. The parkways were blocked at first by the political influence of wealthy estate owners, who preferred to keep the public far from their homes. But Moses cut a deal with the Nassau County Republican machine, letting local politicians skim profits from real estate development at parkway exits. Work then proceeded according to his designs—except for the route of

Robert Moses in 1933 at the opening of Bethpage State Park. The park boasts a championship golf course that was later the site of the U.S. Open.
(Courtesy of New York State Archives.)

the Northern State Parkway, forced onto a southward detour that kept it away from the largest estates.

Moses' vision was distinctly elitist. Even his greatest achievements were very much for, not by, the public, and he held a narrow idea of what that public was. The poor were effectively excluded from Jones Beach. Moses vetoed a plan to extend the Long Island Railroad to the shore, and the parkways were built—when two-thirds of New York's population could not afford a car— with bridges too low for buses to pass through. As his powers grew, he punched highways and redevelopment projects through crowded New York neighborhoods with the same imperious disdain he had shown to Long Island farmers.

Buoyed by popular acclaim for his parks, and loved by mayors and governors with a thirst for getting public works built, Moses won one construction task after another. As the years passed, his credit with the public declined, but by now control of jobs and contracts gave him immense political clout. His powers grew apace. By the 1950s he ran the parks of both city and state; he oversaw highways, bridges, and tunnels throughout the city; he had built one of the world's largest hydroelectric projects at Niagara Falls; he headed New York's slum clearance committee; and without any formal position he controlled the city's public housing. Objecting in 1959 to free Shakespeare plays in Central Park on the grounds that the audience should pay for damage to the grass, he ignored the views of the mayor who was his nominal superior and declined even to return phone calls. Only after a long battle by director Joseph Papp did he agree to the building of the Delacorte Theater for free performances.

The toll bridges and tunnels under Moses' control had grown into a vast money-making machine, and he dominated the spending of even greater sums in federal and state transportation budgets. Subways and commuter trains were falling apart, yet he remained rigidly devoted to the automobile. Not a mile of new rail line was started in New York City between 1933 and 1965. Between 1955 and 1965 alone, the city added 439 miles of highways, and even greater plans were in the works.[8]

It was not just grand engineering works that put postwar America on rubber tires. Actions on a much smaller scale reinforced car dependence. Hidden in obscure engineering standards and in the fine print of zoning codes, new mandates rewove the fabric of local streets and neighborhoods by granting the automobile primacy over pedestrians and transit riders.

The highway engineers applied the means of science, but they used them to serve ends imposed from without. When city engineers first observed congested car traffic in the early 1920s, they were struck by the danger of speeding automobiles and the ability of streetcars to move greater numbers of people. The scarce space of city streets could be used most efficiently, many thought, by placing limits on automobiles. Carmakers and their allies in government road-building agencies saw this as a threat. They reacted as they did to another challenge that faced them in the same years, the poisonous nature of leaded gasoline, by seizing control of the science.

A new profession of highway safety was created under industry control. Studebaker Corporation funded the first traffic research institute in 1926, soon yielding its place to the carmakers' trade association. In 1930 a professional society, the Institute of Traffic Engineers, was formed. Ernest Goodrich, ITE's president, was a civil engineer who had long called for the removal of streetcars from city streets; his deputy was Miller McClintock, the chief of the industry-supported institute. In the hands of this new profession, even local streets were designed above all to move automobiles. Practitioners aimed, in the words of a 1955 textbook, "to achieve efficient, free, and rapid flow of traffic; yet, at the same time, to prevent traffic accidents and casualties." Efficiency was measured by the movement of vehicles; a car and its driver were equal to a streetcar full of passengers. Pedestrians were at best an afterthought, and more often an obstacle.[9]

At the request of federal and state highway officials, ITE in 1942 issued its first *Traffic Engineering Handbook*. The prescriptions of this manual aimed at traffic speed and driver comfort. Lanes were to be 12 feet wide for mixed car and truck traffic and 11 feet for cars alone. For parking lanes on urban streets, 13 to 15 feet were recommended. These guidelines were devised for through streets, but by the 1950s the group had recommendations for subdivisions too. On interior streets, it encouraged curves and dead ends with few access points to the perimeter highway—anyone on foot was sent the long way around. Pavement widths were stipulated as 26 to 36 feet, a far cry from Raymond Unwin's 16 to 20 feet, and sure to induce fast driving. In 1965 the minimum street width was hiked to 32 feet.

By the sixties ITE was giving lip service to pedestrians, but it still designed its standards for cars. Dead ends proliferated, rarely completed with pedestrian cut-throughs. The guidelines merely encouraged sidewalks; most suburbs ignored the exhortation and allowed developers to leave them out. For roads and intersections, however, ITE handbooks were often enforced as if written on stone atop Mount Sinai.[10]

As streets widened, parking lots proliferated. Until the invention of the parking meter in 1935, on-street parking was free everywhere. Downtown parking quickly became scarce, and roadways filled with drivers circling in search of parking spaces. Zoning authorities added minimum parking rules to their ordinances, requiring new buildings to accommodate visiting cars off the street.

As is common in zoning matters, status motivations lie hidden behind the stated rationales for parking minimums. Large-lot subdivisions where curb space is plentiful are rarely exempted. Indeed, early off-street parking rules, which mandated one space per house, could shrink the supply of parking. A one-car garage furnishes one space, but that space goes to waste when the owner is away from home. Its driveway eliminates a curb space that was usable twenty-four hours a day.

Curbside parking was disfavored because it was déclassé, suggestive of old neighborhoods with no garages and cars lining the roads. A 1969 planning text says that homeowners often object to on-street parking "from the purely aesthetic standpoint." Aesthetics, here, is best understood as a euphemism. Parking is still allowed on driveways, and any given car is no better-looking there than on the street. But one's own BMW in the driveway is entirely different from someone else's Toyota at the curb.[11]

In 1946 a survey found that parking mandates were imposed in only 17% of cities. Just five years later, 71% had them in effect or on the way. Parking requirements were calculated to handle the most cars that might ever visit a building, with nothing spilling over onto the street. The ITE eventually chimed in with inflated guidelines, based on measurements of the number of cars parked in places where alternatives to driving are nonexistent.

Parking, available without limit, was provided free to the driver. This was a vast government program promoting the automobile, its cost hidden because it was paid with private rather than tax money. Not only was the car directly subsidized, but parking requirements changed the city, discouraging walking and transit use. With land gobbled up by parking lots, commercial districts were less dense and less walkable.[12]

By the late 1930s it was evident that growth had spread past the legal boundaries of many cities and decline had set in within. Downtown retailers and their landlords, losing customers to stores closer to suburban homes, grew concerned when city neighborhoods slid downhill—something once welcomed as a natural process that cleared the way for expansion of the business district. Declining neighborhoods were afflicted with "blight," an ill-defined condition that sometimes meant simply that the residents were not wealthy enough to be good customers. Planners had long debated cures for slums; now they saw blight as nearly as great a threat. Many thought the remedy was to clear whole districts and rebuild them from the ground up, in accordance with their theories. Government would plan, but rebuilding, all but a few left-wingers thought, should be carried out by private owners.[13]

To rebuild large areas at one time, land owned by many parties must be assembled under a single owner. In the course of the 1940s, many states established redevelopment authorities empowered to use eminent domain for this purpose. A few prominent projects, among them New York's Stuyvesant Town and Pittsburgh's Golden Triangle, began quickly. But there was a problem: blight was worth more in the marketplace than developers would pay for the land beneath it. If "slum clearance" was to go forward, subsidies were needed. The federal government, in the 1949 housing act, stepped forward with these funds.[14]

By now the original rationale for the program had disappeared. Planners of the 1920s and 1930s aimed at decongestion—getting rid of poverty by destroying slums and pushing people out of overly crowded neighborhoods. Removal of housing was a positive good. As late as 1944, when Robert Moses put forward an expressway plan for Baltimore that would have destroyed the homes of 19,000 residents, he argued that "the more of them that are wiped out the healthier Baltimore will be in the long run."[15]

But in the postwar years the city was shrinking on its own. Slum clearance got a new purpose—to bring the middle class back downtown—and the Housing Act of 1954 gave it a new name, "urban renewal." As before, however, the rebuilding would be done by private capital. For renewal to yield a profit, the new structures had to be bigger than what they replaced. The economic logic of the program led not to decongestion but to high-rises.

The federal program began slowly, delayed by court battles and the discovery that few municipalities really had the citywide plans that the law required before land could be condemned. Only in the mid-fifties did it gain momentum. Demolition of urban neighborhoods then moved ahead rapidly, propelled by the backing of powerful financial and real estate interests and greased by machine politicians who saw opportunities to sell their friends valuable real estate at below-market prices.[16]

Urban renewal was a disaster for cities. Livable working-class neighborhoods were torn down along with genuine slums. Low-income residents thrown out of their homes had nowhere to go; the Republican congress of 1954 slashed already small public housing programs while doubling the appropriation for urban renewal. And accompanying the carnage of slum clearance was the destruction of homes in the path of interstate highways and the ongoing damage that the interstates, once built, did to their surroundings.

What replaced the old neighborhoods only multiplied the damage. Architectural fashion had changed since the first talk of slum clearance—modernism, with its disdain for adornment, displaced the classicism of the City Beautiful. But the designers of the new urban quarters turned to their inherited planning principles. Cars came before people, and conspicuous waste was the mark of status. The doctrines of suburban subdivision were applied in the middle of cities.

The areas targeted for renewal were old streetcar suburbs and even older city neighborhoods, with their closely spaced and easily walkable street networks. (Grid streets, in themselves, were seen as a sign of blight.) The dense fabric of houses and stores vanished. In its place came sterile towers surrounded by parking lots, divided into superblocks by high-speed arteries that repelled pedestrians. Windswept plazas imitated the uselessness of front lawns. Suburban sprawl, with fewer trees and less grass, had come to the city.[17]

One thing was clear about slum clearance almost as soon as it got going. It did not get rid of slums.

Philadelphia's Yorktown urban renewal project, a low-density suburban-style neighborhood ten blocks from City Hall.
(Courtesy of Special Collections Research Center, Temple University Libraries.)

Northern cities were seeing a massive population turnover. As white renters and the married children of homeowners moved out into suburban subdivisions, a flood of impoverished blacks arrived from the South. Ethnic transitions in urban neighborhoods had never been free of friction; this one was explosive.

Segregated neighborhoods, their boundaries fixed by thirty years of racial covenants, remained in place even after a 1948 Supreme Court ruling made those restrictions legally unenforceable. "Respectable" real estate agents still refused to sell to blacks. Changing the ethnic composition of a neighborhood violated brokers' ethics codes and was grounds for expulsion from the indispensable multiple listing services. Blacks who did move into an all-white area were often targets of violence. Civil rights groups struggled against these practices; antidiscrimination laws were passed locally and, in 1968, nationally. But enforcement faltered in the face of local resistance. The expanding black population was housed, in its vast majority, by the conversion of all-white neighborhoods to all-black.

Racial turnover was commonly brought about by the ugly process of *blockbusting*. In an all-white neighborhood near the boundary, a single house would be sold to a black, or an apartment rented—sometimes it was enough to pay a black mother to walk down the street with a stroller. Real estate operators, eager to cash in, spread panic among white residents. Homeowners would sell quickly and cheaply. The speculators turned around and sold or rented to blacks, who were forced by their lack of housing options to pay higher prices.

White neighborhoods, often helped along by local real estate agents, banded together to keep blacks out. The reasons for opposition to change are easy to understand. Conversion often brought crowding; new black residents of single-family neighborhoods, struggling to pay mortgages, would take in boarders, or investors would convert homes to boarding houses. In an era of disappearing blue-collar jobs and rising crime rates, the arrival of lower-income tenants raised fears of lawlessness. Sensationalist media fanned these fears with reporting on the crime- and drug-ridden neighborhoods that black buyers were fleeing. Demographics shifted rapidly once a "tipping point" was passed; refugees from urban renewal joined new arrivals from the South to create an immense population pressure. Three or four years after the first black family moved in, a neighborhood would be entirely African American.

Class resentments mixed with racial prejudice in the resistance of white residents. The racial borderlines ran through old neighborhoods where federal lending guidelines had discouraged reinvestment. Houses were old and had low market values; owners feared that after selling out they would be short of funds to buy elsewhere. White supporters of fair housing laws often lived in wealthier sections where single-family houses were protected from change by zoning, covenants, and high real estate prices.[18]

Although times were prosperous and unemployment low, crime and welfare dependency rose. Riots in 1965, 1967, and 1968 heightened racial tensions, and *inner city* became a shorthand expression that meant poor, black, and dangerous. Homeowner resistance to racial change exploded onto the national scene as a *white backlash* that Republican politicians would exploit for decades to come.

Once housing discrimination was outlawed in 1968, the FHA and banks were forced to begin lending in cities. A final explosion of blockbusting ensued. The practice then faded away; there was no money to be made once blacks no longer paid higher prices than whites.[19]

The 1968 housing law tried to solve the problems of public housing projects, by then widely recognized. New varieties of subsidized low-income housing were authorized, smaller buildings that could be sited in suburbs as well as cities. The Richard Nixon administration—which gained great political advantage by stirring up white backlash—at first vigorously promoted the dispersal of low-income housing into the suburbs. By the end of the decade public housing of all kinds was violently unpopular. The entire program expired in

1973 when a presidential order halted construction of subsidized housing for the poor and middle class.[20]

The racial crisis left a strong imprint on the politics of land use, as racism reinforced the already ingrained belief in the importance of the social pecking order. In the white urban neighborhoods that remained, the instinct to resist change congealed into a fierce determination, often given political form by civic associations. The long-standing suburban antipathy to the city persisted, made more intense by school busing orders that left suburban towns alone and integrated schools within the city's legal boundaries. Public transit, already disdained as the vehicle of the less affluent, was now feared as a carrier of black criminals.

Elite opinion and the mass media did much to promote these trends by portraying urban issues, in which race, class, and economics were intertwined, as purely racial. It was much easier for affluent integrationists to pin the blame for center-city problems on the racism of others than to set blockbusting battles in the broader context of zoning and transportation. Their own suburbs, a wider look might show, perpetuated a system of social sorting that pitted blacks against whites in decaying urban neighborhoods. Race, in a backward way, thus joined property values, beauty, and sanitation as a code word for status-seeking.

4

Ticky-Tacky Boxes

The project of remaking the world in the image of the Country Club District of Kansas City never lacked for skeptics. Living, breathing, complex cities had their lovers.

These early lovers were few in number. They did not build, they made no laws or ordinances, and often they barely knew what it was they loved. The men and women who made things happen hardly noticed them. But in the realm of culture they rode high.

The first to be infatuated with the city were artists. In the course of the nineteenth century, a little world of impoverished poets, writers, musicians, and painters began to float around the less expensive districts of great cities. For the bohemians, as they became known, self-expression and rejection of the conventional were high virtues; aesthetic experiment was joined to spiritual and sexual exploration. In Paris and London, where they gathered, their art and their lives were soon celebrated. They burst onto the Parisian scene in 1830 and are still remembered through Puccini's opera.

New York, in the middle of the 1800s, already possessed its own artistic demimonde, but it was one that languished in obscurity. The city's bohemia flitted from here to there until the end of the century, when it found a place to settle down and flourish. It came to pass, as O. Henry recounted it in 1910, somewhat by happenstance:

> To quaint old Greenwich Village the art people soon came prowling, hunt-ing for north windows and eighteenth-century gables and Dutch attics and

low rents. Then they imported some pewter mugs and a chafing dish or two from Sixth Avenue, and became a "colony."[1]

It wasn't just art people. Greenwich Village wished as passionately for the overthrow of the economic order as for the overturning of the old aesthetics. Leftist writers like Max Eastman and John Reed flocked there. The marriage of artistic self-expression to radicalism created an American formula—European bohemia was mostly apolitical—and it is a formula that still endures.

This was a proudly urban combination. Municipal reformers from old New York and Boston families might disdain the cities and their new immigrant populations. For young radicals who flocked to Greenwich Village from small-town America in the years around the First World War, crowded streets and tenements were something to embrace. The juxtaposition of slum and salon was among the chief enticements—for refugees from the stultifying uniformity of small town and suburb, the intellectual and political ferment of the Jewish Lower East Side was an exhilarating change.[2]

Still, a contradiction was buried in the Greenwich Village synthesis of politics and art. Radicals and bohemians both rejected middle-class conformism, but to different ends. One sought to level hierarchies; the other erected its own ranking system to replace the conventional scale. One rejected affluence; the other wished everyone could enjoy it. Bohemian outrage against the bourgeoisie had, perhaps, more in common with aristocratic disdain than with proletarian revolt. Its ethos was akin to the knightly values Veblen identified with the leisure class, disdaining the humdrum, domestic, and routinely productive to exalt self-expression, instinct, and authenticity.[3] The working class aspired, in no small part, to what the Village spurned; what would happen if workers' demands were met? A thin line separated comradeship from condescension.

Greenwich Village and its urban sensibility found a resonance. By the twenties, artistic enclaves had grown up in other cities—in Chicago's Towertown, on San Francisco's Russian Hill, in the French Quarter of New Orleans—and expatriate American writers established a colony in Paris.[4] Nonconformism was their credo, and it hardly escaped notice that uniformity was the governing principle of the emerging suburbia. Writers need not treat urban themes—no one would turn to Ernest Hemingway or F. Scott Fitzgerald to understand the daily routine of city streets—and they might sometimes abandon the city for rural retreats. But by the way they lived they affirmed that urban diversity ranked above suburban homogeneity.

Jesse Nichols was still perfecting his subdivision techniques in Kansas City, yet he and his kind were already in the crosshairs of the arbiters of culture. Sinclair Lewis, a political radical if not a bohemian, fired the heavy artillery. His *Babbitt* was a comic portrait of the suburban conformist of 1922. A firm Republican, of course, and a strict Presbyterian, George F. Babbitt had a clear credo:

> The ideal of American manhood and culture isn't a lot of cranks sitting around chewing the rag about their Rights and their Wrongs, but a God-fearing, hustling, successful, two-fisted Regular Guy, who belongs to some church with pep and piety to it, who belongs to the Boosters or the Rotarians or the Kiwanis....

For the real estate promoters of the time, conformism was the very essence of a successful business strategy. So it was only fitting that Sinclair's protagonist was a realtor, sponsor of a "high-class restricted development." The principles of suburban land use were as self-evident as the canons of the Republican Party and the Rotary Club. Babbitt was, we are told, ignorant of "all landscape architecture save the use of curving roads." America might not be perfect, he was willing to concede, but that was because "we've got a lot to do in the way of extending the paving of motor boulevards."

The educated American middle class, eagerly buying up houses in the Country Club District and its imitations, recognized the man who sold those homes. Readers jumped at the chance to think of themselves as better than him. *Babbitt* was a bestseller, and the name entered the language. Even George F. Babbitt himself, ever a reflection of his surroundings, looked down on the crass materialism he saw in others. He was not, he insisted, one of those who "don't see the spiritual and mental side of American supremacy."[5]

American culture continued in the 1930s to value urban life as American life did not, but it did so in a different way. Bohemianism gave way to economic radicalism, the ordinary man and woman were no longer disdained, and the suburb was made immune from criticism by its very ordinariness.

The New Deal brought the previously excluded into the American mainstream, and the largest group of the excluded was city dwellers—the Catholic and Jewish immigrants and their children. But political inclusion was not matched with cultural recognition. Socially conscious writers and artists favored rural themes—the California migrants of John Steinbeck's novels, the impoverished countryside of Dorothea Lange's photographs, the lumberjacks and fishermen of Rockwell Kent's paintings, the Appalachia of folk singers. New Deal culture welcomed city people, yet the city itself was still somehow less than fully accepted.

New housing tracts rolled outward after the Second World War, and the suburbs quickly came again under critical fire. Not until the sixties would the bombardment be heavy enough to slow the juggernaut of sprawl development, but a steady sniping came from two sides. The academic and literary establishment, turning away from radicalism, still assailed the stifling conformism of the Levittowns of the world. And urban bohemias, by their very existence, questioned the premises of suburbia.

It was indeed an age of conformity, but bohemia maintained itself and even slowly grew. Alongside it, and often overlapping, a new gay subculture emerged among men made conscious of their sexuality by wartime service. Greenwich Village was more than ever a magnet, now not just the home of artists, writers, and activists, but the birthplace of a musical style, folk music. Chicago's Towertown had lost its special character, but the French Quarter of New Orleans remained, protected since 1936 by an amendment to the state constitution. New centers of cultural and sexual dissent sprouted in decrepit corners of big cities: North Beach in San Francisco, Venice in Los Angeles, and elsewhere.

Places like Greenwich Village and the French Quarter were no longer slums. Union wages and postwar prosperity lifted their working-class population out of poverty. The artistic and intellectual "colonies," still minorities, grew in numbers and attracted newcomers who were settled and stably employed. But artistic self-expression remained closely allied to youth and urban poverty. The beatnik, a new edition of an old style, brought rejection of suburban conformism to a new level. Where earlier bohemias had been poor out of necessity or out of devotion to art, poverty was now a preference. For the beats, lack of money was a point of pride.[6]

The beats were no model for established writers and scholars; it was a time when intellectuals were moving from the fringe of society into the mainstream of affluence. Even so, the rise of postwar conservativism drew liberals' attention to the plague of conformism. The seat of this malady was easy to locate—in the dull, undifferentiated suburbs. Social science was now the rage, so the criticism took the form of academic studies as well as fiction. A new literary form, the best-selling work of sociology, brought this message to a wide public.

William Whyte's *The Organization Man*, a detailed study of a new Chicago suburb, was on the bestseller list for a year after its 1956 publication.

Houses in Daly City, California, the suburb that inspired Malvina Reynolds's "Little Boxes."
(Courtesy of Adrian M. Hayes.)

Whyte described his subjects in sympathetic detail, yet the book was read as a deeply critical work. Suburbia was a sink of conformism, dominated by a generation of bureaucrats who worked in large corporations.

Vance Packard's *The Status Seekers*, a more popularly written book, was a number-one bestseller in 1959. Rigid stratification, it warned, was destroying the openness of American society. No treatment of this topic could pass over the pecking order of real estate. "A great deal of thought, on the part of builders, has gone into finding symbols of higher status," Packard explained, and he went on to give a lengthy catalogue of those symbols. The "rather frightening, headlong trend toward social stratification by residential area" particularly bothered him: "Even more oppressive than the uniformity of these new one-layer town developments is the synthetic, manipulated quality of the community life found in many of them."[7]

Many readers of these works were living the life they were warned against, and others were surely thinking of moving to the suburbs. Some, no doubt, wanted only to learn how to acquire the status symbols and move ahead in the organization. Still, the criticism stuck. A foundation was in place for debates to come.

It was in 1962 that the two strands of discontent, the intellectual and the countercultural, came together in a folk song. The sight of houses covering a hillside in Daly City, just outside San Francisco, inspired Malvina Reynolds to compose "Little Boxes." She saw Daly City from the highway, passing through on her way from one bohemia to another. In South Berkeley she lived down the street from an anarchist commune. Her destination was a political meeting in the countercultural outpost of La Honda, where writer Ken Kesey would soon host the LSD parties made famous by Tom Wolfe's *The Electric Kool-Aid Acid Test*.

"Little Boxes," a minor hit after Pete Seeger rerecorded it in 1963, is remembered on the Left to this day. Its target, or at least its intended target, is the wealthy suburban establishment:

> *And the people in the houses*
> *All went to the university,*
> *Where they were put in boxes*
> *And they came out all the same,*
> *And there's doctors and lawyers,*
> *And business executives,*
> *And they're all made out of ticky tacky*
> *And they all look just the same.*
> *And they all play on the golf course*
> *And drink their martinis dry....*

But these short verses, examined closely, are full of ambiguity. As much as "Little Boxes" is on target as cultural metaphor, its lyrics are bad sociology. The tract houses of Daly City were San Francisco's Levittown, built for the working class. Doctors, lawyers, and business executives resided elsewhere, in bigger homes on larger lots. And, even more to the point, they lived in houses that didn't look like those boxes in Daly City.[8]

Someone who listened to "Little Boxes," but not too closely, might hear a song about the sameness of houses rather than the conformism of people. And ears were open to hear that song. In the folk scene of the sixties, as in the Greenwich Village of a half-century earlier, feelings of cultural superiority were buried beneath the Leftism. The satirist Tom Lehrer sang to the same audience, and he knew its weaknesses. "The nicest thing about a protest song," he observed, "is that it makes you feel so good." In "The Folk Song Army" he portrayed a certain type of listener:

> *We all hate poverty, war, and injustice,*
> *Unlike the rest of you squares.*

Is the enemy the boxes or the people in them? Do we seek a better world or to be better than the neighbors? These might be fine distinctions when the antidote to suburban sterility was the music of Malvina Reynolds and the drugs of Ken Kesey. But the "Folk Song Army," like generations before it, would grow older, and soon it would buy real estate.

After a while the counterculture faded from view. But it hardly went away; the memory of the sixties was absorbed into the mainstream of commercialism. While many survivors strove to maintain the ideals of their youth, among some aging hippies and more of their camp followers egalitarianism gradually faded into the snobbery of nonconformity. In an older house, built by an earlier generation, they could stand out from those conformists in new suburbs full of boxes made of ticky-tacky. Never mind that the neighbors were those doctors, lawyers, and business executives. At least the houses didn't all look just the same.

5

Jane Jacobs versus the Planners

Cities in the 1950s were visibly in trouble. Factories closed, downtown stores lost customers, office jobs moved to the suburbs, and residential neighborhoods, with rare exceptions, went downhill as they aged.

That something was going wrong was not in doubt. But established opinion, loath to admit mistakes, placed the blame on natural processes. The housing economist William Grigsby summed up the era's conventional wisdom in words that the next half-century would prove spectacularly wrong:

> With a few notable exceptions, the *residential* real estate market works only once. It creates, alters, maintains, and improves, and eventually discards assets, but seems incapable of providing for their replacement on the site.[1]

The antidote for this supposed market failure was urban renewal. City neighborhoods were rebuilt with separated land uses, superblocks, high-speed roadways, and barren plazas. The solutions for other urban problems were similar: to make cities even more like the suburbs that were strangling them. The cure for traffic jams was more roads. To bring shoppers back downtown, store buildings were torn down and replaced with parking lots.

The technocrats who prescribed these remedies were quick to reject any questioning of their science by the untrained masses. Their discipline was, or so they claimed, akin to engineering. It was not a matter of taste or social convention but the logically determined response to the facts. On this façade of objectivity rested the jobs of credentialed planners, and much more. An edifice of authorities and agencies, along with the politicians who sponsored them, was tightly linked with the developers and contractors who profited from government-subsidized land and large-scale construction.

Critics there were of this commercial juggernaut, but for the most part they shared its basic doctrines. Apostles of the automobile, a Le Corbusier and a Frank Lloyd Wright, dominated the architectural avant-garde. Planners did realize that the new interstate highways would hollow out cities, but even the profession's dissidents were slow to question basic principles.[2] No antidote could be devised for what was poisoning the cities until the underlying causes of the malady were diagnosed.

Jane Jacobs was the one who dared to say the emperor was naked.

She arrived in New York from Scranton, Pennsylvania, fresh out of high school in 1934, and quickly fell in love with the city. She got a job as a secretary and moved with her sister to Greenwich Village, where she would spend the next thirty-four years. Frequent walks took her through Manhattan's extraordinarily specialized business districts, and her acute and readable observations soon made her a magazine writer. She married and with her husband bought a three-story building on Hudson Street. They paid a thousand dollars less than the price of the cheapest house in Levittown.

In 1952 she talked herself into a job at *Architectural Forum*, where she was sent to report on the gathering wave of urban renewal. She didn't like what she saw. The "renewed" neighborhoods were empty of life. A short walk outside showed what was missing—streets full of little stores, children playing, people hanging around. Yet these were the blocks, the planners told her, that were next to be demolished.

Substituting for an editor who took ill, she gave a talk at Harvard in 1956 to an all-star audience of architects and planners. Word of her unconventional views spread, and William Whyte, author of *The Organization Man* and an editor at *Fortune* magazine, had her turn the talk into an article. "Downtown Is for People" brought her ideas to a larger audience. Then came a grant from the Rockefeller Foundation that allowed her to work full time on a book. In January 1961 she completed the manuscript of *The Death and Life of Great American Cities*.[3]

Where others had started from the defects of cities and sought ways to correct them, Jacobs began by asking what makes cities succeed. The simplest level

Jane Jacobs with petitions opposing urban renewal in Greenwich Village, 1961.
(Courtesy of the Library of Congress, World Telegram & Sun collection.)

was a single street. Watching her own block in Greenwich Village day after day, she perceived a complex pattern of order among disorder, what she called the ballet of the sidewalk. The dancers were young and old, shopkeepers and strangers, they lived on the block, they worked nearby, they were visitors from the suburbs. All did their part in making the street a safe, welcoming place. Together they made it truly urban.

Jane Jacobs stood on her Hudson Street sidewalk, an Archimedes whose lever was her power of seeing the everyday things that others missed. She reasoned from one observation to another until she overturned the world of city planning. "Eyes on the street" were what made cities safe. To keep those eyes there all day, uses must be densely mixed, not sorted and thinned out. The street needs attractive uses that draw people onto the sidewalk, with variety that maintains their interest. The streetcorner is especially valuable, the site of human encounters both habitual and unexpected.

She summarized her findings in four principles:

1. The district, and indeed as many of its internal parts as possible, must serve more than one primary function, preferably more than two.
2. Most blocks must be short; that is, streets and opportunities to turn corners must be frequent.
3. The district must mingle buildings that vary in age and condition, including a good proportion of old ones so that they vary in the economic yield they must produce. This mingling must be fairly close-grained.
4. There must be a sufficiently dense concentration of people, for whatever purposes they may be there.

This turned the received doctrines of city-building on their head. Density is good, monotony bad. Automobiles yield to those on foot; superblocks make way for grid streets. Permanence brings decay. And enforced separation of land uses, the principle on which all else rested, is not just unnecessary but actively destructive.

These ideas did not merely dispute the design principles of urban renewal; they challenged the very essence of the planning enterprise. Cities, as Jacobs saw them, are not engineering problems. They are frames for the spontaneous flowering of the human spirit.[4]

Conventional planners were quick to find fault. Jacobs, they alleged, spoke for literary bohemians and not for ordinary folk. It was true that Greenwich Village benefited from an unusual mixture of people and activities. Bars where longshoremen drank in the afternoon were hardly out of the ordinary in those years, but few such establishments could boast the evening literary clientele of Hudson Street's White Horse Tavern. Such complaints issued from the establishment, but not just from there. Herbert Gans, an early opponent of urban renewal, chided Jacobs for failing to understand that the middle class did not share the tastes of intellectuals, artists, and tourists.[5]

This objection was off the mark. Jacobs' ideas rested on a wider inquiry; she put Hudson Street directly under her microscope simply because she lived there. Before she ever organized her own neighborhood, she protested urban renewal in the bohemian-free precincts of East Harlem. Even Hudson Street was a place mostly of shopkeepers and blue-collar workers. The 1950 census, taken a few years after she moved in, counted in her fourteen-block neighborhood 149 apartments that had no kitchen and shared a bathroom in the hall.[6]

For that matter, Jacobs was not the first to point out the sterility of housing projects. Another independent thinker, George Orwell, saw the same

thing two decades sooner. His 1937 account of the life of the English working class, *The Road to Wigan Pier*, condemned public housing without pubs
and corner stores as "monstrously inhuman." In Orwell's judgment, the
new homes were barely better than the Dickens-era slums of Liverpool and
Manchester. Orwell knew that workers are not bohemians—no book could
be clearer on that point. *Wigan Pier* is still remembered for the scorn it pours
on "that dreary tribe of high-minded women and sandal-wearers and bearded
fruit-juice drinkers who come flocking towards the smell of 'progress' like
blue-bottles to a dead cat."[7]

The claim that only intellectuals like diverse and lively streets is still heard
today, but it has long since lost all plausibility. The passage of time has made
clear how widely this taste is shared. Greenwich Village, like other places, has
fallen victim to its own desirability. The house Jane and Bob Jacobs bought for
$7000 was put on the market in 2009 for $3.5 million.

Death and Life did have its shortcomings, even if they were not what its detractors complained about.

For one thing, the book says almost nothing about transit. You walk,
you drive, occasionally you take the bus. The subway, so central to the life of
Manhattan, does not make an appearance until page 467. For all Jacobs' ability
to see what others overlooked, the subway was so much part of the landscape
that she failed to perceive its importance to New York. The further development of public transportation, she wrote, should come only after the revitalization of neighborhoods.[8]

This was, for the most part, a harmless error. In San Francisco, where some
desired to freeze the city in its existing form, opponents of the new subway
could cite Jacobs.[9] But readers elsewhere rarely noticed what was missing.
For several years now, complaints that automobiles were strangling cities and
pleas for new rail lines had flooded newspapers. Outside Manhattan and San
Francisco, lovers of cities knew all too well the insufficiencies of their transit
networks. The New York subway itself had been starved of investment, and
when the book came out it was beginning to fall apart. People who took Jane
Jacobs seriously understood the need for more subways.[10]

Another weakness of *Death and Life* is the defensive nature of its prescriptions. We read much about *unslumming* but little about how to build places
that will never be slums. A chapter about how to make more lively neighborhoods is titled "Forces of Decline and Regeneration"—regeneration but
not creation. Here Jacobs, elsewhere so far ahead of her time, is very much a
thinker of her own day.

Nothing in the book is more prophetic than its warning of the curse of success. So many want to live in a diverse locality that the wealthy, and especially the wealthy and childless, crowd in and destroy what attracted them. "The demand for lively and diversified city areas," Jacobs realized, "is too great for the supply."[11] When these words were written, the pace of change was slow. The bohemian invasion of Greenwich Village was then sixty years old, yet part of the neighborhood had recently been condemned as a slum and more was threatened with the same. Today things move far more quickly. By now nearly every neighborhood Jacobs praised in 1961 has lost or is on the way to losing its diversity of income.

The needed supply of diverse neighborhoods, clearly, has not been forthcoming, but why? This is a question Jacobs does not answer. Her critique of zoning is thorough and pertinent, but she does not explain why the theories she refutes are so attractive. Here Herbert Gans was more perceptive. A major force preserving slums, he pointed out, is that "no one who has any say in the matter wants people of lower income or status in his neighborhood."[12]

As the end of *Death and Life* approaches, oversights accumulate and start to obscure the achievements of the early pages. But then Jacobs leaves us with a parting reminder of her brilliance, a stunning tour de force of intuition.

Her final chapter, about "the kind of problem a city is," leans heavily on an essay by the mathematician Warren Weaver, a founder of information theory. Weaver's paper on science and complexity is now a scientific classic, a groundbreaking effort that prefigured whole fields of research.[13] Jacobs had a research grant and an office at the Rockefeller Foundation, where Weaver was a vice president, and surely she learned directly from him. For someone with no scientific training, merely to recognize the significance of Weaver's concepts was an accomplishment. But she went further.

In an extended discussion of these ideas, Jacobs identifies cities as problems in *organized complexity*. Their behavior cannot be understood by mere addition of component parts or from statistical averages. She then goes forward on her own and lists some habits of mind useful for understanding cities. "Think about processes," she advises, and "seek for unaverage clues." A failed city is a place of low energy where nothing departs from the average; the unaverage, the interesting, what she has been calling the diverse, arises only in high-energy systems.[14]

Here Jacobs anticipates developments in the physics of complexity that were yet to come. She was no student of science. Fractal mathematics and nonequilibrium thermodynamics were surely not things she thought about or even would have understood if she had. She was a writer and thinker of genius.

Death and Life was an instant classic, and it still draws readers after half a century. Yet its message has been very incompletely heeded. Roads are still laid out in superblocks, streets deadened by empty plazas, new buildings kept apart from old. Mixed use and urban density now win the favor of architects and planners, but the public often still resists.

The illnesses that afflicted America's cities were more than the consequence of wrong ideas. The forces of sprawl were deeply embedded in the country's culture and economy. Jane Jacobs' intellectual achievement was only a starting point for change.

6

Saving the City

Ears were open to hear Jane Jacobs' message. The racial and economic illnesses of old urban neighborhoods were growing more acute, and the malady had begun to spread beyond their borders. Chronic psychological and circulatory disorders afflicted even seemingly healthy areas of recent construction.

Burgeoning suburbs offered no worthy substitute for declining cities. The spiritual emptiness of consumerism and conformism was matched by the physical ugliness of public places. A drive down a suburban commercial strip showed that empty space between buildings is no guarantee of architectural beauty.

The relentless spread of subdivisions destroyed time-honored landscapes of farm and forest. Pundits foresaw the growth of a single vast metropolitan area stretching from Virginia to Maine, annihilating vast stretches of countryside.

As the fear of human congestion receded, a new plague of automotive overcrowding took its place. The *New York Times* in 1959 highlighted a commuter crisis of traffic jams and failing railroads in three days of front-page articles. Headlines laid the blame on what was by then well-known as *urban sprawl*. The experts, other than what the *Times* called "a few radical advocates of the automobile," held it impossible to meet the transportation needs of the modern city without vast improvements in mass transit. New York, with its subways and railroads, was far better off than Los Angeles, "a jelly-like glob of humanity, oozing through a sea of smog on creaking wheels."[1]

The champions of suburbanization and road-building were now on the defensive, intellectually if not politically. As early as 1958, a National Health Forum could be told to look past "the well-advertised cracks in the picture windows of the suburbs." In 1960, a Brookings Institution economist felt compelled to stand up for the automobile against critics who said it was "polluting the atmosphere, clogging the highways, and destroying the city." The best case he could make was that it was better than the horse.[2]

Even Richard Nixon, sticking with the suburban status quo in his run for president that year, thought it wise to dress up inaction as a call for change. "We can deal with this so-called 'urban sprawl,'" he declared, "only by steady support of effective and farsighted zoning powers in states and counties."[3]

The well-entrenched sprawl machine, backed by powerful real estate and construction interests, could easily shrug off the complaints of intellectuals. Only the power of an organized political force might slow the juggernaut. But that force was gathering on the horizon. As the pace of highway-building and urban renewal accelerated, the destruction of urban neighborhoods brought forth a massive grass-roots opposition.

The first years of slum clearance, in the late 1940s and early 1950s, had not been without controversy. But the focus of early complaints was on what was built—and on the skin color of the new residents—rather than on what was destroyed. Where most voters were homeowners, as in Detroit and Chicago, opponents of public housing won quick victories. This left a legacy: urban renewal, in these cities, would keep away from white neighborhoods.[4] Only the black sections of town would be "renewed," and before long critics were saying that urban renewal might better be called "Negro removal."

The 1949 housing law, by bringing private developers into the rebuilding process, reinforced the destructive impetus. Land selected to be cleared now had to be capable of being rebuilt profitably. Where New Deal public housing programs had targeted the worst slums, developers wanted to go where new housing would be easiest to sell. Almost any older section of a city could be diagnosed with the vaguely defined malady of blight, so renewal agencies sent their wrecking balls to relatively healthy neighborhoods near downtown.[5]

As the pace of demolition accelerated in the late 1950s, a growing opposition could no longer be dismissed as racially motivated. The Achilles heel of urban renewal was relocation. A federal law that required equivalent replacement housing for the displaced was widely ignored. Renewal projects sent the poor flooding into surrounding areas, sometimes creating more slums than were removed. Blacks suffered doubly: they were the favored targets

South Margin Street in Boston's old West End awaits demolition as suburban-style towers rise behind it in Charles River Park.
(Courtesy of the West End Museum.)

for removal, and the prevailing pattern of segregated housing confined their search for new homes to a few already overcrowded neighborhoods.[6]

The turning point came for urban renewal with the destruction of Boston's West End, an area on the edge of downtown that was almost all white. This working-class neighborhood was designated as blighted based on studies that greatly overstated the amount of substandard housing. In 1954 the city chose as the developer a newly created company that had only $1000 in equity. At the head of this corporation was a twenty-seven-year-old Harvard-educated lawyer. He had gone to work for Mayor John Hines after organizing a "good government" group that delivered key political backing to the mayor's election campaign.

Residents opposed the plan, but they were slow to organize and made no headway in the face of united support for rebuilding from Boston's business, political, social, and religious leadership. In April 1958, eviction notices went out to 2700 households, and a year and a half later all were gone. Forty-eight acres of land were condemned for $7.40 a square foot, revalued at $1.40, and leased to the developer for around 9¢ a year. A singularly sterile assortment of luxury housing towers and institutional buildings replaced the West End; the dispersed residents mourned their loss for decades afterward.[7]

Other sections of the city observed the fate of the West End with horror. In South Boston and Charlestown, redevelopment faced fierce opposition from homogeneous Irish neighborhoods that wielded great influence in local politics. They saw urban renewal as an attack on the city's ethnic communities by the old Protestant elite. The South Boston project was stopped cold; in Charlestown, after a long struggle, rebuilding went forward on a much-reduced scale. Meanwhile, the renewal agency extended the emptiness of the rebuilt West End into the heart of downtown with Government Center, a vast bare plaza flanked by parking garages and a forbidding concrete City Hall.[8]

Urban renewal was already under attack from the grass roots in other cities, and then a series of books made it controversial at the national level. *The Death and Life of Great American Cities* in 1961 was followed a year later by Herbert Gans' description of life in the West End before its demolition, *The Urban Villagers*. The liberal authors of these critiques were joined by a conservative, Martin Anderson, whose *The Federal Bulldozer* pointed to many of the same defects in the program. He argued that renewal should be left to the workings of the marketplace.

The market for luxury high-rise apartments was quickly sated, and developers lost interest in buying large tracts of empty city land. By the early sixties, wholesale demolition became rare. Urban renewal programs then tried to reconstitute themselves by launching initiatives to rehabilitate neighborhoods. The federal program, enmeshed in controversy, finally expired in the Nixon administration. The precedent of using eminent domain to assemble land for private development lives on, used more selectively in the absence of federal subsidy but still a matter of controversy.

Resistance was gathering as well against the march of highway building. The first major victory came in Greenwich Village, won in large part by Jane Jacobs herself. Robert Moses had been trying for years to punch a four-lane extension of Fifth Avenue through Washington Square, which served the Village as its neighborhood park. Jacobs joined the opposition in 1955 and quickly rose to leadership. Thousands signed petitions, and such notables as Eleanor Roosevelt, Margaret Mead, and Lewis Mumford were drawn in. The campaign steadily gained momentum and in 1958 New York's political leadership was won over. The city scrapped the road plan and removed an existing bus turnaround from the park.[9]

But Moses had much bigger ideas. Back in 1929, planners had mapped out no fewer than seven east–west highways through the city. Moses first tackled the Cross-Bronx Expressway. Bulldozing over local opponents, he punched the roadway through seven miles of crowded city blocks. Healthy South Bronx neighborhoods turned into a legendary slum. Next on his agenda were

Malvina Reynolds sings to a rally against freeway building in San Francisco, May 17, 1964.
(Courtesy of The Bancroft Library, University of California, Berkeley.)

two elevated interstates across Manhattan. One, at 30th Street, hit obstacles in the 1940s and never made headway. But after his defeat in Washington Square, Moses moved ahead to build the Lower Manhattan Expressway, a mammoth ten-lane elevated highway through what is now SoHo. An epic ten-year battle ensued, with Jacobs again a leader of the opposition. Only in 1969 was the project finally killed.[10]

In San Francisco, too, resistance surfaced early. The sight of the first downtown elevated interstate, the Embarcadero Freeway along the water-front, horrified the city. A petition drive led the board of supervisors to cancel seven of ten proposed interstates in 1959. Still on the books was the Panhandle Freeway, intended to create a through route for motorists across the heart of the city to the Golden Gate Bridge. It was a road that would not die, despised by the populace but resurrected again and again under state pressure. Even the election of an anti-freeway mayor in 1963 was not enough to kill it. The following May, thousands rallied on threatened park-land; Malvina Reynolds performed a new song written for the occasion, "The Cement Octopus." Two years later San Francisco's freeway-building era finally came to an end when the board of supervisors, by a narrow majority, issued a definitive rejection.[11]

In Washington, DC, the highway builders in 1959 put forward a gran-diose plan for a spider's web of four concentric beltways linked by radial highways. Opposition sprang up immediately along the northwestern arm; the well-connected residents of upscale neighborhoods reached into the White House and managed to slow down the entire program. The radial that headed north traversed low-income black neighborhoods and the emerging bohemian enclave of Takoma Park; there a more radical opposition emerged. Leaflets called for "no more white highways through black bedrooms." In the end, only a piece of the downtown loop was built; nearly all remaining interstates within city limits were taken off the map in 1971.[12]

In Boston there were a dozen years of struggle before two interstates through the city's old streetcar suburbs were canceled in 1971. Here as elsewhere the movement was broadly based, but the order of assembly was the reverse of Washington's. Poor neighborhoods objected first; Harvard and MIT professors joined in later. Eventually the entire spectrum of political opinion from Samuel Huntington to Noam Chomsky could be found among the signers of a single protest letter.[13]

By the mid-sixties, highway battles raged in cities throughout the country, and activists were linking up. The 1966 Transportation Act restricted the destruction of parks and historic buildings by highways, and it downgraded the Bureau of Public Roads inside a new Transportation Department. President Lyndon Johnson appointed expressway skeptic Alan Boyd as secretary and put another reformer, Lowell Bridwell, in charge of its highway programs.[14]

The fight against urban expressways gained impetus when the Highway Act of 1973 allowed money designated for highways to be used for mass transit. Cities could cancel roads without losing federal aid and the jobs it brought. Interstate money saved the Washington Metro when budget shortfalls threatened the project's collapse and built new subway lines in Chicago, Boston, and New York. Still, the federal aid program remained heavily biased—transit projects required far more local matching funds than roads. And many states had their own rules, enacted years earlier at the urging of federal authorities and the highway lobby, that forbade transfer of highway money to transit.[15]

The highway revolts prevented vast destruction. Plans barely imaginable today, such as elevated interstates through lower Manhattan and New Orleans's French Quarter, had once seemed unstoppable. Still, the movement won only partial victories. The fundamental premise that expressways are a good way of moving people in cities was never overturned; highways were blocked by appeals to values that had nothing to do with transportation. And the juggernaut was not halted everywhere. The strength of broad-based movements, reaching across divisions of class and race, was required. Where these coalitions could not be assembled—and they were especially hard to bring together in conservative Southern cities, where black neighborhoods were often deliberately targeted for destruction—road-building went according to plan.[16] To this day, the centers of Houston, Miami, Los Angeles, Detroit, and other cities are choked by dense highway networks that rend their urban fabric into tatters.

Yet another front was opened in the sixties in the war to save cities. This was preservation of historic buildings.

The pivotal event was the destruction of New York's Pennsylvania Station. The great railroad terminal designed by Charles McKim was a masterpiece of the City Beautiful movement, with high-ceilinged waiting rooms surrounded by a grand colonnade modeled after the ancient Roman Baths of Caracalla. The railroad, at the height of its wealth and power when the station was built, came to parlous straits in the sixties. It sought to sell the air rights over its terminal, demolish the edifice, and move its operations to a low-ceilinged train station in the basement of the new structure.

New York's architects were horrified. The city's population, alerted by a protest committee that quickly won the backing of the *New York Times*, agreed. "The city's investors and planners have aesthetic as well as economic responsibilities," the *Times* said, but no law protected old buildings. Penn Station was torn down in 1963, replaced by a bland office building and an even blander sports arena.[17]

The legal gap was soon filled. In 1965 New York empowered its Landmarks Commission to designate historic buildings, which owners were forbidden to demolish. Federal legislation came a year later, establishing a National Register of Historic Places. Cities throughout the country were quick to follow New York's example.

These successes came at a price. The destruction of cities was halted with double-edged swords that protected the suburban status quo as well. Arguments against urban change dovetailed with the suburban insistence that what was built once should remain forever unaltered. Success in preserving city neighborhoods froze the existing pattern of development more firmly into place, driving new building outward into an ever-expanding sprawl.

For one thing, victories were largely defensive; activists struggled to keep what already existed. They brought to light the previously unrecognized merits of old neighborhoods and slowed the pace of their destruction, but what replaced what could not be saved was as bad as ever. This was a failing whose consequences seemed small at first but would bulk larger as time passed. Robert Moses was no more ruthless a destroyer of working-class housing than the nineteenth-century rebuilder of Paris, Georges-Eugène Haussmann—but Haussmann left his city the Boulevard Saint Germain while Moses' legacy is the Brooklyn-Queens Expressway.

With the issue framed as destruction versus preservation, rather than city versus sprawl, the cry of "stop the bulldozers" could be used to protect the exclusivity of upscale suburbs and newly gentrified sections of cities. Battles against highways and urban renewal were succeeded by fights against non-profit housing on empty lots. The striving to keep out people of lower status could be portrayed as a revolt of the oppressed people against rapacious capitalists, status-seeking disguised in a cloak of self-righteous egalitarianism.[18]

Another legacy of the battle to preserve the cities was excessive trust in the remedy of citizen participation. This was an idea in the air in the sixties, much like planning in the twenties. The rising student New Left organized around the slogan of "participatory democracy," and the centerpiece of President Johnson's War on Poverty was a Community Action Program that required the "maximum feasible participation" of the poor. The urban renewal program had explicit community participation requirements as early as 1961, and Secretary of Transportation Boyd, upon taking office in 1967, called for more community participation in highway decision-making.

The pitched battles of the sixties were succeeded by more mundane local skirmishes. The new rules were, for those with skills and time to deploy them, handy tools to use against public action of almost any kind. Few but the nearest neighbors of routine construction projects care enough to devote much time, and the skills to make involvement meaningful are held disproportionately by the affluent and well educated. The new rules thus empowered nearby property owners more than anyone else. The suburban system of land tenure, the right of landowners to control what neighbors build, was now at home in the city.

Citizen participation was conceived as a means of granting influence to the excluded, but in practice it advantaged those with the time and skills to participate. Affluent communities, urban and suburban alike, had a new way to stake an old claim—and they, unlike the urban poor, had wealth and power behind *their* assertions.[19]

Finally, the means used to halt highway-building were mostly procedural. On top of citizen participation, a 1969 law required Environmental Impact Statements for federally supported construction projects. The statute placed no limit on the damage a project did, but opponents could search for defects in the document. If they found any, and they often did, they could sue to delay the project until the paperwork was fixed. In the short run this helped highway opponents greatly; court-ordered delays legitimated their complaints, and they could use the time to build political support for full cancellation. But at the same time these procedural complexities created a new bias toward sprawl. The fewer the neighbors who might object, the easier it was to build. Highways through empty land on the fringes of cities moved ahead while urban projects, trains and roads alike, bogged down in studies and lawsuits.

The defenders of urban life paid a high price for their accomplishments, but it was a price that had to be paid. The victories of the sixties and seventies, however partial, were essential to the health of cities. Fighting uphill battles against entrenched bureaucratic and economic power, the organizers of the freeway revolt could hardly let the perfect be the enemy of the good.

Reformers of the sixties had another remedy for sprawl, one more forward-looking and endowed with more staying power. This was the revival of rail transit. Here again, success required allies, and in this case coalition-building was especially tricky. New rail lines needed the backing of the same urban business interests that were enemies in battles over highways and urban renewal.

Even at the peak of highway-building and streetcar abandonment, some rail transit was built. Chicago used New Deal public works funds to build a downtown subway tunnel in the thirties and forties. In the fifties, Cleveland built its first subway, and Boston added an off-street trolley line. By 1960, downtown business groups were promoting subway plans in Baltimore, Los Angeles, and Seattle as well, but two, three, and even five decades would have to pass before these efforts bore fruit.[20]

The real return of rail began in San Francisco. The city's geography ruled out freeway-building as the remedy for a declining downtown—there was no good place to put a second highway bridge over San Francisco Bay. By the early 1950s everyone outside the state highway bureaucracy dropped the idea of a new bridge, and downtown developers began to push for a rail tunnel to Oakland. A few years later the freeway revolt gained traction, making it clear that a new rail line was the only possible way to bring more people into downtown.

Progress was slow; there was no hope of funding from either Washington or the state. But in 1962 voters approved a bond issue and local sales tax increase to build a new rail network. Bay Area Rapid Transit, or BART, ran through a tunnel beneath the bay and fanned out in three directions across the East Bay. On the San Francisco side, BART went under Market Street in the bottom half of a two-tiered tunnel. Streetcar tracks were relocated from the street into the upper level of the tunnel, where they now bypassed traffic backups. After lengthy delays caused by the use of unproven new technology, the first passengers arrived downtown in 1973.[21]

Next behind San Francisco was Washington, DC. Here the initiative came from highway opponents, and business tagged along later. The city did not yet have home rule and the federal government ran it as a colony, so political connections were crucial. Road opponents had the ear of the John F. Kennedy administration and managed to win appointments to key planning positions. They put together a modest rail plan for the city and got it approved by Congress in 1965. Bigger things were in the works as Maryland and Virginia suburbs joined the city to establish a regional transit authority. In 1968 this body approved a plan for 98 miles of tracks, with three tunnels through downtown and nine arms reaching far into the suburbs, and it broke ground the next year. Enthusiastically supported by the populace, Metro overcame political perils, construction delays, arguments about routes, and almost endless financial tribulations. Trains began to run in 1974, and in January 2001, after thirty-one years of work, the last of the planned stations opened.[22]

Meanwhile, the Urban Mass Transportation Act of 1964 at last made federal money available for transit. By the seventies cities across the country were building "heavy rail" lines that ran in tunnels, elevated, or on fenced-off surface rights of way. Atlanta, Miami, and Baltimore joined San Francisco and Washington in building entirely new subways, and there were substantial expansions in Philadelphia, Boston, and Chicago. Even New York shook off the stagnation of the Moses years, digging a new tunnel under the East River.

As much as the subways of the seventies were a reaction against urban expressways, their designers shared a premise with the highway builders. The goal was to save the city by bringing suburbanites downtown. New rail networks bypassed dense neighborhoods in the urban core and stretched long tentacles out to distant parking lots. Commuters moved swiftly to downtown offices, but city dwellers' travel needs were less well served. Washington broke the pattern—civil rights leaders insisted on service for the urban poor, and its three rail tunnels span the city's inner residential neighborhoods as well as its downtown office core—and its new rail system is by far the most successful. Today the Washington Metro is the nation's second busiest subway, carrying more riders than older systems in Chicago, Boston, and Philadelphia.

When Malvina Reynolds recorded "The Cement Octopus," she put "Little Boxes" on the flip side. Sterile, conformist suburbs and the destruction of cities were two symptoms of a single disease. The suburbs demanded a solution too.

The Washington (left) and Atlanta (right) subway networks, drawn to identical scale. Both systems were designed principally for suburb-to-city commutes; Washington's is far more useful for trips within the city limits (outlined in gray).

The most visible of the suburbs' problems was ugliness, assaulting the eyes on highways lined with billboards and strip malls. This was something the reformist spirit of the sixties would not ignore. President Johnson's wife, Lady Bird, chose highway beautification as her signature issue. After a fierce legislative battle—the billboard industry did not lack for clout in congress— the Highway Beautification Act was passed, removing billboards from rural stretches of interstate highways.

Others sought less superficial remedies for suburban ills. The Garden City was not dead. Lewis Mumford, then renowned as a social critic, ended his 1961 bestseller *The City in History* with a plea for the revival of Ebenezer Howard's ideal. Mumford called for new cities, planned rather than built for profit, to restore the organic relationship of man to nature.

More practical people had similar ideas. By 1964 two idealistic real estate developers were building new towns outside Washington, DC. Reston, Virginia was the brainchild of Robert Simon. Columbia, Maryland, was developed by James Rouse. Both "planned communities" eventually flourished— they now have nearly 150,000 inhabitants between them—but as antidotes to suburban failure they fell far short of their founders' hopes.

What Reston and Columbia show today is how much better the sixties were at identifying problems than at solving them. Simon condemned suburbs in words that that make him sound like one of today's New Urbanists:

Our present zoning ordinances are largely responsible for the diffusion of our communities into separate, unrelated hunks without focus, identity, or community life. They have helped produce chaos on our highways, monotony in our subdivisions, and ugliness in our shopping centers. [23]

As a cure for these diseases, the two new towns offered a purer version of suburbia—a return to the vision of Radburn, where Simon's father had been a major investor. Homes were built for a range of income levels, but townhouses and apartments were separated from single-family houses and set amid seas of parking lots. Covenants enforced by homeowners' associations separated stores and workplaces from living quarters. Wide roads, built with no sidewalks, surrounded superblocks filled with dead-end streets. Pedestrians had paths of their own, hidden behind the houses.

The idealism of the founders lives on among current residents; liberal Democrats win far more votes than in newer developments nearby. And a city-style ethnic succession has begun, with minorities edging toward dominance on the east side of Columbia and in the southern half of Reston. Yet the labor expended in planning these communities yielded little fruit. Trees hide shopping areas from the road—but the view from the parking lot is the usual strip mall. Footpaths bring a few to workplaces and commuter buses; everything else enforces the usual suburban dependence on the car. Far out in the country when conceived, the two new towns have since been engulfed by exurbia. Little different today from their surroundings, they stand as monuments to a mistaken theory.

As more planned communities followed Reston and Columbia, developers dropped the vision and kept the sprawl. The goal of mixing incomes was forgotten. Roads still lacked sidewalks, and pedestrians got nothing in their place.

Still, suburbs were changing. No longer would they be pure expanses of single-family homes feeding commuters into the city. Powerful economic and political forces were bringing jobs to the suburbs, and with them came a demand for less expensive places to live. Land-use rules changed to fit the new market conditions, and dwellings of inferior social rank—row houses and apartments—were allowed into the suburbs. But politicians could not ignore the wishes of their constituents. Profit-seeking builders contended with status-conscious homeowners, reaching accommodations that left both only partially satisfied and led to consequences intended by neither.

Factories and offices were already springing up at the exits of the new interstates. The outward migration began in Massachusetts along Route 128, an expressway opened in 1951 as a bypass around Boston. At the highway's exits a new landform was created when real estate developer Gerald Blakeley set

An early industrial park on Route 128. Reservoir Place, Waltham, Massachusetts (to the left), which opened in 1955, is entered by a single road next to the cloverleaf.
(U.S. Geological Survey photo.)

out to build "garden type industrial parks." These complexes, their buildings surrounded by parking lots and arranged in vast superblocks, were reachable only by car. By 1957, 140 companies had moved out to Route 128; 96% of them came from Boston's old downtown and streetcar suburbs.

Soon the interstate highway program was ringing cities all over the country with beltways, and jobs followed outward as they had in Boston. Federal policy encouraged the new high-tech defense contractors to avoid downtown locations, presumed to be targets in the event of atomic war. Local governments, especially in the new, less expensive suburbs where children thronged the schools, often welcomed industry for its contribution to the property tax rolls.[24]

The rising price of suburban land meant that single-family houses could no longer be sold at the low prices of a Levittown. For residential builders who aimed at the lower end of the market, the only way to produce an affordable product was to put up row houses. At the same time, high-end developers wanted more flexibility in laying out their subdivisions. Both kinds of developers needed to put houses on smaller lots than zoning laws allowed.

Such clustering had to be sold to the existing residents, who controlled zoning boards. In 1960 the developers' Urban Land Institute floated the concept of the *planned unit development*. A buffer zone controlled by a homeowners association would surround new buildings, keeping overall densities low. Prestigious features such as landscaping, tennis courts, or golf courses could be placed on the unbuilt land. Extra protection against loss of status came from covenants that governed the appearance and use of houses in minute detail. The Federal Housing Administration agreed in 1963 to approve loans in such developments—it insisted on highly restrictive covenants that would unalterably fix the character of the future neighborhood—and the idea took off.[25]

Apartments were coming to the suburbs too. In the forties and fifties, more than 80% of new dwelling units were one-family homes, but multifamily construction rose sharply in the early sixties. Most of the new apartments were in the suburbs. The trend was accelerated by the introduction of condominium ownership, a concept previously unknown in American law. By 1967 all fifty states had legalized condos.[26]

Tax law changes and federal subsidies accelerated construction of rentals in the late sixties, and a full-scale apartment bubble followed. In the peak year of 1972, more than a million multifamily housing units were built, almost matching the number of new single-family houses. In 1974 the bubble burst. It left behind a heritage of cheaply built housing, a breeding ground for the suburban slums of the future.[27]

These apartments were built to satisfy zoning rules their single-family neighbors insisted on. Levittown had imitated the separated uses, setbacks, and superblocks of the Country Club District, and now the same features dropped another notch downmarket. The law required them even when they no longer served their original purpose. Budget-conscious developers squeezed in off-street parking as cheaply as possible, building "garden apartments" surrounded by parking lots. Row houses, too, were moved away from the street so that parking could go out front.

The placement of the new housing reinforced the suburbs' dependence on the automobile. With the best land already zoned for single-family houses, apartments were often pushed out to the fringes of existing towns and onto empty land beyond. Far from rail stations and stores, walled off in superblocks where even the bus stop was far away, only the poorest residents would do without a car.[28]

A dingbat in west Los Angeles.
(Courtesy of Eric M. Pietras.)

The dingbat, a California invention, carried automobile-centered design to an extreme. It gave cars the entire surface of the ground. In 1935, Los Angeles adopted a rule that required one covered parking space for each house or apartment. Builders responded by making the housing the roof. Thin-walled apartments were raised on sticks above the tenants' parking spaces. This was a cheap way to build parking anywhere that land was scarce, and by the 1960s dingbats were popping up throughout California's less expensive older suburbs.

Created in direct response to government rule-making, the dingbat served no one's purposes. It increased density while destroying walkable streetscapes. It was more expensive to build than traditional apartments, yet it did nothing—to say the least—to elevate the prestige of its surroundings. Dingbats were a sign of a regulatory apparatus escaping the control of its sponsors. Planners and realtors, like the Sorcerer's Apprentice, could only watch helplessly as their creation took on a life of its own.[29]

The rules that governed land use were still called zoning, but a look at the zoning map was now only the first step in learning what could be built. Through a variety of legal devices, each new construction project received individual scrutiny. The planned unit development allowed the owner of a large tract of land to build things that a zone did not ordinarily allow—not just row houses but also factories or even mixed uses. But this required individual permission, granted only after detailed plans were submitted for public scrutiny. Then there were the *special exception*, the *floating zone*, and the simple expedient of zoning all land for single-family houses and rezoning whenever someone wanted to build something else. By these techniques local government exercised an intrusive and sometimes arbitrary control over what could be built. The result could be systematic exclusion based on race and income. Public hearings were the norm, and the audience—inevitably dominated by neighbors of the proposed project—would be asked on occasion to give its verdict by a show of hands.[30]

Underlying this legal evolution was an implicit bargain between suburban homeowners and developers. The homeowners allowed in something of lower status than their own homes. In exchange, the developers subjected themselves to the suburban mode of land tenure in a particularly stringent form. When anything but classically suburban buildings like strip malls and single-family houses was built, adjoining property owners were empowered to negotiate every detail—down to the specifics of the covenants that would tell future homeowners what colors they could paint their doors and what plants could grow in their gardens.[31]

Even as the long decline of the cities culminated in the race riots of the late sixties, forces were gathering that would turn them around. New urban bohemias emerged from the countercultural explosion of the decade's last years. Small-scale imitations of the drug culture of San Francisco's Haight-Ashbury and New York's East Village sprang up in low-rent sections of cities large and small, attracting young migrants fed up with the boredom of suburbia. The faded walls of former streetcar suburbs erupted with psychedelic coloring; staid university towns like Boulder and Eugene were suddenly on the front lines of cultural revolution.

The hippies faded quickly, their outer markings absorbed into mass culture. As a movement they had only a brief moment in history, but the social consequences of their meteoric passage endured. Most important for our story here, the counterculture upended the ranking of social status. Cool outranked square; authenticity displaced wealth; old houses and old clothes were better than new.

Sex roles were changing rapidly. Young women flooded into the professions and postponed childbearing; gay men emerged from the closet. These singles and childless couples might be ready to settle down, but they had lived the tumult of the sixties. For many, a move back to their parents' suburbs would have been a defeat.

The places hippies had lived were by definition cool, so young people with steady jobs moved in. Elsewhere—around downtown Brooklyn, for example—working-class districts filled with nineteenth-century homes drew professionals in search of authenticity. By the late seventies whole neighborhoods were turning over, their long-time residents displaced by more affluent buyers who carefully renovated the old houses.[32]

Soon a pattern could be discerned. Artists, students, and intellectuals kick things off, arriving in search of low rents and escape from conformity. Once these pioneers gather, bookstores and cafes open—businesses that, like their customers, rank higher in social prestige than on the scale of wealth. As a bohemian enclave emerges, the neighborhood starts to gain status. Plucky homebuyers chance the renovation of old houses. Eventually profit-seeking builders arrive, the ground cleared in front of them by residents and small shopkeepers.

Change came fastest in the citadels of counterculture. Emblematic was the rapid evolution of San Francisco's Haight-Ashbury, hippie ground zero in 1967 and barely a decade later a fancy residential district. Today the commercial strip along Haight Street is a relic of the Summer of Love, a psychedelically painted homage to the sixties. The area around it has morphed into an upscale neighborhood, with the traces of its moment in the sun nearly gone. Visiting in 2011, I walked two blocks up Ashbury Street from Haight and counted four Mercedes and a BMW among the fifty-odd cars parked at the curb.

This trend imported a name from England—gentrification—and its authors, the young urban professionals, became known as yuppies. They were not the first to fix up run-down neighborhoods. Philadelphia's Society Hill, Washington's Georgetown, and the historic centers of some southern cities had preceded them. But for earlier renovators of old houses, bohemian enclaves had no special attraction. In New York after the Second World War, the German working-class neighborhood of Yorkville was rapidly transformed into the elite Upper East Side, while change came slowly to Greenwich Village.[33] The gentrification wave of the seventies was different. The manifestation in wood and brick of a new status hierarchy, it dwarfed what had come before. It washed into nearly every sizable city that possessed old neighborhoods and into some that didn't.

Still confined to select neighborhoods, this return to the city was less than a full-scale urban revival. Its greatest significance was as a sign of what was to come, a harbinger of changing values. Suburbanites might still think they stood at the top of the social ladder, but that ranking was now under challenge.

7

The Age of the Nimby

nto the real estate scene of the 1970s came a new social phenomenon. Neighborhoods across the country sent a message of "Not in my backyard" to, it sometimes seemed, anyone who wanted to build anything anywhere. The behavior was so common that the acronym of NIMBY, coined at the end of the decade, soon lost its capital letters.

Exclusion in itself was nothing new. Suburbanites had long labored to keep less prestigious people and activities out of their neighborhoods. Minimum house price covenants went back to the 1890s, single-family zoning to the 1920s. On occasion the urge to exclude had found potent political expression, as when Detroit voted Republican in the 1949 mayoral election. The sociologist Herbert Gans, writing in 1965, could observe as a matter of course that "middle-class homeowners use zoning as a way of keeping out cheaper or less prestigious housing, while working-class communities employ less subtle forms of exclusion."[1]

But this earlier exclusionism had a narrow focus. It aimed only to protect residential neighborhoods and had no animus against builders per se. In the 1920s, homeowners were commonly on the same side as development interests. Real estate dealers often organized the homeowners, mobilizing them to pass zoning laws and stop racial mixing.[2] Civic associations flourished in the new suburbs after the Second World War, but here they were less political. As late as 1966, an experienced zoning lawyer could write that "the average suburban community believes commercial and industrial developers are desirable suitors while residential developers are not."[3]

Just a few years later, this distinction had vanished. Now any building, of any type, had to be kept out, and nimby homeowners were the scourges of the real estate industry. Where homeowner associations existed under covenants, they took the lead. Elsewhere voluntary civic associations sprang to life. A full-fledged antigrowth movement emerged, equipped with ideology and political leaders. Horizons broadened as development was fought not just nearby but also throughout the town or even the county. City neighborhoods resisted as passionately as suburbs.[4]

Soon "slow-growth" activists were winning control of some suburban governments and gaining influence in many more. Incumbent politicians who managed to fend off the insurgencies found themselves adopting their opponents' agenda. The tide slackened briefly during the recession of the early eighties—the usual trigger for homeowner mobilization was an unwanted development project in the vicinity. The pause came to an end in 1985 when Florida adopted a statewide system of growth control, and the next year a wave of antigrowth activism washed over California from north to south. Growth limits continued to gain in popularity over the remainder of the decade.[5]

New tactics and old were employed in the fight against change. Zoning rules tightened. Whole neighborhoods became historic landmarks. A battery of new tools, advertised as *growth control* or *growth management*, were devised. Only rarely did the growth controls succeed in curbing growth—and, far more often, they gave further impetus to the spread of sprawl.

The slow-growth movement could often accomplish its purposes with the tried-and-true technique of rezoning. As suburbs sprawled outward, they engulfed former farming towns with zoning codes tailored for local landowners eager to cash in on development. The new residents, like suburbanites elsewhere, wanted a more exclusionary zoning.

Built-up places were rezoned too. Often, in neighborhoods built before the onset of zoning in the 1920s, small commercial landowners had dominated the zoning process. Caring more for profit than for status, they left themselves free to build to higher density.[6]

During the years of depression, war, and the single-family housing boom, residents of these less expensive areas paid little attention to zoning. Few apartments were going up anyway. In the most run-down districts, rentals dominated, and homeowners were too few and too impoverished to have much influence. But as city neighborhoods began to revive in the seventies, householders new and old mobilized against development. In southern California, longtime residents led the push to reduce the allowable building size. In Washington and Chicago, gentrifiers were first to call for "downzoning."[7]

Downzoning had its limits, though. Some states required time-consuming studies before land could be rezoned. If property owners objected—and the landowners most likely to build were the ones most inclined to object—they could throw up additional obstacles. On the suburban fringe vacant land was being developed faster than rezoning could stop it, and local governments devised faster-acting techniques that became known as growth controls. Meanwhile, in established suburbs and rebounding city neighborhoods, the new historic preservation rules were seized on to stop change.

Growth controls took many forms.[8] The most straightforward was a cap on building permits. Petaluma, California, and Boca Raton, Florida, pioneered this approach in the early seventies. Petaluma limited the number of permits per year; Boca Raton added a permanent ceiling on the city's population. Both cities' rules were challenged in court. Petaluma's approach was upheld, but the Florida courts struck down Boca Raton's limit (while letting stand a rezoning that banned apartment buildings outright).

Another commonly used technique is the Adequate Public Facilities Ordinance, or APFO. First introduced by Ramapo, New York, in 1969, these laws block new development that could overwhelm local infrastructure. If roads, schools, or sewers are overcrowded, builders must either wait for government to expand them or pay for the expansion themselves. The aim, ostensibly at least, is not so much to limit growth as to get infrastructure built by incentivizing developers. Sometimes the developers pay; more often they use their political power to get the taxpayer to pay. While these ordinances have linked development to many types of public facilities, their main use is for roads.[9]

Although promoted as a means to limit sprawl, the APFO turned out to make it worse. How fast cars move is the measure of whether transportation is adequate. If the nearest supermarket is 10 miles away and can be reached in 15 minutes, developers can build. If the supermarket is 1 mile away and it takes 5 minutes to drive there, they can't. The ordinance pushes new construction outward to where traffic is still light. Destinations spread farther apart require longer drives, and rules designed to limit traffic wind up making more of it.[10]

A common variant of the APFO, known as staging, has similar effects. Permits to build are released in waves, their timing often tied to the completion of new highways.

Among the strongest forms of control was the growth boundary, or greenbelt, which permanently preserves the land beyond a fixed line as farm or forest. Here it was the suburbs around San Francisco that took the lead. Slow-growth forces won control of Marin County in 1968; a general plan adopted in 1973 reserved more than half the county's land for agriculture and recreation. Development came to a near-halt, and the county's population, growing rapidly to that point, stabilized.[11]

Other California counties followed, usually with weaker laws, and the idea spread. Oregon in 1973 required all its counties to establish growth boundaries, and Maryland came close to passing a similar law a year later. Some of Maryland's large suburban counties acted in the absence of state law and reserved substantial portions of their area for agriculture. Toward the end of the decade, a referendum put California's entire coastline under control of a state commission, and New Jersey halted development in the state's Pine Barrens region.[12]

Only rarely did these boundaries succeed in containing growth. States had real power to direct growth, but only Oregon ever really tried. When small municipalities imposed controls, builders easily jumped past the city limits. County growth boundaries had more effect, but eventually the development tide ran past their borders.[13]

As regulation tightened, opportunities to build grew scarce, and grants of permission made property instantly more valuable. Local governments tried to capture this value for themselves by making developers pay for the right to build. Sometimes there was a straightforward tax. More often, an *amenity* or *proffer*—a public benefit built at the developer's expense—was negotiated case by case.

Politicians, caught between developers and homeowners, typically sought compromise. The new regulatory tools slowed the rate of growth; they rarely stopped it altogether. Absolute ceilings were further discouraged by the Boca Raton court decision, although its language did not definitively rule them out. Even the most ardent opponents of development sought to display moderation; they billed their program as slow growth rather than no growth, and growth controls acquired the less threatening name of growth management.

Wealthy city dwellers liked development no more than suburbanites, but calls to limit growth rang hollow in cities that weren't growing. Urban nimbys needed other tools, and they found one close at hand—another of the achievements of the sixties, the landmark preservation laws enacted after the destruction of Pennsylvania Station.

Historic preservation from landmark to parking lot: Pennsylvania Station, New York (top), and Sam's Park and Shop, Washington (bottom), soon after each was built.
(Courtesy of the Library of Congress, Detroit Publishing Company and Matson collections.)

The lost railroad terminal had been valued as a landmark, the monumental gateway to the city. Its defenders fought on aesthetic grounds; the opponents of demolition called themselves the Action Group for Better Architecture in New York. The building was beautiful, and everyone knew that what replaced it would be ugly.

Years before, a different group of activists had begun to struggle in obscurity for legal protection of old buildings. These preservationists, who reaped the fruits of victory after Penn Station, had an agenda much broader than better architecture. They refused to make aesthetic distinctions; for the head of New York's landmarks commission a few years later, the buildings to be preserved were "not merely the best of them, mind you, but the most characteristic." The idea of landmarks—particularly notable structures—faded into the vague concept of historical significance. The purpose of preservation was, as a widely cited 1985 paper put it, the pursuit of "stability, identity, and environmental control" by "retaining diverse elements of the past" and "perpetuating the diverse identities of places." Within these cloudy categories, almost any resistance to change could be justified.[14]

It fell to a suburb-like section of Washington, DC, to test the limits of historic preservation. In 1981, the new Metro reached Cleveland Park. Riders entered down a stairway alongside the parking lot of a fifty-year-old strip mall. The owners of Sam's Park and Shop wanted to replace it with a larger, more urban structure. But the wealthy and influential homeowners who lived nearby liked things as they were—the neighborhood had led the successful fight against freeways two decades earlier—and they didn't want any new construction. Tersh Boasberg, the local leader, told the *Washington Post* that "the central question is, 'Can an urban neighborhood control what happens to it, or is development inevitable?'"[15]

Historic preservation was the community's chosen tool. In the unique political structure of the nation's capital, this offered better prospects of success than zoning. Two federal appointees, unlikely to bend to local pressure, sit on the five-person zoning board. Preservation, on the other hand, is within the full purview of the elected city government.

Sam's Park and Shop, its neighbors thus proclaimed, deserved protection as a pioneering example of strip-mall architecture. But for the historic designation to succeed in blocking new construction, it wasn't enough for the store building to remain intact. The parking lot had to be saved as well.

The residents' case was not an easy one to make. In front of the original Park and Shop were a gas station and a car wash (an "automotive laundry" in the preservationists' inflated prose), later torn down to make room for more parked cars. Nearby stores were built in a hodgepodge of styles, without parking of their own. But no matter:

> It is the integrity of the entire complex which is important...the rhythm created by tall and short, projecting and receding, and the general overall appearance and feel of the streetscape combine to make this a very human and appealing place in which to do one's shopping.

It was a long way from landmarks to human and appealing places to shop, but in 1986 the fight for the parking lot ended in victory. "They paved paradise and put up a parking lot" had been Joni Mitchell's lament in the 1970 hit folk song "Big Yellow Taxi." Now, a few years later in Cleveland Park, a parking lot *was* paradise.[16]

By 2007, twenty-seven historic districts ringed downtown Washington. They contain more than twenty-five thousand structures, all subject to strict control of new construction. The rules have an uncanny resemblance to the architectural review that Frederick Olmsted's sons devised for "high-class" subdivisions. Construction in today's historic districts must match the "massing, size, scale, and architectural features" of its surroundings while being "differentiated from the old"; ninety years ago John Charles Olmsted advised clients to allow only "a single style of architecture and a limited choice of exterior building materials" while avoiding "tiresome monotony." Decisions are made by a board of specialists, but residents have heavy input. Homeowners in these districts now possess the control over their neighbors' land that Tersh Boasberg sought. A third pillar of suburban land tenure stands alongside covenants and zoning.[17]

Unwilling to admit—and often unable to recognize—the status-seeking motivations that lurk behind their agenda, opponents of development search for any convenient excuse to oppose something that might be built nearby. Traffic is a perennial objection, blessed by the Supreme Court in *Euclid v. Ambler* and never since out of favor. Another common tactic is to go after the builder rather than the building. Homeowners appeal to the sympathies of the uninvolved, presenting themselves as innocent victims of oppressive developers.

If roads are empty and the builder is an uninviting target, other arguments are at hand. There's too much parking or too little. If houses are proposed, offices are what the neighborhod needs; if offices, houses would be better. Property values will go down; we will be priced out of our homes.

When all the usual arguments fail, new excuses must be cooked up. In this endeavor the drafters of 1920s zoning rules set a high standard of creative thinking—the ostensible reason to ban billboards in residential zones was to deprive fornicators of opportunities for concealment—but more recent generations have not lacked in imagination. One French bistro in Beverly Hills, wanting to open a second restaurant nearby, found neighbors worried that its patrons would urinate in the street while waiting for their foie gras.[18]

Ever since the 1970s, large-lot suburbs have played the environmental card. When growth controls first blossomed in Marin County, there was an unspoiled ecosystem to protect and such arguments had a real point. But in Los Angeles, complaints of "Eden in jeopardy" came from wealthy retirees who built mansions in the fire-prone desert canyons of the Santa Monica Mountains. Political influence here overcame the deficit of plausibility, and the National Park Service began to buy up land in the vicinity.

Development then spilled over into the next county, and the Santa Monica Mountains homeowners fought back by putting into office an insurgent county supervisor named Maria VanderKolk. The novice lawmaker misperceived the priorities of these suburban environmentalists. Elected on a promise to preserve a mountain tract called Jordan Ranch, she succeeded in making the entire ranch a park, along with two adjacent canyons. This achievement, in her sponsors' eyes, was a betrayal—the deal that saved the ranch authorized urban-style building on nearby flatlands. VanderKolk, when her term expired, became a private citizen again.[19]

When antigrowth homeowners ventured onto the wider political stage, they tended to adopt the political coloration of their surroundings. In most suburbs, that put them on the right. The California civic associations that led the downzoning drive of 1972 were soon the shock troops of tax revolt. Los Angeles homeowners boasted of being the fathers of Proposition 13, a tax-cutting amendment to the state constitution that a statewide referendum approved in 1978.[20]

Elsewhere, fear of housing integration fed lower-middle-class nimbyism. After the Fair Housing Act of 1968 banned outright racial discrimination by homesellers, the civil rights movement turned its attention to the more subtle barriers that still blocked integration. Exclusion by income often amounted to exclusion by race, and even when the victims had the same skin color as the perpetrators it had similarly pernicious effects. With integration of schools and lunch counters fresh in everyone's memory, it was easy to see how talk of "neighborhood character" or "compatibility" could be code words for something else. Massachusetts in 1969 empowered a state agency to overturn "snob zoning" rules that kept subsidized housing out of suburban towns. Similar laws were passed by the Connecticut and New York legislatures, but they fell victim to the governor's veto in one case and repeal in the other.[21]

In New Jersey, lawsuits demanding construction of subsidized housing in all-white suburbs triggered a right-wing insurgency. To fend off court pressure, the state's Republican governor, William Cahill, proposed a law in 1972 to override local ordinances that excluded apartments from municipalities. Fevered opposition arose in the state's white ethnic suburbs. Joining with more affluent areas, they organized as the United Citizens for Home Rule.

Loathing of the bill was so intense that Cahill was defeated in the next year's Republican primary by a defender of local autonomy.

In the general election Republicans were defeated across the board, but new suburban Democrats in the legislature shared their predecessors' devotion to local zoning. A twelve-year tug-of-war followed among courts, local governments, builders, and fair housing advocates. In the end, New Jersey enacted a relatively mild law. It brought apartments to towns that excluded them entirely but delivered little affordable housing.[22]

Racial fears have surely not vanished as a nimby motivation, but they have greatly weakened since the 1970s. Dislike of apartments has not abated with the fading of racial prejudice; instead, the battle to preserve status has broadened. As the years have passed and the civil rights movement faded from memory, the political atmosphere shifted rightward and exclusion could be defended more openly. A second wave of growth control, even bigger than the first, arrived in the late eighties. Townhouse residents now fight apartments while single-family householders battle townhouses. Almost anything at all that might be built near someone's house is a potential target; schools, ballfields, and even nature paths can come under attack.

Closer to downtown, the nimby wave got started on the Left. Its strongholds were the bohemian enclaves, where suburbia was rejected by activists and ordinary residents alike.

Activists had the wind at their back in neighborhoods that had defeated urban renewal and highway-building. But it took time for a full-fledged antigrowth politics to emerge. Early gentrifiers had moved to the city to live among a mixture of races and income levels. Once renewal agencies stopped building the towers of the 1950s, they were willing and sometimes even eager to live with new low-income housing. Jane Jacobs led a campaign for subsidized rental apartments in Greenwich Village.[23]

Attitudes subtly shifted with the rise of the student New Left at the end of the 1960s. Hostile to all large institutions, and to technology in general, every instinct of this movement made it suspicious of official proposals. More specifically, it counted the universities among the main pillars of an oppressive system. For a student movement, the schools were the nearest at hand of those pillars, and thus the first target of attack. Students for a Democratic Society, the main New Left organization, launched a national campaign against expansion of universities into surrounding communities.

SDS burst onto the national scene when Columbia University students went on strike in 1968. The main demand of the strikers was a halt to construction of a gym in nearby Morningside Park, a crime-ridden and decrepit strip of land at the bottom of the slope that led down from the heights where the university stood.

The gym was to be used by the community as well as the students, and neighbors welcomed the idea when first proposed in the early sixties. The area around the university was then anything but upscale, and across the park stood Harlem, one of the city's worst slums. The gym would redeem land that was at best useless, and in many eyes an active danger to its surroundings. Jane Jacobs enthused over the project in *The Death and Life of Great American Cities*. "Columbia University," she wrote, "is taking a constructive step by planning sports facilities—for both the university and the neighborhood—in Morningside Park."

But critics gathered on two sides. Guardians of the city's parks, drawn from New York's old elites, questioned the propriety of selling off grounds designed by Olmsted and Vaux, however much the masters' work had gone to seed. In mid-decade they were joined by the new Black Power movement, which saw the gym as an intrusion of the white power structure into a quintessential urban black turf. Even worse, black youth would go in through a door at the bottom of the hill, while students would use a separate entrance at the level of the heights. In early 1967, with construction near on the horizon, the militant leader Rap Brown threatened to burn the gym down if it were built—not an idle menace in those years of urban unrest. When digging began the following winter, students joined Harlem residents in a series of demonstrations.

On April 23, 1968, SDS gathered to confront the university authorities. Kept out of the school library, they marched down to the park to tear down the fence around the gym foundation. Then they returned to campus and seized university buildings. After a week, the New York police stormed the campus with tear gas and ended the protest. In the aftermath, the gym project was canceled. In 1990 the gym excavation was turned into a pool and waterfall, and today Morningside Park is a pleasant urban refuge, flanked on both sides by gentrified neighborhoods.[24]

The New Left imploded at the end of the sixties. A few of its adherents tried to live out revolutionary fantasies; many more settled down in newly gentrifying urban neighborhoods and strove for a better society by more prosaic means. There they made common cause with moderate leftists and liberals, groups they had not long before derided as sellouts.

Among these former New Leftists, a residue of hostility remained toward anything big and anything industrial. Their new allies joined in the skepticism of giant building schemes. The freeway revolt was on the upswing, and the bitter aftertaste of urban renewal was still on the tongue.

The new urbanites, their numbers greatly reinforced by the changes of the sixties, forged a political program with wide appeal. They brought together tenants, labor unions, left-wing activists, gentrifiers, and homeowners of all income levels in established single-family neighborhoods. This movement, dubbed the "new urban populism," aimed to preserve cities as they were, protecting homeowners with downzoning and tenants with rent control. It made war against highway-building, and even public transit could come under suspicion—in San Francisco, the local "alternative" weekly newspaper warred against BART as a developer plot to "manhattanize" the city. Mayors elected on platforms of this sort (minus, usually, the hostility to downtown office development) included Boston's Ray Flynn, Chicago's Harold Washington, and a host of others in cities large and small.[25]

The program of freezing the urban landscape with rent control and downzoning protected residents when cities were in decline, and it gained political punch by mobilizing renters. But when the pace of gentrification picked up in the late seventies, the homeowner–tenant coalition became harder to sustain. By now the federal urban renewal program was gone, and the battle against urban highways had run its course. Gentrification of existing buildings, rather than wholesale demolition, was the main threat to affordable housing. Tenants and their left-wing allies wanted poorer residents to stay in improving neighborhoods; they sought to build subsidized apartments as stand-alone projects or as "sweeteners" in larger private developments. More conservative homeowners, in newly gentrified districts as in long-affluent neighborhoods, were hostile to any new building and disliked subsidized housing most of all.

It did not take long for fissures to open among the gentrifiers. The first wave of New York brownstoners, drawn to the city in search of a racially and economically mixed environment, were challenged in the late seventies by more recent arrivals who did not share their egalitarian politics. Within a few years, the latecomers were organizing their own political clubs and community groups. A similar breach opened in San Francisco after a 40-foot ceiling height was imposed on residential districts in 1978 and downtown office development was capped in 1986. Soon wealthy neighborhoods battled their erstwhile allies over stores and subsidized housing.[26]

In cities with a more conservative political culture, gentrifiers allied with real estate interests from the outset. Dallas preservationists joined in the ruthless expulsion of low-income black residents from a redevelopment area north of downtown and stood by when the city razed nearby public housing. Phoenix, attempting to fabricate an upscale downtown by means of wholesale demolitions, echoed the urban renewal of the 1950s.[27]

The rightward-trending politics of the gentrifying inner city provided an electoral base for the emergence of centrist "new Democrats" in the 1980s and 1990s. This was a group notable for lack of principle, even by the lax standards of American politics. Dick Morris, who rose from Manhattan's West Side to be Bill Clinton's chief triangulator in the White House, is an extreme case, but keeping closer to home was no bar to opportunism. Mayors like San Francisco's Gavin Newsom and representatives of downtown council districts like Washington's Jack Evans forged de facto alliances between upscale nimbys and real estate interests. New building was kept out of wealthy neighborhoods while the developers, denied the most profitable building sites, were compensated with subsidies for development elsewhere. The city as a whole, its coffers drained of revenue, paid the price when this coalition of the comfortable arranged truces in the development wars.

Left-wing opposition to development did not, to be sure, vanish from the scene. As hippie enclaves aged, sharply etched branding brought slow-growth politics to places like Berkeley, Boulder, and the Washington suburb of Takoma Park. The image here was small-scale funk rather than the grit of Greenwich Village or the glitz of Beverly Hills, but it was protected with no less ardor. For not a few residents, their distinctive neighborhoods were not examples for emulation so much as signs of grace, distinguishing the elect from the ordinary suburbanites around them.[28] As gentrification progressed, development came under stringent control. New apartments were forbidden and commercial building strictly regulated. Today one sees retail strips that look like cryogenically preserved remnants of the 1970s.

In recent years, the rise of the antisprawl movement has put resistance to change in conflict with left-of-center social and environmental goals. The antidevelopment consensus has broken down, and battles now rage over redesign of streets and plans for new apartment buildings in old downtowns. Opponents of urban infill are fewer in number, but they have not abandoned the fight. The rhetoric of the environmentalist Left remains on their lips, but the substance of their agenda has begun to converge with the familiar exclusion of old-line suburbs.

The evolution of left nimbyism is exemplified by Zelda Bronstein, a socialist feminist historian who chaired the Berkeley Planning Commission from 2002 to 2004. Among the numerous construction projects she has fought is

The west parking lot at the Ashby BART station, a valuable open space according to some neighbors.
(Courtesy of BART.)

a plan to replace a parking lot at the Ashby BART station with housing and stores. She and other opponents contend that the area around the station— occupied by less than eight dwelling units per acre—is too dense and needs more open space and recreational facilities. "The Ashby BART west parking lot," their manifesto argues, "is, in its funky way, the largest open space in the area."[29]

When Left nimbyism first emerged in San Francisco, the opponents of BART suggested that satellite cities should be built so that downtown would not have to grow. Neither mass transit nor freeways would be needed, they argued, because jobs would be so close to housing that "many people can even walk or ride a bicycle to work." Forty years later, Zelda Bronstein has emerged as Berkeley's leading opponent of bike lanes.[30]

What set off the slow-growth explosion of the early seventies? Some frequently cited explanations don't hold water. Economists frequently think of nimbyism as a means of protecting property values,[31] but homeowners resist commercial rezonings that would raise the value of their land manyfold.[32] Nor are traffic jams the underlying issue; opponents of development projects who complain about overcrowded roads often ask as well for more free parking— hardly a means to discourage driving. And neither congestion nor property values explains why the slow growth movement emerged in the 1970s and not earlier or later.

Neighbors who opposed this hotly contested development in Chevy Chase, Maryland, surely did not fear that their property values would decline.
(Photo by author.)

Other suggested causes have more plausibility. To some degree, the rise of growth control was a reaction to the suburban apartment boom. In southern California, for example, the proliferation of dingbats provoked a wave of opposition. In 1972, slow-growth forces there won control of many towns and put a halt to apartment construction. Parsippany, New Jersey, saw its population double between 1962 and 1967 as five thousand low-end garden apartments were built; it then banned all new apartments.[33]

Another factor was the growth of environmentalism, which emerged as a mass movement in the fifties out of struggles to protect wilderness from dams. Rachel Carson's 1962 bestseller *Silent Spring* raised the stakes. Pesticides, pollution, and overdevelopment were not mere nuisances but a threat to the planet, and preservation of undeveloped land now seemed far more urgent. Upscale San Francisco suburbs, where the slow-growth movement built on earlier campaigns for parks, pioneered growth controls in the early seventies.[34]

The new ecological consciousness gathered influence through the sixties, reaching a peak in 1970 when millions turned out for Earth Day protests across the nation. Joni Mitchell, lamenting parking lots in "Big Yellow Taxi," reached back to Rachel Carson: "Hey farmer farmer, Put away that DDT." Poisons, parks, and parking were all tied together.

Other social forces were at work too, and in retrospect they seem more influential. The sixties upended the hierarchy of social status, giving authenticity a prestige to rival wealth. This reversal outlasted the counterculture that gave birth to it; the new rankings had an economic function to fulfill. In *The Conquest of Cool*, Thomas Frank describes how American capitalism in this period shifted away from mass marketing and tailored its products to distinct market segments. Advertisers aimed to make their brand somehow different from what the conformist masses bought. Customers looked for the designer label; the clothing was an afterthought.[35]

With housing such a large part of the economy and so closely tied to its consumers' self-image, this transition was inevitably reflected in the real estate market. Homeowners sought psychological differentiation in neighborhoods as in soft drinks, clothing, and automobiles. Large suburban houses and their carefully groomed lawns were no longer unambiguous badges of success; the owners risked being classed with the reviled conformists. In one wealthy Silicon Valley suburb, the "semi-rural Los Altos streetscape image" became so important that the city now requires new houses to have plain fronts and look smaller than they really are.[36]

Social status was more precarious than before, threatened from every side. Upscale suburbs already had images worthy of protection; elsewhere new brands were brought to life. By means of house tours, block parties, and civic associations, gentrifiers undertook mental renovations that carved out distinct neighborhoods from featureless stretches of urban decay. Brownstoners resurrected long-forgotten local history to turn pieces of South Brooklyn into Cobble Hill and Carroll Gardens. Districts with polyglot populations gained narrow ethnic identities—the more exotic the ethnic group, the more authentic and the more desirable the new brand. In Chicago's Argyle, a once-thriving Jewish center that now has an Asian flavor, a rabbi promotes Vietnamese shopping and wants kosher delis to go somewhere else.[37]

Run-down suburban subdivisions, too, could assert their unique character. Anything that might carry lower status had to be excluded, and even a big new house, something that formerly only added prestige, might threaten the brand image. The only safe course was to resist all change.

The neighborhoods with the strongest brands were most opposed to growth. The nature of the brand mattered little; expensive old-line suburbs and gentrifying bohemian enclaves were swept up alike in anti-development fervor. In 1970s California, growth control was embraced in both liberal San Francisco and conservative San Diego, but rejected by the characterless Central Valley. Oakland, the place of which Gertrude Stein said "there is no there there," bucked the nimby tide that swept over the rest of the Bay Area.[38]

The apartment boom surely was a trigger, and environmentalism was a genuine force; however, the shift in status hierarchies is the fundamental reason that nimbys flowered in the seventies. Wealth was still something to flaunt in 1967, when a Connecticut town defended its four-acre zoning by saying

"Greenwich is like Tiffany." Three decades later, the similarly upscale suburb of Chevy Chase, Maryland, was fighting against a commercial development that Tiffany would anchor.[39]

Another fifteen years have now passed, and the battle for suburban prestige is waged as tenaciously as ever. Apartment houses are no more welcome than in the 1920s, but authenticity has replaced exclusivity as the rationale for keeping them out.

"How many more generic, developerville town centers do we need?" This, according to the leading opponent of development in the affluent suburb of Kensington, Maryland, is why six-story buildings should not replace gas stations and run-down strip malls. Brand name, for the post-sixties nimby, is better than generic, no matter how shabby the brand might be. "We," our Kensington friend explains, "are just battling for the soul of a place that *already is different from the surrounding area.*"[40]

The new nimbyism, essential to stopping downtown highways and urban renewal, proved a very mixed blessing for city life once those battles abated. Opposition to development on the suburban fringe helped limit sprawl; when similar movements gained strength near city centers, they only pushed building outward. And the form of what was built was altered too. While growth boundaries did encourage clustering, other controls made suburbs even more dependent on the automobile.

Quite aside from the specifics of individual disputes, the politics of not-in-my-backyard work against urban vitality. Nimbys are strongest in the most distinctive and unconventional places. Bland, boring suburbs with no brand image let builders in. What gets reproduced is what no one cares about enough to want to keep the same.

8
Spreading like Cancer

D espite the struggles of the 1970s, or perhaps because of them, sprawl moved on. It spread over wider territories. It mutated into new forms. The eye was assaulted by landscapes never seen before. Fields of McMansions sprang up in the countryside, gated communities cowered behind stucco walls, office towers were sprinkled among parking lots.

The outward wave was now propelled by its own momentum. New homes and workplaces, reachable only in a car, dumped traffic back into older neighborhoods. There the fight against change was fought even more fiercely, as the urge to wall out the automotive flood reinforced the sentiment of status-seeking. Development was driven out onto the fringe; highways, widened to carry ever more traffic, became unwalkable; sprawl begot more sprawl.

Planners had come to reject the old orthodoxies. But the new theories, when they made their way into rules at all, were heavily watered down, and what got built seemed little better than what came before. Advertised cures like growth controls and cluster zoning all too often made things worse. Sprawl seemed immune to all attack. It grew like a cancer, ever changing, leaping over whatever obstacles were set in its path, swelling even as the city that gave birth to it shriveled.

By the 1980s the interstate highway system planned in 1956 was nearly finished, aside from canceled urban segments. Yet this gargantuan feat of engineering had hardly banished traffic jams. Housing tracts spread outward along the new interstates, their inhabitants compelled to drive farther and more often. Cars sat interminably on crowded downtown expressways, and backups spread to once-empty suburban streets. More roads, it could be seen, only brought more traffic.

Congestion worsened, but highway construction went on. Interstates got wider and new expressways appeared on maps. Road builders, closely allied with the oil, automobile, and trucking industries and powerful suburban real estate interests, had enormous clout. New roads brought new sprawl and even more driving. The average American drove two-and-a-half times as far in 2000 as in 1960.[1]

The highway lobby did face resistance. The urban freeway revolt had faded, but environmentalists remained on the attack. The Clean Air Act of 1970 empowered the Environmental Protection Agency to block new highways that threatened to pollute the air. Still, even after the law was strengthened, state highway agencies found ways to get around the rules. They claimed, for example, that road widenings would purify the air by getting rid of stop-and-go traffic. They built carpool lanes as a way to clean up. These arguments, however dubious, won acceptance from public agencies reluctant to confront the well-connected road interests.

The new roads had to be paid for, and gasoline taxes rose steadily. The highway lobby, initially opposed to the gas tax, reversed course and went along with a jump to 3 cents a gallon in 1956 to pay for the interstates. After President John F. Kennedy hiked the tax another penny in 1961, increases were avoided for years. But the inflation of the late seventies drove up the cost of new highways, and repair bills mounted as the interstates aged. States were raising their tax rates, and in December 1982 Congress approved an increase to 9 cents in a federal transportation bill proposed by President Ronald Reagan.[2]

The federal gas tax was raised twice more in the early 1990s, but it has not gone up since. In the states, too, increases have lost popularity. Between 1998 and 2008, more than half the states did not raise their gas tax at all, and only five states increased it faster than the rate of inflation.[3] Other trends squeezed revenues as well. As cars got better gasoline mileage, drivers paid less tax per mile. And the spread of suburban superblocks forced traffic onto major arteries and off the local streets built by city and county governments. The indirect subsidy of state highways by real estate taxes shrank, because state highway departments derived a smaller portion of their tax revenue from gasoline consumed on roadways they did not pay to maintain.

As suburbs spread and highways could no longer punch through open countryside, the cost of new roads exploded. Price tags now reach two or three billion dollars for roads that serve just one sector of a metropolis. By the 2000s, highway budgets were in a tight pinch.

The highway lobby was no more deterred by lack of money than by air pollution or its failure to reduce congestion. Money went into new roads, while old ones were allowed to fall apart. States issued bonds to be paid back with future federal aid. New toll roads, rare in the years when federal funds were pouring in, once again made their appearance.

The road builders had largely given up on the centers of big cities, but they still wanted to lay asphalt in built-up suburbs. Here they faced a thorny problem when they tried to justify their plans. When traffic backs up, people drive less than they would if the roads were clear. New lanes added to the highways quickly fill up with trips that no longer have to be forgone, and cars move no faster than before. Spending money on highway construction seems a waste if it doesn't make traffic move faster.

To maintain the promise of congestion relief, highway backers came up with the idea of adding toll lanes next to toll-free expressways. Tolls in these lanes vary from hour to hour. As traffic thickens, the rate goes up so that more drivers will be unable to pay. If you can still meet the price, you get to drive the speed limit.

These toll lanes were quickly dubbed Lexus lanes, and they deserve the name. A study showed that drivers with incomes above $100,000 were four times more likely than those who earn less than $40,000 to have used the toll lanes on their last trip. Tolls can reach levels that seem astronomical to drivers accustomed to free interstates, yet they rarely bring in enough money to pay back the cost of construction. Most Lexus lanes need heavy subsidies.

Highways are thus segregated by economic class, much like suburban neighborhoods. Lexus lanes, by design, serve a minority—if most of the cars were in the pay lanes, the free lanes would move at the speed limit and there would be no reason to pay. The tolls are primarily an allocation mechanism, and only incidentally a source of revenue. Their purpose is to deter those less able to pay from using the new lanes. Those wealthy enough to afford the tolls bypass the traffic jams, while everyone backed up on the free lanes gets to pay the bills.[4]

Not only did the interstates and their clones proliferate, but lesser roadways were dedicated ever more exclusively to automotive use. Those who still tried to walk found little welcome. Children's games were no longer tolerated, even where dead ends and closed loops ensured that traffic would not be blocked. Some states banned street play by law, and there are suburbs where even play on sidewalks is forbidden. In 2000, the Federal Highway Administration announced that "children at play" signs would no longer be allowed—because they might encourage play.[5]

For a new suburban generation, the only way to get around was in a car. In 1969, 49% of elementary school pupils still walked or biked to school; by 2009 the figure was 13%. Instead of walking to friends' houses, children were chauffeured to prearranged play dates. A Rockville, Maryland, mother who allowed her ten-year-old to take the public bus to school risked an investigation for child abuse. Other parents complained to the principal that her behavior was dangerous—in a place where car keys are routinely handed over to seventeen-year-olds.[6]

The layout of new suburbs and redeveloped downtowns reinforced the primacy of the automobile. Wide lanes encourage cars to speed. Pedestrians, forbidden to cross on one side of an intersection, need three green lights to get to the other side. If they reach a corner when the light is green, they face "don't walk" signals timed to pen them in so cars can turn faster. At one suburban intersection—in an area designated for transit-oriented development—crossing the street is a journey of 8½ minutes across twenty-eight traffic lanes.

The curved roadways that Lewis Mumford and George F. Babbitt had so insisted on were now ubiquitous. Even residential streets that carried little traffic widened—room is needed, it is argued, for fire engines to turn around.[7]

There was a subtle but profound alteration in the way street corners are built. Curbs no longer meet at right angles; they swing around in broad curves. It became standard even in cities for the curb to start bending back 25 feet from the cross street. On busy suburban roads, the bend begins even farther from the corner. Those on foot must choose between dangerous crossings of broad asphalt expanses and annoying zigzags to where the road narrows. Cars round the turn at highway speed. The simple act of walking down the street is so perilous that pedestrians are sometimes warned to wear reflective clothing, as if they were in the woods during hunting season.[8]

These changes were no mere whim of car-loving traffic engineers. Behind them stood the lobbying might of the trucking industry.

The truckers had fought for decades to put bigger vehicles on the roads, but they were long stymied by the railroads. A major battleground was Pennsylvania, where the Pennsylvania Railroad held sway over the legislature and limits on trucks were especially strict. A few weeks before the 1950 election, the Pennsylvania Motor Truck Association divided $76,000 between the chairpersons of the state Democratic and Republican parties. It was, the association's treasurer later conceded under oath, like betting on both teams at

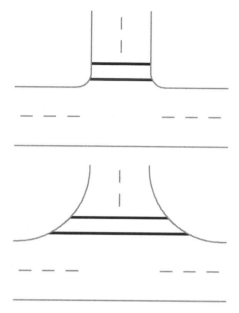

Pedestrian crossings on streets with sharp (top) and broadly curving (bottom) corners.

a baseball game, but he countered that "nothing was hidden, it was all out in the open."[9]

The truckers gained ground in the 1970s as their old antagonists weakened. But they still faced strenuous opposition from local governments and the American Automobile Association. Even highway engineers objected; they worried that bridges weren't built to carry the weight of big trucks. Just before the 1974 election, the Truck Operators Nonpartisan Committee made last-minute campaign contributions to 117 congressional candidates from both parties. Six weeks later, the House of Representatives reversed an earlier vote, and weight limits were raised on interstate highways.[10]

In December 1982, the truckers won full victory. The Reagan administration agreed to their demands in exchange for the industry's acceptance of a tax increase that hit trucks harder than autos. Weight limits were raised again, and state limits on the length and width of trucks were overruled. Tractor-trailers could have trailers up to 48 feet long; soon the limit in most places was 53 feet.[11]

A key provision, not fully understood by critics when the law was rushed through a lame-duck Congress, legalized the big trucks on many local roads as well as on the interstates. Road-builders had a new justification for designs that encourage cars to speed; pedestrians, ignored when the issue was under debate, were the victims. Lanes grew wider; curbs were pushed back at inter-sections so that extra-long vehicles could make the turn. And, because it was written into the statute, the neighbors had no way to object.[12]

As the years went by, builders put up fewer apartments. From 1969 to 1973, apartments were 38% of all new housing. The ratio dropped sharply when the bubble burst in 1974, and it never recovered. A smaller multifamily housing boom came in the mid-eighties, but even at its peak apartments did not exceed 32% of new homes, and in the post-2000 housing bubble they were only one out of every six units. In 1972 900,000 apartments went up; in the best years after 2000 the number barely reached one-third of that.

Why did builders switch from apartments back to one-family houses after moving so eagerly the other way in the sixties? There was no lack of demand. Economic trends, demographics, and shifting tastes all favor apart-ments. Single-family houses are less affordable; since 1973 real income has gone down for people in the bottom half of the income distribution, who make up the majority of apartment dwellers. There is no greater demand for yards for children's play; nearly half of all households had children in 1960 but only a third in 2000. And gentrifying neighborhoods, with their row houses and apartment renovations, show that multifamily living is hardly losing popularity.

Only the tightening of land use regulation in the nimby era can explain the falloff in construction of apartment houses. Their builders face stricter zoning, growth controls, and aroused neighbors.

A telltale sign that regulation is at work is the near-disappearance of the two-to-four–family house. If dislike of urban living were causing the drop in apartment construction, two-family houses would stay in fashion—they are much more like single-family homes than high-rises are. But when rules are tightened, small rental properties cannot bear the cost of lawyers and paper-work. Census data show that the construction of two-to-four–unit dwell-ings has fallen off even more than that of larger buildings. In 1972 more than 140,000 new dwelling units of this kind came onto the market; in the best year after 2000, the number is 43,000.

The latest housing market collapse has hit small multifamily buildings espe-cially hard. In 2010, just 11,400 apartment units of this type were built—only 5000 or so new two-to-four–family structures in the entire United States. Yet there are willing buyers and able builders for such homes. Even after the bust, gentrifiers snap up this kind of house in dilapidated neighborhoods. The small construction firms that did mansionizations during the boom would have no trouble building two-family houses. The demand is there; only the law stops them.[13]

Homeowner associations, once rare outside the wealthy neighborhoods that could bear their operating costs, moved downscale after the FHA issued its endorsement in 1963. Some localities forced developers to set up associations that would maintain streets, sewers, and parks. The current residents wanted more tax revenue without the cost of maintaining new infrastructure. Only five hundred subdivisions had homeowner associations in 1962; in 1975 the figure rose to twenty thousand; and by 1994 80% of all new housing was subject to these private governments. Architectural review, imposed only by a few high-end developers in the early part of the century, became a routine feature of suburban life. Covenants, never expiring and nearly impossible to change, embalmed neighborhoods with a permanence that the developers and zoners of the 1920s could only aspire to. Constitutional protections of free speech and free assembly vanished when streets and parks were privately owned.[14]

The privatization of the suburban public realm advanced another step with the gated community. By the end of the century, fenced-off subdivisions were ubiquitous in suburbs of the south and west, their walls sometimes lining both sides of a highway. The design impulse behind the superblock was taken to an extreme, with entry limited to a few openings where uninvited visitors could be turned away. Inside the fence, the homeowners association was more powerful than ever, controlling physical access as well as land use and design. And the automobile held residents in a tight grip; with so few gates open, travel by any other means was a near impossibility.

The sales pitch for these subdivisions appealed to emotions of fear and snobbery. The biggest market was retirees. They had lived the suburban migration of the 1950s and watched, usually at a distance, the urban troubles of the 1960s. Retirement communities let no one under fifty-five reside within the gates; those compelled by the vicissitudes of life to raise their grandchildren must move out. Another target group was parents of young children, who had grown up in a tightly controlled world of tract houses and play dates. Observers of gated communities noted the unusual homogeneity of their population, not just economically but racially as well.

Walls and fences provided little real protection against lawbreakers—the crime rate in ungated neighborhoods of similar nature was already low, and barriers did little to lower it. But a vague dread of the different and unfamiliar took hold. Such fear was behind the much-debated death of seventeen-year-old Trayvon Martin in 2012. Martin's killer, George Zimmerman, patrolling an

The central portion of Tysons Corner, the country's largest edge city, in 1980.
(Photo by Scott Boatwright, courtesy of Fairfax County Library, Virginia Room.)

economically hard-pressed gated subdivision in Sanford, Florida, may or
may not have been guided by racial animus. But there is no dispute about
Zimmerman's first explanation of what made him call the police: "This guy
looks like he's up to no good or he's on drugs or something. It's raining and
he's just walking around looking about." The gated community was so thoroughly suburban that "just walking around looking about" could be seen as a
criminal act.[15]

Workplaces moved steadily out from the city center. Factories had been leaving the cities since the 1940s, eager to avoid city-based unions and in search of
more room for spread-out assembly lines. Offices now followed, with corporate headquarters joining high-tech businesses in the flight to suburban office
parks. By 1998, only 23% of the jobs in the country's hundred largest metropolitan areas were within 3 miles of the center.[16]

What was happening here? Jobs began moving into the suburbs somewhat
later than the spread of residences; it is tempting to think that the purpose
of the exodus was to shorten commutes. But the jobs did not go to the same

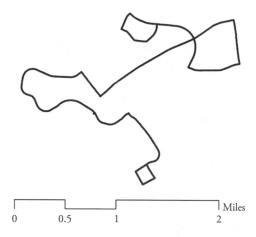

0   0.5   1   2   Miles

A slow bus in and out of suburban superblocks. Montgomery County Ride-On route 83 takes 21 minutes (more in traffic) to travel 2 miles of straight-line distance.

places as the homes. Population spread out fairly evenly around the cities; employment clustered where the housing was highest-priced, in what real estate experts call the "favored quarter." Big shopping malls moved in the same direction; department stores were attracted to people who had spending power.[17]

The most important factor determining where a corporate office moved was proximity to the chief executive's home and golf club.[18] Jobs concentrated near the fanciest houses. In places like Stamford, Connecticut, Mountain View, California, and Bethesda, Maryland, old town centers near rail stations blossomed into urban downtowns. More often, "edge cities" grew up on left-over land near freeways, vast agglomerations of office towers and shopping malls set among parking lots. Tysons Corner, the biggest edge city, borders the expensive Virginia suburbs of McLean and Great Falls; Houston's Post Oak is next to River Oaks; Los Angeles' Century City is across the road from Beverly Hills.

Edge cities forced nearly everyone into cars. They were so dense that cars were unavoidably stuck in traffic, but nearly impossible to reach by any other means. Buses ran, at best, once or twice an hour. They took long detours in and out of superblocks, following routes so twisted that they sometimes looked like they needed tomato sauce. Few but those too poor to own an automobile would put up with the delays.

Even within the superblocks, six- and eight-lane roads ran between the parking lots, nearly impassable on foot. To cross the street to buy lunch, you got in your car. The CEO had a short drive home on back roads and an assistant who ran errands during the day. The lower ranks sat in traffic jams.[19]

It was the market that jammed jobs into a favored quarter, but the consumer was not sovereign in this market. The consumers of office space are the people who work there—and they had no say. Their bosses forced them into long commutes on overcrowded highways. Indeed, when jobs moved to the suburbs to escape unions, the employers' very purpose was to *deprive* workers of a voice in decisions.

As these trends came together, house-building accelerated. Restrictions drove up the price of land, and a self-reinforcing dynamic set in. Houses came to be seen as a financial investment as much as an object of consumption. Rising prices no longer curbed purchasers' demand for dwelling space, as conventional economic theory holds, but stimulated more of it. Financial bubbles emerged in the housing market as prices in many cities soared in the late 1970s and again a decade later. Both booms were cut short by economic recession, but by the late 1990s prices were shooting upward even faster than before.[20]

By now suburbs were no escape from urban ills. Tract housing aged and did not always age well. Traffic often was worse than downtown. Poverty and crime plagued run-down garden apartments.

With unions largely banished, suburbs abounded in low-wage service and construction jobs, and immigrants flocked to them. The working poor, hardly able to afford a car even when they qualified for a driver's license, led a precarious life amid the landscape of strip malls and subdivisions. From a rented room, a dangerous walk along the side of the highway led to a long wait for the bus.[21]

Affordable rentals were scarce, and homeowners struggled to pay their mortgages. Yet it was illegal to divide houses into apartments. In earlier generations, idle construction workers could make up for lost wages by adding rental apartments onto small houses. Now this escape route was shut off. Declining neighborhoods, still zoned single-family long after their veneer of prestige had worn off, were unable to upgrade by the residents' own efforts. They were dragged down by rules meant to uphold their social standing.

Elsewhere, the old formula for escape was still in use. Workplaces leapfrogged to the outer edge of the favored quarter; real estate was cheap, and the boss's drive to work would be against traffic. People moved outward too; the population was whiter, the houses newer, the roads not yet filled up. Exurban subdivisions sought to stand out from the Levittowns, and the average size of a newly built house ballooned from 1785 square feet in 1974 to 2582 in

2008. Large lots and thick foliage created an illusion of rural isolation. Homes were harder to walk to, they were farther from the city, and they were more restricted than ever.

Middle-income buyers, their incomes stagnant, needed generous financing to pay for the big houses, and the pace of building went up and down with changes in the lending market. Savings and loan associations, earlier the main source of private mortgage loans, could no longer meet the demand; they had sought quick profits in commercial real estate after a 1980 deregulation allowed them to diversify and were crushed by the bursting of the speculative bubble that followed. Fannie Mae and Freddie Mac, federal agencies that had been privatized in the sixties, wanted to keep growing, and they filled the gap. They bought up mortgages with money borrowed cheaply thanks to taxpayer backup. The mortgages, in a process called securitization, were packaged into bonds and sold.[22]

Fannie and Freddie could push things only so far. Still somewhat tied to the government, they had rules that deterred overly risky lending. To really blow up the housing market, private enterprise had to work its magic. Wall Street did not shy from this challenge. It took securitization a step further, slicing and dicing loans and sorting the pieces into bonds that were said to be much safer, thanks to the magic of statistics, than the original mortgages.

Repeal of the Glass-Steagall Act in 1999 deregulated banks, allowing mortgage lenders to merge with stockbrokers. New financial giants arose, seeking growth at all costs. The faking of paperwork became routine; lenders and homebuilders had sales targets to meet. Bonuses were paid on what you did this quarter, and, when disaster struck, banks that were too big to fail would be bailed out anyway. The flood of new capital fueled a vast construction boom. By the time it peaked, unscrupulous bankers were encouraging bad loans so they could place bets against them.[23]

Before the bubble ended in disaster, it gave one more push to suburban sprawl. There were few bankers left with the local knowledge to judge the value of a small parcel in a city neighborhood. Wall Street had squeezed them out. A big downtown office tower could still borrow on its own merits, but lesser mortgages had to be assembled into packages and sent out into the financial marketplace.

The rationale for this process rested on large numbers—whether an individual mortgage will be paid is unpredictable, but if bond buyers took the average of enough loans and compared them to similar loans that have already paid off, they could know what to expect. So the securitizers needed mass-produced mortgages, resembling as much as possible the mortgages of years past. To write mortgages that all looked just the same, the big banks wanted little boxes—and not-so-little ones—that all looked just the same. Developers were happy to supply the copycat buildings that eager lenders demanded. Strip malls and office parks lined the highways, all built in the same pattern. South Carolina, seen from the road, could have been California. Stores, offices, and houses were financed by Wall Street number-crunchers who cared only for cookie-cutter buildings that fit the established car-centered mold. The bankers' bonuses rose and fell with their deal-making, so how easily a loan could be packaged mattered more than the value of the property behind it.[24]

Fueled by speculation and financial fraud, the wave of building gathered force and grew to a mighty crest. In the twelve months of 2005, 1.7 million one-family houses were built, a quarter-million more than any year before or since. The houses of the new outer suburbia were bigger and more spread out, and their inhabitants had no choice but to drive more.

In 2008 the flood began to retract. The real estate bubble, already letting out air for three years, collapsed so suddenly that the world's financial system nearly went down with it. Barely a quarter as many houses were built in 2009 as four years before. Prices tumbled, falling most in the new subdivisions farthest from downtown. Some developments were abandoned, half-finished, when builders went bankrupt. Others were awash in foreclosures and empty houses.

The ever-bigger houses of the boom years had been matched with ever-stricter covenants and ever-tighter zoning. Architecture and governance alike were designed for perpetual affluence, and the aftermath of a popped bubble brought troubles no one had prepared for. Soon vigilante patrols were mounted to keep squatters out of empty McMansions. Mosquito control officers sprayed abandoned swimming pools; Lee County, Florida, had so many foreclosures that it used helicopters to find the pools. A gated community outside Atlanta, in the habit of fining residents $250 for planting unauthorized flowers, discovered that it lacked means to shut down a bordello operating in one of its houses.[25]

The great migration was over. A half-decade after the crash, suburban building has resumed, but it will never again be the same inexorable outward surge. The landscape created by the migration remains, embodied in houses, stores, roads, habits, and laws. What we do with that landscape will determine what kind of country we make in the century to come.

9

The War of Greed against Snobbery

At the edge of the metropolis, where tract housing intrudes into farm and forest, local politics falls easily into a time-honored pattern of consensus. Once the houses go up, neither homeowner nor developer wants anything to change. Builders have room to do their work and little need to disturb their neighbors. Keeping past customers happy brings buyers to new subdivisions. Planners do their work in peace, laying out house lots and strip malls.

But the land fills up, the development frontier moves on, and this happy state of affairs comes to an end. The interests that had thrived in harmony now conflict. Zoning constrains the builders who earlier profited from it. Homeowners come to think that new construction injures them: even when there is no physical intrusion, it takes a psychic toll.

Soon one side or the other upsets the political equilibrium, and the pendulum swings sharply back and forth. There are midnight rezonings by lame-duck pro-growthers after election defeats, "temporary" building moratoriums that never reach an end, and the contentious lawsuits that such maneuvers trigger.[1] Builders jump to take advantage of sudden reversals while they can, spraying structures across the landscape in a patchwork that adds to sprawl.

Eventually the balance of forces reaches a stable equilibrium, and the wild oscillations settle down into a steady orbit. New systems of control emerge to reconcile the quest for profit with the striving for social status. Neither free market nor central planning, these arrangements blend law, politics, and economics. Five patterns of governance will be sketched out in this chapter: snob zoning, industrial cities, tollbooth regulation, fiscal zoning, and bureaucratic "paralysis by analysis."

These are pure models, only approximations to a fluid reality. Mixtures are common, and as communities evolve their regulatory systems change with them. Greed and snobbery, moreover, are hardly the only human motivations. Unselfish civic activism, omitted here for clarity, can have great influence. Still, these pure cases are well worth study. Stripping off complexity makes it easier to see underlying mechanisms.

The simplest stable pattern of land use governance is snob zoning. A small locality excludes almost everything other than single-family homes on large lots. Here snobbery trumps greed; the residents' overriding concern is the elevated status of their neighborhood. They do desire higher property values, of course, but not if it detracts from the prestige of the locality.

This works best when the territory is small enough to make internal conflict rare. Elections are rarely contested, and the administrative burden is so light that there is little need for a bureaucracy that might develop interests of its own. The governing body—a town council, zoning board, homeowner association, or historic commission—faithfully executes the wishes of its constituents.

Close approximations to this ideal type are easy to find. They are common in upscale suburbs and in suburban-style neighborhoods within city limits. Locally controlled snob zoning is the dominant form of governance in the wealthy areas around older cities like Boston, New York, Philadelphia, St. Louis, and Chicago. It has proved a reliable tool for resisting change, enabling elite subdivisions to preserve their original appearance for a century and more.[2]

The affinity of small municipalities for snob zoning is on display in the suburbs of New York. In the first years of the twentieth century, the robber barons whose heirs would later frustrate Robert Moses built opulent estates on the North Shore of Long Island. They pushed a law allowing municipalities to incorporate with as few as fifty residents through the obedient New York legislature in 1911, and tiny villages sprang up whose only inhabitants were the estate owners and their house servants. The initial purpose of the maneuver was to keep taxes low and repel outsiders—the villages forbade parking on the few public roads allowed to penetrate their territory.

The children of the nouveau riche mansion-builders had neither the bank-rolls of their forebears nor their passion for ostentatious social climbing, and as the properties were passed on the North Shore began a slow decline. By the late 1930s, the land was worth more as house lots than as estates. The little municipalities then enacted zoning ordinances that forbade construction on lots smaller than 1, 2, or even 5 acres. Today the estates are gone but the villages survive, preserved by zoning rules as heavily wooded enclaves of upper-middle-class privilege.[3]

Other affluent suburbs rushed to incorporate, in states where the law allowed it, as soon as the new zoning powers became available in the 1920s. By the late 1930s, middle-class subdivisions near New York and St. Louis were imitating them. The postwar years saw neighboring communities fighting "border wars" over control of land use and tax revenues, using incorporation and annexation as weapons of battle.[4]

This technique of restricting land use took another step down the social ladder in mid-century California. What was called the Lakewood Plan let owners of the new assembly-line houses run skeletal governments on a tight budget. Lakewood, when established in 1954, was a city of 17,500 newly built houses on small lots next to a Douglas Aircraft plant. The motive for incorporation was to avoid annexation by the adjoining city of Long Beach. Inspired in part by study of Long Island, Lakewood's leaders escaped the burden of paying for a separate administration by contracting with Los Angeles County for fire, police, and other services. Zoning powers they kept for themselves. The device proved effective and was copied across the state.[5]

Houston, often hailed as an outpost of the free market because it lacks a zoning ordinance, is understood more realistically as an extreme instance of snob zoning. Under the Texas statute passed in 1965, covenants may be imposed by majority vote, and they are enforced by the city government. This law makes an unparalleled transfer of power to small districts. Elsewhere only neighborhoods outside the boundaries of the central city can incorporate to gain control of land use; Houston grants this prerogative, clothed in another legal form, even to subdivisions within its borders. The city's affluent districts have not been shy in making use of it.[6]

Long Island's robber barons were not the first to incorporate tiny municipalities and run them as private fiefs. A few clever entrepreneurs preceded them, profiting by the creation of low-tax havens for factories. Some of these cities, like Teterboro in New Jersey and industrial cities around Los Angeles, persist to this day.

Here the profit motive governs, and zoning laws reinforce its rule. Nearly all human habitation is forbidden; only a select few are granted admittance. The residents are carefully chosen, reliable voters picked to ensure reelection of the incumbent officeholders.

Operating like private businesses, these entities market their advantageous legal status to industrial companies. Manufacturers who buy in escape taxation for schools, social programs, and other inconvenient costs of human existence. Factories also avoid the bother of satisfying sometimes exacting neighbors, and they can try to bypass even minimal obligations to public health and safety. When smog first struck the Los Angeles basin in the 1940s, the industrial cities refused to join the remainder of the region's governments in imposing air pollution controls. Only an act of the state legislature that created a county-wide air pollution control district could overcome their recalcitrance.[7]

Vernon, the largest of the California cities that resisted smog control, bears the words "exclusively industrial" on its city seal. Established in 1905, it now contains 1800 businesses and has a budget of $300 million. The founder's grandson, mayor from 1974 to 2009, resigned shortly before being convicted of election fraud. Other top officials, paid salaries running from $800,000 to well over a million dollars, were charged with various diversions of public money and forced out.

Nearly all of the city's fewer than one hundred residents live in city-owned housing, an arrangement that allows the city administration to handpick the voters who keep it in office. The entrenched incumbents take no chances with the composition of the electorate. To ensure that security guards who work the night shift will not claim residence, the city zoning ordinance bans the possession by these workers of even a cot to recline on.[8]

Greed and snobbery, more commonly, are both contenders on the political battlefield. Local politicians are then most comfortable maintaining a steady balance. They can operate the apparatus of land use regulation as if it were a tollbooth where payment, in cash or in kind, is exacted from developers as the price of passage through the barrier of neighborhood objections.

Landowners have a theoretical right to use their land, so payment is not explicitly required. But in zoning as on the highways, routes that bypass the toll plaza are arduous and unpleasant by design. The most common technique for forcing developers through the tollbooth is to zone for much less density than anyone really wants—on land intended for high-rises, single-family houses or strip malls might be prescribed. When someone wants to build, they either apply for rezoning or seek approval of an "alternate" use of the land.

These requests are voluntary in legal form, so the governing body has discretion in granting them. But for the landowner, gaining approval is a practical necessity, because the buildings that the property is zoned for are too small to repay the purchase price of the land.

The amount collected at the tollbooth depends on the wealth and influence of the objecting neighbors; the manner of payment and the identity of the beneficiary vary with the local political culture. Benefits may flow to the public at large, to the objectors, or to the gatekeepers themselves. Concessions to demands issued by the neighbors are normal. A donation, in cash or in kind, is often made toward the expense of local government. Campaign contributions are almost always in the mix, and flat-out graft is hardly unknown. Developers make sure to hire a well-connected lawyer—even when there is no influence involved, an experienced guide is needed to emerge unscathed from the maze of local governance.

The neighbors can be propitiated by a multitude of means. Structures shrink—property owners, knowing that concessions will have to be made, frequently begin by seeking approval for something bigger than what they really want to build. There can be an added measure of prestige: rentals become condos; Safeway gives way to Whole Foods; fine dining displaces drive-throughs. The developer may pay for playgrounds or otherwise improve nearby subdivisions. A zoning lawyer in Philadelphia reports that civic associations sometimes come to him and say, "We like the project, but we don't know what to ask for."[9]

The mechanics of tollbooth regulation vary with the structure of government and the relative strength of the contending forces. Where builders have the political upper hand, the entire process can be scripted. A political consultant's how-to manual for developers offers practical advice along those lines:

> It usually also makes sense in proposing a controversial project to let the mayor appear to wring concessions from the developer, thereby creating political cover for officials to grant project approval. This involves a preexisting *sotto voce* agreement on what the developer will provide, followed by a public demand in the newspaper from the mayor that the developer provide it. After an orchestrated closed-door meeting at which the mayor ostensibly lectures the developer on the project's shortcomings, the developer sheepishly emerges and reluctantly agrees to the mayor's demands, to the applause of the citizenry and local news media.[10]

When greed and snobbery are more evenly matched, government officials find it easier to stand aloof. They handle disputes in much the way Britain once managed wars on the European continent. The zoning board and city council, burdened by heavy workloads and wary of public criticism, hold back while the battle rages fiercely. They keep their powder dry and intervene only when one side is about to collapse. On those rare occasions, they step in to restore the balance of power. This ensures that both parties are tied down in the struggle and neither has enough freedom of action to disturb the overseers' peace. Otherwise they wait until the warring armies reach exhaustion and ratify whatever settlement the adversaries negotiate among themselves.[11]

Yet another variant of tollbooth regulation grows out of the practice of *district courtesy*, common since the earliest years of zoning. Where local legislators are elected by districts, they agree to vote on land-use matters according to the wishes of the member who represents the property in question. This habit, once entrenched, is nearly impossible to eradicate; someone who refuses to go along loses control of what happens in his own district without gaining any influence over decisions elsewhere.

Inherent in district courtesy is a grant of arbitrary power, a temptation even for those of unblemished character. Prince George's County, Maryland, where the practice has a long tradition, illustrates the consequences. In 2010 the FBI raided the home of the outgoing county executive and found $79,000 in cash stuffed in his wife's bra. This might have happened anywhere, but the county's next scandal was peculiar to the district courtesy system. A council member of unquestioned personal honesty went regularly to developers and demanded contributions to community organizations. "You have these people making millions, and all this density and all the traffic [we'd] absorb on Route 1. You mean to tell me you have nothing to help out our schools?" he explained when the practice was exposed.[12]

For many local politicians, continued strife serves self-interest. When every future development approval is at risk in the next election, the continued flow of campaign contributions is assured. Pro-development members of city councils will appoint a resolute slow-grower to the zoning board. This shows impartiality to the electorate, and at the same time it keeps a fire lit under campaign contributors. Less scrupulous legislators have been known to maintain captive civic organizations that spring suddenly to life as indignant nimbys if a builder resists the usual shakedown.

It might seem that tollbooth zoning would not favor any particular kind of development, but this political arrangement tends in practice to promote sprawl. For one thing, district courtesy empowers local interests, and especially nimby homeowners, at the expense of outsiders who want houses or jobs. Beyond that, the magnitude of the toll exacted often depends on the strength of homeowner objections. The fewer the neighbors, the less the expense—a substantial incentive to build near empty land.

The slant toward sprawl affects the nature of new buildings as well as their location. Concessions are negotiated not with the entire community but with the portion that objects most actively. Not only is this group usually composed of near neighbors, but it is also almost always the segment of opinion most hostile to density and most attached to traditional suburban life.

A developer's first priority is to get the project approved; maximizing the saleable square feet comes second; design is where it is easiest to yield. When the negotiation is concluded, the shape of new urban areas has been dictated by the most anti-urban section of the population. Housing becomes less affordable, front doors face away from streets, buildings sit behind a moat of empty parking lots. In the declining industrial suburb of Dundalk, Maryland, for instance, neighborhood activists blocked a street-front mixed-use, mixed-income redevelopment project as they welcomed a plan for a gated enclave of luxury apartments and a marina.[13] The outcome, here as elsewhere, was a de facto collusion of builders and neighbors against the wishes of the larger community.

Avarice is not, of course, a trait peculiar to real estate developers and public servants. Homeowner politics seeks pecuniary advantage along with higher status, and low real estate taxes are a recurrent theme. From California's Proposition 13 in the 1970s to today's Tea Party, tax revolts have found a mass following among the defenders of snob zoning.

The desire for low taxes manifests itself in land-use regulation as *fiscal zoning*.[14] Towns approve only those new buildings that will yield more in real estate taxes than the cost of the public services they demand. This logic favors one-bedroom apartments, unlikely to send children to public schools, over larger apartments, and high-price McMansions over affordable housing. Where local governments depend on sales tax revenues, they subsidize high-volume retail operations. Planners put strip malls and office buildings next to boundary lines, dumping the cost of access roads onto the adjoining town.

Fiscal zoning is a particular temptation for medium-sized localities, with populations of a few tens of thousands. Large enough to have their own schools and services, and thus bear the financial costs of the choices they make, they are still sufficiently small that unwanted uses can be pushed off into the next town.

Recent years have seen an upsurge of fiscal zoning. Inner-ring suburbs, their budgets stretched by economic decline and loss of state and federal aid, are hungry for revenue. Towns compete for cash cows like department stores and factories, offering financial incentives on top of favorable zoning. Bidding wars can grow so intense that the eventual winner gains little new revenue, merely shifting the burden of its taxes from business to residences.[15]

Zoning is now approaching a century in age. As time passes, the rules accumulate detail, and the effort needed to administer them grows unceasingly. Beyond a certain point, the very complexity of the system begins to determine outcomes. Big bureaucracies have tendencies that are independent of the purpose of the apparatus. The most extreme example of central planning, the former Soviet Union, developed characteristic pathologies, and American zoning bureaucracies, when they grow large, exhibit many of the same traits.[16]

Montgomery County, Maryland, although by no means a purebred specimen, vividly displays the behaviors of bureaucratic land use regulation. The county first adopted zoning in the 1920s, closely tracking Herbert Hoover's model legislation. Beginning in the 1960s, an expanding consensus of the county's residents recognized the need for a different pattern of growth, and the county moved gradually away from the suburban model of single-use zones and automobile dependence. Mixed-use downtowns around Metro stations in Bethesda and Silver Spring are outstanding examples of successful transit-oriented development.

To legalize this evolution, the county had to make substantial changes in its land use rules. But single-use zoning was never abandoned. It remains on the books, encumbered with a maze of added rules for approval of large buildings. The system thus created has strong elements of the tollbooth model. What the county wants to see built is specified not in the zoning ordinance but in master plans drafted by a planning board and approved by the county council. When a landowner wants to build, she must return to the planning board for approval of the size and design of each building and the nature and amount of amenities she will provide. Studies, reports, neighborhood meetings, and public hearings multiply—the county's characteristic style is called *paralysis by analysis.*

As the county introduced more urban design concepts, new categories emerged alongside the old ones and an ever-increasing number of exceptions made their way into the rules. When developers and neighbors reached compromises not envisaged in the regulations, still more exceptions and categories appeared. Each step along the way added new complexity. A half-century of this evolution has brought forth a confusing tangle of rules, fully understood by none but a few insiders.

A county of a million inhabitants keeps a large staff of planners busy reviewing new buildings. There is not enough time to keep all the plans up to date, and major revisions occur only when developers' eagerness to build overwhelms the system's inertia.

The saga of a shuttered Dodge dealership shows paralysis by analysis in full inaction. The property is in a mixed-use zone next to the Shady Grove Metro station. But when the area's master plan was adopted, the car dealer was happily selling vehicles and housing was assigned to other parcels. A few years later, Dodge went bankrupt and put the dealer out of business. The land found a buyer who was eager to put up a 417-unit apartment building. This proposal won the support of the neighbors, and it clearly conformed to the county's smart growth policy. But the planning board, its staff reduced by budget cuts, didn't have time for the studies and hearings required for master plan amendments. Even hundreds of new apartments near a subway station were not enough to justify the effort.[17]

The county's steady flow of construction generates so much paperwork that the planning board and county council cannot possibly absorb all the detail. As in Soviet central planning, power inevitably flows downward to the people directly concerned, the only ones with enough information to make intelligent judgments. Overworked low-level staff are happy to accept decisions negotiated between the developer and the neighbors, and no one higher up knows enough to overrule them. Paralysis by analysis empowers the directly interested parties to collude against the wider public, and the same deleterious effects emerge as in the tollbooth model.

Soviet planning is mirrored as well in a bias toward large-scale investments. Buildings on small lots rarely yield enough revenue to repay the cost of studies and hearings needed for approval, and small parcels can't be chopped up into enough pieces to meet all the requirements. Large developments are preferred by regulators, too, because it takes more time to review and approve many little projects than one big one.

As Jane Jacobs emphasized, diversity of ownership helps create lively urban centers. By making urban-style building impossible on small lots, the county forces small landowners to sell out to large developers. New developments arrive in a corporate style, and the public—often the same people who insisted on the lot-size restrictions—complains about their sterility.

The defects of this system come together in Montgomery County's parking rules. The ordinance announces that every housing unit must have two off-street parking spaces and follows with a long list of ways to have fewer. Some reductions are voluntary and some mandatory; all involve expensive paperwork. A builder of apartments above a supermarket near the White Flint Metro station ran into rules that directly contradict each other. Traffic has to be controlled by limiting the number of arriving cars. Yet off-street parking is still required. The owners wind up counting cars entering the garage to prove that no one parks in spaces the county made them build.

In recent years, financial pressures and changing public attitudes have challenged this way of doing things. A rewrite of the zoning code is under way. And an ambitious plan for the White Flint area, adopted in 2010, sweeps away many older rules to replace superblocks and strip malls with high-rises fronting on a grid of streets.

Suburban construction is not the only sector of the economy where status sells. Nightclubs, like neighborhoods, thrive on exclusivity, and both employ gatekeepers to maintain the desired aura. These functionaries—bouncers, doormen, and planners—bring diverse credentials to their work, but they all have the same task. Their job is to keep the riffraff out while carefully trading off revenue against cachet. The balding hedge fund manager with a taste for champagne gets seated in the VIP section for the same reason the office building is allowed to go up along the interstate.

Restricting access to nightspots does little substantial harm. No one is compelled to visit them, and getting shut out brings no physical detriment beyond the loss of time. Clubs, moreover, fill only a small part of the demand for alcohol. If all you want is a beer, there is no need to wait behind a velvet rope.

Housing and jobs, on the other hand, are necessities of life. Land-use controls crop up everywhere, and no one who needs to earn a living or find a place to sleep can escape their grasp. At the zoning board as in the nightclub, the coupling of snobbery and greed fosters wasteful extravagance and unnecessary humiliation. But to be put out on the sidewalk by the sheriff is a very different matter from being detained there by the doorman.

10

A New Thirst for City Life

America, at the end of the millenium, could seem like one big subdivision. The suburban status-seeking impulse had acquired a life of its own. As it marched down the social totem pole, each layer of society in turn imitated those above. Fed by a vast complex of vested interests, it had swatted away the scorn of intellectuals and the lawsuits of integrationists. It overpowered even the political muscle of the real estate developers who first set it in motion. In city and town alike, single-family houses and automobiles were the unquestioned normal; any other mode of life seemed somehow deviant.

A formidable apparatus of covenants, zoning ordinances, and historic districts protected the residential pecking order. These devices preserved more than neighborhoods; they maintained status distinctions inherited from long-past eras. The 1890s, when city folk looked down on the agricultural masses, lived on in rules against farm animals. The 1920s motorist's disdain for streetcar suburbs imposed off-street parking minimums. Preservation boards continued the 1960s search for authenticity.

But status symbols lose their power when everyone has them. The prestige of suburbia failed to impress those who grew up knowing no other life, and the values of a new generation clashed with inherited institutions. The first challenges to the suburb's superiority over the city came in the sixties with the apartment boom[1] and the beginnings of gentrification. By the end of the millennium, suburban living was clearly losing cachet. Highway builders still poured concrete and zoning boards chased away apartments, but the emotional foundation of the entire structure was rotting away.

Shifting status rankings were reflected in popular culture. The late fifties and sixties were the years of TV sitcoms like *Leave It to Beaver* and *Ozzie and Harriet*. Suburban families lived the only life that was truly normal. A partial return to the city accompanied the gentrification wave of the seventies and similarly petered out in the Reagan years. Then in the late nineties, following the success of *Seinfeld*, Manhattan was glamorized in *Sex and the City* and a flood of other shows.[2] The suburbs were hardly forgotten, but they had a new image; it was a long way from the family in *Father Knows Best* to the one in *The Sopranos*. By 2010 the return to the city could be taken for granted; Manhattan was almost passé as Brooklyn turned trendy.

Status symbols were eroding right in front of the house. On midcentury lawns, homeowners labored to keep lawns carefully mowed and to exclude broad-leafed crabgrass from their precious turf. The intrusive species was such a symbol of suburban living that Kenneth Jackson's history of the suburbs, published in 1985, was titled *Crabgrass Frontier*.

Once sod grew in front of rich and poor alike, it lost prestige. Manicured lawns have hardly disappeared; many homeowners like the look. But they are no longer a national obsession. The war against crabgrass has ended in surrender; people under thirty barely know what Kenneth Jackson's title means. Google in 2009 rented a herd of goats to nibble down the turf around its headquarters, and this once-forbidden practice[3] has become a fad. Cities are changing their laws to allow grazing in residential zones.[4]

Even the quintessentially suburban game of golf is losing its allure. In 2011 in the United States 11% fewer rounds were played than in 2000. The number of golf courses peaked in 2005 and began to decline.[5]

Yet the norms of suburbia remain deeply ingrained. Homeowners still wedded to the old values—among them most civic association leaders and many government officials—find it inconceivable that others might want to live differently. Affluent city dwellers, when too numerous to be ignored, are dismissed as hipsters acting out a soon-to-be-outgrown stage of immaturity.[6]

Suburban nonconformity still meets stiff resistance, with concessions made only grudgingly. Nature lovers let their lawns go to seed, and neighbors demand strict enforcement of grass-cutting ordinances. A Michigan woman, in 2011, was threatened with three months in jail for growing vegetables in front of her house.[7]

Bitter battles erupt between adherents of the now-fashionable "locavore" movement and defenders of the long-standing exclusion of farm animals from residential zones. When Montgomery County moved to legalize backyard henhouses, sharp criticism came from both wealthy Chevy Chase and more modest neighborhoods. At a public hearing, one witness called the proposal "a cultural slap in the face" at African Americans who had grown up poor. With success, she said, "they left behind the poverty and the stigma of racism associated with the chickens. For many that achievement included a suburban single-family home and neighborhood."[8]

Elsewhere zoning boards debate at length the fine distinctions between unproductive pets, which homeowners may harbor, and useful livestock that are proscribed. This last issue came to a head in Belmont, California, which advanced the cause of scientific land use planning by pioneering the separation of pet goats from farm animals. The city's lawmakers adopted a 1600-word ordinance laying down conditions under which pygmy goats of the species *Capra hircus* may be raised in residential zones.[9]

The growing popularity of cities was felt most of all in real estate markets. After a pause of a decade or so, gentrification resumed in force in the mid-nineties. It was now the rule rather than the exception in cities that enjoyed prosperity and good transit. A decade into the new millennium, waves of upscale newcomers had washed across the entire island of Manhattan; reached through San Francisco, Boston, Chicago, and Portland, Oregon; and touched nearly every corner of Washington, DC. In places like Denver and Salt Lake City, a skimpy light rail network was enough to spark a new flowering of downtown, and a few smaller cities like Portland, Maine, managed vigorous revivals with no rail at all. Even in Detroit, where the local economy was worst, residential districts near downtown began to revive.[10]

Once the return of the affluent was a mass phenomenon, city living lost its subversive overtones. Upscale neighborhoods now attract families along with the childless. Lower Manhattan is awash with children; turf battles in Brooklyn bars pit singles against stroller-pushing parents.[11]

Gentrification, as the public sees it, is still the progression from starving artists to granite countertops that urban bohemias experienced between the mid-fifties and the nineties. But that image is out of date; today real estate interests often take the lead. Speculators may jump in first, buying up property even before the neighborhood begins to improve. New apartment buildings can precede renovation of the existing housing stock. The developer, in a gesture to tradition, may kick things off by renting loft-like apartments to

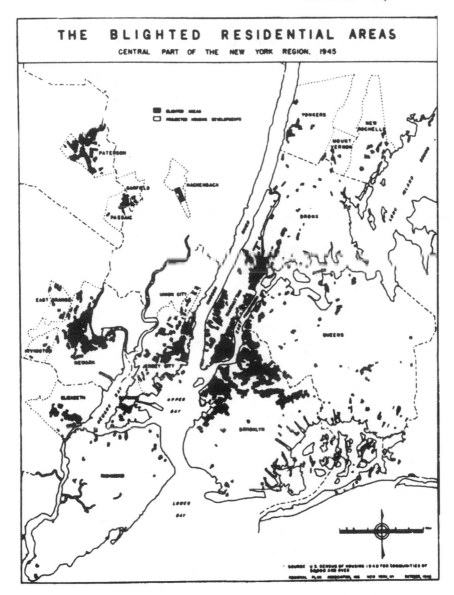

What are today the expensive sections of New York, Jersey City, and Hoboken were the cities' blighted areas in 1945.

(National Housing Agency map reproduced in Scott, American City Planning.)

artists at a loss. Or the bohemian phase can be skipped entirely—an omission concealed by real estate promoters' habit of decorating their merchandise with status markers that have lost their original function. One comes across "arts districts" whose residents are no more likely to earn their living with paintbrush and easel than a McMansion with a carriage driveway is to have a coach-and-four stabled in the back.[12]

And cities have found another way to revive. New ethnic neighborhoods spring up, often replacing concentrations closer to downtown. New York's Chinatown now has fewer Chinese residents than Flushing, Queens; Little Tokyo, near downtown Los Angeles, has been supplanted by Gardena; the center of Washington's Salvadoran community moved out of Mount Pleasant and settled beyond the city limits in Maryland. New York's outer boroughs have seen a burst of construction activity; immigrants built so many small multifamily buildings that the city's population, in decline for decades, made up its losses and rose to new highs in the 2000 and 2010 censuses.

The bursting of the real estate bubble in 2005 devastated exurban tract housing, but it brought only a hiccup to the urban market. The time was past when a house was an investment; now city living was cheaper as well as cooler. No longer could homebuyers "drive til you qualify" into distant suburbs where house prices were low and then live off the growth in home equity. It made sense to move closer in for a shorter and less expensive commute. In the early nineties, the central city's share of new housing had been 11% in the Chicago area and 18% in New York. By 2008 the figures were 51% and 67%.

Urban housing prices fell a bit after the crash and then resumed their upward course. Condos were hard to sell—prospective buyers lost their appetite for investing in real estate—but downtown buildings could be remarketed as rentals. By 2009 apartment rents were moving up sharply. Urban high-rises sprouted from the earth wherever the economy retained some strength—the construction of big apartment buildings did not drop at all after 2005.[13]

The popularity of gentrified urban districts inspired an obvious thought. Why not build new neighborhoods like the old ones? It was a simple question to ask but not so easy to answer. The nature of the city had been changed irrevocably by the automobile and by zoning; the conditions that let streetcar suburbs grow naturally could not be replicated.

A new planning paradigm was needed; architects were the first to frame one. Andres Duany and his wife, Elizabeth Plater-Zyberk, won a commission in the 1980s to design a resort from scratch on the Florida panhandle, with the freedom to write their own zoning code. Kentlands, a suburban community outside Washington, soon followed. The success of these projects led to meetings with like-minded architects around the country. In 1993 they founded the Congress for the New Urbanism and issued a twenty-seven-point manifesto.[14]

At the heart of the New Urbanism was a root-and-branch rejection of the doctrines that created suburbia. Planning is art, not engineering. Districts of varying density and style, purposefully arranged along a "transect," replace

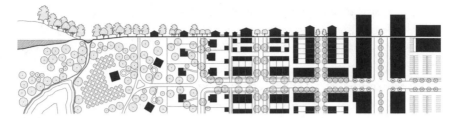

New urbanist transect.
(Courtesy of Duany Plater-Zyberk and Company.)

sprawl. The struggle against "human congestion" is no more; houses are built on small lots close to sidewalks. Walking and transit are preferred to the automobile. Workplaces, stores, and homes stand side by side; all ages, races, and incomes live together.

The creators of the first New Urbanist communities were in no position to take on nimby neighbors and zoning codes. They located in outer suburbs or even in rural areas, giving up the chance to build near transit. But the success of these pioneers showed that money could be made. Other developers followed, men and women with the patience, the political savvy, and the financial strength that it took to redevelop built-up areas.

The capital markets were still set up to finance cookie-cutter buildings, and it did not take long for a standardized, dumbed-down New Urbanism to emerge. By the late nineties, lenders and investors had bought into two conventional varieties of urban-style development.

One was the downtown apartment building with, perhaps, a shop or two on the first floor. In big cities with expensive land, it would be ten to twenty stories high with underground parking. In suburbs and smaller cities, a parking structure would hide behind four or five floors of wood-frame apartments. Where the surroundings were right, such buildings contributed to a genuinely urban setting, and if near a railroad station they added riders.

The other new standard was an odd hybrid, the "lifestyle" shopping center. Its stores were arranged along a pseudo–Main Street with wide sidewalks. The shopping area was surrounded by parking, and buses, if allowed onto the property at all, were kept out of the shopping area and made to stop on the far side of the garage. Still, the owners had at least begun to recognize what the market was looking for.[15]

Developers and architects were learning as they went, and after 2000 their work came closer to the goals of the New Urbanists. Apartment houses filled out the ground floor with stores; lifestyle shopping malls added offices or housing upstairs; infill was built near rail lines instead of subdividing empty land; new streets opened up suburban superblocks; excess parking was cut back. The new showpieces of the movement, like the Bethesda and Clarendon stations of the Washington Metro, had the access to transit that a Kentlands and a Seaside lacked.

The urbanism delivered by trend-following developers was still of varying quality. West Broad Village, launched in 2009 outside Richmond, Virginia, is more than two miles from the nearest bus stop. The row houses that builders advertise as "urban brownstones" are made of wood and plasterboard. A little patch of grid streets is marooned inside a superblock, with houses and stores fronting roadways that dead-end in grass and parking lots. West Broad Village may be no more than a life raft adrift in a sea of sprawl, but it delivers something the subdivisions around it lack. The condos are selling briskly.[16]

Far more successful was the transformation of older suburban downtowns. Market trends brought mixed uses to what had been mostly commercial centers. During the housing bubble, condo prices rose much faster than office rents. Apartment houses were put up on empty lots between the office towers. Here was the diversity of uses that, as Jane Jacobs observed years earlier, somehow works better when it comes spontaneously than when it's planned.

The builders of the new mixed-use areas were carried forward on a current of popular demand, but they swam with weights tied to their ankles. Only after a safe passage through the treacherous waters of negotiations and approvals could they put a shovel in the ground. Along the way they invariably had to compromise urbanist visions to meet the demands of traffic engineers, zoning boards, and suburban neighbors.

So great was the risk and expense of this journey that few embarked on it without the promise of large profits. New Urbanist projects went up, for the most part, in the wealthiest sectors of the metropolis. In less affluent areas— where prospective residents had far more need for the lower cost of living that jettisoning one's automobile brings—developers still adhered to the tired suburban formulas of setbacks and parking lots.

The automobile, once a luxury and now a necessity, suffered the same loss of status as the lawn. Pleasure driving gave way to the killer commute. Carhops were a memory preserved in films like *American Graffiti*; drive-throughs were everywhere. Drive-in movies were nearly extinct. The magic carpet to glamor and prestige had become a ticket to drudgery.

In time, the altered values led to changes in behavior. The miles Americans drive, after rising steadily for a half-century with only brief interruptions for recessions and gasoline price spikes, leveled off in the prosperous years after

2004. Ridership on transit, which stagnated in the eighties and fell during the recession of the early nineties, took off in 1995. The biggest increases were on subways and light rail lines.

Economic factors, especially rising gas prices, helped these trends along, but the underlying causes were cultural and generational. Carpooling continued a long-term decline, the opposite of what would happen if cost were the main reason people drove less. The drop in automobile use, moreover, was almost entirely among drivers under forty.[17]

For a sizable minority of young adults in the new millenium, living without an automobile ceased to carry shame. With fear of global warming growing, it could even be a badge of environmental honor. It was easier, too; car-sharing services offered the convenience of driving a car now and then without the cost and bother of owning one. Some now boasted of being "car-free."

The most dramatic transit revival took place in Washington. In 2000, barely a quarter-century after the city's first Metro line opened, the number of rail passengers surpassed the sum of Boston's subway, light rail, and commuter trains. The city was now second only to New York in total rail ridership. Auto registrations in the District of Columbia dropped 6% between 2005 and 2008, although the population grew 2% and gentrification was driving income levels upward. The downtown commercial office district, confined before the Metro opened to the seven or eight blocks west of 15th Street, spread eastward as far as the Capitol and then leapfrogged south. In-town residential neighborhoods, where auto use had been the norm, evolved into a walking city, and new apartment districts sprang up on the edges of downtown.[18]

The biggest growth in transit use was not for traditional commuting into downtown but for nonwork travel. This reflected a shift in lifestyle as people no longer organized their lives around the automobile. Between 1999 and 2010, the number of people boarding the Washington Metro during the morning rush hour—a good measure of commuting travel—increased 34%. Over the same period, ridership increased 64% on Saturdays and Sundays.[19]

Train travel from city homes to suburban jobs spiked upward. Reverse commuting on New York's commuter rail lines doubled within ten years, while the number of such trips taken by car barely budged. This was cultural change, not demographics. Affluent new residents of downtown neighborhoods could easily have afforded cars and suburban houses, but they chose city life and trains instead. By 2011, the international banking firm UBS was thinking of relocating its offices from Connecticut back into Manhattan. In the suburbs, explained a city landlord, "they just can't hire the bankers and traders they need."[20]

By the end of the 1970s the destruction of old trolley lines was nearly complete. Less than 200 miles of track in seven cities remained. Most survivors were routes that ran in tunnels beneath downtown streets; this was the case in Boston, Philadelphia, Newark, and—after the 1973 completion of the BART subway—San Francisco. Cleveland's trolley ran through downtown in a trench; Pittsburgh's passed through a tunnel south of town. Only in New Orleans did streetcars still run entirely at ground level.

Northern Europe had not abandoned its streetcars, and its cities, like San Francisco, were upgrading old networks by moving them off the street. American transportation planners, troubled by the high price tags of the subway systems then under construction, saw these hybrid systems as a less expensive alternative. They coined a new term, *light rail*, to describe them. Powered like streetcars by overhead wires, light rail would be separated from car traffic as much as possible, but costs would be held down by running, most of the time, at ground level with traffic lights at street crossings.[21]

The first new light rail line in the United States was in San Diego. This rapidly growing city had studied transit options for years, but in a heavily Republican region that was still building freeways there wasn't enough money for anything like San Francisco's BART. An opportunity to do something more affordable arrived suddenly in 1976. A tropical storm destroyed a freight rail line that ran from near downtown to the Mexican border, and the local transit agency quickly bought the right of way. It rebuilt the single track and opened service in 1981. The "Tijuana trolley" was an immediate success, and within three years a second track was needed. Extensions to the east and north followed.

The San Diego model—trains moved slowly on downtown streets but sped up in the suburbs where they had their own right of way—was an attractive compromise between cost and speed. It found many imitators, especially in western cities with little tradition of transit use and few of the dense old streetcar suburbs that could generate walk-on riders in large numbers. A succession of cities opened lines that expanded into networks: Portland in 1986; Sacramento and San Jose in 1987; Los Angeles in 1990; and Denver, Dallas, and Salt Lake City later in the nineties. By 2010 there were twenty-six cities with light rail systems; route mileage had nearly quadrupled in three decades.

Congress gave transit a victory in 1991 by allowing the transfer of highway money to rail projects virtually without limit. But almost nowhere did states use this new authority. Denver, Dallas, San Diego, and Salt Lake City still built freeways; they paid for light rail with sales tax increases pushed through by alliances between downtown business interests and environmentalists.[22] The new rail lines revived these cities' fading downtowns and stimulated New Urbanist development around outer stations, and they were immensely popular. Yet they only modestly deflected the overall direction of growth. The bulk of new jobs and housing still went to the car-dependent suburban fringe.

In Portland and Sacramento, light rail lines took the place of canceled freeways. The greatest change in urban form occurred in Portland, where the growth boundary constrained sprawl. Los Angeles, too, turned in a more urban direction as the force of demographic change and the public's craving for rail overcame the frictional resistance of endlessly squabbling politicians. Immigrants remade former automotive suburbs, and riders poured onto trains and buses.[23] But California lacked Oregon's state-level land-use controls, and the real estate boom brought an explosion of exurban sprawl alongside the downtown revival. Los Angeles and Sacramento are now cleaning up after burst bubbles of McMansion-building in their outer reaches.

New light rail lines were built in older eastern cities too. In Jersey City and Hoboken, where light rail connected to older rail tunnels under the Hudson to New York, a high-rise boom town rose on a decrepit old waterfront. In St. Louis and Buffalo, with much weaker economics, new rail access supported a modest gentrification in neighborhoods near downtown.

Transit would not remake a city if you couldn't walk to the station. But the traffic engineers' premise that roadways were for cars was by now a widely held belief. The idea that streets should be designed for other purposes was slow to take hold.

The earliest corrections of past mistakes were removals of urban expressways. The first highways to go actually collapsed on their own—New York's corroded West Side Highway in 1973 and San Francisco's Embarcadero Freeway, trigger of the revolt against the interstates, in a 1989 earthquake. Voters saw that the absence of the highway did not bring traffic gridlock, and after pitched political battles the elevated expressways were replaced with surface boulevards. These examples were contagious—highway demolition led to neighborhood rebirth—and after 2000 cities began to experiment gingerly with the removal of highways that still functioned.[24]

But lesser streets were slow to change. Outside the densest cities, those who walked had little voice. In old automotive suburbs with rapidly changing populations, immigrant pedestrians risked life and limb on roads engineered for the rapid movement of native-born drivers. New suburban transit stations were often ringed by parking lots and high-speed roadways, discouraging all but the poorest or most committed from reaching them on foot.

Bicyclists were far better organized than pedestrians, and they had worked for decades to have their needs recognized. They succeeded, at first, mostly in getting off-road bike trails that were designed for recreation and served few commuters. John Forester in the 1970s had introduced the concept of vehicular cycling—the idea that bicycles could often move faster and more safely by sharing traffic lanes with cars rather than on separate pathways where they were vulnerable to collisions with turning cars. Cyclist organizations pursued this idea, but they made little headway in getting traffic engineers to accept the idea of designing streets for nonmotorized users.

In 2003, bicycle advocates broadened the idea of bicycles in traffic lanes into the "complete street," a roadway designed for all of its users, pedestrians as well as cyclists. The slogan took hold far faster than the reality. By 2010, more than a hundred places had written policies endorsing complete streets.[25]

These ideas were put only slowly into practice. It took two high-profile city transportation commissioners to shake things up. Janette Sadik-Khan took charge of New York's streets in 2007, and Gabe Klein followed a year later in Washington. Soon cars were giving up space downtown to make room for wide sidewalks, and new bicycle lanes were fenced off from moving cars. Klein trumpeted the new approach with a high-profile bike lane down the middle of Pennsylvania Avenue from the Capitol to the White House.

Even more visible was Sadik-Khan's remaking of Broadway, for the previous century a four-lane avenue where the car was king. Through most of midtown, cars were now limited to one through lane. One lane was reserved for bikes, and pedestrians got space to walk and sit. Times Square, long renowned for its jammed sidewalks, became a vast pedestrian plaza that cars could enter only when passing through on cross streets.[26]

Elsewhere change rarely went as far. Palm Beach County, Florida, which did more than most suburbs, shows how far there is to go. The county calmed traffic in a few of its scattered downtowns, but these are small corners of a sprawling suburban domain. Elsewhere it continues to build six-lane highways with no on-street parking, 50-mile speed limits, and turn lanes at nearly every corner. Sidewalks jut up against the roadway, separated from stores, homes, and hospitals by walls and ditches. Narrow bike lanes painted next to high-speed traffic are little more than a futile gesture.

In the nineties these trends—the return to the city, New Urbanism, the transit revival—converged with long-standing worries about sprawl.

Broadway at 41st Street, with former traffic lanes now used by pedestrians and bicycles.
(Photo by Jim Henderson.)

Bicycle lanes are a futile gesture when placed amid forty-five lanes of motor vehicle traffic. Forest Hill Boulevard and State Route 7 in Palm Beach County, Florida.
(U.S. Geological Survey photo.)

Environmentalists, facing the menace of global warming, desired more than ever to curb the use of cars. To escape from the political trap created by the failure of growth controls, they sought a new synthesis.

They dropped the slogans of "no growth" or "slow growth" in favor of a new theme of "smart growth"—the idea of accepting new building and directing it into compact, ecologically sustainable nodes where people can get around without driving. The smart growth advocates reached out in two directions, building coalitions with rural preservationists and urban real estate interests. Seeing how sprawl had leapfrogged over local growth controls, they made their push at the state level.

The idea, but not the name, was pioneered in Oregon. State planners, given a veto over local zoning rules by the 1973 growth boundary law, insisted that cities allow at least half of new housing to be apartments and townhouses. In the Portland area, home to half the state's population, rules promoting multi-family housing were further strengthened in 1990 and 2000.[27]

Maryland put smart growth on the national agenda. In 1997, Governor Parris Glendening proposed an initiative of that name, aimed at controlling sprawl by concentrating growth in older neighborhoods. Growth boundaries and state review of land use rules were out of the question politically—local zoning was defended by rural development interests and suburban home-owners alike—but Glendening managed to push a weaker concept of "priority funding areas" through the legislature. As in Oregon, each county would draw a line around the areas designated for development, and the state would pay for roads, schools, and other infrastructure only within the boundary. Glendening held office for another five years, and state funds were redirected toward urban centers.[28]

The smart growth movement has spread around the nation, winning support from both left and right. But its legislative achievements have been modest. Advocates have secured the passage of growth management laws in many states. But in Maryland and elsewhere, politicians hesitate to challenge local control of zoning. It is now three decades since any legislature empowered state planners to overturn snob zoning rules.

The political climate is not hospitable to new directions. The public openness to social reform of the 1960s and 1970s is long gone. With growth controls under constant assault from the right, environmentalists hesitate to grant power to unelected state officials; they fear it will be used not to promote urban revival but to override protections of rural land. Conservative office-holders fear to pit their business backers against homeowning constituents. Change in laws comes far more slowly than in the marketplace.

11

Backlash from the Right

By the end of the millenium planners and downtown developers had embraced smart growth. People in their twenties and thirties flocked to cities. But urbanism did not lack for enemies.

A long-established principle, the social superiority of single-family houses, was in question. Neighborhood activists, wedded to the status quo, were numerous and vocal; the nimby worldview had deep roots in the branded neighborhoods of the postindustrial economy. In a world of growing income inequality, the wealthy strove to separate themselves from the merely well-off, and the marginally affluent struggled to stand apart from the poor.

New Urbanists tried to mollify their critics by pointing out that no one wanted to get rid of traditional suburbs. They insisted that they sought only to open up additional choices for those who wanted them. But this missed the point. A world of smart growth might let owners of single-family houses keep their structures, but it deprived them of their privileged place in the residential pecking order.

Economic interests that profited from sprawl were at risk as well. They had money, and they knew how to use it in politics. The highway lobby, always dependent on government contracts, was adept at keeping those contracts coming. The developers of tract subdivisions lived by their ability to influence local governments and their land-use rules.

These two forces—homeowners and politically connected businesses—could be stronger joined together than either could on its own. Neither grass-roots protest alone nor backroom influence-peddling could turn back the smart growth tide; lobbying needed electoral backing. Protecting the status quo of sprawl required an alliance, and the alliance would need a political program to mobilize the homeowner masses.

Experienced partisans were at the ready, prepared to fill this demand. Beginning in the 1970s, foundations and research institutes funded by the Mellons, the Kochs, and other wealthy conservatives had nurtured a cadre of far-right public policy experts.[1] For these ideologues for hire, smart growth was a business opportunity. The real estate industry had already turned to them for arguments against growth control. They now jumped at the chance to target public transit too.

A separate group of anti-transit consultants was already in the field—they had entered the market niche opened up by referendum battles over light rail. Once the Smart Growth movement took off in the late nineties, the right-wing network invited the rail critics in. Sam Staley became deputy director of the Reason Foundation; Wendell Cox received part-time appointments with both the Heartland Institute, a center of global warming denial, and the Heritage Foundation; Randal O'Toole wound up on the staff of the Cato Institute.[2]

How would these advocates frame the issue? Development battles, up to then, had been fought largely on local issues. Without any general principles to call on, opponents of smart growth had no good way to explain what they disliked. Open avowals of status-seeking had always been rare, and other rationales had problems of their own. The ecological argument for growth controls in particular had to go; environmentalists were now on the other side.

Defenders of suburbia could still say that a "way of life" was under attack. But the argument had to be made carefully—the way of life must be something loftier than keeping people with less money out of the neighborhood. The right-wing think tanks, specialists in protecting wealth and privilege by waging culture war, knew what to do. They drew up a case for sprawl that rests overtly on population statistics and economic theories but conveys an underlying cultural and emotional message. The single-family suburb embodies true Americanism, under attack by an alien cultural elite.

There was nothing new in this maneuver; appeals to conformism and nativism have long buttressed the single-family neighborhood. Already in 1922 George F. Babbitt, Sinclair Lewis' fictional realtor, denounced long-haired professors and invoked American supremacy. After World War II, Senator Joseph McCarthy held lengthy hearings where builders denounced public housing as un-American and contended that rental apartments breed communists. For Governor Thomas Kean of New Jersey in 1983, a court decision that allowed lower-income housing in exclusive towns was moving toward "a socialistic country, a communistic country, a dictatorship."[3]

Now that the prestige of suburbia is past its peak, the same themes play to anxieties of declining status. Cox, trained as a demographer who calculates numbers, calls his book on sprawl *War on the Dream*. Robert Bruegmann, himself a professor of art history, disparages the smart growth movement as an elitist revolt against the healthy masses. Joel Kotkin tells us that California is waging "war against single-family homes" on behalf of "aging hippies who made their bundle during the state's glory days and settled into places like Mill Valley."[4]

The conservative defenders of sprawl were adept at pushing these emotional buttons, but they had a logic problem to deal with. The fundamental tenet of their libertarian think tanks is that government may not tell property owners what to do with their property. But suburbia has little to do with the free markets that libertarians claim to believe in. Covenants, zoning, subsidies, and exclusions created it and kept it alive.

It wasn't just principles that libertarians had to ignore when they made the case for sprawl—there were facts, too. In gentrifying downtown neighborhoods, and at transit stations in upscale suburbs, property values have spiked upward and apartment construction has surged. This puts the critics of smart growth in a bind. In the market worldview, it is an article of faith that prices reflect consumer preferences. The rising price of urban real estate irrefutably contradicts the claim that suburban sprawl is where people want to live. It's hard to argue that the market's wrong when you start from the premise that it's always right.

The core of the problem is suburban land tenure—the homeowner's power to control what happens on a neighbor's land. The entire edifice of free-market economic theory rests on the supremacy of consumer choice. But in the single-family suburb a collectivized status-seeking apparatus overrides the preferences of individual property owners.

To be accepted in the conservative network, writers must defend suburban land tenure yet appear to uphold the doctrine of the sovereign consumer. It isn't easy. Robert Bruegmann tries to justify zoning as an exercise of consumer sovereignty, empowering people to choose how and where they live. Liberal critics of suburbia, as he sees things, fail to appreciate how much ordinary people value choice.

This point is illustrated with the example of a woman who takes three buses from a trailer park in central New Jersey to a low-paid job at Newark Airport. Sprawl, Professor Bruegmann argues, gives her the benefit of choosing to live in the trailer park. The reader can only guess what he would think if the woman's hometown outlawed mobile homes. The professor has no grounds for objecting to the change of rules—the rezoning would be an exercise of consumer sovereignty, just like the snob zoning that first made the bus odyssey necessary. Now that the airport worker is homeless, his logic would suggest, she has more choice, and so she's better off than before. Before there was only one trailer park—now she can choose among so many trees to sleep under![5]

Bruegmann at least makes an effort to reconcile land-use controls with consumer sovereignty; many of his cothinkers simply ignore the contradiction. Randal O'Toole tells us that he first turned against smart growth out of outrage that his neighbors might be allowed to build multifamily housing on land they owned—when government failed to impose a ban, he contends, it was impermissibly telling people how they should live. Wendell Cox denounces nimbyism and exclusionary zoning when they stop suburbs from being built and lets them pass unnoticed when they keep suburbs from changing into something else.[6]

Joel Kotkin, as he looks fifty years ahead, takes more pains to cover his tracks. "In the 21st century," he assures us, "families and businesses will have ever more freedom to locate where they wish." Kotkin goes on to denounce urbanists who want Americans to be "crammed into high-density communities." The good news, he reports, is that the future will be Phoenix and not Boston; "resistance from largely lower-density communities close to the core" will save the cities from cramming. Kotkin carefully navigates around the means by which this resistance makes itself felt. In a 243-page book about land use, the word *zoning* never appears.[7]

Prosprawl theorists could get only so far by ignoring zoning. Their mass constituency, the preservers of the single-family neighborhood, expected an active endorsement of their most powerful weapon. Yet the thinkers could not abandon the deregulatory agenda of their funders. They needed a supple doctrine, one that condemns antisprawl land-use rules as intolerable interference with the free market yet explicitly endorses exclusionary zoning.

It was no mean feat to devise a coherent argument in support of two propositions that so manifestly contradict each other, but the right-wing think tanks specialized in this sort of intellectual gymnastics. A 2001 manifesto called the Lone Mountain Compact laid out the orthodox defense of sprawl. The leading transit opponents joined academics and a scattering of right-wing luminaries as signers.

The manifesto starts out, as expected, with ringing affirmations of the free-market faith. "The most fundamental principle is that…people should be allowed to live and work where and how they like," and "Densities and land uses should be market driven, not plan driven." Such principles might logically have led into a defense of property owners' right to build as many apartments near transit stations as tenants want to rent.

But here it takes a detour. The Lone Mountain Compact does not reject all constraints on landowners' right to develop their property—it condemns only those that are "centrally directed." It's just fine for small wealthy enclaves to infringe on property rights by zoning out apartment buildings. Even better if renters are denied the right to vote on these rules: "Local neighborhood associations and private covenants are superior to centralized or regional government planning agencies."[8]

This was a deft maneuver. As libertarians, the compact signers could distinguish deed covenants, agreements entered into voluntarily, from growth controls imposed by law. But after carefully drawing a sharp line between private contract and government fiat, they immediately rubbed it out. Zoning, they decided, is acceptable when imposed by small townships where everyone owns property, because there it works in practice like a covenant. There was no need to spell out what it is the two have in common—the denial of voting rights to the people who are kept out. Land-use regulation, Lone Mountain doctrine holds, is not evil per se. It's wrong only when it's enacted democratically for the benefit of the whole community.

Peter Gordon, a more systematic thinker than other Lone Mountain signers, makes the exclusionary logic explicit. Gordon concedes that individual landowners cannot always be free to use their property as they want; some form of collective governance is unavoidable. What he objects to, as a matter of principle, is democracy; dollars, not people, deserve to vote. "The very features that may give political institutions strength at the same time create severe problems," he complains. "Voters are often not landowners (e.g., the 80 percent renter population in the politically active city of Santa Monica, California). Many zoning decisions negatively affect landowners."[9]

In any case, the libertarian distinction between laws and covenants hardly stands up to scrutiny. Consider the buyer of a house in the planned community of Columbia, Maryland. The deed she signs binds her to rules James Rouse established in 1963. That is a free consumer choice, the doctrine holds, while growth controls elsewhere in that state are an assault on liberty. But this is a difference in form alone. The Columbia homeowner association can be escaped only by leaving town, and the same remedy is open to those who dislike the land use rules of local governments.

For that matter, Maryland itself was established as a private enterprise. Lord Proprietor Cecil Calvert and his heirs ruled the colony, granted to them by the king of England. Settlers who bought their land became subject to their government. These purchases, for white residents at least, were as voluntary as any other real estate transaction; the colonial government rested on the same basis of consent as today's Columbia Association. Today Cecil Calvert and James Rouse are equally dead. After Calvert's passing, however, the events of 1776 intervened, and only Rouse's government still operates under the law of real estate. That, if you follow the libertarian reasoning to its logical conclusion, is a misfortune; the people of Maryland would be freer if George III had won the war and the state was administered as a private corporation.

The arguments might be frail, but they serve their purpose. The political and legal campaign against growth controls under way since the 1980s has a rationale. The movement's slogan is property rights, and its central aim is to win compensation for landowners prevented from developing their land. But its targets were carefully marked off—single-family zoning was left alone.

The political ground zero of this campaign was Oregon. Landowners outside the state's growth boundaries organized as Oregonians in Action to overturn the rules. Large timber interests paid many of the bills, but the message was the populism of the right-wing think tanks. Growth control backers, the group's lawyer said, "are intellectual elitists, driving with their tops down in their Saabs, drinking Chardonnay." [10]

When Oregonians in Action went into action, the principle of property rights had only selective application. In 2001 the organization tried to overturn zoning rule changes that, by allowing more apartments to be built on vacant land within the growth boundary, enlarged the rights of landowners. Its 2004 property rights referendum, approved by the voters but overturned in court, explicitly exempted from its scope all zoning rules older than the state's 1973 growth boundary law. The right to property, in practice, was the right to build single-family houses and nothing else. [11]

The property rights movement's legal strategy yielded mostly losses, but the courtroom successes it did achieve had the same selective effect as its political action. One partial victory was the 1992 case of South Carolina developer David Lucas. The Supreme Court decided that while no compensation is due when government restricts the way land is used, owners must be paid if no use at all is permitted. This ruling left local governments free to promote sprawl with single-family zoning but limited their power to restrain it by stopping development altogether. The limitations were not severe—later cases narrowed the impact of this ruling—but they were one more obstacle in the way of sprawl control.[12]

The movement pressed on in the face of legal defeats, and it was able to score political wins. Some western states passed laws that required compensation for "partial takings"—regulations that limit the use of land. The Republican tide of 2010 brought further gains. In Florida, a new right-wing governor and conservative legislature repealed very mild growth controls that had been enacted in 1985.

The rise in 2009 of the Tea Party, which married dislike of cities to fervor against government, enlarged the grass-roots base of the campaign against growth control. A movement where calls were heard to keep government out of Medicare was hardly bothered by the inconsistency between deregulation and tight suburban zoning. Donna Holt, the leader of Ron Paul's Campaign for Liberty in Virginia, worried that rural landowners will not be able to sell their farms to developers if housing is built in cities. "Infill development and vertical sprawl are overtaxing urban environments," she warned. Holt urged fellow believers in the free market to oppose "restrictive zoning" that forbids tract housing. At the same time, she encouraged bans on the building of apartment houses—such zoning, somehow, is not restrictive.[13]

The Tea Party's attention soon turned to a 1992 United Nations resolution called Agenda 21. This lengthy document, little known until it drew the ire of Tea Party activists, exhorts member nations to conserve open space through denser growth. It suddenly came under attack as a nefarious plot. As one activist describes it, Agenda 21 is "the action plan implemented worldwide to inventory and control all land, all water...all information, and all human beings in the world."

Exposés spread through Tea Party networks and made their way onto Fox News. Glenn Beck wrote a novel titled *Agenda 21* that starts out, "They took Mother away today." Denunciations of apartment houses and bike lanes as elements of a worldwide conspiracy flooded into zoning boards and town councils.[14]

By 2012 the outcry became Republican Party dogma. In January the party's National Committee passed a resolution that denounced Agenda 21 as a threat to "the American way of life of private property ownership, single family homes, private car ownership and individual travel choices." Later in the year the party's election platform denounced the Barack Obama administration for "replacing civil engineering with social engineering as it pursues an exclusively urban vision of dense housing and government transit." Residents of apartments and townhouses were, by implication, un-American, especially if they went to work on a bus.

Here the cultural agenda of the Tea Party was manifest. As much as the campaign against Agenda 21 advertised itself as a property rights movement, what it really sought is enforced uniformity of living arrangements. Zoning rules are good when they force people to live in single-family houses by denying landowners the opportunity to build other kinds of homes. Only regulations that keep land undeveloped are evil.

Not all right-wingers place political convenience above intellectual rigor. In the last decade a school of libertarian urbanists has emerged, propounding a free-market case against sprawl. Harvard economist Edward Glaeser, a paragon of careful empirical research, sees density as almost a cure-all for urban problems. For others in this group, such as Michael Lewyn and Stephen Smith, deregulation allows a variety of living arrangements to emerge and frees consumers to pick whichever pleases them.[15]

These writers offer trenchant critiques of current land-use rules and useful suggestions for reform, but their version of libertarian theory shares an underlying flaw with the prosprawl variety. Both ignore status-seeking. The premise of free-market economics is that markets are efficient because they set people free to choose what they buy and how they use what they buy. But the market for land and buildings is full of people who choose to deny their neighbors choice by excluding buyers and preventing use. Such markets free some by fettering others.

The libertarian urbanist vision, in its pure form, is even less plausible than the left-wing dream of a world without acquisitiveness. To reach either utopia, human motivations must change. Socialists can make a moral argument for "share and share alike." What rationale can libertarians offer for "greed is good, snobbery bad"?

In any case, the market urbanists' independent thinking is of little interest to the conservative establishment. In the right-wing research-propaganda complex, nothing is more important than staying on message. Discipline is enforced so strictly that the Heritage Foundation shut out its own founder's point of view. Paul Weyrich, until his death in 2008, was a fervent advocate for railroads and especially for light rail. A cultural conservative rather than a libertarian, he argued that neighborhoods built around train stations would "foster a sense of community...to uphold morals and maintain standards of behavior." Weyrich had to advocate for light rail from his Free Congress Foundation, not much more than a one-man operation; Heritage promotes the views of Wendell Cox.[16]

Smart growth threatened road builders as much as subdividers. The highway lobby had long taken a decidedly nonideological approach to politics, relying on a shower of campaign contributions that fell generously on incumbents of both parties. But as circumstances changed, the pavement people began to find right-wing religion. As early as 1977, conservative writers had complained of a war against the car. "The war against automobiles is never-ending," the political scientist James Q. Wilson wrote in 1998, and from then on the slogan repeated in a steady drumbeat.[17]

Where the property rights movement was at first orchestrated from top down, the defense of the automobile was more spontaneous. After seven decades of suburbanization, the idea that motorists possessed an exclusive right to use streets was built into the landscape and inculcated in public consciousness. Everything in the suburban environment said that roads were made for motor vehicles alone. Drivers were quick to pick up the theme of "war on cars" and run with it whenever they felt inconvenienced.

The cultural subtext of the automotive backlash is easiest to discern in the vehemence of attacks against bicycles. It is hard to make a reasoned case against bikes; they waste no one's money and abridge no one's freedom. The most one can say is that cyclists violate traffic laws, but it would be hard to find a complaining driver who never exceeds a speed limit or rolls through a stop sign. Deprived of rational argument, the various strands of anti-urbanism erupt in an explosion of status anxiety. Each uses its own language to express the same disdain for the lower orders who want to share the public roads.

Urban cyclists are belittled as "hipsters"—low-income immigrants make up a large share of cycle commuters, but they pose no threat to social standing and thus are invisible to the critics. When bike riders fail to show motorists the expected deference, they are "smug" and "self-righteous." The only motorists so labeled are Prius owners, as if no one buys a Mercedes or Cadillac to show off.

According to a Tea Party Republican candidate for governor of Colorado, short-term bicycle rental in Denver is part of the Agenda 21 strategy to rein in American cities. From a more cosmopolitan starting point, a Jaguar-driving *New Yorker* business writer reached a similar conclusion. Admitting an "emotional reaction to the bike lobby's effort to poach on our territory," he justified his animus with the complaint that bike lanes were making it impossible for him to find free parking near Manhattan restaurants.[18]

Bicyclists were not the only intruders whose presence aroused the fury of motorists. Bus lanes, speed cameras, and even pedestrians legally crossing the street in crosswalks drew angry criticism.[19] In Seattle, charges of a war on cars rained down on environmentalist mayor Michael McGinn. It was an effective mobilizing device, appealing to drivers' unthinking certainty of their possession of the roadways.

This feeling of entitlement was on clear display in 2011 when a jury in Cobb County, Georgia, found Raquel Nelson guilty of vehicular homicide. A car struck her four-year-old son and killed him while the family was crossing a five-lane highway to get from the bus stop to their garden apartment. The mother was a criminal, according to prosecutors in the wealthy Atlanta suburb, because she did not walk, with two young children and an armful of packages, a quarter-mile to the nearest crosswalk and a quarter-mile back. None of the jurors who convicted her had ever ridden a local bus.[20]

Right-wing publicists might ignore a Raquel Nelson and leave their followers to think of her as an aggressor in the war against the automobile. But they still face a problem of inconsistency when they hitch a ride on motorists' belief in the divine right of cars. Their free-market theory has little in common with reality. Suburban roads, even more than suburban neighborhoods, are made by government.

And the devotion of the automobile culture to free roads and free parking poses another even greater problem for these writers. It clashes directly with the agenda of the people paying the bills.

In an era when the highway lobby's old funding formulas have stopped working, road builders hope that toll lanes will save the day. The Reason Foundation is a center of toll road promotion; Peter Samuel, the editor of a newsletter for the toll road industry, was a signer of the Lone Mountain Compact. These and other prohighway publicists marshal economic theory to justify tolls as user fees that simply make drivers pay for the roads they drive on.

But at the grass roots, the motorist's sense of entitlement says just the opposite. Paid parking and tolls are just as much a war on drivers as bike lanes and crosswalk signals. Careful steering is required to keep the heavy artillery of the culture war pointed away from the economic interests of the sponsors.

The congestion charge, a daily fee assessed on anyone who drives into a congested downtown, brings this contradiction into the open. The issue first flared up when London's left-of-center Mayor Ken Livingstone imposed a $15 per day charge. American rightists seconded the criticism levied by British conservatives, with Wendell Cox weighing in loudly if inconsistently.[21]

The Reason Foundation, as the main center of agitation for privately operated toll roads, has no choice but to endorse user fees in principle. But when a city actually tries to impose a congestion charge, the foundation joins Cox in finding reasons to say no. Excuses were not easy to find when New York Mayor Michael Bloomberg proposed a fee on drivers in Manhattan. The best Sam Staley could do was to complain, under the headline "Bloomberg vs. the Car," that enforcement by photographing license plates raised "legitimate and troubling questions about the surveillance systems needed to implement these programs." When toll road operators three years later sought to use the same surveillance system, Staley enthused that "video license plate reader technology eliminates most of the hassle for consumers and users."[22]

Caught between their doctrine and motorists' attachment to the subsidized status quo, the road warriors keep finding reasons to reject in practice what they support in principle. Randal O'Toole wants to get rid of rules that require off-street parking in new buildings—but not now, only after public parking rates go way up. Marc Scribner of the Competitive Enterprise Institute endorses the concept of deregulating land use in Virginia—but he opposes an attempt to actually do so. The reason he gives is that streets with narrower lanes, shorter blocks, and sharp corners will somehow "force inclusion." These writers are the St. Augustines of the free market—end government regulation and make me chaste some day, they pray, but don't take away my subsidy just yet.[23]

When all else fails, conservatives raise the issue to the level of philosophy. "The real reason for progressives' passion for trains is their goal of diminishing Americans' individualism in order to make them more amenable to collectivism," writes George Will. Randal O'Toole wants to "give people freedom to choose what they want" by turning city neighborhoods into gated communities. "The war against suburbia reflects a radical new vision of American life which, in the name of community and green values, would reverse the democratizing of the landscape that has characterized much of the past 50 years," adds Joel Kotkin.[24] The battle to preserve sprawl is a defense of freedom.

12

The Language of
Land Use

Freedom and democracy, George Orwell once wrote, are words
that are "often used in a consciously dishonest way. That is,
the person who uses them has his own private definition, but
allows his hearer to think he means something quite different." Such, surely, is
the freedom of the gated community and the democracy of snob zoning.

"Politics and the English Language" was Orwell's topic,[1] and politics has
done much to debase the language of land use. The day is long past when the
buyers and sellers of houses boasted openly of their restricted communities.
Old-school homeowners, here and there, still speak frankly among themselves,
but they do better to dissemble when they make their case to the electorate as
a whole.

In more enlightened circles, status-seeking is frowned upon, and here
self-deception is the rule. Pretenses are maintained in closed conversation and
even private thought. Orwell understood this too—rote phrases, he wrote,
"perform the important service of partially concealing your meaning even
from yourself."

The law shares blame with politics for this corruption of language. Suburban land tenure, the right of a property owner to obstruct building on nearby
land, is not a recognized legal doctrine. While commonly asserted and often
successfully exercised, it invariably comes disguised as something it is not.

The Supreme Court ruled that zoning, the main enforcement mechanism of suburban land tenure, is constitutional. But it upheld it as an exercise of the "police power" and not a property right. Under this doctrine, the legitimate basis for restricting owners' use of their land is the protection of concrete, tangible interests of the larger community—there must be, in Alfred Bettman's words, "a motive related to safety or comfort or order or health." Reality, from the beginning, has been otherwise. Zoning mainly serves an intangible interest, the social status that accrues to the neighborhood through the intentionally wasteful nonuse of property.

A second chasm soon opened between fact and legal theory. The courts used the rationale of convenience to connect zoning to the police power. Dividing land into zones for designated uses, they said, gives property owners advance warning against building something that would interfere with neighboring properties. Landowners, knowing from the beginning what could and could not be built, would avoid wasting time and money on infeasible projects. Society would gain too by avoiding costly and disruptive disputes.

The promise of simplicity and certainty has, to say the least, not been fulfilled. As zoning has evolved, anything but a tract of single-family houses on large lots, or maybe a strip mall, is judged case by case. The outcome, hanging on the whims of neighbors or the push and pull of local politics, is often unforeseeable. Yet the law still conceives zoning as an exercise in systematic forethought to avoid identifiable hazards. To withstand judicial scrutiny, a city council or zoning board must justify its verdict before the courts as a rational application of fixed criteria.

Historic preservation brought yet more purposeful confusion. Nimbys who pose as preservationists speak of why they like the old building, when their real passion is dislike of the new one.

Social convention and legal fiction weigh down heavily on those engaged in land use matters, leaving them unable to speak frankly about basic concepts. If you don't want something built, an honest statement of objections invites defeat in court. Developers and their lawyers have equally compelling reasons to engage in self-censorship. When your aim is to get the project approved before the money runs out, it makes no sense to question the whole system. Straight talk is unlikely to convince the judge or the zoning board, and it risks offending neighbors who might otherwise agree to a compromise.

Now and then, in the aftermath of utter defeat, builders openly vent their feelings. Richard Babcock quotes a developer's letter to a wealthy New York suburb that did not let him put up an apartment house for the elderly. In Briarcliff, the spurned builder wrote, zoning aims to guarantee "that each newcomer must be wealthier than those who came before, but must be of a character to preserve the illusion that their poorer neighbors are as wealthy as they."

Babcock himself was an attorney of such eminence that he had license to unusual frankness. The paramount purpose of zoning, he wrote, was "the protection of the single-family house neighborhood....As might be expected, such a motive is rarely articulated as a rationale for this popular device, either by the supporters or critics of zoning."[2]

Such plain speaking is rare indeed. Developers and nimbys, although everyday antagonists, share a common interest in the prestige of the neighborhood, and both use words as tools to that end. One party directs its linguistic creativity into salesmanship. Row houses turn into *townhomes; garden apartments* grow parked cars in the gardens; dead ends are translated into French as *cul-de-sacs.* The other side, hiding its aims from the world at large and often from itself, has a weakness for phrases whose meaning slips away when carefully examined.

Land use disputes thus come before the public veiled in a thick fog of evasion, euphemism, and flat-out falsehood. From this miasma rises a plague of obscurity that infects the language itself. Terms devised to conceal reality become so familiar that they are uttered without thinking. Critics find themselves unable to question received dogmas for want of words to express their thoughts.

A tour of this vocabulary must begin with *compatibility.* The concept is at the heart of land-use regulation. In the narrow sense, incompatible uses are those that cannot coexist, like a smokehouse and a rest home for asthmatics. But the word has taken on a far broader meaning.

Compatibility, in the enlarged sense, is often thought of as a sort of similarity. But the nature of the required resemblance is hard to pin down. At times, the concept seems to disguise circular reasoning. Incompatible land uses are forbidden in the zone. What is compatible? Land uses of the kind that are allowed in the zone.

The key to deciphering this word lies in a crucial difference between compatibility and similarity. If two things are similar, they are both similar to each other, but with compatibility it is otherwise. A house on a half-acre lot is compatible with surrounding apartment buildings, but the inverse does not follow. An apartment building is incompatible with houses that sit on half-acre lots.

Compatibility, in this sense, is euphemism. A compatible land use upholds the status of the neighborhood. An incompatible one lowers it. Rental apartments can be incompatible with a neighborhood that would accept the same building sold as condos. An apartment house and a ten-room mansion are both incompatible with an older subdivision of small expensive homes: the one because apartments are inferior to houses; the other because its yard, overshadowed by the structure, fails to manifest the conspicuous waste of land that gives such areas their special cachet.

The euphemism is so well established that the narrow meaning has begun to fall into disuse. Neighbors who object to loud noises or unpleasant odors just lay out the specifics; incompatible has come to mean "I don't like it and I'm not explaining why." The word is notably unpopular with New Urbanists. Faced with such an obvious case of incompatibility, in the literal sense, as a parking lot in a walkable downtown, they call it a "disruption of the urban fabric" or a "wasteful use of land."

Compatibility may be the most pervasive linguistic deformation, but it is hardly the only one. Homeowners will complain about the *impact* on their neighborhood when basement apartments are rented out or high-rises are built nearby. This word conflates purely psychological desires, among them the wish to keep away from people with lower incomes, with physical detriments like smell and shade. Its value lies in its vagueness—objectors can make a case without saying concretely what their objection is.

The term *growth controls* refers in common usage only to rules enacted after the magic year of 1969. A law passed in 1972 that limits a 1000-acre village to 250 houses is a growth control. A zoning ordinance that went into effect five years earlier is not, even if it accomplishes the same thing by specifying that every house must sit on a 4-acre lot.

Another slippery phrase is *public use*. Here the word *use* conveys almost the exact opposite of its common meaning. Montgomery County has a definition: *public use space* is "space devoted to uses for public enjoyment, such as gardens, plazas, or walks." A common example is the plaza that sits empty between an office building and the street, elevating the status of its surroundings through the display of conspicuous waste.

The operative word in the definition is not *use* but *enjoyment*. In other words, no productive work can be done in the space. By this definitional sleight of hand, disuse becomes a kind of use, and indeed the only kind allowed. In one case in 2011, the planning board forbade the placement of a barbecue in a public use space when a neighbor complained that it would encourage the public to use the space.[3]

A similar shell game shifts the meaning of *exemplary*. In its ordinary dictionary definition, the exemplary is something fit to serve as an example for others—in other words, a thing of unusual value. This, surely, is how the public understood it when laws were passed to protect exemplary buildings. But once those laws were in effect, buildings and districts were called exemplary simply as examples of something old.[4] The intent of designating exemplary buildings as historic was to preserve the outstanding. The practice, with this linguistic trick, is to embalm the ordinary.

The word *plan* retains its original meaning, but it can conceal more than it reveals. In plain English, a plan represents an intention for the future. Plans often do express the intentions, or at least the hopes, of city leaders. But many master plans merely describe current land uses, providing a legal justification for zoning. Elsewhere plans remain on the books long after they become obsolete; no one takes the trouble to update them until a developer is ready to move. It is not rare that the intended future use of land is altogether different from what is written in the plans.

Our linguistic tour would hardly be complete without a visit to the *greedy developer*. The key to decoding this phrase is that the word *greedy* lacks semantic content. Antipathy to developers has no relation to their degree of avarice; if anything, nonprofit builders of low-income housing encounter more hostility than the truly greedy. The ostensible target is the wealthy entrepreneur who builds new houses; the real one is the people who will live in them.

The builder stands accused, often enough, of the sin of *manhattanization*. When first used in San Francisco in the late 1960s by opponents of downtown skyscrapers, this was a vivid and descriptive coinage. But just as the developer's first name lost its connection to avarice, manhattanization became unmoored from New York City. The term, in current usage, can refer to almost any structure that rises above its surroundings.

A campaign against manhattanizing Menlo Park, California, objects to a proposed master plan that would allow two-, three-, and four-story buildings around the train station. The movement's leader explains her goals by asking, "Are we going to remain a small town, with low-density development, or are we going to be more like Redwood City and Palo Alto?" Manhattanize might seem an odd choice of word to convey the meaning of "make it look like Palo Alto," but stale metaphor, as Orwell pointed out, does a service. It releases the speaker from the need to explain, or even figure out herself, exactly what she means to say. The premise of the argument against density is left unstated and thus immune from challenge.[5]

A somewhat different illness afflicts the terminology of transportation. Vocabulary again impedes critical thinking, but the problem here is not what words conceal as much what they unconsciously express. It is what is called

A rebuilt El Camino Real, the central artery of Menlo Park, California, as envisioned in a plan seen by detractors as manhattanizing the town.
(Courtesy of Perkins + Will.)

windshield perspective, the penchant of elected and unelected policymakers to see streets exclusively through the eyes of a driver.

Streetcorners, the places where Jane Jacobs found the life of the city lived, become *intersections* whose only function is to move you someplace else. When turn lanes are added it's called an *improvement* even though pedestrians find the street harder to cross. Walking, bicycling, and transit are *alternative* transportation.[6]

This windshield worldview is ingrained in the technical terminology of traffic engineers. An intersection is deemed to *fail* if cars need too much time to get through. It doesn't matter how long those on foot must wait to cross. If a car stops because a pedestrian is in the crosswalk, it is a *conflict*—something the engineers abhor. But no conflict occurs when heavy traffic keeps that same pedestrian from making a legal midblock crossing.[7]

Built into such language is the idea that nothing but cars belongs on the roads. Talk and write this way long enough, and it starts to be taken for granted that automobiles are the only normal way to get around. This becomes the unthinking assumption even when everyone knows the facts are otherwise. Thus, in Washington, DC, where only 41% of employed residents drive to work, the American Automobile Association complains that the city is being unfair to motorists because it wants to make cars optional.[8]

A brief interlude of frank discussion of zoning began around 1965. Twenty years had passed since the postwar building boom began, long enough to bring to light the weaknesses of the new suburban system. Meanwhile, the success of the civil rights movement in breaking down formal barriers of separation had turned attention to informal ones. Books appeared like Richard Babcock's *Zoning Game*, Seymour Toll's *Zoned American*, and Michael Danielson's *Politics of Exclusion*. Laws that challenged snob zoning were enacted in a few states and debated in many others.

The window closed after a decade and a half. The sixties were fading into the past, and the national mood swung rightward. On what remained of the left, moreover, egalitarianism gave way to relativism. Authenticity was now what mattered,[9] and whatever else one might think of nimbys, they certainly express an authentic strand of neighborhood opinion. Questioning the declared intentions of grass-roots groups, always a risky political maneuver, became intellectually suspect as well. Even critics of suburban land tenure found it easier to take the arguments of the system's defenders at face value. Few probed beneath the surface of words like incompatible and impact. With issues understood in such categories, the right to exclude again seemed a natural part of the background of life.

"If thought corrupts language, language can also corrupt thought," Orwell warned in his famous essay. For half a century and more, deformed language has made it hard to think clearly about the communities we live in. Our system of land use will be the easier to understand the more we use words that say plainly what we mean.

13
Breaking New Ground

Americans have long since lost their love for sprawl, yet they struggle to put something in its place. The urbanist movement has turned for inspiration to a few communities that succeeded in swimming against the current. Portland, Oregon and Arlington, Virginia, embraced smart growth before the name existed. In Maryland, grass-roots activists revived a light rail project that powerful nimbys had struck down and left for dead. Advocates and scholars have carefully studied the planning and architecture of these groundbreakers to see what worked and what did not. Their politics and governance deserve the same attention.

Portland leads the nation in smart growth policies. It has a booming down-town, an expanding light rail network, policies that promote infill develop-ment, and streets rebuilt for sharing by pedestrians, bicyclists, and drivers. Portland's success is often seen as a triumph of good planning, and it is; how-ever, years of political organizing and coalition-building made the planning possible. Oregon voters laid the groundwork for the city's transformation with three choices they made in the 1970s.

First came the election of Neil Goldschmidt as mayor of Portland. In the sixties, the city was a magnet for the young and hip, and low-key ver-sions of bohemian enclaves had emerged in old streetcar suburbs on its east side. Through these very neighborhoods, highway engineers planned to drive the 5½-mile-long Mt. Hood Freeway. In the politicized atmosphere of the times, residents new and old rose up against the threat. Goldschmidt, a twenty-nine-year-old antipoverty lawyer who had helped organize the Freedom Summer civil rights campaign in Mississippi, was elected city commissioner in 1970. He was among the first of the new urban populists to win office. Two years later he ran for the city's highest office and rode a wave of protest to victory over fierce opposition from the city's business elites.[1]

The young mayor proved adept in the exercise of political power. Taking the helm of a city in decline, he perceived the need for a program of economic revival that went beyond the concerns of the neighborhood activists who had elected him. To that end, he immediately set about building coalitions with the business interests that had opposed his election. Consensus emerged rapidly on a new land-use policy. Business got a vigorous promotion of downtown development, with the city's dense core encouraged to expand outward. For neighborhoods, there was a new emphasis on housing rehabilitation; money for parks; streets rebuilt to make room for pedestrians, buses, and bicycles; and a formal role for neighborhood associations in local governance.

The new direction in transportation was slower to emerge. Plans for more downtown parking were quickly axed, but the Mt. Hood Freeway kept moving ahead. Only in 1994 did the city and county vote to scrap the interstate. Even then there was no agreement on what to do with the money that decision freed up, and other road projects remained in dispute. The dominant power in state transportation planning was Glenn Jackson, the prohighway president of the local electric utility and chairman of the Oregon Transportation Commission. Goldschmidt forged a close personal relationship with the much older Jackson. In 1975 the two of them worked out a plan not fully revealed to the public for another two years. Jackson accepted the loss of the Mt. Hood Freeway and another planned expressway; Goldschmidt would allow a third contested interstate on the east side of the city to go forward. The freeway money was divided between the new multipurpose streets, the widening of yet another expressway, and a new transitway running east from downtown.

What kind of transit would go in the transitway was still up in the air. Goldschmidt's staff was taken with the new concept of light rail; their boss, whose downtown bus mall was then under construction, inclined toward rubber-tired vehicles. Grass-roots activists and county officials favored rail, but state highway bureaucrats were skeptical and their studies focused on busways. Then, as the mayor was fending off a profreeway challenger to his reelection, he reversed course behind the scenes. By the start of 1977, light rail was suddenly the favored option. Goldschmidt went to Washington in 1979 and served two years as federal secretary of transportation, construction of light rail began in 1983, and the line opened in 1986. The former mayor came back to

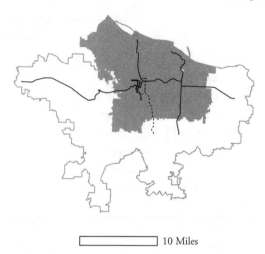

10 Miles

Portland, Oregon; city shaded, growth boundary shown as gray line. Light rail network in black, with line under construction dashed.

Oregon, served a term as governor in the late eighties, and remained the state's premier power broker until felled by a sex scandal in 2004.[2]

The second choice that shaped Portland came the summer after Goldschmidt became mayor. A moderate Republican governor, Tom McCall, pushed through the legislature a plan to draw growth boundaries around all metropolitan areas. The law established a new state agency with a veto over local land-use regulations. Its main aim was to preserve farmland in the rapidly urbanizing Willamette Valley, and its core backers were slow-growth environmentalists; McCall famously invited outsiders to "visit, but don't stay." Support came as well from farmers in the valley.[3]

In initial inspiration, Oregon's growth boundary plan differed little from the rural land reserves established elsewhere in the 1970s. But it had two key features that controls in other states lacked. Because the law applied statewide, development could not leapfrog past the boundaries into friendlier jurisdictions. Even more important, perhaps, was a rule that originated as a concession to opponents. Urban areas had to be enlarged to make room for twenty years of future population growth. This gave environmentalists, who wanted above all to keep the boundaries from moving outward, a strong stake in urban density. The more infill development was allowed, the less land would be gobbled up on the fringe.[4]

The third crucial vote came in 1978. The Portland area created an elected metropolitan government, known as Metro, with power over land use. Metro's structure, proposed by academic experts, sailed through a low-key referendum. In other states such a proposition would have triggered fierce resistance to the loss of local control over zoning. Here, where the power to oversee land use had already been centralized and suburbanites had little fear of a minority population that was small even in the city, the arrival of this new governing body seemed a mere administrative rearrangement. It turned out to be much more than that; direct elections gave Metro the independence and legitimacy it would need to override local zoning rules.[5]

The growth control law left many issues unresolved, and the new system emerged slowly; Portland did not draw its boundary until 1979. Yet the plan was hotly contested from the beginning. Three times in its first decade, opponents forced statewide referenda; the voters upheld it each time. McCall, when he left the governor's office, founded a new environmental organization called 1000 Friends of Oregon. The name went quickly out of date as the membership climbed past five times that number. Set up to protect the new growth boundaries against legal challenges, 1000 Friends broadened its horizons as time passed. By the end of the century it was defending growth control on many fronts—in referendum battles, in the courts, in the legislature and in county seats, and with its own research and planning studies.[6]

While the leadership of Neil Goldschmidt and Tom McCall launched Portland on its new course, the structure of the Oregon economy opened the way for them. For one thing, housing costs were low—this was one of the city's attractions for the bohemian influx of the 1960s. Portland rents were under the national average in 1970 and were far lower than in New York, Boston, and San Francisco. They went up little faster than inflation in the seventies and hardly at all in the eighties. Movements for rent control gained little traction, and an issue that could have gotten in the way of Goldschmidt's neighborhood-business alliance was never on the table.[7]

A second factor was the collapse of Oregon's lumber-dependent economy at the beginning of the 1980s and the political consequences that ensued. Bad times continued through most of the decade, and real estate prices plunged—adjusted for inflation, the average house in Portland lost more than 30% of its value between 1979 and 1989. Gentrification, which took hold in Portland's bohemian neighborhoods as elsewhere in the late seventies, halted when the turnover of population did not raise prices. The city's east side stayed affordable while its population changed. Portland had yet to see the dilution of its bohemian flavor that was already perceptible in Brooklyn and San Francisco, and newcomers to the city were slow to generate the sort of conservative nimby politics seen elsewhere. This political current emerged only a dozen or so years later, and in the interim linkages between infill development and growth boundaries were set in place.[8]

The local economy returned to health after 1990, propelled by a rapidly growing semiconductor industry in the affluent western suburbs. Older sections of the city shared in the prosperity, bringing the same social and economic pressures that afflicted other healthy urban areas. But the institutions that Portland had created over the previous two decades gave the city a unique ability to control its land use.

Metro's planners, required to look twenty years ahead, faced two challenges. One was the need to update the growth boundary to make room for future growth. The other was a new state rule aimed at curbing the use of cars, imposed under pressure from 1000 Friends. It mandated a 10% cut in miles driven per person and an equal reduction in parking spaces.

Planners of the early 1990s did not foresee the shifting preferences and soaring gas prices that curtailed automobile use after 2004. They judged the target of 10% less driving to be nearly unreachable. Businesses revolted against the loss of parking. The only way to cut car use, all sides agreed, was to concentrate future development at transit stations. But this would not satisfy the law unless someone could demonstrate that it would work.

The planners' computer models were capable of making the needed predictions, but only if a specific menu of land-use changes was plugged in. Local governments, fearing an eruption of public anger if they even thought about massive rezonings, were unwilling to draw up the needed menu. 1000 Friends stepped into the breach. It obtained a federal grant for its own study and hired the consulting firm doing Metro's modeling to carry out the work. The 1000 Friends report, known as LUTRAQ (for Land Use, Transportation, and Air Quality), concluded that if light rail expanded and dense urban areas were built at the stations the amount of driving would come down substantially. This combined strategy could accomplish much more than either land-use rules or new transit lines alone.

This planning process put big-picture decisions about the future of the region before the public. It left the details of what would happen on particular parcels of land to be worked out later. With the issues framed this way, LUTRAQ won wide support. Metro adopted plans that minimized expansion of the growth boundary by promoting dense transit-oriented development. Portland, in 1998, amended its zoning code to allow apartment additions on houses even in areas zoned for single-family homes.[9]

By now Oregon's growth control laws were under attack again. The concept of urban growth boundaries was too well accepted to be taken on directly.

The opponents, organized as Oregonians in Action, adopted a strategy that was the reverse of the other side's—they drew attention away from the overall policy choices and tried to undermine the structure of growth control by calling referendums on individual rules that were less popular. An appeal to Portland-area nimbys came up empty—a rollback of the zoning changes that allowed mixed-use development was beaten at the polls. But they had better luck when they stressed the rights of property owners and personalized the issue with stories of small landowners just outside the growth boundaries. Voters approved two statewide referendums that required local governments to compensate landowners when growth controls lowered property values. Courts overturned the first, in 2000; voters drastically trimmed back the second when they saw local governments hit with large compensation bills for popular rule changes—but smart growth advocates knew they were under political siege.[10]

Coalitions shifted back and forth as the two sides struggled to define the battleground. The homebuilding lobby was closely allied with 1000 Friends when infill was the issue, but it backed the Oregonians in Action property rights referendums. Homeowner groups in the Portland suburbs swung the other way.

Still, the basic contours of conflict were static. Loggers in southwest Oregon and ranchers in the east opposed growth control for economic reasons. Within the metropolis, election returns reflected clashing status hierarchies. Backing for urbanism was strongest in Portland's new downtown and the walkable neighborhoods around it. In built-up areas close to the growth boundary—where, economists found, controls exerted the most upward pressure on property values—calls went out to halt smart growth and "let the suburbs be suburbs." Oregonians in Action drew votes from expensive auto-oriented neighborhoods as it mocked the elitism of the newly fashionable district just north of downtown.[11]

If property rights were smart growth's greatest political vulnerability, light rail with its promise of jobs and real estate profits was its strength. The rail network, from its first days, aimed not just to carry people on trips they were already taking but also to create a new pattern of travel by changing land use. In 1998 a tunnel punched through to the city's prosperous western side, extending the line that already ran east from downtown. With tracks now reaching the city's favored quarter and neighborhood nimbys undercut by growth control rules, dense town centers rose around suburban stations. The light rail system added more suburban branches in 2001, 2004, and 2009, and the city built slower-moving streetcars to serve growing neighborhoods close to downtown.

Light rail was now Portland's point of pride. Its renown as the symbol of the city's renovation surpassed its role in the region's transportation network. (The Portland light rail trains carry six trips a day for every hundred residents; Washington's Metro, built just a few years earlier, carries seventeen.) In 2011 construction began on the most ambitious expansion since the tunnel to the west, a 7-mile line that will run south on the east side of the Willamette River after crossing on a new bridge.[12]

The Washington suburb of Arlington, Virginia, follows Portland on most lists of smart growth success stories. Along five stations of the Metro Orange Line between Rosslyn and Ballston, high-rise mixed-use development has remade a 3-mile-long commercial strip. The corridor has gained twenty thousand housing units and more than fifty thousand jobs, yet many roads carry less traffic now than forty years ago: 40% of the residents take transit to work, and fewer than half drive.[13]

Arlington's unique geography set the stage for this makeover. A city-sized county, it was created in 1846 when the section of the District of Columbia lying south of the Potomac River was returned to Virginia. Expansion of the federal government in the 1930s and 1940s brought rapid suburban growth, given an extra boost by the construction in Arlington of the world's largest office building, the Pentagon. By the mid-fifties single-family houses and garden apartments blanketed the county, and the tide of suburbanization swept outward past its borders.

As elsewhere, Arlington's initial infatuation with transit grew out of a fight against highways. Opposition to I-66, connecting Washington to western suburbs, was near-unanimous—the interstate cut through local neighborhoods and benefited only those who lived beyond the county's borders. In need of a substitute, Arlington gave enthusiastic backing to plans for Washington's new Metro. But Congressman William Natcher of Kentucky, who chaired the subcommittee that controlled Metro's funding, warned that he would kill the subway project if any interstates were canceled. Highway opponents in the District of Columbia overcame Natcher after a long struggle, but Arlington conceded and agreed to build both Metro and I-66. As a compromise, the road was narrowed to four lanes, with only carpools allowed during rush hour.[14]

At first Metro's planners wanted to run the Orange Line down I-66, the least expensive route. But the county insisted on putting the tracks underground beneath Wilson Boulevard, a downtown-style commercial strip that was losing business to newer shopping malls. And Arlington wanted as many stations in this corridor as possible; it wound up with five. Voters gave strong

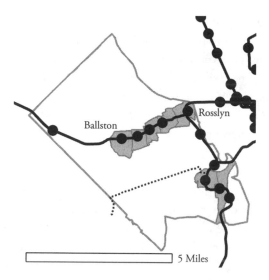

Arlington, Virginia, with areas zoned for transit-oriented development shown in gray. Metro is solid line; planned Columbia Pike streetcar route dashed.

support to these decisions. A referendum on a bond issue to pay for Metro won 70% of the votes.

Soon after the first spade went into the ground, Arlington began planning for its new subway. The nimby wave arrived on schedule here; a Committee on Optimum Growth, organized in 1971, argued that stations should be surrounded by parking lots instead of high-rises. But redevelopment around the new transit stations was a given—the county had chosen the Wilson Boulevard route for that purpose. Neighborhood associations reconciled themselves to the coming redevelopment as an unavoidable evil that could at best be constrained. The county protected most of their territory from change; it restricted new buildings to a quarter-mile radius around the stations and made no changes in single-family zones elsewhere.[15]

Lessons from an earlier failure profoundly influenced the design of the new urban centers. In the 1960s, high-rise office towers had sprouted in an old industrial area known as Rosslyn, across the Potomac from Georgetown. The county laid the district out in the spirit of 1950s urban renewal—single-use office towers amid roads designed for high-speed traffic. It pushed pedestrians off the streets, shunting them onto elevated walkways that led into buildings through unmarked doors at the end of second-floor corridors. Planners and residents, whatever their other differences, were united in revulsion at Rosslyn's ugliness and sterility, and they resolved not to repeat its mistakes.

A decade before the New Urbanist architects would begin their work, plans for the corridor above the Metro line insisted on mixed uses and walkability.

In December 1975, four years before the Orange Line opened, the county board adopted a growth program for the next quarter-century. At its heart was the rebuilding of the Orange Line corridor. Detailed plans for the areas around the stations followed over the next eight years. These documents emerged from lengthy negotiations involving neighborhoods, landowners, planners, and elected officials and won at least grudging assent from all sides.[16]

When the county adopted its new plans, it left low-density suburban zoning in effect. It rezones land only after a developer submits an acceptable design for each building and agrees to pay for a supposedly voluntary "proffer." The voluntary character of the payment is a legal fiction made necessary by Virginia law. The state severely limits local governments' power to impose conditions on developers; the procedure of last-minute rezoning evades this restriction by making the builder choose between "volunteering" to do what the county wants and winding up unable to build at all.

Decision-making in Arlington has avoided the bureaucratic deadlock of Montgomery County. Negotiations focus on the size of the proffer and what it will pay for—the plan already spells out what the developer will be allowed to build. And the builder negotiates directly with the ultimate decision-maker, the county council. Arlington is fairly small—a population of around two hundred thousand—and routine approvals of suburban subdivisions ceased years ago, so the number of new buildings is small enough that council members have time to scrutinize each project individually. Stable land-use policy is also promoted by the continuity of Arlington's liberal Democratic Party leadership; after Ronald Reagan carried the county in 1980, it swung sharply to the left and gave 72% of its votes to Barack Obama in 2008.[17]

As time passed, opposition to growth along the corridor faded away. By 2009, the former leader of the Committee on Optimum Growth insisted that his organization had been not for no growth in the corridor but just for slow growth. The county now intends to urbanize a second run-down corridor, along Columbia Pike, building a streetcar line to make up for the absence of Metro.[18]

In 1989 Maryland governor William Donald Schaefer called for building two light rail lines with state funds. One would cross Baltimore, where Schaefer had long been mayor, from north to south, and the other would run on a recently abandoned 3-mile stretch of freight tracks in Montgomery County outside Washington. The governor, whose motto had always been "do it now," rushed forward headlong to build light rail in his beloved Baltimore. Montgomery County politicians wanted their line too, and they had already purchased the old railroad right of way for that purpose. However, the county's famously protracted planning processes delayed an official decision. By the time they said yes, the funds set aside by Governor Schaefer had disappeared in Baltimore cost overruns and an economic downturn.

The Montgomery light rail route was a transportation planner's dream. Not only did it run between the urban-style downtowns of Bethesda and Silver Spring, the county's two largest job centers, but at each end it would connect to a branch of the new Washington Metro. It could be built at ground level without running into traffic—three major roads crossed over the old tracks on bridges. But the proposal faced lavishly funded opposition. The right of way ran beside wealthy Chevy Chase neighborhoods and, worst of all, through the middle of the golf course of the exclusive Columbia Country Club.

The state, having given up on the idea of building with its own money, began environmental studies to qualify for federal grants. But in 1994, a light rail opponent was elected county executive and the new county council was closely split. Planning work halted and most observers thought the project was dead.

A small group of activists, myself among them, did not give up. The Action Committee for Transit (ACT) had organized in 1986 when the freight line closed. Its few dozen members proselytized for light rail before any audience they could find, relying on elected officials to provide political firepower. After the election setback, Harry Sanders, the group's founder and a former leader of the state's Common Cause, realized a new strategy was needed. He set about organizing a broader alliance in support of the transit line. Only a threadbare coalition could be assembled at first. Business groups gave merely token support; their attention was elsewhere, on a long-running struggle over whether to build an expressway called the Intercounty Connector farther out in the suburbs. The most active allies were recruited among homeowners living near the Washington Beltway—there had been talk for years of widening this crowded highway that runs parallel to the light rail route, and neighborhood leaders feared the project would resurface unless transit was built in the corridor.

The battle over light rail settled into a war of attrition. Opponents sought to turn a bicycle trail, planned from the beginning to run alongside the tracks, into an obstacle to light rail. They convinced the county to build an "interim" graveled trail and then made their slogan "save the trail." The two sides battled for support of environmentalists and bicyclists. Retired ACT members haunted the state capital, watching for killer amendments hidden in the state budget by Columbia Country Club's lobbyists.

Activists were drawn to the light rail issue by the sheer injustice of the situation. The merits of the project first led them to sign on as supporters and attend an occasional meeting. Learning more about the issue, they realized that this transit line, which would benefit so many, had been stopped by the power and money of a country club that was carefully keeping itself out of the limelight. I was one of those who gradually became more committed. When Harry Sanders decided to spend his time on coalition organizing, he asked me to serve as president of ACT. I accepted on the soon-forgotten promise that I wouldn't have to do much work.

It was clear that overcoming the country club's money and connections would require not just majority support—that already existed—but a near-consensus strong enough to overwhelm the opposition. Coalition-building was one part of that; another was winning the battle of public opinion. This required moving beyond a "good government" appeal and making light rail a populist issue by putting Columbia Country Club in the spotlight.

Over the next dozen years, the country club's role was highlighted with leaflets, signs, and media events in front of the "members only" entrance. After research uncovered behind-the-scenes string-pulling, this message reached a large audience through high-profile exposés in the *Washington Post* and *New York Times*. At one point I ran into the club's lobbyist at a political event. "My mother doesn't like what you say about me," he said with a half-smile. For perhaps the only time in my life, I came up with an instant comeback. "Your mother should love what we say. All we ever talk about is how highly paid you are."

Another element of the strategy was countering the opponents' campaign contributions by mobilizing the prorail majority among the voters. The success of the Washington Metro system gives transit proponents a great tactical advantage—supporters can be targeted by passing out leaflets at the stations. Before the 1998 primary election, ACT members distributed twenty thousand scorecards that rated candidates on light rail and other transit issues. The new county council had a six-to-three majority for the light rail line, with one member crediting the scorecard for his margin of victory. The day after the new council was sworn in, it voted to ask the state to resume planning work.

Meanwhile, the State Highway Administration had restarted studies of adding more lanes to the Beltway. Required by federal law to consider transit alternatives, the study in early 1997 added an additional option suggested by ACT. This was an extended version of the Bethesda-Silver Spring light rail

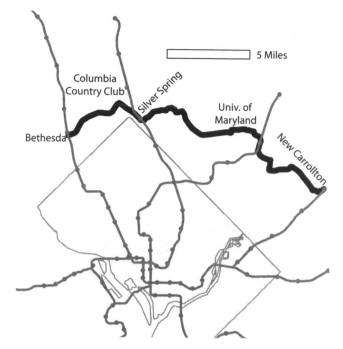

5 Miles

Columbia
Country Club

Silver Spring

Univ. of
Maryland

Bethesda

New Carrollton

The planned route of the Purple Line outside Washington, DC.

line, continuing eastward into neighboring Prince George's County and passing through the campus of the University of Maryland. The terminus of this
route was soon fixed at New Carrollton, where it could connect to Amtrak
trains to New York as well as another Metro branch. With five other colors
already spoken for on the map of the Washington Metro, the project became
known as the Purple Line.

As the Beltway study proceeded, transit options became its focus. Engineers
were finding that widening the highway would be difficult and extraordinarily
expensive, and Governor Parris Glendening's pursuit of his smart growth
agenda brought a higher priority to transit. A political battle was raging over
the Intercounty Connector after the governor stopped work on the highway
in 1999; environmental groups that had earlier hesitated to offend their members in Chevy Chase now lined up behind the light rail line as a major transportation project they could favor.

Expanding the smaller proposal into the Purple Line made light rail even
more popular among the electorate, but the noisy opposition of the county's
most affluent precincts drowned out this quiet support. Even the Purple Line's
most ardent backers underestimated the public's enthusiasm for it. A flyer

showing its route inserted into Washington's iconic five-color subway map was well received, so in March 2001 ACT threw all its resources into passing out thirty thousand copies at Metro stations. Hope that the flyer would attract a few new members turned into astonishment when 120 coupons were clipped out and mailed back with $10 dues checks.

This success inspired a turn to the Purple Line's other established base of grass-roots support. Volunteers distributed the leaflet door to door in communities along the Beltway. Accompanying each copy was a letter from a leader of the neighborhood's civic association, explaining why light rail was needed to stave off the threat of highway widening. The favorable response from homes close to the noisy interstate was expected, but surprisingly just as many new members joined at the far end of the neighborhoods. So the campaign moved on to other areas, reaching more than fifty thousand homes over five years and recruiting over a thousand new members.

Seeking to assemble the widest possible majority, advocates avoided portraying the Purple Line as a social justice issue and emphasized that it would help nearly everyone. It was easy to personalize the benefits. Transit riders saw instantly that they would gain access to attractive destinations. Others could identify with drivers stuck in Beltway congestion; the light rail would give them a way to bypass the traffic jams.

Governor Glendening now swung strongly behind the Purple Line. In October 2001 he gave the route along the old tracks a high-profile endorsement, rejecting alternatives that opponents had put forward to obfuscate the issues. Business no longer saw the transit project as pie in the sky and entered the fray in force. Planning went into high gear, but the victory was short-lived. In 2002 Maryland elected a Republican governor, Robert Ehrlich, who opposed the light rail line.

Ehrlich, under heavy pressure from business lobbies, did not kill the project outright. He chose instead to "obfuscate, alter, study and delay," as his own appointee to the Metro board later put it. Planners put light rail on hold and looked at a low-cost bus route that would bypass the country club. At the same time, the new governor moved quickly ahead to build the Intercounty Connector at a cost of more than $2 billion. This expensive roadway gobbled up funds that might have been used for the Purple Line, but at the same time it strengthened the project's political position. With the highway no longer in question, the transit line became the top transportation priority of suburban business groups.

In 2006 Governor Ehrlich was defeated for reelection by Martin O'Malley, mayor of Baltimore and a Purple Line backer. By now an extraordinary coalition

Gov. Parris Glendening announces plans to build the Purple Line in 2001. Behind him is an Action Committee for Transit banner reading "We don't travel in golf carts and Mercedes—We need the Purple Line."

had lined up behind the project. It included business, labor, environmentalists, ethnic minorities, and many neighborhood associations. Outspoken support emerged even in the Chevy Chase neighborhoods where opposition was strongest. An endorsement from the Washington Area Bicyclist Association undercut the "save the trail" slogan. Most of the few remaining opponents among elected officials now reversed their positions, and the councils and executives of both counties gave their unanimous backing.

The consensus was reinforced in 2010 by a rematch election for governor. By now Columbia Country Club's place in the Purple Line debate was firmly fixed in the public mind. Ehrlich had allowed himself to be quoted saying that "it will not go through the Country Club," and O'Malley had the rare political pleasure of championing a populist cause that won him business support. The Purple Line was at the center of the election campaign, the only specific issue that Washington-area business groups pointed to in their out-of-character endorsement of the Democratic candidate. O'Malley swept to a landslide victory.

Planning for the new light rail line now moved ahead, as swiftly as complex engineering problems and an equally complex federal approval process allowed. In March 2013, the Maryland legislature raised the gasoline tax by 20 cents per gallon, ensuring that the state could pay its share of construction costs. In June, Columbia Country Club dropped its opposition, settling for a shift of the tracks 12 feet to one side so that tees can stay where the golfers want them. The project still needs federal funding, but signs are favorable; the Purple Line is expected to carry 74,000 riders per day, far more than competing projects of similar scope. If all goes according to plan, the Purple Line will break ground in 2015 and go into full operation in 2020.[19]

Portland, Arlington, and the Purple Line were smart growth successes in years when efforts elsewhere often fell short. Do these narratives have common features that might explain their outcome?

Each of these stories begins with initiatives led both from above and from below, from elected leaders and the grass roots. But they then take different courses. In Portland and Arlington, elites were the strongest backers of smart growth; the battle for the Purple Line was long led from the grass roots. Oregon's growth boundaries have been vulnerable to referendum challenges when opponents personalized the issue in ways that voters identified with. In Maryland, it was the supporters of light rail who succeeded, after much struggle, in framing the benefits of light rail—and the motives of the opponents—in vivid, easily understandable images.

But all three share one crucial element. Smart growth advocates win by thinking big. The larger vision inspires the public to override parochial objections. The entire polity chooses its future course; smaller localities lose the veto rights that suburban land tenure ordinarily grants. In Portland, the growth boundary created a coalition for infill development. In Arlington, it was the rejuvenation of an entire corridor. The struggle for the Purple Line summoned enthusiasm that a shorter rail line could not muster, mobilizing a new generation of advocates for urbanism. Harry Sanders of the Action Committee for Transit loved to quote Daniel Burnham: "Make no little plans...."

14

The Politics of Smart Growth

As the experiences of Portland, Arlington, and the Purple Line show, big ideas do not bring change by themselves. For the activism of the committed few to overcome an entrenched status quo, it must be backed up with mass support. Only a political movement, with a practical program and the strength to put it through, can turn vision into reality. Democracy is the means for moving smart growth from aspiration to reality.

Majorities, in a democracy, are not made by altruism alone; they gather when idealism is harnessed to self-interest. The victories of the New Deal and the civil rights movement rested on the organization of workers and African Americans behind demands for justice. Urbanists, likewise, can succeed only by mobilizing constituencies that link their prosperity and social standing to the fulfillment of their vision.

Even a majority achieves little unless its numbers are translated into political power. In our unequal society, there are many things the majority wants and does not get. Raising the minimum wage, making the rich pay more taxes, and putting Wall Street bankers on trial—all are more popular than urbanism. Urbanists, often, are surprised and frustrated by the slow pace of progress. They are entitled to frustration but not to surprise. Change requires politics, and politics requires strategy.

A winning coalition may seek to change the world, but it must be put together in the world as it is. Today's movements for urban revival cannot be launched, as those of an earlier generation were, off the momentum of antifreeway and environmental campaigns. The ideology of localism that propelled the movements of the 1970s was well suited to those negative goals, but it is a poor fit to the positive vision of smart growth.

Portland and Arlington succeeded by building new coalitions. It was not easy; they faced a twofold challenge after their freeways were canceled. There was the difficult intellectual task of developing a new model of growth, one that defied long-established doctrines of city planning. Then came an equally daunting political task. The new course, which bore fruit only slowly, had to be sustained by enduring political majorities.

Many others now seek to copy the achievements of these two cities. In some ways, the imitators have an easier job. With the flowering of the New Urbanism, the design principles that Arlington worked out by trial and error can be learned from textbooks. The market demand for city living has brought the political backing of business interests. And a mass constituency for urbanism has grown in a postsuburban generation. But there are new obstacles as well. Nimby sentiment has hardened since the seventies, and an organized opposition to smart growth has emerged from right-wing think tanks.

How advocates will organize depends on circumstances. The mass urbanist politics of a Portland can sprout where there is fertile soil. Big cities often have urbanist constituencies in waiting, capable of becoming an electoral force. San Francisco cyclists came together when "critical mass" rides filled the streets in the early 1990s. Ten years later, they had a five-thousand-member association that politicians feared to offend.[1]

Where the political climate is conservative and nearly everyone drives, activist organizations are likely to stay small. Yet small advocacy groups can have influence far out of proportion to their numbers when their ideas excite bigger constituencies. Rachel Flynn, the imaginative planning director of Richmond, Virginia, won wide support among residents for a pedestrian-oriented revival of the city's central neighborhoods.[2]

In suburbs, smart growth proponents occupy a strategic political position. The constant battle between developers and neighborhoods keeps local officials in a bind, forcing them to choose between resistance to growth and the need for a healthy local economy. Giving each side half a loaf satisfies no one. A middle way based on a positive program can be an attractive alternative to unsatisfactory compromises based on raw power.

With the backing of a disinterested organization of local residents, politicians find this approach much easier to pursue. Here the advocates' greatest asset is not numbers but credibility. Independence, presence in the community, and transparent finances are the foundations of that credibility. Ongoing associations, even with just a few members, are more effective than ad hoc campaigns. Support for "good" development is more believable when there is a track record of opposing the "bad," and vice versa.

Whatever the political environment, smart growth advocates find it tricky to maintain alliances. The need to fight on two fronts forces them to negotiate their way between two overlapping coalitions. When working to curb sprawl development and highway-building, they join with environmentalists and rural and exurban nimbys. Then they turn to builders, business groups, and low-income housing advocates to overcome nimby opposition to transit and infill.

Such maneuvers pose problems for established organizations with wider agendas than land use. Environmental groups, especially, face inner tensions when they work with builders. Their staff and leadership see nimbys as an obstacle to weaning suburbs from the automobile, but the membership—much of it housed in expensive suburban subdivisions—can be reluctant to follow. A volunteer citizens group, running on a small budget but free of these constraints, is sometimes more effective than a well-funded project run by an existing organization.

Direct limits on the building of automobile-dependent sprawl remain on the smart growth program. The outward push of development continues, albeit with greatly weakened force after the collapse of the real estate boom. Successes may be limited in the short term, but the movement relies on an alliance between urbanists and opponents of outer-suburb growth in the outer suburbs.

In the long run, the partisans of urban revitalization and rural preservation are natural allies. Those who seek to preserve farms and forests are sure to be accused of strangling the economy; they need to be able to say where housing and stores should go instead. Urbanists, similarly, need to demonstrate their independence of developer allies by working against "bad" projects. Beyond that, coalitions give both sides a reason to look beyond the issues at hand and broaden their thinking.

The program of these coalitions must be carefully crafted. The fallout of the clampdown of the 1970s shows that growth controls can backfire if not well designed. Statewide growth boundaries have been proven effective in

Oregon, but they seem beyond reach elsewhere at the moment. Local ordinances will be easier to enact, but they have their limitations. Curbs on office parks are hard to enforce at a time when governments, desperate for jobs and tax revenue, eagerly yield to the desires of employers. Restrictions on stores and housing lose their punch when development leaks across town and county boundaries. Still, merely slowing building in the exurbs may be enough to stop it, by buying time until long-term market trends take effect. And even when the prospects of victory are dim, taking a stand has educational value.

The reverse side of the sprawl control coin is infill development. Of all the elements of smart growth, it may be the most popular in the abstract. In brick and concrete, however, it is often fiercely controversial.

The politics of infill depends on location. Big-city downtowns almost always welcome new buildings—the economic benefits are vast, and the neighbors are few. Where the overflow from downtown can be channeled into empty old industrial districts, things for the most part still go smoothly. But when new structures are to be inserted into neighborhoods near existing homes, infill becomes a much more complicated matter.

It is in the favored quarter, where jobs cluster near expensive housing, that the economic incentives for new urban-style development are greatest. Here the promise of large profits puts the political muscle of big real estate developers behind smart growth. In jurisdictions large enough that near-neighbors are not the only voters, the developers usually find friends among politicians—not just conservatives but also liberals who see an opportunity to win business backing that they would otherwise seek in vain.

But the politicians seek to strike a balance. Favored-quarter neighborhood activists are rarely willing to endorse new buildings—in wealthy suburbs, the residents who like growth least rise to the top of homeowner groups. Even when nimbys are politically outmatched, there is a strong desire to appease them with concessions. The dominant political coalitions will be endangered if disputes become so inflamed that elections turn on development issues.

Arlington's Rosslyn-Ballston corridor runs along the edge of the favored quarter, and its political strategy has often been emulated. It amounts to a bargain between neighborhoods and developers. Big new buildings can go up, but they are carefully confined to small districts around the rail stations. Single-family homeowners far from transit are "protected" because development is channeled away from them. Neighborhoods closer in get amenities paid for by the builders, and the new arrivals are often forbidden to park on streets within their boundaries. Arlington introduced residential permit parking in the 1970s, with districts carefully gerrymandered to exclude apartment buildings.

With this program, local officials reach out to rank-and-file homeowners over the heads of civic association leaders. Civic activists, like most believers in a cause, are inclined to think that what they want for themselves is good for everyone, and even if they live far from train stations they instinctively ally themselves with nimbys closer in. Their followers, however, are more likely to take the self-interested tack of "better over there than near me" and support infill development that isn't in their own back yards.

Infill plans do get support from some neighborhood leaders. Some of them simply agree that smart growth is for the good. Others remain unconvinced by urbanist arguments but see development as inevitable. They resign themselves to what they cannot stop and seek to negotiate what concessions they can from the developers

The Arlington compromise squeezes growth into a tight radius. High-rises near the station are surrounded by single-family houses on suburban lots. This does not reproduce the old streetcar suburbs, where side streets lined with one- and two-family houses packed closely together feed customers to stores along the trolley line. New urbanist planners would surely prefer to build fewer high-rises and spread the same floor space over a larger area by scattering row houses and apartment buildings through neighborhoods.

But the political forces at work in upper-income suburbs rarely allow such mixing. Advocates and planners who might want to insert small apartment houses into single-family neighborhoods face fierce opposition from well-organized homeowner groups. Proponents of change have only the force of their convictions; scattered-site development spreads its profits too thinly to generate a self-interested lobbying force. From the urbanist point of view, the dense high-rise nodes that go up in these suburbs are a second best, but they are usually the best attainable in the circumstances.

In less affluent suburbs, infill does not have big-business muscle behind it and must find a different path. Here Portland is the outstanding success story. The impetus was the state's growth boundary law, which requires the border to be moved out if zoning rules inside the boundary do not allow enough building to house all the new residents expected within the next twenty years.

Portland did not have Arlington's opportunity to limit its smart growth to the vicinity of rail stations. The favored-quarter suburbs to the city's west did rezone some land around the new light rail line, but they were willing to take only so many newcomers. The only area with enough room to house the city's growing population was the old streetcar suburbs on the less affluent east side. In that part of the city, high-rise building was not an option. There the light rail stations, built alongside interstate highways, were not attractive sites for dense urban centers.

To preserve its growth boundary, Portland had to squeeze more people into low-rise residential neighborhoods. The city did this by allowing smaller lots and two-family houses in one-family zones. New rules were pushed through by an unlikely coalition of urbanists, environmentalists, and homebuilders, driven together by the state's growth boundary law.

Other cities have found it hard to duplicate this alignment of forces. Some have added row houses and apartments to middle-income neighborhoods— New York City in particular gained population the same way in the 1990s. But there the zoning was already in place, left over from the permissive past. Portland's rewrite of its zoning code was, in its time, unique.

In the 2010s Portland has begun to find imitators. So far changes elsewhere are more modest, and they still prove highly controversial. But there may be a wider political opening for this model of urbanization in the aftermath of the crash of 2008.

In the wake of the housing bubble, many declining inner suburbs face a situation like Portland's east side during the lumber recession of the 1980s. Despite economic stress, they remain attractive places to live, and close-in locations make it practical to commute by bus. Dividing houses into two apartments would help owners pay their mortgages and give tenants affordable rentals. But duplex conversion, when not banned altogether, is made difficult and expensive by zoning obstacles like requirements for added off-street parking and house-by-house approval.

As urbanists seek to ease these rules, they may be able to build alliances that extend beyond the transit riders and young city dwellers who constitute their usual political base. Immigrants, by definition newcomers, are among those disadvantaged by exclusionary zoning. But the effects of zoning on the overall housing market are slow and indirect; immigrants face difficulties nearer at hand, and they rarely get involved in land-use matters. Duplex conversion, which offers immediate relief for the pressing problem of housing affordability, could be the one zoning issue that rouses low-income ethnic constituencies.

In city centers as on the fringe, the larger the area that makes a decision, the more easily a majority for smart growth can be assembled. When built-up areas allow nearby neighbors to decide on infill, they deny any voice to the beneficiaries of the development—the people who would live, work, shop, and walk around in the newly urbanized areas. Farther out, the grant of zoning power to small towns yields similarly undemocratic results. Farmers allow themselves to sell their land to tract developers, and the buyers of the expensive new houses then keep out the less affluent who would like to follow them.[3]

Local governments zealously defend their zoning powers, and full transfer to a higher level of government is rarely feasible and often undesirable. But the antisnob zoning laws passed by a few states in the 1970s had a real effect in forcing single-family suburbs to let in less expensive housing and allow apartment buildings. In recent years more modest reforms have again proved possible. Some states encourage recalcitrant suburbs to accept transit-oriented development, and others penalize towns that allow too much sprawl.

Statutes need not be as strong as Oregon's growth boundary law to recast local political debates. California's Napa Valley wine country provides a striking example. A strongly antigrowth electorate defeated a 2008 referendum aimed at derailing a New Urbanist development on an old factory site. A state law that dates to 1980 requires every county to accept its share of affordable housing, and voters feared that rejecting the project would undermine rules that protect vineyards from development.[4]

Another route to change is through federal laws that encourage more rational land use. These laws work through regional bodies known as Metropolitan Planning Organizations, or MPOs. The MPOs are supposed to coordinate land use with transportation planning. But they are typically governed by a board composed of local elected officials, and they rarely challenge local land-use decisions.[5] Portland is the one city where voters elect the MPO, and its experience shows that an elected regional body, once it exists, tends to attract more power. Direct election of MPOs might be an attainable reform elsewhere, especially as the growing affluence of urban downtowns and the changing racial composition of both cities and suburbs calm suburban fears of metropolitan government.

15

Democratic Urbanism

C reating denser cities is just the beginning of the unmaking of sprawl. What fills in the urban spaces must be truly urban.

The needed changes are many, and they will not be easy. The roots of sprawl go deep, permeating the subsoil of American life. Thousands of mundane decisions about streets, sidewalks, houses, schools, stores, and civic buildings shape the suburban landscape. Some are made under the watchful eyes of snob zoning, others are negotiated at the regulatory toll booth, and not a few reflect the profit-and-loss calculations of fiscal zoning.

Policy directives will only slightly shift the outcome of these choices—the landowners, neighbors, and government officials who make them will continue to pursue their own agendas. Nor can public participation exert much influence—activists and volunteers, unless they live in the immediate vicinity, rarely find the time to inject themselves into these everyday decisions. Only structural change—altered institutions and incentives that give rise to different systems of control—can transform the behavior of the interest groups concerned with local real estate.

Our inherited patterns of land-use governance mix different economic systems, and new arrangements will involve new mixtures. A helpful way to think about reform is to list the elements that might go into those mixtures.

The economist János Kornai classified the ways economic activity is organized into five mechanisms. The market, where buyer and seller negotiate as equals before the law, is of course one. Another is bureaucratic coordination, which passes information up and down a hierarchy. This was Kornai's main concern; his scholarly aim was to understand Soviet communism. He adds three other mechanisms: self-governance, with decisions made by voting; ethical coordination, gifts given without expectation of return; and family coordination.[1]

In the organization of American land use all five mechanisms are present, and the common stable patterns combine elements of more than one. Even in the snob zoning of a small suburb, self-governance lays out the zones and the market decides whether anything gets built in them. On the scale of a metropolis, economics, politics, law, and sociology are entangled in an intricate net.

Weaknesses in the governance of land use are widely recognized, and there is no lack of proposals for change. But reformers, all too often, seek only to perfect the mechanism closest at hand. Planners put forth better plans, economists rail against overregulation, and local activists insist that nearby property owners should have the last word. Isolated changes can bring unexpected consequences as a tug at one thread ripples across the web.

A restructured governance of land use would, ideally, set each mechanism to the tasks it does best. Markets are most effective in catering to a diversity of tastes; owners of buildings should be able to alter their use as consumers make new demands. Only bureaucrats can do the boring work of making sure potholes are patched and sewers don't overflow; they need the budgets and the authority to get their jobs done. Voting gives everyone a say in policy choices; the people as a whole have the right to make the big decisions.

In all the complexity of land use governance, this last principle stands out: the reestablishment of popular sovereignty. All deserve a voice in determining the common future. The principle of one person, one vote must replace the restricted voting of suburban land tenure. The vagaries of a war of snobbery against greed should not shape our cities.

Zoning, covenants, and historic preservation, as now organized, all function to maintain the status quo. Of the three, zoning has the most pervasive influence.

One basic element of reform is the elimination of zoning's openly undemocratic features. When the public votes on rezoning, suffrage should be based on residence rather than landownership. Tenants should receive the same notice of proposed changes as landlords. Associations should be recognized as representing neighborhoods only if they accept renters as equal members with homeowners. The more zoning boards are democratic in form, the greater the ability of the unrepresented to organize politically and change their practice.

But that is only a beginning. New Urbanist planners have undertaken a fundamental rethinking of zoning. They call for complete replacement of current ordinances with what they call the form-based code. It regulates the size, shape, and placement of buildings instead of specifying the uses inside them as a zoning code does.[2]

On the surface the form-based code aims at the substance of the rules rather than procedure, but in practice it alters power relationships. The bureaucracy and the neighbors lose control of the insides of buildings and gain more influence over their outsides; builders and their customers make the opposite exchange. Mixed-use buildings, no longer exceptions, are no harder to approve than single-use buildings and are no more liable to neighborhood obstruction. Citizens who wish to preserve sprawl no longer possess means of influence that those who wish to challenge it lack.

Charles Siegel, a transit activist in Berkeley, California, would take the democratization of zoning much farther. Siegel has an anarchist streak, but he is also a pragmatist and among the few who have thought carefully about governance and sprawl. If cities were left to grow without rules, he points out, today's automotive dominance would only perpetuate itself. Instead of abolishing regulation entirely, he therefore seeks to replace prescriptive rules with a framework that enables spontaneity and complexity to flourish. Instead of leaving planning to experts, he would have the political process set limits on the nature of development.

Siegel has some specific suggestions for his grass-roots legislators. He would limit the number of floors in buildings—three or four stories where we wish to imitate streetcar suburbs, six for urban neighborhoods—and require a little bit of empty space for light and air. He insists on small blocks and would put a cap on how much land one owner could control. Most of all, rules are needed to tame the automobile and prevent it from corroding the fabric of the city. He would do this with area-wide speed limits. In city centers, cars might be banned entirely; urban neighborhoods would limit speed to 10 or 15 miles an hour; suburbs would allow drivers to go 20 or 25. A centrally planned network of rapid trains would tie the entire city together.[3] Even if this sketch seems utopian, it has value in showing a coherent direction for change.

Especially pertinent is Siegel's call for divided ownership of land. It offers a practical cure for the lack of character that plagues even the best New Urbanist projects. A single owner who controls an entire shopping district can offer tenants immunity from nearby competition in exchange for higher rents. Each store on the property winds up in a distinct market niche. The merchant who can afford to pay the most rent is the one who fills the niche most efficiently, and that is usually a chain store with standardized merchandise. Thus the stultifying sameness of enclosed shopping malls—and the eerie mall-like feeling that even well-designed New Urbanist suburbs can exude.

A contrasting dynamic sets in when adjoining buildings have different owners. Stores in the same line of business are let in. Head-to-head competition drives merchants to cut prices, raise quality, and add distinctive traits to their goods. Trades cluster into specialized centers that draw customers from throughout the metropolis. Competition and proximity are potent drivers of innovation, infusing a far wider area with economic vitality.[4] And the rich fabric of differentiated neighborhoods makes the city much more than the sum of its streets—it was the supremely specialized business districts of mid-twentieth-century Manhattan that turned Jane Jacobs into an urbanist.

Current planning practice, even among New Urbanists, tilts strongly toward unified control. Master plans promote *land assembly*. When cities condemn land for redevelopment, they most often seek a single buyer for the entire property. If the project is too big for one company, a *master developer* is put in charge. Landowners are not the only decision-makers enticed by the monopoly profits that single ownership can bring—local government is relieved of infrastructure costs, neighbors appeased by suburban-style amenities, politicians showered with campaign contributions. But the city itself, economically weaker and deprived of urban texture, is the worse.

Even when common ownership is not imposed by fiat, zoning laws encourage it. Some places allow mixed-use development only on large lots. Elsewhere, the expense of seeking approvals is so great that small-scale projects are unfeasible. If rules were friendlier to diversity of ownership, infill projects could be more like old downtowns, given life and color by their smaller property owners. Simpler rules can build more complex cities.

Simpler, as Siegel emphasizes, is more democratic as well. When the public has clear choices, it can decide among them. Complexity transfers power away from voters, either to planners or to the private interests most directly concerned. Streamlining approval processes democratizes zoning.

More often than not, when infill is built in today's suburbs, each building is a political decision. Either a locality waits to rezone until the owner is ready to build, or the zoning requires a case-by-case approval to build anything big enough to give the builder a profit. This, in large jurisdictions especially, yields a profoundly undemocratic governance of land use. The near neighbors have leverage to extract concessions, and citizens with a less direct interest lack motivation to counter them.

The more democratic practice is to adopt area-wide plans after public debate and immediately rezone all land for its intended use. Because plans attract the interest of a broader public than single buildings, the landowners and neighbors must share their influence. Power flows to the voters of the larger area.

A practical objection to this procedure is that governments lose the power to make developers pay for infrastructure and amenities. But there is another way to extract money from developers: taxation. Taxation is more democratic because the money raised is spent in the open, as part of the city budget. The entire population has a voice. When developer contributions are worked out behind the scenes, the biggest benefits go to the people with the power to say no. These, most often, are small groups of wealthy homeowners who live near the most profitable new buildings.

If anything in the world of land use is an affront to democracy, it is the private government of the homeowner association. At best, those too poor to own real estate are denied a vote; at worst, future generations are bound irrevocably by the whims of the developer who created the association. Always, the rights of residents to free speech, artistic self-expression, and free movement are at risk.

The "planned communities" of the 1960s and 1970s are aging, and the dead hands of deed covenants now weigh down on their inhabitants. They fix land uses in place; they ban mixed uses and upstairs apartments. These rules, often nearly impossible to alter, preclude the infill strategies that enlivened the inner-ring suburbs of Arlington and Portland.

The homeowner associations, designed for permanent prosperity, are ill fitted for economic decline. Distressed homeowners stop paying fees, and assessments go up on the neighbors. Foreclosure, the association's ultimate remedy to collect unpaid assessments, is useless when houses are mortgaged for more than they are worth—the bank, which normally gets paid before the association, will take all the money if the property is sold. Rising fees squeeze the owners who keep paying, and the entire community falls into a cycle of decay.

Obsolete rules and straitened budgets are symptoms of a fundamental defect. Homeowner associations are governments, not private organizations. The principles of constitutional government, arrived at through centuries of struggle, should apply to them. Mandatory payments for the upkeep of common services should be treated as taxes, worthy of priority payment before private debts like mortgages. Covenants on land use, density, and design of buildings should expire after a fixed lifetime, replaced by zoning regulations that can be kept up to date. (This seemingly radical innovation is a return to the legal doctrines of the nineteenth century, put in place to prevent just the sort of problem associations now face.) And community governments, whatever their form or origin, should be controlled by their citizens, with fundamental freedoms protected and voting rights extended to tenants and homeowners alike.[5]

Critics of homeowner associations are many, but their focus tends to be narrow. They limit their complaints to the most obnoxious rules or get bogged down in the minutiae of individual disputes. Incumbent board members and the for-profit management firms that associations hire to run their operations defend the status quo. With heavy lobbying in state capitals, they have managed so far to stave off reform by agreeing to cosmetic changes. But there is a large constituency for change among homeowners who revile the unresponsive, nitpicking boards of their associations. Framing the issue within the broader debate over smart growth and democratic control of land use would encourage state legislatures to remedy the underlying defects of private government.

Historic preservation is the third pillar of suburban land tenure. Its prevailing doctrines are an open invitation to thinly disguised nimbyism. Vaguely defined categories can, with enough ingenuity and political influence, be stretched to fit almost any old building. In Santa Monica, California, civic groups tried to make a half-empty trailer park a historic landmark. Their goal was to block a 486-unit apartment complex near a future light rail station. This was the rare case where the Landmarks Commission had no choice but to turn them down. Its jurisdiction was limited to the concrete pads, the commission declared; it was powerless to protect the trailers.[6]

The preservationists' core concept, historic and architectural "significance," is a catch-all that lumps together two distinct categories: the landmark and the merely old. There are good arguments for protecting both sorts of buildings, but they are of different orders.

True landmarks are places of such exceptional importance—sites of historic events, great works of architecture, and such—that total protection is merited. But divorcing significance from artistic merit leaves no basis for identifying architectural landmarks. In the end, aesthetic judgments are still made—they are unavoidable—but they are made behind the scenes by insiders, allowing criticism from the public to be brushed off.

Old things that are not landmarks deserve protection too, but of a different sort. The heritage of the architectural past lies in ordinary-looking styles—what architects call *vernacular*. To preserve a style, buildings must survive, but what matters is how many and not which ones. No single structure is essential.

Because cities are living organisms and not architectural museums, some old buildings must be torn down. This imperative is recognized in practice by preservation authorities, but their theory distinguishes only the historic from the not historic. Without a basis for choosing among old structures, they fall back on the rule of first come, first served. The wealthiest and most influential neighborhoods show up first, and it is their old buildings that stay. Urbanist theory suggests the opposite—demolish the ordinary when it sits on expensive real estate and preserve architectural styles on less valuable land. The old buildings that remain would be what Jane Jacobs thought they should be, low-rent settings for the economic diversity that makes cities thrive.

There are old neighborhoods where the historic fabric itself merits preservation, but even here some new building should be allowed. The current preservation system creates dead zones that wall off the past—even when, as in the case of Washington's Cleveland Park district, the defining characteristic said to make it historic is a mixture of different ages and styles. Rapid change can destroy the distinctive traits of city neighborhoods, but stopping construction hardly ensures the survival of historic character. Today's upscale Greenwich Village is not the place that drew in the John Reeds and Jane Jacobses.

The heritage of the past is most alive when it is embedded in a living environment. One way to mix old and new might be with quotas on destruction of threatened building styles. A city would limit how many Victorian frame houses could be demolished each year, how many Sears Craftsman houses, how many buildings in each historic district. The permits might be given out first come, first served, or if demand were high they could be auctioned off. In each category, a minimum number of structures would have to be preserved— no more permits when the limit is reached. Setting quotas in the open balances the aesthetic judgments of the entire city against the political pull of nimby neighborhoods. San Francisco would surely retain most of its wooden Victorians, Los Angeles might get by with some dingbats here and there, and the entire country could probably make do with just a handful of original McDonald's golden arches.

Many of the changes suggested here would run afoul of the legal principles that now underpin land use regulation. The status quo rests on a series of legal fictions—the police power, the master plan, voluntary consent to covenants, historical significance—that make reform hard to discuss rationally and harder to enact. The persistence of these doctrines, in the face of their patent unreality, reflects the need to reconcile the system of suburban land tenure with the law's obsolete concept of private property.

As the law sees it, land is something with value in itself. In the days when real estate was bought to grow corn or cut lumber, this was an eminently sensible doctrine. But today life is otherwise. Urban land, as distinct from useful buildings that might sit on it, has little intrinsic worth. It acquires value to the extent that the rules allow something to be built there or that a buyer thinks the rules can be changed to let something be built.

In legal theory and public consciousness, owners still have an inherent right to use their land. But in practice that right disappeared years ago and was replaced by suburban land tenure. Today no one seeks to reverse that evolution—those most insistent on protecting property rights are often the fiercest partisans of snob zoning. Legal doctrines should be based on facts and not obsolete theories.

This does not mean that judges can step back and let governments do whatever they wish—but they should protect the underlying purposes that private property serves rather than any abstract right. Rules that bar interference with the zoning that happens to be in place purport to protect property owner against arbitrary actions of government, but they do so by freezing in place the equally arbitrary decisions made years before. The balance between a farmer's desire to subdivide land and city dwellers' wish to limit sprawl should be struck by today's electorate rather than the voters who lived in a small town long ago. The rights of landowners, like the rights of neighbors, must be weighed against the will of the majority.

A real need that property rights serve is to protect against unfairness of local governing bodies. A perfect balance between the individual and the public interest will be impossible to find. But the goal of improving on the current situation is hardly daunting. Ensuring that homeowner associations can no more abridge rights than local governments would be a good start.

Another useful function of land ownership is to create markets that offer choice to consumers and promote economic growth. In the mixed economy of land use, some markets serve these ends and others don't. Property rights serve no larger social purpose when they restrict consumer choice and protect status at the expense of economic activity. This, most often, is the effect when homeowners enforce rules written by long-dead developers.

When good policy collides with legal fiction, it is the law that should change. Suburban land tenure is deeply rooted in the American psyche and will not soon disappear. But the law should recognize it as a political claim that can be outvoted. It should not be a legal entitlement.[7]

Reconciling a new legal structure with existing constitutional law will require ingenuity. But lawyers are rich in ingenuity. Those who undertake this task will have to reconcile conflicting goals, and imperfections are inevitable. Still, it will not be hard at all to do better than the current arrangement. Jurisprudence that reflects reality could enlarge popular sovereignty and at the same time offer more choice to consumers and more rights to individuals.

The democratization of land use is only the end of the beginning of the battle against sprawl. Even with form-based codes, new street design standards, and better governance, the detailed work of building will remain to be done by specialists. Architects, planners, builders, and engineers can be empowered to create more livable cities, but how well they do it will be up to them.

Humanizing the landscape of strip malls and edge cities is not a simple task. Fortunately, many thinkers are at work on solutions. A good introduction for general readers is *Suburban Nation* by Andres Duany, Elizabeth Plater-Zyberk, and Jeff Speck. Professionals can turn to books like Galina Tachieva's *Sprawl Repair Manual* and *Retrofitting Suburbia* by Ellen Dunham-Jones and June Williamson.

The worse the sprawl, it turns out, the harder it is to fix. Successful transit-oriented downtowns, in Arlington, Portland, and elsewhere, take advantage of existing grid street patterns. New buildings can arrive one by one, and sidewalks that are already walkable become livelier as more people walk on them. In more recently built suburbs, where the superblock layout funnels traffic onto six- and eight-lane arterials, this sort of gradual upgrade is nearly impossible. There are few pedestrians on the unpleasant highways, so the existing structures face away from them and occupants of new, more urban buildings have nowhere to walk to. When someone suggests a new road connection, objections are swift and loud. In this environment any through street becomes a traffic sewer—a complete grid would be better for everyone, but no one benefits by going first.

To overcome the twin hurdles of politics and traffic, entire neighborhoods must be redesigned at once. In the automobile-era suburbs of Washington, where superblock road designs predominate, this work has already begun. Under Montgomery County's White Flint plan, a new street grid will criss-cross what are now parking lots. Across the Potomac River, planners have undertaken the formidable task of rebuilding Tysons Corner after the Metro arrives there in 2014.

The street network around the White Flint Metro station (entered at dots), Montgomery County, Maryland. Left in 1988 and right as planned for 2020 (with pedestrian connections dashed).

These thorough makeovers are so expensive that only wealthy sections of the favored quarter can afford them. The new street networks are never as dense and well connected as in older cities, and they emerge only over decades. White Flint got a head start from an earlier master plan that began to open passageways through the superblocks. Even so, the grid will take a dozen years to fill out, and it will not connect to adjacent subdivisions. The new Tysons, with two wide roads through its heart that are already nearly impassible for pedestrians, could be stillborn. Its planners were unable to overcome local traffic engineers' insistence that more people always need more roads, and they agreed to add more lanes of speeding traffic to its already wide central highways.

Such hindrances continue to obstruct urban transformation, even where the manifest need to rebuild has opened purses. In places the way forward is known but the will is lacking; elsewhere planners face conundrums that no one has yet solved. And rebuilding edge cities is only part of the task; less costly fixes will have to be devised for the exurbs of the last housing boom, whose premature decay has already begun.

If the citizenry continues to demand change, these intellectual roadblocks may be overcome along with the political and economic obstacles. Unsolved problems will find answers and better responses will emerge to difficulties thought already overcome. Public mobilization does not just erect a political framework; it inspires further progress. Democracy has a way of unleashing human creativity.

16

Affordable Housing in an Ownership Society

Affordability is an issue that bedevils urbanists. When neighborhoods revive, say critics of smart growth, the people who live in them are the losers. Rents shoot upward, forcing out low-income tenants. Soon the middle class is priced out too. Home values skyrocket, and their owners can't afford the tax bills. Stores stocked with everyday necessities are replaced by trendy boutiques, and then the boutiques give way to chain stores. Diversity fades into the stodgy uniformity of rootless affluence.

This is a familiar story, and it has elements of truth. But what drives up the cost of urban living is not revitalization so much as the obstacles in its way. Good transit reaches only a small portion of the metropolis, and there good schools and safe streets are often lacking. Affluent neighborhoods near rail lines keep housing scarce with single-family zoning, parking minimums, and height limits. Where sections of the city improve, pent-up demand collides with scarcity, and prices rise.

Whatever the trigger for gentrification may be, moreover, the damage it does is less severe than critics claim. It helps residents in some ways as it hurts them in others. Homeowners troubled by higher taxes still gain wealth from rising house prices. Many renters live in public housing or are under rent control, and others stay on in aging apartments while landlords resist the lure of redevelopment to hold out for even higher prices. In the meantime, renters and homeowners alike enjoy the improvements that come with the arrival of more affluent neighbors.

But if affordability is a weak argument *against* smart growth, it is still a problem *for* smart growth. Tenants can be victims of a process that creates enormous value for others. In a world of zoning, covenants, and historic districts, this is hardly the natural working of a free market. Land use law takes pains to shelter homeowners from the intangible "impacts" of nearby stores and apartments, yet it gives tenants no protection against the very tangible harm of higher rents.

The disappearance of affordable housing from reviving neighborhoods hurts the poor most, but the whole city suffers with them. The demand for urban living, in many cities, is dammed up between the barriers of poverty and crime on one side, and suburban land tenure on the other. It has great force when it breaks through. Once an area begins to improve, housing prices shoot up and the population turns over rapidly. A zone of affluence emerges, separated by invisible walls from the surrounding poverty. Gentrification, bottled up in small spaces, destroys the mosaic of mixed uses and mixed incomes sought by many of those who initiate the process. Active intervention on behalf of affordability preserves diversity. It makes for a more livable city as well as a fairer one.

The most direct and efficient way to keep housing affordable is rent control. Rent control is of course less popular among landlords than among tenants, so it has long been a subject of fierce debate.

Mainstream economists tend toward skepticism about price controls of any sort, and rent control has been a particular target of the conservative wing of the profession. The case against rent control has changed little over the years. It is, in essence, that fixing rents destroys the incentive to create more affordable housing by building new homes or splitting up existing ones. The classic statement is a 1946 pamphlet commissioned by the National Association of Real Estate Boards and written by Milton Friedman and George Stigler. Writing at a time of postwar housing shortage, Friedman and Stigler laid heavy stress on the splitting. "Until there is sufficient new construction," they argued, "this doubling up is the only solution."[1]

Whatever merit such contentions may have in the abstract—and there are strong counterarguments—they have little relevance to the housing market as it actually exists. The logic of unfettered competition presupposes that owners of capital assets seek to maximize their property's value and utility. This theory breaks down when the goal is to gain prestige by letting fewer people live on each acre of land. The competitors aim not to use their own assets more productively but to prevent their neighbors from using theirs.

Thus, competition in the real estate market is tightly fettered. The very purpose of zoning rules is to reduce the supply of apartments. The realtors' trade association, which paid for the Friedman and Stigler pamphlet, also helped draft the model planning act of 1928. Their open intent, in promoting planning, was to raise house prices by limiting supply. The realtors' passion was not free markets, but high rents.[2]

Zoning, with its insistence on single-family "character," steps in with particular force when someone tries to follow Milton Friedman's advice. Homeowners with unused rooms break the law if they create another dwelling unit. New entrants into the housing market—demobilized soldiers in 1946, immigrants and recent college graduates today—have no access to empty living space.

When houses cannot be divided, removing rent controls adds nothing to the supply of homes. The only legal way to double up is to move in with your parents, and rent ceilings don't stop parents from taking in their children. All deregulation does is take money from tenants and put it in landlords' pockets.[3] A vote on rent control, with single-family zoning on the books, does not decide whether the government will set rents. It chooses whether to raise them up with one law or hold them down with another.

When shortages are most severe, tenants are most in need of protection, but that is when rent control is least effective. It is a dam that protects only when the flood does not rise too high. If the market rent climbs far above the controlled rent, tenants and landlords alike exploit the gap. They sublet, pay "key money," and otherwise do business off the books. To keep controls working, new housing must satisfy the demand.

Most of the world today, and the United States in the past, have believed that the profit motive cannot produce an adequate supply of affordable housing. Many countries initially responded as the New Deal did, with housing built by cities or by public agencies. With the passage of time, it became clear that ownership by centralized government agencies brought problems of its own. While the sterility that George Orwell and Jane Jacobs observed in public housing can be blamed on modernist planning theories, the remedies for that ill—variety, flexibility, and personal initiative—are not easily applied by large bureaucracies.

In the years since the 1970s, western Europe has sought to combine the virtues of individual and common ownership. The urban housing market has

Nonprofit housing in the Netherlands, built at the sidewalk with stores on the ground floor.
(Courtesy of Pamela Lindstrom.)

evolved in the direction of market socialism. Apartments are rented and sold in an open market, while cooperatives and nonprofits compete in the building of new structures. The land under the buildings remains in government hands, owned by the city or controlled to limit the scope of individual profit.

Public attitudes and power relationships would need to change enormously before the United States could move toward such a system. And there is a further obstacle. Even if the federal government offered funding for public housing on the scale of the past, the problem of siting the housing in a city of status-seeking neighborhoods would remain to be overcome.

But urbanists cannot neglect government and nonprofit housing. The existing stock of public housing is irreplaceable for those who live there. And the neighborhoods around housing projects benefit too, by retaining economic diversity as they gentrify. When buildings must be torn own, due to age and wear or to insufficient density, new public housing should replace them. And, however distant the prospect, the country needs a revived national program of housing construction.[4]

Prosperous communities, if they have the political will, can add to their affordable housing even without federal aid. The rent on apartments for the middle class (but not the poor) can usually pay for construction and upkeep. The reason apartments are so expensive in upscale neighborhoods is not so much the cost of construction as the scarcity of opportunities to build. Scarcity value is embodied in land prices, but local governments own much land and can deploy their regulatory powers to obtain the use of other land. The vast demand for less expensive housing can hardly be sated by such means, but what is built is immensely valuable to its inhabitants and the neighborhoods around them.

In few places are tenants numerous and well organized enough to enact rent control, and in the absence of federal money only so much new affordable housing can be built. It can be hard even to preserve what now exists.

This issue comes to the fore in rapidly gentrifying neighborhoods. Here urbanist thinking offers some potential remedies. A flat-out ban on new off-street parking would channel new housing away from the top end of the market.[5] Unrestricted conversion of single-family houses to duplexes would let owners stay in place and benefit from rising values while adding to the supply of less expensive rentals. Both measures would guide change rather than trying to halt it altogether.

Tenant advocates often fall back instead on a purely defensive approach and oppose new construction in the neighborhood. This strategy rests on a seemingly straightforward logic. Real estate prices are always a matter of location—buildings are expensive because they're near expensive buildings—so keeping out new buildings, which will always charge a higher rent than the older ones around them, helps keep housing affordable.

The means of stopping development is a political coalition of tenants and nimby homeowners. This alliance is surely an odd basis for left-wing politics, but a school of academic theory justifies it as such. The idea is that neighborhoods are defending themselves against an exploitative and nearly all-powerful "growth machine." The fuel that drives the machine is profit, derived from the excess of the "exchange value" realized when land is redeveloped over the "use value" enjoyed by its current residents.[6] This logic dovetails nicely with the greedy developer mantra of more conservative suburban homeowners.

Growth machine theory has the merit of focusing on the exercise of political power, something that is glossed over in much establishment writing about land use. It explains, moreover, why urban renewal and downtown expressways were so hard to stop in the 1950s and 1960s. But the theory is less useful in current circumstances. For one thing, it exaggerates the power of the growth machine. Developers would surely, if allowed, build their high-rises in prestigious close-in neighborhoods like Beverly Hills, Grosse Pointe, and Georgetown. Condos would be easier to sell there than in the run-down areas where local governments now let them build.[7] For another, the concept of use value misconstrues the motivation for resistance to growth. Nimbys acquire higher status by means of conspicuous waste; what zoning protects is not the use of land but its disuse.

A variant of this theory that emphasizes the role of lower-income neighborhoods as centers of resistance to capitalism is popular among neo-Marxist writers. Aiming to understand the global forces behind recent economic trends, they focus on the role of banks and real estate developers in urban change and downplay the role of individual gentrifiers. The single-family zoning of suburban homeowners has little relevance to their concerns and is often taken for granted.

The focus on gentrification shifts the political base for affordable housing. Tenants themselves do not mobilize on the abstract issue of future land use as they do for the immediate protection of rent control. Meanwhile, support grows more intense among the gentrifiers themselves—for some grass-roots advocates of affordable housing, opposition to gentrification begins with a desire to keep the neighborhood just the way it was when they moved in. Sympathy for low-income residents comes only afterward.[8]

At their worst, local struggles against gentrification have less to do with the poor than with protecting the brand image of poverty in a newly hip neighborhood. Local activists seize on neo-Marxist theory to denounce all change as the evil machinations of the multinational elite. Here there is an echo of prosprawl libertarians like Randal O'Toole and Joel Kotkin. One group hails nimbys as enemies of the urban cultural elite; the other welcomes them as partners in the struggle against global capital. Either way, the rhetoric serves a similar purpose. It provides a rationale for alliances that would otherwise be hard to square with the locally fashionable political ideology.[9]

Identifying gentrification as the underlying issue brings the issues of transportation and development to the fore. Other things in poor neighborhoods keep wealthy newcomers out too—crime and bad schools, for example— but it is hard to argue for their preservation. An activist may think, as one Chicagoan told an interviewer, that crime helps keep his neighborhood from becoming "too nice," but few longtime residents agree.[10] Targeted instead are light rail lines and new buildings on vacant land. In themselves they displace no one, but as triggers of change they seem as threatening as condo conversions and they are much easier to stop.

For tenants, who certainly have a direct concern for affordability, coalitions with nimbys lead to a dead end. Changing city neighborhoods cannot be preserved as low-rent refuges unless the demand for urban living is soaked up somewhere else. New urban downtowns would have to be built in the wealthy areas where CEOs live and jobs cluster. But the alliance with nimbys makes it impossible to challenge snob zoning within the same political jurisdiction. And by legitimating resistance to change, it reinforces the status quo elsewhere.

The wealthy inevitably play the exclusion game more effectively than the poor. Pent-up demand is funneled into the surviving remnants of an older urbanism. The price of the existing housing stock soars. This dynamic of gentrification has gone furthest in San Francisco, where soaring housing costs accompany tight building limits. The best-paid jobs are in Silicon Valley office parks, so reverse commuters' cars crowd the streets of once-poor neighborhoods.

Housing is least affordable in the wealthiest suburbs and city neighborhoods, which price out the middle class along with the poor. Minimum-wage workers are not the only ones forced into long commutes; teachers and firefighters can't afford to live near their jobs either.

A common remedy in such areas is what is known as inclusionary zoning. These rules require builders to rent or sell a certain portion of new housing at prices that middle-income people can pay. More than one hundred localities have adopted them. Some places require affordable housing in all new housing; elsewhere builders who comply earn a *density bonus*—the right to put bigger buildings on their land."

Inclusionary zoning is usually an add-on to existing zoning codes, and that has been a weakness. Zoning's original purpose was to keep low-priced dwellings out, and pasting in new text does not undo the exclusionary workings of the rest of the ordinance. Parking minimums are a particular burden; an affordable apartment near a subway station has no need for a $50,000 underground parking space. Exempting affordable housing from such rules—or repealing them altogether—builds more homes at less cost.

Condominium fees are another obstacle. In high-end condos, doormen, athletic clubs, and such extras drive up the monthly charge. Here again, car-free living can be the remedy. The condo association might own the garage and finance itself by renting out spaces, or it could assess fees on parking spaces rather than living spaces. Residents of affordable units would escape paying for unneeded luxuries if they went without a car or parked off the premises.

The number of affordable apartments inclusionary zoning can build is small compared to the need, but its political significance is great. By allowing people of modest means to live everywhere, it breaks through the suburban cycle of competitive exclusion. The real estate market, driven by the cost of land and the influence of local nimbys, when left to itself pushes low-income housing toward less expensive sections of town. Absent inclusionary zoning, homeowners in those areas will complain that they are stuck with what no one else will take. Giving all areas a share of officially designated affordable housing smooths the way for other means of mixing income levels and combining land uses.

Inclusionary zoning has little point unless houses are expensive and new buildings are going up. After the housing bubble, such success is more the exception than the rule. Cleveland, Detroit, and Buffalo are full of walkable neighborhoods where the supply of housing exceeds the demand. There no one worries about affordability.

There are, too, places in the middle, where the boom is long gone yet housing remains maddeningly expensive. Decay and affordability can be problems simultaneously. Such middle-range neighborhoods can be found in inner suburbs of relatively prosperous cities. Here the legalization of two-family houses would help deal with both threats.

Another type of middle-income suburb, the McMansion exurb, poses a less tractable problem. Although their economic settings vary, ranging from relative prosperity to the calamities of Las Vegas, Phoenix, and southwest Florida, all are at risk of the cycle of decay endured by inner cities in the 1950s and 1960s. House prices fall, public services go downhill as tax revenues decline, and an influx of lower-income residents magnifies the resulting loss of status. Some areas on the outskirts of San Francisco and Washington may soon see a flight of the affluent in search of good schools and safe neighborhoods in the inner city.

Exurban decline, if it starts to feed on itself, may prove hard to stop. When streetcar suburbs went downhill, they still offered an inexpensive place to live. With stores in walking distance and buses to downtown, no one needed a car. Zoning was permissive and covenants long forgotten, so big old Victorian houses were broken up into affordable apartments and rooming houses. Slums like the South Bronx did collapse, but many neighborhoods built before the First World War sustained themselves as healthy, livable working-class communities.

Failed exurbs will find this path hard to follow. Expensive commuting cancels out low rents. Zoning forbids the breakup of big houses into rental apartments, and covenants occasionally forbid rentals altogether. Some subdivisions are already half-empty, and complete abandonment could become a long-term trend.

One California exurb, the city of Merced, may have stumbled into a way out of this dilemma. A new state university with 5200 students has room for only 1600 in the dorms, so the students have taken to renting empty McMansions. These living arrangements do not run afoul of zoning rules because the structure is not divided into separate apartments. Five students may pay $200 a month each and share a five-bedroom house that once went for more than half a million dollars. A sophomore does his homework in the Jacuzzi; a senior fills a walk-in closet with baseball caps and T-shirts. The university sends free buses to student-heavy subdivisions.[12]

Few outer suburbs are endowed with Merced's student population, but many have families of modest means in search of better homes. If the law allowed it, five- and six-bedroom houses could be split into two or three apartments. Long-distance commutes will never be cheap, but their cost can be kept within reason by running commuter trains or buses from park-and-ride lots. Where affordable housing is scarce and the destination is a dense downtown full of jobs, subdividing may be a way out in the exurbs too.

Tenants, in a country where most people own their homes, enter politics in a position of weakness. For owners, housing affordability is a two-edged sword. They are both sellers and buyers, and as sellers they like high prices. They want, moreover, their neighbors' houses to be expensive—it is a matter of status and of real estate prices too.

Advocates for affordable housing are left with a stark political choice between two strategic alliances.

One approach is to preserve the existing stock of low-cost housing with strict rent control that blocks demolition of affordable units. Only when new supply cushions it against market demand can such a system endure. The supply can come from public or nonprofit housing built on vacant land or, in the absence of federal housing subsidies, by opening up residential neighborhoods to construction of new housing. This strategy has had successes, in cities from New York to Santa Monica, but they require the right political and ideological circumstances. Public debate must be open to ideas of the left. And low-income voters must be well organized, in unions or political parties, strong enough to be the senior partners in the inevitable alliance with the nimbys.

When tenants don't have enough strength to make rent control a realistic possibility, alliances with nimbys can easily boomerang. Tenant votes go to slow growth candidates who, when elected, make new housing harder to build. In the absence of new urban places, affluent would-be urbanites flood into the walkable neighborhoods that already exist and bid up prices there.

Renovations and condo conversions eat up the affordable housing in these old city districts.

Affordable housing proponents can avoid this outcome by dealing with the other side in the developer–nimby wars. They lend their support to new development in exchange for inclusionary zoning and easing of limits on rental apartments in houses. This strategy promises much less to renters than the benefits of rent control. But it has a chance of success in many more places.

Neither local strategy can promise more than partial success. Before affordable and livable housing can be built for all, the political environment must change both nationally and locally. Financing must come from the federal government, and zoning boards must allow infill development without arm-twisting by developers. Both are long-term quests. But they are goals that cannot be abandoned.

17

On Track toward Livable Cities

Great cities, Daniel Burnham understood, are built from plans with "magic to stir men's blood." A century after his passing, that maxim has lost none of its force. Today it is the inheritance of sprawl that stalls the renewal of cities and stymies the renovation of suburbs. Change comes only when the public is roused to impose its will.

Trains, like nothing else in cities, possess Daniel Burnham's magic. When discussion of new rail lines starts, ideas bubble up from the grass roots. Fierce debates erupt over where the tracks should go. The public joins the discussion because change is not abstract. Those near the route see how their daily lives will be affected, and others can put themselves in their shoes.

If a project is put to a public vote, volunteers mobilize. Supporters living along the future tracks counter the inevitable nimbys. Environmental groups, slow to speak out when infill development is at issue, wax enthusiastic. Coalitions of unusual breadth come together, uniting labor, business, ethnic neighborhoods, and conservationists. Polls show that trains are popular.

Trains provoke this interest and engagement because they are much more than transportation. The urban rebirth of the last thirty years has been a rail renaissance. New York, Boston, Chicago, and Philadelphia have revived around their subways; change comes fastest not to the prettiest or safest neighborhoods but to those with the best rail connections.[1] Washington and

Portland have been remade by their new train lines. In Los Angeles, Denver, and San Francisco, skimpy rail networks that reach suburbs just here and there have sufficed to revive once-fading downtowns.

As they remake cities, rail lines bring rethinking. By elevating public space, they reject the suburban ideal of isolation. A visible challenge to the driver's ingrained belief that a car is the only normal way to move around, they affirm in steel and concrete that city dwellers no longer rank below suburbanites. Grass-roots advocacy for urbanism begins, almost always, with a railroad.

Rail transit is not merely a conveyance. It is the political and mental key that opens the door to urban change.

In economics, as in politics, rail transit is central to urban revival. Financing alone cannot revive the ailing postbubble housing market, because the supply of dwelling places is ill-matched to the demand. Suburban McMansions are a drag on the market; what consumers seek are apartments and townhouses in the new transit-oriented urban centers. But there are simply not enough places to build the housing that is in demand; few cities have a transit network large enough to open up the needed land.

Money spent on new urban rail lines thus stimulates the economy twice. The direct impact of construction dollars is followed by the redevelopment that transit brings.

Rail construction is important, too, for housing affordability. New homes near train stations are expensive, in many cities, simply because there are so few places they can go. The demand for apartments near transit exceeds the supply of places to put them. If land near rail stations loses scarcity value, new transit-oriented housing will be more affordable for the middle class.

Nothing else the federal government could do would help cities as much as a drastic increase in funding for subways and light rail. Beyond the direct benefits of transportation, jobs, and pollution control, rail transit has a multitude of political and economic spinoffs. Urban trains are good for the body, the spirit, and the pocketbook, and they should be a top priority of national policy.

Rail transit has its critics, and not just among the right-wing defenders of sprawl. One persistent line of attack is technocratic. Proponents of *bus rapid transit*, or BRT—buses that board like trains and move faster than other traffic by running in their own lanes or getting more green lights—assert that they can provide the same quality of transportation as light rail for much less money. They point to successes in Latin America and elsewhere overseas.[2]

These claims run up against a strong public preference for rail over bus, and they have come under withering criticism from light rail proponents. When there are stops at traffic lights, busways carrying heavy passenger loads are slower than light rail.[3] Rail advocates also dispute the claims of cost savings, and they point out that the ride is smoother and more comfortable by train. Americans, they argue, will not accept the crowding that enables buses in low-income countries to carry large passenger loads.[4]

Cost, speed, and ridership all matter, but urban revival depends on what is outside the vehicle as much as who is inside it. Here busways fall short; they do not fit as well on city streets. To move as many people as three-car trains that are five minutes apart, buses have to run every minute or so. It is easy to cross the street between trains that pass by every five minutes; a bus lane that carries the same number of riders has frequent traffic that is a barrier to those on foot. And if the passenger load is too heavy for downtown streets, the trains can be put underground, while bus tunnels are hard to build, expensive, and unpleasant. Flexibility is touted as an advantage of busways—buses can leave the reserved lane when convenient and enter traffic—but in densely built-up places with many transit riders it is trains that are more adaptable.

In any case, the debates of specialists about the tangible pros and cons of transit modes do not shape public opinion. The intensity of the public preference for rail has a different cause. Rail has high status. Buses do not. Second-class transportation, people feel, will only make their city second-class.

As the bus proponents see it, these attitudes are irrational prejudices that should not distort public policy. But status shapes cities just as money does; ignoring it is the opposite of realism. No one would tell Los Angeles and Washington that they are wasting money by redeveloping old factory districts, because high-rises could have been built without subsidies by rezoning Brentwood and Georgetown. Comparing a light rail line that emerges from a contentious political battle to a bus route no one asked for is like picking the spot for a new office tower without checking whether neighbors will object to the zoning change.

Yet that is what transit planners are required to do. The federal bureaucracy, hostile to rail since the Ronald Reagan administration, helps lead the push for bus rapid transit. Until the rules were changed in 2010, it ranked projects solely on their cost-effectiveness as means of transportation.[5] The Federal Transit Administration now gives some weight to the potential of a project to spur land development, but the bias toward buses remains.

At the local level, where the politics of transportation planning mostly play out, rail-bus debates are unavoidable. Budgets are always limited, and spending too much money on rail lines with too few riders can cripple transit agencies. But here the rationale for bus rapid transit is usually to spend less, not to get more for the same money. Once this choice is made, flexibility becomes BRT's Achilles' heel. A city decides to cut costs by building a rail-like busway; the engineers go to work; the savings turn out less than hoped. The easy way out is to drop the train-like features of the bus lane. The promises are rapid, but the bus is slow.

Some BRT advocates disown the run-of-the-mill bus lines that emerge from this sequence of bait and switch; Robert Poole, of the libertarian Reason Foundation, embraces them. "BRT," he writes, "aims to provide performance and service qualities comparable to those of rail transit but at a cost that is considerably lower than that of light rail systems." But bus rapid transit, he tells those who are thinking of actually building it, does not need to move rapidly. He advises cities to operate what he calls "BRT-lite"—a bus painted a special color, running in regular traffic lanes but making fewer stops.[6]

A similar reversal of positions occurs when transit agencies try to move regular buses faster. The arguments for what are called *bus priorities* are based on efficiency—crowded roadways carry more people when buses get lanes to themselves and traffic lights let them through first. This is the same kind of thinking that recommends BRT as a substitute for rail. But the right-wingers who laud BRT when light rail is on the agenda have little interest in this kind of efficiency. Quick to condemn wasteful spending when it goes to rail, they fall silent when motorists benefit from waste. They now put status ahead of efficiency; buses may be a cheaper way to move, but they rank low in the suburban pecking order.

On those infrequent occasions when bus rapid transit does come to pass, the vehicle's inferior standing quickly asserts itself. Cleveland built a high-profile BRT on Euclid Avenue with traffic lights that turned green when a bus approached. As soon as the line opened, drivers on cross streets complained, and the "signal preemption" was turned off within weeks. Boston, in the 1970s, relocated its aging Orange Line on land cleared for a canceled interstate. The low-income neighborhoods traversed by the old elevated tracks were promised light rail as a replacement. Instead they got a pair of bus lanes dubbed the Silver Line. When it snows, which is not a rare event in Boston, plows clear the car lanes and pile up snow where the buses go—the opposite of what happens on the light rail Green Line.[7]

Another group of rail critics concern themselves with equity rather than efficiency. They willingly concede that rail provides a better quality of travel—in

Boston's Silver Line bus rapid transit route after a snowstorm, with buses in mixed traffic because bus lanes are not plowed.
(Courtesy of Jeremy Marin.)

fact, the premise of their argument is that buses are transport for those who can't afford to drive. New rail lines, they contend, draw off money better spent on the poor and give the middle class a luxury ride at the expense of the more deserving.

This thinking crystallized when the Bus Riders Union of Los Angeles was formed in 1993. The city's rail revival was faltering in the face of construction problems and political infighting, while a swelling population of immigrants jammed buses. The regional transit agency faced a giant budget hole and chose to plug it by raising fares and cutting bus service. The new organization sued, charging a violation of civil rights laws, and won a settlement that brought new buses, less rush-hour crowding, and lower fares.

The Bus Riders Union's hostility to rail transit emerges from a broader political analysis. Its founders believe that white America is hopelessly corrupted by racism. They thus put race at the center of their politics and treat economics as secondary. This perspective offers little prospect of creating a majority within this country for change, and they therefore give priority to supporting Third World revolutions by mobilizing the minority poor.[8] They have no desire to elect allies to office—that would only reinforce the illusion of American democracy—but seek to extort concessions from the power structure by means of lawsuits and disruption.[9]

From this point of view, conflict between bus passengers and middle-class commuters is not something to avoid. It mirrors the larger struggle between oppressed racial minorities and the white population. The Bus Riders Union has no use for vehicles where poor and middle class ride together. It blurs the cleavages of race and poverty that it organizes around.

The hard work of the Bus Riders Union and the buses its lawsuits have put on the street have won it admirers across the country. Few imitators share the group's ideology, but many copy its transit program by setting buses against trains.

But bus instead of rail is a false choice. Trains, in the long run at least, are rarely financed at the expense of buses. Rail lines are paid for with higher taxes or fewer roads, and they help finance buses by winning political support for transit. Once the stations open, bus routes feed into them and their newly walkable surroundings. This attracts the middle-class ridership that buses lack elsewhere.

And trains appeal to drivers as well as their own riders, assembling majorities that buses cannot achieve on their own. In Virginia's sprawling Hampton Roads region, the planning body asked residents what kind of transport tax dollars should be spent on. Light rail was supported by 57% of those who answered the poll, slightly more than highway construction, although only 2% said they usually get around on transit. Heavy rail got 37% and buses only 22%.[10] Even the Bus Riders Union in Los Angeles piggybacked on rail—the improvements its lawsuit won were paid for by a tax passed to build Metro lines.

New York, San Francisco, and Washington, with their subway and streetcar lines, show the spinoff effect of trains. Buses crowd the streets, much more so than in cities without rail. In transportation, as in other domains, the poor do best when they share public services with the middle class. Social Security and Medicare thrive; even their enemies pretend to be their protectors. Welfare programs wither away, political punching bags for their opponents, and buses that serve only the poor suffer the same fate.

Few states finance transit as they do roads. The entire state bears the burden of rural highways, but outside the highly urban states of New Jersey and Maryland the cost of trains and buses is borne disproportionately by big-city taxpayers. New rail lines require local tax increases which, very often, go before the voters in a referendum.

This hurdle—one that highways are rarely made to cross—is not a low bar. A strong case must be presented to an electorate that is inevitably suspicious of higher taxes. Success comes easiest when a route and budget are on the table—voters, very sensibly, want to know what they will get for their money. As transit grows more popular, majorities are easier to assemble. In 2000 and 2001, local taxes for transportation won passage about half the time; a decade later three-quarters were approved.

Winning these elections requires a broad coalition of support. Most successful transit campaigns bring together labor, business, and environmentalists. Labor almost invariably supports new rail lines in principle, but its active mobilization does not always follow; firm commitments to union construction and operation of the future rail system are needed up front. Business backing is crucial because money is so powerful in American politics. Few transit referenda win without the help of downtown real estate interests, and blessings by business umbrella groups can deter funding of the opposition. Environmentalist endorsements, while not always essential, are valuable too. They add votes, they can bring volunteers, and they defuse the arguments of nimby opponents. Grass-roots transit advocacy groups, although they rarely match the numerical strength of their allies, play a central role. Their track record of disinterested advocacy adds credibility that backers with a financial interest lack, and they are often the backbone of volunteer efforts.[11]

These diverse coalitions can be hard to hold together. The most troubling question, usually, is whether to combine transit and highway spending in a package. This is a choice that must be approached pragmatically. How much of the money does transit get, and will the money bring real change? The perfect should never be the enemy of the good, but some spending packages merely perpetuate the status quo.

New rail lines are the centerpiece of transportation reform, but they are hardly the end of it. Transit does not compete with the automobile on a level playing field when cars get enormous hidden subsidies. No subsidy is bigger than free parking, something suburban zoning codes effectively require. All the parking spaces in the United States, taken together, are worth more than the country's cars and trucks, and 99% of them are given away.[12]

Parking is a core element of sprawl. Not only does free parking subsidize driving, but it also makes it hard to create walkable downtowns. Parking lots and garages deaden sidewalks and gobble up land. Density can be preserved by putting parking underground, but that drives up the price of city housing and may not be affordable at all.[13]

Change is difficult. Drivers' instincts and emotions rebel against it; the car culture demands free and easy parking. Former Santa Monica planning commissioner Frank Gruber marvels at local nimbys who detest five-story apartment houses yet enthuse over plans for a seven-story public garage. "Parking is like sex," he observes. "If you have to pay for it, it's not right."[14]

Still, many motorists have parking fears that are rationally grounded, and this segment of opinion can be won over. As Donald Shoup shows in his book *The High Cost of Free Parking*, the key reform is setting the price of parking at a level that makes it easy to find a space—what has become known as *performance parking*. Drivers gain in convenience as they lose in cash. Shoup has put his theories into practice by successfully repricing parking meters in Pasadena, Redwood City, and other California suburbs.[15]

But performance parking is only a first step. Limiting demand so that it matches supply does not stop the creation of too much supply. Pressure to build excess parking comes from many sources.

Single-family neighborhoods often ask for extra parking when high-rises go up nearby. They want assurance that newcomers won't park on "their" streets. In old streetcar suburbs, parking is scarce and this is a practical concern. Elsewhere the issue is social status; there are plenty of spaces along the curb, but the prestige of the subdivision would suffer if alien automobiles were allowed into them.

Underground parking can appease these demands, but it is expensive and only attracts more traffic. Instead, homeowners are often given exclusive rights to park on neighborhood streets. Occupants of new buildings are denied parking permits, either by rule or by gerrymandering the borders of the parking districts. A policy that in effect marks apartment dwellers' cars with a scarlet A is surely discriminatory. But it is much less unfair to be forbidden to park in the neighborhood than not to be allowed to live there at all. If people are more important than cars, parking discrimination is a price worth paying to overcome housing discrimination.

Parking at stores is another tricky issue. Merchants in the new suburban mixed-use developments love cheap parking for their customers. Some pay for it themselves and give it away; others push for public garages. Either way, customers who arrive on foot subsidize those who drive. And the pedestrians have no choice but to pay; they are a captive market that has nowhere else to go. This is one more subsidy for motorists, unfortunate but often necessary. Driving to suburban malls is massively subsidized, and storefront businesses must compete. As the suburban downtowns grow into true urban centers, they will eventually have to be weaned from their dependence on excess parking. It will be a difficult task, and one that must await its proper time.

What can be done now is to remove parking minimums from zoning codes. That would be significant progress; everyone loses when money is spent to build parking that the builders don't want. But deregulation is no panacea—the forces that push for subsidized parking are strong, so even the parking the builders want is too much.[16] Thus, much remains to be learned about parking policy. Are maximums a good idea? Should parking be taxed to recover the street-building costs it imposes on local governments? Should merchants be forbidden to bundle it with other goods they sell and required to add a charge for customers who park? Research into such questions has scarcely begun.

Streets are not just transportation arteries. As Jane Jacobs understood, they are stages for the most human of all activities—living together as social animals. At their best, people on foot crowd them, meeting by plan and by chance with neighbors, acquaintances, and strangers. New Urbanist designers have learned to fit buildings comfortably into cities, but the streets have not kept up with the structures. Roadways are still built for the automobile, with wide lanes and fast-moving cars.

The obstacle here is not ignorance but lack of will. A new breed of traffic engineers has figured out the design of walkable streets. Portland, with its bike lanes and traffic calming, gave an early demonstration of their art, but imitators have been few and sluggish. Even the cities with the highest subway ridership in the country, New York and Washington, were slow to follow suit. Only after 2005 did they begin to redesign downtown streets for bicycles and pedestrians. Elsewhere the car is still king. There is at most a grudging bow to "complete streets"—bike lanes on the sides of roads, brick crosswalks, and here and there a "pedestrian zone" that proves everyplace else is an automobile zone.

The problem here is political, and rail is the political remedy. The bureaucrats who control road design fear the consequences if they rock the boat too soon, and they fear them with reason. Sharing roadways with pedestrians and bicycles challenges motorists' sense of entitlement. Only when voters pour out of trains on foot, matching the drivers in vehemence and number, can the demand for walkability be heeded without dread of electoral revenge.

The long drive into sprawl has reached a dead end. America needs trains to carry it back out. For our cities to fulfill their urban potential, winning a new transportation policy—in the nation, in the states, and locally—is the central political task.

Transit advocates come to that task with special burdens, but also with unusual strengths. They begin at a disadvantage when they try to convince politicians of the rightness of their reasoning. Elected officials drive constantly to visit with their constituents, and this experience inclines them to see things from the motorist's point of view.

But in politics the force of argument counts for less than the force of votes. And train riders have built-in advantages when they come together to exert political power. The driver, traveling alone, is pushed toward individualism and consumerism, while mass transit brings people to a common place where they can discuss their problems and join forces. Places where people walk and ride the train are places that stimulate political activism.[17]

Once riders organize, they have strength beyond their numbers. Activists connect easily with their base—when they pass out flyers at the station, they are targeting their supporters with laser-like precision. Rail commuters, some evidence suggests, even vote more often than drivers in low-turnout local elections. An auto commuter may not know there's an election, while someone who takes the train regularly probably shook the hand of all the candidates.[18]

The strengths of the train rider, when seized on, far outweigh the weaknesses. Railroads are much more than steel and concrete. They build cities by growing their economies, by enlivening their streets. They empower us all to break our national addiction to sprawl and take our future into our own hands.

Afterword

The desires for worldly goods and for the respect of others are basic human urges that few individuals can overcome. Neither impulse, surely, will soon vanish, but each can be made to serve good ends or bad. They can find an outlet in destructive egoism, or they can be channeled so that the striving of each contributes to the welfare of all.

The quest for material gain contributes most to the common good when it is a collective rather than an individual enterprise. Large business organizations have brought the world vast improvements in productivity and advances in technology. In unions, the push for higher wages creates industrial civilization's greatest force for equality, democracy, and mass enlightenment.

But the last forty years have seen a shift away from cooperation and toward individual money-making. Organized labor grows weaker. Businesses operate, more and more, to enrich their managers alone.

The search for honor and prestige, by contrast, is most socially useful when it is a quest for individual prominence. Then it inspires philanthropy and innovation, motivating the talented to be creators of the arts and sciences and the merely wealthy to be their patrons. In a collectivity, the desire for respect easily goes astray. It leads to invidious distinctions of race, wealth, or ancestry.

Today we privilege the worst side of both these urges. Suburban land tenure empowers zoning boards, homeowner associations, and historic districts in the pursuit of collective status-seeking. The quest for permanence and exclusivity imposes conformity, stifles self-expression, and discourages the display of excellence.

Meanwhile, individual gain supplants common prosperity as a motive force for building. Immediate profit matters more than long-term value. The shopping mall and the master developer replace the business district of small landowners who cooperate as they compete. Bond-market manipulation finances real estate, and houses become assets to flip rather than homes to grow old in.

The making of the places where we live is far too complex an undertaking to be other than a social endeavor. How we oversee it determines what and where we build. Today our governance of land use sanctions individual greed and collective snobbery and denies us the power to mold the human landscape to our intentions. The selfish motives of gain and preferment can never be banished from human life, but we must harness them to work for the betterment of all. Surely we can do that, if we organize ourselves to build the communities we desire.

Acknowledgments

My greatest debt for the development of the ideas in this book is to my colleagues in the Action Committee for Transit. Its members have been a constant support, balancing idealism with practicality while working together in harmony and mutual support. I could not possibly name all who deserve thanks, but among those worthy of special mention are Nick and Carole Brand, Jean Buergler, John Carroll, Jim Clarke, Ronit Dancis, Bee and Brian Ditzler, Jon Elkind, John Fay, Ruth Fort, Tom Fuchs, Greg Gagarin, Bruce Gilson, the late Ted Gordon, Neil Greene, Jon Gubits, Carl Henn (whose premature loss continues to be felt), Kathy Jentz, Tracey Johnstone, Quon Kwan, Alan Lauer, Richard McArdle, Jessica Mitchell, Harvard Morehead, Kristen Mosbæk, Rodolfo Perez, Dan Reed, Richard Reis, Eleanor Rice, Hans Riemer, Barbara Sanders, Greg Sanders, Miriam Schoenbaum, David Sears, Tina Slater, Tom Stecher, Ed Tennyson, Ted Van Houten, Wes Vernon, Cavan Wilk, Bill Wilson, and especially Cindy Snow. I learned much from Richard Hoye, and I owe most of all to ACT's founder Harry Sanders, whose loss we all regret constantly.

I must also thank the activists in other organizations that I have worked with on the issues of transportation and land use. Among them are David Alpert of Greater Greater Washington; Webb Smedley, Ralph Bennett, and Wayne Phyillaier of Purple Line Now; Cheryl Cort, Kelly Blynn, and Stewart Schwartz of the Coalition for Smarter Growth; Craig Simpson, Jimmy Allen, and Jackie Jeter of Amalgamated Transit Union Local 689; Karren Pope-Onwukwe and Todd Reitzel of Prince George's Advocates for Community-Based Transit; Robbyn Lewis of the Red Line Now PAC; Dolores Milmoe, Diane Cameron, and Neal Fitzgerald of the Audubon Naturalist Association; John Wetmore of Perils for Pedestrians; and Dru Schmidt-Perkins of 1000 Friends of Maryland. I learned much from civic activists in Montgomery County, including Richard Arkin, Jack Bonsby, Peter Galvin, Margo Kelly, Dan Wilhelm, and the late Stuart Rochester. No less deserving of gratitude are the dedicated public servants who have overseen the Purple Line in its long odyssey: Glenn Orlin, Henry Kay, Ernest Baisden, and Mike Madden. The ideas here are, of course, mine, and I am sure all of those I thank will find things to disagree with.

Another source of ongoing inspiration has been *Dissent* magazine. Many of the ideas in this book were first developed in articles, from which some text has been adapted. These include "Bureaucracy and Markets" (Fall 1995), "Suburbs, Status and Sprawl" (Winter 2001), and "Stuck in Traffic" (Summer 2006).

I am obliged as well to many for help directly in the writing of this book. I had useful discussions with Arlington County Supervisor Chris Zimmerman, Nick Caston, Pamela Lindstrom, and my daughter Estye Fenton. Rick Rybeck, Cavan Wilk, Steven Amter, and Wes Vernon read and commented on sections of the manuscript, and David McBride and Sarah Rosenthal of Oxford University Press did much to help perfect it. Terry Owens of the Maryland Transit Administration; David Kessler of the Bancroft Library, University of California; and Duane Lucia of the West End Museum helped me locate photographs. Dan Malouff earns special thanks for drafting all the maps.

Notes

Chapter 1

1. Carl J. Guarnieri, *The Utopian Alternative: Fourierism in Nineteenth-Century America* (Cornell University Press, Ithaca, NY, 1991); Morris Hillquit, *Socialism in the United States* (Funk & Wagnalls, New York, 1903), pp. 76–88.
2. The original source for this quotation, attributed to Mary Ellen Russell, daughter of the "sailor preacher" Father Edward Taylor who was close to Emerson and other transcendentalists, is Thomas Wentworth Higginson, *Part of a Man's Life*, (Houghton Mifflin, Boston, 1904), p. 12. Mrs. Russell's dates are given in her grandson's memoir, Thomas Russell Ybarra, *Young Man of Caracas* (I. Washburn, New York, 1941).
3. Kenneth T. Jackson, *Crabgrass Frontier: The Suburbanization of the United States* (Oxford University Press, New York, 1985), pp. 84–85; Dolores Hayden, *Building Suburbia* (Vintage, New York, 2003), p. 52.
4. Roger Wunderlich, *Low Living and High Thinking at Modern Times, New York* (Syracuse University Press, Syracuse, NY, 1992).
5. John Humphrey Noyes, *History of American Socialisms*, (J.B. Lippincott & Company, New York, 1870), esp. pp. 449–511; Guarnieri, *Utopian Alternative*, pp. 322–326; Hayden, *Building Suburbia*, pp. 52–53; Susan Henderson, "Llewellyn Park, Suburban Idyll," *Journal of Garden History*, vol. 7, pp. 221–243 (1987).
6. Henderson, "Llewellyn Park"; Hayden, *Building Suburbia*, pp. 54–61; Robert Fishman, *Bourgeois Utopias: The Rise and Fall of Suburbia* (Basic Books, New York, 1987), esp. p. 125.
7. Henderson, "Llewellyn Park"; Michael Kazin, *American Dreamers: How the Left Changed a Nation* (Alfred A. Knopf, New York, 2011), p. 55.
8. Henderson, "Llewellyn Park."
9. Henderson, "Llewellyn Park."
10. Jackson, *Crabgrass Frontier*, pp. 79–81.
11. Jackson, *Crabgrass Frontier*, p. 79; Robert M. Fogelson, *Bourgeois Nightmares* (Yale University Press, New Haven, CT, 2005), pp. 40–42; Hayden, *Building Suburbia*, p. 65.
12. Jackson, *Crabgrass Frontier*, pp. 95–97; Fogelson, *Bourgeois Nightmares*, pp. 35, 88–90, 131–137; Fishman, *Bourgeois Utopias*, pp. 144–148; Mary Corbin Sies,

"Paradise Retained: An Analysis of Persistence in Planned, Exclusive Suburbs, 1880–1980," *Planning Perspectives*, vol. 12, pp. 165–191 (1997).

13. Sam Bass Warner Jr., *Streetcar Suburbs: The Process of Growth in Boston (1870–1900)*, 2nd ed. (Harvard University Press, Cambridge, MA, 1978); Hayden, *Building Suburbia*, pp. 71–88.

14. Warner, *Streetcar Suburbs*, pp. 46–66, 75–79.

15. Henry James, *The Bostonians* (Penguin Classics edition, London, 1986), pp. 52, 55.

16. William M. Offutt, *Bethesda: A Social History* (Innovation Game, Washington, DC, 1995), pp. 74–77; Carl Abbott, *Greater Portland: Urban Life and Landscape in the Pacific Northwest* (University of Pennsylvania Press, Philadelphia, 2001), p. 87.

17. Warner, *Streetcar Suburbs*, pp. 144–151.

18. Warner, *Streetcar Suburbs*, p. 122; Fogelson, *Bourgeois Nightmares*, pp. 40–41.

19. Warner, *Streetcar Suburbs*, p. 122; Fogelson, *Bourgeois Nightmares*, pp. 54–59.

20. Fogelson, *Bourgeois Nightmares*, pp. 60–66; William S. Worley, *J. C. Nichols and the Shaping of Kansas City* (University of Missouri Press, Columbia, 1990), pp. 30–36.

21. Worley, *J. C. Nichols*, pp. 61–70, 78–80, 116–117, 122–144, 164–174, 232–263; Fogelson, *Bourgeois Nightmares*, pp. 108–109; J. C. Nichols, "Subdivision: The Realtor Must Anticipate the Future Needs of His City," *National Real Estate Journal*, Oct. 24, 1921, quoted in Jane Holtz Kay, *Asphalt Nation* (University of California Press, Berkeley, 1997), p. 180; J. C. Nichols, "Subdivision Practices," *National Real Estate Journal*, Nov. 4, 1938, http://www.umkc.edu/WHMCKC/publications/JCN/JCNPDF/JCN053.pdf, accessed December 21, 2011.

22. Worley, *J. C. Nichols*, pp. 91–93; Fogelson, *Bourgeois Nightmares*, pp. 118–130. Inspired: Cheryl Caldwell Ferguson, "River Oaks: 1920s Suburban Planning and Development in Houston," *Southwestern Historical Quarterly*, vol. 104, pp. 191–228 (2000).

23. Fishman, *Bourgeois Utopias*, pp. 146–147; Sies, "Paradise Retained." Quotation from Charles Cheney, quoted in Robert Fogelson, *The Fragmented Metropolis: Los Angeles 1850–1930* (Harvard University Press, Cambridge, MA, 1967), p. 324 fn.

24. Thorstein Veblen, *The Theory of the Leisure Class*, chapter 6.

25. Michael Jones-Correa, "The Origins and Diffusion of Restrictive Covenants," *Political Science Quarterly*, vol. 115, pp. 541–568 (2001); Fogelson, *Bourgeois Nightmares*, pp. 95–103, 125–131.

26. Jackson, *Crabgrass Frontier*, pp. 160–171, 174–177; Hayden, *Building Suburbia*, pp. 115, 118–120, 127.

27. Marc A. Weiss, *The Rise of the Community Builders: The American Real Estate Industry and Urban Land Planning* (Columbia University Press, New York, 1987), pp. 73, 114–116; John Kenneth Galbraith, *The Great Crash, 1929* (Houghton Mifflin, Boston, 1955), pp. 3–7.

28. Weiss, *Community Builders*, pp. 70–72.

29. Weiss, *Community Builders*, pp. 12, 54–58, 65–72, 79–87; Marc A. Weiss, "The Real Estate Industry and the Politics of Zoning in San Francisco, 1914–1928,"

Planning Perspectives, vol. 3, pp. 311–324 (1988); Mel Scott, *American City Planning Since 1890* (University of California Press, Berkeley, 1969), pp. 76, 152–163.

30. Christopher Silver, "The Racial Origins of Zoning in American Cities," in June Manning Thomas and Marsha Ritzdorf, eds., *Urban Planning and the African American Community: In the Shadows* (Sage Publications, Thousand Oaks, CA, 1997), pp. 23–42; Jones-Correa, "Racial Covenants"; Fogelson, *Bourgeois Nightmares*, pp. 98–99; Seymour I. Toll, *Zoned American* (Grossman, New York, 1969), pp. 262–263.

31. Keith D. Revell, "Regulating the Landscape: Real Estate Values, City Planning, and the 1916 Zoning Ordinance," in David Ward and Olivier Zunz, eds., *The Landscape of Modernity: Essays on New York City, 1900–1940* (Russell Sage Foundation, New York, 1992), pp. 19–45; Toll, *Zoned American*, pp. 110–116, 143–166, 172–184; Scott, *American City Planning*, pp. 153–160.

32. The anticipation cannot be documented directly for obvious reasons, but for the behavior following immediately on the adoption of zoning ordinances see Scott, *American City Planning*, pp. 197; Weiss, "Zoning in San Francisco"; Toll, *Zoned American*, pp. 207–210. When zoning arrived, the machines were losing a major source of graft as a result of the slowdown in streetcar expansion.

33. Scott, *American City Planning*, pp. 160–161, 192–198, 227–228.

34. Fogelson, *Bourgeois Nightmares*, pp. 155–159; Kenneth Baar, "National Movement to Halt the Spread of Multifamily Housing, 1890–1926," *Journal of the American Planning Association*, vol. 58, pp. 470–482 (1992); William M. Randle, "Professors, Reformers, Bureaucrats and Cronies: The Players in *Euclid v. Ambler*," in Charles M. Haar and Jerold S. Kayden, eds., *Zoning and the American Dream* (Planners Press, Chicago, 1989), pp. 31–59, see pp. 49–50. For an anthropological description of the animus against apartments, written in the 1970s but reflecting long-persisting attitudes, see Constance Perin, *Everything in Its Place: Social Order and Land Use in America* (Princeton University Press, Princeton, NJ, 1977), pp. 32–70.

35. Baar, "National Movement"; Marc A. Weiss, "Urban Land Developers and the Origins of Zoning Laws: The Case of Berkeley," *Berkeley Planning Journal*, vol. 3, pp. 7–25 (1986); Scott, *American City Planning*, pp. 161–162, 192–193; Richard F. Babcock, *The Zoning Game: Municipal Practices and Policies* (University of Wisconsin Press, Madison, 1966), pp. 3–6, 115; Raphael Fischler, "Health, Safety and the General Welfare—Markets, Politics and Social Science in Early Land-Use Regulation and Community Design," *Journal of Urban History*, vol. 24, pp. 675–719 (1998).

36. Jones-Correa, "Racial Covenants"; Evan McKenzie, *Privatopia: Homeowner Associations and the Rise of Residential Private Government* (Yale University Press, New Haven, CT, 1994), pp. 56–74.

37. Fogelson, *Bourgeois Nightmares*, pp. 206–207; Weiss, *Community Builders*, pp. 68–72; Worley, *J. C. Nichols*, pp. 126, 132–139.

38. Michael Lewyn, "How Overregulation Creates Sprawl (Even in a City Without Zoning)," *Wayne Law Review*, vol. 50, pp. 1171–1207 (2004); Teddy M. Kapur, "Land Use Regulation in Houston Contradicts the City's Free Market

Reputation," *Environmental Law Reporter*, vol. 34, pp. 10045–10063 (2004); John Mixon, "Four Land Use Vignettes from Unzoned(?) Houston," *Notre Dame Journal of Law, Ethics & Public Policy*, pp. 159–185 (2010); Babcock, *Zoning Game*, pp. 25–28; David G. McComb, *Houston: A History* (University of Texas Press, Austin, 1981), pp. 96–97, 99, 156–160.

39. See McKenzie, *Privatopia*, pp. 122–149.

40. Conservative economists who interpret zoning as a collective property right include Robert H. Nelson, *Zoning and Property Rights* (MIT Press, Cambridge, MA, 1977); William A. Fischel, *The Economics of Zoning Laws: A Property Rights Approach to American Land Use Controls* (Johns Hopkins University Press, Baltimore, 1985); Peter Gordon, F. Frederic Deng, and Harry W. Richardson, "Private Communities, Market Institutions, and Planning," in N. Verma, ed., *Institutions and Planning* (CUPR Press, New Brunswick, NJ, 2007).

41. Babcock, *Zoning Game*, pp. 12, 140–142.

42. Only a few scholars have asked why there is such fine sorting by social status in American suburbs. The question is usually addressed, when it is, in the context of a comparison with Europe. The most plausible answer, other than historical accident, comes from Ernst Freund, quoted in Toll, *Zoned American*, pp. 266–267; Herbert J. Gans, "The Failure of Urban Renewal," *Commentary*, April 1965, pp. 29–37. They suggest that greater sorting occurs here because the more fluid class structure of this country leaves Americans deprived of other markers of status. Another European inheritance from feudalism may also be relevant; the lord's manor was surrounded by peasant hovels, so bourgeois residences that imitated it did not need spatial separation from the urban poor. Other deterministic explanations are less convincing. Robert Fishman, *Bourgeois Utopias*, pp. 104–107, 118–121, contends that the bourgeoisie had the same urge for social separation in Europe as in America. He explains the suburbanization of the middle class in the United States and Britain, but not in France, by political democracy and inherited legal doctrines. These factors do not account for the early twentieth-century revolution in American land tenure law. Michael N. Danielson, *The Politics of Exclusion* (Columbia University Press, New York, 1976), p. 23, points to the local control of zoning in the United States; this does not explain restrictive covenants and exclusionary zoning within cities. Perin, *Everything in Its Place*, esp. pp. 32–44, 108–124, looks not to Europe but to pre-industrial societies. She suggests that American culture associates different housing arrangements with different stages of life and that taboos against mixing of life stages are universal features of human culture.

Chapter 2

1. Babcock, *Zoning Game*, pp. 30–31, 116–120, 185; Fogelson, *Bourgeois Nightmares*, p. 112.

2. Fogelson, *Bourgeois Nightmares*, pp. 158–159; Scott, *American City Planning*, p. 154.

3. Randle, "The Players."

4. Toll, *Zoned American*, pp. 122–140; Scott, *American City Planning*, pp. 95–100, 117–127.

5. Weiss, *Community Builders*, pp. 54–67; Worley, *J. C. Nichols*, pp. 89–92.

6. Scott, *American City Planning*, pp. 84–88; Toll, *Zoned American*; Herbert Gans, *People, Plans and Policies* (Columbia University Press, New York, 1991), pp. 124–130.

7. Scott, *American City Planning*, pp. 97, 152; Weiss, *Community Builders*, pp. 56–60, 64–72.

8. Randle, "The Players"; Baar, "National Movement"; Toll, *Zoned American*, pp. 199–200.

9. Scott, *American City Planning*, pp. 192–195; Toll, *Zoned American*, pp. 203–204, 268.

10. Toll, *Zoned American*, pp. 168–171; Scott, *American City Planning*, pp. 152–153.

11. Michael Allan Wolf, *The Zoning of America* (University Press of Kansas, Lawrence, 2008); Arthur V. N. Brooks, "The Office File Box—Emanations from the Battlefield," in Haar and Kayden, *Zoning and the American Dream*, pp. 3–30; Randle, "The Players"; Scott, *American City Planning*, pp. 238–240. Quotation from *Euclid v. Ambler*.

12. Scott, *American City Planning*, pp. 193–195, 242–248; Weiss, *Community Builders*, pp. 72–78; Marc A. Weiss, "Planning Subdivisions: Community Builders and Urban Planners in the Early Twentieth Century," in *Planning and Financing Public Works* (Public Works Historical Society, Chicago, 1987), pp. 21–46; Toll, *Zoned American*, p. 164.

13. Sinclair Lewis, *Babbitt* (Dover, Mineola, NY, 2003), quotations from pp. 30, 51, 58.

14. Peter D. Norton, *Fighting Traffic: The Dawn of the Motor Age in the American City* (MIT Press, Cambridge, MA, 2008), esp. pp. 72–85, 139–141, 185–193, 207–235.

15. Mark S. Foster, *From Streetcar to Superhighway: American City Planners and Urban Transportation, 1900–1940* (Temple University Press, Philadelphia, 1981), pp. 71–78, 110–111, 113; Robert M. Fogelson, *Downtown: Its Rise and Fall, 1880–1950* (Yale University Press, New Haven, CT, 2001), pp. 102–108, 160–182; Ruth Knack, Stuart Meck, and Israel Stollman, "The Real Story Behind the Standard Planning and Zoning Acts of the 1920s," *Land Use Law & Zoning Digest*, February 1996, pp. 3–9.

16. Zachary M. Schrag, *The Great Society Subway: A History of the Washington Metro* (Johns Hopkins University Press, Baltimore, 2006), p. 35.

17. Scott, *American City Planning*, pp. 31-39, 44-57; Charles Moore, *Daniel H. Burnham, Architect, Planner of Cities* (Houghton Mifflin, Boston, 1921), vol. 2, p. 147.

18. Scott, *American City Planning*, esp. pp. 117–127; Foster, *Streetcar to Superhighway*, pp. 33–36, 70–72.

19. Scott, *American City Planning*, pp. 232–237. Country Club District: Fogelson, *Bourgeois Nightmares*, p. 74.

20. Southworth, "Street Standards."

21. Scott, *American City Planning*, esp. pp. 197–198, 214–215, 255–256; Nathan Glazer, *From a Cause to a Style: Modernist Architecture's Encounter with the American City* (Princeton University Press, Princeton, NJ, 2007), p. 175.

22. Weiss, "Planning Subdivisions"; Scott, *American City Planning*, p. 285.

23. Babcock, *Zoning Game*, pp. 32–38.

24. Scott, *American City Planning*, pp. 278–279.

25. Scott, *American City Planning*, p. 250. Mumford developed the same themes in *The City in History* (Harcourt, Brace & World, New York, 1961), esp. pp. 426–434.

Chapter 3

1. Rosalyn Baxandall and Elizabeth Ewen, *Picture Windows: How the Suburbs Happened* (Basic Books, New York, 2000), pp. 46–49; Scott, *American City Planning*, pp. 259–260; McKenzie, *Privatopia*, pp. 45–51. Worley, *J. C. Nichols*, p. 107, points out the similarity of Radburn to the design of the Country Club District fifteen years earlier.

2. Jackson, *Crabgrass Frontier*, pp. 195–203.

3. Jackson, *Crabgrass Frontier*, pp. 203–225; Weiss, *Community Builders*, pp. 141–158; Southworth, "Street Standards." "Retain stability" and "park area": Jackson, p. 208. "Messianic fervor": Weiss, p. 148. Detroit wall: Thomas J. Sugrue, *The Origins of the Urban Crisis: Race and Inequality in Postwar Detroit* (Princeton University Press, Princeton, NJ, 1996), pp. 63–65.

4. Jackson, *Crabgrass Frontier*, p. 195; Baxandall and Ewen, *Picture Windows*, pp. 67–74.

5. Jackson, *Crabgrass Frontier*, pp. 219–230; Sugrue, *Urban Crisis*, pp. 72–88; Joshua B. Freeman, *Working-Class New York: Life and Labor Since World War II* (New Press, New York, 2000), pp. 105–120; Arnold R. Hirsch, "Less than *Plessy*," in Kevin M. Kruse and Thomas J. Sugrue, eds., *The New Suburban History*, (University of Chicago Press, Chicago, 2006), pp. 33–56.

6. Jackson, *Crabgrass Frontier*, pp. 231–240; Baxandall and Ewen, *Picture Windows*, pp. 117–139; Hayden, *Building Suburbia*, pp. 136–137.

7. Kay, *Asphalt Nation*, pp. 212–214, 241–242.

8. Robert A Caro, *The Power Broker: Robert Moses and the Fall of New York* (Alfred A. Knopf, New York, 1974), esp. pp. 172–220, 896–972, 1026–1039. Owen D. Gutfreund, "Rebuilding New York in the Auto Age: Robert Moses and His Highways," in Hilary Ballon and Kenneth T. Jackson, eds., *Robert Moses and the American City: The Transformation of New York* (W. W. Norton, New York, 2007), suggests that the stoppage of rail expansion was entirely a consequence of federal policy and local public opinion, but as discussed in Chapter 6, other large cities did expand their rail systems during these years.

9. Norton, *Fighting Traffic*, pp. 159–171, 202–206, 234–241; Michael Southworth and Eran Ben-Joseph, "Street Standards and the Shaping of Suburbia," *Journal of the American Planning Association*, vol. 61, pp. 65–81 (1995). Leaded gasoline: Benjamin Ross and Steven Amter, *The Polluters: The Making of Our Chemically Altered Environment* (Oxford University Press, New York, 2010), pp. 33–34.

10. Southworth and Ben-Joseph, "Street Standards."

11. Donald C. Shoup, *The High Cost of Free Parking* (Planners Press, Chicago, 2005), pp. 21–23, 380–382, 607. "Purely aesthetic": Clan Crawford, *Strategy and Tactics in Muncipal Zoning* (Prentice-Hall, Englewood Cliffs, NJ, 1969), p. 84, quoted by Shoup, p. 433.

12. Shoup, *Free Parking*, pp. 21–23, 129–141.

13. Fogelson, *Downtown*, pp. 317–320, 341–350; Scott, *American City Planning*, pp. 285–287, 379–385.

14. Fogelson, *Downtown*, pp. 358–364, 371–377; Scott, *American City Planning*, pp. 380–385, 426–428.

15. Owen D. Gutfreund, *Twentieth Century Sprawl: Highways and the Reshaping of the American Landscape* (Oxford University Press, New York, 2004), pp. 25–59. Moses: Raymond A. Mohl, "Stop the Road: Freeway Revolts in American Cities," *Journal of Urban History*, vol. 30, pp. 674–706 (2004).

16. Fogelson, *Downtown*, pp. 365–370, 378–380; Scott, *American City Planning*, p. 501.

17. Fogelson, *Downtown*, pp. 237–238, reports that downtown real estate interests, when they first became concerned about urban decline, turned to Miller McClintock and Harland Bartholomew for advice. Hilary Ballon, "Robert Moses and Urban Renewal," in Ballon and Jackson, *Robert Moses*, pp. 94–115, recounts Moses' acceptance of the "modernist paradigm of superblock urbanism." Gregory Heller, "The Power of an Idea: Edmund Bacon's Planning Method Inspiring Consensus and Living in the Future," B.A. thesis, Wesleyan University, 2004, pp. 97–101, 107–112, describes the suburban inspiration of the design concepts developed by Philadelphia's influential planning director.

18. Sugrue, *Urban Crisis*, pp. 181–258; Danielson, *Politics of Exclusion*, pp. 125–126; Jim Sleeper, *The Closest of Strangers: Liberalism and the Politics of Race in New York* (W. W. Norton, New York, 1990), pp. 80–90, 116–152.

19. Alyssa Katz, *Our Lot: How Real Estate Came to Own Us* (Bloomsbury, New York, 2009), pp. 1–15; Hillel Levine and Lawrence Harmon, *The Death of an American Jewish Community: A Tragedy of Good Intentions* (Free Press, New York, 1992), pp. 164–180, 194–224.

20. Danielson, *Politics of Exclusion*, pp. 79–106, 213–236.

Chapter 4

1. "The Last Leaf."

2. Christine Stansell, *American Moderns: Bohemian New York and the Creation of a New Century* (Metropolitan Books, New York, 2000), esp. pp. 16–18. In Russian exile communities in Europe, there were forerunners of the Greenwich Village synthesis of advanced politics and art, but they are less relevant for our purposes here than they are in political history.

3. This is explored by Cesar Grana, *Modernity and its Discontents* (Basic Books, New York, 1964), pp. 163–171.

4. Towertown: Harvey Warren Zorbaugh, *The Gold Coast and the Slum: A Sociological Study of Chicago's Near North Side* (University of Chicago Press, Chicago, 1929). Russian Hill: Richard Walker, "Classy City: Residential Realms of the Bay Region," http://oldweb.geog.berkeley.edu/PeopleHistory/faculty/R_Walker/ClassCity.pdf, pp. 20–21. French Quarter: Scott S. Ellis, *Madame Vieux Carré: The French Quarter in the Twentieth Century* (University Press of Mississippi, Jackson, 2009), pp. 24–30.

5. Lewis, *Babbitt*, quotations from pp. 143–144, 30, 33, 139, 65.

6. Ellis, *Madame Vieux Carré*, pp. 43, 71–73; James Albert Gazell, "The High Noon of Chicago's Bohemias," *Journal of the Illinois State Historical Society*, vol. 65, pp. 54–68 (1972); John d'Emilio, *Sexual Politics, Sexual Communities: The Making of a Homosexual Minority in the United States, 1940–1970* (Chicago: University of Chicago Press, 1983), pp. 31–33, 38–39; 180–182; Paul Goodman, *Growing Up Absurd* (Random House, New York, 1960), pp. 63–69.

7. Vance Packard, *The Status Seekers* (David McKay, New York, 1959), quotations from pp. 66, 305, 90.

8. Walker, "Classy City," pp. 20, 29.

Chapter 5

1. William G. Grigsby, *Housing Markets and Public Policy* (University of Pennsylvania Press, Philadelphia, 1963), p. 251. Emphasis in original.

2. Scott, *American City Planning*, pp. 536–541, 592.

3. Anthony Flint, *Wrestling with Moses* (Random House, New York, 2009), pp. 3–28, 90–92; Alice Sparberg Alexiou, *Jane Jacobs, Urban Visionary* (Rutgers University Press, New Brunswick, NJ, 2006), pp. 39–50, 57–65.

4. Jane Jacobs, *The Death and Life of Great American Cities* (Modern Library Edition, New York, 1993). Ballet: pp. 65–71. Four principles: pp. 196–197.

5. Gans, *People, Plans and Policies*, pp. 33–43 (article originally published in 1962).

6. Alexiou, *Jane Jacobs*, pp. 43–50, 68–70; Flint, *Wrestling with Moses*, pp. 22–25; Charles Grutzner, "Shopping Scarce in City Projects," *New York Times*, June 16, 1957; John Sibley, "Village Housing a Complex Issue," *New York Times*, March 23, 1961.

7. George Orwell, *The Road to Wigan Pier* (Harcourt Brace Jovanovich, New York, 1958), pp. 65–74, quotations from pp. 71, 182.

8. Jacobs, *Death and Life*, p. 482.

9. Bruce Brugmann and Greggar Sletteland, *The Ultimate Highrise: San Francisco's Mad Rush Toward the Sky...* (San Francisco Bay Guardian, San Francisco, 1971), esp. p. 223.

10. See, e.g., Charles Grutzner, "Rise of the Urban Region: A Study of New Way of Life," *New York Times*, January 27, 1957; "City Told to Aid People, Not Cars," *New York Times*, April 21, 1958; Harrison E. Salisbury, "Study Finds Cars Choking Cities as 'Urban Sprawl' Takes Over," *New York Times*, March 3, 1959; Cabell Phillips, "Capital Uneasy on Traffic Plan," *New York Times*, October 22, 1961. Subway collapse: Caro, *Power Brokers*, pp. 930–933.

11. Jacobs, *Death and Life*, pp. 325–326, 334.

12. Gans, "Failure of Urban Renewal."

13. Warren Weaver, "Science and Complexity," *American Scientist*, vol. 36, pp. 536–544 (1948).

14. Jacobs, *Death and Life*. Habits of mind: p. 574. High-energy: p. 577.

Chapter 6

1. Salisbury, "Cars Choking Cities". History of word: George R. Hess, "Just What Is Sprawl, Anyway?," *Carolina Planning*, vol. 26, no. 2, pp. 11–26; Bruegmann, *Sprawl*, p. 119.

2. Emma Harrison, "Rebirth of Family Seen in Suburbs," *New York Times*, March 21, 1958; Wilfred Owen, "In Defense of the Automobile," *New York Times*, October 16, 1960.

3. "Statement by Nixon on Housing Program," *New York Times*, September 29, 1960.

4. Sugrue, *Origins of the Urban Crisis*, pp. 57–88; Martin Meyerson and Edward Banfield, *Politics, Planning and the Public Interest* (Free Press, Glencoe IL, 1955).

5. Fogelson, *Downtown*, pp. 239–240, 318–320, 340–380; Herbert J. Gans, "The Failure of Urban Renewal," in James Q. Wilson, ed., *Urban Renewal: The Record and the Controversy* (MIT Press, Cambridge, MA, 1966), pp. 537–557; Ballon, "Moses and Urban Renewal."

6. Caro, *Power Broker*, pp. 965–983; Chester Hartman, "The Housing of Relocated Families," *Journal of the American Institute of Planners*, vol. 30, pp. 266–286 (1964).

7. Herbert J. Gans, *The Urban Villagers: Group and Class in the Life of Italian-Americans* (Free Press, New York, 1962), pp. 282–287, 291–304, 308–318; Thomas H. O'Connor, *Building A New Boston: Politics and Urban Renewal, 1950-1970* (Northeastern University Press, Boston, 1993), pp. 26–28, 50–52, 61–65, 125–137, 141–142; Walter McQuade, "Boston: What Can a Sick City Do," in Wilson, *Urban Renewal*, pp. 259–277.

8. Barry Bluestone and Mary Huff Stevenson, *The Boston Renaissance: Race, Space, and Economic Change in an American Metropolis* (Russell Sage Foundation, New York, 2000), pp. 82–86; O'Connor, *New Boston*, pp. 182–188, 215–219.

9. Flint, *Wrestling with Moses*, pp. 61–92; Robert Fishman, "Revolt of the Urbs: Robert Moses and His Critics," in Ballon and Jackson, *Robert Moses*, pp. 122–129.

10. Flint, *Wrestling with Moses*, pp. 138–178; Caro, *Power Broker*, pp. 850–894.

11. William Issel, "'Land Values, Human Values, and the Preservation of the City's Treasured Appearance': Environmentalism, Politics, and the San Francisco Freeway Revolt," *Pacific Historical Review*, vol. 68, pp. 611–646 (1999); Mohl, "Stop the Road"; Katherine M. Johnson, "Captain Blake versus the Highwaymen: Or, How San Francisco Won the Freeway Revolt," *Journal of Planning History*, vol. 8, pp. 56–83 (2009); Joseph Rodriguez, *City against Suburb: The Culture Wars in an American Metropolis* (Praeger, Westport, CT, 1999), pp. 21–46.

12. Schrag, *Great Society Subway*, pp. 36–44, 119–128, 134–141.

13. Alan Lupo, Frank Colcord, and Edmund P. Fowler, *Rites of Way: The Politics of Transportation in Boston and the U.S. City* (Little Brown, Boston, 1971), pp. 1–111; Chester Hartman, *Between Eminence and Notoriety: Four Decades of Radical Urban Planning* (Center for Urban Policy Research, New Brunswick NJ, 2002), p. 19.

14. Mohl, "Stop the Road." Other cities in which plans for urban interstate networks were drastically cut back include Baltimore, Cleveland, New Orleans, and Philadelphia. There were more limited highway cancellations in many other cities, including even Houston, Los Angeles, and Detroit.

15. Schrag, *Great Society Subway*, pp. 180–182; Federal urging: Gutfreund, *Twentieth-Century Sprawl*, pp. 32–34.

16. Mohl, "Stop the Road"; Lupo, *Rites of Way*, pp. 162–166, 215–218; Jacob Kobrick, "Let the People Have a Victory: The Politics of Transportation in Philadelphia, 1946–1984," Ph.D. thesis, University of Maryland, 2010, pp. 193–227, 254–292; Tom Lewis, *Divided Highways: Building the Interstate Highways, Transforming American Life* 2nd ed. (Cornell University Press, Ithaca, NY, 2013), pp. 179–210.

17. Eric J. Plosky, "The Fall and Rise of Pennsylvania Station: Changing Attitudes Toward Historic Preservation in New York City," M.S. Thesis, Massachusetts Institute of Technology, 1999.

18. See Suleiman Osman, *The Invention of Brownstone Brooklyn: Gentrification and the Search for Authenticity in Postwar New York* (Oxford University Press, New York, 2011), pp. 220–230, 253, 262–265, 273–275.

19. Jewel Bellush and Murray Hausknecht, "Planning, Participation, and Urban Renewal," in Bellush and Hausknecht, eds., *Urban Renewal: People, Politics, and Planning* (Anchor Books, Garden City, 1967), pp. 278–286; Susan S. Fainstein, *The Just City* (Cornell University Press, Ithaca, NY, 2011), pp. 65–67, 75–78; Lupo, *Rites of Way*, pp. 161–162. Boyd: Mohl, "Stop the Road."

20. Lupo, *Rites of Way*, pp. 220–222; information from transit systems' websites. Bus-only lanes were also introduced on the streets of many cities in the late 1950s and 1960s; only some of these have survived. See Asha Weinstein Agrawal, Todd Goldman, and Nancy Hannaford, "Shared-Use Bus Priority Lanes on City Streets: Case Studies in Design and Management," Mineta Transportation Institute, Report No. CA-MTI-12-2606, April 2012, pp. 6–9, http://transweb. sjsu.edu/PDFs/research/2606-shared-use-bus-priority-lanes-city-streets.pdf, accessed April 25, 2012.

21. Stephen Zwerling, *Mass Transit and the Politics of Technology: A Study of BART and the San Francisco Bay Area* (Praeger, New York, 1974), pp. 20–31, 39–44, 65–68; Office of Technology Assessment, "Assessment of Community Planning for Mass Transit: Volume 8-San Francisco Case Study," Report OTA-T-23, February 1976; Johnson, "Captain Blake"; Rodriguez, *City against Suburb*, pp. 47–54.

22. Schrag, *Great Society Subway*.

23. Gulf Reston Inc., "A Brief History of Reston," http://www.restonmuseum.org/main_/rht_briefHistory.htm.

24. Margaret Pugh O'Mara, "Uncovering the City in the Suburb," in Kruse and Sugrue, *New Suburban History*, pp. 57–79; Jon C. Teaford, *Post-Suburbia: Government and Politics in the Edge Cities* (Johns Hopkins University Press, Baltimore, 1997), pp. 50–54; Bluestone and Stevenson, *Boston Renaissance*, pp. 92–94.

25. McKenzie, *Privatopia*, pp. 81–93.

26. Max Neutze, *The Suburban Apartment Boom: Case Study of a Land Use Problem* (Resources for the Future, Washington, 1968), pp. 8, 86–90; McKenzie, *Privatopia*, pp. 94–96.

27. Data from U. S. Bureau of the Census, "New Privately Owned Housing Units Started: Annual Data," http://www.census.gov/const/www/newresconstindex. html, accessed July 8, 2011.

28. Neutze, *Suburban Apartment Boom*, pp. 52–57, 67–72, 84–85; Danielson, *Politics of Exclusion*, pp. 103–104.

29. Shoup, *Free Parking*, pp. 142–143; Mike Davis, *City of Quartz: Excavating the Future in Los Angeles* (Vintage, New York, 1990), p. 176. The term dingbat first appeared in print in Reyner Banham, *Los Angeles: The Architecture of Four Ecologies* (Harper & Row, New York, 1979), pp. 157–159.

30. Babcock, *Zoning Game*, pp. 6–11, 91; Patricia Burgess, "Of Swimming Pools and 'Slums,'" in Mary Corbin Sies and Christopher Silver, *Planning the Twentieth-Century American City* (Johns Hopkins University Press, Baltimore, 1996), pp. 212–239; Alan Mallach, "The Tortured Reality of Suburban Exclusion: Zoning, Economics, and the Future of the Berenson Doctrine," *Pace Environmental Law Review*, vol. 4, pp. 37–130 (1986).

31. Danielson, *Politics of Exclusion*, pp. 72–74; Babcock, *Zoning Game*, pp. 9–11.

32. Osman, *Brownstone Brooklyn*, pp. 8–9, 82–118, 189–219.

33. Cameron Logan, "The Constituent Landscape: History, Race and Real Estate in Washington, D.C, 1950-1990," Ph.D. thesis, George Washington University, 2008, pp. 97–108; John F. Bauman, "The Paradox of Post-War Urban Planning: Downtown Revitalization versus Decent Housing for All," in Daniel Schaffer, ed., *Two Centuries of American Planning* (Johns Hopkins University Press, Baltimore, 1988), pp. 231–264. Yorkville: Glazer, *From a Cause to a Style*, pp. 167–168, 172–173. Society Hill: Alan Ehrenhalt, *The Great Inversion and the Future of the American City* (Alfred A. Knopf, New York, 2012), p. 142. Osman, *Brownstone Brooklyn*, pp. 82–102, describes artists and writers, some complaining that Greenwich Village has been taken over by tourists and poseurs, in the lead when gentrification of Brooklyn Heights peaked in the 1950s, but he notes that the first arrivals in the 1940s were bankers and insurance managers. The non-bohemian style persisted in the South; the revival of downtown Wilmington, North Carolina, in the 1960s and 1970s is described by Julia Anne Yannetti, "From Downtown Revitalization to Suburban Preservation in Wilmington, North Carolina," M.A. Thesis, University of North Carolina, Wilmington, 2010, pp. 45–56. In New Orleans, in the first half of the twentieth century, bohemians and elite gentrifiers were sometimes allies and sometimes opponents; see Ellis, *Madame Vieux Carré*, pp. 18–19, 22–26, 42–44.

Chapter 7

1. Gans, "Failure of Urban Renewal."
2. Jones-Correa, "Racial Covenants"; McKenzie, *Privatopia*, pp. 70–75; Davis, *City of Quartz*, pp. 161–163; Spear, *Black Chicago*, pp. 208–212; Weiss, "Zoning in San Francisco"; Sugrue, *Urban Crisis*, pp. 44–45; Kevin Fox Gotham, "Urban Space, Restrictive Covenants and the Origins of Racial Residential Segregation in a US City, 1900–50," *International Journal of Urban and Regional Research*, vol. 24, pp. 616–633 (2000).
3. Whyte, *Organization Man*, pp. 287–291; Babcock, *Zoning Game*, p. 42.
4. Numerous observers, coming from different points of view, agree on the occurrence of a qualitative change and its timing: Davis, *City of Quartz*, pp. 174–180; Danielson, *Politics of Exclusion*, pp. 37–39, 64–66; Brugmann and Sletteland, *Ultimate Highrise*, p. 92; Michelle J. White, "Self-Interest in the Suburbs: The Trend Toward No-Growth Zoning," *Policy Analysis*, vol. 4, pp. 185–203 (1978); Teaford, *Post-Suburbia*, p. 173; Christopher B. Leinberger, *The Option of Urbanism: Investing in a New American Dream* (Island Press, Washington, DC, 2008), p. 131; William A. Fischel, "An Economic History of Zoning and a Cure for its Exclusionary Effects," *Urban Studies*, vol. 41, pp. 317–340 (2004). Peter Siskind, "Suburban Growth and Its Discontents," in Kruse and Sugrue, *New Suburban History*, pp. 161–182, puts the change slightly earlier, in the late 1960s.
5. William Fulton, *The Reluctant Metropolis: The Politics of Urban Growth in Los Angeles* (Johns Hopkins University Press, Baltimore, 1997), pp. 51–62; Davis, *City of Quartz*, pp. 188–210; Teaford, *Post-Suburbia*, pp. 174–186; Madelyn Glickfeld and Ned Levine, *Regional Growth... Local Reaction: The Enactment and Effects of Local Growth Control and Management Measures in California* (Lincoln Institute of Land Policy, Cambridge, MA, 1992), pp. 5–8.
6. Scott, *American City Planning*, pp. 240–241.
7. Davis, *City of Quartz*, pp. 170–180; Logan, "The Constituent Landscape," p. 133; Robert Bruegmann, *Sprawl: A Compact History* (University of Chicago Press, Chicago, 2005), p. 241, n. 15.
8. Glickfeld and Levine, *Regional Growth*, pp. 13–14, provide a more detailed catalog of growth control techniques.
9. S. Mark White and Elisa Paster, "Creating Effective Land Use Regulations through Concurrency," *Natural Resources Journal*, vol. 43, pp. 753–779 (2003).
10. Montgomery County, the home of the most-studied APFO, had to exempt the area around the White Flint Metro station in 2011 to make transit-oriented development possible there. See also Charles E. Connerly, Timothy Stewart Chapin, and Harrison T. Higgins, *Growth Management in Florida: Planning for Paradise* (Ashgate, Aldershot, UK, 2007), pp. 211–223. Pendall, "Do Land-Use Controls Cause Sprawl?," finds that APFOs promote density, but his definition of APFO appears to be different from that used here, and his evidence, a statistical analysis, is less than definitive.
11. Louise Nelson Dyble, "Revolt against Sprawl: Transportation and the Origins of the Marin County Growth-Control Regime," *Journal of Urban History*, vol.

34; pp. 38–66 (2007); Richard A. Walker, *The Country in the City: The Greening of the San Francisco Bay Area* (University of Washington Press, Seattle, 2007), pp. 88–95.

12. John M. DeGrove, *Planning Policy and Politics: Smart Growth and the States* (Lincoln Institute of Land Policy, Cambridge, 2005), pp. 11–15; Richard F. Babcock and Charles L. Siemon, *The Zoning Game Revisited* (Lincoln Institute of Land Policy, Cambridge, 1985), pp. 135–157, 235–254; Maryland Association of Counties, "PlanMaryland: 1974 Land Use Legislation Fights Still Echo Today," http://conduitstreet.mdcounties.org/2011/07/11/plan-maryland-1974-land-use-legislation-fight-still-echoes-today/, accessed August 20, 2011.

13. R. Pendall, "Do Land-Use Controls Cause Sprawl?," *Environment and Planning B: Planning and Design*, vol. 26, pp. 555–571 (1999).

14. Compare Plosky, "Pennsylvania Station," pp. 33–45, to Logan, "Constituent Landscape," pp. 120–134. Logan, p. 252, states that "historic districts were quite explicitly designated in the 1970s to control the rate and nature of change." Quotations from Plosky, p. 51; Robin Elizabeth Datel, "Preservation and a Sense of Orientation for American Cities," *Geographical Review*, vol. 75, pp. 125–141 (1985).

15. Wendy Swallow, "Group Seeks to Save Park and Shop," *Washington Post*, November 9, 1985; Elizabeth Kastor, "Panic in Cleveland Park," *Washington Post*, April 23, 1986.

16. Cleveland Park Historic District, National Register of Historic Places Registration Form, March 19, 1987, quotation from Section 8, p. 40; Logan, "Constituent Landscape," pp. 294–296; Swallow, "Save Park and Shop"; Kastor, "Panic in Cleveland Park"; Eve Zibart, "Cleveland Park Given Historic Designation," *Washington Post*, November 20, 1986.

17. Logan, "Constituent Landscape," p. 7; "Introduction to the Historic Preservation Guidelines," District of Columbia Historic Preservation Office, n.d.; Fogelson, *Bourgeois Nightmares*, pp. 89–92, 161–164; Worley, *J. C. Nichols*, pp. 135–137, 142.

18. Babcock, *Zoning Game*, p. 116; Davis, *City of Quartz*, p. 204.

19. Fulton, *Reluctant Metropolis*, pp. 177–199; Davis, *City of Quartz*, pp. 171–172.

20. Davis, *City of Quartz*, pp. 180–185.

21. Danielson, *Politics of Exclusion*, pp. 88–92; Kenneth Forton, "Expanding the Effectiveness of the Massachusetts Comprehensive Permit Law by Eliminating Its Subsidy Requirement," *Boston College Environmental Law Review*, vol. 28, no. 4 (2001); John J. Tarrant, *The End of Exurbia* (Stein and Day, New York, 1976), pp. 61–63. A somewhat similar law was enacted in California in 1980.

22. David L. Kirp, John P. Dwyer, and Larry Rosenthal, *Our Town: Race, Housing, and the Soul of Suburbia* (Rutgers University Press, New Brunswick, NJ, 1996), pp. 112–118; Siskind, "Suburban Growth."

23. Flint, *Wrestling with Moses*, pp. 131–135.

24. Stefan Bradley, *Harlem vs. Columbia University: Black Student Power in the Late 1960s* (University of Illinois Press, Champaign, IL, 2009), pp. 39–62, 67–101; http://morningsidepark.org/park/history.php, accessed September 25, 2013. Quotation from Jacobs, *Death and Life*, p. 143.

25. Peter Dreier, John Mollenkopf, and Todd Swanstrom, *Place Matters: Metropolitics for the Twenty-First Century*, 2nd ed. (University Press of Kansas, Lawrence, 2004), pp. 180–183; 204–206; Brugmann and Sletteland, *Ultimate Highrise*, esp. pp. 58–59, 194–202.

26. Osman, *Brownstone Brooklyn*, pp. 226–231, 272–280; G. William Domhoff, "Why San Francisco Is Different: Progressive Activists and Neighborhoods Have Had a Big Impact," September 2005, http://sociology.ucsc.edu/whorulesamerica/local/san_francisco.html, accessed July 4, 2011; Japonica Brown-Saracino, *A Neighborhood That Never Changes: Gentrification, Social Preservation, and the Search for Authenticity* (University of Chicago Press, Chicago, 2009), pp. 51–79, 189–192.

27. Marsha Prior and Robert V. Kemper, "From Freedman's Town to Uptown: Community Transformation and Gentrification in Dallas, Texas," *Urban Anthropology*, vol. 34, pp. 177–216 (2005); Jason Hackworth, *The Neoliberal City: Governance, Ideology, and Development in American Urbanism* (Cornell University Press, Ithaca, NY, 2007), pp. 153–163.

28. Brown-Saracino, *Neighborhood That Never Changes*, gives a perceptive portrait of what she calls "social preservationists."

29. "Neighbors of Ashby BART Statement of Principles," http://nabart.com/nabart.html, accessed July 4, 2011.

30. Brugmann and Sletteland, *Ultimate Highrise*, p. 201; Zelda Bronstein, "The Stealth Plan to Bicycle-ize Marin Avenue," *Berkeley Daily Planet*, December 10, 2004; "Save the Alameda," January 14, 2010.

31. See, e.g., William A. Fischel, "Why Are There NIMBYs?," *Land Economics*, vol. 77, pp. 144–152 (2001); Gordon, "Private Communities."

32. Perin, *Everything in Its Place*, pp. 137–144. Edward L. Glaeser and Bryce A. Ward, "The Causes and Consequences of Land Use Regulation: Evidence from Greater Boston," *Journal of Urban Economics*, vol. 65, pp. 265–278 (2009) show empirically that zoning in the Boston area greatly reduces property values. Robert Cervero and Michael Duncan, "Neighbourhood Composition and Residential Land Prices: Does Exclusion Raise or Lower Values?," *Urban Studies*, vol. 41, pp. 299–315 (2004) similarly find that separation of land uses lowers property values in California's Silicon Valley.

33. Davis, *City of Quartz*, pp. 174–180; Danielson, *Politics of Exclusion*, p. 55.

34. Walker, *The Country in the City*, pp. 92–94, 99–107.

35. Thomas Frank, *The Conquest of Cool: Business Culture, Counterculture, and the Rise of Hip Consumerism* (University of Chicago Press, Chicago, 1998).

36. "City of Los Altos Single-Family Residential Design Guidelines, New Homes & Remodels," http://www.ci.los-altos.ca.us/commdev/planning/documents/ResidentialDesignGuidelines.pdf, accessed May 27, 2013.

37. Osman, *Brownstone Brooklyn*, pp. 195–202, 205, 209; Logan, "Constituent Landscape," pp. 122–131, 159–160; Brown-Saracino, *Neighborhood That Never Changes*, pp. 8, 145–179.

38. Glickfeld and Levine, *Regional Growth... Local Reaction*, pp. 21–27.

39. Greenwich: Danielson, *Politics of Exclusion*, pp. 59–60. Chevy Chase: Manuel Perez-Rivas, "Posh Md. Area In Throes of Growing Pains; Friendship Heights' Future Is Subject of Intense Debate," *Washington Post*, July 1, 1996.

40. Lydia Sullivan, quoted by Dan Reed, *Just Up the Pike*, http://www.justupthepike.
com/2011/02/plan-preserves-kensingtons-assets-while.html, accessed July 14,
2011, emphasis in original.

Chapter 8

1. Vehicle miles traveled from http://www.fhwa.dot.gov/policyinformation/statis-
tics/2009/vmt421.cfm, accessed July 15, 2011.

2. James A. Dunn, Jr., *Driving Forces: The Automobile, Its Enemies, and the Politics
of Mobility* (Brookings Institution, Washington, DC, 1998), pp. 35–39; Brian D.
Taylor, "Public Perceptions, Fiscal Realities, and Freeway Planning," *APA Journal*,
vol. 61, pp. 43–56 (1995); Martin A. Sullivan, "Gas Tax Politics—Part I," Tax
Analysts, September 22, 2008, http://www.taxhistory.org/thp/readings.nsf/Art
Web/5DDB79194769C2BF852574D5003C28D5?OpenDocument, accessed July
13, 2011.

3. Federal Highway Administration, "Highway Taxes and Fees—2008" and
"Highway Taxes and Fees—1998," available at http://www.fhwa.dot.gov/ohim/
hwytaxes/2008/index.cfm, accessed July 13, 2011. The Consumer Price Index
increased by 32% from 1998 to 2008.

4. Benjamin Ross, "Stuck in Traffic: Free-Market Theory Meets the Highway
Lobby," *Dissent*, vol. 53, no. 3, pp. 60–64 (Summer 2006).

5. "Effectiveness of 'Children at Play' Warning Signs," Wisconsin Dept. of
Transportation, April 27, 2007, http://wisdotresearch.wi.gov/wp-content/
uploads/tsrchildrenwarningsigns.pdf, accessed December 12, 2013; Russell Carter,
"Kids Cited for Playing on Sidewalk in OK Town," KFOR-TV, September 18, 2010,
http://www.kfor.com/news/local/kfor-news-mustang-ordinance-story,0,5279078.
story, accessed July 2, 2011.

6. Norreen McDonald, Austin Brown, Lauren Marchetti, and Margo Pedroso, "U.S.
School Travel 2009: An Assessment of Trends," *American Journal of Preventive
Medicine*, vol. 41, pp. 146–151 (2011); Lenore Skenazy, "A Principal Calls CPS
after Mom Lets Daughter, 10, Ride City Bus to School," *Free-Range Kids* blog,
http://www.freerangekids.com/a-principal-calls-cps-after-mom-lets-daugh-
ter-10-ride-city-bus-to-school/, accessed November 18, 2012.

7. Andres Duany, Elizabeth Plater-Zyberk, and Jeff Speck, *Suburban Nation:
The Rise of Sprawl and the Decline of the American Dream* (North Point,
New York, 2000), pp. 66–69. 8½ minutes: Benjamin Ross, *Greater Greater
Washington*, January 14, 2013, http://greatergreaterwashington.org/post/
17341/8half-minutes-to-cross-the-street/.

8. Duany, *Suburban Nation*, pp. 69–70. Reflective clothing: http://www.walkinginfo.
org/why/tips_walking-safely.cfm; http://www.harttma.com/Community/Road
Safety/PedestrianSafety.aspx, accessed August 20, 2012.

9. "Truck Lines Gird for Rail Combat," *New York Times*, June 28, 1953.

10. "Capitol Delivery," *New York Times*, January 20, 1975; Robert Sherrill, "Raising
Hell on the Highways," *New York Times Magazine*, November 27, 1977.

11. Dunn, *Driving Forces*, p. 38; Ernest Holsendolf, "Legislation to Raise the Gas
Tax by 5 Cents Is Introduced to Senate," *New York Times*, November 30, 1982;

Jerry Knight, "A Tradeoff for the Truckers," *Washington Post*, December 12, 1982; Matthew L. Wald, "The Bigger the Truck, the More Controversy," *New York Times*, July 18, 1997.

12. Stephen Kinzer, "New York Fights U.S. to Exclude Longer Trucks," *New York Times*, January 27, 1983; Federal Highway Administration, "Federal Size Regulations for Commercial Motor Vehicles," FHWA-HOP-04-022, October 2004, pp. 1–2, 12.

13. Bureau of the Census, "New Privately Owned Housing Units." Apartments are defined by the Census Bureau as buildings with five or more units; townhouses count as single-family homes.

14. McKenzie, *Privatopia*, pp. 11–12, 103–105, 127, 129–132, 164–165; Paula A. Franzese and Steven Siegel, "Trust and Community: The Common Interest Community as Metaphor and Paradox," *Missouri Law Review*, vol. 72, pp. 1111–1157 (2007).

15. Edward J. Blakely and Mary Gail Snyder, *Fortress America: Gated Communities in the United States* (Brookings Institution, Washington, 1999); Rich Benjamin, "The Gated Community Mentality," *New York Times*, March 29, 2012.

16. Teaford, *Post-Suburbia*, pp. 87–96; Elizabeth Kneebone, "Job Sprawl Revisited: The Changing Geography of Metropolitan Employment," Brookings Institution, April 2009. Union avoidance: Dreier, *Place Matters*, p. 118; Sugrue, *Urban Crisis*, p. 128; Fogelson, *Downtown*, p. 195.

17. Robert Lang, *Edgeless Cities: Exploring the Elusive Metropolis* (Brookings Institution, Washington, DC, 2003), pp. 90–94; Harry J. Holzer and Michael A. Stoll, "Where Workers Go, Do Jobs Follow? Metropolitan Labor Markets in the US, 1990–2000," Brookings Institution, December 2007; Leinberger, *Option of Urbanism*, pp. 35–40; Teaford, *Post-Suburbia*, pp. 162–172.

18. William H. Whyte, *City: Rediscovering the Center* (University of Pennsylvania Press, Philadelphia, 2009 [first published 1989]), pp. 286–289; Jackson, *Crabgrass Frontier*, pp. 268–269; Leinberger, *Option of Urbanism*, pp. 37–38; Joel Garreau, *Edge City: Life on the New Frontier* (Anchor, New York, 1992), pp. 91–93. See also Danielson, *Politics of Exclusion*, pp. 141–148; O'Mara, "Uncovering the City."

19. Leinberger, *Option of Urbanism*, pp. 42–44; Hayden, *Building Suburbia*, pp. 154–158.

20. Barry Ritholtz, "Case Shiller 100 Year Chart (2011 Update)," http://www.ritholtz.com/blog/2011/04/case-shiller-100-year-chart-2011-update/, accessed November 12, 2011.

21. Alan Ehrenhalt, *The Great Inversion and the Future of the American City* (Alfred A. Knopf, New York, 2012), pp. 90–112; Sugie Lee and Nancey Green Leigh, "The Role of Inner Ring Suburbs in Metropolitan Smart Growth Strategies," *Journal of Planning Literature*, vol. 19, pp. 330–346 (2005).

22. Katz, *Our Lot*, pp. 54–73.

23. Yves Smith, *Econned: How Unenlightened Self Interest Undermined Democracy and Corrupted Capitalism* (Palgrave, New York, 2010), pp. 236–240, 247–251, 253–263; Katz, *Our Lot*, pp. 78–128.

24. Leinberger, *Option of Urbanism*, pp. 49–62.

25. Katz, *Our Lot*, pp. 130–131; Associated Press, "Pools Become Mosquito Havens in Foreclosure," April 22, 2009, http://www.msnbc.msn.com/id/30344932/ns/technology_and_science-science/t/pools-become-mosquito-havens-foreclosure/, accessed July 16, 2011.

Chapter 9

1. Siskind, "Suburban Growth," describes sharp political swings in the 1960s and 1970s in Montgomery County, Maryland, Fairfax County, Virginia, and the Town of Ramapo in New York. Similar accounts can be found for Marin County, California, in the 1960s in Dyble, "Revolt against Sprawl" and for Loudoun County, Virginia, in the late 1990s and early 2000s in Anthony Flint, *This Land: The Battle over Sprawl and the Future of America* (Johns Hopkins University Press, Baltimore, 2006), pp. 186–188.
2. Sies, "Paradise Retained"; Teaford, *Post-Suburbia*, pp. 18–24.
3. Dennis P. Sobin, *Dynamics of Community Change: The Case of Long Island's Declining "Gold Coast"* (Ira J. Friedman, Port Washington, NY, 1968), pp. 29–38, 99–104, 108–110, 151–156.
4. Teaford, *Post-Suburbia*, pp. 14–18, 60–69, 96–108, 201–204.
5. Hayden, *Building Suburbia*, pp. 138–141; "John S. Todd, Father of the City of Lakewood, A History," http://www.lakewoodcity.org/civica/filebank/blob-dload.asp?BlobID=3305, accessed Aug. 28, 2011, esp. p. 33.
6. Kapur, "Land Use Regulation in Houston"; Mixon, "Land Use Vignettes."
7. Ross and Amter, *The Polluters*, pp. 78–81. Berkeley, California, had a similar motivation when it established industrial zones within its boundaries in 1916. The zones enabled Standard Oil and other polluting industries to ignore the objections of working-class neighbors when they located their factories. See Weiss, "Case of Berkeley."
8. Hector Becerra, "Vernon Mayor and Ex-official Are Indicted," *Los Angeles Times*, November 15, 2006; "A Steep Fall for Patriarch of Tiny, Industrial Vernon," *Los Angeles Times*, May 29, 2009; Hector Becerra, Sam Allen, and Kim Christensen, "Vernon a Tightly Controlled Fortress," *Los Angeles Times*, September 18, 2010.
9. Steve Volk, "Turf Wars: Neighbors Gone Wild," *Philadelphia Magazine*, June 2010.
10. P. Michael Saint, Robert J. Flavell, and Patrick F. Fox, *NIMBY Wars: The Politics of Land Use* (Saint University Press, Hingham, MA, 2009) p. 116.
11. Whyte, *City*, p. 241 has a similar description of planners who stand aside.
12. Babcock, *Zoning Game*, p. 141; Paul Schwartzman, Ruben Castaneda, and Cheryl W. Thompson, "Jack Johnson, Prince George's County Executive, and His Wife, Leslie, Arrested," *Washington Post*, November 13, 2010; David Daddio, " 'Dernoga Money' Stymied College Park Growth," *Greater Greater Washington*, http://greatergreaterwashington.org/post/10191/dernoga-money-stymied-college-park-growth/, accessed January 21, 2012.
13. Christopher Niedt, "Gentrification and the Grassroots: Popular Support in the Revanchist Suburb," *Journal of Urban Affairs*, vol. 28, pp. 99–120 (2006).

14. The large and muddy academic literature on this subject has much confusion between snob zoning and fiscal zoning. Economists, professionally concerned with money, often mistake status-seeking for defense of property values.

15. Dreier, *Place Matters*, pp. 111–112; Fulton, *Reluctant Metropolis*, pp. 255–281.

16. János Kornai, *The Socialist System: The Political Economy of Communism* (Princeton University Press, Princeton, NJ, 1992), esp. pp. 127–130, 176.

17. The project is now moving forward by annexing the land to the adjoining city of Rockville, which has simpler approval processes.

Chapter 10

1. Babcock, *Zoning Game*, p. 47 suggested at the time that cultural change was an element in the 1960s apartment boom.

2. For a comprehensive count of sitcom settings, see Michael Ray Fitzgerald, "Sitcoms and Suburbia: The Role of Network Television in the De-Urbanization of the U.S., 1949–1991," M.S. Thesis, University of Florida, 1997, esp. pp. 68–74, 87.

3. See Veblen, *Theory of the Leisure Class*, chapter 6.

4. Dan Hoffman, "Mowing with Goats," http://googleblog.blogspot.com/2009/05/mowing-with-goats.html, accessed July 23, 2011; Marty Englert, "Goats the New Chickens," *United Press International*, January 29, 2010.

5. Data from National Golf Foundation, http://secure.ngf.org/cgi/faqa.asp, accessed December 17, 2012.

6. Perin, *Everything in Its Place*, pp. 42–44, 55–59, analyzes this attitude from an anthropological perspective.

7. Bret Rappaport, "Green Landscaping: Greenacres," *John Marshall Law Review*, vol. 26, no. 4 (1994); Steven Kurutz, "The Battlefront in the Front Yard," *New York Times*, December 20, 2012.

8. Montgomery County Council, June 11, 2013, http://montgomerycountymd.granicus.com/MediaPlayer.php?view_id=6&clip_id=5289, accessed June 14, 2013, quotations from testimony of Hessie Harris at 28:02.

9. Belmont, California, Municipal Code, Chapter 5, Article IV, "Regulation of Pygmy Goats."

10. Ehrenhalt, *Great Inversion*, esp. pp. 3–8, 40–88, 137–144.

11. Ehrenhalt, *Great Inversion*, pp. 67–71; Soni Sangha and Vivian Yee, "As Beer Garden Extends Welcome to Juice-Box Set, Some Barflies Jeer," *New York Times*, August 2, 2012.

12. Jason Hackworth and Neil Smith, "The Changing State of Gentrification," *Tijdschrift voor Economische en Sociale Geografie*, vol. 92, pp. 464–477 (2001).

13. John Thomas, "Residential Construction Trends in America's Metropolitan Regions, 2010 Edition," U.S. Environmental Protection Agency Report, January 2010, pp. 10, 19. Big apartment buildings are those with at least twenty units. Figures for New York City exclude Staten Island, which is more suburban than the rest of the city.

14. Flint, *This Land*, pp. 61–78. Manifesto: http://www.cnu.org/charter, accessed August 3, 2011.

15. Leinberger, *Option of Urbanism*, pp. 106–112.

16. Edwin Slipek, "Inward and Upward," *Style Weekly* (Richmond, VA), January 29, 2013.

17. Matthew Dickens and John Neff, *2011 Public Transportation Fact Book* (American Public Transportation Association, Washington, 2011), Appendix A, pp. 1–2; Steven E. Polzin, Xuehao Chu, and Nancy McGuckin, "Exploring Changing Travel Trends," http://onlinepubs.trb.org/onlinepubs/conferences/2011/NHTS1/Polzin2.pdf, accessed August 27, 2011.

18. Kytja Weir, "Vehicle Registrations Drop in District," *Washington Examiner*, April 14, 2009.

19. John Pucher, "Renaissance of Public Transport in the United States?," *Transportation Quarterly*, vol. 56, pp. 33–49 (2002); Washington ridership based on unpublished data furnished by WMATA.

20. Sam Roberts, "More Commuters Are Going against the Flow, and Out of the City," *New York Times*, November 7, 2005; Charles V. Bagli, "Regretting Move, Bank May Return to Manhattan," *New York Times*, June 8, 2011. The Washington Metro has ridership trends similar to the New York commuter rail lines.

21. Gregory L. Thompson, "Defining an Alternative Future: Birth of the Light Rail Movement in North America," *Proc. 9th National Light Rail Transit Conference*, Transportation Research Circular E-C058, November 2003, pp. 25–36; Robert C. Post, *Urban Mass Transit: The Life Story of a Technology* (Greenwood, Westport CT, 2007), pp. 137–139; John W. Schumann, "Status of North American Light Rail Transit Systems: Year 2009 Update," *Proc. Joint International Light Rail Conference*, Los Angeles, April 19–21 2009, Transportation Research Circular E-C145.

22. Dunn, *Driving Forces*, pp. 42–43; Jack McCroskey, *Light Rail and Heavy Politics* (Tenlie Publishing, Denver, 2003), pp. 65–107.

23. Gregory L. Thompson, "Taming the Neighborhood Revolution: Planners, Power Brokers, and the Birth of Neotraditionalism in Portland, Oregon," *Journal of Planning History*, vol. 6, pp. 214–247 (2007); Ruth Hultgren, "How It Happened," http://www.friendsoflightrail.org/history/documents/How%20It%20Happened.pdf, accessed August 7, 2011; Fulton, *Reluctant Metropolis*, pp. 135–150.

24. Jason Henderson, *Street Fight: The Politics of Mobility in San Francisco* (University of Massachusetts Press, Amherst, 2013), pp. 54–86; http://www.preservenet.com.

25. Barbara McCann, *Completing Our Streets: The Transition to Safe and Inclusive Transportation Networks* (Island Press, Washington, DC, 2013), pp. 22–29, 32–33.

26. Michael M. Grynbaum, "New York Traffic Experiment Gets Permanent Run," *New York Times*, February 11, 2010; "Broadway Is Busy, with Pedestrians, if Not Car Traffic," September 5, 2010.

27. DeGrove, *Planning Policy and Politics*, pp. 20–23, 27–28.

28. DeGrove, *Planning Policy and Politics*, pp. 262–275; Gerrit-Jan Knaap and John W. Frece, "Smart Growth in Maryland: Looking Forward and Looking Back," *Idaho Law Review*, vol. 43, pp. 445–473.

Chapter 11

1. David Brock, *The Republican Noise Machine: Right-Wing Media and How It Corrupts Democracy* (Crown, New York, 2004), pp. 44–67.
2. Flint, *This Land*, pp. 153–163; Bruegmann, *Sprawl*, p. 157.
3. Lewis, *Babbitt*, p. 65; Baxandall and Ewen, *Picture Windows*, pp. 90–96; 103–112; Babcock and Siemon, *Zoning Game Revisited*, p. 215.
4. Wendell Cox, *War on the Dream: How Anti-Sprawl Policy Threatens the Quality of Life* (iUniverse, New York, 2006); Bruegmann, *Sprawl*, p. 153; Joel Kotkin, "California Wages War on Single-Family Homes," *Forbes Magazine*, July 26, 2011.
5. Bruegmann, *Sprawl*, p. 87. Bruegmann's justification of zoning is on pp. 105–107.
6. Cox, *War on the Dream*, pp. 128–130; Flint, *This Land*, p. 157. Criticisms of Cox and O'Toole are summarized by Tod Litman, "Evaluating Rail Transit Criticism," http://www.vtpi.org/railcrit.pdf, accessed August 22, 2011, and Todd Litman, "Rail Transit In America: A Comprehensive Evaluation of Benefits," http://www.vtpi.org/railben.pdf, accessed March 2, 2012, pp. 44–55.
7. Joel Kotkin, *The Next Hundred Million: America in 2050* (Penguin, New York, 2010), pp. 35, 38–40, 77–78, 233–234.
8. http://www.perc.org/articles/article402.php, accessed August 10, 2011.
9. Gordon, "Private Communities." See also Peter Gordon and Harry Richardson, "Exit and Voice in U.S. Settlement Change," http://www-bcf.usc.edu/~pgordon/pdf/exit_voice.pdf, accessed July 3, 2012, which lauds newly incorporated suburban governments as "less likely to be prompted to extend standing to large numbers of 'stakeholders' at the expense of property owners." Gordon and Richardson try to justify their rejection of democratic governance by contending that economic welfare will be maximized by local governing bodies that compete to supply "collective goods." But their argument contradicts itself. After conceding that free-market competition among individuals is inefficient, they reason from the premise that competition among local governments *will* necessarily be efficient. No justification is offered for this premise, even though competition among governments faces the problems of agency in addition to the problems that affect competition among individuals.
10. Flint, *This Land*, pp. 182–184.
11. Flint, *This Land*, pp. 172–173; 182–184; 202; Nancy Chapman and Hollie Lund, "Housing Density and Livability in Portland," in Connie P. Ozawa, ed., *The Portland Edge: Challenges and Successes in Growing Communities* (Island Press, Washington, DC, 2004), pp. 206–229.
12. Flint, *This Land*, pp. 136–139.
13. Donna Holt, "Smart Growth—Is It Really Smart?," http://www.rightsidenews.com/2011031522005/life-and-science/energy-and-environment/smart-growth-is-it-really-smart.html, accessed December 12, 2013.
14. Leslie Kaufman and Kate Zernike, "Activists Fight Green Projects, Seeing U. N. Plot," *New York Times*, Feb. 3, 2012. Quotation from http://www.postsustainabilityinstitute.org/what-is-un-agenda-21.html, accessed September 25, 2013.

15. See Edward Glaeser, *Triumph of the City: How Our Greatest Invention Makes Us Richer, Smarter, Greener, Healthier, and Happier* (Penguin, New York, 2011); Michael Lewyn, *A Libertarian Smart Growth Agenda: How to Limit Sprawl Without Limiting Property Rights* (Lambert, Saarbrücken, 2012); and Stephen Smith's blogging on *Market Urbanism*.

16. Paul M. Weyrich and William S. Lind, *Moving Minds: Conservatives and Public Transportation* (Free Congress Foundation, Alexandria, VA, 2009), quotation from p. 15.

17. B. Bruce-Briggs, *The War against the Automobile* (E. F. Dutton, New York, 1977); James Q. Wilson, "Cars and Their Enemies," *Commentary*, July 1997; James Q. Wilson, "The War on Cars," *Slate*, January 15, 1998, http://www.slate.com/id/3670/entry/24043/, accessed August 14, 2011; Randal O'Toole, "The Coming War on the Automobile," *Liberty*, vol. 11, no. 4, pp. 25–30 (March 1998); Stephen Moore, "The War against the Car," *Wall Street Journal*, November 11, 2005; Wendell Cox, "Washington's War on Cars and the Suburbs," Heritage Foundation Special Report SR-79, June 17, 2010; Eric de Place, "The 'War on Cars': A Brief History of a Rhetorical Device," http://www.grist.org/article/2011-01-06-war-on-cars-a-history, accessed August 14, 2011.

18. Christopher N. Osher, "Bike Agenda Spins Cities toward U.N. Control, Maes Warns," *Denver Post*, August 4, 2010; John Cassidy, "Battle of the Bike Lanes," http://www.newyorker.com/online/blogs/johncassidy/2011/03/battle-of-the-bike-lanes-im-with-mrs-schumer.html, accessed December 12, 2013.

19. Speed cameras: Petula Dvorak, "In Montgomery County, Cameras Are Frequent Victims of Accelerated Tempers," *Washington Post*, November 5, 2011. Permit parking: Joel Kotkin, "The War against Suburbia," *American*, January 21, 2010, http://www.american.com/archive/2010/january/the-war-against-suburbia, accessed August 15, 2011. Crosswalks: Dan Neil, "Pedestrian Detection," *Wall Street Journal*, January 21, 2011.

20. Elise Hitchcock, "Pedestrian Convicted of Vehicular Homicide in Own Child's Death," *Atlanta Journal-Constitution*, July 14, 2011; David Goldberg, "Protect, Don't Prosecute, Pedestrians," *Washington Post*, August 4, 2011. After her case got national attention, Nelson was eventually allowed to plead guilty to jaywalking and pay a $200 fine.

21. Wendell Cox, "The Real Test for Congestion Charging is Whether It Will Choke Off Jobs," *Telegraph*, February 17, 2003; Wendell Cox, "The London Congestion Charge: Separating the Hype from Reality," *Public Purpose*, June 2005, http://www.publicpurpose.com/pp87-lcc.pdf, accessed August 14, 2011. In the first article, written before the charge was imposed, Cox wrote that "congestion pricing makes all the economic sense in the world, but it remains to be seen whether it makes economic sense in central London." In the second, he wrote that "the problem is that the conditions that have produced traffic reduction and modest public transport impacts in London exist in few other places in the world."

22. Sam Staley, "Bloomberg vs. the Cars," http://reason.org/blog/show/bloomberg-vs-the-car; Sam Staley, "Is the End of Transponders Near," http://reason.org/blog/show/is-the-end-of-transponders-near, accessed August 14, 2011.

23. Randal O'Toole, "Using Markets to Enhance Mobility," http://www.cato-unbound.org/2011/04/06/randal-otoole/using-markets-to-enhance-mobility/, accessed August 14, 2011; Stephen Smith, "Virginia Land Use Law: Marc Scribner from CEI Responds," http://marketurbanism.com/2011/02/07/virginia-land-use-law-marc-scribner-from-cei-responds/, accessed August 21, 2011. Scribner also fears that allowing dense development will cause condemnation of private land for redevelopment, something not authorized by the legislation at hand.

24. George Will, "High Speed to Insolvency," *Newsweek*, February 27, 2011; Kotkin, "War against Suburbia"; Randal O'Toole, *The Vanishing Automobile and Other Urban Myths: How Smart Growth Will Harm American Cities* (Thoreau Institute, Bandon, OR, 2001), pp. 481–492.

Chapter 12

1. George Orwell, "Politics and the English Language," in *Orwell: A Collection of Essays* (Houghton Mifflin Harcourt, Orlando, FL, 1981), pp. 156–170.

2. Babcock, *Zoning Game*, pp. 48, 115. Perin, *Everything in Its Place*, pp. x, 81–83, emphasizes the lack of frankness in discussions of land use.

3. Site Plan 82004005A, Gables Rothbury Square, heard by Montgomery County Planning Board, July 14, 2011.

4. Exemplary at one time could refer to any example, but this usage was essentially extinct a century ago.

5. Sean Howell, "The Manhattanization of Menlo Park?" *Almanac* (Menlo Park, CA), October 20, 2009.

6. The city of West Palm Beach, Florida, has issued a policy on neutral transportation language: http://www.8-80cities.org/Articles/City%20Transportation%20Language%20Policy.pdf, accessed October 5, 2011.

7. Researchers use a variety of definitions of conflict and rarely state them explicitly. A pedestrian prevented from leaving the sidewalk by a legal automobile movement never counts as a conflict.

8. John Townsend, quoted in Courtland Milloy, "Speed Cameras: Traffic Enforcement or Highway Robbery?" *Washington Post*, September 11, 2012.

9. This line of thinking is taken to an extreme by Tara Roeder, who argues that New Urbanist efforts to mix income levels are a racist attack on minority and working-class communities. "American Spaces: New Urbanism's Fascist Rhetoric," *Consortium: A Journal of Crossdisciplinary Inquiry* (2011).

Chapter 13

1. Abbott, *Greater Portland*, pp. 79–97, 140–142, 148–149; Gregory L. Thompson, "Taming the Neighborhood Revolution: Planners, Power Brokers, and the Birth

of Neotraditionalism in Portland, Oregon," *Journal of Planning History*, vol. 6, pp. 214–247 (2007).

2. Carl Abbott, "Centers and Edges: Reshaping Downtown Portland," in Ozawa, *Portland Edge*, pp. 164–183; Thompson, "Neighborhood Revolution."

3. "Introduction," in Carl Abbott, Deborah Howe, and Sy Adler, eds., *Planning the Oregon Way: A Twenty-Year Evaluation* (Oregon State University Press, Corvallis, 1994), pp. xi–xiv; Gerrit Knaap, "Land Use Politics in Oregon," ibid., pp. 3–23; Abbott, *Greater Portland*, pp. 161–162.

4. Ethan Seltzer, "It's Not an Experiment: Regional Planning at Metro, 1990 to the Present," in Ozawa, *Portland Edge*, pp. 35–60; Abbott, *Greater Portland*, pp. 166–170; DeGrove, *Planning Policy and Politics*, pp. 19–22, 26.

5. Abbott, *Greater Portland*, pp. 157–160; DeGrove, *Planning Policy and Politics*, pp. 23–24.

6. William G. Robbins, *Landscapes of Conflict: The Oregon Story, 1940–2000* (University of Washington Press, Seattle, 2004), pp. 293–301; Knaap, "Land Use Politics."

7. Deborah Howe, "The Reality of Portland's Housing Market," in Ozawa, *Portland Edge*, pp. 184–205. Howe reports that the median inflation-adjusted rent in the city grew by 8.8% in the 1970s and 2.2% in the 1980s. Individual tenants saw even smaller increases, if not decreases—if the rent in every existing unit stays the same, the average rent will go up because new units, which typically have much higher rents than old ones, enter the market. Of the total Portland rental housing stock, approximately 18% was less than ten years old in 1979 and 5% was that new in 1989.

8. Howe, "Portland's Housing Market"; Steven Johnson, "The Myth and Reality of Portland's Engaged Citizenry and Process-Oriented Governance," in Ozawa, *Portland Edge*, pp. 102–117.

9. Seltzer, "Not an Experiment"; Sy Adler and Jennifer Dill, "The Evolution of Transportation Planning in the Portland Metropolitan Area," in Ozawa, *Portland Edge*, pp. 230–256; Nancy Chapman and Hollie Lund, "Housing Density and Livability in Portland," ibid., pp. 206–229; DeGrove, *Planning Policy and Politics*, pp. 23–30.

10. Flint, *This Land*, pp. 172–186, 202.

11. Abbott, *Greater Portland*, pp. 175–176; Chapman and Lund, "Housing Density"; Flint, *This Land*, p. 182.

12. Adler and Dill, "Evolution of Transportation Planning"; "Building Future Transportation Leadership Seminar Proceedings: Success Factors from Portland," TriMet, January 24, 2008, esp. pp. 12–22. Ridership in Portland and Washington is calculated from unlinked trips reported to the American Public Transportation Association for the first quarter of 2011.

13. Robert Brosnan, "30 Years of Smart Growth: Arlington County's Experience with Transit Oriented Development in the Rosslyn-Ballston Metro Corridor," July 2008, http://www.arlingtonva.us/departments/CPHD/planning/power-point/rbpresentation/rbpresentation_060107.pdf, accessed October 15, 2011.

14. "Arlington's Smart Growth Journey," http://arlington.granicus.com/Media Player.php?view_id=4&clip_id=1206, accessed October 15, 2011; Schrag, *Great Society Subway,* pp. 122–127, 134–141.

15. Schrag, *Great Society Subway,* pp. 130–131, 223–227; Mark R. Parris, "The Rosslyn-Ballston Corridor: Early Visions," Arlington County Planning Department, February 1989.

16. Parris, "Early Visions"; "Arlington's Smart Growth Journey."

17. Brosnan, "30 Years of Smart Growth." This analysis is also based on discussions with people active in Arlington politics.

18. "Arlington's Smart Growth Journey."

19. This section is written mostly from the author's experiences. Written sources on the history of the Purple Line include a newsletter archive at http://actfortransit. org/archives/publications/; Jo-Ann Armao, "Montgomery Trolley Plan Travels on a Bumpy Track," *Washington Post,* October 15, 1989; Josh Kurtz, "Purple Line Has Taken a Circuitous Path," *Gazette* [Gaithersburg, MD], March 24, 2000; Katherine Shaver, "Glendening Stokes Rail Fight; Decision to Build Purple Line Inside Beltway Fires Up Duncan," *Washington Post,* October 30, 2001; Gretchen Morgenson, "With a Gift, Fannie Mae Puts on Golf Shoes," *New York Times,* September 29, 2002; Catherine Dolinski, "Ehrlich Drawing the Line," *Gazette,* August 27, 2003 ("will not go through"); Katherine Shaver, "Fortunes Shift for East-West Rail in Md.: Purple Line Stalled as Connector Hums toward Construction Under Ehrlich," *Washington Post,* January 16, 2005; Robert J. Smith, "Will the Purple Line Be Built?" *Washington Post,* July 6, 2006 ("obfuscate, alter"); Katherine Shaver, "Purple Line Foes Offer No Ideas, and No Names," *Washington Post,* July 13, 2008; Katherine Shaver, "Format of Purple Line Up to Voters," *Washington Post,* October 8, 2010.

Chapter 14

1. Henderson, *Street Fight,* pp. 115–120.

2. Thad Williamson, "Justice, the Public Sector, and Cities," in Clarissa Rile Hayward and Todd Swanstrom, eds., *Justice and the American Metropolis* (University of Minnesota Press, Minneapolis, 2011), pp. 177–197.

3. See Fischel, *Economics of Zoning Laws,* pp. 209–216.

4. Louisa Hufstader, "Pipe Dreams," *Northbay Business Journal,* December 2008. According to rumor, the referendum was initially financed by developers who wanted to overturn the ban on building on vineyards.

5. Elisabeth R. Gerber and Clark C. Gibson, "Balancing Regionalism and Localism: How Institutions and Incentives Shape American Transportation Policy," *American Journal of Political Science,* vol. 53, pp. 643–658 (2009); Arthur C. Nelson, Thomas W. Sanchez, James F. Wolf, and Mary Beth Farquhar, "Metropolitan Planning Organization Voting Structure and Transit Investment Bias: Preliminary Analysis with Social Equity Implications," *Transportation Research Record,* vol. 1895, pp. 1–7 (2004); Fulton, *Reluctant Metropolis,* pp. 155–174.

Chapter 15

1. Kornai, *Socialist System*, pp. 91–109.
2. Duany, *Suburban Nation*, pp. 221–224.
3. Charles Siegel, *Unplanning: Livable Cities and Political Choices* (Preservation Institute, Berkeley, CA, 2010), esp. pp. 69–92.
4. Glaeser, *Triumph of the City*, makes this point strongly and perhaps overstates it.
5. Franzese and Siegel, "Trust and Community," offer a more detailed program of reform that addresses these problems without making homeowners associations into governments.
6. Jason Islas, "Santa Monica's Village Trailer Park Gets Celebrity Boost," *Lookout News*, May 23, 2012, http://www.surfsantamonica.com/ssm_site/the_lookout/news/News-2012/May-2012/05_23_2012_Santa_Monicas_Village_Trailer_Park_Gets_Celebrity_Boost.html. For anti-growth basis of opposition to this project, see http://www.smclc.net/PDF/VTP/VTP5-21-12.pdf. Both accessed July 15, 2012.
7. Fischel, *Economics of Zoning Laws*, recommends moving in the opposite direction by making zoning a property right that can be bought and sold. Fischel is realistic and thoughtful in his analysis of zoning as it is now, but his recommendations for change too often rest on the unexamined premise that the object of zoning is economic welfare.

Chapter 16

1. Milton Friedman and George Stigler, "Roofs or Ceilings? The Current Housing Problem" (1946), http://www.fee.org/library/books/roofs-or-ceilings-the-current-housing-problem/, accessed November 12, 2011; Brian Doherty, *Radicals for Capitalism: A Freewheeling History of the Modern American Libertarian Movement* (Public Affairs, New York, 2007), pp. 191–193.
2. Weiss, "Planning Subdivisions."
3. Another objection to rent control is that it gives incumbent tenants an unfair advantage over newcomers to town, who wind up paying a higher price for their own apartments because so much housing has been kept off the market. But the same argument can be made against homeownership, which also grants preferential use of houses to their incumbent occupants. Critics of rent control rarely call for the abolition of private property.
4. See Glazer, *Cause to a Style*, pp. 165–191.
5. Henderson, *Street Fight*, pp. 91, 99–104.
6. John Logan and Harvey Molotch, *Urban Fortunes: The Political Economy of Place* (University of California Press, Los Angeles, 1987) is the basic source for this theory. Similar analyses are found in Jason Hackworth, *The Neoliberal City: Governance, Ideology, and Development in American Urbanism* (Cornell University Press, Ithaca, NY, 2007); Sidney Plotkin, *Keep Out: The Struggle for Land Use Control* (University of California Press, Berkeley, 1987), esp. pp. 7–11.

7. Logan and Molotch, *Urban Fortunes*, pp. 120–123, suggest that these areas are protected by mutual solidarity among the builders and that doing so is functional to the growth machine because the availability of fancy places to live makes the city more attractive to outside investors. A city's fancy neighborhoods are surely an economic asset, but it does not follow that developers avoid building in them for that reason. Many upscale neighborhoods have had to work hard to stop development.

8. Brown-Saracino, *Neighborhood That Never Changes*, pp. 118–120, 127–130.

9. Brown-Saracino, *Neighborhood That Never Changes*, pp. 252–253, discusses political motivations for the reticence of neo-Marxists about nimbys.

10. Brown-Saracino, *Neighborhood That Never Changes*, pp. 93, 234–235.

11. Heather Schwartz, "Housing Policy Is School Policy: Economically Integrative Housing Promotes Academic Success in Montgomery County, Maryland," Century Foundation, 2010, p. 4, http://tcf.org/assets/downloads/tcf-Schwartz.pdf, accessed November 11, 2011.

12. Patricia Leigh Brown, "Animal McMansion: Students Trade Dorm for Suburban Luxury," *New York Times*, November 13, 2011.

Chapter 17

1. Ehrenhalt, *Great Inversion*, pp. 40–88.

2. Annie Weinstock, Walter Hook, Michael Replogle, and Ramon Cruz, "Recapturing Global Leadership in Bus Rapid Transit: A Survey of Select U.S. Cities," Institute for Transportation & Development Policy, May 2011, http://www.itdp.org/documents/20110526ITDP_USBRT_Report-HR.pdf, accessed November 29, 2011.

3. Alan Hoffman, "Advanced Network Planning for Bus Rapid Transit: The 'Quickway Model' as a Modal Alternative to 'Light Rail Lite,'" Federal Transit Administration report, February 2008, pp. 57, 77–78.

4. Litman, "Rail Transit in America," pp. 40–43; "'Bus Rapid Transit' or 'Quality Bus'? Reality Check," Light Rail Now, http://www.lightrailnow.org/facts/fa_brt007.htm, accessed November 29, 2011; "Bus Rapid Transit—Not for New Jersey," New Jersey Association of Railroad Passengers, http://www.nj-arp.org/Assets/bus%20rapid%20transit%20-%20not%20for%20nj.pdf, accessed December 12, 2013.

5. ."Success Factors from Portland," pp. 51–60; Yonah Freemark, "US Government Plans Overhaul of New Start Funding Guidelines, Reducing Importance of Cost-Effectiveness," *Transport Politic*, http://www.thetransportpolitic.com/2010/01/13/us-government-plans-overhaul-of-new-start-funding-guidelines-reducing-importance-of-cost-effectiveness/, accessed November 26, 2011.

6. Robert Poole and Kenneth Orski, "Hot Networks: A New Plan for Congestion Relief and Better Transit," Paper 305, Reason Foundation, 2001, www.rppi.org/ps305.pdf,; Robert Poole, "Better Busways Don't Require Exclusive Lanes," *Gwinnett Gazette*, December 2, 2011.

7. Karen Farkas, "HealthLine Buses Moving Slower Than Expected on Euclid Avenue," *Cleveland Plain Dealer*, July 6, 2010; Massachusetts Sierra Club,

"MBTA's Silver Line—Taxpayers Get Less for More," http://www.sierraclubmass. org/issues/conservation/silverline/slreport.pdf, accessed March 4, 2012.

8. In its organizing strategy, the group's leader Eric Mann wrote, "the focus has been on building 'independent social movements' that are antiracist, rooted in the working class of color, and fighting various manifestations of racism and national oppression." Eric Mann, "A Race Struggle, a Class Struggle, a Women's Struggle All at Once: Organizing on the Buses of L.A.," *Socialist Register*, vol. 37, pp. 259–263 (2001); Eric Mann, "Building the Anti-Racist, Anti-Imperialist United Front: Theory and Practice from the L.A. Strategy Center and Bus Riders Union," http://www.thestrategycenter.org/article/2009/03/12/building-anti-racist-anti-imperialist-united-front, accessed November 25, 2011 (source of quotation); Eric Mann and Manuel Criollo, "Grassroots Organizing for a World Revolution," http://www.zcommunications.org/grassroots-organizing-for-a-world-revolution-by-eric-mann, accessed November 25, 2011; Tom Wetzel, "Organizing Around Transit: At the Intersection of Environmental Justice and Class Struggle," http://www.uncanny.net/~wetzel/ecoclasstransit.htm, accessed November 25, 2011.

9. Tactics shifted somewhat in 2008 when the BRU leadership worked hard for the election of Barack Obama. The underlying political analysis centered on race did not change.

10. "Hampton Roads Long-Range Transportation Plan: Visioning Survey Report," Hampton Roads Transportation Planning Organization, September 2013.

11. Peter J. Haas and Katherine Estrada, "Revisiting Factors Associated with the Success of Ballot Initiatives with a Substantial Rail Transit Component," Mineta Transportation Institute Report 10-13, June 2011, http://transweb.sjsu.edu/PDFs/research/2911-Ballot-Initiatives-Rail-Transit.pdf, accessed November 24, 2011; Weyrich and Lind, *Moving Minds*, pp. 131–142; "Transportation Finance at the Ballot Box," Center for Transportation Excellence, 2006, http://www.cfte.org/CFTE%20Election%20Trends%20Report.pdf, accessed November 24, 2011.

12. Shoup, *Free Parking*, pp. 205–223.

13. Shoup, *Free Parking*, pp. 129–141.

14. Frank J. Gruber, "Seduced by Parking," *Lookout*, June 30, 2003, http://www.surfsantamonica.com/ssm_site/the_lookout/columns/FrankGruber/FG-2003/06_2003/06_30_03_Seduced_by_Parking.htm, accessed August 3, 2012.

15. Shoup, *Free Parking*. Pasadena: pp. 238–245. Redwood City: Donald Shoup, "Cruising for Parking," *Access*, Spring 2007, pp. 16–22.

16. Henderson, *Street Fight*, pp. 87–111.

17. Thad Williamson, *Sprawl, Justice, and Citizenship: The Civic Costs of the American Way of Life* (Oxford University Press, New York, 2010), pp. 217–241.

18. Williamson's analysis of survey data reports no correlation between transit use and voting. However, he focuses on national elections, where almost everyone is aware that there is an election and few have shaken the candidates' hands. My own review of election returns in Montgomery County found that in low-turnout elections, precincts near Metro stations have much higher voting rates than sociologically similar precincts far from them.

Index

THE DRIFTERS

CHILDREN OF DISORGANIZED
LOWER-CLASS FAMILIES

THE DRIFTERS

CHILDREN OF DISORGANIZED
LOWER-CLASS FAMILIES

BY
CHARLES A. MALONE, M.D.
ELEANOR PAVENSTEDT, M.D.
ILSE MATTICK
LOUISE S. BANDLER, M.S.W.
MAURICE R. STEIN, PH.D.
NORBETT L. MINTZ, PH.D.

EDITED BY
ELEANOR PAVENSTEDT, M.D.
CLINICAL PROFESSOR OF PSYCHIATRY, BOSTON UNIVERSITY SCHOOL
OF MEDICINE; STAFF CHILD PSYCHIATRIST, TUFTS-
COLUMBIA POINT HEALTH CENTER, BOSTON

FOREWORD BY
BERNARD BANDLER, M.D.
PROFESSOR AND CHAIRMAN OF THE
DEPARTMENT OF PSYCHIATRY, BOSTON
UNIVERSITY SCHOOL OF MEDICINE,
BOSTON

LITTLE, BROWN AND COMPANY
BOSTON

LIBRARY OF CONGRESS CATALOG CARD NO. 67-27513

FIRST EDITION

Second Printing

The names of participating families
and their children have been
changed to protect confidentiality.

*Published in Great Britain
by J. & A. Churchill Ltd., London*
British Catalogue No. 7000 0103 4

PRINTED IN THE UNITED STATES OF AMERICA

DEDICATED TO

THE PROJECT FAMILIES

NORTH POINT FAMILY PROJECT MEMBERS AND CONTRIBUTING AUTHORS

CHARLES A. MALONE, M.D. *Director*

Formerly: Assistant Professor of Psychiatry, Department of Psychiatry, Boston University School of Medicine, Boston

Presently: Associate Professor of Clinical Child Psychiatry, University of Pennsylvania Medical School; Training Director, Philadelphia Child Guidance Clinic, Philadelphia

ELEANOR PAVENSTEDT, M.D. *Codirector*

Formerly: Professor and Director of Child Psychiatry, Department of Psychiatry, Boston University School of Medicine, Boston

Presently: Clinical Professor of Psychiatry, Boston University School of Medicine; Lecturer, Tufts University School of Medicine; Staff Child Psychiatrist, Tufts-Columbia Point Health Center, Boston

BERNARD BANDLER, M.D. *Consultant*

Professor and Chairman of the Department of Psychiatry, Boston University School of Medicine, Boston

Formerly indicates at the time of the project.

NORBETT L. MINTZ, PH.D. *Research Psychologist*

*Formerly: Assistant Professor of Psychology, Department of Psychology,
Brandeis University, Waltham*

*Presently: Associate Psychologist, McLean Hospital, Belmont, Mass.;
Associate Psychologist, Department of Psychiatry, Harvard
Medical School, Boston*

MAURICE R. STEIN, PH.D.
Consultant Sociologist

*Associate Professor of Sociology and Chairman, Department of Sociology,
Brandeis University, Waltham*

ILSE MATTICK *Director of Nursery School*

*Formerly: Research Associate, Department of Psychiatry,
Boston University School of Medicine, Boston*

*Presently: Associate Professor of Education,
Wheelock College, Boston*

LOUISE S. BANDLER, M.S.W.
Director of Family Casework

*Formerly: Lecturer in Casework,
Simmons College School of Social Work, Boston*

*Presently: Assistant Professor of Social Economy,
Simmons College School of Social Work, Boston*

Poverty, illness, and disorganization have been the traditional lot of man. Only in recent years have our knowledge, technology, and abundance made their conquest seem a feasible goal. The dynamics of democracy in turn have transformed the feasible into an imperative. We are now embarked on a massive national program to eradicate poverty, illness, and disorganization, which today are seen to be interrelated. Good will, optimism, a drive for action, and a tendency to oversimplify are typical of the American character. If all our energies were deployed in programs for action without a concomitant increase in our detailed knowledge of the complexities with which we are dealing, skepticism of our ultimate success would be justified. An awareness of complexity and study in depth, however, are also part of the American character; pragmatism rests on inquiry and experiment.

Multiproblem families, while not necessarily limited to any socioeconomic group, represent the hard core of poverty, illness, and disorganization. Much is known about them—enough to justify large-scale action programs. Much is still unknown about these families—enough to jeopardize the success of such programs unless we deepen our knowledge of their nature, their natural history, and our techniques for dealing with them.

This demonstration study by Drs. Pavenstedt and Malone, Mrs. Mattick and Mrs. Bandler, and their co-workers represents four years of intensive work with only thirteen families. They have,

I believe, added greatly to our basic knowledge of these families, particularly of the mothers and of the children. As a result of their work, we understand the members of these families. We understand them across generations and through their life spans. We understand them in their struggling humanity and in the appealing-repelling Dickensian panorama of their methods of survival. We see and feel the mirrorlike reciprocity of individual, family, and social disorganization. We are persuaded, if we needed persuasion, that the mothers can be involved. Their "lack of motivation" represents the rationalization for our past failures and for the inadequacy of our traditional institutionalized techniques for meeting their needs. We are shown, if we needed showing, that mothers want to be good mothers and that they can learn better child-rearing practices as part of felt motherhood. We see how much can be accomplished in the therapeutic-educational nursery school, in forwarding the growth and development of the children, so ignorant and so overwise, so retarded emotionally and so impoverished intellectually, and yet so overdeveloped in guile.

The authors of this book share a common orientation and perspective, namely, that of psychoanalytic understanding. It is that understanding, not psychoanalytic theory or technique, which permits such rich communication among the social worker, psychiatrist, and educator. The developmental, adaptational perspective is a cornerstone of behavioral science. Psychoanalytic understanding here makes it truly dynamic. It enables us to add to our previous knowledge of multiproblem families the enormous dimension of the human personality seen longitudinally in familial and social interaction.

One special value of this volume is the vistas it opens for further studies in depth. Precise knowledge and analysis carry with them a precise awareness of where knowledge stops and where research begins. Every chapter in this book contains both implications and specific suggestions for advancing our understanding of multiproblem families.

Since this study is a demonstration project, the authors were aware from the beginning of its potential implications for social action. They have fully realized that the manpower and funds necessary for a study in depth of multiproblem families cannot be reproduced in large-scale programs. They have also thought extensively and made many suggestions about how their knowledge, experience, and practices can be feasibly implemented through social action.

This book should be of significant value to many people: to psychiatrists, psychologists, social workers, educators, social scientists, public health workers, civic and political leaders, and urban planners. The problems of poverty involve housing, health, welfare, education, job training, and race relations, which all commingle in the human soil of the multiproblem family. By what it tells us of the mothers and the children, this volume reminds us of the necessity for keeping the human dimension, the personality dimension, in the foreground lest our solutions become too abstract, oversimplified, and superficial, and result only in social manipulation and engineering. In spite of our great resources the war against poverty, like any other war, can be lost if we neglect the complexities of human nature.

BERNARD BANDLER, M.D.

ACKNOWLEDGMENTS

THE NORTH POINT PROJECT was undertaken as a reaching-out effort into the community from the Boston University–Boston City Hospital Guidance Clinic, in the Department of Child Psychiatry of the Division of Psychiatry, Boston University School of Medicine. It was supported by the National Institute of Mental Health's Community Research and Services Branch through demonstration project grants #5-R11-MH445-1,2,3 and #5-R11-MH445-4S1, 1960–1965.

We are deeply grateful to the families who participated in the project for admitting us into their lives and entrusting us with their children.

We wish to acknowledge our indebtedness to and thank the many staff members whose devoted and persevering service, as well as sharp powers of observation, made available the data upon which much of this book is based. Among the family workers were Joseph T. Devlin, M.S.W., who was with the project from its earliest phase; Elizabeth J. White, R.N.; Jane Wiesenbarger, M.S.W. (now Mrs. William Reeves); and Sarah Smith, M.S.W. (now Mrs. Lloyd Spain). The teachers were Ann Coolidge, B.S.Ed., Takako Salvi, R.N., and Richard Liebowitz, A.B. Ann Ross, Ed.D., served as consultant observer to the Nursery School; Maxwell Schleifer, Ph.D., was for a limited time research consultant. Amelia Blackwell, Ph.D., was responsible for testing all the children and for play therapy with some. Jane Hulek, Ph.D., did a splendid analysis of the test results; we regretted not being able to locate her for permission to include the report in this book.

Our thanks to the many social and community agencies, both public and private, who referred families and in other ways cooperated with us. We are greatly indebted to the recreational facility that graciously housed the project.

We thank the editor and the publishers of the *Journal of the American Academy of Child Psychiatry* (see Vol. 4, No. 4, April 1965) for permitting us to reprint large sections of "Adaptations of Nursery School Techniques to Deprived Children" by Ilse Mattick.

Our special thanks go to Mrs. Ruth Knee of the National Institute of Mental Health for her constant encouragement and support.

We are grateful also to Mrs. Myrtle Orloff, a devoted secretary, who did more than was required throughout the project.

To Mrs. Beatrice Taplin we add our heartfelt thanks for her patient attention to our secretarial needs and for her accurate transcript of the manuscript.

E. P.

CONTENTS

II. THE CHILDREN

III. THE FAMILIES

IV. THE ENVIRONMENT

V. THE PROBLEM OF ASSESSMENT OF CHANGE

THE DRIFTERS

CHILDREN OF DISORGANIZED
LOWER-CLASS FAMILIES

INTRODUCTION

Eleanor Pavenstedt

Now that an all-out assault on poverty is under way, conditions in 1955, when we timidly began our pilot project to assist children of disorganized, maximally deprived families, seem almost unreal. Publications were beginning to come through from the New Haven study (10) regarding the preponderance of mental illness in the lower class but had not yet made sufficient impact to lead to modifications in psychiatric care.

It was later that a succession of writers aroused us, as a nation, out of our complacency. Michael Harrington (8), by vividly portraying lives that public welfare and private social agencies were failing to render more endurable, was the standard-bearer. John Kenneth Galbraith's *The Affluent Society* (5) brought home to a more intellectual group our failure to provide for the poor. By 1965 society was no longer able to deny that a considerable proportion of its population lived under substandard conditions and in a state of deplorable mental health. Middle-class society was primed for public action and President Johnson successfully appealed to our national conscience with his demand for legislation to eliminate mass poverty.

Simultaneously the growth of delinquency and of gang warfare was attributed to a steadily growing number of high school dropouts, of unemployable young people. Educators, sociologists, and

the mental health professions became increasingly concerned with
the failure of our "middle-class schools" to teach and prepare large
groups of the nation's children for employment. We were clearly
confronted by our failure and the awareness that expanding auto-
mation and scientific discoveries would compound the problem.
"The economy of the late twentieth century requires trained
minds, educated judgment, and conceptual skill" (7) and only a
fraction of Americans were receiving the necessary training and
education.

GOALS AND PHILOSOPHY OF THE PROJECT

This is not another book on poverty nor on the "culture of poverty." We have been concerned with a small group of the poor—
perhaps the most disadvantaged. We became alerted to their plight
when, in a city hospital-guidance clinic, we found ourselves powerless to deal with the failure-to-thrive syndrome, the multiple
learning problems, the delinquent acting out, the abortive suicidal
attempts, and the premarital conception of children of a large
group of the children and adolescents who came to the hospital
from disorganized homes. We recognized the need for a new child-
guidance program to serve as an arm into the community. Bradley
Buell (2) had recently published his findings from a survey of 108
public and private agencies in St. Paul, Minnesota, showing that 6
percent of all the families absorbed 46 percent of the health services and "55 percent of all the adjustment services, including psychiatric service, casework, and protective supervision." It was our
impression that this was the group we had become concerned
about and that a multidisciplinary program of investigation and
service for families of small children who were not making constructive use of existing agencies was overdue. Section I of this
book will provide a history of the project in the setting of other
similar projects.

Since 1955 preschool educational programs of all kinds have
been promoted with predominant emphasis on *cognitive* development. We understand education to mean what its roots imply: *e
ducere,* to lead out of. It is our tenet that *in order to lead out of*

misery, as well as out of intellectual dearth, intervention must begin very early and be concerned with total personality development.

Misery as we found it meant feeling cheated and rejected by society at large and becoming distrustful and suspicious; the danger from uncontrolled impulses within and from the environment led to a state of chronic subthreshold anxiety; impulsive acts dissipated the limited job opportunities and feelings of worthlessness followed; this in turn contributed to an absence of purpose and goal and resulted in being deprived of most of the advantages and privileges of our society. Alienation, danger, deprivation, absence of purpose and goals, and self-abasement existed not only in relation to society but in personal and family life as well.

The children who were studied at the age of 3 and 4 were already damaged. When we set ourselves the task of bettering their early upbringing, we wanted to prepare them for the competitive struggle with which their parents were incapable of coping. Our goal was to help them to become self-respecting, productive members of society, capable of relating to and communicating with others, with the energy, initiative, and factual orientation to stand up for themselves.

In Section II, on the children, our psychological frame of reference will be described in some detail. It will become clear why we are convinced that *cognitive development is an inseparable part of a broader learning process,* and that *only by supporting overall developmental maturation can children be helped to attain the personality and cognitive tools with which to build satisfactory lives for themselves.*

The children studied in nursery school were already so retarded and deviant in their development that corrective, rather than preventive, measures had to be introduced. Fundamental areas of learning and attitudes basic to normal development were stunted and skewed. Functions necessary for survival in their pathological environment had been prematurely developed and were hypertrophied. How their personality in some measure had become rigid and resisted reorganization will be discussed in Chapter 6.

A description of these preschool children when they entered nursery school (Chapter 4), our understanding of their developmental lags and precocities (Chapter 6), as contrasted with development in an "average expectable environment" (9) (Chapter 5), the measures devised to help them make up for their deficiencies (Chapter 7), the changes observed as well as the barriers to change (Chapter 8) will be the prime subject matter of this book. The important work with the families which helped the reparative process to take place will be discussed in Section III. Section IV consists of a brief report on an anthropological survey of the sociocultural environment. A final chapter will deal with our recommendations for implementation of similar programs and for future avenues of research.

THE PROJECT POPULATION

The North Point Project dealt with 13 families who among them had 45 preschool children, 21 of whom attended the project's special nursery school. Quarters of both school and project were in a recreational facility operated for many years in the slum where the families lived. Criteria for selecting the families were as follows: gross social and psychological pathology, failure to work constructively with community services while availing themselves consistently only of public welfare, children only below the age of five, and domicile within walking distance of the project. The existence of a child-rearing unit (at least mother and child or children) and some expression of interest in the continuance of care were further conditions for acceptance.

Although the families had many similar psychological and social characteristics and problems in their daily functioning, there was a range of disorganization and pathology. This range, to be described in the section on the families, permits a broader perspective and may make this study more useful clinically to others who work with disorganized families in different settings. These are the so-called hard-to-reach, hard-core, multiproblem families that are represented in all community agency case loads. They invariably ceased coming to the agency after the immediate crisis had been met and were usually designated as failures until recently, since more of an effort is being made now to reach out to them and to maintain a supportive contact.

Our aim was to improve the conditions under which children, still in their most formative years, grew up, since it is our hypothesis that *the children's early experiences are the most decisive influence in the perpetuation of the maladaptations of these families over generations.*

This *repetitive pattern of disorganization and failure* (18) came to light as we explored the past histories of the families. In social agency, hospital, and court records, alcoholism, unemployment, marital discord, divorce, neglect of children with transient state placements, prostitution, extramarital partnerships, crime, and mental illness recurred as far back as we could trace.

In contrast to the general literature on cultural deprivation only a few of the project families were members of a racial minority. (Only three Negro families participated in the project.) One of the unique findings was that the father and mother were usually from different ethnic and religious backgrounds. Although many of them lived in public housing projects, they preferred the anonymity of private lodgings. Distrustful and evasive in their dealings with agencies, they remained isolated from the mainstream of our society and defended themselves against "caretakers."

Medical personnel was less threatening since they probed less into people's lives and did not invoke moral censure. The nursing profession, both public health and visiting nurses, who brought physical care to them in their home, often were and are able to establish an enduring and meaningful contact. Social workers associated with home care services provided by some hospitals in or near deprived areas are often successful in maintaining supportive contacts and in manipulating the environment favorably. The mental health professions, in the sporadic instances when they tried, were until quite recently unsuccessful in modifying the individuals' or the families' way of life. Much of this, as indicated above, has undergone a change in the last few years since everyone's attention has been drawn to the needs of the poor.

Some social service groups in St. Paul and in several other large cities have successfully carried out special projects with these families, having access to them via one or more older children who had aroused public concern.

The Pine School Program (15) alone by 1955 had begun to work with a similar kind of preschool child and his family. The report on this program escaped our attention until recently because of its emphasis on mental retardation. Many of its findings confirm ours.

RELATED POPULATIONS

Although our subjects were drawn from an urban slum, we would venture to guess that rural shanty dwellers have many of the same characteristics. The disorganized group in this part of the country is not primarily composed of families from racial minorities. Many of the latter, however, when dislocated, may suffer from the same isolation and self-devaluation, the same absence of cultural ties.

Another socially disorganized group are the migrants. Despite Robert Coles' findings (4) on Mexican migrants, migrants less tied to their church deserve to be studied and may turn out to be like the project families.

Only careful research can determine whether the disheartened and apathetic families in the large poverty areas, who lacked the initiative and courage to move as opportunities for sustaining a reasonable livelihood faded away (for example, Appalachia), may belong to the group we studied.

Few people have ventured to estimate the size of this population. "This group," Frank Riessman (14) writes, "despite the disproportionate public attention it receives, is surprisingly small." Herbert Gans (6) puts it at 5 percent of the working class. Dorothy Barclay (1) quotes Dr. Havighurst as estimating "that half of all children in school today need more stimulation and personal attention—most disturbing of all is the final one-eighth who certainly qualify for the designation 'deprived.' Coming from seriously inadequate homes—disturbed, disorganized, destructive—they are both intellectually undernourished and emotionally starved." This certainly describes our group. It is our impression that many characteristics of the families and children we studied exist also in fringe groups, perhaps a little less disorganized and alienated.

PLACE OF DISORGANIZED FAMILIES
IN THE BROADER POVERTY SEGMENT
OF THE POPULATION

Work with these families has taught us, particularly in contrast to the stable working-class families, many of whom lived on a "poverty income" in the same slum (13) (the subjects of a longitudinal child-development research project), that a slum population is anything but the homogeneous group so often encountered in the rapidly growing literature on educational enrichment of the culturally deprived. Nor is the "poverty group" homogeneous. Catherine S. Chilman (3), in summarizing studies on "significant cultural patterns of the poor," speaks of "sub-cultures" of poverty. She goes on to say that "criteria must be precise to differentiate the working class, the employed poor, the unemployed poor, or the chronically dependent. It is highly probable that there are more differences between the very poor . . . and the skilled labor groups than between the latter and the middle class." To this we heartily subscribe.

Almost all the families worked with were chronically on and off public relief, if not steady welfare clients on one or another program. Kermit Wiltse (17) in a description of ADC (Aid to Dependent Children) families writes: "Their behavior seemed a reasonable response to the buffetings of a series of singularly destructive environmental experiences coming on the heels of poor ego formation. . . they were on relief in a society where that carries clear connotation of inadequacy, immorality, and worthlessness."

All of the families were not fatherless and many mothers on the Aid to Dependent Children (ADC), now Aid to Dependent Families and Children (ADFC), program provide their children with a far healthier child-rearing experience than was the lot of the children from the disorganized group. However, the chronic relief atmosphere may well have affected these mothers, as it did Wiltse's clients, for their feelings of self-devaluation were insistently pervasive and carried over onto the children.

Although disorganized families akin to those to be described in this book have many ties to their extended family, these are tenuous, stormy, and unreliable. Nor do they provide the affection, support, and comfort, the source of gratification and security, as well as of shared concerns and responsibilities, available to the larger, more stable working-class group.

One of the criteria of selection, that there be serious social and/or psychological pathology, puts the project families into John Kenneth Galbraith's (5) category of "case poverty." They do not belong to a "culture," having neither traditions nor institutions. No ethnic ties nor active religious affiliations hold them together. In fact we speak of them as a group only because of certain common patterns of family life and a form of peripheral social existence. Their antisocial behavior consists more in their failure to abide by certain social institutions—which results in prostitution, child neglect, bigamy, and so on—and in a tendency to yield to impulsive, unsophisticated, delinquent acts, than in espousing a criminal way of life.

OUR REASONS FOR CONCENTRATING ON THIS GROUP

The background of our staff was in clinical psychology, which dictated our interest in this group of grossly pathological families. In order to treat the children in our clinic we needed to know a great deal more about their development.

The discovery that the maladjustment of these families was self-perpetuating was a further stimulus. We agree with Galbraith's statement (5) that "the first and strategic step in an attack on poverty is to see that it is no longer self-perpetuating. . . . to eliminate poverty efficiently we should invest more than proportionately in the children of the poor community."

From earlier work with women of this group in a reformatory, it was clear that they were repeating the same miserable conditions for their children that they complained about bitterly in their own childhood. No efforts on the part of the staff to modify the women's impulsive behavior after their discharge were successful. Furthermore there was no social institution to which one could turn for help with this group. Everyone had become discouraged with their failure to follow through and adhere to any plan of treatment.

It was imperative that the vicious circle be broken into at some point. We believed that the most modifiable age at which to intervene was the nursery school age, 3 to 5. By this time it is essential to expose children to influences they otherwise lack. We wanted them to experience a relationship with trustworthy, consistent, and benevolent people from the middle class that they were growing up to fear and suspect. We believed that a simple predictable daily routine would help them learn to anticipate and plan, to postpone gratification and gradually tolerate frustration. We were convinced that devoted teachers with sufficient time could open up to them new worlds of communication and knowledge and skills.

In order to find preschool children we had to look for their families. The task of involving them in a relationship with our staff and of gaining their confidence sufficiently to permit us to have their children in our nursery school will be documented. It was arduous and for this reason children from the group have not been entered in Head Start nursery schools except in a few areas where social workers or nurses had already gained access to the homes before the program opened.

Although children in nursery school can be exposed to new influences, they continue to live in their families the major portion of their time. Unless the parents can be helped to deal with their children in a more controlled, protective, and nurturant fashion, to communicate with them and to relate to them as immature beings in need of patient training, school influences will lead to only relative success.

We realize that many people believe that the really essential change in these families will come about through broad economic and social measures. Everyone on the project staff agrees that this is essential but not sufficient. Others will protest that we are approaching these lower-class families with middle-class norms and standards. In regard to the latter we can only agree with Suzanne Keller's statement (11) that "cultural relativism ignores the fact that schools and industry are middle-class in organization and outlook."

Before the "Great Society" will be able to boast a drastic reduction of its poor and unemployable, much finer differentiations in the range of developmental deviancies and failures will have to be drawn (16). The potential advantages and pitfalls of the different patterns of adaptation of the many subgroups require exploration. *Chronic fears fed by recurrent situational stress and danger* (12), *inconsistencies and noxious overstimulation interfere as seriously with the normal development of the children of the poor as do the deprivations—cultural or economic—that have been so widely emphasized.*

Only when we have such detailed information will we be able to devise pertinent preventive and educational policies and practices that will prepare all lower-class children for the livelihood to which citizens of this country are entitled. In view of the complex adaptations that will be required of men in a progressive country where rapid changes are now anticipated, we have no blueprints for the education that will be needed to hold a job and maintain family life. It is all the more important that child rearing in the early years promote overall maturity which provides for *flexibility of adaptation.*

The North Point Project was conceived in order to explore in depth one small segment of the children and families of the poverty group—to devise a service and treatment methods and then to explicate our findings. We have reason to believe that these findings can be generalized to this segment of the population throughout the country.

REFERENCES

1. Barclay, Dorothy. Family Business in Brief. *New York Times Magazine,* May 1962.
2. Buell, Bradley, and Associates. *Community Planning for Human Services.* New York: Columbia University Press, 1952.
3. Chilman, Catherine S. Child-rearing and Family Relationships: Patterns of the Very Poor. *Welfare in Review* (U.S. Department of Health, Education, and Welfare, Welfare Administration) 3:9, 1965.
4. Coles, Robert. The Lives of Migrant Farmers. *American Journal of Psychiatry* 122:271, 1965.

5. Galbraith, John Kenneth. *The Affluent Society.* Boston: Houghton Mifflin, 1958.
6. Gans, Herbert. *The Urban Villagers.* Glencoe, Ill.: Free Press, 1962.
7. Gordon, Edmund. A Review of Programs of Compensatory Education. *American Journal of Orthopsychiatry* 35:640, 1965.
8. Harrington, Michael. *The Other America.* New York: Macmillan, 1962.
9. Hartmann, Heinz. *Ego Psychology and the Problem of Adaptation.* New York: International Universities Press, 1958.
10. Hollingshead, Augustus B., and Redlich, Frederick G. Social Stratification and Psychiatric Disorders. *American Sociological Review* 18:163, 1953.
11. Keller, Suzanne. The Social World of the Urban Slum Child: Some Early Findings. *American Journal of Orthopsychiatry* 33:823, 1963.
12. Malone, Charles. Safety First: Comments on the Influence of External Danger in the Lives of Children of Disorganized Families. *American Journal of Orthopsychiatry* 36:3, 1966.
13. Pavenstedt, Eleanor. A Comparison of the Childrearing Environment of Upper-Lower and Very Low-Lower Class Families. *American Journal of Orthopsychiatry* 35:89, 1965.
14. Riessman, Frank. *The Culturally Deprived Child.* New York: Harper & Row, 1962.
15. Roll, Marlin H. A Study of Retarded Young Children. In National Conference on Social Welfare, *Social Work Practice.* New York: Columbia University Press, 1962.
16. Srole, Leo. Poverty and Mental Health. Unpublished manuscript presented to American Psychiatric Association Regional Research Conference, Boston, 1966.
17. Wiltse, Kermit. Orthopsychiatric Programs for Socially Deprived Groups. *American Journal of Orthopsychiatry* 33:806, 1963.
18. Wooton, Barbara. *Social Science and Social Pathology.* London: George Allen & Unwin, 1959.

I

BACKGROUND

1

A SURVEY OF REMEDIAL PROGRAMS
FOR MULTIPROBLEM FAMILIES AND
THEIR PRESCHOOL CHILDREN

Norbett L. Mintz

A N Y R E V I E W must establish criteria which make the survey
of remedial programs in the social welfare field incomplete in some
respects. We restricted our survey to programs for (or including)
multiproblem families and their preschool children, although the
programs might not have been so defined; their own definitions
will be quoted in the summaries. Besides operating a preschool
program for the children, the projects had to include some structured work with parents (not merely observing or interviewing);
they had to deal with the child and family unit on an outpatient
rather than on an institutional or day-care basis; and they primarily had to be educational-therapeutic rather than clinical-psycho-
therapeutic programs (casework or group therapy with parents was
included, but not a psychotherapy program for children with the
nursery school ancillary to it). Some programs were excluded because all we had available was a vaguely worded abstract or a letter
from a project director with only a few sentences of description.
Indeed, there often was a guardedness about releasing information,
an attitude which should be alien to scientific research but which
nonetheless exists. Finally, we did not include foreign programs,
nor unpublished programs in this country unless the various scien-

tific exchange services were able to provide minimally detailed abstracts.

Thus, the well-known projects at the University of Chicago (35) and at the New York Institute of Developmental Studies (10, 11) were excluded because structured work with parents has not been an integral part of their programs. Hunt's study (18,19) and the work of Hess (16, 17) were not included because they have been basic or preliminary to an actual nursery school program. The University of Wisconsin project (28) has worked only with kindergarten children. We excluded such day-care centers as the Children's Hospital, Washington, D.C. (25), and the State University of New York in Syracuse (4). Also not included were the clinical programs of New York's Child Development Center (26, 27), of Cleveland's University Hospitals (14, 20, 21), and of the Merrill Palmer School (7, 8). The most complete report of these kinds of programs, excluded both because it was primarily clinical and because it dealt only with children of kindergarten age or older, was that of the Educational Therapy Center of Richmond, Virginia (32).

REINFORCEMENT AND PROGRAMMED INSTRUCTION

The programs that most depart from modern nursery school practice are those staffed by psychologists who see the need of "culturally impoverished" children as essentially being one of perceptual or cognitive "enrichment." From this point of view, programmed instruction and reinforcement procedures offer themselves as one possible method of remedy. While many studies seem to be experimenting along these lines, two projects appear to have built these procedures into the center of their work.

University of North Carolina. Baughman, Dahlstrom, and Long, (1, 2, 24) have been collaborating on a series of projects concerning "impoverished" southern rural children, Negro and white. The program, started in 1962, mostly has studied kindergarten to eighth-grade children. Recently, 25 preschool children have been visited in their homes twice weekly for a period of three months, so that workers can introduce programmed instructional material designed to enrich their environment. To evaluate the effects, they will send some children to an experimental kindergarten in the project and not others. This research differs from all others in this survey in that the entire preschool experience takes place in the child's home rather than in a nursery school.

Murfreesboro (Tennessee) City Schools. Klaus and Gray (15, 23) started this program in 1961, with 87 Negro preschoolers, divided into four groups—two experimental and two control. Behavior reinforcement and other special experiences have been introduced to offset the progressive retardation that ordinarily transpires as "culturally deprived" children go through school. As indices of cultural deprivation, the project used income (well below $3000), occupation (semi-skilled or unskilled), education (eighth grade or below), and housing (poor). Many mothers were on ADC; half of the families had missing fathers; and most families were large. The control children had no program other than testing. The experimental children had the same special programs, except that one group went for two years, and the other for one year, prior to public school. The experimental programs had two parts: a ten-week summer school, followed by contacts in the home during the rest of the year. The summer school was designed so as to "manipulate four variables"—attitude to achievement (motivation, persistence, delay), aptitude for achievement (perceptual, language, and conceptual development), social and personal development, and physical condition—although it appears that only the first two received concerted attention. Behind these variables lay a set of conceptualizations about differences in stimulation and in reinforcement between deprived and nondeprived children. In order to give as "immediate reinforcement of behavior" as possible, there were four assistants and one head teacher for each class of 20 to 22 children. During the rest of the year, specially trained teachers visited the homes once a week. These home visits were an attempt to promote continuity with the summer sessions and to get parents to engage children in cognitively stimulating experiences. A psychiatric consultant advised home visitors and summer school teachers about activities that would stimulate emotional growth for the children; he also guarded against possible ill effects of the intervention program.

Results so far show that the experimental group had a significant gain in I.Q. scores compared to the controls, with the greatest gain obtained for the experimental group that ran a year longer. Similar results were found for experimental versus control groups on the Peabody Picture Vocabulary Test and on the Illinois Test of Psycholinguistic Ability, although with these tests the two experimental groups did not show a difference from each other. When the project children entered public school, they did "conspicuously better" than the controls on entrance tests, including tests of reading readiness, "approximating" scores of ordinary children. Observational data on behavior changes apparently support the test results. Follow-up through the early grades is planned.

NUTRITIONAL STAFF

The studies in this survey generally used a multidisciplinary approach. However, while they mention the need to change health practices, most have provided neither a *specialized* staff nor a concerted program for such change. Two studies differ from all others in that they incorporated a nutritional program.

Pine School, State University of Iowa. This study appears to have been the first preschool program specifically designed to offset retardation engendered by "cultural deprivation." It paralleled the style of the North Point Program in that it dealt intensively with relatively few multiproblem families and their children, more than one child from a family was in school during the project period, and social workers visited the homes. However, it differed from our own study in that children were kept in school for a longer time during the day, and the treatment staff included home economists.

The program began in 1957, under the directorship of Carr, as a joint project of the State University's College of Education and Department of Pediatrics (29, 33). It contained 43 "endogenous, mentally retarded, deprived children" coming from 20 "inadequate, deprived, multiproblem families." The aims were to record the development of these children for a period of at least five years, and to make an interdisciplinary effort at environmental manipulation which would not involve disruption of the family unit and which would alter the unfavorable course of development in these children. The criteria for selection of children were chronological age between 3 and 6, I.Q. between 50 and 80, no evidence that would suggest organic etiology of the retardation, some evidence of mental retardation in at least one other family member, and parents in the lower socioeconomic status group.

All but two families had been known to the county welfare office prior to their acceptance, and 13 of the 20 families received public assistance some time during the project. Two of the fathers were classified as semiskilled, and the rest were unskilled. The staff portrayed the parents as lonely people, socially alienated, needing acceptance, and having a desire for social participation if acceptance were felt. The parents seemed to be aware of middle-class symbols and had some desire to emulate them, but in addition they came to the project with strong evidence of hostility, frustration, feelings of rejection, and an awareness of their social inadequacy and resultant dependency. These characteristics presumably determine the parental responses to children and result in transmitting to the next generation a repetition of these same social inadequacies. What follows is the project's observation of the child-rearing practices of their families:

The most striking characteristic . . . is the inconsistency with which the parents manage the children. They rarely promote acceptance of any general principles of behavior or of ethical conduct. It is obvious that children are permitted to behave very differently, for example, when they are home alone with the mother and when there are visitors. At times the presence of the father demands a different pattern of behavior. The mother often expresses her awareness of other social values by direct means, telling the children that their teachers will expect certain behavior, or that the "cops" will not permit certain acts. The children are more apt to be punished for "getting caught" or annoying an authority figure than for committing an act which is wrong or generally disapproved. If there is a consistent approach, it would seem to be inculcation of the theory that adult displeasure should be avoided in any given situation. It would appear that children are rarely rewarded for a correct response per se. The attitude of the adult present becomes an important variable in every situation. This seems to promote, in the children, attitudes of servility toward authority figures, a reluctance to respond spontaneously, and a general feeling of uncertainty about expectations. (33)

The treatment program aimed at establishing orthodox routines that normally already would exist for middle-class children. "[To] succeed in competition with middle-class children in a school taught by middle-class teachers, some commonality of experience with their competition seems imperative" (33). The school had two classes of 10 children each. A full-time teacher was assigned to each room; assistants and student teachers were added when available. The children were picked up at their homes between 8:30 and 9:00 A.M. and returned between 3:00 and 3:30 P.M. They were offered milk three times a day and a high-protein, low-carbohydrate lunch. The nursery program provided stimulation and experiences designed to increase the children's fund of general information, familiarity with the elementary tools of learning and language, acquaintance with the atmosphere of a school, and an opportunity to develop the ability to form more adequate interpersonal relationships.

Public health nurses, pediatricians, and home economists all cooperated in the care of children and their families. Two part-time social workers assisted the families to go to community agencies and provided casework when community agencies were not available or were unable to be used. Toward the end of the program the social workers mainly acted as consultants for community agencies, helping them take on a more active role with these families. The home economists and nurses met twice a month with groups of mothers. They gave instruction on child management, health procedures, and homemaking. In addition, the home economists visited mothers at home and helped design a program of marketing and budgeting, so as to improve nutrition.

The results show a significant gain in I.Q. scores for children in the program. The major gain was accomplished during the child's first year, although a group of children who came into the program at a relatively young age seemed to derive benefit over both years.

Of 27 children who had left the school at the time of the published report, 16 entered regular public school with satisfactory adjustment. Nine of these 16 were reading in the highest or the middle reading group of a three-group system. Three of the 27 children attended regular school but had special programs (to counteract slight retardation); 6 attended classes for the mentally retarded; and 2 children became emotionally disturbed and did not attend regular schools.

Hawaii Department of Mental Health. This study by Dean and Yanagi (9) was started in 1961 for children of "subcultural" backgrounds, that is, from families that were below average in socioeconomic and nutritional ratings. The children ranged in age from 3 to 5½ years. All were free of organic or emotional complications but had been shown to be functioning below their intellectual potential. Intervention was of two types: in-home and in-group training of families by a social worker and a nutritionist, and in-group training of children. This intervention continued for three years, but social work and nutritional help ended after the second year. A unique feature of this program is that matched control groups as well as experimental subgroups were designed to assess the contribution of combined family and child intervention, in contrast to child intervention alone.

NEGRO POPULATIONS

In several programs the study population consists wholly or largely of Negro families. As already mentioned, this was the case for the Murfreesboro and for the University of North Carolina programs. In addition, three other studies fall into this class. We suspect there may be more, but most of the studies reviewed did not specify the ethnicity of their population.

Howard University. This project for "culturally deprived" preschool children and their parents began in 1964 under Kittrell's direction (22). The experimental group consisted of 38 three-year-olds and their parents, while 67 three-year-olds and their parents comprised a control group. The nursery experience specifically was designed to foster school readiness. A parent-education program was aimed at encouraging parents to support the readiness skills developed through the nursery program. Evaluation included standardized situations, teacher ratings, tests and observations, and focused on changes in the children as well as parental modification of home and child management.

Ypsilanti Public Schools. This community program was started by Weikart in 1962 (36), with a population of Negro preschool children. All children were diagnosed as having functional mental retardation, presumably a result of their "culturally deprived" environment. The children attended a nursery school with an experimental program of cognitive enrichment. Parents were visited in their homes once a week by teachers, who encouraged them to foster this type of enrichment. In addition, groups of parents met regularly to discuss mutual problems. Children were tested and parents interviewed. A matched control group of children was tested, their parents interviewed, and the children sent to non-experimental nursery schools. All children will be followed up into the early grades.

New Haven Public Schools. Started in 1963 under the directorship of Phillips (30, 31), this program tries to provide "culturally deprived" children with experiences needed for them "to approach the regular school situation with some assurance of success." Its population is 85 percent Negro, 5 percent Puerto Rican, and 10 percent white. Sixteen program centers, serving 480 children, currently are in operation, with more to be started. One hundred and fifty children and families already have been served. The preschool experience runs one year, with the children entering the city's kindergartens the following year. The nursery school provides sensory-rich experiences and an ordered and structured environment, within the context of established nursery school practice. In addition, counselors mediate between children, parents, and teachers, to strengthen home-management procedures and to stimulate a parental desire for education of their children. Parent counseling is continued up until third grade in school, and the teachers are asked to participate in this. Prolonging counseling after the end of the nursery program seems to be unique to this project.

Preliminary results (31) show that children tested after four months in nursery school had a significant increase in I.Q. scores. Qualitatively, many children starting out with scores in the "retarded" range scored in the "average" range after four months. Behavioral changes also were noted in the direction of greater ability to communicate, more spontaneity, and more assertiveness and/or negativism. Considering the passivity often found with these children, the staff interpreted even negativism as a positive development.

PUBLIC SCHOOL PROGRAMS

As is already apparent, many of these projects are being run in conjunction with, or directly by, public schools. We have reviewed, under other categories, Murfreesboro, New Haven, and Ypsilanti. In addition, several other school systems have initiated special programs. We closely followed one of these (Boston) and know that although it was provided for children in poverty areas, its classes had only a very few children (if any) as handicapped as the ones that will be described in Chapter 4. The enrollment procedures required motivation and initiative on the part of the families, while our disorganized families needed modified intake procedures and considerable work in the homes to overcome their resistance and to make it possible for them to allow their children to participate (see Chapter 7.) It is difficult to say how many other project populations differed from ours in this important respect.

Boston School Department.   This program, directed by Beahan, was started in 1964 in conjunction with a community agency, Action for Boston Community Development (12). Its aim was to improve the academic outlook for "culturally deprived and disadvantaged" children, who ordinarily would fail in school. One hundred and sixty children, 80 from each of two economically and socially disadvantaged areas, were chosen for study. Half were randomly assigned to a control group and half were sent to nursery school. Four classes were operated, with 20 children per class. Control and experimental groups will continue to be tested up through their third grade in public school.

The nursery program ran two hours per day and used the ordinary curriculum as its base. Special group activities were introduced to foster language development, sensory awareness, muscle control and coordination, and social behavior. In addition, children who were ready for further experience were taken aside, singly or in small groups, for special activities and simple games. Teachers were responsible for holding conferences with parents as a regular part of the program. Home visits and group meetings helped to air feelings about aspirations for children, child-rearing practices, and other concerns. Mothers were encouraged to visit classes and to volunteer as assistant teachers.

Baltimore Public Schools. This preschool program for four-year-old, "culturally deprived" children began in 1962 by Brunner and Furno (3, 34). Their nursery schools placed particular stress on individual differences, as well as on the need for firsthand experiences, for sensory-rich opportunities, and for language and self-concept development. The program also assisted parents to understand and accept responsibility for their children's education, and facilitated communication between the school system and other community agencies working with these children and their families.

Englewood (N.J.) Public Schools. This program, directed by Fischel, was designed to improve language, cognitive, and motor skills by introducing manipulative and creative experiences into a nursery school setting (13). The school ran four days a week for two hours a day. The fifth day was devoted to parent-staff conferences. Eight groups of children, with a maximum of 20 per group, were serviced. The groups were not exclusively culturally deprived, but were a "cross section" of all socioeconomic and ethnic groups in the community.

Pennsylvania Public Schools. This program, started in 1963 under Hartman, is operated in cooperation with local school boards as well as the Department of Public Welfare and Health (5,

6). The program offers enrichment in language development, cognitive skills, perceptual development, and self-image for children from "educationally and culturally disadvantaged" families. Criteria for these families are semiskilled or unskilled occupation and one parent a school dropout. Two quite different and structurally independent programs are being operated: one is a regular academic-year nursery school, coordinated with special programs up through the third grade; the other is a series of three summer-school programs, starting the summer prior to nursery school and running through the summer after kindergarten.

The summer school runs for six weeks each summer. In the fall following the first summer session, the teachers spend afternoons working in the home with parents and children, or at a school site with groups of parents. Since the summer-school children do not attend nursery schools in the fall, but do attend kindergartens a year later, the work with parents the first winter helps to acquaint them with the materials their children will encounter the following year. Social workers help develop inter-agency cooperation on treatment plans and assist teachers with their home visits and with their group meetings. This summer-school program continues to serve several hundred children.

The academic-year program appears to have involved 20 children in each of two classes, with another group of 40 children serving as controls. This program did not depart radically from traditional nursery school curricula, although more stress was placed on "promoting greater environmental awareness, sharpening various sensory qualities, improving language fluency, and enhancing social attitudes." Apparently, these families also were served by social workers. An ambitious program of yearly testing and evaluation is planned for all program children, with special comparison testing for the 40 experimental and 40 control cases. The project will attempt to measure change in family functioning, and to follow children as they enter the primary grades.

PROGRAM VARIATIONS

In the four preceding sections we have described all of the programs falling within our review criteria. One additional feature that differentiates the various studies is the use of experimental comparison groups to evaluate alternative strategies. The Murfreesboro project systematically varied length of exposure to their program by having some groups go a year longer, which meant entering the children a year younger. The Hawaii study also varied the length of exposure for the children, but this was achieved by having some stop a year later rather than entering a year younger. They apparently also varied the type of program, such as preschool experience with or without work with the children's parents. The Pennsylvania project, as explained in detail in the section immediately above, ran two quite different programs in order to answer the economic question of just how expensive a remedy is needed to produce at least minimally adequate results. The University of North Carolina program, with a similar objective, sent only a part of the experimental preschool group to the experimental elementary school program.

Of course, variations such as these are hardly possible when a small group of families is being studied intensively, as was the case for the Pine School group or for our own project. However, with many more projects now beginning to process hundreds of children (although many of these projects may contain relatively few children from hard-core multiproblem families), it would seem that program variations would become feasible as well as useful.

REFERENCES

1. Baughman, E. Earl. Personal communication, 1965.
2. Baughman, Emmett E., Dahlstrom, William G., and Long, Eugene R. Abstracts. In Braun, Samuel J. The Nursery School

in Preventive Mental Health: A Listing of Bibliography and Programs (mimeographed), 1964.

3. Brunner, Catherine, and Furno, Orlando.   Abstract.   In Braun, Samuel J.   The Nursery School in Preventive Mental Health: A Listing of Bibliography and Programs (mimeographed), 1964.

4. Caldwell, Bettye M., and Richmond, Julius B.   Programmed Day Care for the Very Young Child. *Journal of Marriage & the Family* 26:481, 1964.

5. Commonwealth of Pennsylvania, Department of Public Instruction.   The Pre-School and Primary Education Project (mimeographed), 1964.

6. Commonwealth of Pennsylvania, Department of Public Instruction, Welfare and Health.   A Comprehensive and Long Range Attack on the Drop-Out Problem: Pre-school and Primary Education Project, Progress Report (mimeographed), 1964.

7. Cook, Marianne.   Personal correspondence, 1965.

8. Cook, Marianne, and Doerring, Paul L.   The Teacher in a Therapeutic Pre-School Project (mimeographed).

9. Dean, Sidney I., and Yanagi, Garret H.   Abstract.   In U.S. Department of Health, Education, and Welfare, Welfare Division, Children's Bureau, Clearinghouse for Research in Child Life, 1964.

10. Deutsch, Martin.   Nursery Education. *Journal of Nursery Education* 18:191, 1963.

11. Deutsch, Martin.   Facilitating Development in the Pre-School Child. *Merrill-Palmer Quarterly of Behavior and Development* 10:249, 1964.

12. Edwards, Esther P.   An Interim Report on the Boston School Department: ABCD Pre-Kindergarten Program (mimeographed), 1965.

13. Fischel, Maxine.   Abstract.   In Braun, Samuel J.   The Nursery School in Preventive Mental Health: A Listing of Bibliography and Programs (mimeographed), 1964.

14. Furman, Erna.   Treatment of Under-Fives by Way of Their Parents. *Psychoanalytic Study of the Child* 12:250, 1957.

15. Gray, Susan W., and Klaus, Rupert A.   An Experimental Preschool Program for Culturally Deprived Children (mimeographed), 1964.

16. Hess, Robert D.   Educability and Rehabilitation. *Journal of Marriage & the Family* 26:422, 1964.

17. Hess, Robert D.   Maternal Teaching Style, Social Class and Educability (mimeographed), 1964.

18. Hunt, J. McVicker.   The Psychological Basis for Using Pre-school

Enrichment as an Antidote for Cultural Deprivation. *Merrill-Palmer Quarterly of Behavior and Development* 10:209, 1964.

19. Hunt, J. McVicker. The Implications of Changing Ideas on How Children Develop Intellectually. *Children* 11:83, 1964.

20. Katan, Anny. Personal correspondence, 1965.

21. Katan, Anny. The Nursery School as a Diagnostic Help to the Child Guidance Clinic. *Psychoanalytic Study of the Child* 14:250, 1959.

22. Kittrell, Flemmie P. Abstract. In U. S. Department of Health, Education and Welfare, Welfare Division, Children's Bureau, Clearinghouse for Research in Child Life, 1964.

23. Klaus, Rupert A., and Gray, Susan W. The Early Training Project. In Proceedings of Section II, Division of School Psychologists of the American Psychological Association: Today's Educational Programs for Culturally Deprived Children (mimeographed), 1962.

24. Long, Eugene R. Abstract. In U. S. Department of Health, Education, and Welfare, Welfare Division, Children's Bureau, Clearinghouse for Research in Child Life, 1964.

25. Marans, Allen E. The Prevention of Culturally Determined Mental Retardation (mimeographed), 1964.

26. Neubauer, Peter B., Alpert, Augusta, and Bank, Barbara. The Nursery Group Experience as Part of a Diagnostic Study of a Preschool Child. In Esman, Aaron H. (Ed.), *New Frontiers in Child Guidance*. New York: International Universities Press, 1958.

27. Neubauer, Peter B., and Beller, Emanuel K. The Differential Contribution of the Clinician and the Educator to the Diagnosis of the Pre-Latency Child. In Krugman, Morris (Ed.), *Orthopsychiatry and the School*. New York: American Orthopsychiatric Association, 1958.

28. Olson, James L., and Larson, Richard. A Pilot Study Evaluating One Method of Teaching Culturally Deprived Kindergarten Children (mimeographed), 1962.

29. Parsons, Mabel. A Home Economist in Service to Families with Mental Retardation. *Children* 7:184, 1960.

30. Phillips, Adelaide. The Pre-Kindergarten Program of New Haven, Connecticut (mimeographed), 1964.

31. Psychologist's Report, Pre-Kindergarten Program of New Haven, Connecticut (mimeographed), 1965.

32. Riese, Hertha. *Heal the Hurt Child*. Chicago: University of Chicago Press, 1962.

33. Roll, Marlin H. A Study of Retarded Young Children. In Na-

tional Conference on Social Welfare, *Social Work Practice*. New York: Columbia University Press, 1962.

34. Spodek, Bernard. Poverty, Education, and the Young Child. *Educational Leadership* 22:593, 1965.

35. Strodbeck, Fred L.   Progress Report (mimeographed), 1963.

36. Weikart, David P.   Abstracts. In Braun, Samuel J. The Nursery School in Preventive Mental Health: A Listing of Bibliography and Programs (mimeographed), 1964; and in U.S. Department of Health, Education, and Welfare, Welfare Division, Children's Bureau, Clearinghouse for Research in Child Life, 1964.

2

OVERVIEW OF THE
NORTH POINT PROJECT

Eleanor Pavenstedt

OPENING PHASES, 1955-1959

Our awareness of the existence of the kinds of families
that were selected for the project, of their serious self-perpetuating pathology, and of our failure to deal with them appropriately,
sprang from consultative psychiatric work in a women's reformatory, child-guidance work in two clinics bordering on a slum area
—one in a city hospital—and finally from a special teaching program for fourth-year medical students.* In the latter, comprehensive care was given to women selected at random from a city hospital prenatal clinic. The students explored the socioeconomic, medical, and psychological aspects of the women's lives in their homes
and in the clinic. The finding, that in attempting to assist them
beyond our four-month program we were repeatedly blocked by the
inability of the families with the most stringent needs to cooperate
with social agencies, finally brought home to us the necessity of
initiating some new and different way of reaching these families
and particularly their children—children who, by the very fact
that they were born into one of these disorganized, socially mal-

* Supported by the Commonwealth Fund.

adapted families, appeared doomed to follow in the footsteps of their antecedents.

In 1955 the work of the initial phase was designed to determine whether women who had been cared for during the student teaching program but were not sufficiently motivated to secure help actively would accept it if it were to be brought into their homes.

Although the project was undertaken to explore the possibility of rendering service to these families of young children, we were impelled to do this work just as much by our interest in deviant child development. In order to discover how to adapt child-guidance procedure and techniques to deal with this pathological group of families, we needed to know practically everything about them: how they lived, what their attitudes were beyond the initial distrust and suspicion toward middle-class people, what (if any) aspirations they had for themselves and for their children, how they talked, who their close associates were, what their immediate and extended family ties were, what degree of maturity they had achieved, what particular areas had remained at an infantile and/or childish level, and how all this affected their child-rearing practices. In order to work constructively with the children we needed to know what age-inappropriate experiences they had been exposed to, what support they received from their parents and older siblings in times of special stress, whether and how much personal attention, affection, and education they received at home. We really wanted to know about them and their development from pregnancy on, as we were simultaneously carrying out a longitudinal study of child development in a much more stable working-class family group. We seriously doubted that the mothers of this project would tolerate bimonthly observations of themselves with their infants and toddlers; but we had no idea, when we began, how extremely difficult it was going to be to study the development of these grossly deprived children. During the opening phases of this project the family workers were so engrossed in the needs and demands, the constant crises of the adults in the families, that we could only form a sketchy—and, as it turned out, much too optimistic—impression of the children.

From October 1955 to August 1957. During the initial phase of this work our staff consisted of only one full-time worker, provided by the Division of Mental Hygiene of the Massachusetts Department of Mental Health. He was assisted by consultants in child psychiatry, psychology, and social work. We found a man, with a personal background of work in a protective agency (the Society for the Prevention of Cruelty to Children) and a family background in probation, already familiar with the group of families about which we were concerned. Going into homes, unsolicited, was at that time called "aggressive casework"! Administratively his introduction to the families was probably optimum, as he either joined the staff of the teaching project at the city hospital—which was well, although warily, accepted by most of them—or declared himself a follow-up worker from that program. In keeping with a principle in psychotherapy, he took the families where he found them and allowed them to use him as they wished, within reality limits. His personal devotion to every one of his clients was quite unusual. It was possible for him, eventually, to gain access to their homes and to become acquainted with their lives. He saw more than they were usually willing to expose to an outsider from middle-class society, and a social worker. Other members of the family besides the mother soon entered into a relationship with him. It was possible to establish a casework relationship with most of the families followed intensively, and some gradually called upon the social worker for assistance, at times on their own initiative. A few made regular office visits. Furthermore, it was possible to implement a few preventive mental health principles because of the social worker's presence on the scene at certain crucial moments as a result of his continual close contact with several members of the family. He was of assistance to some of the older children, but the picture of the younger ones, who were of greatest interest to us, remained dim.

From September 1957 to July 1959. During this period the staff was augmented by another full-time social work position, a part-time social work supervisor, a public health nurse with special training in mental health, and a half-time psychologist. The child psychiatry consultant remained and was joined by a social scientist. Quarters were provided by an old and respected settlement house in the heart of the slum. In order to test out a less sophisticated avenue of approach, since hospitals as a source of referrals might be accessible to very few family workers elsewhere, we now began to solicit referrals from the Department of Public Welfare, from the housing authority of a housing project, and from the home medical service of a private hospital. In each case great attention was given to the process of referral and transfer.

A special scheme, set in motion at that time, concerned the use of multidisciplinary personnel. We encouraged workers from each discipline to learn and borrow particularly appropriate concepts and skills from the other disciplines. For this reason several staff members were assigned to the same family. Sometimes each one focused his attention on a different member of the family; sometimes it was the nature of the current problem that called for the particular skills of a certain profession. In view of inevitable turnover of staff, it seemed essential that the affiliation of the families to us be, as far as possible, to the entire project staff. Parties for all of the families and the entire staff, inaugurated during this phase, were planned to promote the families' relationships to the project rather than to a single worker.

An interesting example demonstrates the impact of one profession on the other when both are in the home at the same time. In one of the families the social worker had observed that the baby lay in his crib in diapers that were soaked and soiled, and that he was surrounded by flies. She had not felt that it was within her role to change the diaper. One day when the nurse was at the home with her, bandaging the mother's leg, she experienced not a moment's hesitation in changing the baby's diaper. Such concrete experiences of active help were of the greatest importance in dealing with this group.

It became current practice to accompany family members to medical facilities and to interpret medical recommendations. It was quite a revelation to some mothers to see the nurse being given such summary treatment—being kept waiting, for instance—as she had been accustomed to receiving herself. Heretofore this had been just another proof of her worthlessness.

In these families, where actual needs were so pressing, the workers made every attempt to meet those that were realistic by directing the parents to the appropriate agencies and mediating between the latter and the families.

Another concrete form of help was simple education about pregnancy, childbirth, the different developmental stages, balanced
food for a family, healthy disciplinary attitudes, and so on ad infinitum. We do not want to give the impression, however, that most of
the talking was done by the staff. Although intrafamilial communication was usually so disrupted, the family members, when they
began to feel secure with the staff, poured out their woes and needs
in a never-ending stream. So much so that it was impossible for the
workers really to observe the children and to familiarize themselves with them at different ages.

Findings of the Opening Phases.   The children were tested during both initial phases. It is noteworthy that *we really did not
grasp the marked and general developmental retardation and deviance of the group from testing alone.* In fact, the children who
were able to cooperate with the tester, who in turn adapted to their
special needs, usually accumulated a score that gave them at least
an average intelligence rating.

Some of the mental health principles that we invoked for our
work during the opening phases with the few children we handled
individually—that is, individual therapy in connection with a very
recent trauma to prevent undue repression, denial, projection, and
displacement—proved to be far too ambitious. We came to understand the reasons for our failure in the demonstration phase when
we had a nursery school where we saw that the children had a very
tenuous ego development. The requirement of tolerating the pain
and anxiety subsequent to a trauma was far more than they were
capable of. (It is precisely this sort of thing that psychiatrists need
to know in order to work with a child on a pediatric service or in
consultation with an agency.)

We grasped the impact of separation anxiety during this early
phase, but did so more fully in regard to the parents than the children. We saw mothers whose children had gone away behave as
though the children no longer existed; we wondered whether they
failed to recognize that people out of sight continued to exist (the
concept of object constancy). But we had such brief and widely
spaced contacts with the children while they were away from home
that we did not learn how separation affected them. What we were

unaware of was the pervasive use of the mechanism of denial that we observed over and over again in both mothers and children when the latter first came to nursery school.

When we began the North Point Demonstration Project in 1960, we brought to it a good understanding of the adults, partly from our direct experience with them and partly from the vast literature on narcissistic or borderline personalities (that is, borderline between neurotic character disorders and psychosis). Following is a summary of what we learned:

1. The initial distrust and suspicion can be dealt with by perseverant evidence of reliability, but never totally allayed.

2. These people think concretely with little grasp of abstract concepts.

3. Consequently acts have far more meaning for them than words.

4. In their great deprivation they are need-oriented and hence almost completely egocentric. (Therefore we planned not to tell them initially that our major interest was in their children.)

5. They tend to have a craving for possessions; a woman's children are often her only possessions and are clung to accordingly.

6. The boundaries of the self seem fluid, so that a child might be experienced as part of the self and separation then amounts to an amputation.

7. Their lives are dominated by impulse.

8. Their aggression is poorly modified. (Probably their early libidinal development was stunted so that love was not available to fuse with aggression.)

9. They are hampered by phobic restriction—which we also found in the stable working-class group. It often impedes a mother's active pursuit of health measures both for the children and herself, and is usually interpreted by health personnel as neglect or lack of cooperation.

10. They are overcome by a feeling of isolation. This may lead to uncontrolled sexual behavior as the only means of making a contact.

11. They occasionally indulge in fantasies of intellectual prowess and cultural interests to overcompensate for their deep feelings of inferiority.

However, our endeavors to help them become more organized and trusting were largely based on the intuitive ability of the individual staff member. We learned that besides going out to these people in their homes, we had, in order to cross class barriers, to share personal experiences with them, exchange information about food and clothing sales, recipes, and our own attempts to deal with children. This sort of exchange allowed them gradually to feel genuinely accepted.

Many of the traits observed in the adults can be linked to their early emotional deprivation. In order to alleviate this process in the children it was obviously essential to move them at as early an age as possible into an environment where there were trustworthy, nurturing, responsive adults. Furthermore, we recognized the importance of brief separations so that both mother and child could learn that they remained whole, continued to exist, and would be reunited.

THE NORTH POINT DEMONSTRATION PROJECT, 1960–1965

Whereas we had learned about the psychosocial characteristics of the parents, the development of the children and their level of functioning at any age remained obscure. Our staff had observed them drifting about the house, seldom engrossed in any activity, drawn to the visitor, courting his or her favor and readily climbing into any available lap.

The demonstration project was undertaken to explore the personality make-up of preschool children from disorganized families. Our purpose was to evolve methods for supporting and building upon any achievements, for strengthening adaptive functions that would be required upon entry into essentially middle-class schools, for gradually dispelling the fear and suspicion of people in authority, for buttressing the usual development of children between 3 and 5.

In order to facilitate this the directorship of the project was given over to a child psychiatrist who added to it a nursery school teacher and nursery school facilities. A research anthropologist

joined the staff to study the impact of the milieu on family functioning and child development. The psychologist's time was
doubled to permit exploration of early child development in the
home. An experienced social worker, skilled in the assessment of
interpersonal process, directed the work with the families.

Referrals and Selections.   Since the staff had been cut to a minimum during the year preceding the demonstration phase, several
families were lost. Others no longer met our age criteria for their
children. Consequently the selection process had to be revived.
The disappointment of referring agencies over the inability of the
project to accept new families during the previous year and a half
had to be recognized and dealt with. Repeated personal reaching
out to directors and staff members of referring agencies, willingness to accept any referral for a thorough intake study during
which feedback to the agency was sustained, and finally a conference in the presence of both directors eventually set the referral
process in motion again.

Once a family fitted our criteria, we were not concerned how
problem-ridden it was, as long as our intake study did not uncover
circumstances that made it imperative for the children's welfare to
separate them from their parents. Serious difficulties arose because
disorganized hard-core families are seldom identified in the community as long as their children are preschoolers. Only four of the
twenty-five community resources referred families that turned out
to meet our criteria. Seventy percent of these were referred by the
nursing group—public health and visiting nurses' organizations
who followed the practice of keeping in touch with families in
need. Contact with the referring agency was maintained throughout the duration of the project in the expectation that the families
would revive their ties and work more constructively with community agencies upon termination.

The Work of the Staff.   Besides these problems concerning referrals and selections, it became apparent that the project staff was
unconsciously prolonging the period of preparation for their involvement with the families. It was only after the relationship between this reluctance and their anxiety about the difficulty of the

uncharted character of the work ahead was made explicit and was explored that the workers began to look actively for referrals.

Daily morning work meetings and weekly interdisciplinary conferences were important in sustaining morale and counteracting the frustration and discouragement that is inevitably involved in providing service to multiproblem families. The need for open communication and sharing had to be constantly reaffirmed, with some members more able and willing than others to participate in this process.

The next hurdle was overcoming the resistance of the families to bringing their young children to nursery school. The cooperative effort of the teachers and the family workers in dealing with this issue will be described at some length in Chapter 7.

Soon after the nursery school began to operate, the deviant behavior of the children became apparent. The importance of delineating the developmental characteristics of the children now assumed first place since we had to identify and understand the source of their strengths, retardations, and deviancies in order to evolve methods and techniques to assist them. Our nursery school took on a therapeutic character far beyond our anticipation.

Work with the families also progressed in the direction of further evaluation of the adults' functioning as well as the development of a clearly conceptualized structured approach to them.

Developmental observations in the home were, as foreseen, difficult to carry out. Our original plan to experiment with modifications and cross-fertilization of the roles and techniques of the different disciplines also had to be abandoned. Both of these attempts met with a certain rigidity of disciplinary indentifications and some resistance to intrusion into their accepted fields of activity.

The presence of the anthropologist at our staff meetings contributed to our awareness of danger and disorganization, lack of purpose and shiftlessness in the environment. His suggestion that the project represented to our families a miniature community to which they gradually related, in contrast to their previous absence of ties to any culture or institution, led to our conscious efforts to present them with the opportunity of making this encounter as frequently as possible.

Testing. Psychological testing* of 28 children was inconclusive due to the difference in chronological age when tested, the variable number of tests completed per testing session, and variable frequencies and types of longitudinal tests administered. Among them were the Stanford-Binet Form L.M., Merrill-Palmer, Draw-A-Person, Children's Apperception, Rorschach and Thematic Apperception tests. Many children at times were difficult to test because of "short attention span and distractibility, hyperactivity, acute separation anxieties and other fears, needs to control and manipulate the adult, negativism and other aggressive behaviors."

However, *the majority of the children "were judged† to have average intellectual potential with only a few at either higher or lower potential levels. For a significant number it appeared likely that everyday functioning was below the level attained on formal testing."*

Their willingness to accompany the examiner was related in part to the stage of their relationship to the teacher. Cooperation "could not be depended upon due in part to a tendency to regress rapidly" under the stress of performing upon demand. Willingness to go with the examiner and subsequent testability were also affected by "the extent and manner in which they were involved in one of the repeated family crises characterizing their home life."

The finding, frequently reported in the literature, of test items involving language and thought scoring lower than those involving performance skills was not substantiated throughout the sample. However, there was "deviant instability of test function throughout our sample in both these functional categories."

"Cognitive processes tended to be literal, unimaginative, and poorly organized to varying degrees among the children. One or more of the capacities to utilize symbolic representation for purposes of labeling objects, designating their characteristics, and noting similarities, differences, or interrelationships among objects tended to be unstable and/or immature and/or defective for the developmental level. . . . In a significant number of cases there was a tendency for memory to range from poor to only fair."

---

* The following section has been adapted by the editor from a report by Jane Hulek, Ph.D.
† The tests were administered by Amelia A. Blackwell, Ph.D.

The sensory motor drawing tasks "tended to trigger too readily mobilized regressions from age-appropriate concepts to amorphous primitive ones."

"As one method of coping with environmental stimuli, some children seemed at times preoccupied with 'not looking,' manifested by shutting their eyes, . . . defining the function of eyes as closing them, threats to 'erase' anxiety-provoking test pictures, threats to turn the light off so the examiner 'won't see nothing,' refusal to look at test material, throwing 'awful-looking' test material on the floor, and so on. In some cases not listening also served to shut out the overwhelming environment." The "longitudinal data suggested that this blocking mode of defense through 'not looking' and/or 'not listening' was in some cases the forerunner of coping with the environment by 'not knowing' and thus contributory to the arrest of cognitive function. . . . Attempted mastery of both vague and specific fears through flight, manifested by general evasiveness toward outside objects and people, was a common mode of adaptation."

TERMINATION OF THE PROJECT

Unfortunately the work with the families and our concentration on trying to remedy, via the nursery school, the ill effects of their environment on the children was drastically reduced after only three years of effort. With the accentuation of interest, nationally, on the poverty group and particularly on the preschool education of children, pressure to share our experiences with others and to communicate them in writing precluded further deepening of understanding and exploration of concepts.

The basic plans for working with each family and each child emerged in supervision, staff conferences, and in discussions based on our day-to-day experiences with our subjects. Every member of the staff contributed to our speculations and innovations which were tested and re-examined before they were eventually formulated. The development of theoretical formulations and educational-therapeutic techniques that crystallized out from the shared observations and ideas of our clinically well-trained staff, from six different disciplines of the social sciences, proved to be an exciting and rewarding experience. Ours was an experimental approach and our findings require confirmation and validation.

3

THE SOCIOCULTURAL SETTING*

Maurice R. Stein

I T I S C L E A R that the North Point neighborhood has been a slum and a skid row for a long time. Research carried out in 1898 (3) showed that the slum was holding its own against the skid row. This was a neighborhood where first-generation immigrant Jews, Irish, and Italians, as well as Negroes, coexisted with the skid-row bums who were far more like the American hobo described by Nels Anderson (1) than the present-day crowd of lonely alcoholics. Along with the hobo this neighborhood has suffered continual loss of status in the community at large, even when compared with its position fifty years ago.

THE EFFECT OF VERTICAL MOBILITY ON THE NEIGHBORHOOD

In historical terms, the increasing dominance of the skid-row bums, and of the older roomers who shade off into the bums, should be stressed, as should the departure from the neighborhood

* Abstracted from Maurice Stein's final report on the demonstration project to the National Institute of Mental Health and arranged by the Editor.

45

of all of the first- and second-generation immigrants who were capable of upward mobility. This filtering-upward process has continued, leaving behind a hard core of depressed Irish, Italian, and Jewish families. Even the Negroes have moved outward, so that only the most hard-pressed remain near the center of skid row. This area then picks up the alcoholic and geriatric failures as they filter down from slightly more privileged regions, while at the same time housing a population that has been filtered out from upwardly mobile immigrants and a population of recent immigrants from the most deprived situations, especially unmarried Southern Negro women and, recently, desperately poor Puerto Ricans.

There are at least two kinds of vertical mobility in the neighborhood. First, there are the families and individuals who organize their affairs in such a way as to get out into better lower-class or even lower-middle-class neighborhoods. At least one ethnic group, the Greeks, have worked out a very stable relationship with an area of second settlement, in this case the Greek community in another part of town. They are tied to these middle-class Greeks in myriad ways. The older Greeks who have chosen to remain do not lose status by staying here and can easily maintain contact with relatives and friends in the area of second settlement. The Greeks show difficulties between generations found among Jews in an earlier period. This is a form of upward vertical mobility. Downward vertical mobility occurs among persons forced into this area, usually for social reasons like alcoholism, extreme poverty, isolation, ethnic discrimination, or any combination of the foregoing.

We can learn something about upward mobility from the families in the child-development project (2), most of whom have moved out of the area since the study began. And we have tentative outward motions from a few of the disorganized families. We would suspect that there will prove to be relationships between the capacity to accomplish developmental tasks as measured by child-development criteria and the capacity to achieve upward mobility since these developmental tasks all point toward autonomy and individuation. The fact that the child-development families could pay for services and could meet appointments demonstrates important social and psychological differences from our families. We suspect that they are families who regard their presence in the neighborhood as a temporary necessity as opposed to families who pretty much accept their position as do multiproblem families.

LIFE ON SKID ROW

The institutional arrangements of skid row dominate the visible life of the neighborhood. The bus, the bars, the pawn shops, the old-clothes shops, the garbage, the broken glass, the broken windows all interweave with and override the islands of "respectability" that appear. One of the reasons for this is simply that skid-row dwellers tend to spend far more time in the streets than most other people. They slop over, so to speak. In fact, the bums tend to regard the entire area as their stamping ground. They are more attached to street corners and to doorways than to any indoor sleeping places that they find. In the fullest sense, they live in the neighborhood.

There are several studies of "bottle groups" in skid row. The pattern of drinking seems to be that of bottle groups in doorways at the lowest level and of regular barroom drinking at higher levels. The bars are quite specialized according to quality, age, and ethnic background as well as according to drinking styles. One bar has regular customers consisting of older men, all semirespectable, all either pensioners or with small incomes, and all dependent upon this bar for their major social contacts. Other bars specialize in family groups while the "tough" bars specialize in bums, sailors on the town, pick-ups, and the like. One can play the numbers in almost any bar in the neighborhood without difficulty if one is known to the bookie or bartender; pick-ups can be arranged in all but the most respectable bars, and various kinds of illegal gambling and dope can be found if one has the proper connections.

Once we recognize the dominance of skid-row alcoholics and older roomers who live on the periphery of the skid-row subculture, we can begin to understand the atmosphere in which other residents of this area live. The opportunities for making money off the bums, or the temptation to go on the bum, are omnipresent, and in fact constitute the most visible and accessible way of living for men, women, and children alike. Yet at the same time, there is

considerable fear of and derogation of the skid-row bums. Unlike
the rest of the city, which can ignore alcoholism as a social problem, in this area alcoholism is both problem and pattern for everyone. The bums constitute a negative reference group for everyone
in the neighborhood. The Old Men's Bar is operated by the owner
and bartenders who pride themselves on keeping the bums out. The
Greeks that we interviewed have profound contempt for other ethnic groups, especially Negroes, but bums are placed in an even
lower category.

The other group in the neighborhood, which as we said earlier
shades off into skid row, is that of old people who room here because it is cheap and can provide undemanding companionship. As
far as contributing to the atmosphere of passivity, poverty, and a
kind of hopeless waiting goes, one must credit the rooming-house
oldsters almost as much as the bums.

THE SOCIAL POSITION OF OUR MULTIPROBLEM FAMILIES

The social context in which our families live can be identified as
one in which a large segment of the visible population engages in
activities alien to the legitimate work life of the middle class. The
bums and the old men spend their time lounging around, the prostitutes and criminals are likely to do the same during the day, and
only storekeepers, bookies, and the police engage in anything that
looks remotely like work.

One great division in the neighborhood would consist of the several kinds of "respectables" on the one hand and the several kinds
of "disreputables" on the other. A main distinction would be the
maintenance of a minimum middle-class front, as well as the maintenance of careful distance from all forms of disreputability. The
bums and some of the old men fall at the lower extreme of the
respectability continuum. The Greeks and a small group of Negro
families living around Circle Park constitute the upper end of the
same continuum. The disorganized families fall somewhere between these two groupings. They maintain a façade of middle-class

respectability in specific areas, but this façade is always cracked at crucial points.

The multiproblem families display the same kinds of oscillating identity themes as do skid-row alcoholics, struggling with at least two of the same image-constellations. They certainly have the tendency to see themselves as Total Failures at various points, and they have the tendency to see themselves as Temporary Victims and Prospective Reformees at others. They present and feel the former when they want sympathy, while they present the latter when they want to convince agency workers that they are doing their best. But far more central to the multiproblem adults is their repertory of familial subidentities.

Another version of the same hypothesis is to state that *members of multiproblem families are people who have never been able to, or have never been allowed to, develop a consistent sense of self or identity; instead they have developed a plurality of inconsistent identities* which accommodate them to differing elements and differing social systems within the skid-row complex.

REFERENCES

1. Anderson, Nels. *Hobo: The Sociology of the Homeless Man* (1923). Chicago; University of Chicago Press, 1961.
2. Pavenstedt, Eleanor. A Comparison of the Child-rearing Environment of Upper-Lower and Very Low-Lower Class Families. *American Journal of Orthopsychiatry* 35:89, 1965.
3. Woods, Robert. *The City Wilderness.* Boston: Houghton Mifflin, 1898.

II

THE CHILDREN

4

DESCRIPTION OF THE CHILDREN
Ilse Mattick

T H E D E S C R I P T I O N that follows is based on observations of the children in the nursery school and at home when they were picked up and returned by the teachers. The small size of the groups gave us the opportunity for careful study and for intensive work with individual children. This was particularly important in view of the fact so little was known about preschool children from multiproblem families. During their brief, often unsuccessful, appearances in day care centers they usually have proven to be too difficult for teachers to feel confident in handling them. Consequently teachers have tended to use their energies to help the more reachable child while these children "get lost" in the class or remain on the periphery. As a group they constitute a large proportion of our preschool dropouts, if indeed they dropped in at all. (Of our 21 nursery school children, 6 had previously made brief, unsuccessful appearances in play groups.) The North Point Project provided an opportunity to really get to know these children.

There is always the danger of approaching such children with a set of assumptions said to be typical of slum children. The notions that they "fight all the time," that "they don't talk," that they have neither the "perceptual skills for listening" nor are able to "pay attention," that they are "peer-oriented," and other notions may all have some validity in specific instances. We found, however, that these can just as easily be shown to be incorrect or even beside the point. To avoid acting upon such stereotyped assumptions we approached the children with an open-minded research attitude.

A NOTE ABOUT DATA COLLECTION

In order to meet the children with an open mind and to objectify our findings we used the following procedures for collecting data about the children's functioning in nursery school:

1. Teachers' reports of individual play sessions (during mother's interview), of visits to school, and of home visits.

2. Daily process recordings by the teachers (consisting of notes taken during session and of detailed observations dictated immediately following each session).

3. Focused observations of individual children and of groups engaged in specific activities.

4. Regularly scheduled all-morning recordings by nonparticipant observer (followed by tape-recorded discussions).

5. Structured daily reports focused on issues relating to interaction of the child with the environment—separation from home, relationship to peers and to teacher, and so on.

6. Behavioral observations by psychologist. (Psychological test reports were analyzed separately from the nursery school data.)

7. Observations by various team members.

These data were summarized as follows:

1. A detailed first-impression summary (after about six weeks of school attendance).

2. A comprehensive progress report (at the end of each school year).

3. Summary reports concerning special events in a child's life.

During the write-up phase of the project all of the nursery school data were organized into categories, encompassing various areas of functioning, that would yield relevant information about the children when they first entered nursery school as well as about the extent and limits of progress made by them over time. The categories relating to nursery school behavior will be used here.

FINDINGS OF PREVALENT TENDENCIES IN THE CHILDREN'S BEHAVIOR*

Because of the necessity of condensing our findings there is a risk of creating misunderstandings through oversimplification. It is important to keep in mind that what follows represents a summary of many findings that point to *prevalent tendencies* in the children's behavior.

A casual look revealed nothing unusual or distinctive about these children. Anyone familiar with children can tell at once that retarded or atypical children look and act differently and need to be taught differently from other children. It is a little more difficult to see the deviance in the children of multiproblem families. To the superficial observer these usually charming, bright-eyed children, with their wide smiles and friendly ingratiating manner, look like any average group of children. On the whole they are responsive to people, usually alert, and many of them are particularly well coordinated.

This may well be the reason why so little concern has been shown about them until later school failure or delinquency focuses attention on them. They do not "look like" children who are in trouble, who need help immediately, who are severely disadvantaged.

However, as soon as we were able to move beyond a superficial impression and watched the quality of the children's interaction with people as well as their daily functioning and play behavior, it became apparent to us that these children were different.

Obviously the children were not all alike. In fact they ranged from the lively, outgoing, boisterous child to the severely withdrawn child, from the adroit manipulator to the type of child who

* I thank the International Universities Press and the Editor of the *Journal of the American Academy of Child Psychiatry* for permission to borrow sections of my article entitled: "Adaptation of Nursery School Techniques to Deprived Children" (16) for this and other chapters in the book.

would look vaguely into space or plead with his eyes. There were those who ranged all over the room unable to contain themselves within any given space, and others whose use of space was restricted to a very small area. Anxiety was reflected by rigid immobility or by random motoric discharge. Similarly, conflicts could be overreacted to or avoided by denial by the various children. In their struggle over toilet training one child turned frequently to the use of paint and of water play, while another pointedly avoided exactly these materials. Thus, as in any nursery school group, there were as many individual characteristics as there were children.

However, while treating them as the individuals they were, we were nonetheless impressed by some common characteristics. Many of these are familiar from the work with disturbed, psychotic, retarded, or institutionalized children, but their particular combination seems to distinguish them from any of these groups and to be peculiar to the children from grossly deprived homes.

It is of particular interest that these shared characteristics differed little along the continuum of chronological age (2½ to 6 years at time of admission to the program). Although age differences were revealed by some aspects of their behavior and by formal testing, their developmental deviancies were strikingly similar, regardless of age.

OUTWARD APPEARANCE
AND MOTOR ABILITIES

As noted above, the children were generally well built and had a sturdy appearance. They had an appealing manner and were superficially friendly. In brief encounters they effectively hid their unhappy, frightened, and defeated attitude toward the world. Yet at times, particularly when they thought themselves unobserved, they also had "old" or frightened expressions, and frequently their smiles were merely a motor automatism.

Their motor coordination showed developmental anomalies. In some ways the children evidenced superior gross motor coordination for their ages. They were sure-footed, quick, and capable of many advanced motor feats. They had an astonishingly good sense of rhythm. Motoric activity was preferred and would produce an occasional expression of fleeting happiness on a child's face. But most of the time it appeared to be primarily a vehicle for tension discharge. Wild motor activity or its opposite, a withdrawal to repetitive, mechanical movements, went hand in hand with an impaired capacity to control or to modulate impulsivity. They showed a lack of motoric caution which resulted in frequent falls and injuries. Thus we had 4-year-old children who would pump themselves on the swing like 8-year-olds, but fell off backwards like 2-year-olds. With remarkable skill they would climb to the top of the jungle gym but they might miss the bottom step and fall on their heads. They seemed to lack any self-protective measures, being careless with the use of their bodies and seemingly not trying to prevent injuries. The most dramatic incident was that of a 3-year-old girl who fell down a flight of stairs and upon being offered a dime by a stranger to repeat this, threw herself down the stairs once more.

Accidents and injuries were usually not accompanied by expressions of appropriate affect. Pain was rarely expressed; even after a severe fall a bland or smiling expression would persist. The children did not easily learn from past disasters. Falling off the top of the climber by letting go did not prevent a subsequent fall off the swing by taking hands off again. In general, their motor activity tended to be diffuse rather than focused. Frustration, pain, displeasure, all would bring aimless movement.

Motoric discharge frequently served to avoid meeting a challenge directly. For instance, instead of working on finding the right space for a puzzle piece, a child would slide under the table and then creep around the room for a long period; another child, about to paint, would pick up the one paint jar that had no brush in it, and, instead of looking for a brush, would quickly set it down and run wildly back and forth through the room.

In summary, the children often used their bodies for diffuse discharge and avoidance, with little focus on the pleasures of attaining mastery.

Viewed superficially, their high motility made the children appear active and aggressive. But when this diffuse motoric discharge was observed closely and its behavioral sequences traced, it became apparent that this was in fact used to avoid facing situations directly. It had the quality of "flight" rather than of "fight." This recognition may point the way to a more understanding handling of "hyperactivity" in deprived children; that is, rather than respond to the motor behavior, we might focus our efforts on helping the child deal actively with whatever it is he does not feel able to handle and is therefore avoiding.

SELF-IMAGE

The contrast between children who are comfortable with themselves, who feel, at least to some degree, worthy, important, capable, successful, and children who predominantly think poorly of themselves, who have difficulties in defining themselves and accepting their capacities and limitations, is very apparent when one observes children's activities in a nursery school room. One can easily pick out the child whose self-esteem needs boosting and who needs assistance in coming to terms with himself. All available data seem to indicate that there is a close connection between environmental deprivations and the ratio of children with poorly developed self-systems in any group. In the accounts of preschool programs for disadvantaged children that have sprung up since our project began (2, 7, 10, 12, 28) there is repeated mention of the children's poor self-image. In day-care centers many more children show signs of insufficiently positive feelings about themselves than in most suburban nursery schools. In our nursery school the behavior of the children indicated strongly that low self-esteem and marked self-devaluation were characteristic of them. They had little confidence in themselves or in their abilities. A lack of pleasure or satisfaction in doing, or in expectation of accomplishment, was a shared characteristic of all the children. There was no discernible drive toward goals or toward completion of anything. A child's standard response to the teacher's attempts to engage him in activities was "You do it—me can't."

Deprecating comments about themselves and their activities were common, such as "I don't know nottin' " or "Dat dopey shit pitsha" (referring to a boy's own picture just completed), accompanied often by curses, particularly those denoting dirt or smell.

We looked for, but could not find, signs of pride in anything the children made. They just walked away without so much as a glance. When a teacher would voice her appreciation or try to comment—for instance, on colors used—the child would look puzzled at best; more often he would disclaim any connection with the activity. A girl who had spent the better part of the morning baking cookies would shrug her shoulders and proclaim she didn't know who made them.

Although young children are generally far more interested in the process of doing than in the end product, most of those who have attained some degree of self-awareness and feel good about themselves express satisfaction with their ability to gain mastery in the use of materials. This is such a common occurrence in nursery schools that frustrating experiences calling forth dissatisfaction and anguish stand out against them. Here, however, it was difficult to judge capacities, as the threshold of frustration appeared to be too low to allow for involvement; self-derogation rather than self-esteem permeated the children's image of themselves. Whenever the children gave indications of having any expectation of themselves, it was of failing, of being incapable. Where other children would rise to a challenge, these children would quickly give up.

There were many signs of confusion on the part of the children about who they were. It was expressed by rapidly shifting behavior between infantile and adult mannerisms, by referring to themselves as "me" or in the third person, often by confusing sexes (even at age 5). Very few children said I when talking about themselves. Instead, a nonspecific her was used frequently, in talking about mother, father, themselves, other children, toys, clothing, anything at all. This nonspecific designation often made it impossible to figure out who or what the child might be referring to. The absence of clear self-differentiation and self-acceptance was demonstrated when a child was confronted with a positive statement about himself. The response to "pretty girl" or "What nice clean hands you have!" (after washing up) would be a puzzled look on the child's face. A direct question such as "Who are you?" would be more likely to bring a reply of "Nobody" or "A baby, no a mommy, the sister, me don't know," than the expected calling out of the child's name or "A girl" or "A boy" or a playful assumption of fantasy roles in which young children usually delight.

Most of these children could not bear to look into the mirror nor identify themselves on a photograph; they tended to avert their eyes. Several children, when led to the mirror by the teacher, would claim to see the teacher only, not themselves.

These manifestations of uncertainty about themselves were constantly reinforced at home. The parents frequently acted in a childlike, dependent, impulsive, irresponsible, need-oriented manner. They tended to compete with their children and to turn to them for support, even asking them to make important decisions. It was hard to tell at times who was the "child" and who was the "parent." In reversing roles with their parents, the children often took on responsibilities far beyond their years. They could go shopping across dangerous intersections, baby-sit, feed babies at night, and engage in a variety of other adult activities. But these advanced feats would be coupled with a delayed ability to perform such self-help items as dressing themselves, even at age 5 or 6. Their role confusions and adaptive use of imitation thus resulted in behavior that was both more and less mature than expected for their age group.

In the nursery school they were constantly overreaching themselves by attempting tasks that young children could not possibly be expected to do. On the other hand they would feel themselves incapable of even the most simple task, well within their reach of accomplishment. One minute they seemed to act like grownups, the next regress into very immature behavior, at neither time being comfortable with themselves. This uncertainty about themselves and the poor judgment of their own capacities seemed to work counter to any motivation for achievement that they may have had. They displayed a kind of pseudo autonomy, a show of professed independence from adult help which always broke down rapidly with the inability to actually trust themselves to achieve on their own. This could not but further undermine the already devalued self-concept of the children.

This devalued self-concept was strikingly shown by the low level of enjoyment. They approached everything with a combination of greed, suspicion, and lack of self-confidence rather than with the expectation of pleasure. It was not only that they could not show pleasure, they seemed devoid of childlike fun. There simply was no exuberance, no enthusiasm, no spontaneity. Laughing, when it did occur, in most cases amounted to shrill hysterical shrieks, denoting hyperexcitement and fear; crying occurred very rarely and might be either soundless or take the form of desperate shrieks or an infantile type of wailing that afforded no relief to the child.

COPING WITH DAILY LIVING

The disparity between precocious ability and helplessness resulting in pseudo as against functional autonomy, was a serious deterrent to effective coping with daily living for the children. A pervasive passivity was their main coping response. They acted upon cues or in direct imitation of others rather than on their own volition. Where other young children use initiative to respond to tasks and challenges of the daily nursery school program, these children proceeded passively, reacting to demands as best they could, without inner commitment, satisfaction, or pride in their ability.

Routines and other situations calling for action on the part of the child were typically carried out in an overly obedient, joyless, submissive, and rigid manner, with only token negativism and with signs of strong fear of retaliation when this negativism appeared. This would be true whether the routines involved toileting, washing hands, putting items of clothing into their cubbies, walking to the playground, or resting on their blankets. More positive interest was shown in routines involving eating; at least here there were signs of excitement, urgency, and inner participation. However, even this situation was marked not by gratification but by dissatisfaction and suspicion. The children were worried that there might not be enough food; and in fact there could not be enough food to assuage an almost bottomless need to be given. Along with the hunger for attention, this greediness for food seemed to be the expression of unsatisfied needs. Most of them paid little heed to what it was they were stuffing into their mouths. Resentment at other children or adults getting any part of the food seemed to outweigh the pleasure of participating in the snack.

Certainly the most difficult of school routines for the children were transitions. It is during these times when the children are terminating one type of activity and preparing for another that a number of tasks need to be taken care of in sequence by them. The teacher is usually occupied with cleaning up. Transitions in nursery school make the highest demand on self-direction and on inner resources. Not surprisingly the children were unable to cope well with these demands. They revealed an inability to direct themselves effectively; they were easily confused and distraught. It was at transition times that the children were most apt to regress, become disoriented, helpless, and "unreasonably" demanding.

Of course, disadvantaged slum children have no monopoly on this difficulty. They share this with other children who for some reason or other are insufficiently self-directed. However, in most nursery schools such children are the exception; here they were the rule.

Because of the children's inability to initiate their own activities or to maintain them on their own, their attempts to act independently were frequently unsuccessful and they would collapse in misery when faced with a task. A child would run away from a block structure if one block did not "fit," instead of searching for a way of placing the block more securely; washing doll dishes, a child would load the entire sink with objects so that she could no longer manipulate any of them and instead of removing some pieces her "coping" would consist of collapsing on the floor and making pathetic infantile sounds. Symbolic representation, such as play and verbalization, did not appear available to the children as an effective coping device.

Auditory and particularly visual hyperalertness, with excessive focusing on the actions of adults, existed alongside their striking unresponsiveness to large segments of the external world. It is generally said that disadvantaged children do not "pay attention." We found that the children paid attention with high concentration to external cues of their own choosing rather than to those items the teacher would have preferred. With suspicious alertness the children were skillful in reading visual cues and readily oriented themselves to the obvious externals of a situation. They had learned to outguess the intentions of adults and were particularly skillful in knowing when to remove themselves speedily to avoid potential pain. This orientation included their ability to mimick, to parrot, and to memorize by rote external observable patterns even though they might not know or understand their substance.

We noticed that the children relied so heavily on external cues, patterns, and safety considerations, that once they had learned to do something one way they could not be taught or persuaded to learn to use another way. They were often perceptually apprehensive, watching and listening intently and reacting impulsively, as if by proper reading of cues they could forestall trouble for themselves. For instance, a teacher walking across the room about to turn on the light would have several children preceding her to the switch. Or the teacher mentioning casually that soon it would be time to have juice would find the children jumping up frantically, pouring juice into cups. It did not have to be words that would signal the teacher's intentions; the children were equally good or even better at "reading" facial expressions, gestures, movements. It was virtually impossible for the teachers to communicate visually with each other without being imitated by several children. Of course, the children often misread cues and reacted inappropriately.

It is very difficult to convey the flavor of these quick responses. An observer described it most accurately when she likened the children's actions to the performance of marionettes. Young children love to imitate and much learning takes place in this way, particularly if these imitations set up a back-and-forth response. With these children, however, neither their eager reaction to what they conceived to be the intention of others nor their token mimicry appeared to provide the pleasure and satisfaction that we have come to associate with the active learning process (20). Imitation served primarily the function of securing and regulating contact. After all, if a child imitates a teacher's smile without knowing what she is smiling about, it is hard to know what kind of information is being transmitted; if the child picks up and merely carries about the scissors that the teacher was about to reach for to cut out a picture, this can hardly be seen to lead to the child's mastery in the use of tools.

As to unresponsiveness, these children showed little knowledge or curiosity about things in their surroundings. They often avoided stimulating experiences by "deliberately" not paying attention to new objects. The children walked right past the most attractive toys, they ignored a table full of shiny papers or of brightly colored playdough. The urge to investigate, feel, smell, taste, manipulate, explore, test out, master, and use in their own way, according to their own needs and desires, obviously had not been encouraged. These children displayed a kind of oblivion to stimuli quite different from the tentative guardedness shown by other timid children.

Expectation of calamity and guarded fearfulness permeated all aspects of coping with daily life in school. The slightest accident in the nursery school seemed to paralyze the entire class. When, for instance, a toy rolled off the table, the expectation of some disastrous punishment, not only by the child nearby, but by all the children in the room, would regularly disrupt all play and send the children into a frenzy of random motor activity, and occasionally out of the room and even out of the building. When the school car had to stop for a red light the children assumed that it was because "Us goin' to bump." The clatter of the garbage truck was assumed to be "outa get ya." Disaster, or potential disaster, was always expected to be just around the corner. When a mother did not open the door at the first knock, she was assumed to be "dead," "in de hospital" or "in jail." Equally, a baby brother with a minor illness was expected to get worse, "He die an' de cops take 'em."

Obviously, these children had experienced their surroundings as essentially dangerous and unpredictable. As Minuchin noted: "He experiences a violent world that he cannot modify by his own actions." (18) They appeared to have no confidence of being protected or of being able themselves to differentiate between realistically dangerous aspects and those that they could master.

In short, the children's prevalent mode of coping with daily living was a defensive one. Keenly alert to the intentions of others, they reacted rather than acting upon their own initiative. Denial and the avoidance of conflicts or of commitments were the children's major coping devices.

CAPACITY FOR RELATIONSHIPS

The children's characteristic relationships to people were need-oriented, distrustful, shallow, and nonspecific. They had a facile friendliness combined with an appealing and endearing manner which aided them in their "getting along" orientation to people and to the world around them.

They were past masters at manipulating things for themselves with a minimum of conflict. While waiting for a child to come to the car in the morning, for instance, the other children would repeatedly get candy or pennies from adults in the street in so skillful and unobtrusive a manner that, at the time, it escaped the notice of the teacher.

In the classroom we became aware of how frequently the children were apt to get their way with adults and peers in an alarmingly smooth manner. It quickly became apparent that this ingratiating and manipulatory approach to people—repeated endlessly, with little variation—was the only social approach available to most of them. Nearly everything they did seemed to be geared to securing the teacher's ears or eyes and to obtaining tangibles for themselves. For a long time *Gimme* and *Look at me* were the main verbalizations.

This eager search for attention was usually without specific focus; it showed a relentless, indiscriminate longing to be given to. A child would point at a shelf and urgently call, "Gimme," without being able to settle on any one object, even when the teacher produced every single thing on that shelf. Sometimes the request would involve whatever another child had gotten hold of—particularly if "given" by the teacher. Whatever was given by an adult, or cleverly manipulated away from another child, was just as quickly dropped again; getting, not possessing, seemed to be the urgent need.

To be in contact with the adult took precedence over anything else. When painting, for instance, a child would shout, "Look at me," turning toward the teacher. Only when the teacher would show interest in the painting did the child, too, pay attention to his or her own activity. In the beginning, this attentiveness, and frequently the activity itself, would only last as long as the teacher demonstrated her focused interest; for many of the children activity ceased if the teacher as much as shifted her eyes. Nor did it seem to matter who provided the attention. People appeared to be interchangeable for these children. Not only would a child move from one teacher to another quite indiscriminately, children would turn as readily to total strangers, or walk off with anybody. Their approaches were need-oriented and showed a lack of experience with consistently satisfying back-and-forth relationships.

It is difficult to describe the lack of carry-over of the interactional experiences with the teacher. Usually a child shows that cumulative pleasurable experiences with a teacher increase his feeling of comfort and trust. His greeting, his verbalization, his ways of relating become increasingly more specific and more personal. But with these children there was, for a long time, hardly any change from one day to another, as though past experiences with a teacher had no lasting impact. After five weeks in school, a child might rush into her teacher's arms, all smiles and eagerness, and immediately—with the identical facial expression—rush into the arms of a startled lady, a total stranger who just happened to walk into the building and who had not as much as glanced at the children.

Yet while constantly on the lookout for contact, the children demonstrated that they did not really trust the adult, nor could they tolerate being helped. They were apparently quite unused to adults showing an interest in them, and they were startled when it was offered. Requesting an object, they would turn away when the adult offered it; clamoring for help, they would go through the motions of helping themselves, disregarding the teacher's efforts to aid them. A child who would wail to be read to, for instance, would, at the approach of the teacher, set up the book in front of himself, thus blocking her out. Distrust and suspicion were expressed by selective unresponsiveness and by gestures such as averting the eyes on being contacted. A few of the children used gestures typical of protecting themselves from physical abuse, such as shielding their heads with their arms, regardless of the unmistakably benevolent nature of the adult's approach.

Even those children who did not so obviously expect blows were fearful of aggression or retaliation. They expected blame for the most farfetched occurrences—a napkin blown off the table by the wind, a child tumbling out of a wagon at the other end of the room, another child dropping a ball.

They were particularly fearful of retaliation for shouting, crying, and for uncovering their bodies. On the other hand, we found unconcern, on the part of most of the children, about wetting their pants.

The high degree of apprehension of the children was perhaps

revealed most clearly by their inability to "talk back," to show signs of normally expected self-assertion and occasional displeasure in response to other people's actions or demands. Anger was rarely directed toward the teacher. For example, the setting of limits for safety or for routine reasons, which frequently may call forth angry responses from other young children, would be reacted to with a defeated air, as if the mere setting of limits spelled total rejection. Even the few instances of passive resistance and an occasional protective outcry of "Do it myself" were hardly ever translated into action. Rather, there was too great a readiness to submit passively in order to avoid conflicts, to show token obedience, to nod agreement, at times without even understanding what was being requested.

The few children who went through a period of throwing tantrums did so less in reaction to specific interactional situations than as an expression of mounting, unmanageable frustration caused by their difficulties in controlling themselves and in manipulating their environment in a satisfying manner. The anger, when expressed at all, was characteristically directed toward the self.

When distressed, the children not only did not spontaneously turn to the teacher for comfort or help, they did not allow the teacher's sympathetic approach and became virtually unreachable.

Both separation and closeness tended to terrify the children. They struggled to keep the teacher from being too far, as well as from being too close, at any time. We did not see the usual expressions of stranger and separation anxiety. Hardly any child showed overt distress or anxiety over leaving home with teachers he hardly knew. There was avoidance of the issue of separation on the part of the parents also. When children were leaving for nursery school, the parents would frequently turn away and would not even say goodbye to them. Likewise, the children failed to ask about their mothers or about going home while they were in school. There was a similar reaction to the teacher's or a child's absence from the room. It took several weeks—in some cases months—before these anxieties became manifest.

The strangeness of a new situation itself is known to heighten separation anxiety (29). However, these children did not seem to have experienced predictable reciprocity in their early relationships (25), so that they lacked the expectation of predictability in the school, or in any environment. Anyone or anything that was gone appeared to be totally gone for the child, with little expectation of reappearance. Children did not search for toys that fell under the table, nor dig up a shovel covered with sand. For that matter, even their own hands covered with sand brought an anguished shout or frightened stare, devoid of the usual humorous reaction which such situations are apt to trigger off in other children. One child stared at a teacher each time she had put on tights. After weeks the child finally asked, "But where's you legs, her gone?" Not one child could name a simple object, well known to them, when covered in their presence with a cloth, without looking at or at least feeling the object. It took several months in nursery school before the children could express in dramatic play, or by direct verbalization, their preoccupation with the problem of separation, loss, and abandonment.

For a long time, we did not appreciate just how central this question of separation was for the children. Teachers tend to take "the ability to separate" at face value. Secure children tolerate separation more easily, as they bring their separation anxiety into the open and deal with it successfully (30), while insecure children will find separation more difficult; angry protests, crying, clinging, and other manifestations of overwhelming anxiety reveal some disharmony in the mother-child relationship. We may have failed to show enough awareness toward the children for whom the process of separation is so painful and threatening that they have to deny its occurrence by giving no outward sign of their massive anxiety. If in addition the parents, with their own histories of painful separations, can supply no reassurance for the child and in fact must engage in denial as well, we may witness the most casual parting between parents and children. A teacher's effectiveness in building relationships with deprived slum children may well hinge on an understanding of this issue.

These children's behavior with adults did not indicate the usual predictable sequence in the establishment of a trusting, reciprocal relationship between children and teachers (8, 22). The interaction here had a quality of timelessness, a lack of sequential progression. It was a moment-to-moment encounter, with the teacher used by the child as an extension of himself in his relentless and dissatisfied search for immediate gratification.

Nor were relationships with peers on a more trusting, mutually satisfying level. Fear, distrust, and the need for immediate gratification characterized peer relationships as well, and there was little indication of the usual age-expected spontaneous interest in each other. Avoidance of involvement was characteristic. There was hardly any spontaneous conversation between the children, other than to secure tangibles, and even then only a few words were used. However, covert attentiveness to each other could be inferred from the immediate reaction of other children to a particular child's gaining the teacher's attention. Facile imitation of each other's activities, expressions, and gestures was frequent. This was noticeably disconnected from any meaningful activity on the part of the children. Conflicts were largely avoided, with aggression expressed only indirectly, such as by sudden, impulsive grabbing away of toys.

It is generally assumed that children deprived of adult interaction and guidance have strong sibling bonds. We did not find more meaningful interrelatedness among the siblings when they were placed in the same groups. Rivalry between them was even stronger. The only cohesive interaction we observed was dependence of the younger children on the oldest siblings. This had the same quality as the attention seeking behavior toward adults and was responded to by the older sibling as though he or she were an adult at the particular instant the younger ones turned to him, to revert immediately after to fierce competitiveness for attention or to regressed behavior that seemed to obliterate chronological age differences. Spontaneous protectiveness, support, help with accomplishments or explanations were not forthcoming, nor could siblings be identified through behavior indicative of any special bond between them.

It would be misleading to refer to the children's mode of relating to people simply as "immature." While the dependency and need-orientation were certainly those of much younger children, the dimensions of distrust, fear, and hyperattentiveness represented a complex pattern of adaptation to their interactional experiences. The basic trust which Erikson (9) postulates as an essential factor in the course of healthy development was conspicuously missing.

It needs to be pointed out that with very few exceptions (and these involved specific traumatic experiences) the children were neither bitter nor hostile; nor had they "given up"; they relentlessly and with single-mindedness kept making contact and searching for gratification. They showed in this a tenacity bordering on stubbornness which we learned to recognize as an essential ingredient of the children's hold on reality. Stubbornness can have high survival value in the midst of circumstances as confusing and painful as are the daily experience of these children.

Thus, they showed determination in their efforts to secure continuous attention from adults, but their inexperience with consistent responsiveness posed serious difficulties for the teacher.

The problems of communication alone were formidable. The children were not used to engaging in back-and-forth conversation. Typically, a boy would run to the teacher, looking very upset, and say, "De doggie don't find de modder," running off again before the teacher could have a chance to reply. But even as the teacher would then seek out the child, all efforts on her part to solicit more details would only bring forth the same sentence again. Unless the teacher happened to have been in the school car and had noticed this boy's concern about a dog standing alone on the street that morning, there was no way for her to "tune in" on his thinking, except to perceive his separation anxiety. Or a girl indicates an interest—without a word, but with longing glances—in an Easter basket another child had just made. A teacher's suggestion— "Would you like to make a basket? Here is some construction paper; pick the color you want, and over here are scissors and paste" —would be more than sufficient to get most children encountered in nursery schools started on their work. This little girl, as was typical of these children, regardless of their age, nodded her head, smiled, and ran off. How great the temptation for a teacher then to simply let it go at that, or else to compel all of the children to sit down and make baskets, whether they care to or not!

Perhaps the most confusing dimension of the children's relationship with people was the unpredictability of their behavior. Just as they showed by their anxious hyperalertness that they were unsure of what to expect of others, they themselves did not give discernible indications of what they wanted or were about to do. It is most difficult to foster learning opportunities when each child's behavior is unpredictable and there is little basis for establishing meaningful ongoing relationships.

LANGUAGE AND COGNITIVE DEVELOPMENT

Even prior to the recent concern with the lags in cognitive development of many slum children (3, 7, 10, 12, 14, 23, 26) it was known that early stimulus deprivations were apt to produce obstacles in children's learning processes (see especially 1, 5, 11, 21, 24, 27). The "dullness" (despite possible high endowment) found so often among neglected or institutionalized children is the despair of all the various well-meaning people trying to help them acquire knowledge.

With children whose behavior seemed primarily oriented toward gaining tangible gratification and avoiding pain, it was difficult for some time to assess just what was the extent of their cognitive development and of the availability of language with which symbolically to express their thoughts. Nor was it easy to test, not only because tests tend to be "culture-loaded" but also because of their suspicion of people and their high anxiety in dealing with direct questions and requests. Our observations revealed that the children appeared far more knowledgeable in the nursery school setting than they did in structured tests. But even when we came to know them well and could encourage them to engage actively in many learning situations, insufficient self-esteem tended to keep their achievements on a lower level than we knew them to be capable of.

A picture has sprung up characterizing slum children as practically incapable of speech. This we did not find true. Except for one 2½-year-old who did not speak at all when she started in nursery school, the children had quite a number of words at their disposal and used them to varying degrees. One 5-year-old spoke at home, but restricted speech markedly everywhere else. Another made monosyllabic responses when spoken to and did not volunteer verbalization. Several children spoke incessantly; some children would burst into speech when anxious, others only when relatively free from anxiety.

In spite of these differences in range the children's language use had certain features in common. Their vocabularies were small, much below what would be expected of children in day-care centers (6). Communication was frequently effected by means other than the use of language—gestures, pleading looks, appealing or fixed smiles, whimpering, whining, and so on. There were many nonspecific demands which seemed to express a vague longing for contact rather than an identifiable communication. Minuchin (19) has observed that in these families "language is not treated or used as an autonomous medium for the exchange of information but is used rather as an instrument to establish a rare sense of contact . . ." The children vaguely identified objects with *dis,* even when the name of the object was perfectly familiar to them. Poor pronunciation, reversal of pronouns, distortions of meaning, or simply incorrect usage often made their speech incomprehensible. Compared to data on other children in the same age range (17) significant qualitative differences emerged. In talking of her younger brother, a 5-year-old girl said, "Her pushed all bloody." Subsequent inquiry brought further confusion so that the teacher could not determine who had pushed whom. A child calling "Me pour dis," may have been inviting the teacher to pour his juice, or perhaps was asking permission to do so himself.

The children had at their command a number of simple words and sentences relating to their immediate needs. In addition, they repeated adult statements heard at home, such as angry curses, threats, ridicule, demands, and other expressions frequently used in the environment. These phrases usually were reproduced in fragments, frequently out of context. One 3½-year-old would say repeatedly in a conversational tone of voice, unrelated to anything specific, "Get out of my sight. I'll break your neck." "Her stupid bastard" was heard as frequently as "Shut up 'n get out" (these being the more benign type of exclamations). One 4-year-old girl sat on top of the climber and sang in a very high voice, "Step right up and say you love me," to be followed immediately by a string of curses, shouted in a low, menacing voice.

The children demonstrated that they did not trust the teacher to answer or even listen to their verbal demands by usually repeating them even while they were already being responded to. In addition, the teacher's verbal responses were often not acted upon nor sometimes even understood by the children. For example, a 4½-year-old girl, when told by the teacher that the pocketbook that she was looking for was on the *dresser,* merely played with her *dress* and looked bewildered. Another 4-year-old, after the teacher finally discovered that the "thing" she was clamoring for referred to chalk and said that the chalk was behind her on the windowsill, stood there bewildered, saying over and over, "But where?" Sometimes the children would seem to understand, but lacked confidence in the reliability of verbal communication.

Frequently children would repeat verbal directions, but had pronounced difficulties in translating them into action, until the words were accompanied by a physical demonstration. A 4-year-old boy, told he could secure the top of his puppet show curtain on the table by putting a heavy object on it, repeated the words but could not act upon them until the teacher demonstrated. Needless to say, this difficulty in conceptualizing and in using language for symbolic representation and problem solving made communicating with the children exceedingly difficult.

When the children initially came to nursery school there appeared to be little interest in names and properties of objects. Colors, numbers, sizes, shapes, locations, all seemed interchangeable. There was a lack of exploration of language and an absence of the usual play with words which facilitates increasing communicative skills and serves to extend knowledge. As a result the children's language tended to have a constricted, as well as monotonous, quality. The tone was rather flat (confirmed by comparing their recorded voices with those of another nursery school), and there was little variation in verbalization. (As found also by Bernstein [4].) Most of the children could say something in only one way, without being able to elaborate or find alternate ways of expressing themselves. "Exploration and clarification of meaning [were] almost invariably absent." (19)

An interest in books or stories was minimal to nonexistent. While the children liked being talked to and read to, it was another way of getting attention. They hardly seemed to listen to what was being said. Yet, bits of stories and particularly bits of songs were memorized rapidly and repeated for a short time.

Concomitant with the language impairment, these children also showed marked deviations in cognition. As already stated, there was an overreliance on concrete action, with a paucity of abstract thought. The children's capacity to generalize was minimal, as was their ability to integrate multiple stimuli. Whatever they saw or did appeared to exist in isolation and a newly learned skill would not be readily applied in another context. For instance, a child who had succeeded in controlling his pouring of juice from a pitcher into his cup could not manage to do this when watering flowers, using the very same pitcher. If a child learned to attach the ladder to one side of the climber this did not mean that he could attach it to the other side, or that he would know how to go about attaching similar objects to one another. Likewise, the similarities and differences between making playdough and baking cookies could not be grasped. Going to one playground did not seem to prepare them in any way for another, although the same standard equipment was found in both. Even more surprisingly, the experience of successfully hammering nails into wood to make an "airplane" in no way seemed to provide the knowledge of how to hammer nails into wood for some other purpose.

Illustrative of these serious limitations in cumulative integration of learning experiences was the children's behavior on trips to places they were well familiar with. We deliberately chose to provide experiences that were based on the children's regularly repeated activities in their home environment—for instance, going to the neighborhood store in order to buy juice and cookies for their snack at school. One would have expected children who had gone shopping there daily for a year or two to have learned something about the store, such as where the various foods were to be found, what they were called, and how to conduct themselves in the setting. Instead, these 4- and 5-year-old children were totally disinterested and uninformed, running about heedlessly and sidling up to strangers. While they readily agreed with the teachers that they had come to buy cookies, they made no attempt whatever to find them. The children could neither name any of the objects in the store nor point to those the teacher named, but they were ready to pick up anything the teacher showed them. When the cookies were finally "found" and each child carried a box, on the way back to school not one could name what was in his bag without opening it and peering inside.

Rather than assume that the children did not "remember" the store, the cookies, or other previously experienced objects or episodes, it appears to us more likely that each incident was experienced by them as quite separate and not easily combined to form generalized and reapplicable knowledge. It was as though they reacted to each situation without inner commitment or comprehension.

The inability to move beyond literal designations was demonstrated consistently. For example, a 4-year-old boy placing two blocks on his tall block structure was asked what he was building. The only answer that could be elicited was "blocks, on top." Pictures would be referred to by such phrases as "wid de paint" or "color on de paper." In contrast most young children encountered in nursery schools have the ability to abstract from the activity itself and to designate the application of paint on paper as "a painting," or a picture of something definite, and to give name and description to a block building.

The very literal designation of their own activities appeared to be connected with their difficulties in comprehending the relationships of parts to whole and of common denominators of separate experiences.

Demarcation between reality and fantasy appeared unusually poor. While some reality-fantasy confusion would have been age-expected, the children's lack of differentiation and the extent of their animation of inanimate objects was astonishing. Pictures of animals in books, for instance, were seriously stroked, hit, or feared; cups were said to be fighting, a seashell to be searching for his mother. A 3½-year-old boy, looking at a picture depicting three kittens on a table, handed the book to the teacher with the earnest plea "Take 'em down, put 'em on de floor." Not only realistic-looking puppets but even a small piece of a puzzle might cause a child to suddenly shriek and flee to the top of the climber, expressing fear. A 4½-year-old boy who feared dogs showed the same panic reaction to animal crackers.

In addition, there were many signs of unfamiliarity about the simplest aspects of the world around them, knowledge that most young children bring to nursery school. Manipulations of everyday objects, such as unscrewing a jar, opening a faucet, stopping a toy from rolling off the table, were new even for 4- and 5-year-olds. Skills such as counting and familiarity with the names and discriminating properties of objects (hot-cold, sour-sweet, soft-hard, big-small, and the like) and their whereabouts were hardly present. When confronted with a problem such as how to open a salt container or how to fasten a board to a sawhorse, they seemed to be without any resources for solving the problem. They had apparently not experimented sufficiently nor did they have the expectation of being able to find solutions.

Beyond protecting themselves to some extent—they knew for instance how to spot and avoid a drunk on the street or in their doorway with a nonchalance that could not be matched by the teacher —and beyond fulfilling their parents' demands, which also seemed a matter of "survival," they appeared to know very little about themselves and about their surroundings. Remarkable as these survival skills were for coping with certain aspects of their surroundings, they appeared characteristically in response to the environment rather than as activities initiated by the children. Energy seemed to go into avoidance rather than into active self-directed manipulation.

The organizing of facts, the experimenting, labeling, differentiating, classifying, questioning that one sees going on relentlessly and through a variety of avenues, and that can be aided significantly in the nursery school setting, here did not seem to be actively engaged in. The children not only solicited no information nor voiced questions, they also failed to explore independently in order to find solutions for themselves. Undoubtedly, even in their passive manner, the children had learned to categorize and generalize certain facts: how else could they have managed to adapt to their complex environment in some functional manner? However, with so much energy going into self-protection and with the availability in the environment of only minimal amounts of meaningful stimuli and guidance, the process of cognitive organization was bound to be seriously affected.

Capacity to Focus on Activity. Initially, most of the children did not seem to know how to play, beyond a cursory uninvolved fingering of toys. No objects in the nursery school room seemed to have any meaning for a child, separate from the fact that another child had approached or handled it. Even this rivalry-dominated choice of objects was quite directly related to the teacher's presence and the degree of her availability. If the teacher helped one child to put shoes on a doll there was a sudden interest by many of the children in dolls with shoes. When the teacher rolled a ball back to a child, other children would drop whatever toys they happened to be handling and urgently request balls to play with. The children's interest in play activities appeared not to go beyond their relation to immediate gratification. Thus a child wanted to have the puzzle another one was using but didn't investigate the puzzle itself, neither the picture on it nor the possibility of putting the pieces together. Or a boy would pick up the sponge with which the teacher had just cleaned off the play sink but do nothing but squeeze it over and over, only to drop it in fear and run off when water dripped on his shoe.

Whenever we saw even brief play it was with very direct and intensive support from the teacher. Even then, there was little investment, but rather brief exploration, predominantly tactile. Play disruptions were frequent and it was difficult to speak of an attention span in these children. As already mentioned, because of their extremely low frustration tolerance they very quickly gave up and fled the task. They did not plan nor did they seem to anticipate an outcome. Play was a moment-to-moment affair, grabbing hold indiscriminately of whatever was to be gotten, or using materials in order to attract attention to themselves.

These children simply did not become deeply involved in their activities. Not only did they seem to be ever alert, watching for the intention of other people, but many aspects of play which other children take in their stride appeared to frighten the children. Over and over we saw children run in fright when a clothespin fell off the table, a piece of puzzle fell out, a bead dropped off the string, and so on. Characteristically, such items were not recovered. This fearful reaction suggests an expectation of being blamed. The children's persistent tendency to treat such objects as pictures, puzzles, and beads as though they were real and could act on their own added to the threats of their environment.

The children's use of material appeared "dull," chiefly because their investigation of the potentials of any given object was so limited. The conspicuous absence of spontaneous imaginative involvement with materials was striking. In spite of the fact that most of the children rushed around incessantly, picking up this or that toy, using one piece of equipment or another, there was no sustained or even momentarily focused interest in anything. The concentrated efforts on securing the exclusive attention of the teacher initially did not include responsiveness to her suggestions, explanations, or efforts to invoke interest in nursery school materials.

In contrast to the usual nursery school, where some children initially hesitate to immerse themselves in play, for this group of children the uninvolved manner was not a temporary but rather the customary way of handling toys. No doubt their high level of anxiety contributed to their difficulties in settling down. There were, however, no signs that most of them had ever actually known how to settle down or how to play.

We did not expect to find this, as we assumed that children, thrown early on their own devices would have developed the capacity to play by themselves and even with others. As we learned more about the child-rearing patterns in their homes we realized that stimulation and responsiveness by the parents to a child's exploration of objects was minimal. Most of them did not know how to enjoy playing with children and in all probability nobody had ever played with them or had encouraged them to play. Appropriate toys were found in few of the homes and even these were mostly mere fragments. As the parents reported—and this was borne out by our own observations—the "play" of the children consisted chiefly of jumping on the furniture. We also observed that very many of the young children said to be "playing" on the street were in fact mostly standing around, perhaps poking a can with a stick or intermittently running back and forth in an aimless manner. The impact of ever-blaring television in the homes appeared to be different from that on other young children (13). These youngsters reported exclusively incidents of injury and disaster involving children; that is, their danger orientation permeated their selection of items remembered. Thus fantasies served to reinforce reality.

During the registration interviews we had been surprised when, in response to questions about their children's preference for toys, mother after mother gave us only the vaguest information. No child appeared to have "a favorite toy" nor show any particular interest in any activity. At the time we chalked it up to the mother's busy life that left little time for observing her children. In fact the accounts they gave of the children rushing from one object to the next, wanting "whatever is around," was a most accurate description. Add to it the parents' expectation of failure and their proneness to ridicule or devaluation of their children's activities. For example, "Here comes de airplane," says a boy entering his home, proudly holding a piece of woodwork constructed in school. "Oh yeah, big deal," responds Father, laughing derisively; "What a piece of junk!" Older and younger siblings pull the airplane apart within minutes, while the boy stands by silently. In another home a doll brought by a relative as a birthday present to one girl was carried off at once by a younger brother and never seen again. There was no protection of a child's "rights" or feelings, no manifestations of positive interest in and reaffirming response to a child's activity. It is really not surprising, then, that so many of the children literally had to be taught to play when they first came to nursery school.

There were nonetheless some preferences in activity. These were first of all for gross motor equipment and then for objects that lent themselves to repetitive and rather infantile modes of play (such as pull toys). Toys that involved fine motor skills and required problem solving were by and large avoided or merely bandied about. Self-initiated play was seen rarely; responding to the intentions of others was the rule. We never heard the familiar "I want to do . . ." nor did they show by their actions that they knew what they wanted or could make choices. One toy seemed to be as good or indifferent as another. Only quantity seemed to be of some import. If, for instance, four jars with blue paint happened to be well filled, each child would want all four of those rather than a selection of different colors.

The closest to actual play involvement that we could move the children, in the first few months, was in the form of meager, constricted bits of fantasy play that would emerge with some encouragement, rarely spontaneously. These were dominated by portrayals of hunger, abandonment, and fighting (child demanding food, mother feeding or withholding, child looking for mother, child lost, mother leaving, mother screaming angrily). There were few variations, no attempts at playing out alternative solutions, no elaborations, no flights of fantasy; rather a painfully literal portrayal of specific home experiences. In and out of play there was a strong pull toward regression (creeping, baby talk, demands for immediate gratification). The children would shift rapidly and unpredictably from one role to another; from the helpless, searching baby to an angry, demanding, often withholding, mother. This constant shift was emphasized by a pronounced shift in voice also. They overdramatized, and often it was difficult to ascertain whether they were engaged in play or play-acting in reality. They did not engage in other kinds of role play (such as pretending to be an animal or a car).

Thus, for many reasons, the capacity of these children to focus on activities was very limited. The real challenge for teaching did not lie just in introducing new kinds of activities conducive to learning, but in motivating the children to become engaged at all, to develop initiative and the ability to make choices, to approach play actively with eagerness, curiosity, and joy in doing, to move the children toward wanting to gain increasing knowledge and mastery of the world around them.

The "intrinsic motivation" which Hunt (14) postulates to be identical with spontaneous interest in doing and learning appeared buried beneath the need to secure and manage contact with a caretaking person. Any hope of uncovering it within the nursery school setting was contingent on our ability to provide these children with consistently trustworthy relationships. In other schools, where by and large the children come with basically trusting attitudes, the teacher can build upon existing relationships, knowledge, interests (8, 15, 22). Here, however, we had to devise methods that might compensate for crucial deprivations in social, emotional, and intellectual areas, in order to help these passive and frightened children develop toward becoming active, self-directed and self-confident children.

REFERENCES

1. Alpert, A. (Chairman). Institute on Programs for Children Without Families. *Journal of the American Academy of Child Psychiatry* 4:163, 1965.
2. Baltimore Public Schools Early School Admission Project. Progress Report, 1963–64 (mimeographed), 1964.
3. Bereiter, C., Engelman, S., Osborn, J., and Reidford, P. A. An Academically Oriented Pre-school for Culturally Deprived Children. In Hechinger, F. (Ed.), *Pre-school Education Today*. New York: Doubleday, 1966.
4. Bernstein, B. Social Class and Linguistic Development: A Theory of Social Learning. In Halsey, A. H., Floud, J., and Anderson, A. (Eds.), *Education, Economy and Society*. Glencoe: Ill.: Free Press, 1961.
5. Bruner, J. S. The Cognitive Consequences of Early Sensory Deprivation. In Solomon, P. (Ed.), *Sensory Deprivation*. Cambridge: Harvard University Press, 1961.
6. Cazden, C. B. Subcultural Differences in Child Language: An Inter-disciplinary Review. *Merrill-Palmer Quarterly of Behavior and Development* 12:185, 1966.
7. Deutsch, M. Minority Group and Class Status as Related to Social and Personality Factors in Scholastic Achievement. *Society for Applied Anthropology*, Monograph 2. Ithaca, New York: Cornell University Press, 1960.
8. Doak, E. *What Does the Nursery School Teacher Teach?* Chicago: National Association of Nursery Education, 1951.
9. Erikson, E. H. Identity and the Life Cycle. *Psychol. Issues,* Monograph 1. New York: International Universities Press, 1959.
10. Feldmann, S. A Pre-school Enrichment Program for Disadvantaged Children. *The New Era* 45:3, 1964.
11. Goldfarb, W. Emotional and Intellectual Consequences of Psychologic Deprivation in Infancy: A Re-evaluation. In Hoch, P., and Zubin, J. (Eds.), *Psychopathology of Childhood*. New York: Grune & Stratton, 1955.
12. Gray, S. W., and Klaus, R. *Early Training for Culturally Deprived Children*. George Peabody College and Murfreesboro, Tennessee, City Schools, 1963.

13. Hartley, R. Personal communication on current research in children's response to TV, 1966.
14. Hunt, J. McVicker. The Psychological Basis for Using Pre-school Enrichment as an Antidote for Cultural Deprivation. *Merrill-Palmer Quarterly of Behavior and Development* 10:3, 1964.
15. Johnson, H. *School Begins at Two.* New York: New Republic, 1936.
16. Mattick, I. Adaptation of Nursery School Techniques to Deprived Children. *Journal of the American Academy of Child Psychiatry* 4:670, 1965.
17. Menyuk, P. Syntactic Structures in the Language of Children. *Child Development* 34:407, 1963.
18. Minuchin, S., Auerswald, E., King, C. H., and Rabinowitz, C. The Study and Treatment of Families Who Produce Multiple Acting-out Boys. *American Journal of Orthopsychiatry* 34:125, 1964.
19. Minuchin, S., and Montalvo, B. An Approach for Diagnosis of the Low Socio-Economic Family. *Psychiatric Research Reports of the American Psychiatric Association* 20:163, 1966.
20. Piaget, J. *Play, Dreams and Imitation in Children.* New York: Norton, 1951.
21. Provence, S., and Lipton, R.C. *Infants in Institutions.* New York: International Universities Press, 1962.
22. Read, K. *The Nursery School.* Philadelphia: Saunders, 1960.
23. Reissman, F. *The Culturally Deprived Child.* New York: Harper & Row, 1962.
24. Sachs, L. Emotional Acrescentism. *Journal of the American Academy of Child Psychiatry* 1:636, 1962.
25. Sander, L. W. Issues in Early Mother-Child Interaction. *Journal of the American Academy of Child Psychiatry* 1:141, 1962.
26. Smilansky, S. Progress Report on Program to Demonstrate Ways of Using a Year of Kindergarten to Promote Cognitive Abilities, Impart Basic Information and Modify Attitudes Which Are Essential for Scholastic Success of Culturally Deprived Children in Their First Two Years of School. Israeli project presented to Research Conference on Education of Culturally Deprived, University of Chicago, 1964.
27. Spitz, R. A. Hospitalism: An Inquiry into the Genesis of Psychiatric Conditions in Early Childhood. *Psychoanalytic Study of the Child* 1:53, 1945.
28. Strodbeck, F. L. Project Report: The Reading Readiness Nursery: Short-Term Social Intervention (mimeographed). University of Chicago, 1963.

29. Yarrow, L. J.   Maternal Deprivation: Toward an Empirical and Conceptual Re-evaluation. *Psychological Bulletin* 58:459, 1961.
30. Yarrow, L. J.   Separation from Parents During Early Childhood. In Hoffman, M. L., and Hoffman, L. (Eds.), *Child Development Research,* Vol. I. New York: Russell Sage Foundation, 1964.

GUIDEPOSTS DERIVED FROM NORMAL DEVELOPMENT

Charles A. Malone

Having presented a detailed description of what the children were like when they came to the nursery school, we will now focus on our efforts to understand them by putting their qualities and characteristics into a meaningful framework. In doing this, we are retracing the steps we took in the project work. The foregoing description represents in an organized form the challenge which the young children of disorganized low socioeconomic families present in the nursery school. In order to meet this challenge, we spent many hours discussing and reviewing their behavior so that we could modify and adjust the therapeutic and educational methods used in the nursery school to meet their needs more effectively. Over time, our efforts to understand the children became more organized and conceptualizations emerged. Our thinking about these youngsters focused on developmental issues—on comparing them explicitly and implicitly with "ordinary" children of the same age. The normative frame of reference we used (derived mainly from studies of middle-class children) was modified by our experience with lower-class children in day-care nursery schools and in the developmental study of another segment of the lower class (16, 17, 21).

It is our intention in this chapter to communicate the general view of early child development which served as a background for us in recognizing different or deviant trends in the development of the multiproblem-family children we observed. We wish to describe the leading features of development in preschool children and to put forward generalizations regarding the processes by which "healthy" development occurs. Our purpose in doing this is clear. Ordinary 3-year-olds in a preschool setting appear different from the preschool children in our nursery school. Since we attempted to adapt the nursery school to the developmental needs of the low socioeconomic children in our care, communication of the developmental framework employed becomes necessary in order for the reader to appreciate the basis on which we estimated the appropriateness and age-adequacy of the childen's development.

In order not to oversimplify and schematize the subtlety of early development to such an extent as to be misleading, we will attempt to summarize the leading steps and processes by which ordinary 3-to-4-year-olds attain a level of functioning and adjustment that is described as "normal" without losing sight of the complexity that is involved.

The word *ordinary* raises questions. To expect low-income-family children to develop like "ordinary" children may involve hidden biases. We have attempted to counteract this possible skewing effect by relying on our experience with lower-class children who grew up in the same neighborhood (16) as the youngsters in our project. We also will be describing issues and features of early development which we believe to be important for *all* children, regardless of socioeconomic background. We wish to stress the fact that low socioeconomic status and poorly organized or disorganized family-life patterns produce a child-rearing environment which contributes to deviant trends in the development of the children.

There are many different models or conceptual views of normal child development which we have not the space to review here. Actually the various ways of organizing and viewing development overlap and share certain common ground, and are not mutually exclusive. The viewpoint (or bias) which we hold involves psychoanalytic concepts of child development, modified and enriched by naturalistic observations which stress maturational and biological sequences and concepts involving psychosocial adaptation. In this view, there is an assumption that the various leading features of a child's development, and the learning that is an integral part of it, are a result of dynamic interaction between his constitutional endowment (including his drives and inborn maturing systems) and his environment. In the early years, the family (especially the parents and particularly the mother) represents the major part of a child's environment. It is in the child's growing and increasingly subtle relationship with his parents that social, cultural, educational, and economic as well as vitally important psychic forces impinge upon him and shape his growth. In this process, what the child brings into the interaction with his environment in the various stages of his development has strong, at times dominant, biological roots. Early in a child's life, these biological roots and their psychological expression are more easily distinguished and followed. Later, as a child's personality emerges and becomes increasingly complex, features that appear more closely related to dynamic interaction with the environment (acquired) are more easily distinguished. Nevertheless, we assume that the inherent and the acquired are continually in dynamic balance with each other, so that at any point the range of age-appropriate development depends on harmony between the two. Conversely, unmet or newly accentuated biological needs (drives) produce disequilibrium between the environment and the growing child which can impede and delay the maturational sequence.

In the interaction between the immature human organism and his environment, the epigenetic model and psychosocial theory of Erikson (1, 2) hold great appeal because they emphasize maturational unfolding, psychosexual stages, interpersonal relationships, and social as well as personal adaptation. The epigenetic view emphasizes that successful negotiation of phase-specific developmental tasks is prepared in previous developmental phase solutions and carried on and worked out further in subsequent tasks. It also stresses the idea that deficiencies, defects, or delays in relation to a given developmental phase distort and are continued in subsequent stages. Erikson's psychosocial theory builds upon the ego psychology of Freud and other psychoanalysts (6, 11), and provides an important bridge between the influence of the drives and intrapsychic developments on the one hand and interpersonal relationships (object relationships) on the other in the process of personal and social adaptation to reality.*

In the process of adaptation so critical in a young child's development, learning has a featured role, but is not viewed by us solely in a stimulus-response context, nor simply as an independent unfolding of innate cognitive processes. Where development progresses smoothly, however, one is impressed by the maturational unfolding of intellectual functioning according to the assimilation-accommodation model described by Piaget (18). At the same time, in the process of the child's adaptation to reality, one is impressed by his innate urge to grow, explore, investigate, manipulate, and to develop mastery over and capacity to effect his environment. Thus, the idea of inborn ego roots advanced by Freud (10), elaborated by Hartmann (11, 12), and more recently emphasized by White (27), is most congenial with our view of normal development.

THE FIRST YEAR

When we consider the earliest development of the human organism during the first months of life, there is little that we can call mental (5). The meager information that we have regarding the newborn infant comes from direct observation. At this point, the infant reacts, behaves, and operates on an instinctive basis, and in relation to physiological needs and patterns of rising or diminishing tension. Sensorimotor reflexes are present (such as sucking, grasping, and rooting), and a baby can follow visual stimuli briefly, but there is no evidence of memory (that the infant will seek or respond to stimuli or people on the basis of recall of previous experience). We assume that the newborn infant lives in a "fluid, unbounded, twilight sort of world" (4) in which objects swim into view or recede, appear and disappear. It seems, however, that the patterns of tension accumulation and tension reduction, and the corresponding occurrence and sequence of pleasure-displeasure experiences affects the manner in which awareness of outer reality comes about. Although the baby does not "know" his

---

* The more recent work of Sander (22, 23) extends and deepens Erikson's views in meaningful ways.

mother in the first weeks, he receives a great many sensorimotor impressions of her around his feeding and care that will gradually lead to the formation of his visual, and later his mental, image of her. The mother's face and the support, comfort, and gratification of her body are associated with the hunger-reducing, pleasurable experience of nursing. Feeding is emphasized because it is so central to the very young infant's physiological needs, but diapering, bathing, soothing, cuddling and rocking—indeed, the whole range of maternal care—contribute pleasurable, tension-reducing experiences.

Escalona believes that early development is more complex than the sequence of rising tension, discomfort or pain, gratification and relaxation described by Freud. She points out (4), for example, that there are considerable variations and differences in very young infants regarding patterns of sucking, sleep and wakefulness, and degree of skin irritability. Thus, mothers are called upon to modify and adapt their care to the particular needs and patterns of their babies. Similarly, infants are called upon to make many responses and adaptations beyond those connected with feeding. The very young baby experiences certain discomforts which he is unable to discharge through his own immature somatic and mental apparatuses. The soothing, tender, nurturing care of his mother provides relief and gratification.

Thus, we are reminded that there is variability in infants' ability to communicate cues regarding their needs and in their response to caretaking efforts to comfort them. Similarly, there is a range within normal "ordinary devoted" mothers in regard to their child-care attitudes, preferences, styles, and ability to read and respond to the cues of their babies. Nevertheless, the sequence described above does provide the schematic model of a basic process in the development of the very young child. The first months of life can be considered to be focused on the adaptation achieved between mother and infant in relation to meeting basic body needs (21). In this mutual adaptation, initially the infant is primarily a cue-giver and secondarily a cue-receiver, and the mother is primarily a cue-reader and secondarily a cue-giver. As reciprocal adjustment occurs in the early months, the patterns of the mother's care becomes stabilized and she distinguishes different states in her baby, qualities in his cry, and expresses the conviction, "I know my baby." At the same time, one can observe stabilization in the infant's feeding, elimination, sleep, and wakefulness patterns. Concomitantly, early signs of the baby's response to his mother, or another consistent caretaker, are noted.

At around two months, the response smile appears and is a significant milestone. At first, this is an instinctive response and not yet a response to a human face. As the mother, however, becomes involved in the delightful experience of stimulating and responding to the smiling behavior of her baby, it becomes a social response. This back-and-forth reciprocal exchange of smiles characterizes the early phases of human attachment in an infant. It soon broadens to involve play and vocalization and becomes an example of reciprocal, mutually enjoyable interaction which is a vital quality in the mother-child relationship and the basis for developing *basic trust* (1). This reciprocal, physical, social, and emotional interaction with the mother provides consistent, predictable experiences, so that with the maturation of his inborn equipment the infant begins to recognize the cues that signal need-satisfying experience and the mother who is responsible for it. Gradually the attachment to the experience shifts to the person responsible for it and the baby's first love for someone outside himself begins. With this, we see early signs of the infant's capacity to respond to the sight and sound of his mother and wait for his feeding. This is another milestone, for it indicates the beginning of several important interrelated capacities—to anticipate, to delay gratification, and to accept, at least temporarily, substitutes for immediate need satisfaction. These capacities are very limited at first but this is a turning point and heralds future developments.

This kind of satisfying exchange between mother and child stimulates emotional and cognitive development. Provence (19) feels that the physical handling involved in daily care is significant for the infant's development of certain motor skills, the sense and image of his own body, and the capacity to act. In this mutual adaptation, the mother is a stimulator, energizer, organizer, regulator, and protector, keeping a certain sense of balance between discomfort and comfort, stimulation and quiet, activity and passivity which she feels (through her learning and adaptation as a mother) is optimal for *her* child.

This interaction provides yet another highly significant stimulus for development—an appropriate balance between gratification and frustration. The word *appropriate* is the key one, since this balance is different for different children and for the same child over time and at different hours of the day. Children need frustration in measured amounts. Winnicott (28) and Kris (14) point out that frustration is a stimulus for a child's mental and physical activity to meet, cope with, and master the discontent. This begins the process of a child's developing the ability to accept disappointment and tolerate inevitable frustrations, to negotiate discontent and to manage through his own ability to affect people and things. Kris indicates that masterable frustration stimulates "initiative for independence" in the young child.

Around three months, maturation makes possible the coordination of motor movements with vision. Now the infant can bring his hand to his mouth or into his sight *purposefully*, whereas previously it occurred by chance. This early capacity for purposive action opens up a whole range of sensorimotor experience—a series of visual and tactile experiments in a baby's initial discovery of his world and differentiation of himself which Freud (9) identified as a key to normal development. From this point on, the child with increasing activity and range explores and investigates his world. Initially, his eye-hand coordinations are aimed at bringing objects into his mouth to be sucked and mouthed and he begins to organize his experience and sense of himself through these means (13). Gradually, his coordinated hand and eye explorations become "emancipated" from his mouth and he grasps things with his fingers and his eyes and investigates them with a satisfaction that was earlier connected with his mouth. The infant "conducts" a series of experiments: touching, mouthing, and manipulating *his* hand feels different from the same activity with his mother's hand or a toy. Through a variety of such experiences and in the mutual interaction with his mother, the infant organizes his early sense of himself, and gradually differentiates self from "not self." In the sphere of intellectual development, Piaget (18) distinguishes a series of steps by which the infant uses, organizes, integrates, and differentiates his reflex equipment through sensorimotor experience as maturation makes possible new levels of experimentation. In this adaptive process of assimilation and accommodation, the young child learns about the world of phenomena and things.

Something that is new and different, but not too different, will stimulate new sensorimotor adaptations.

Beginning in the second half of the first year, and continuing into the early months of the second year, there is a rapid increase in a child's motor development and he achieves various motoric milestones: crawling, standing, cruising, and walking. As he attains each milestone, he receives parental acclaim. The shift from passivity to activity thereby gains increased impetus and thrust. As he becomes increasingly mobile, the young child needs space but also protection from excessive stimulation and physical harm.

The infant's increased activity raises an important issue in the mother-child relationship (21). The infant now begins to initiate social and other interchange with his mother, to show preferences and desires, and to attempt to affect the stimulations reaching him. His degree of success in stimulating her to respond to him has implications for his further development in relation to activity and initiative.

Sometime in the second half of the first year of life, usually around eight or nine months of age, as the infant's love for his gratifying mother becomes established and he develops a sense of a separate self, and of the person outside the self, separation and stranger anxiety appear. Now the baby reacts to other people substituting for the mother with dismay, anxiety, crying, or protests. The child now distinguishes his mother from strangers and expresses distress and demand for his mother. We believe that an infant at this age fears losing his loved one, and that he does not yet know that people and things, and most importantly his mother, have an independent existence whether he can see them or not. This concept will develop around one year of age. Sander (21) observes that in this latter part of the first year and continuing into the second, a young child shows clear preference for his mother and attempts to use his activity and initiative to focus on her as *the* person to meet his increasingly specific demands. The youngster's demands during this period are intense and unremitting. At the same time he is able and does move away from the mother only to return to her side or her lap for "refueling" (15). It seems that the appearance of focalized demand, the gradual mastery of separation anxiety, and the development of object constancy go hand in hand with the process of gaining an early level of "independence." Satisfactory negotiation of these issues depends upon "the mother's ability to yield or to compromise by keeping the baby in her awareness while she pursues her own interests" (21). Negotiation of these issues has important consequences for the further separation-individuation process (15) and development of autonomy which characterize the second and third years of life.

THE SECOND YEAR

In the second year of a child's life the "areas of most rapid development involve locomotion and the refinement of motor skills, socialization, language and speech, and autonomy and selfhood" (17). During the second year, the child will progress to steady walking, climbing, and running. He will coordinate his gross and fine movements. Play with toys provides a wide range of stimuli, challenges, and satisfactions, and as Provence points out (19), they are useful as objects upon which the child can discharge feelings *without* evoking a response." Examination and exploration of toys and household items enhances cognitive development and the child engages in many investigations with absorption and concentration.

In the increasingly important exploratory behavior of young children at this time, curiosity and increasing skill and control in motor development aid them in the investigation of the properties of their physical world as well as the relationships between people and things. In addition to seeking new experience a child will also become absorbed in the familiar and in repeating well-established patterns. Wenar (25) describes this investigative behavior in the second year of life as "executive competence" which relates to White's concept of competence, whose underlying motivation is the desire to produce effects upon the environment, termed *effectance* (26).

There is some disagreement as to the degree to which this exploration is essentially maturational and independent of interpersonal factors (and social learning). For some students of development, the relationship to the mother is of central importance in the child's growth toward independence. Not only is this relationship vital in terms of providing emotional security for the child in his exploratory excursions, but it is considered that without the stimulation of adequate mothering, a child lacks interest in things and invests minimally in manipulative investigations, although he is maturationally capable of engaging in them (20). For other students of development (such as Gesell and Piaget) interest in exploring objects occurs in relation to a natural unfolding of maturational capability. These views are not mutually exclusive. In a healthy child-rearing environment, one is struck by the stage-by-stage unfolding of interests and the child's investigations appear quite independent of direct social influence. For a young child, however, such an environment means an appropriately satisfying, regulating, and frustrating relationship with the mother.

The broad concept of adaptation to reality (as a function of the child's ego or self) is useful here. During the second and third years of his life, a child is exploring personal and interpersonal fields as well as the impersonal; he is making discoveries which assist him in placing and relating himself and his own body to people and to things. In this process, he is learning to adapt himself to various actualities (3). The child's investigations have a personal stamp and involve a fitting together of inner perception and outer reality experience.

While the toddler is engaged in this process of exploration and learning about his world, developing competence and mastery, and asserting his emerging independence and active wish to affect his environment, certain related developments are also taking place.

The parents (especially the mother) are placing limits on the activities of the toddler. At the same time that a new world of motor experiences and learning is opening up for him, the possibilities of harm or damage and infractions of parental standards of acceptable behavior are also increasing. The parents are making decisions about what and how much to allow. They are deciding where and in what ways to curb the impulses and seemingly boundless energies of their young child. In part, they do this according to their own personal life style and social values and in part they are transmitting general societal and cultural standards. They are exerting their influence in order to promote appropriate socialization of the child to their social and personal values.

The toddler needs to learn to curb his wants, gain control over his body, and develop habits and behavior in line with his parents' attitudes and wishes, and in response to their approval and disapproval. It is also important for him to learn that his loved parents can limit him firmly and that he can occasionally transgress prohibitions and incur their anger without losing them or their love (17).

This period is often described as the period of negativism because the assertiveness of the toddler may run counter to the parent's wishes and an open struggle may arise. Fraiberg (5) emphasizes, however, that the main characteristic of this phase is a powerful striving to become a person. "It is a kind of declaration of independence," she points out, "but there is no intention to unseat the government." Sander (21) also stresses the positive aspect of this period which he describes as a further expression of the child's initiative and as a basic part of the emergence of autonomy. Often the struggle occurs in relation to toilet training, but it involves other functions as well.

Toilet training is such an important component of habit training and socialization that it warrants being discussed separately. As Fraiberg (5) points out, the process of toilet training is a gradual one and needs to be if a child is going to resolve actively the issues which attainment of voluntary control involves. The young child enjoys various pleasures in relation to elimination which he is reluctant to give up. He is apt to regard his bowel movements as a valuable part of himself. The height and size of the toilet and the process of flushing away may arouse anxiety in him. He does not yet have an accurate concept of relative size, and he may imagine that the toilet could make him disappear. Thus, there are a number of steps involved in the mastery of bowel training which the child negotiates with the assistance of his parents. Ultimately, as with most of the socialization process, a child's success is motivated by his love for his parents and wish to please them, and his own pride and satisfaction in accomplishment.

For many children and parents, bowel training is a decisive encounter and there is a struggle of wills in the process of gaining voluntary control and further autonomy. Erikson (2) stresses this when describing bowel training: "The matter of mutual regulation between adult and child now faces its severest test. If outer control by too rigid or too early training insists on robbing the

child of his attempt gradually to control his bowels and other functions willingly and by his free choice, he will again be faced with a
double rebellion and a double defeat."

Another important set of developments which are taking place
in the latter part of the second and in the third year involves the
acquisition of language. Even before the development of speech,
the child needs the stimulation of being spoken to. Mothers pick
up and respond to the vocalizations of their children, reinforcing,
interpreting, and clarifying it in such a way that his repertoire
of sounds with specific meaning steadily increases (19). This enhances the acquisition of language and its organization into a system of meaningful communication. Through language a child is
able to label, categorize, and organize knowledge and ultimately to
use information to think through and solve problems (19). Speech
makes possible symbolization which is essential for intellectual
processes and the growth of logical thinking (18).

At the end of the second year (often coinciding with achievement in socialization), there is a surge in language use. This is
fostered by adult encouragement and a child's being talked with
on the level of his interests and comprehension. Feedback from
parents assists the child in gradually elaborating his vocabulary,
making simple sentences, correcting his pronunciation, and ab-
sorbing some notions of syntax.

Speech lures the child into a world in which laws of thinking
and realistic considerations oppose the child's previous world view.
Heretofore, the young child functioned in a pleasure-seeking egocentric way. He held belief in the power and magic of his own
actions, feelings, and wishes. The child gradually abandons this
egocentric view in favor of communication through the words and
the meanings of those around him (18). It will take a while before
logical thought and functioning according to reality will become
dominant, but the process is under way and moves along steadily
from this point on.

As part of its vital relationship to thinking and mental organization, language has profound influence on a child's development of
inner controls and socialization. Soon after a youngster begins to
acquire language the whole task of child rearing becomes easier.
Improved communications facilitate the process of conveying and
reinforcing parental standards, values, and attitudes. A child can

sometimes control his impulses or avoid danger situations by uttering the parental prohibition to himself. Language makes it possible for a child to take in his parents' verbal prohibitions and make them his own. Words begin to substitute for acts and contribute to the child's increasing ability to delay and even renounce direct gratification. Words provide a means of influencing and effecting the environment and offer a sense of reliable control and power. New and increasingly elaborate possibilities of experiencing himself as competent open up for the child and enhance his self-esteem.

Almost all that we have discussed in relation to a child's second year is relevant to the issue of developing *autonomy*. Because he is or can become a voluntary partner in the socialization process, the fact that the young child with his strong efforts at self-determination is obliged to adapt himself to consistent limits does not threaten but rather enhances his autonomy. Autonomy, as we have seen, has its earliest beginnings in the first year in the child's increasing activity and efforts to initiate interaction with his environment and influence the stimuli impinging upon him. The autonomy issue reaches its height in the second and third years. Erikson (2) describes this phase of development most meaningfully when he says, "This stage, therefore, becomes decisive for the ratio between love and hate, for that between cooperation and willfulness, and for that between self-expression and its suppression. From a sense of *self-control, without loss of self-esteem* comes a lasting sense of autonomy and pride."

THE THIRD YEAR

Various features of the child's development during this year culminate in a fullness of language use and symbolic representation, competence, mastery of aggression, inner control, socialization, and individuation that we call autonomy. This broader autonomy is the cornerstone for much subsequent growth. The child's development now becomes increasingly subtle and we can only point to highlights and allude to their interdependence in the developmental processes which occur in the third year.

The socialization which begins in the second year of life involves more than the development of inner controls and voluntary response to the limits, prohibitions, and standards of personal behavior of the parents. It also involves important steps in becoming a social being and learning responsiveness in respect for others. These are early steps, but they are fundamental. As with locomotion, or any area of development for that matter, the toddler will stumble and fall, slip back and move forward, but the dominance of egocentricity is broken and will gradually give way to interpersonal considerations in the child's social learning. Pavenstedt (17) brings this out in an understanding way as she describes various emotional encounters of young children. She points out that through patient explanations and demonstrations young children can be helped to recognize feelings, understand when they are hurting, gain some notion of solicitude, and develop awareness of "the other guy."

However, sudden mood swings, petulant demands, and breakthroughs of anger, rage, and destructiveness will inevitably occur and one cannot introduce young children to social considerations with unrealistically high expectations. They still tend to be selfish and as yet unready to fully internalize and live by parental values. They are ready to experience emotional responsiveness to others, however, and they need models of sympathy, empathy, and respect for others.

An important part of this aspect of socialization involves children learning to control their own aggressive feelings. Ego or self-mastery over aggressive impulses and ability to modify the destructive element of aggression greatly enhances the child's autonomy and has important effects on his relationships with people. Throughout the period of training and socialization, the child's aggression, in the form of stubborn balkiness, spoken anger, occasional temper tantrums, and destructiveness is regularly in evidence. Timidity and fears at this age may arise because a child projects his aggressive destructive impulses onto people and things in his environment. Anna Freud (7) observes: "Whoever has dealt with toddlers knows the peculiarly clinging, possessive, tormenting, exhausting kind of love which they have for their mothers." At this age, loved toys or pets are occasionally maltreated as well as frustrating objects or persons. Since the frustrating parent toward whom the child expresses his aggressive feelings is also the loved parent, a state of *ambivalence* exists. Gradually, through repeated experiences with his parents and with the assistance of their patient guidance, the child learns to bring his aggressive feelings under control. In the interest of his love relationships he modifies the expression of his aggressive feelings. The learning and mastery process here involves conscious experimentation by the child in holding in check or modifying destructive and hurtful expressions of hostility while searching for inventive and more constructive ends. With this development, relationships become less ambivalent and tender feelings become more dominant. Ideally, the vigor and energy of the aggressive tendencies are retained as the goals of aggressive activity are slowly shifted.

Language development progresses rapidly in the third year and the functions, processes, and influences associated with its development take giant steps forward. The child rapidly absorbs ideas and these ideas are gradually organized in an interrelated hierarchical structure and employed in increasingly logical and rational ways (secondary process thinking). He rediscovers and reinvents using the symbolic representation which is now available to him (18). He builds up a repertoire of words to describe feelings, actions, intentions, relationships, and properties. He develops, elaborates, and symbolically represents concepts about his phenomenological experience.

At this age fantasy also becomes increasingly available to children, to be utilized and to play upon and modify activity and experience. In fantasy play a child can assimilate experience (including painful or frightening events) by transforming passive experiences into active ones, adopting new or different roles, and changing the outcome of reality events (24). Thus, in the third year speech becomes an even more significant resource for problem solving, coping, and adaptation. In addition to using play, language, and fantasy to assimilate experience and cope with situations children also use these means to protect themselves against danger, particularly danger which arises in relation to their impulses (6).

Interwoven with and supported by the development of autonomy in the third year is the child's developing and increasingly refined *sense of self*. This begins in the second year when the child learns that people continue to exist when out of sight (object permanence) and develops a capacity to form mental representations of people and things. He learns to ascribe separate existence to others and to separate himself off from them. This separation-individuation process (15) culminates in the third year in a feeling of identity in which the various differentiated aspects of the self are united. At this time, the child senses himself as active, competent, and desirable. Indeed, the whole range of his self-experience and activities which he regards as his "own" become integrated into the sense of self.

The nucleus of the child's self-concept is his sense and representation of his body, his physical self. The more conscious the child is of himself as a person, as an "I" (and indeed, use of the personal pronoun reflects the child's sense of self), the more he values his body. It is of interest that in the third year as the concept of the "I" emerges, children often go through a period of concern about bruises or scratches, even imperceptible ones, and frequently resort to that cure-all, the Band-Aid. It is as though the child's sense of integrity and completeness as a personality is intimately bound with his sense of the intactness and wholeness of his body.

Emerging out of the "autonomy crisis" (2) and the whole decisive alternative of being an independent person and being a dependent one, the child develops a new sense of self-awareness. This early establishment of identity focuses our attention on the important topic of identification. Identification is a process through which the characteristics, attitudes, functions, values, and defenses of another—in short, the widest possible range of human qualities —become part of the self. Although many identifications begin with imitation (which is a more voluntary and conscious process than identification), not all imitation leads to identification in the sense of becoming a permanent component of the personality.

Freud (8) postulates that experiences of gratification and frustration are operative in the laying down of memory traces which make the child seek the person who brought gratification. As maturation makes it possible, a child's efforts to deal with inevitable frustrations become more active, including his attempts to recreate the gratifying early mother-child unity; hence, a more active form of early identification develops in the child's increasing efforts to imitate the smiling, sounds, facial expressions, movements, and ac-

tivities of his love object. Freud (9) speaks of the child's development as largely determined by the general tendency to repeat actively what has been and is being experienced passively in infant
and child care. Imitation of the parents which leads to identification with them fosters this shift from passivity to activity.

In the whole process of developing a firm sense of self, the child
is assisted by the speech and intellectual developments which are
occurring simultaneously. Language is the principle vehicle by
which a child organizes and communicates his awareness of himself
and others and through which he receives the recognition by adults
of the accuracy of his perceptions. Through a mutual feedback
process, a child confirms, clarifies, and refines his perception of
himself and others and represents them accurately internally.
Through language he achieves separateness from his parents in
their presence. He still uses direct, concrete experience and he still
needs to have direct, physical contact (such as comforting, gratification, reassurance) but increasingly he is able to be assured of
himself in relation to his parents and other important people
through language and thought and to represent self and others and
their complex interrelationships symbolically in his mind.

With the satisfactory negotiation of the autonomy phase and
the development of a distinct individuality the child approaches
his fourth year as an increasingly complex and resourceful personality capable of a considerable amount of self-reliance and initiative. Bolstered by various developments in regard to control and
modulation of impulse, socialization, language, and thinking, he is
equipped with a variety of problem-solving capacities and coping
strategies. He is ready to meet new situations and actively explore
new experiences. Among the new worlds he may enter at this time
is the nursery school. Against the continuing background of their
supportive, guiding home life, many children at age three are
ready to negotiate their separation concerns and enter into meaningful relationships with peers and teachers. They are ready to
broaden their base of operation and learning. They are able to engage in parallel and shared play with some respect for their peers.
They can learn the important social skills of cooperation and compromise, and the even more important experience of friendship.

With this description of readiness for nursery school, we have covered the highlights of ordinary childhood development up to roughly the age of the preschool multiproblem-family children when they entered our nursery school.

REFERENCES

1. Erikson, E. H.   *Childhood and Society.* New York: Norton, 1950.
2. Erikson, E. H.   Identity and the Life Cycle. *Psychological Issues,* Monograph 1. New York: International Universities Press, 1959.
3. Erikson, E. H.   Reality and Actuality. *American Journal of Psychoanalysis* 10:451, 1962.
4. Escalona, S.   Emotional Development in the First Years of Life. In Senn, M. E. (Ed.), *Transactions of the Sixth (1952) Conference.* New York: Josiah Macy, Jr. Foundations Series, 1953.
5. Fraiberg, S.   *The Magic Years.* New York: Scribner, 1959.
6. Freud, A.   *The Ego and the Mechanisms of Defense* (1936). New York: International Universities Press, 1946.
7. Freud, A.   Aggression in Relation to Emotional Development: Normal and Pathological. *Psychoanalytic Study of the Child* 3/4:37, 1949.
8. Freud, S.   The Interpretation of Dreams (1900). In *Basic Writings of Sigmund Freud.* New York: Basic Books, 1950.
9. Freud, S.   On Female Sexuality (1931). *Collected Papers of Sigmund Freud.* London: Hogarth Press, 1950, Vol. 5, p. 252.
10. Freud, S.   Analysis Terminable and Interminable (1937). *Collected Papers of Sigmund Freud.* London: Hogarth Press, 1950, Vol. 5, p. 316.
11. Hartmann, H.   *Ego Psychology and the Problem of Adaptation* (1939). New York: International Universities Press, 1948.
12. Hartmann, H.   The Mutual Influences in the Development of the Ego and the Id. *Psychoanalytic Study of the Child* 7:9, 1952.
13. Hoffer, W.   Mouth, Hand and Ego-Integration. *Psychoanalytic Study of the Child* 3/4:49, 1949.
14. Kris, E.   Neutralization and Sublimation; Observations on Young Children. *Psychoanalytic Study of the Child* 10:30, 1955.
15. Mahler, M.   Thoughts about Development and Individuation. *Psychoanalytic Study of the Child* 18:307, 1963.
16. Pavenstedt, E.   A Comparison of the Child-rearing Environment of Upper-Lower and Very Low-Lower Class Families. *American Journal of Orthopsychiatry* 35:89, 1965.

17. Pavenstedt, E.   The Second Year of Life. Working paper (mimeographed) for N.I.M.H. Conference, 1965.
18. Piaget, J., and Inhelder, B.   *The Growth of Logical Thinking* (1955). New York: Basic Books, 1958.
19. Provence, S.   Developmental Needs of Children and Their Relation to Group Care—The First Year of Life. Working paper (mimeographed) for N.I.M.H. Conference, 1965.
20. Provence, S., and Ritvo, S.   Effects of Deprivation on Institutionalized Infants: Disturbances in Development of Relationships to Inanimate Objects. *Psychoanalytic Study of the Child* 16:189, 1961.
21. Sander, L. W.   Issues in Early Mother-Child Interaction. *Journal of the American Academy of Child Psychiatry* 1:141, 1962.
22. Sander, L. W.   Adaptive Relationships in Early Mother-Child Interaction. *Journal of the American Academy of Psychiatry* 3:231, 1964.
23. Sander, L. W.   Interactions of Recognition and the Developmental Processes of the Second 18 Months of Life. Text of paper presented to Tufts, New England Medical Seminar Series on Community Psychiatry, 1965.
24. Waelder, R.   Psychoanalytic Theory of Play. *Psychoanalytic Quarterly* 2:208, 1933.
25. Wenar, C.   Competence at One. *Merrill-Palmer Quarterly of Behavior and Development* 10:329, 1964.
26. White, R.   Competence and the Psychosexual Stages of Development. In Jones, E. (Ed.), *Nebraska Symposium on Motivation.* Lincoln: University of Nebraska Press, 1960.
27. White, R.   Ego and Reality in Psychoanalytic Theory: A Proposal Regarding Independent Ego Energies. *Psychological Issues,* Monograph 11, 1963.
28. Winnicott, D.   Transitional Objects and Transitional Phenomena: A Study of the First Not-Me Possession. *International Journal of Psycho-analysis* 34:89, 1953.

6

THE PSYCHOSOCIAL CHARACTERISTICS OF THE CHILDREN FROM A DEVELOPMENTAL VIEWPOINT

Charles A. Malone

THE FOREGOING detailed description of what the multi-problem family children were like when they entered nursery school indicates that at an early age they already had a notable deviation in their development. This developmental deviation will be the central focus of this chapter. We shall endeavor to summarize our understanding of the children's psychosocial characteristics in relation to environmental influences and developmental processes.

Consideration of the children's psychosocial characteristics has importance beyond its significance in relation to the adaptation of our nursery school techniques. Young children of disorganized families had not been studied before and therefore our findings and views have exploratory value. Although the deviations in development noted in the children are similar to developmental deviations of other groups of preschool children reported in the literature, *they are also different.* More importantly, the multiproblem families with whom we worked represent a segment at the more disorganized end of the continuum of low-income families (32,

35). There is increasing country-wide concern regarding the manifold problems of children of slum families. Ultimately, all therapeutic and/or educational programs for these children (and their first or second cousins from less disorganized low-income families) can benefit from an understanding of their development, much the same way that child welfare and placement programs have benefited from studies of the effects of maternal deprivation. Thus, our efforts to conceptualize about the group of children in our sample should contribute to gaining perspective on a sizeable segment of the low socioeconomic group of children. Without this kind of perspective the planning and evaluation of programs for the low-income group may be led into needless errors or erroneous conclusions.

This is perhaps best seen in relation to the educational needs of this group. Concern for the educational needs of underprivileged youngsters is justified by the large numbers of them who follow a pattern of poor school adjustment, underachievement and early school failure and dropout (47, 54). The increasingly high incidence of school failure among lower-class children, which is in turn linked with increasing rates of unemployment, delinquency, and crime, has led to the general recognition of this as one of the most serious problems currently confronting our society. Inasmuch as low socioeconomic families are a heterogeneous group, there is a corresponding range of educability as well as psychosocial pathology among the children of this group. We believe that our work, aimed at clarifying as explicitly as possible the characteristics of the multiproblem-family children observed in nursery school, will establish one distinguishable group at the lower end of this range and will contribute to the process of viewing more clearly the range of learning problems, as well as the range of special therapeutic and educational techniques (with both children and parents) that are needed to meet these problems.

We therefore will undertake the task of clearly setting down our current understanding of the children's characteristics, in spite of certain limitations. To begin with, our data are descriptive and come from relationship-oriented services to the children in the nursery school and to the families in their homes. They derive mainly from the observations made by the teachers, and to a lesser extent by the child psychiatrist and the educational psychologist on the project team. Consequently they lack the depth in cross section and over time of analytic and child-developmental studies. We do not actually know, firsthand, the detailed early histories of the children whom we observed. Rather, we must infer the gross outline of these histories from the children's current home lives and relationships, the past history obtained by the family workers, and our home-visit observations of the mother's child-rearing practices. Another qualification that needs to be emphasized is the fact that we are generalizing about trends which appear in the children as a group. Among the children there are variations in the degree to which our general observations are true; but, despite divergent individual histories, native endowment, and temperament, the group of children from multiproblem families share most of the qualities and characteristics which were described in the preceding chapter. Finally, we have not had available to us comparable studies of preschool children of low socioeconomic families, and have had to rely on studies of deprived children reared in other settings (institutions and foster homes) and developmental studies of children from less disorganized families. Thus, the literature can only provide us with gross analogies, similarities and differences.

In view of the limits of our data, it should be clearly understood that the views, formulations, and generalizations to be found in this section are suggestive and rather speculative in nature. However, we feel strongly that efforts to conceptualize must be made now, before this general field becomes bogged down further in descriptive reports of individual experiences which are not organized and abstracted to the point that they can be compared, argued, and challenged on the basis of the experience of others.

Part of the problem of communicating our understanding of the children relates to the difficult task of conceptualizing the mutual influences of social, economic, and psychological forces on developing, changing human beings who have multiple interrelated tasks in accomplishing a "life adjustment." Hartmann (21) attempts to simplify the problem by discussing development in the context of an "average-expectable" environment; we are limited in doing this because the environment of the children was neither average nor expectable. Piaget (59) describes stages in intellectual development by, in effect, assuming an average-expectable environment and disregarding instinctual drive influence; however, at home or in the nursery school the children were rarely in a conflict-free state. Others (27) discuss the culturally deprived child's intellectual functioning in sociological terms; we believe the functioning can best be understood in psychological terms. Still others (5) address themselves to the psychic effects of maternal deprivation; we are convinced that maternal excesses, as well as maternal deprivation, are formative in the lives of the children. Finally, there are no norms of development based on studies of children from the poverty group and the very instruments used to make psychological or developmental assessments may be biased.

Having acknowledged our dilemma and certain limitations of our data, we will now discuss the leading qualities of the children from a psychosocial and developmental point of view, attempting to relate what the children are like to outstanding features of the environment in which they have been reared. In doing this, we will focus almost exclusively on pathology. It would, of course, be misleading to the reader if we were to emphasize only this aspect of multiproblem families. The children, it should be pointed out, besides showing delays in their development, are also in certain ways healthy. They are appealing, alert, sturdy, and attractive. They are well coordinated and capable of a wide range of age-appropriate gross motor feats. They are engaging and succeed in drawing people's interest. Although they do so at some cost, by virtue of their cue-reading skills the children orient themselves quickly and they are able to accomplish some rather grownup tasks. Above all, they are able to get along in a world in which most children would be hard pressed to survive. Similarly, the children's parents, for all their inconsistent, neglectful, seductive, and aggressive behavior toward their offspring, cannot be categorized solely as "bad" or "rejecting." They struggle to raise their children well and to provide for them. They want their children to have a better life, to obtain an education, and to get someplace in the world. Even in their harshness the parents try, albeit unsuccessfully, to prepare their children for a life of hardship and disappointment. Though they may be selfish, confused, and ambivalent, the parents are concerned about their youngsters and often blame themselves for the children's difficulties.

In attempting to relate what the children are like to environmental influences, especially intrafamilial relationships, we are aware that many factors impinge on the youngsters and combine to shape their growth, that the principle of overdetermination is constantly at work. In relation to a number of their characteristics, we perceive multiple actual or potential influences from intrapsychic, interpersonal, and environmental sources. From among the many influences on the children's development, we have chosen three—deprivation, devaluation, and danger—because they stand out and appear highly significant. There are others which we might have selected, such as the socializing effects of the families' organization and life patterns (2, 25). Minuchin, Montalvo and their co-workers (34) have pointed out that the patterns of communication, relationship, and power status organization that emerge and operate in disorganized low-income families are models for the children, and that they are learned in the course of family life. This socializing effect is so important that we do try to bring it into focus from time to time in our discussion. Thus, it should be stressed that while we have elected to focus on the interrelated effects of three environmental influences, we do so at the expense of considering other significant factors. In the discussion which follows, wherever an environmental influence is isolated and referred to separately, it is simply to identify a facet in a complex field, not to point to specific cause-and-effect relationships. Similarly, wherever overlapping influences are repeatedly described, the sole purpose is to emphasize the fact that many interrelated and interdependent effects may derive from the same set of influences.

In discussing the children's characteristics in a developmental framework, we will rely on the guideposts from normal development which we employed in evaluating the disorganized-family youngsters. Our consideration of the children's psychosocial qualities will be divided into two parts. First, maternal deprivation, devaluation, and external danger as formative environmental influences will be described separately for heuristic purposes. Secondly, leading features of the youngsters' make-up will be discussed as illustrations of the interrelated effects of these three influences.

Environmental Influences. Bowlby (5), in reviewing and summarizing the effects of maternal deprivation on children's development, concludes that if mental development is to proceed smoothly, it would appear to be necessary for the child's undifferentiated psyche to be exposed during certain critical periods to the influence of the psychic organizer—the mother.

Clearly, Bowlby's work has done us a great service in calling attention to the vital importance of the child's relationship to a consistent mothering person and to the profound developmental deficits which occur in children deprived of mothering in their early years. His viewpoint, however, contains a distorting element in that it places the child's relationship to his mother in the position of being equated with *all* the organizers of embryological development. This tends to leave out of the picture other psychic stimulators, regulators, and organizers, such as less-permanent mothering figures, fathers, siblings, and environmental events. Further, Bowlby speaks of *the* mother, leaving unsaid the complex range of mothering, or lack of it, which would provide adequate stimulation for a child's growth.

In life situations, other than certain institutions, the presence or absence of deprivation is not so clear-cut; consequently the role of this factor and its relationship to other gross influences on a child's development is complicated and indistinct. Among the various influences that impinge on children of disorganized multiproblem families are several that appear to have far-reaching effects. The three factors we stress are deprivation, devaluation, and external danger. These leading qualities of the environment appear particularly in the children's disturbed relations with their parents, but they are also present in other aspects of their family and neighborhood life experience.

MATERNAL DEPRIVATION.   Of the three environmental factors influencing the children's development, maternal deprivation is the best known and most thoroughly documented through a number of independent studies (5). Gesell and Amatruda (17) summarize the adverse reactions of institutionalized infants in the first two and a half years of life in terms of lowered interest and reactivity (especially social, such as relating to people and vocalizing), reduced integration of total behavior, diminished exploration and manipulation of toys, resistance to new situations, impoverished initiative, and retardation of language behavior. Goldfarb's follow-up studies (18, 19, 20) of children institutionalized from infancy to three and a half years, and then reared in the same foster home, indicates that certain areas of retardation persist. He stresses particularly the prolonged effects on intellectual functioning, language development, and capacity for sustained relationships.

Without reviewing the studies of institutionalized children further, it is already clear that many of the leading characteristics of the preschool children in our study are similar to those reported in the literature on maternal deprivation. This raises the possibility that qualities noted in the children, such as delayed intellectual and language development, shallow nonspecific relationships, reduced investment in and enjoyment of themselves, diminished initiative, and docile behavior (despite poor capacity to control and modulate impulses) may be related to the effect of deficient maternal care, which exists for children of multiproblem families as a dynamic process, in spite of their being family-reared.

Although the children of such families are not raised in the quiet, orderly, sterile atmosphere of a well-run orphanage, the regular home visits which our staff made revealed that the children nevertheless lack consistent care from the same mothering person. They grow up in an environment in which the lack of care, consistency, and predictability add up to considerable personal, emotional, and social deprivation. Growing up in a noisy, hectic apartment with a mother whose physical and emotional presence is unreliable, and who is frequently overwhelmed by the manifold burdens of the household and the care of many children, the young children are frequently left alone for hours; they may be put off by themselves in a crib or a room, isolated from stimulation and with only a few toys for many hours each day (35). They are fed with propped-up bottles, often without being checked regardless of their cries. If they lose the nipple, or are unable to retrieve it or to hold the bottle, their needs may go unattended. When the mothers are around, their own needs may interfere with their capacity to give to their children. Diapers may not be changed, and, in general, there is little holding, comforting, and handling involved in the mother's infant and toddler care. A quiet baby is considered a "good baby" and self-activation and motor capacity is fine if this answers the mother's need and expectation to have her child grow up fast, and does not place any demands upon her. Thus, paradoxically, while the children are allowed to fend for themselves, the mothers dress them until or beyond school age, probably because it is easier. They also feed them bottles for years, often up to nursery school age. In other ways as well, the early care which the children experience is rather passivity-inducing in nature. Along the same lines, self-help, initiative, exploration, and manipulation are often restricted, and may be punished as "aggressive" or because they make "demands" or are seen as "controlling." Toys are minimal, usually kept out of reach and often age-inappropriate. More importantly, the children are rarely played with. Similarly, vocalizing and smiling often do not receive response from the busy mothers and reciprocal exchange is rare.

The deprivation which these youngsters experience, however, is not uniform, nor is it their sole experience. Not being held or cuddled may alternate with passionate hugging and kissing, or with impulsive teasing. For all the premium placed by the mothers on their offspring being passive, quiet, and good, they delight in and laugh at naughtiness. The mothers "expect," or at least respond to, behavior that meets their needs, and at times only shouting and crying (intensity of noise rather than appropriateness of request) succeeds in gaining their attention.

Thus, there is a mixed picture of stimulation (at times excessive and inappropriate) and deprivation, although the latter catches and holds our attention more. In relation to deprivation, what is particularly lacking during the first years are the many varied physical and emotional stimulations that are ordinarily involved in a reciprocal, mutually enjoyable relationship with the mother. At a later age being talked to and given explanations is almost equally vital. The important energizer and regulator functions of the mother in a process of reciprocal exchange are limited and weakened. Care is inconsistent and left to chance or impulse in the families. It is not geared to the children's needs or communications. Pleasure, play, exploration, and practice are at a minimum.

Some of the complex interrelated ramifications of the impact of these conditions on the early development of the children were touched upon indirectly in the foregoing chapter. The child-care conditions described above impede the children's shift from passivity to activity and do not provide the experience of *appropriate levels of discontent* (masterable frustration) which is such an important stimulus to mental activity and promotes "initiative for independence" (28). As maturation makes it possible for the children to be capable of purposive action and to develop a concept of the self as active, this capacity (except in the gross motor sphere) is not encouraged or offered opportunity for expression or practice. Finally, since care is insufficiently geared to the children's inner needs, there is not enough opportunity for them to perceive that their communication of inner needs has been understood and responded to. Thus, the prestages out of which competence and effectance develop (56) are thwarted. There is insufficient experience on the children's part of enduring frustration, of closing the gap between desire and actuality, of negotiating discontent through their own activity and their ability to effect their environment.

The illuminating study by Provence and Lipton (41) is of particular interest because their data emphasize the effects of inadequate mothering without the complicating influence of other factors (such as danger and devaluation) which must be taken into account with our sample. Their study is also of special interest because they provide a follow-up report on the children at age 3 and 4 after one to two and a half years of placement in a foster home. Their more specific and focused report on the effects of deprivation highlight those of our findings which are more strongly related to the influence of deficient maternal care, while at the same time emphasizing those which cannot be accounted for in this manner. Comparison of Provence and Lipton's findings to ours, therefore, proves interesting and valuable.

Although the children we studied were already 3 or older, they show a number of characteristics described in institutionalized children up to the age of 2. It can be postulated that some of the deficits of multiproblem-family children go back to the first two years of their lives, and that little in the subsequent year assists them in repairing the deficiencies and recovering the normal pace of development. For example, Provence and Lipton found delay in differentiation between the attendant and the stranger. The institutionalized children were amiable and bland, and there was an absence of anxiety in relation to strangers. They were more upset when they were moved from the familiar setting of the large room in which they lived than they were in the presence of strangers. It appeared that sameness of physical environment and their presence in the group were dominant factors in their *feeling of security,* and that they took comfort from the situation rather than from a relationship to an adult.

In relation to maintaining a feeling of security, it seems to us that whatever his experience has been, a child will make some effort to find security in some kind of sameness or predictability. In our sample we found that in nursery school the children experienced considerable difficulty making changes or transitions from one situation to another. They relied considerably on reading external cues in order to orient themselves and provide security. Since this involved literal following and imitation of external patterns, shifts and changes were distressing to them. It also appeared that the youngster's repetitiveness and desire to have things repeated in the same way were also part of their need to produce sameness and to assure predictability of situation and stimuli. In this regard, the way in which the children relate to people is of interest. It seems that they relate to people visually far more than emotionally and in this sense treat people like "the situation" in their need to assure themselves of sameness.

Of even greater interest to this discussion is Provence and Lipton's follow-up study of their sample after one to two and a half years in a stable foster home. After many months in a foster home, institutionalized children appear very much like the children in our sample. Like the children we studied, institutionalized children later exposed to good home environment do best developmentally in relation to gross motor skills. They show capacity to be engaging and attractive but appear indiscriminately friendly. They reveal impairments in thinking, especially in relation to their literalness, concreteness, and difficulty with tasks involving problem solving. Finally, the area of language is the slowest to improve, and within the language sphere the children's greatest gains involve learning by imitative repetition and rote, learning best words related to needs and routine matters of everyday life.

Despite the undoubted significance of the similarity between the children of multiproblem families and institutionalized children, the deviant development of children reared in disorganized problem-ridden families cannot be completely ascribed to, nor fully understood, in terms of deprivation alone. It is not only delayed and deficient; it is also uneven and anachronistic. This disparate feature of the children's development led us to consider other formative influences in their environment and relationship experiences. In this quest certain qualities of the children not previously emphasized in studies of deprived children caught our attention: the children's orientation to danger and their skill in manipulating; their high anxiety level, driven action-oriented quality, and trend toward diffuse motor discharge; their pseudoautonomy and proclamations of an independence they do not possess; their reliance on visual and auditory hyperalertness to orient and protect themselves; and, finally, the literalness of their imitation, learning, and thinking. Although institutionalized children after their foster home experience appear quite similar to disorganized-family children, Provence and Lipton do not emphasize these qualities. These differences in the children in our sample, particularly the uneven quality in their development, led us to consider the influence of other factors. In this process, the effects of devaluation and especially those of external danger stand out.

DEVALUATION.   Children of multiproblem families grow up in an environment in which there is a strong and pervasive sense of devaluation. It is a profound feeling which surrounds the children and invades their interactions and therefore has a continuing effect on their personal growth. As a general ingredient of life and relationships, devaluation is inextricably interwoven with other environmental forces and does not appear as an isolated factor in the children's milieu; thus, it is for conceptual purposes solely that this important environmental influence is discussed separately here.

In the particular slum neighborhood in which the children live there is an atmosphere of defeat and despair. Drifters, alcoholics, and derelict men and women reveal their sense of devaluation. They gravitate toward and submit to defeat, exploitation, and degradation. They demonstrate inability to achieve and perform vital personal, moral, work, and social-role functions by which human beings establish and maintain their self-esteem.

Low socioeconomic families in general, and multiproblem families in particular, experience devaluation by the larger society. These families *are* dispossessed. Although this is most evident along racial lines, the sense of being derogated by and alienated

from the dominant society cuts across color lines for this socioeconomic group. Not only are various important life opportunities
deficient but their second-class citizenship even lacks certain
human or civil rights. Police raids in the middle of the night to
prove cohabitational abuse of public assistance funds is but one
example of this devalued civil rights status.

This negative feedback of devalued status in the eyes of the community is particularly evident and depressing for disorganized low
socioeconomic families. Dependence on public welfare (which was
the case for most of the families we studied) illustrates this. Starting with the demeaning "means test" and carrying through many
of the families' contacts with public welfare, they experience derogation in the manner in which they are treated (57) and are often
the objects of suspicion and hostility. This negative, devaluing
feedback process is reciprocal in the sense that many times the families themselves succeed unwittingly in inducing others to treat
them with disrespect which is similar to and reinforces their own
lack of respect for themselves.

Within the disorganized families themselves, low self-esteem and
self-devaluation are repeatedly in evidence. The parents' sense of
hopelessness regarding their future lot in life and helplessness to
deal with personal concerns or environmental forces pervades family life. The parents reveal little sense of capacity to achieve or
produce or be something valuable in personal, child rearing, marital, learning, or work terms. Most damaging of all for the children's feelings of self-worth is their own mother's tendency to de-
value them. Rank (43) observes: "What is most evident to me is
not that the mothers were detached and 'not there' but rather that
the mothers' control over their own emotions was shaky and unstable, that the devaluation of the child fluctuated with the degree of
her own self-esteem, that she thus transmitted her own worthlessness to her child."

At home the children had few enduring possessions. The clothes
of one child were put on another. In the nursery school, we saw
little or no evidence of property rights or sense of possession. Nor
were the children able to fight for their rights. We did see the
strong but transient *gimme* or *I want* and *mine*. We did see the
urge to have, but without the strong concomitant desire to hold on
to and use. In the children the most important possession of all,

possession of the parents and their love, did not appear strong enough. The children did not have sufficient experience in relation to being their parents' valued possession, yet loved as a separate person for their own sake. We feel that there must be some continuing basic experience in a child's life of being loved because "I am" before and in order that a child can achieve the experience of being loved for "what I am" (that is, for personal values, like being decent, thoughtful, generous) or for "what I do" (achievements, skills, moral behavior).

The children's achievements or products are often ignored or deprecated. They seldom experience praise or appreciation for their efforts, and at times their attempts to attain recognition appear to threaten their parents. Mothers have been heard to say in front of others, "Who is he? He's a nobody," or derogatorily, "She thinks she's somebody."

We feel that these observations are correlated with what we see in the nursery school. Initially, the children show little confidence in themselves, interest in making things, or esteem for their products or themselves. Importantly, in relation to their intellectual functioning, the children show little regard for the products of their minds. The whole range of mental activity (thinking, imagination, learning, asking questions, expressing ideas, developing knowledge and capacity to solve problems) is not valued by them nor encouraged by their parents. The implications of this for the children's school functioning is clearly evident in their approach to learning situations.

These children may pretend a confidence and independence they cannot demonstrate or sustain, only to suffer humiliation when their lack of capability is exposed. Reduced to helplessness by such realizations, they reveal strong feelings of self-devaluation and their controls may collapse, whereupon they dash around wildly or regress to infantile displays or appear crushed and give up. Loss of control is accompanied by deterioration of their body control. Thus, devaluation and lowered self-regard can be seen throughout the children's milieu and its effect on their growth is obviously far-reaching.

EXTERNAL DANGER. Early in our experience with the preschool offspring of problem-ridden low socioeconomic families, we were impressed with the fact that the children and their parents were not suffering solely from a deficiency disease. Although there are important deficiencies in their lives, we are struck by features and qualities which are present in the personal make-up and family-life patterns of this group. This is particularly notable in the children's development, which involves more than deficit and delay; it is also deviant in its uneven quality. This disparate quality drew our attention to the role of external danger as a shaping influence in their growth. They are regularly exposed to real dangers in their family and neighborhood lives. From the first months of life on, actual or potential harm poses a threat to them. The kinds of danger which surround them involve the fact that they must bear the brunt of harsh punishment and parental loss of control. They are yelled at, slapped, and beaten in inconsistent, confusing ways. They are punished for accidents as well as intentional naughtiness, for things they haven't done as well as things they have, even for things that previously and on other occasions they have been encouraged to do. These children witness parental drunkenness, battles, and sexual activities, and experience neglect and abuse. Alcoholism, violence, promiscuity, and prostitution are not abstract concepts, but home and neighborhood life experience for them. Unpredictably, their mothers leave them alone or in the unreliable care of others, and threatened desertion, homelessness, and police action continually hang over their heads.

Gradually, as we reflected on the impact of these ubiquitous dangers on the children, a conceptual framework emerged. This framework differs from past conceptions in the emphasis it places on the role of outer danger in the children's life adjustment. We tend to emphasize external danger because it generally has not received much attention in the literature on hard-core or multiproblem families, whereas, by contrast, deprivation has been given considerable recognition as the dominant or sometimes sole etiological factor. As we have emphasized before (32), our findings lead us to postulate that external danger in the children's lives mobilizes early and continuous self-preservative interests and emphasizes survival first and foremost. Hence, the children develop an early coping orientation to life, and show considerable efforts toward compensation. They use what they have developed to make up for their own deficiencies and to cope with their dangerous family and neighborhood environments. They develop early facility to know well what adults like, dislike, or fear, to manipulate the environment, and to present themselves endearingly if need be (4).

External danger and survival considerations appear to influence the children's growth on a number of levels:

1. They seem to contribute to a thwarting of the children's instinctual life. In the interests of managing to please, getting along, and avoiding harsh punishment, the children appear to ignore or relinquish instinctual interests and virtually any expression of direct resistance in the form of defiance and anger. One has the impression that they dare not express aggression, resentment, and hostility openly. Consequently, they are compliant. This compliance substitutes for voluntary control achieved through mastery. In the nursery school, aggression, which was only occasionally expressed openly, gained indirect expression in the children's imitative reenactments in play of their parents' aggressiveness and in the carry-over to others of their sadomasochistic orientation toward their parents (4). Similarly, it seems that the children dare not insist that their needs be met nor acknowledge dependency yearnings lest this open the floodgates of inner longing and make them victims of their own painful feelings of unmet needs. Such expressions at home run the risk of displeasing their parents and make them liable to further painful rejection. The children's dependency continues in other forms. After a while in nursery school some of the children are repeatedly caught up in expressions of their fear and wish to be babies. They are often so dominated by their need for attention that their various efforts at learning and developing skills are disrupted by their intense rivalrous feelings when they happen to see the teacher turn to another child.

The children are exposed to confusion and inconsistency as well as to excessive frustration of their instinctual needs. For example, holding and being cuddled are excessively frustrated at times. On the other hand, they may be hugged and kissed intensely in keeping with their parents' transient need. They are often allowed prolonged overindulgence, such as having bottles until they are three or four years of age. Besides being overstimulated, they are often stimulated out of phase when they are regularly exposed to sexual and aggressive sights and sounds and when they become the target of their parents' sadism in the form of teasing and impulsive cruelty. These all contribute to persistence of the children's craving for pleasure which a child ordinarily learns to postpone or give up.

For the children of problem-ridden families, the important gains that normally accrue via ego mastery (through a gratifying relationship experience which also helps them to endure disappointment) are unfortunately weakened. They do not have enough experience in expressing intense urges and feelings which their mothers meet but also regulate. They come to fear such intense feelings and drives. Observers of child development feel that such passive experience with a mother who regulates and comes to the child's aid is of vital importance. In this way, the child experiences intense fears, feelings, and urges that he is able to tolerate with parental aid. Later, the child goes through a process in which he is increasingly able to meet and cope with such strong urges through his own efforts in collaboration with his parents. In multiproblem-family children the outgrowth of this partnership, the stepwise internalization of the model of the parents' protective regulation, fails to occur. Without this internal aid the children tend to externalize their intense urges and feelings and to fear them in others. Danger adds to the effect. Since expression of intense feelings may be harshly punished by their mothers, the children tend not to entrust and direct their needs toward their mothers (a process so fundamental in the partnership that leads to internalization). The general skill which the children acquire in protecting themselves from outer danger adds to this tendency to externalize, since they appear to have better barriers to outside threats than they do in relation to inner ones.

2. Outer danger also appears to influence development in terms of the children's inner regulating mechanisms and the stages of conscience formation usually noted in children of preschool age (11, 22). There are several areas where we believe survival considerations affect the children's ability to control their behavior and may in turn affect the adequacy and nature of their later conscience formation.

To begin with, the real dangers in the children's lives foster facile compliance and obedience in which the children parrot or follow rules they often do not understand. They apply controls mainly through fear, and rely too heavily on reinforcement from an outside agent instead of from internalized prohibitions. Secondly, in relation to the harsh treatment which they receive, these youngsters tend to cope with the fearful and aggressive aspects of their parents by imitative "identification with the aggressor." They yell, shout, and swear. The mothers often cannot tolerate these reflections of themselves and punish the children. They try to teach the children to "do as I say, not as I do." These factors of confusion and contradiction will lead to later faulty conscience formation or will impede the process of internalizing standards of behavior. Without predictable responses from their parents, the children have difficulty assessing what is approved or disapproved, right or wrong. Finally, the children's focus on danger plays a part in the delay in their capacity for concept formation and abstraction. Abstraction is essential to the process of forming ideals (49) and the concept of intention is vital in a child's developing a sense of responsibility, both of which are important in later healthy functioning of the conscience.

3. It is, however, in relation to the self particularly that the influence of external danger and self-preservative needs is most far-reaching in the lives of multiproblem-family children. Four interrelated sets of qualities which we observed in them illustrate this influence.

a. Danger Orientation. Despite their facile friendliness and appealing manner, we are struck by their tension and guardedness. Their distrustfulness seems more than the absence of trust, it is also a vigilant watchfulness to avoid threats. Despite surface contentment, their furtive looks betray their high level of anxiety and danger orientation. Their bland, amiable smile appears to be part of the defense against danger in the sense that, in spite of their guardedness, they present a friendly façade which experience has proved to be safest and most successful when meeting strangers. In nursery school, if something happens suddenly or unexpectedly (if the juice spills or a block building is bumped into), all of the children react as though they are guilty and will be punished. There is no such thing as an accident. The concept seems as foreign to them as the idea of intention. Even passing events are reacted to as dangerous and they are ever on the lookout for the worst to occur.

b. Visual and Auditory Hyperalertness to Some Stimuli and Hypoalertness to Others. They are alert to the sounds and sights of the street, to the teacher's whereabouts and attention, whom she is with, and who is getting something. Everyday nursery school stimuli, or even the teacher's spoken direction, cannot compete for the children's attention in view of their preoccupation with the task of avoiding potentially noxious situations. A feature of this hyperreactivity is their use of vision to protect themselves; they show intense visual scanning of the environment in any new or uncertain situation. They attempt to use visual recognition and sizing up as a means of orienting themselves and show particular adeptness in reading observable cues. It appears that the children "navigate" through life situations by triangulation rather than by a built-in guidance system.

Nevertheless, while they attempt to prevent the teacher's being too distant, they also do not let her get too close. It is as though they have to protect themselves against both painful distance (like loss of the teacher's attention or being exposed to her leaving) and painful closeness (such as intrusion, unexpected punishment, rejection, or devaluation). Either extreme is too dangerous.

Clinical experience reveals the frequency with which children who are maladjusted have difficulty establishing a comfortable balance between closeness and distance in their interpersonal relationships. The distinctive feature in this area for multiproblem-family children is the fact that they seem to need to negotiate this interpersonal problem of keeping a safe closeness and distance through geographical means, wherein they can use their special senses, especially vision. This is in sharp contrast to the more frequent clinical experience with children who use emotion, ideation, or fantasy to negotiate the closeness-distance issue in interpersonal relations, when this is for some reason distressing to them.

Silberman (54), referring to the work of Martin Deutsch (7), emphasizes that slum children lack the auditory discrimination that is essential to reading. He feels that due to the noise level at home the slum child develops the ability to wall himself off from his surroundings and fails to develop an ability to distinguish between relevant and irrelevant sounds and to screen out the irrelevant. If, for instance, a truck rumbles by while a teacher is talking, the lower-class pupil pays more attention to the noise of the truck.

In considering this observation, one must note that for multiproblem-family children spoken words do not have the meaning or reliability that they have for ordinary middle-class children. Apart from language, however, Silberman's comment involves *his* definition of relevance and irrelevance, not the slum child's. Aside from the children's low attention and concentration span and their distractibility, it seems to us that the noise of the truck rumbling in the street is relevant to children of lower-class families because it presents a threat. On the other hand, initially the teacher's words are not very relevant and do not have to be guarded against. Gradually, as the children feel safer in nursery school, their hyperalertness to environmental noise diminishes; more importantly, as they develop a more meaningful relationship to their consistent and trustworthy teacher and her reliable language, their capacity to discriminate what she says against background noises improves.

c. *The Use of Many Forms of Denial, Such as Avoidance, Evasion, Obliviousness, and Ignoring.* Anna Freud (12) speaks of the likelihood that children develop defenses in relation to real external danger which are comparable to the defenses they develop in relation to intrapsychic danger. We believe the primitive forms of denial seen in multiproblem-family children illustrate this. The children avoid particularly noxious outside stimuli by not being aware of them. For example, they handle the major and repeated threat of actual separation from their mothers by being oblivious of its existence. Similarly, although they keep careful track of the teacher's whereabouts when she is in the room, they ignore her when she leaves the room. These are examples of denial by not perceiving. It appears that when the children are about to be overwhelmed by a threat and feel helpless to deal with it, their coping devices are called into play, but instead of visual alertness they defend themselves by nonrecognition and nonperception.

d. *Certain Areas of Advanced or "Precocious" Ability.* The term *precocious* is placed in quotation marks because it should be distinguished from Anna Freud's use of the term to describe advanced ego development and functioning in children who later tend to have rather severe obsessive-compulsive characters. These precocious abilities have high survival value for the children. The kind of above-age-expectancy functioning that we have in mind in using this term is, for example, the children's role reversal with their parents. They are pushed into shopping, stalling bill collectors, making decisions for their parents, and caring for younger siblings. These areas of advanced function appear to be quite similar to Redl's description (46) of hypertrophied ego functioning in delinquent children. In this role reversal, several of the children's coping capacities stimulated by survival considerations are combined—their use of observable cues to orient themselves and their facility at imitation and learning by rote. The process is further reinforced by the high premium placed by the parents on having their own needs met.

These areas of precocious functioning do not appear to be as indicative of fragility in development as they are of unevenness and disparity. They are strengths which are also weaknesses. The children's early and in some ways premature coping patterns and above-age-expectancy functioning play an important role in their efforts to accommodate to their deviant milieu, but they also contribute to the children's inflexibility and literalness. The pseudo independence thus created substitutes for and undermines the development of later fuller independence.

REFERENCES

References for Chapters 6 and 7 begin on page 158.

DEVELOPMENTAL DEVIATIONS CONSIDERED IN THE LIGHT OF ENVIRONMENTAL FORCES

Charles A. Malone

IN CONSIDERING the leading psychological and social characteristics of the multiproblem-family children we studied, we are cognizant of the fact that the children in our sample are of preschool age, and therefore still in their formative years; strong inner and outer developmental forces will continue to shape their growth. We are not describing a finished product, but simply distinctive trends of deviant development in children who are still growing, changing, and developing. Nevertheless, the children appear to have started on a definite path in development, and they are "off course" in their journey thus far. It is important to consider the deviations in their development at the preschool age, not only because they formed an important basis for our therapeutic-educational nursery school program, *but also because recognition of these deviations is essential to understanding and gaining perspective on a whole group of low socioeconomic preschool children.* (Section III will illustrate the extent to which many of these deviant trends persist into adult life.) Our approach to the children's developmental deviation will be to consider leading features and characteristics of their make-up as observed in the nursery school in the light of the effects of deprivation, danger, and devaluation.

THE USE OF VISION

It is clear from the material presented and discussed earlier that one of the distinguishing qualities observed in the children from problem-ridden, low socioeconomic families is their *use of vision*. Certain aspects of their use of vision seem to illustrate a relationship between environmental influences and the children's attempts to compensate for deficiencies in themselves or their social reality by using what they have at their disposal. We have already underscored, in relation to the effects of external danger, their alertness and focus on outside signals. A fundamental feature of their use of vision involves efforts to protect and orient themselves. In this process, they orient themselves to *the form* of an observable pattern, even though they may not recognize or understand the *substance* of that pattern. For instance, in the nursery school the children see and reflect imitatively the facial expressions of others although they do not appear to have a sense or inner recognition of the person's feelings. They imitatively, and even compliantly, follow patterns and routines without evidence of having an understanding of their meaning and purpose. The children make "perceptual identifications" (6) or imitative kinds of identification with the visible, concrete qualities of the teacher instead of with her emotionally experienced qualities. They frequently repeat in a rote manner patterns and behavior learned by this process of visual recognition and imitative reflection as though needing to reinforce them by repetition. Similarly, they request repetitions, often of a "carbon-copy" nature, from the teacher as though to reassure themselves that something is so or exists or will be repeated. It is our impression that in this manner the children's use of vision plays a role in their compensatory efforts aimed at providing themselves with some degree of security.

Sandler (51) discusses children's use of perception to provide a background of safety. He contends that the act of perception is an act of mastery through which the child copes with excitation and is thus protected from being overwhelmed by excessive sensory stimulation. He postulates that this process is accompanied by a feeling of safety which provides a background of security for everyday experience. Sandler, however, speaks of perception as though it takes place uniformly and is a totally integrated process. In relation to normal children this is probably a reasonable assumption, but in relation to multiproblem-family children it seems to us that perceptual development follows disparate lines which are reflected in the uneven perceptual capacities (for instance, hypoalertness to some stimuli and hyperalertness to others) which we observe in nursery school. The children appear to utilize certain kinds of perceptual skill involving vision to cope with excitation and provide some degree of safety, but this is insufficiently coordinated with and supported by other aspects of personality organization and integration.

The idea of disparate lines of development in relation to particular areas of a child's functioning is not new. Freud and Burlingham (14) called attention to the fact that children reared in isolation from their parents have good or even advanced motor development whereas their language and social development lag behind. On the other hand, Provence and Lipton (41) report that coordinated utilization of fine motor skills in accomplishing manipulations of toys lags behind in institutionalized children reared in isolation from their mothers. Thus, young children raised in an institution appear to be advanced in one area of motor development and retarded in another.

It seems reasonable to us to suppose that differences similar to those reported in relation to motor development obtain in regard to the development of perceptual capacity and organization. For example, in the children in our sample, perceptual development is anachronistic in that advanced or at least age-appropriate capacities exist side by side with undeveloped or weakly developed capacities. Disparate features of a child's development (that is, motor skill or perception) may be related to the degree to which the functional skills involved are dependent on social learning. Thus, we note that in nursery school the children use visual capacities which are more dependent on maturation to substitute for weakly developed empathic perceptual skills which are more dependent on social experience. This is illustrated when the children observe and imitatively reflect the facial expressions of others in lieu of perceiving and having an inner sense of the feelings of another person. Of course, having an inner sense of the feelings of others involves more than perceiving and organizing perceptions. It also involves cognitive-affective operations, memory, internal representation, and other ego functions that are integrated into a meaningful whole. This is just the point we are making, namely that the children use skills in vision and imitation (coping capacities stimulated by external danger and survival considerations) to compensate not only for weakly developed perceptual skills and organization, but also for other deficiencies in their development.

Along the same lines, we noted that the children make imitative "identifications" with the observable qualities of another person rather than with the felt qualities of that person. *The imitative perceptual process which the children make use of lacks the experience of shared feelings and a history of a meaningful love relationship.* As a result, the type of "identification" which they make appears shallow and seems easily given up and replaced by another.

Nevertheless, one can presume that their use of vision supplies the children with an increased feeling of safety. This hard-earned security, unfortunately, may not be long-lasting, however, because there is not sufficient stable internalization. Consequently, we observe that the children frequently repeat patterns and behavior acquired by this process of visual recognition and imitative reflection and request similar literal repetitions from the teacher in order to reassure themselves. Apparently, they do this as an expression of their need for sameness and in order to reaffirm and reinforce the perceptual substitution which they have made. This type of process appears to be related to the literalness and need for regular reinforcement which we observe to be major handicaps in the children's progress in learning and development of independence over the course of their nursery school experience.

Certainly the fact that the children grow up in a dangerous environment, a world which shifts and changes in unpredictably painful ways, contributes to the accentuation of vision as a means of self-protection. Studies of child development carried out at Yale by Ritvo and Solnit (48) suggest that such accentuation of vision begins early and is intimately connected with discomfort or "danger" in the mother-child relationship. They describe the development of a preschool child whose relations with her mother were dominated by discomfort. They point out that the child's development, while lagging behind in certain areas, was accelerated in three areas—capacity for visual recognition, use of imitation, and motor skill. The child used her skills for self-protection and in particular used vision for sharper awareness and control of the threatening environment. In strange or new situations this child used her visual acuity to scan the environment for signals of danger. Rather than form a close, trusting bond with her mother this youngster relied primarily on her own skills and developed a premature emphasis on "do it myself" and control. It appeared to Ritvo and Solnit that due to discomfort and danger experienced in relation to her mother, this child had shifted her investment away from people to the mental act of visual recognition. The similarities at the preschool age between the children in our sample and the child described by Ritvo and Solnit suggest that it may be that the children's experiences with their discomforting, inappropriately overstimulating, punitive, and at times frightening mothers have prompted them to turn away from their mothers and invest in themselves and their own equipment and capacity to avoid pain. We suspect that this type of experience promotes distrust of others wherein keeping a safe distance and manipulative control of the situation interfere with and substitute for close affective relations. Thus, the children tend to turn away from certain experiences that involve entrusting oneself completely to another which would provide a cornerstone for certain critical inner development.

THE USE OF IMITATION

Closely related to the accentuation of vision in multiproblem-family children is their emphasis on imitation. They imitate gestures, words, facial expressions, activities, and choices—indeed, the widest range of observable phenomena. There are, however, distinctive characteristics noted in the children's imitation. Imitation of the teacher occurs before a relationship with her is established. Imitation has a "carbon-copy," literal quality in that what is imitated most readily are the concrete features of a person or situation. Therefore, imitation often occurs out of context or devoid of specific personal meaning. For instance, the teacher's verbalized caution at a street crossing is parroted without regard for her intention or what she is warning against. Thus, Susan, age 4, repeats the teacher's "Watch out for the cars, kids" but blithely crosses the intersection herself without care. At times, imitation appears to have a defensive purpose in the sense that it may be used as a means of coping with a new situation or when the children are anxious or under stress. With their mothers, the teacher, and with strangers imitation occasionally appears to have the function of holding off. It is as though imitation is used to please people (such as mother or teacher), to keep them interested and gain their attention while also keeping them at "arm's length." Finally, in the frequency with which imitation is noted in the children, one is aware of the degree to which they expend their energies in imitative rather than in independent, self-directed ways.

The children's marked use of imitation and its distinctive characteristics appear to us to be related to different aspects of their environmental experience. *Both what is lacking and what is present in the environment seem to combine to produce similar effects.* To begin with, in the children's early experience various aspects of activity, exploration, and self-help have been discouraged. The parents do not encourage the children to feel that their lead will be followed; rather, they indicate their own desire to have the children follow their lead and meet their needs. The mothers, particularly, tend to reveal their self-love by treating the children as extensions of themselves and showing pleasure when the children gratify them or entertain and perform for them. Thus, in the interest of avoiding rejection or harsh criticism and holding onto gratification they have in their relations with their parents, the children learn to imitatively follow the parents' lead.

Imitation as a way of relating and a means of self-protection is carried over into nursery school. Although demanding of attention and things from the teacher, the project children did not turn to her for help and closeness. Yet they readily imitated her gestures, parroted her words, and followed her lead. In other words, they bring into nursery school an important mode of relating to their own mothers—to perform, follow, please, and avoid punishment *by using imitation.* They bring their means of maintaining contact while keeping at a safe distance, their means of pleasing and doing what they think is expected.

For most of the children there is the added confusion of being cared for by multiple mother substitutes or unreliable caretakers who have differing child-rearing attitudes and who make different demands on the children. What is "expectable" in their environment is that it changes. In view of their mothers' shifting moods and the contradiction of being cared for by unreliable mother substitutes, it behooves the children to shift their behavior imitatively to suit external changes.

The very unreliability of the environment which at least partly deprives these youngsters of adequate nutriment (stimulation, regulation, and support) for developing selfhood and individuality is what they must take into account. In a sense, active self-direction would be a handicap in their type of environment and would lead to repeated conflicts. The "danger" for disorganized-family children is to deviate from what adults expect. They do not have inner confidence that they will not suddenly be whacked or humiliated or deserted, or that the situation will not unexpectedly change. They must somehow do what avoids pain and hopefully will be pleasing, or at least get them by. Lacking certain inner security, resourcefulness, and direction, and pushed by the environment to focus on what is outside, the children lean heavily on environmental cues. They are quick to "learn" the form without seeming to grasp the substance. They are ill-equipped personally and environmentally unsupported to attend to the subtle, relatively hidden aspects of interpersonal exchange; in a sense they cannot afford such luxury. They must match what they can as quickly as they can, being ready to shift adroitly to a new match at a moment's notice.

In this task of *accommodation,* the children are assisted by skills and abilities (danger orientation, hyperalertness to adults, visual and auditory sensitivity) apparently stimulated by external danger. Such capacities do provide them with tools which aid them in their imitative adjustment to people and situations. The children's abilities and compensatory efforts and, indeed, the whole orientation of the process of accommodation, however, increase their dependence on outside cues and further the degree to which they are *bound to external stimuli.* The literalness and rigidity of the children's imitative behavior reflects the degree to which they are bound to outer stimuli and to which they are tied to observable, externally-directed patterns. While imitation assists these young-sters to adjust to their deviant milieu it also increases their depend-ence on *manifest* patterns, signals, and behavior.

IDENTIFICATION

This discussion of imitation leads us to consider the topic of identification. Ordinarily, certain kinds of imitation in children are considered to be an early form or prestage of the process of identification. The term *imitation identification* is used to describe early or intermediate forms of identification in which imitation is rather strongly evident and internalization does not appear to have taken place. Our observations of disorganized family children do not indicate that they form reasonably lasting identifications; they do not seem to take over the characteristics of others in the inte-grated fashion usually observed in the identification of preschool children. What we note instead are imitative identifications with the teacher and others which precede a meaningful relationship to that person. Before discussing the children's imitative or percep-tual identifications, however, a few comments about the process of internalization (of which identification is a part) are in order.

In an earlier publication (31) stemming from the work of the project, we stressed that one of the most important delays in the children's development, contributing to their problems, is the lag in developing stable internalization. Further experience and work with the children in our sample only adds to our sense of the im-portance of this lack of stable internalization. Appreciating the nature of internalization in the children is critical to understand-ing not only their psychological characteristics and deviant devel-opment, but also their efforts at compensation. For many of the children's efforts are directed at compensating for deficiencies in their internalizations.

Internalization is defined most broadly by Hartmann and Loew-enstein (22): "We would speak of *internalization* when regula-tions that have taken place in interaction with the outside world are replaced by inner regulation." Ritvo and Solnit (48) state: "internalization is a term used to describe the process by which the ego forms inner or psychic representations of object persons to whom the child is attached that originally (and still) influence the child from without. The process is a continuum from perceptions to imitations to taking over a characteristic of an object in ego identification. The more developed the internalization process, the more subtly and intimately blended is that attitude or characteristic as part of the ego."

The discussions in Hendrick's paper on early identification (24) and in Sandler's paper on the process of internalization (52) imply, although they do not specifically state, that stable internal models arise under the influence of an "average-expectable" environment (21). The confusing, unpredictable features of the social reality of multiproblem-family children betray the lack of an average-expectable quality and underscore their handicap in forming stable internalizations. The inconsistent quality of the children's environment impedes and limits the process of internalization which depends upon matching between inner anticipation and outer reality. Thus, we can readily point to inadequate or incomplete internalization in the children. They have difficulty relying on inner regulatory mechanisms in regard to processes involving assessment, anticipation, and planning.

It is easy enough to identify handicaps and deficiencies in salient features of internalization in these children, but at the same time it should be noted that whatever does have some degree of consistency and reliability in their environment will be taken in or at least "taken on" by them. Even when the fact that impresses itself upon the children is that you can expect change, this will be learned in the socialization process they go through. For instance, in lieu of relying on inner cues or a process of self-assurance, the children learn to depend on outside signals in a process of nimble "other assurance."

What we mean to stress is that in the children's environment, where confusion and inconsistency predominate, there are qualities of relationship experience and features of the environment that have some or a fair degree of constancy and that are reinforced. The children latch on to such elements, particularly those which occur in relation to the parents or other significant persons, when they are able to recognize them. They cling to them all the more tenaciously because these young children have gained so little emancipation from their environment. They seek to repeat these more reliable encounters in a rather unyielding way. The limited experience of predictability and "fitting together" with their environment they do achieve are models for their future. As all children do, these children carry the history of their relationship experiences in their identifications (immature and imitative though they may be) and repeat past relationship experiences with new people. (See discussion of identification with the aggressor, below.) The very constricted nature of the children's inner repertoire of alternatives or detailed and elaborated models makes the models which they do have, and the repertoire of choices which they do learn, all the more important.

The degree of imitation in the children's identification, as well as its defensive quality and the fact that internalization processes related to identification appear incomplete, lead us to conclude that the children are fixated at an early stage in the identification process. Knowledge of normal identification (22, 24, 26) quickly sharpens our focus on the developmental delay present in the identifications of children of disorganized low socioeconomic families.

Identification, as we understand it, requires a *sufficient* degree of specific attachment to a loved person, self-nonself differentiation, capacity to tolerate frustration, and the stimulation of masterable discontent (24, 58). These ego-developmental elements (and the numerous personality growth factors which contribute to them) must be present in a degree sufficient for a young child to resolve the pain and distress of loss (of a loved person) by the process of identification. By *loss* we mean relative loss such as is involved in disappointment, temporary separation, and frustration of instinctual wishes, as well as complete loss through death or permanent separation.

When one considers the weakness of the children's capacity for strongly felt specific attachment to a loved one, self-nonself differentiation, tolerance of frustration, and their insufficient experience with masterable discontent, one is not surprised that their identifications are predominantly immature and imitative, or that they are easily formed and as readily abandoned.

The knowledge of identification provided by the literature contributes to our awareness of what is missing or deficient in the children's identifications, but it does not provide much information about what is present. What we are struck by in the children is the prevalence of imitation, imitative forms of identification with the aggressor, and the defensive quality of their perceptual identifications.

The work of Ritvo and Solnit (48) sheds some light on the problem of understanding the qualities which are present in the children's immature identifications. Clinicians are familiar with the fact that an extreme gratification-frustration imbalance, characteristic of a grossly disturbed mother-child relationship, profoundly distorts the identification process. Ritvo and Solnit, however, suggest that even less extreme imbalance in a more ordinary mother-child relationship than has previously been postulated may interfere with identification and produce deviation in development. They propose that when a child's early experience with his mother is predominantly discomforting and frustrating, the identification with her is defensive in nature, internalization is incomplete, and the child does not show the gains in adaptive activities and functions which normally accrue from identification. They believe that the child's experience of pain and discomfort in relation to a parent (such as aggressive treatment) makes the parent at least partially dangerous. As a result the child is not receptive to the mother, but rather wards off and keeps her at a safe distance. They conclude that "When internalization proceeds by way of a predominantly positive tie to the love person, it is more likely to proceed to completion than the internalization that develops from the predominantly aggressive tie."

Identification with the Aggressor. The issue of discomfort and aggression in the children's relationships with their parents, and the question of identification which develops from a predominantly aggressive tie to parents focuses our attention on a particular aspect of the children's play, namely their play reenactments of adult roles and their imitative identifications with aggressive figures (12).

In nursery school, we note the numerous indications that these youngsters attempt to cope with the threatening aspects of their parents by imitative identification. In imitating the parents' aggression, they are doing actively what they have experienced and continue to experience passively. In play, they assume adult roles in which they yell, curse, and punish as an outlet for their poorly mastered aggressive drives. The real or imagined transgression of another child in such play is an "acceptable" or "safe" excuse to swoop in and denounce, criticize, and punish that child. It appears that they use such identification with the aggressor as part of their repetitive efforts in play to master and assimilate hurtful and threatening aspects of their relationships with their parents, much in the manner described by Freud (16) and Waelder (55). To judge from the persistence of this play and its rather stereotyped quality, however, the children do not seem to be able to work through their distress and assimilate the threat.

It is a sad and unhappy fact that being aggressively treated—punished, devalued, yelled at, and controlled—*is* the way in which these children have experienced relationship and closeness with their parents. Aggressive behavior is a means of communicating and contacting in their families. Hence, they tend, by their repetition of this experience, to recreate in nursery school the aggressive relationship they have known at home. Thus, there is little comforting, protecting, or tenderness in their caretaking play with dolls. Should their imitation be continued in their later behavior as adults, the children will, to some extent at least, become poorly controlled, angry, punitive, dissatisfied adults and parents like their own.

It is of importance that the children tend to perpetuate this type of aggressive relationship by repetition. Not only do they hit and punish the "bad" one, but they also provoke being chased, hit, criticized, or punished by others through teasing, grabbing, or naughtiness. The aggression that they have experienced has been exciting and in some ways gratifying so that we see some of the children attempting to provoke the same sadomasochistic relationship with the teacher that they have known with their parents.

The defensiveness of this process and the fact that aggression is otherwise usually expressed covertly and impulsively, and is generally guarded against (such as denial of or relinquishment of aggressive wishes in the service of self-preservation), reduces opportunities for mastery of the aggressive drive in behavior and human relations. Interpersonal relationships tend to remain too closely tied to power struggle and control issues. The issue of who has power and who is in control dominates whereas affection and tenderness are interpersonal experiences that are more foreign to the children.

THE ISSUE OF SEPARATION

One of the most striking things about the children noted in their early nursery school experience was the absence of separation anxiety. Indeed, it was as though the fact of leaving their mothers and traveling to a new place with a stranger (teacher) or the fact of leaving the nursery school and returning home was not noticed. The parents also did not appear to recognize the fact of separation. It seemed that the families ignored leave-taking and returning. This seeming obliviousness and nonrecognition of separation, as we said earlier, is one of the interesting manifestations of a primitive form of denial by not seeing.

Later, in nursery school, as the children developed a meaningful attachment to the teacher, anxiety and distress over separation, loss, and aloneness were expressed repeatedly toward the teacher and in their play. Sometimes it appeared as dread of abandonment. The children appeared to be concerned about helplessness and the total loss of a loved person which is an early developmental issue. Many of the children worked on the issue of separation with the teacher in games and play revolving around coming and going, and in verbal exchange. These are familiar means similar to those younger children employ in relation to their mothers. Although all of the children were eventually able to bring out their fear, only some felt sufficiently secure to express to their mothers their feelings of anxiety over separation. When this occurred, only some of the mothers were able to respond to their children's expression of fear with reassurance and support. Some of the mothers then developed more responsibility about not leaving their children unexpectedly or in the unreliable care of others. Other mothers, however, were not able to respond supportively because of their own separation difficulties or because of feeling overburdened. When the mothers did not respond to or even rejected expressions of separation anxiety and when unexpected separation or temporary abandonment continued to occur, the children's efforts at surmounting their fears were greatly handicapped.

Provence and Lipton (41) report that when placed in foster homes institutionalized children showed minimal evidence of upset. Only after they revealed signs of developing a meaningful relationship with their foster mothers, did they begin to manifest typical separation anxiety specifically in relation to their foster mothers. Shortly afterward, however, these children stopped showing separation anxiety and reverted back to their former general nonspecific friendliness. Their response to strangers was again hardly different in intensity or meaningfulness from their response to their foster mothers. These observations appear quite similar to our findings concerning multiproblem-family children who also seem to avoid expressing and focusing on their separation fear with their parents and at the same time maintain a nonspecific friendly approach to everyone. Unless given considerable support and provided with corrective relationship experience (such as occurred in the nursery school), the children apparently withdraw from coping with this painful issue and thereby lose the usual high degree of specificity found in children's attachments to people. Instead, they relate superficially (and in the same manner) to everyone, and their capacity and willingness to weather frustrations and separation is undermined.

LITERALNESS AND INFLEXIBILITY

Among the leading characteristics of children from problem-ridden families, literalness and inflexibility stand out. These qualities are seen in relation to the children's imitation, language, thinking, and affective responses. Their importance, however, goes beyond the frequency with which they are noted as qualifying features in the children's make-up; it derived mainly from the fact that they persisted virtually unmodified in the children despite one and a half to three years of attendance in the nursery school and several years of concomitant intensive work with the families. Since literalness and inflexibility impede the youngster's adjustment in certain distinctive ways (especially in relation to learning), their practical significance is notable.

In nursery school, the teacher's efforts to introduce variety were often frustrated by the children's sticking rigidly and rather tenaciously to one way of doing things. The youngsters welcome simple, well-structured, reasonably predictable routines. Although we expected that predictable structure would be more important to these children than to ordinary preschoolers, we did not anticipate how much they would depend upon the external structuralization of the program. We soon became aware that learning the simple order of the nursery school day or of the school routines brought relief to them. The importance of reliable outer structure is seen in the tenacity with which the youngsters hold onto the "proper" order of nursery school routines. Any flexibility or variation introduced by the teacher led to distress and confusion.

Confronted as they are with the lack of inner assurance and direction and with surroundings which change and hold threatening possibilities, multiproblem-family children cling to what works and proves useful. Sameness increases their feeling of security. A known pattern (usually because it is observable or it is one of the few things that is reinforced with some consistency in their experience) is held on to rigidly in their efforts to manage. Early overemphasis on coping as a protective and defensive maneuver seems to lead to inflexible clinging to what works, rather than to searching for new or interesting possibilities or alternatives. Accommodation is the goal, and assimilation appears to fall by the wayside. These are considerations which lead us to conclude that the children pay a considerable price in the range, variety, resourcefulness, and plasticity of their development for the early coping and compensatory patterns by which they accommodate to their deviant milieu. A strong tendency to literalness and inflexibility is part of this price.

REPEATED FALLING AND
LACK OF BODY CARE

Earlier in this section we underscored the children's tendency to feel devalued and criticized. Under such conditions, or when they are confronted with their inability to do what they announce they can do, their controls appear to deteriorate. Related to this, we are impressed with the children's general lack of body care, their *heedlessness* and *lack of caution* in relation to themselves. Early in their nursery school experience we observed the children carelessly careening around the room, stumbling and bumping into things, tripping over chairs or toys, and falling off the climber, slide, or swings. The fact that the children's heedlessness in relation to their bodily safety occurred in spite of their generally good, or even advanced, gross motor skills, and in spite of their general danger orientation, made it seem all the more significant. The children's lack of care regarding their bodies also appeared to be part of their generally deficient spatial orientation, as well as a dramatic example of their difficulty in controlling and modulating impulses.

The teacher's response to the children's repeated tripping, falling, and bumping into things was to intercede actively and protect them from harm despite the fact that the children showed no emotion when they fell and did not cry or seek consolation. It was a novel experience for them when the teacher comforted them and repeatedly expressed her concern for their physical welfare. The teacher tried to protect them through holding and guiding. She attempted to counter their heedlessness by substituting her own caution and verbal admonitions regarding possible injury.

At first the number of accidents seemed to decrease only in relation to the teacher's physical agility and ability to anticipate possible falls. Gradually, however, during the development of what appeared to be an increasingly meaningful attachment to the teacher, who encouraged them to be careful of themselves, the children's tendency to trip and fall began to decrease. Instead, they began, in their gross motor play, occasionally to place themselves in "danger" of falling or hurting themselves and by their looks in

the teachers direction make an implicit call for help and solicitude. Later, under the teacher's consistent encouragement to ver-
balize, the children learned to ask for her "help." These, at times
shouted, requests had dual meaning since they asked for protection
and concrete manifestations of the teacher's concern and interest.
At this point the noticeably decreased number of falls and accidents appeared to result from the children's increased regard for
their own safety.

Subsequently in times of stress (such as separation from their
parents, harsh punishments, or criticism from their parents), as a
feature of their regression, the children might again show heedlessness regarding their body safety. Although they appeared to
learn a new attitude toward themselves and their bodies through
their relationship to and imitative identification with the teacher,
this new attitude was not as autonomous and resistant to regressive
influences as one would like. It was an attitude taken on in relation
to the teacher in the familiar pattern of imitative identification
which requires continuing reinforcement and relative freedom
from stressful conditions.

In our efforts to understand these observations we have come to
place increasing emphasis on the role of self-esteem and its effect
upon the children's capacity for caution and body care. In relation
to their self-esteem certain aspects of the youngster's social reality
should be mentioned. The children are let out on the street at a
very young age, without anyone or with only slightly older siblings
to care for them. Discomfort from blows or falls may go unheeded
and they often realize that no one is sufficiently concerned to comfort them. The lack of predictable experience regarding parental
protection and concern for their well-being interferes with the
children learning similar self-directed attitudes. Most stressful and
damaging of all, in this regard, is their parents' harsh, devaluating
criticism. Under the impact of parental criticism the children's
skill, care, and control in the use of their bodies may deteriorate.
Ritvo and Solnit (49) made a similar observation in relation to a 4-
year-old boy whose skill in using his body would deteriorate under
the impact of parental scolding and whose subsequent regression
was accompanied by heedlessness in regard to his own safety.

Freud (15) comments on the relationship between the child's
self-esteem and his capacity for caution and heed. He says, "The

feeling of self-regard appears to us as a measure of the ego. What components go to make up that measure is irrelevant. Everything we possess or achieve, every remnant of the primitive feeling of omnipotence that experience has corroborated helps to exalt the self-regard." Freud's formulation of the vital psychic ingredients of the parents' love and praise in the promotion and maintenance of self-regard points to the deficit in the children's development and emphasizes the undermining effects of devaluation. When a child experiences mastery through achievements, skills, and functions, he is aware of real ability to exert control over his impulses, himself, and things, and sometimes over other people. The child will gradually be capable of relinquishing unrealistic wishes for magical control if he has real means of control which can be reliably repeated and which bring him the praise and respect of his parents. A child must not only learn progressive mastery but also receive tangible social recognition for the mastery he achieves (10).

It is our impression that the heedlessness and lack of caution which we observed in the project children are not just concomitants of regression under the impact of criticism and/or punishment in the children, but are also the result of the lowering of their self-esteem which occurs when their parents or other important adults harshly scold them. We feel that the lack of sufficient love and protection (deprivation) as well as the experience of criticism and derogation (devaluation) and the presence of seductive overstimulation, harsh punishments and threats (danger) in their relations with their parents combine to produce the profoundly lowered self-regard and concomitant heedlessness which was characteristic of them.

LEARNING HANDICAPS

As we stressed in the introduction to this book and do again in this section, perhaps the most significant area in which the children of disorganized low-income families are handicapped in their development is in relation to learning. Without benefit of rather long-term therapeutic and special educational intervention, we believe these children will suffer from significant impediments to learning and ultimately experience failure. This probable lack of success at school will, of course, further handicap the children in their lives, and in turn their own families when they become parents, in the most far-reaching ways.

Perhaps the most important finding of the project was that many of children's educational handicaps are to an extent remediable through the combined therapeutic-educational techniques used in our nursery school (described in detail in the following chapter). Though the children still appear to have definite limitations in terms of their ultimate school success, early preschool intervention for this group of low socioeconomic children has proved successful, at least up to a point.

Certain qualities in the children and features of their learning difficulties seem particularly important. In the early months of nursery school there were a number of aspects of the children's play, behavior, and reactions that alerted us to the likelihood that learning would be a more difficult process for them than for an ordinary group of 3- and 4-year-olds. They were observed to be listless and inattentive. The children did not play much nor did they gravitate to the doll corner or the blocks; they only fingered the toys or puzzles for brief periods. They were readily distracted and often disrupted their aimless mechanical play to seek the attention of the teacher or a stranger who had entered the room. These youngsters showed little capacity for *focal attention* (33). Along with this, there was a low frustration tolerance and a tendency to discharge tension in diffuse motor activity. Although they were compliant and could manage to exert control for fear of punishment, they found it difficult to control and modulate impulses under ordinary circumstances. They had difficulty in keeping out internal or external interferences, so that their concentration and attention span were low and their play and work was vulnerable to regression and disruption.

The children showed little interest, curiosity, initiative, and enjoyment in relation to play. They lacked preferred toys or a sense of possession. Choices tended to be imitative or rivalrous. Along with their low levels of investment, there was little experimentation, exploratory manipulation, practice, or development of new skills in the use of toys. Fantasy expression tended to be minimal, and later when it did appear, it was often dominated by repetitious restatements of the same theme of loss, hunger, or abandonment, or else used as a vehicle to control or punish other children.

We have repeatedly described the fact that the children showed initially a shallow, nonspecific approach toward the teacher. They were hyperalert to her whereabouts, seeking her attention, yet maintaining a distance. They appeared to long for a relationship with the teacher, while at the same time they were distrustful. Toward their peers they were rivalrous and could barely engage in parallel play, let alone become involved in mutual activities.

In the neighborhood which the children know, learning and education, as we usually understand them, are not much in evidence nor are they valued. Alcoholics, drifters, older single rooming-house dwellers, teenage school dropouts, and unemployed youths hang around in doorways or on street corners, displaying neither industry nor achievement but rather school and work failure. Of course, the neighborhood does teach "lessons" about things like alcoholism and petty crime, but these run counter to the children's interest in school.

Within the family environment, in spite of rather nebulous aspirations for education and school success, *there is a history and evidence of poor education and school failure in the parents and siblings.* Books are rarely present and even more rarely read and enjoyed. Newspapers and occasionally a magazine are the reading fare that competes unsuccessfully with television for the parents' attention. The parents have little general information on current events, but more importantly there is not much evidence of using learning for the purpose of solving problems, and a thirst for knowledge is lacking. *Spoken language is limited, and words are not regularly used to explain or convey information.* Oftentimes the children are not listened to. In addition, in the children's family environment, language and explanations are often confusing and contradictory. Their curiosity tends to be discouraged and their products and their productivity—their schoolwork—are disparaged and devalued.

The environment in which the children grow up thwarts and delays their intellectual development as well as their capacity to learn. Beyond this, however, in their homes they do *learn* styles of cognitive functioning and communication, modes of approaching ideas, school, and teacher, values and attitudes toward learning and achievement, which further impede their intellectual functioning, especially in schools which are a product of the larger society's social and economic values and organization. Though it is surely difficult to picture, in view of the disorganization and deficiency of these low socioeconomic families, the children are socialized into family and neighborhood subcultural patterns (29) and styles (25). What the children bring with them to school is a product of what they have lacked in the way of emotional and psychological stimulation of their intellects, and what they have had in terms of psychological and emotional input. Consideration of the language and cognitive styles and development of the children, as well as their lack of impulse control, reveals rather clearly the descriptive bases for the view we hold.

Language Development and Communication Style. The children's difficulties in communicating and the immaturity of their verbal development is rather striking. In nursery school, the children revealed vocabulary and spoken language levels well below age expectancy. Language was seldom used to communicate or to seek information, to gain knowledge, or develop skills (2, 7, 25). Instead, communication was frequently effected by nonverbal means—gestures, facial expressions, whimpering. Their speech was often infantile in pronunciation and used imitatively or to gain attention or to express babyish desires. Requests such as "Gimme" or "Do dat" were used without specific reference to what was to be given or done. The children had particular difficulty with words which convey spatial, time, or cause-and-effect relationships (for instance, *over, under, behind,* and *later*). There was little expectation that the teacher would answer or even listen and they quickly repeated their demands even while they were being responded to. They seemed to talk at someone rather than with and to someone. There was a literalness and inflexibility regarding language (3). Concomitantly, they were concretely action-oriented and understood concepts that were physically demonstrated far better than those which were explained verbally. Importantly, the children were often more oriented to the relationship and affective content of verbal messages than they were to the informational content (33); the attention and interest of the teacher far outweighed in importance what she was saying.

In attempting to gain perspective on the children's language development, the influence of deprivational factors is, of course, prominent. Provence and Lipton (41) and others place emphasis on language as the most significant area of retardation in institutionalized children. The learning of language is not simply a matter of teaching a child words by repetition and reinforcement (30). The process begins much earlier, when a child seeks to solve problems before language is even possible. It starts with the gaining of mutuality in which a child learns, through his mother's predictable, sequential response to his cues, that her cues are meaningful and his own are too. If signals such as these are not responded to and do not solve problems, a child does not experience enough satisfactory "fit" between his inner-state perceptions and communications and the response of his environent. When the ability to communicate verbally is present, it should lead to broader and more focused problem-solving capacity. If, however, the lack of appropriate fit persists it may lead to increased misunderstanding.

We must, however, also take into account the influence of growing up in a low-income family and neighborhood. Minuchin (33) observes that interpersonal transactions in the families lack shared rules and that intensity of sound often dominates over making sense. Bernstein (3) points to the restricted language code of low socioeconomic people which limits verbal elaboration of meaning and intention, and which is geared to communication of global descriptive relationship messages rather than information and problem-solving tools. These observations correspond to our own. We are familiar with homes in which there is a continuing distraction of high noise levels from radios and television sets and parents assert themselves by yelling; in the few conversations that do occur, subjects are often not carried to conclusion and interruptions are multiple.

What is being emphasized here is the fact that in addition to the profound effects of deficient maternal care on language development, the children of multiproblem families are introduced to modes of language use in their homes. The language styles that arise from this intrafamilial learning process are at the very least different from, and in some ways antagonistic to, the styles of communication that the children encounter and are expected to use in

school. Their communication styles, to some extent at least, interfere with reciprocal verbal exchange with the teacher.

Most importantly, the children's capacity to treat language and
communication autonomously for purposes of gaining knowledge
and solving problems is grossly interfered with. The use of language as an all-important means to higher levels of abstraction,
reasoning, and logic (40) is at least delayed and probably partially
blocked for these children. Some of the vicious-cycle effects of the
children's language difficulties relate to the vital role of reliability
in personality growth. Reliable meanings of words are essential to
reality testing and to other areas of psychosocial functioning, since
without words to categorize, organize, and represent experience,
the children live in a relatively structureless world (30). Lag in
the acquisition of valid meanings via language impedes concept
formation and abstraction and the development of self control.
The language that is acquired is often diverted from learning purposes to attention-getting maneuvers.

Cognitive Development and Intellectual Style.   A number of
important delays in cognitive development and handicaps in intellectual style were noted in the children during the early months of
their experience in the nursery school. They lacked interest in
learning the names and properties of toys and equipment; colors,
numbers, sizes, shapes, locations, all seemed relatively interchangeable. In view of the fact that the children had average or better
intellectual endowment by testing (which is known to have a bias
against less verbal children) this lack of interest was all the more
striking and alarming. In general, the children's thinking appeared to have remained immature and on a magical, egocentric
level with excessive concreteness as its most notable quality; they
were quite tied to direct, immediate sensory experience and the
use of "action units" in their thinking. Related to this concreteness, the tendency toward literalness noted in other areas was also
apparent in their thought processes.

Many of the children revealed primitive modes of thinking, such
as animation of the inanimate (stroking and patting the picture of
a cat), which appeared more often than one would expect in children of this age group. Vital concepts such as intentionality, spatial

relations, and causality were weakly developed at best. When the teacher put on gloves, the children wondered where her hands had gone. Similarly, legs "disappeared" in tights, and toys that were dropped out of sight seemed lost. For these children, the absence of a reliable system of causality and a lack of knowledge about their surroundings combined with a low frustration tolerance to make thinking through and solving problems extremely difficult for them.

In considering the children's intellectual handicaps in the light of their environmental and child-rearing experiences, we note that in many ways the thinking difficulties described represent the persistence of early modes of thinking, normally present in very young children. The detailed naturalistic observations and theories of Piaget allow us to make certain rough comparisons with the preschool children we observed, and thereby to focus our attention on particular areas of cognitive delay.

Piaget's work (37, 38, 39) traces the development of rational thinking in children from its earliest reflex beginnings. He describes four stages in the course of which action is transformed into thought. The first or sensorimotor stage is the experiential level in which a child initially organizes his growing awareness of the world. As maturation and development make it possible, a child uses his own activity and sensory encounters with his world and his developing language to form concepts about spatial relations, time, conservation, causality, intentionality, and object permanence. The weakness of concept formation in these areas in the children we studied has already been noted. However, the areas of the object concept (of object permanence) and the concept of intentionality deserve particular attention.

The Object Concept. The children, indeed, appear to have little confidence that a person or thing will continue to exist and eventually be available again, if it cannot be seen or touched or if they cannot for the time being make it reappear. They have a weak capacity for holding someone or something in thought when that thing or person is not available. The maintenance of interest in and belief in the existence of objects that are beyond the reach of the senses is essential for personal and intellectual growth. For children to pursue things that disappear involves a sense of permanence and the capacity to form and maintain focal attention on the mental image of objects while pursuing and exploring means of recovery. The children's difficulties with these important cognitive processes appear to us related to their relatively weak emotional investment in people and things, and this in turn seems connected to their experience with their mothers. The mothers' own narcissistic needs and deprivations make it extremely difficult for them to give to their children in a consistent way. Provence and Ritvo (42) propose that deprived, institutionalized infants fail to make use of their maturing potentials because of the lack of interest and investment in toys and in the exploration of inanimate objects. The capacity to manipulate objects and thereby acquire knowledge and skill was shown to be present in the infants, but they did not make use of it. They suggest that the specific deprivation which was causal in this condition in the children was the lack of stimulation from a mothering person. They postulate that interest in inanimate objects stems from the strength of a child's interest in and satisfaction from his mother. We believe that the marked retardation in regard to play which we saw initially in the children derives from a similar source. As their nursery school experience progresses, the stimulation which the relationship to the teacher provides in school leads the children to increased investment in and enjoyment from, as well as use of, play.

The Concept of Intentionality.   In terms of cognitive functioning, the concepts of intentionality (which involves means-ends behavior) and of causality counter belief in the magic of action by introducing cause-and-effect behavior. It prepares the way for more truly representational forms of thought. The confusing and capricious world in which the children live militates against their developing a secure sense of cause and effect and intentionality. In their family lives, the child nearest at hand oftentimes receives the blow whether or not he is the culprit who committed the "crime"; they are punished for things that on other occasions they have been encouraged to do. Their active explorations are often misread by their parents as aggressive demands or attempts to control, and therefore restricted. These various factors (and, perhaps, the form of language used in their families) combine to impede the children's developing a meaningful concept of causality and intentionality. In the nursery school, we saw numerous examples of the children's difficulty in recognizing the intentions of others and in perceiving and expressing their own intentions (3). Of course, it is particularly at what Piaget terms the preoperational stage (usually 1½ to 7 years of age) that we note the children's delayed concept development. At this stage, Piaget describes the shift from a sensorimotor level to a language-representational level of intellectual functioning. As emphasized earlier, this point of language representation of concepts and capacity to use language to act upon and solve problems involving concrete phenomena is especially handicapped in these youngsters.

The concept of intentionality is closely related to the area of ego development encompassed by the term *initiative* (8). Throughout our description of these children we point out their relatively weak capacity for self-direction and initiative. In relation to this deficiency, the role of deprivational factors seems clear, in the sense that a low level of initiative is a repeated finding in the various studies of maternal deprivation. Kris (28), in discussing institutionalized infants, makes an observation similar to our own. He emphasizes: "The investigators feel the absence of 'driving power.' What lacks is the initiative. Imitation comes easier than self-initiation of action." This lack of driving power, which initiative expresses and represents, seems crucial. Observers (23, 56) of healthy preschool children are impressed with the young child's urge to grow up. A child's incentive toward growth, his initiative, his urge toward independence arise out of the same ground—the stimulation for mental and personal activity which *masterable frustration* provides.

Many observers (28, 41, 44, 58) have pointed to the fact that deficient maternal care fails to stimulate a child's early mental processes adequately. Our study of multiproblem low socioeconomic families broadens this viewpoint. For the children of these families self-activation is thwarted or punished, passive responses are encouraged and rewarded, and following and responding to the cues of others has survival value and is to a certain extent learned in the family environment. The children's ability to cope by adroit passive response to the signals of controlling authority figures is reinforced not only by their experiential success in avoiding pain and attaining some pleasure, but also in the degree to which it provides them with a sense of competence. However limited, in an ideal sense, this sense of capacity to effect their environment is hard-earned and certainly offers them some semblance of effectance (56).

Learning and Impulse Control. Consideration of the children's difficulties in learning would not be complete without giving some attention to their difficulties in controlling and modulating impulses. It is clear in reviewing aspects of normal development, as we did earlier, that in learning and mental functioning it is necessary for a child to think through a problem in order to solve it. This thinking task requires concentration, attention, tolerance of frustration, and capacity to traverse in his mind various possible solutions and to find the correct one. This kind of problem solving depends at least in part upon the capacity to delay discharge and to substitute thought for action. Capacity to delay discharge and to find higher levels of discharge in thought inherently depends upon impulse control. The children's difficulties in controlling and modulating impulses have already been discussed at some length by us elsewhere (31).

Although the children do not display the hyperactive, extremely aggressive, and destructive behavior usually thought of as characteristic of a predelinquent pattern, they do show a tendency to act upon impulse, to discharge tension and feelings when frustrated or under stress in diffuse, motoric behavior. This tendency, when combined with the model of their parents' impulsivity and the influence of the asocial patterning of the neighborhood, may lead the children to later asocial behavior, including forms of delinquency (alcoholism, promiscuity, illegitimate pregnancy, and so on).

It should be pointed out that at least early in grade school, the children's difficulty in modulating and controlling impulses probably will not lead to behavior problems. Perhaps later these will appear. What is more likely in our view is that they will be compliant and docile but show restlessness, inattentiveness, and poor frustration tolerance in the classroom. They are likely to fidget and squirm, shift their eyes around the room, and in general have difficulty maintaining the kind of modulation and channelization of impulses that is necessary in sustaining focused attention. Nevertheless, their quietness and compliant manner may lead to a superficial appearance of adjustment. We see this later behavior as part of a general picture of what we consider to be *pseudoautonomy* in children.

PSEUDOAUTONOMY

As described previously, the issues involved in the training or autonomy period (8, 10) have far-reaching significance for a child's later development. Rapaport (45) defines personal and mental autonomy in the broadest manner as relative freedom from the demands of internal drives on the one hand, so that one can apply one's energies to reality problems, and from the demands of external reality on the other hand, so that inner needs can be heeded if necessary. It is clear that the children of disorganized families do not have this freedom. The fact that they lack sufficient autonomy is repeatedly demonstrated in our findings. The stimulus which having to fend for themselves provides, however, leads to a certain kind of independence and competence which assists them in trying to overcome this lack of full autonomy. This latter process is also fostered by the fact that the parents encourage the children to perform certain tasks in advance of their years in order to meet the parents' needs and make a difficult life easier for them. The mothers particularly place a premium on such "grown-up" behavior, as well as on their children being able to "stand on their own two feet."

The children, in an effort to meet their parents' expectations, try to appear grown up without feeling grown up. They portray capabilities that are not bolstered by inner experience of self-reliance. In spite of difficulty controlling and modulating impulses, the children nevertheless develop substitutions for autonomy by which they attempt to compensate, often with a fair degree of success, for their inner deficiencies. We term these substitutions *pseudoautonomy*. We use this term to refer to the children's compliance, manipulativeness, imitativeness, areas of advanced ability, and efforts to appear more mature than they are. The comparison between the genuine autonomy of normal children and the pseudoautonomy of multiproblem-family children interests us and is summarized in schematic form in the following chart:

Pseudoautonomy		*Autonomy*
Compliance.	*versus*	Voluntary control over impulses, drives, wishes (to have one's own way regarding habits, cleanliness, bowel training, etc.).
Docile obedience.	*versus*	Voluntary response to limits, prohibitions, and expectations of parents.
Impulsivity and tendency to discharge tension in movement and activity which is not goal-directed, but generally diffuse and random. Lack of control and an air of defeat.	*versus*	Sphincter and basic body motor control established. Able to direct energies toward specific goals. Self-control without loss of self-esteem.
Difficulty in regard to both "holding on" and "letting go" (10), especially in terms of giving up too easily and relinquishing possessions too readily. Difficulty sharing and negotiating simple social situations with adults and peers, such as through cooperation or compromise (taking turns). Instead the children substitute *manipulation* of people and situations in order to transact interpersonal business.	*versus*	Early basic social skills. Able to hold on to possessions and what is "mine" and yet able to share, take turns and cooperate in simple ways for periods of time. Able to reach simple compromises and to show persistence and perseverance in tasks and in relation to interests and desires.
Areas of above-age-expectancy functioning, "precocious" abilities, attempts to appear independent.	*versus*	A growing appearance and sense of independence and selfhood within the context of the supportive, guiding, reinforcing relationship with parents in which the child is

Pseudoautonomy		*Autonomy*
		developing motor, language, social, and intellectual skills and a sense of mastery, competence, effectance.
Imitativeness.	*versus*	Self-direction and assertiveness.
Aggression is poorly mastered; it is expressed in covert forms, via identification with the aggressor (reenactment in play of harsh controlling and punitive figures), in impulsive outbursts of "wild" shrieking and running around, or in tantrums. Power and control struggles and ambivalence remain strong in interpersonal relationships.	*versus*	Basic steps in mastery of aggression, especially in relationships, so that aggression comes increasingly under ego control and is subordinated to "love interests" and "ego interests." Issues of dominance *versus* submission, power and control are secondary to social and personal goals.

The contrast between the children's pseudoautonomy and the autonomy of ordinary preschool youngsters emphasizes that their efforts at independence fall short of their mark. The children of disorganized families do not give up but, on the contrary, actively attempt to conserve their parents' love by meeting their needs via pseudomature behavior. At the same time the children's activities often have a driven quality, the main goal of which is to gain attention, and this attitude hinders the acquisition of skills and mastery and by the same token hampers the children in elaborating and consolidating their capacity for independent task completion. The children's efforts at self-control are used to overcome dependency feelings or avoid punishment and are not matched with or supported by the experience of genuine self-confidence. Compliance substitutes for voluntary control and their lack of self-control is accompanied by an air of discouragement and defeat.

The children in our sample, lacking mature means of dealing with others (such as sharing, taking turns, persuasion, cooperation and compromise), substitute *manipulation*. Beyond the frequent use of manipulation to get their own way and to get around adults, to wheedle a toy away from another child or candy from a grown-up, it is also used by the children in attempts to control situations and people and to master anxiety. In spite of proclamations that they can "do it myself" they portray inability or exaggerate their difficulty in accomplishing a task in order to entice the teacher to do it for them. However, if confronted with "failure" they may become upset. One way this anxiety may express itself is by a child's becoming "helpless" and bidding for further support from the teacher.

STRENGTHS ARE ALSO WEAKNESSES

One final topic of consideration—those areas of ability which are beyond the children's years and give the impression of precociousness and independence. These areas, discussed earlier, involve the children's ability to ward off bill collectors at the door, make decisions for their parents, baby-sit, feed and protect younger siblings, and in other ways reverse roles with their parents. (This reversal of roles between parents and children is a rather striking example of a general indistinctness and confusion between generations (34) among disorganized, low socioeconomic families.) These areas of "precious" functioning are extremely important because, however much they may convey an appearance of independence which is more apparent than real, they do provide the children with some level of coping and some sense of being able to "affect my environment." As we have said elsewhere (32) these patterns of coping and above-age-expectancy functioning contribute to the children's often successful efforts to deal with their deviant milieu and at the same time to compensate for lacks in themselves or others. The children are able to sustain elements of security in their lives through their "getting-along" orientation. They are able to size up and accommodate to situations via alert visual and auditory scanning of their environment for signals of possible danger. Through these means they are to some extent protected from the real dangers which surround them. The children are, therefore, less vulnerable to the frequent traumata of their existence. Considering the disorganization, confusion, and danger which surrounds them, this is no insignificant accomplishment.

The children's areas of precocious functioning and ability to cope are clearly strengths. We would emphasize, however, that *they are also weaknesses.* We believe that while survival considerations, stimulated by external danger, assist these youngsters to accommodate to their special kind of life space, they pay a price for this assistance. In the final analysis, the early coping patterns and advanced ability of these young children contribute to their inflexibility and literalness and to fixation at early levels of development.

Several illustrations clarify what we mean. To begin with, although these children are not withdrawn or autistic and do not relinquish a certain contact with people, they also cope by not investing too much or counting too much on people or things. They are wary of taking a chance. Being left to their own devices, the children develop an early protective orientation geared to adults' external cues and to other aspects of reality. To an extent this guards them against autism and is a barrier against psychotic retreat from reality, but it also interferes with aspects of their potential for further development and occurs at the cost of the deepening of their emotional life which depends upon receptivity and responsiveness in intimate human closeness.

Along the same lines, the children's heavy reliance on vision to read cues, reflect imitatively, and be on the lookout for danger is most useful in their lives, but they pay a price for this capacity in the degree to which they are further bound to outside stimuli. As we have already stressed, we believe that the children's being bound to external stimuli contributes to the rigid literalness and concreteness of their thinking, imitation, and learning.

Finally, as young as 3 years of age, the children are sent to do the family shopping in order to relieve their mothers' burdens. This is clearly an accomplishment, involving many skills, which is beyond the average 3- to 5-year-old. When the nursery school teacher took the children to the neighborhood store, however, she discovered that they did not seem to know their way around the store, nor the names of common items on the shelves. Instead, they rattled off the names of a few everyday items which obviously came from memorized lists. This example reveals that the children's capacity to shop for their mothers was not an adaptive one, but rather a premature coping pattern learned by rote.

As we have emphasized before, our descriptive findings suggest that in the process of managing to accommodate to their environment and learning to carry burdens beyond their years, the children of poorly organized, multiproblem, low socioeconomic families attain an early independence which is more apparent than real, one which does not lead to later full independence. Our observations suggest that under the pressures of external danger and the need to grow up fast (and lacking the support and guidance of adequate parental care and esteem), the children grow up too fast and thereby relinquish their childhoods too early. It is our view that the children's premature ability to compensate for deficiencies in themselves and others and to defend themselves leads to early closure of their development whereby flexible adaptability and genuine mastery are forfeited. The children, under the influence of the need for self-preservation and in an effort to counteract and compensate for inner developmental deficits, use what they have at their disposal in themselves, and in their family and neighborhood lives. They do manage to accommodate and protect themselves in certain ways, but at the cost of certain distinct limitations in their growth and a certain foreclosure in their development.

It may be, as Ritvo and Solnit (48) suggest, that experience with discomforting and at times frightening mothers prompts children to turn away from them and to invest in themselves and their own equipment and capacity to avoid pain. This speculative proposition is of interest because it provides a link between the multiple developmental influences impinging on disadvantaged children and the outcome that can be observed in such children during their preschool years.

Whether or not subsequent clinical studies support this proposition, it does seem clear that a number of factors beyond the important and well-known influence of deprivation need to be taken into account in relation to the development of multiproblem-family children. In our project work we did attempt to take into account the children's psychosocial characteristics and deviant trends in development as we evolved modifications and adjustments in the nursery school program that were necessary in order to meet their needs more effectively. The process and results of this adaptation will now be described in detail.

REFERENCES

1. Axelrad, S., and Maury, L. Identification as a Mechanism of Adaptation. In Wilber, G., and Meunsterberger, W. (Eds.), *Psychoanalysis and Culture.* New York: International Universities Press, 1951, p. 168.
2. Bernstein, B. Social Class and Linguistic Development: A Theory of Social Learning. In Halsey, H., Floud, J., and Anderson, A. (Eds.), *Education, Economy and Society.* Glencoe, Ill.: Free Press, 1961, p. 288.
3. Bernstein, B. Social Class, Speech Systems and Psychotherapy. In Riessman, F., Cohen, J., and Pearl, A. (Eds.), *Mental Health of the Poor.* Glencoe, Ill.: Free Press, 1964, p. 194.
4. Blos, P. Discussant in Reiser, D. E., Observation of Delinquent Behavior in Very Young Children. *Journal of the American Academy of Child Psychiatry* 2:68, 1963.
5. Bowlby, J. *Maternal Care and Mental Health.* Geneva: World Health Organization Monograph Series No. 2, 1951.
6. Deutsch, H. Some Forms of Emotional Disturbance and Their Relationships to Schizophrenia. *Psychoanalytic Quarterly* 11:301, 1942.
7. Deutsch, M. The Disadvantaged Child and the Learning Process. In Riessman, F., Cohen, J., and Pearl, A. (Eds.), *Mental Health of the Poor,* Glencoe, Ill.: Free Press, 1964, p. 172.
8. Erikson, E. H. *Childhood and Society.* New York: Norton, 1950.
9. Erikson, E. H. Growth and Crisis of the Healthy Personality (1950). *Psychological Issues* Monograph 1. New York: International Universities Press, 1959, p. 50.
10. Erikson, E. H. Identity and the Life Cycle. *Psychological Issues,* Monograph 1. New York: International Universities Press, 1959.
11. Fraiberg, S. *The Magic Years.* New York: Scribner, 1959.
12. Freud, A. *The Ego and the Mechanisms of Defense* (1936). New York: International Universities Press, 1946.
13. Freud, A. Introduction to Sandler, A. M., Daunton, E., and Schnurmann, A., Inconsistency in the Mother as a Factor in Character De-

velopment: A Comparative Study of Three Cases. *Psychoanalytic Study of the Child* 7:209, 1957.

14. Freud, A., and Burlingham, D. *Infants without Families*. New York: International Universities Press, 1944.
15. Freud, S. On Narcissism: An Introduction (1914). In *Collected Papers of Sigmund Freud*. London: Hogarth Press, 1950, Vol. 4, p. 30.
16. Freud, S. Beyond the Pleasure Principle (1920). In *The Standard Edition of the Complete Psychological Works of Sigmund Freud*, tr. and ed. by J. Strachey and others. London: Hogarth Press and the Institute of Psycho-Analysis, 1955, vol. 18, p. 7.
17. Gesell, A., and Amatruda, C. S. *Developmental Diagnosis* (1941). New York: Hocber, 1947.
18. Goldfarb, W. Infant Rearing and Problem Behavior. *American Journal of Orthopsychiatry* 13:249, 1943.
19. Goldfarb, W. The Effects of Early Institutional Care on Adolescent Personality. *Child Development* 14:213, 1943.
20. Goldfarb, W. Psychological Deprivation in Infancy and Subsequent Adjustment. *American Journal of Orthopsychiatry* 15:247, 1945.
21. Hartmann, H. *Ego Psychology and the Problem of Adaptation* (1939). New York: International Universities Press, 1948.
22. Hartmann, H., and Loewenstein, R. M. Notes on the Superego. *Psychoanalytic Study of the Child* 17:42, 1962.
23. Hendrick, I. Instinct and the Ego during Infancy. *Psychoanalytic Quarterly* 11:33, 1942.
24. Hendrick, I. Early Development of the Ego: Identification in Infancy. *Psychoanalytic Quarterly* 20:44, 1951.
25. Hess, R., and Shipman, V. Early Experience and Socialization of Cognitive Modes. *Child Development* 36:869, 1965.
26. Jacobson, E. The Self and the Object World: Vicissitudes of Their Infantile Carthexes and Their Influence on Ideational and Affective Development. *Psychoanalytic Study of the Child* 9:75, 1954.
27. John, V. The Intellectual Development of Slum Children: Some Preliminary Findings. *American Journal of Orthopsychiatry* 33:813, 1963.
28. Kris, E. Neutralization and Sublimation: Observations on Young Children. *Psychoanalytic Study of the Child* 10:30, 1955.
29. Lewis, O. *The Children of Sanchez: Autobiography of a Mexican Family*. New York: Random House, 1961.
30. Lidz, T. Discussant in Rexford, E., A Developmental Concept of

the Problems of Acting Out. *Journal of the American Academy of Child Psychiatry* 2:19, 1963.

31. Malone, C. A. Some Observations of Children of Disorganized Families and Problems of Acting Out. *Journal of the American Academy of Child Psychiatry* 2:22, 1963.

32. Malone, C. A. Safety First: Comments on the Influence of External Danger in the Lives of Children of Disorganized Families. *American Journal of Orthopsychiatry* 36:3, 1966.

33. Minuchin, S. Psychoanalytic Therapies and the Low Socioeconomic Population. In J. Marmon (Ed.), *Frontiers of Psychoanalysis.* New York: Basic Books, 1966.

34. Minuchin, S., Montalvo, B., Elbert, S., Guerney, B. G., Jr., Rosman, B., and Schumer, F. *Families of the Slums: An Exploration of Their Structure and Treatment.* New York: Basic Books, 1967.

35. Pavenstedt, E. A Comparison of the Child-Rearing Environment of Upper-Lower and Very Low-Lower Class Families. *American Journal of Orthopsychiatry* 35:89, 1965.

36. Pavenstedt, E. The Second Year of Life. Working paper (mimeographed) for N.I.M.H. Conference, 1965.

37. Piaget, J. *The Origins of Intelligence in Children* (2nd Ed.). New York: International Universities Press, 1952.

38. Piaget, J. *Play, Dreams and Imitation in Childhood* (1945). New York: Norton, 1951.

39. Piaget, J. *The Construction of Reality in the Child* (1937). New York: Basic Books, 1954.

40. Piaget, J., and Inhelder, B. *The Growth of Logical Thinking* (1955). New York: Basic Books, 1958.

41. Provence, S., and Lipton, R. C. *Infants in Institutions.* New York: International Universities Press, 1962.

42. Provence, S., and Ritvo, S. Effects of Deprivation on Institutionalized Infants: Disturbances in Development of Relationships to Inanimate Objects. *Psychoanalytic Study of the Child* 16:189, 1961.

43. Rank, B. Discussant in Malone, C. A., Some Observations of Children of Disorganized Families and Problems of Acting Out. *Journal of the American Academy of Child Psychiatry* 2:46, 1963.

44. Rank, B., and MacNaughton, D. A Clinical Contribution to Early Ego Development. *Psychoanalytic Study of the Child* 5:53, 1950.

45. Rapaport, D. The Theory of Ego Autonomy: A Generalization. *Bulletin of the Menninger Clinic* 22:13, 1958.

46. Redl, F., and Wineman, D. *The Aggressive Child* (1951). Glencoe, Ill.: Free Press, 1957.

47. Reissman, F. *The Culturally Deprived Child.* New York: Harper & Row, 1962.

48. Ritvo, S., and Solnit, A. J.   Influences of Early Mother-Child Interaction on Identification Processes. *Psychoanalytic Study of the Child* 13:64, 1958.

49. Ritvo, S., and Solnit, A. J.   The Relationship of Early Ego Identifications to Superego Formation. *International Journal of Psycho-Analysis* 41:295, 1960.

50. Sander, L. W.   Interactions of Recognition and the Developmental Processes of the Second 18 Months of Life. Text of paper presented to Tufts, New England Medical Seminar Series on Community Psychiatry, 1965.

51. Sandler, J.   The Background of Safety. *International Journal of Psycho-Analysis* 41:352, 1960.

52. Sandler, J.   On the Concept of Superego. *Psychoanalytic Study of the Child* 15:128, 1960.

53. Sandler, J., and Rosenblatt, B.   The Concept of the Representational World. *Psychoanalytic Study of the Child* 17:128, 1962.

54. Silberman, C.   Give Slum Children a Chance: Excerpts from *Crisis in Black and White. Harper's* 228:37, 1964.

55. Waelder, R.   Psychoanalytic Theory of Play. *Psychoanalytic Quarterly* 2:208, 1933.

56. White, R.   Ego and Reality in Psychoanalytic Theory: A Proposal Regarding Independent Ego Energies. *Psychological Issues,* Monograph 11. New York: International Universities Press, 1963. P. 3.

57. Wiltse, K.   Orthopsychiatric Programs for Socially Deprived Groups. In Mental Health Programs for the Socially Deprived Urban Child — 1962 Panel. *American Journal of Orthopsychiatry* 33:806, 1963.

58. Winnicott, D.   Transitional Objects and Transitional Phenomena: A Study of the First Not-Me Possession. *International Journal of Psycho-Analysis* 34:89, 1953.

59. Wolff, P.   The Developmental Psychologies of Jean Piaget and Psychoanalysis. *Psychological Issues,* Monograph 5. New York: International Universities Press, 1960.

8

NURSERY SCHOOL ADAPTATIONS AND TECHNIQUES

Ilse Mattick

COMPOSITION OF THE NURSERY SCHOOL

D URING the four years of the nursery school's existence, there was a total enrollment of 21 children who were between the ages of 2½ and 6 years at the time of admission. The children were divided by age into small groups, averaging six children, and they attended for two or three mornings a week. Overall length of attendance varied considerably: ten children participated for a year or less and eleven children attended for a year and a half to three years.

Unlike many preschool projects which control for age, sex distribution, and length of attendance, intake procedures in this nursery school were more akin to those of day-care centers, as we admitted children at any age, at any time during the four years, and for any length of attendance.

We thus were faced with challenges in addition to those posed by the children's deviant development. These circumstances of necessity limited the educational impact and rendered comparability of outcome data more difficult. On the other hand, the small size of

the groups allowed for a continuous individualized approach.
There is no doubt that insights about the children and about the
teaching process were enhanced by the staggering of admissions.
Furthermore, the periodic addition of children to the groups
yielded information about the impact of the arrival of "new" children on the "old" and vice versa. We would have liked to have
increased our groups over time, added more hours and days to
their weekly attendance, and to have had a better balance of boys
and girls. We occasionally experimented by having both groups
attend together, and we scheduled periodic visits by children from
a different psychosocial background to observe the possibilities inherent in introducing better-organized children to the group. The
latter gave us a glimpse of the great benefits that can accrue from
mixed groups, providing these are carefully guided. (Our findings
regarding this process of random entry into the school and the impact of "early," "late," and "other" children on each other will
need to be discussed separately.)

INTRODUCING THE NURSERY SCHOOL TO THE FAMILIES

Our first task was the facilitation of the children's regular attendance in nursery school. This was contingent on our ability to
involve the parents in this venture.

As might have been expected, the families were not self-motivated to enroll their children. Even the assumption made frequently, that a caretaking service would appeal to the parents' wish
to have some relief from their children, was not at all realistic.
These parents had long learned to protect themselves from having
to cope with the children's constant presence by shutting themselves off, either physically (by sending children out on the street
or going out themselves) or, if in the house together, by not "hearing" them, by ignoring their presence. On the contrary, sending
children to school imposed more demands: they had to be dressed
and fed, which involved planning, laundry, food preparation, and
timing of waking. School attendance imposed a rhythm on the

family which did not fit in with their style of living. Unless adjustments are made which take this fact into consideration, the best-planned, most attractive programs for children in slum neighborhoods are bound to draw only the more self-motivated, better-organized group in the community, not the children who need these services most desperately.

We proceeded by allowing time for letting the parents become interested in the nursery school. We quickly learned that if we tried to hurry the process we had to start again from scratch.

As the family worker was the first one to establish a relationship with the parents, her (or his) work preceded and assisted nursery school involvement. Enrollment and continuous attendance were accomplished by modification of the usual nursery school procedure and by careful coordination of the family worker's and teacher's efforts. They planned together how best to introduce the teacher to the parents and children.

For some families this was accomplished during a project party. For others a casual home visit by the teacher, with the family worker, was called for; and with yet other families a school visit with the worker was the important first step preceding actual enrollment.

ADMISSION INTERVIEW

Some parents *appeared* very eager to start their children, and readily made an appointment, maybe to please the family worker or perhaps because they genuinely wanted to "do the right thing" for their children. But we frequently found a wide gulf between the desire to do something and the ability to follow through. Thus, whether the parents seemed eager or reluctant, only one mother managed to come in on the day the first appointment was set. All others were either not at home when the family worker called for them or had a "compelling reason" to postpone the appointment.

We came to expect these delays and accepted them as part of our regular work. In some cases we had only to make a new appointment, and with the family worker's support and transportation, they came in for an interview. Others required more extensive encouragement—participation in some festivity in the nursery school, or the teacher's repeated visits.

Even then most of the mothers seemed more ill at ease than usual during nursery school interviews. This might be expressed by silence or a push of speech, by sitting on the edge of the chair, by clutching a coat tightly around the body, or even by arriving drunk. Some mothers "forgot" the application blanks or inoculation records. It was obvious that schools and teachers were distrusted, perhaps even feared. As the visits or interviews proceeded the mothers became noticeably more comfortable. It was a recurrent experience that it took the combined effort of the teacher and the family worker (who always joined the parent and teacher again at the end of the session) to terminate the visit.

Their quick response to our efforts to put them at ease was indicative of potential responsiveness. Intake interviews and home visits, while allowing for observation of the child, were primarily focused upon establishing a positive contact with the family. Rather than gather specific information we tried to lay the foundation for the parents' cooperation within the limits of their ability. Their obligations were scaled to their capacity, with realistic demands made as they showed increasing ability to fulfill them.

A transportation service was instituted with the teacher taking responsibility in assisting parents to ready the child and receive him back from school. We consider this an essential service for multiproblem families. We maintain that it is unrealistic to ask poorly organized, overburdened mothers to bring their children to school. The only other alternative to providing a pick-up service is to expect the children to come by themselves. This is a poor plan for many reasons, of which an important one is the undesirability of forcing yet one more unchildlike responsibility on a young child.

At the same time it is of the utmost importance that the school not "take over." By setting up definite intake procedures for parents (such as filling out an application form, coming to the office for a registration interview, taking the child to a clinic for a physical examination) we made quite clear that it was the parents' decision to provide nursery school education for their children. This was our way of supporting parental functioning. We stressed our reliance on them, as parents, for working with us in providing a good school experience for each child. This is a viable and honest basis for working with all parents, particularly of young children.

FACILITATION OF REGULAR
NURSERY SCHOOL ATTENDANCE

The teacher further took responsibility for maintaining ongoing contacts with the families. The difference from usual nursery school practice lies in the need for the teacher to take the initiative. It was essential that she go to the families, visit them, and call for the children. Sometimes she helped dress the children, or looked for them all over the neighborhood. Bringing them home from school at the end of the morning sometimes involved searching for the parents. The teacher helped to build a bridge between home and school life. This was of particular importance since the nursery school milieu was essentially different from anything the children had previously experienced. The almost daily contacts with the entire family were instrumental in building a meaningful relationship with the children and in assuring regularity of attendance.

The family's attainment of the necessary time orientation was facilitated by the establishment of clearly defined minimal requirements that provided a structural basis for attendance and a flexible approach in keeping with their individual capacity to adjust and change over time. Our expectation here was that mothers would learn to get their children ready for a specified time (washed, dressed, and fed), receive them when the school car returned at noon, inform the teacher of illness or other reasons for absence, and so forth. These are minimal requirements for most nursery schools and met by most parents as a matter of course. For our families, however, this was an entirely new experience.

When teachers witnessed parents behaving impulsively and engaging in childlike competitiveness with their children it was not always easy to remain objective and accepting. However, increasing understanding of the parent's own deprivations and their truly heroic attempts to cope with the many complications and just plain misery in their life, facilitated empathy and aroused a certain admiration. We also came to enjoy their straightforward responses which frequently showed sensitivity and a sense of humor. With this appreciation a comfortable relationship could develop.

It was important to respect the need shown by most of these mothers to preserve self-esteem by dressing their children impeccably, even when this hampered the children's freedom at play. This prompted us to include a clothes brush, spot remover, shoe polish and slipcoverlike aprons in our equipment; the shift from emphasis on primarily external respectability could not take place until the parents felt that we valued them and their children for themselves. Even then most mothers washed school outfits daily, ironing even the T-shirts. Likewise we accepted money from a mother who asked the teacher to buy her 3-year-old daughter doughnuts and candy, although she knew that this would be against school rules. The teacher respected the mother's attempts to provide breakfast for her child in the only way she could figure out, during a severe family crisis. This was an advance in mothering over earlier times when the child remained hungry or was obliged to ask other people for food.

With each family there was a gradual shift from an often inappropriate use of the teachers to a teacher-family relationship in which the needs of the child became a major focus. The attitudes of the teacher as demonstrated by her consistent behavior gradually served as a model, an alternate one, to child-rearing practices in the family.

The attendance rate in our nursery school, which was significantly higher than is usual in day-care centers and in community nursery schools, particularly in slum areas, can be attributed to the teacher's constant reaching-out, active participation in the children's families' lives.

There was no difficulty in assuring the attendance by the children. At first their hunger for attention in a benevolent setting seemed to override their distrust of new people and places. After adjustment, their eagerness and enthusiasm for attendance was only rarely interrupted, and then usually by a particularly traumatic home crisis. Even sickness seldom kept a child at home; in case of serious illness the combined efforts of the nurse, the family worker, and the teacher were often required to help the child and his parents accept the advisability of missing school.

THE TEACHING PROCESS*

The problems that presented themselves to a teacher of these children can be seen to be manifold. Notwithstanding the fact that one or another feature of the children's behavior can be found in any socioeconomic group and may occasionally be seen even in the most privileged and healthy child as part and parcel of his development, the pervasive anxiety and passivity and the distrustful orientation of these children necessitated modifications of usual nursery school practice. Whenever feasible we attempted to borrow from a variety of experiences in other settings, with other preschool children, where similar but not at all identical problems and needs for specific intervention presented themselves (1, 2, 9, 29, 40, 46). In this first attempt at exploratory work with severely deprived preschool children of multiproblem families we did not "invent" new techniques, but rather tried to adapt the skills available to us to evolve a number of modifications.

The function of a nursery school is primarily educational. However, to the extent that the school deals with children exhibiting developmental deviance it must include therapeutic ingredients. On the other hand, therapeutic measures are educative in effect, since they foster the child's learning process and teach him about himself and the world around him. For the children of multiproblem families, deprived of appropriate stimulating experiences and with many lags in ego functioning, a nursery school program has to be heavily supported by therapeutic measures.

According to the different philosophies of education subscribed to by various teachers, preference may be given to the dynamic child development approach or to teacher-directed or programmed methods, as in the present-day extensions of modified Montessori

* I thank the International Universities Press and the Editor of the *Journal of the American Academy of Child Psychiatry* for permission to borrow sections of my article entitled: "Adaptation of Nursery School Techniques to Deprived Children" (16) for this and other chapters in the book.

(28) or other didactic systems. It has become increasingly clear to open-minded educators that while there are fundamental differences in these approaches there is also much to be learned from each (see, for example, Baldwin [3]).

Our theoretical framework belonged to the general orientation of dynamic child psychology. It took into account the educational implications of recent insights into personality development (6, 7, 13, 17, 24, 49) and also of our emerging knowledge of the psychosocial realities of the children's environment (21, 27, 47). This approach to education, in the tradition of Bank Street College philosophy, is open-ended rather than prefixed.

Our goal was to learn as much as we could about the children and to look for every possible way to assist them toward healthy development. We did not spell out beforehand a set of detailed goals. Nor did we concentrate on helping these children to "catch up quickly" with their middle-class mates. We assumed that the experience of children living in multiproblem families in a slum environment had brought about adaptations sufficiently divergent from children reared in other settings to make the efficacy of such goals highly questionable. They presupposed a value judgment as well as the notion that stimulus deprivation leaves children with a vacuum, that they only need to be properly "filled up" with the right substance in order to be able to function as presumed desirable.

Furthermore, while certain effects of psychosocial deprivation could be seen as characteristic for this group, the children were by no means all alike. The recognition of individual differences and a respect for each child's unique way of exploring and discovering, of preferred perceptual style, mode and capacity for learning called for flexibility in planning and ongoing shifts in the program. Consistent with present-day knowledge of early childhood development we strove to provide optimal opportunities for the children actively to experience the environment in a wide variety of ways.

While it was our aim to find avenues for remediation of developmental lags and deviance in these children, we planned for them, as Biber says, as "children whose fundamental drives, curiosity and capacities are the same as all children's but whose development has been deflected by hampering life circumstances." Biber states succinctly what we specifically tried to avoid: "Programs developed with over-emphasis on compensation for specific deficits, without sufficient investment in providing the stimulation and experience considered optimal for all children, represent a new kind of deprivation" (8).

A dynamic point of view of early childhood development precluded a narrow "training" approach; instead it called for understanding of the particular dimensions of these children's way of functioning in order to set immediate and long-term goals supportive of all aspects of development.

This is not to say that we responded to the children in random fashion, without plan. An organized approach, flexibility, and inventiveness are integral parts of the nursery school teacher's equipment; they were merely called upon to a larger extent than usual. Over time, as a clearer picture of the children's characteristics emerged, a more definite pattern of teaching methods began to evolve. We found that the process of teaching, despite individual variations, became clearly discernible and could be defined.

Teaching Strategies.   These teaching methods had many facets but fell roughly into three main strategies. The first concerned the establishment of an objective structure, to render the school environment safe, predictable, and conducive to active involvement. The second might be called the establishment of a corrective relationship in an attempt to compensate for interrelational deprivations. We saw the strategy of providing experience with consistent, reliable, frequently gratifying relationships, supportive of self-differentiation, initiative, self-assertion, anticipation of satisfaction, and the growing capacity to tolerate frustration, as leading to motivation to focus on and become involved in activities, to explore, and to learn.

The third strategy concerned the provision of optimal opportunity for actively experiencing the environment. We aimed at an educational program, in the broadest sense of the term, that might promote integration rather than the compartmentalization of cognitive, social, and emotional aspects of development. This strategy included exposure to experiences available to most other children as a matter of course and deemed important to healthy development (7, 19, 36, 48).

These three strategies are deeply interrelated. While they are discussed separately, it should be kept in mind that it was precisely their *combination* that helped the children progress.

THE ESTABLISHMENT OF
AN OBJECTIVE STRUCTURE

A reliable, predictable structure of routines was established to create an atmosphere of safety and permit the children to relax their excessive apprehension and hyperalertness.

We had, of course, planned on definite routines, but we had not known that so much would depend on external structuring of the program. Beyond its reassuring qualities, the predictable order of the day served to acquaint the children with sequential events and helped them to plan and to anticipate. For many of them it was perhaps the first time in their lives that they could depend on something happening in a certain order. It should be emphasized that this structure was provided, not "enforced." There were no expectations of rigid adherence; the child was always more important than the schedule. But, one child after another responded to this ordering of daily experience with relief and with pleasurable anticipation of what was to come next.

Its importance could be seen by the tenacity with which the children held on to the "proper" sequence of routines. Any flexibility suggested by the teacher was apt to bring confusion and upset. Even after five months of nursery school attendance, the teacher's suggestion to skip rest and go for a walk in the warm sunshine—a suggestion eagerly responded to in the usual nursery school—resulted in severe disorientation and bewilderment. "We can't have no rest?" a 5-year-old asked unhappily, while another claimed not to be able to find her jacket. A third child got his blanket as though he had not heard, a fourth ran around shrieking in a frightened manner, and a fifth rushed back to the snack table and hastily grabbed for every last cracker crumb. It was not until well into the second year of a child's attendance that he would accept a little flexibility in the routines. Even then these deprived children tended to feel left out when minor changes in the routine were suggested. For instance, a girl who had washed her doll during the entire morning and was therefore reminded that she did not need to wash her hands before snack, ran to another teacher and complained bitterly about not being allowed to wash.

Structuring extended as well to establishing an order in the room, conducive to spatial orientation. While activity areas are well defined in most nursery schools, we had to establish an even more deliberate ordering of definite places. The fluidity of play space established by carrying over activities from one place to another in nursery school rooms only served to bewilder and frighten these children, at least in the initial months. When the easel was being used on both sides and a third child wanted also to paint, for a while it would not do to spread paper on a table or on the floor. This demanded more inner flexibility and purposefulness than the children were capable of. For a time, our children needed simplification of the nursery school "field"; a definitely circumscribed space was both a relief and an inducement to explore.

This ordering was important for establishing differentiation of the objects and of their uses, and served to bring about a certain relatedness between the various materials and their purposes or potentials. In the beginning the children hardly distinguished between different toys. They were just so many things to be collected and dropped again or thrown into a carriage or a box. Naturally, a child was not discouraged from "loading" her carriage; this was, after all, recognized as at least the beginning of self-initiated play and involved random acquaintance with various toys. But since this was not necessarily carried forward to sustained play, and since the children became confused by the chaos they created in no time, the teacher was obliged to help them by identifying and demonstrating some of the inherent uses of materials.

We sought to create an atmosphere that would spell pleasurable predictability yet encourage flexibility and a wide variety of alternatives. Structure was provided but not insisted upon, aside from necessary limits such as those pertaining to staying within the school or playground.

In practical terms, beyond those already indicated, modifications of usual teaching techniques included five points. First, more verbalizing about routine procedures. With these children it was not enough to state, "It is time to clean up"; they also needed to be told, many times over, what to expect subsequently. Second, the teacher participated much more actively and directly and offered her help with routine matters. It was important not to be fooled by the pose of pseudo autonomy that the children were apt to display (15). If you leave such a child to his own devices, merely because he protests that he can take his own snowsuit off (although he makes no move to do so, and in fact has no practice in doing so), his misery may be enormous. We found repeatedly that the children will perform to the best of their abilities any routine demands made on them; they will, for instance, clean up the entire doll corner, but perform these routines without pleasure or pride in accomplishment. By subjecting them to more pressure we tend only to deepen their resentment, fear, and distrust of people and diminish further the chances for developing spontaneous interests and vital curiosity. On the other hand, we found that a helping hand served to induce an interest in the activity itself and eventual commitment to it.

A third modification of teaching techniques concerns the encouragement of individual styles of coping with routines. It was important to help these children lose their deep fear of retaliation and to allow them to experiment with alternate ways of dealing with reality demands. This means that we presented choices and were accepting of the children's testing-out behavior and other timid attempts at self-assertion. A fourth modification concerns the provision of supportive directiveness during transition periods. Simple, clear directions, and in particular the availability of an adult to help whenever children could not manage on their own, served to avoid the frequent upsets and the extraordinary regressive behavior that the lack of structure in transition periods tends to trigger off in such children.

One final modification concerns the arrangement of the room. Because of the heightened motility of the children we found it imperative that space be provided for running, and equipment for climbing. We chose movable accessories, such as ladders, boards, and sawhorses, that encourage active structuring by the children. The doll corner, or "housekeeping corner," as it is frequently called, also needed to be larger than usual. A great deal of learning went on in this particular area, containing as it did the items most familiar to the children and of greatest significance in their lives. As for other activity areas, we found mainly that we had to simplify and frequently avoid too frustrating equipment for a time, as well as build bridges, in concrete terms, between the children's past experiences and the equipment, in order to invite exploration. For instance, the quality of block building increased considerably after we, by chance, made the addition of a realistic-looking cardboard "house" to the block shelf. Representational play materials of a higher order of abstraction needed to be fed in gradually along with more concrete presymbolic toys. The proportion of structured and unstructured materials had to be consciously balanced differently from that required for other nursery school children. Whereas most of the latter make imaginative use of basic unstructured materials, these children's predisposition to concrete thinking made them shy away from them until a link was found, making them comprehensible. Thus the room contained both very simple objects which the children could easily relate to and the less structured basic nursery school material.

The children could be relied upon to give us clues for changes. In time less space was needed for running; the climber was used more frequently for dramatic play than for aimless motoric discharge. Toddlers' toys were ignored and increasingly more challenging activities could be introduced.

THE ESTABLISHMENT OF A CORRECTIVE RELATIONSHIP

It soon became clear to us that the building of a corrective relationship with the teacher was the crucial factor in the children's nursery school experience without which learning was not even seen to begin. This meant the bringing about of a relationship between each child and the teacher which would significantly alter the child's expectations of adults as capricious and untrustworthy.

In working with these children it is important to keep in mind that their expectations of people are different from those usually found in nursery schools. Unlike many young children with whom the establishment of meaningful relationships with the teacher and with peers is soon carried over from basically trustful home relationships, these children had to slowly develop the capacity for them. We noticed that the building and developing of this compensatory relationship proceeded through specific, quite distinct phases. The children's progress in general functioning and their shift to a more active mode of approaching objects and challenges coincided with their capacity to relate. Deeper and more constructive involvement in activities, with an increase in frustration tolerance, curiosity, and problem-solving ability, was contingent on these phases.

The First Phase. Close examination of the initial four to six months of each child's attendance reveals that in the first phase the teacher concentrated almost completely on finding various avenues to provide the foundations for object constancy in a consistently reliable and gratifying setting. Within our predictable structure a great deal of leeway was given to encourage the children to express their wants. The teacher had to learn to pick up their intentions and, by the quality of her response, establish the preconditions for the development of trust and the emergence of initiative. In the beginning this involved constant attentiveness to the children. Responding to their hunger for attention took precedence over anything else. We could not expect even colorful projects to excite a child who did not differentiate between objects or between people and who was confused about differentiating himself from others. Learning could not proceed without the motivation to learn, without trust, without at least a beginning of a sense of self, without some degree of self-confidence and an inner sense of continuity. Play needed to be taught, self-protection promoted through the child's experience of finding himself valued and protected. We could not expect meaningful communication before the children were sure that somebody would listen and respond.

In the beginning demands on the children had to be minimal. Only by tuning in, much as a mother does with a small infant (42), could the teacher search out the cues to their wants and feelings and respond appropriately. This was the prerequisite for getting to know each child, and for developing a sense of timing, of when to step in unobtrusively and provide attentive support without overwhelming or threatening these vulnerable children.

The consistency of interactional gratification provided by the teacher in this phase bespoke unconditional acceptance of the children. She showed appreciation for even the most minute efforts. When a child scattered the pieces of a puzzle she would put it together for him; when he could be persuaded to sit by her and put a piece in himself, she would praise his intentions (even though his actual performance was very poor) and express her conviction that he would learn how to complete it. In every way possible the teacher tried to demonstrate that their efforts were worth while and that play could be enjoyable and satisfying.

The children's need for maintaining distance was respected in the midst of meeting their demands. Some of the most intimate interchanges with the children seemed to be carried on while they were sitting under the table, or had turned their back to the teacher; except for an occasional smile, the teacher made no attempt to come closer. At times the teacher had to pretend to be busy otherwise, while a child would peer into her face; or in the guise of a "kitten," would suddenly hop on the teacher's lap or sit by her feet, only to just as suddenly screech "Shut up!" and turn away.

The teacher shielded the children from painful experiences as much as possible. "Take care of yourself" was combined with "I'll help you take care of yourself. I would not want you to get hurt." She showed them how to climb safely. When a child fell, sympathy was expressed even if the child himself disregarded or even denied being hurt. After such repeated incidents the children finally acknowledged their distress, showed appropriate affect, and began to use caution.

To draw the children's attention to their bodies, the teacher would often stand before the mirror with a child who would, more often than not, indicate that he saw the teacher, not himself. She would move her arms, flex hands, nod, and so on, duly imitated by the child, who seemed both astonished and fascinated by his own body movements and facial expressions.

The teacher commented on their actions, much as a young child usually does for himself. Numerous times during the day she would put the child's gestures into words and respond to his poorly verbalized or unverbalized communications. Usually we could guess somehow what they were trying to convey, but when we could not understand we would persist in our efforts by showing concern for not understanding.

Of course, even the slightest signs of genuine independence were respected and fostered. However, in the early months the teacher often needed not only to start the child in play, but to remain in contact in order for him to maintain his interest. We saw many instances when a teacher had only to lift her eyes and look to another part of the room, while still physically close to a child, for him to suspend his activity until he again had the focused attention of the teacher.

Even by following the daily records it is not easy to ferret out how the teacher went about helping the children behave in a more childlike manner. It was no small feat to encourage them to become more assertive about their rights (including a child's right to protection and care) without their losing the ability to perform the precocious task the environment demanded of them. We found, for instance, that as the children became more self-protective, they were no longer so eager to cross dangerous avenues to shop for mother. Since refusal was not tolerated, a way had to be found to manage the tasks as well as the self-protection. In time several children were able to persuade their mothers to go shopping with them.

Likewise, it was very important to recognize that much of the children's danger orientation was legitimate and served to protect them. It certainly would not have been helpful if they had become trusting of the many untrustworthy aspects of the environment. It was our task to help the children discriminate between trustworthy situations that they could learn to handle and those that were unmanageable for them. It was precisely this discrimination that began to develop when the child began to respond to the consistent trustworthiness of the teacher.

Separation, though not acknowledged by the children, was frequently brought up by the teacher. While the children initially did not seem to pay any attention when the teacher left the room or returned, the teacher herself would announce that she was leaving, and why, and also gave reassurance about her return. This was picked up again when she came back. The same held for going home daily.

We played little hiding games. At first, playing peek-a-boo, the children would simply walk off as soon as the teacher was no longer visible, but gradually this became a favorite game, shifting to symbolic representation, such as hiding toys and recovering them.

The duration of this first phase in the teaching process varied with individual children. It never seemed to take less than four months, and it might require the better part of the first nursery school year.

Obviously, gaining trust in people is a slow process. Once the children realized that the teacher was genuinely interested in them, they needed to test her out mercilessly. They needed to see how the teacher would react if they timidly tried to assert themselves and to ascertain if the teacher would really stick by them and not abandon them. They became very demanding and clinging. If the teacher walked across the room, there would be a small group following her; if the teacher wrote, they had to have pencils, and so on. Once this testing phase was passed the children then began to settle down and engage in many activities.

At this point, the teacher no longer had to be quite as attentive. Frustrations no longer had to be guarded against, provided they were mild at first and well timed. Frequently now, the children could be asked to wait and to express themselves in words rather than by pulling at one's sleeve. They began to anticipate gratification and were thus enabled to delay.

The Second Phase. We now come to the second phase of work with the children. A "repertoire of reciprocal predictability" (13) was established; that is, the children were understood by the teachers and the reliability of the teachers' responses had become predictable to the children. The teacher's function now included helping them discriminate their demands to distinguish between genuine needs and whims and to develop an awareness of alternatives, instead of the expectation of "all or nothing."

We now could encourage more independent action without causing the children to feel rebuffed. Praise became geared to realistic accomplishments. We expected the children to engage in more complex activities and to be capable of increasingly higher frustration tolerance. Requested help continued to be responded to, but we indicated that independent action was valued. In every way possible, we supported their emerging initiative.

The children gradually developed the ability to select and show preferences. They began to experiment a little with new materials and they could be expected to follow simple instructions. They enjoyed listening to stories and telling stories, relating their own experiences to the subject under discussion. They also began to find increasing pleasure in associating with peers. Since the need for rivalry had diminished, the children could be helped to develop the social skills of shared play.

It was during this period that the children began to differentiate between people; they turned to a specific person with a definite request and they were reluctant to leave the classroom for testing or other experiences with a relative stranger. Now separation anxiety came into the open, expressed first in school. They refused to leave at the end of the morning, or clung to the teacher, finding it insufferable to share her for a minute. When she left the room they shouted "Stay here!" or demanded to know when she would return. Bits of paper were brought from home and put in her pocket or even sent to her via the family worker.

These signs of self-assertion in the pursuit of maintaining constancy were then expressed at home. Mothers complained that their children followed them around, asked them not to leave, and objected when they did. Suddenly children showed hesitation about coming to school. Some parents were able to tolerate this, others could not. The children appeared to know quickly what was permissible and rather than seeming confused they brought out in school what they knew they could not express at home. After their separation anxiety had come into the open and was acknowledged the whole process of leaving and returning became far more relaxed.

Demands on the teacher became more definite. "How about get me dat purple paint?" or "Take my picture off and be quick about it," or "Hold me, I might fall."

The children now drew the teacher into their dramatic play, thereby opening the way for her to aid them in moving beyond repetitive literal portrayals of painful experiences toward facing their feelings and playing out alternative solutions (26, p. 694).

SELF-ASSERTION AND IMPULSE CONTROL. As they became more trusting the children also increased their experimentation in asserting themselves. We welcomed rather than inhibited the children's testing-out behavior, because it was important for them to bring their aggression out into the open so that they could then be helped to bring it under voluntary control. It is a common experience, in nursery schools, to have passive children—when given a chance—"come out with a bang," revealing openly their immaturity in the development of impulse control. It was reasonable to expect that the pent-up aggression of these impatient children, with their low frustration tolerance, would emerge as they felt less fearful. With the ready availability of adults and the teacher's sensitivity to a child's limits in bearing frustration, aggression rarely became as prominent an issue in this nursery school as it is in many day-care centers. Certainly there were occasional outbursts, temper tantrums, destructiveness, and these were difficult to handle. But when the teacher's aim is to help the children develop inner control while channeling outer expressions of aggression into acceptable outlets (20, 30, 31), such outbursts can be anticipated and handled positively, even in groups with a larger ratio of children to adults.

Because these children are harder to reach and their outbursts more primitive, teachers are more easily provoked by them and feel threatened by the possibility of losing control of the group. They then tend to retaliate, which only feeds the angry feelings, although it may temporarily drive them once more underground. To break this vicious circle it is important that the handling of aggression become freed from such devices as blame or rewards. If the teacher will adopt a truly helpful attitude of unconditional acceptance of the child, in other words be aligned *with him,* he will eventually acquire self-directed socially acceptable behavior (23). This accepted nursery school technique is particularly important for the development of children from disorganized families (39, 41).

Through our home visits we gained a new perspective on some of the manifestations of the children's so-called aggressive behavior. For example, the children's frequent indulgence in "sneaking" took on new meaning in light of our observations. In one family grandpa had to sneak into the back room so the "man from housing" wouldn't know he had moved in. In another, father sneaked the recently sneaked-in television rapidly out again when a stranger came to the door. Even the children's cat had to learn to sneak out at night, since pets were forbidden in the housing project. We saw a mother unsteadily sneaking next door to "sleep it off" while her 4-year-old daughter covered up for her with a story about her mother having gone to work. And what of the father who has to sneak out the back as the welfare worker comes in the front, simply because the welfare check depends on his absence? With this in mind, when can we call "sneaking" aggressive and when defensive? We had no intention of taking from the children their ability to cope with the demands of their environment and render them more helpless. But we could open up *alternatives* for dealing with various situations.

IMPORTANCE OF ASSISTANT TEACHER.   Having two trained teachers in the room was a necessity even for a small group, particularly during the second phase. There was no end to the demonstrating and explaining called for once the children showed an active interest in exploring. Talk needed to be initiated and maintained; the many activity projects that were now possible had to be carefully prepared and steadily supported. In particular the children's fragile self-esteem had to be bolstered all the time. Maintaining an ongoing and productive relationship with the teacher while sharing her with others was more difficult for these children at 4 and 5 then it usually is for a 15-month-old toddler to share his mother.

The children's tendency at this time to test out the teacher's reliability by deliberately endangering themselves necessitated prompt attention. It also would not have been possible for one teacher alone to attend to the physical needs of the children in the unhurried relaxed manner that was a prerequisite for more autonomous self-care.

Most importantly, two teachers demonstrated that there are alternatives. It was a novel experience for the children to discover that people could have different preferences and implement them without anything disastrous happening.

The demonstration of respect for the opinions and actions of another person was not lost on the children. They began to compare and to remark on the differences with wonder and sometimes with anger. Eventually a child could say amidst self-conscious giggles, "Mrs. A. likes white bunnies, I make 'em pink—you don't have to have to make white, do you?" This was a big step forward for a child who had not ventured an independent opinion before, but simply imitated others.

ADVANTAGES OF THE GROUP.   The extensive efforts made by the teachers in establishing viable relationships are techniques more familiar to the field of individual play therapy (1, 2, 29, 34). However, they are well adapted to work with the more disorganized children one finds in many day-care centers, Head Start groups, and other community schools.

Although these children often need individual attention, there are definite advantages to working with them in small groups. First of all, the group setting dilutes the intensity of the adult-child interaction. Since the need is intense but closeness threatening, it helps that they can "take you or leave you."

A second advantage is that the children can vicariously experience the interaction between the teacher and any other child. While she is attentive to the individual child, the teacher is simultaneously geared to the group. Her reassurance to one has an effect on the rest.

A third advantage the group offers is that it gives the children a chance to work on their rivalry problem. The experience of having a teacher maximally available while sharing her with others, demonstrates continuously that they do not lose the adult even if another child has her attention.

A fourth advantage is that it gradually facilitates satisfying interactions among peers. This experience of mutual pleasure among children is irreplaceable. Also, as is well known, a child will attempt a task more easily after he has watched another child succeed. Imitation of meaningful tasks enhanced problem-solving ability, thus serving an important aspect of the learning process.

FOSTERING PEER RELATIONSHIPS.   In order for social skills to develop naturally the children had to acquire some self-awareness and adequate self-differentiation. The usually observed sequential shifts from solitary to parallel to associative to cooperative play took place less in accordance with specific age levels but was rather related to the degree of solidity of the child-teacher relationship. Frequently, the children's first approach to each other was by imitating the teacher. Thus, a child might help another with a task or involve a child in play as the teacher had done with him. The children also frequently used the teacher as a mediator before venturing more direct approaches to each other. During this phase they required more assistance with social interaction than is usual in nursery schools.

Once relieved of the need to compete for the attention of the adult these children were found to be more generous and less competitive than most middle-class children. They needed no prompting to allow a child just back from the hospital to "hog" the doctor set. A 4-year-old boy spontaneously gave up a newly painted chair to an impetuous little girl, remarking to the teacher, "Her needs dis chair too greedy."

The Third Phase. This was entered when the children were moving toward greater mutuality in their relationship with the teacher and showed a more active interest in their peers. The increase of self-initiated, focused activity reflected growing self-esteem and a more organized, purposive mode of approaching the world. The children had shifted from "Look at me, look what me doing" to "Look what I can do." We now saw glimpses of curiosity; questions were asked and information seemed to be retained and utilized. (The teacher's role in promoting language development will be described below.) The repeated experience of the trustworthiness of the teacher, together with success in their endeavors, brought about the frustration tolerance needed for improved problem solving ability. It paved the way toward greater openness to new experiences and challenges.

The third phase of the teacher-child relationship came closer to that which a teacher maintains in any good nursery school, involving the steps conducive to supporting the child's growing autonomy and supplying guidance, information, and an expanding field of stimulation. However, even during this phase these children required far more intensive individual guidance than is called for in most nursery schools. The continued tenuous quality of the children's trust in others and themselves necessitated a great deal of support, particularly reassurance.

While they knew all too quickly when they failed, they did not always show good judgment about their achievements. It therefore was one of the teacher's tasks to confront the children with their own growing capabilities, to help them function on a level commensurate with their developing abilities.

During this phase, the children still had many expressions that gave voice to their lingering distrust: "You kiddin'," "Oh yeah," "Like hell you will," and the like. (A 4-year-old told by a visitor to her home, "Your teacher sends her love," replied suspiciously, "Where is it?") It is not generally customary for children to greet something with "You said you would and you really got it." When a child ordinarily wants a pencil sharpened or asks for red paint he just takes it, perhaps looks pleased or maybe preoccupied with what comes next, and would not, as our children did, make a big affair of it. For these children the main issue always remained the acknowledgment of their wish by the teacher. Conversely, limitations, although steadily better tolerated, remained a personal deprivation, indicative of disapproval and rejection. Typically, one 4-year-old, painting her seventh picture, each one having been duly appreciated, was reminded that it was time to clean up. She quickly messed up her picture, painted her hands, and then in the bathroom screeched for the teacher's help, help she had not needed for several months.

In other words, the children continued to be very vulnerable, and while their behavior showed increasing anticipation of equitable treatment they could easily be "thrown" when they feared that it might not be forthcoming.

However, as they now had moved toward greater self awareness and therefore could give more well-defined cues, the teacher could gauge more easily when to step in and when to keep her distance, when to "ignore" a given situation and when to respond with silent or verbal support or take specific action. The emergence of increasing autonomy now allowed for experimentation with alternatives in thought and behavior. Every attempt was made to promote more flexibility in the children's approach to things and people. By encouraging greater elaboration in symbolic representation through play and by verbal communication we sought to increase the effectiveness of the ongoing learning experience. With the teacher's guidance age-appropriate peer relationships developed during this phase. Shared play experiences now led to meaningful involvement with one another on a continuing basis.

PROVIDING OPTIMAL OPPORTUNITIES
FOR ACTIVELY EXPERIENCING
THE ENVIRONMENT

Since our aim was to build ego strength and to guide the child "towards increasingly objective mastery of reality without sacrificing the idiom of his own perceptions and transformations" (7), our curriculum represented basic nursery school practices with modifications specific to the experiential differences of the children. The emphasis was on learning by exploration and discovery, on fostering initiative and self-awareness, rather than on didactic presentations of teacher-imposed goals and standards (10, 12, 45). We set the stage, using careful "judgment as to when children have learned all they can from free exploration and are ready for cues, leads, guidance, and direction" (6).

First of all, we had to find ways to move these passive children into activity, to help them find satisfaction in play engagement. Initially they approached even familiar toys (dolls, teddy bears, cars, balls) with little interest, not to mention their avoidance of the strange new nursery school equipment. It did not suffice to provide a relaxed as well as stimulating classroom atmosphere and to make appropriate materials freely available; the teacher had to assume a more active role.

We learned quickly that when she involved herself in an activity nearly all children were at least superficially responsive, if at first only to the extent of watching the teacher. Frequently her presence appeared to constitute a permission to touch and otherwise explore.

Of course, the teacher was selective in the activities she chose to evoke interest in, relating these to her close observations of a child's being drawn more to one activity area or another, returning to look at or handle a particular type of object, or appearing to be watching another child's activity. She demonstrated the inherent *pleasure* and *safety* involved in exploring materials. When a girl, in her clumsy attempts to "set the table," repeatedly pushed dishes off the edge of it and ran off in alarm, the teacher not only assured her that plastic dishes do not break easily, but also that they can be recovered and placed more securely.

These reassurances and demonstrations constitute modifications of usual nursery school techniques. This is not to say that other children do not also occasionally need reassurance in relation to their play, but that the inner resources with which many other children come to nursery school serve them to cope independently with some of the challenges and frustrations that incapacitated these children.

Dramatic Play. We were well aware of the importance of play for the young child as an outlet for feelings, as a source of stimulation for thinking and reasoning, and as a facilitator of social maturation and of self-discipline (18, 20, 32). We therefore considered it progress that within a short time we were able to launch the children in play (particularly dramatic play that involved their home experiences). This needed only to be started or "approved" by the teacher to continue for some time with decreasing need for her immediate attentiveness.

The props used in their dramatic play were not many: sink, bed, carriage, bottles, and sometimes dolls or dishes. The few additional items were often directly traceable to home experiences we knew about or had observed. A 3-year-old boy, for instance, included a lock and key in his "house"—he sometimes found himself in front of a padlocked apartment, not knowing where his mother had gone or when she would return.

However, even the inclusion of meaningful items did not lead to variation or elaboration of play. A "shopping trip" to the "store" involved pushing the carriage or wagon over to the shelf and dumping in everything in sight, without selectivity and without other elements of play ever developing spontaneously. Day after day, the same meager sequence was repeated. The teacher was obliged to demonstrate alternatives, to introduce the possibilities inherent in using various materials, without however imposing her ideas on the children.

The difficulty was always in involving the children's interest. They watched the teacher with fascination; for most children it was probably the first time in their lives that somebody actually

showed concern for their interests. Occasionally we used to catch a
sidelong, bemused look as though it was amazing to a child that a
grown-up could enjoy seeing him play. But to become truly involved in the activity itself, beyond the interest in being with the
teacher, necessitates an internal commitment, and this was slow to
develop.

Manipulation and Problem Solving. This was particularly noticeable with play calling for manipulative skills. Demonstration,
doing for the child and with the child, frequently had to precede
their involvement, as they did not seem to have enough self-
confidence to attempt and follow through on their own on a task
demanding problem solving. Here again we took our cues from
their tentatively expressed intentions.

While we used whatever opportunities presented themselves to
offer appropriate intellectual stimulation to the children, the
teacher was careful not to isolate this aspect of learning from
the many other avenues which foster cognitive development in
young children. Intellectual components of learning were not
treated as separate but rather—just like its social and emotional
components—as an integral part of the active process of attaining
knowledge and skills through a wide choice of manipulative, dramatic, creative play activities. If these children were ever to have a
chance to develop into independently thinking and acting, self-
confident people they needed not only a supportive and "enriched" environment, but also one where they could learn to use
their initiative.

Our emphasis on helping children become self-motivated in selecting their activities may be considered as related to certain aspects of Montessori's (28) educational philosophy as it is to Dewey
(11), Johnson (25), and other educators who recognized the value
of firsthand experiences and individualized active approaches to
learning. (On the other hand, the programmed aspects of the
Montessori method, the insistence on the performance of tasks in a
predetermined manner was antithetical to our aim of promoting
initiative and creativity.)

As already noted, many children had to start on a level far below
their chronological age, and learn to manipulate first very simple
toys designed for toddlers. (We discovered this by chance. A num-

ber of such toys were stored in the same room where we prepared snacks, and one child after another, following the teacher into the room, explored them with such fervor that we included them in the nursery school room.) Typically, a 4-year-old boy, who had been particularly passive and disinterested in play, spent the better part of each day for weeks lying on the floor, rolling a small pull toy back and forth, cooing and smiling as he investigated the wheels, trying to pull it upside down, replacing the removable pieces, and so on. When his manner of playing with the toy became less infantile the teacher introduced Tinkertoys and eventually he moved to the workbench where he chose to make his own wagon. In the course of this development toward acquisition of manipulative skills, he could be helped to branch out in many directions, using paint, clay, and blocks with increasing involvement and pleasure.

Anticipation of Defeat: One of the Obstacles to Progress. Until these children learned to anticipate success the slightest challenge sent them scurrying away. If, during the early phase of teaching, the screwed-on top of the ring tree did not come off at a fierce tug, or a bead slid off the string, this was already too much frustration to handle—regardless of the child's age. Even later on, when a wheel came off that boy's wagon, it did not occur to him to simply return to the workbench to put the wheel back on. When the teacher suggested this, he dismissed her with, "It will break, throw it away, I can't." Even when they were engaged in successful endeavors the children expected that somewhere they would fail or their efforts would be canceled out.

This tendency toward a feeling of inadequacy and futility was repeatedly reinforced by actual experiences. As we frequently observed, a girl going home with a beautiful painting would see it being torn to shreds by her siblings; a child's carefully pasted collage was met with ridicule by mother and then destroyed by sister; a boy's gingerbread man, baked by himself, was immediately broken up by the family members—including mother—and eaten by all of them. It is a wonder that we were able to interest the children in achieving at all! Despite intensive work with the parents, discouragement, ridicule, deprecation, and rather cruel teasing remained an important ingredient of parent-child interaction, particularly when the parent was under a strain, which in such families is frequent.

Building Self-Esteem. With the handicap of the child's tendency toward self-devaluation and his lack of confidence in his ability to achieve, we had to emphasize very simple satisfactions. One piece placed in a puzzle was celebrated for the major achievement it was; a painting, no matter how smeary, was hung up and referred to with enthusiasm; a piece of clay punched with a fist was saved to serve as tangible proof of the child's efforts. With more structured activities, we found it important for the teacher to offer her help before the child became too frustrated, and to retreat at any sign of effort to find his own solution.

Young children are far more interested in the process of work than in the results and it was not our aim here to lay undue stress on "products." These children, however, needed tangible proof that their activities were valued, in order to bolster their low self-esteem.

In the course of time we introduced the children to all of the usual educational materials and encouraged their exploration in a progressively more mature manner. With greater capacity for involvement they developed wider interests and special abilities.

However, such interests frequently had to be bolstered and enriched. The teacher needed to help them focus and express their interests. For some time it was up to her to formulate their quests for them, or at least solicit them. (Rather than being considered an asset, the children's curiosity at home tended to make the parents uneasy or even angry. This is understandable, since there is much to hide in daily life, in order to get by.) Spontaneous verbal exploration as an extension of their investigations seemed to be most available to those children who had acquired considerable self-confidence. However, all of them discovered the pleasures inherent in expressive and manipulative activities, in shared experiences, and in acquiring some skills through self-directed play involvement.

A Casual Way of Presenting Stimuli and Information. Modifications were called for in the usual nursery school techniques for presenting stimuli, since the "spontaneous interests" of children, which usually guide the teacher in program planning (38), were most conspicuously lacking in this group.

An example of information introduced by the teacher would be the casual way of acquainting the children with the names of colors. While the children did not for a long time show any interest in learning colors, the teacher would name them, as a matter of course, such as saying, "How well you pour from the red pitcher."

We also used the children's heightened motility to extend their learning experiences. While teaching them to find ways to gain satisfaction from the skillful use of their bodies, the teacher gave simple explanations about the physical properties of the slide, the climber, and so forth, promoting investigation. To bring some purpose into the aimless running and to use this opportunity to teach the children to cope better with a real necessity in their lives, we made, for instance, a large traffic light. While this was initiated by the teacher, the children were encouraged to take the project over and develop it in their own way.

Not only was it difficult to find the right "dosage" in supplying the kinds of stimulation which most other children have been exposed to at home, but timing also appeared to be of utmost importance. To find the right moment when receptivity was high and information or new materials might have meaning demanded close observation of the children's behavior, particularly in play. It obviously makes a difference whether a "name" is supplied at the time when the teacher so decides or when actual experience has created the possibility for a concept to emerge. Thus, the teacher gave no lengthy lecture about the stapler on the shelf, but when a child returned it on outstretched arm with "Here—dis," she responded by involving the child in a brief discussion about his activity, perhaps comparing stapling with pasting, or whatever appeared of interest to the child. (These attempts to aid the children in clarifying and differentiating were in contrast to home experiences where a girl's repeated question to her mother about where to put the groceries brought the typical answer "Put it.")

As it is for all young children, it was of utmost importance that these youngsters have ample opportunity to explore objects repeatedly and to be able to come back to them repeatedly. "One-shot" exposures to new objects, ideas, or sights are worse than useless as they deepen the children's already considerable confusion.

Exposure to number concepts also proceeded in a casual manner in the course of everyday classroom living and was built upon the children's experiences. While none of the children could count, many knew the values of coins and could give an account of the different amounts to be had from pawnshops for steam irons, vacuum cleaners, watches, and so on. With growing specificity in their relationships with people and to objects they could be acquainted with number sequence and the process of counting.

The materials and manifold experiences available in the nursery school milieu are well covered in the literature (10, 12, 20, 30, 37, 38). Others (14, 18, 31, 33, 35, 44) have described for us the learning potential inherent in the young child's play, its contributions to perceptual, social, and emotional development. The importance of various types of creative, dramatic, manipulative, and gross motor play for the progress of these children has been mentioned throughout and need not be taken up here.

In addition to encouraging full use of nursery school equipment and materials, we provided a wider range of experiences, in the hope that as interpersonal relationships became more meaningful, the children would be able to develop more varied interests.

Facilitating Conceptual Development. One successful method of introducing activities and involving these children was to make structured projects available. One morning a week a table was set up for a special activity. Of course, no child was obliged to join and the usual activities were also available. At first the children would ignore the projects and barely glance at the things laid out for them. When, however, we switched to preparing food: making pudding, baking cookies, and the like, we met with eager response. This again proved the importance of starting with something familiar and immediately satisfying.

Projects like these are standard procedure in many nursery schools. We planned carefully for each activity with the interests and capabilities of the children in mind. But we had to think also of including well-timed exposure to new experiences.

In time these projects could be broadened to include a number of related experiences. To give a concrete example: before making applesauce, the children discussed what was needed, made a shopping list, counted the money, bought apples and sugar at the neighborhood store, and went to fetch the utensils from the kitchen. We read stories related to the subject, and finally went to a farm, wandered through an orchard and saw a cider mill. For most of the children, who had rarely been out of their immediate neighborhood, this encompassed many new experiences indeed.

We then discovered that the children were familiar with apples and oranges only. They had never held or tasted lemons, grapefruit, or any other fruit, nor could they name them or tell them apart. Cutting up and tasting such fruit further revealed that the children could not give names to the taste sensations involved—they literally did not know sweet from sour. We provided, of course, many other experiences that would sharpen sense perception.

While food preparation, particularly baking for family parties, remained a popular type of project, we related projects to seasons, impending vacations, and other occasions. At a time when there was much interest in dress-up in a group, the children made accessories; when we acquired a rabbit, they created a variety of animal things.

It was important to prepare the material thoroughly so that the project could be completed within a very short period. In time, with greater anticipation of success on their part, the children's attention span increased. But by and large they quickly lost their investment if the task was too complicated or involved too many operations.

The children who attended for a second year frequently carried the projects over into other play periods. A boy followed the pasting of a fall leaf collage by bringing in leaves from home and making another collage on his own. A "mural" of spring flowers was added to spontaneously from time to time. However, it needs to be noted that even this spontaneous carry-over was marked by extraordinary rigidity. The boy, for instance, had to have just exactly the same kind of paper plate for his leaves as he had used previously. Although inventiveness and variation of procedure were encouraged throughout, we saw little sign of either.

To aid the process of labeling and systematizing information we played identification games. A favorite with the children involved placing a few objects on the table, naming them, and then covering them and trying to remember their names. For some time the children had to feel the objects through the cloth but eventually they not only rose to the challenge but set themselves more difficult tasks, for instance, classifying objects in pairs, by color, by size, or even rearranging objects to symbolize a story sequence.

Aiding Language Development. The process of promoting language development was one of our most important and difficult jobs, and one that went on continuously. (It demands more detailed description and a more thorough discussion than is possible within the framework of this book.) We had to promote verbal communication, make explicit the meaning and uses of words, their relationships to real objects and to activities. We had to teach the children that there were many things one could talk about and many ways one could do so. They needed to learn that one could use words to describe real things as well as thoughts and feelings.

The challenge was to motivate an interest in learning to use words and to care about their meaning. If it makes no difference to a child whether what is in the jar is "dis" or has a name—*paint*—if it does not matter to him if it is blue or red paint, even the most skillful manner of teaching falls on barren ground. Unless a child is sure he is listened to, there is little impetus for learning to say anything well. Ingratiating manipulation had paid off in the past; other communication apparently had not. So our whole approach to language had to be to make proficiency in verbalization worth while.

It was the teacher who supplied missing words and posed the questions the children indicated but did not ask. She gave explanations in order to acquaint them with her reasoning, to encourage questioning, and to promote interest in causal thinking.

This was brought as close as possible to what the children were familiar and comfortable with. With children so oriented toward the concrete, touchable, and visible, and lacking in experience in abstract thought, words had not only to be simple, but also brought together with physical demonstrations. A request to children to "bring chairs over to the piano so we can sit here and sing together" produced bewildered looks until the teacher showed what was meant, thus joining demonstrable action to verbal communication on a level congruent with the children's conceptual and linguistic grasp.

The teacher's way of commenting on the children's activities led gradually to a greater awareness by the children of their actions, which they then verbalized to the teacher or to themselves in a running commentary accompanying play. This is customary among young children; it was new for this group. To avoid misunderstanding, it may be well to emphasize that we did *not* talk a great deal but that the children's unfamiliarity with what Bernstein (4) terms "formal" or "elaborate" linguistic code necessitated more careful verbalization than is called for in the usual nursery school. (For examples see p. 690 of reference 26.)

The introduction to stories and books called for inventiveness and patience. We not only had to acquaint children with picture books from scratch, we had to demonstrate that looking at a book, listening to a story, can be pleasurable. Only three of our 21 children came from homes where any books at all were to be seen, and only one mother took books to read to her children from the library bus that stopped by her house. Most of the children literally did not know what to do with a book. They joined the reading table reluctantly and flipped the pages in imitation of the teacher or another child who had been in school for some time, but without themselves looking at the book. A 6-year-old girl did not know how to turn the pages; she turned the book instead, from one cover to the other, back and forth. A 5-year-old rapidly turned the pages without a glance inside and beamed when she completed the process, "Me did it."

We encouraged manipulation of books and gradual "discovery" of their inherent interest for the child. But solitary perusal is no substitute for the warm interpersonal experience of reading together with an adult. The children needed both, the freedom to explore books independently and the satisfaction of shared pleasure.

Story content posed another problem. The majority of books written for middle-class children not only take a larger and different vocabulary for granted, they also depict situations totally unfamiliar to these children: families own little houses with trees and lawns around them, enter their car to go shopping or drive to the country; a boy comes down the stairs from his room to greet his

daddy just back from the office; or, a nurse takes the baby for a
walk. The children responded in keeping with their own experience. The policeman helping children across the street was said to
arrest them; the father coming home was said to be "de guy yellin'
for money." Mother calling from the door was "mad"; or if not
seen was "gone." All animals were "doggies," and frequently we
heard, "Doggies lost no Mommy." Obviously the stories in these
books were remote and not particularly relevant to the children's
understanding of life.

So we started by making up stories about the children themselves and their intimate world, as mothers usually do for children.
They quickly learned to give cues as to what they wanted to hear.
The child, for instance, who had suffered many hospitalizations
wanted a story containing: "Then the doctor said to the mommy,
'Your little girl is all better now and she can come home with you
again.' " By actively involving the children in storytelling we were
able to foster more elaborated and expressive use of language.
From these favorite stories we moved to books with more neutral
or general topics and to reading to several children together, and
finally to the whole group. (However, we continued to provide the
intimacy of reading to individual children as well.) While the response to stories never became as lively and enthusiastic as with
children from more fortunate backgrounds, it did improve to the
point, at least, where nearly all the children understood the content of a number of books and could participate in the discussion.
Like other children, they often remembered a large sequence of
the text and would notice the minute the text was changed. But
unlike other children, the tendency to be inflexible about change
was here also a great deterrent to openness to new language experiences. If the children had had their way, we probably would have
read the same book all year. Once they liked a book, that was all
they wanted to hear. If, in a story, a boy riding a bike greets his
mother, he was asserted to be riding a bike to his mother in another book, although (1) that boy was running, (2) there was no
bike in any picture, and (3) the mother did not figure in this part
of the story. Nor could they ever really enjoy stories that dealt with
more complicated themes further removed from their own immediate experiences. There were a few exceptions (such as the book

Caps for Sale) but most of the stories remained way over their heads, as did poetry other than little rhymes about themselves.

A High Receptivity for Music.   Nearly everything that had a melody attached to it was remembered and quickly reproduced by the children with surprising accuracy. The children had an extraordinarily good sense of rhythm, and the majority of them could sing in tune. Once they had been helped to overcome their reluctance (particularly when they realized that no one in school ridiculed them), the pleasure and ability they showed in music was remarkable. Not that all children always participated. But over time they developed an adequate repertoire of songs, danced freely, and enjoyed using—and even making—preschool instruments. The piano was always open and used frequently by the children for the sheer enjoyment of producing sounds. A teacher could often get something across to a child by turning her words into songs.

We do not feel that we have explored sufficiently the potentials of using various forms of music with these children. The high incidence of unusual receptivity to musical experiences among them (see Foster [16]) called for a far wider range of experimentation than we were able to undertake.

The Outside World Becomes More Manageable.   This group of children was not only "culturally deprived"—that is, had not been exposed to the experiences available in our culture for young children—they were not even encouraged to explore and understand their own immediate surroundings. Knowledge appeared to have been fostered insofar as it served expediency. Although children went shopping at three, they had not been taught when it was safe to cross the street. Several 3-year-olds knew how to fill and warm a baby bottle and feed an infant at night; they did not know at 5 what a bottle was made of or where the milk came from. It is doubtful that they even wondered about it; curiosity appears to have been discouraged much earlier in their lives. Some children began to investigate more actively toward the end of the first year in school, but only in the second year of attendance did some others begin to ask "why" and "how."

By and large the outside world was a frightening and dangerous place for the children, an extension of their own primarily threatening surroundings with the added apprehension about the unknown. For the first few months in school nearly all children kept a fearful ear cocked for noises outside the classroom. Only repeated explanations, reassurance, and guided investigations gradually turned this apprehension into watchful interest and even fascination. A garbage truck rattling by, for instance, produced near panic at first; gradually it was identified by sound and watched through the window with appropriate comments as to its function.

Before we could actually come to the point of making the outside world more manageable through firsthand experiences, the children had to become comfortable in the nursery school itself. Even the walk to the nearby playground seemed fraught with dangers for these children: they might lose the teacher; every car on the road was assumed to be there to hurt them; and if a police car went by, the reaction ranged from outright fear to asserting that, "Dey pickin' up de dead guys." Only after the children began to rely on the teacher's protectiveness and trustworthiness could they venture out with some interest in things outside their own narrow surroundings.

Furthermore, they had much exploring to do in relation to themselves, their play materials, their unfolding capabilities; interest in the outside world could not be expected very quickly. However, we did deal with it as it intruded itself naturally on the children's lives at school. We explained, reassured, gave ample time for discovery, and also introduced new experiences when these had a reasonable chance of finding a reception. Our aim was to demonstrate to the children that although they lived in a realistically dangerous world—and there is no doubt that they were surrounded by real dangers and unpleasantness—there were worthwhile and enjoyable aspects to the world that they could learn to master.

In practice this meant that we used every opportunity to introduce firsthand experiences that were meaningful to them, such as exploration of the building, trips to the many interesting places in the neighborhood, all entirely new to most of them, although easily accessible from their homes. The children lived with and cared for rabbits and fish, planted flowers and vegetables in window boxes, investigated seashells, rocks, plants, prisms—whatever caught their interest.

Trips were followed up with related stories and play activities and we usually saw to it that there was something to carry home. By encouraging the children to tell details about these trips to parents (standing by to make sure they would be listened to and adding facts of interest specifically for the parents), we assisted communication between parents and child and gave emphasis to the importance of the experience for the child.

It can hardly be considered a novelty to take nursery school groups on trips. They have long been found to be an effective technique for progressively widening the children's horizon by providing them with direct acquaintance with many facets of their surroundings. Usually the trips taken by a school are supplementary to those of the family. For these children, most of whose parents rarely moved beyond a few square blocks, trips became an even more important experience as a technique for building a bridge to the outside world. Particularly because of the children's difficulties with the comprehension of abstract concepts, it was helpful to give them repeated concrete experiences in and out of school on which to base their growing ability to gain understanding about their surroundings.

Needless to say, it was at first quite difficult to take such frightened, motoric, disinterested children on trips. They were totally unused to walking with others, to holding anyone's hand, and to feeling comfortable about observing the sights. The threat of being lost, of losing something tangible, or losing control of themselves —combined with their pronounced disaster orientation—focused their interests not on the pleasurably informative aspects of the surroundings but on unpleasant, or potentially dangerous, ones.

However, we soon found, just like Bettelheim, that "walking with a child offers many occasions for marginal talks that help him understand his own behavior, to overcome fears through reality testing and to correct false impressions he has gathered about the world at large or about human relations" (5). Without this kind of interactional support for the children who need it, I question seriously the educational value of the frequent trips taken by Head

Start and other preschool groups. With it, however, we found that trips provided additional opportunities for enhancing the child's understanding of himself and his environment.

CONTINUITY AND
CONSOLIDATION OF GAINS

The problem remained of helping these children assimilate their widening field of knowledge. There was no doubt that once they opened up to new experiences the majority of them reacted to stimuli in an alert and intelligent manner. They had become more alive and they showed pleasure in their activities. They demonstrated increasing persistence in their investigations, and their exploratory skills became at least close to age-adequate for a number of them. There was evidence that they remembered much of what they had seen and learned. But could they apply this knowledge to new situations? Could they explore on their own, away from the teacher's encouragement? Could we expect active curiosity and quest for information to continue outside of the nursery school situation?

We know that some of the children tried to involve their parents, and while over time many parents did learn to listen to their children and to reply, on the whole the response and stimulation which these children received were minimal.

This opens up the question of continuity and of consolidation of gains, as the children move from nursery school to grade school. Would their budding ability to explore actively and learn be supported and increased or would rote learning, management from above, and other measures calling for passive modes of responding undo their tentative and shaky move toward autonomy? Would the children's emerging initiative be respected and given ample opportunity? Would their growing self-esteem be supported and achievement valued for the progress it represented rather than be judged in comparison with "age norms"? Would feelings be "allowed" and would there be acceptance of regression caused by environmentally determined tensions? Would school be a place where imaginative play could continue to serve as a clearinghouse for experiences, conflicts, and ideas?

In the nursery school setting we could but open up opportunities for the children to actively experience themselves and the environment, to develop more adequate skills, to organize some of their badly confused impressions, thoughts, and feelings, to experience pleasure in doing, knowing, and relating. This was a start. It needs to be continued, at the children's own pace, regardless of their chance of ever becoming as knowledgable, as flexible, as creative as some other children with a very different start in life. As Holt (22) says: "There must be a way to educate young children so that the great human qualities that we know are in them may be developed."

REFERENCES

1. Alpert, A.   The Treatment of Emotionally Disturbed Children in a Therapeutic Nursery. *American Journal of Orthopsychiatry* 25: 826, 1955.
2. Axline, V. A.   *Play Therapy: The Inner Dynamics of Childhood.* Boston: Houghton Mifflin, 1947.
3. Baldwin, A.   A is Happy—B is Not. *Child Development* 36:583, 1965.
4. Bernstein, B.   Social Class and Linguistic Development: A Theory of Social Learning. In Halsey, A. H., Floud, J., and Anderson, A. (Eds.), *Education, Economy and Society.* Glencoe, Ill.: Free Press, 1961.
5. Bettelheim, B.   *Love Is Not Enough.* Glencoe, Ill.: Free Press, 1950.
6. Biber, B.   Integration of Mental Health Principles in the School Setting. In Caplan, G. (Ed.), *Prevention of Mental Disorders in Children.* New York: Basic Books, 1961.
7. Biber, B.   Pre-School Education. In Ulich, R. (Ed.), *Education and the Idea of Mankind.* New York: Harcourt, Brace & World, 1964.
8. Biber, B.   The Place of Theory of Development and Existing Models of Pre-School Education in Evaluating "New Trends." Paper presented at American Orthopsychiatric Association, 1965. Revised and published as: Biber, B., and Franklin, M. B.   The Relevance of Developmental and Psychodynamic Concepts to the Education of the Pre-School Child. *Journal of the American Academy of Child Psychiatry* 6:5, 1967.
9. Buehler, C.   Play Therapy. *Child Study* 4:155, 1941.

10. Christianson, H. M., Rogers, M. M., and Ludlum, B. A. *The Nursery School: Adventure in Living and Learning.* Boston: Houghton Mifflin, 1961.

11. Dewey, J. *Lectures in the Philosophy of Education,* ed. by R. D. Archambault. New York: Random House, 1966.

12. Doak, E. *What Does the Nursery School Teacher Teach?* Chicago: National Association for Nursery Education, 1951.

13. Erikson, E. H. Identity and the Life Cycle. *Psychological Issues,* Monograph 1. New York: International Universities Press, 1959.

14. Erikson, E. H. Industry Versus Inferiority. In Haimowitz, M. (Ed.), *Human Development.* New York: Thomas Y. Crowell, 1966.

15. Foster, F. P. Premature Independence in Pre-Schools for the Disadvantaged. In *Teaching the Disadvantaged Young Child.* New York: National Association for the Education of Young Children, 1966.

16. Foster, F. P. The Song Within: Music and the Disadvantaged Pre-School Child. In *Teaching the Disadvantaged Young Child.* New York: National Association for the Education of Young Children, 1966.

17. Fraiberg, S. *The Magic Years.* New York: Scribner, 1959.

18. Gardner, D. E. M. Emotions—A Basis for Learning. In Rasmussen, N. (Ed.), *Feelings and Learning.* Washington: Association for Childhood Education International, 1965.

19. Gordon, I. J. *Human Development.* New York: Harper & Row, 1962.

20. Hartley, R. E., and Frank, L. *Understanding Children's Play.* New York: Columbia University Press, 1952.

21. Havighurst, R. J. Who Are the Socially Disadvantaged? *Journal of Negro Education* 33:210, 1964.

22. Holt, J. *How Children Fail.* New York: Pitman, 1964.

23. Hymes, J. *Behavior and Misbehavior.* Englewood, N.J.: Prentice-Hall, 1955.

24. Issacs, S. *Intellectual Growth in Young Children.* London: Routledge and Kagan, 1930.

25. Johnson, H. M. *School Begins at Two.* New York: New Republic, 1936.

26. Mattick, I. Adaptation of Nursery School Techniques to Deprived Children. *Journal of the American Academy of Child Psychiatry* 4:670, 1965.

27. Minuchin, S., Auerswald, E., King, C. H., and Rabinowitz, C. The Study and Treatment of Families Who Produce Multiple Acting-out Boys. *American Journal of Orthopsychiatry* 34:125, 1954.

28. Montessori, M. *The Montessori Method.* New York: Stokes, 1912. (See also *The Montessori Method,* Introduction by J. McVicker Hunt. New York: Schoken Books, 1964.)

29. Moustakas, C. *Children in Play Therapy.* New York: McGraw-Hill, 1953.

30. Moustakas, C., and Berson, M. *The Young Child in School.* New York: Whiteside and Morrow, 1956.

31. Murphy, L. B. *Personality in Young Children.* New York: Basic Books, 1956.

32. Omwake, E. B. The Child's Estate. In Solnit, A. J., and Provence, S. A. (Eds.), *Modern Perspectives in Child Development.* New York: International Universities Press, 1963.

33. Omwake, E. B. Basic Learning Begins with Play. *Teaching and Learning. Journal of Ethical Culture Schools of New York, 1964.*

34. Pavenstedt, E. History of a Child with Atypical Development and Some Vicissitudes of His Treatment. In Caplan, G. (Ed.), *Emotional Problems of Early Childhood.* New York: Basic Books, 1955.

35. Piaget, J. *Play, Dreams and Imitation in Childhood.* New York: Norton, 1951.

36. Prescott, D. A. *The Child in the Educative Process.* New York: McGraw-Hill, 1957.

37. Rasmussen, M. (Ed.). *The Nursery School Portfolio.* Washington: Association for Childhood Education International, 1961.

38. Read, K. *The Nursery School* (4th Ed.). Philadelphia: Saunders, 1966.

39. Redl, F. *Controls from Within.* Glencoe, Ill.: Free Press, 1952.

40. Rexford, E. The Role of the Nursery School in a Child Guidance Clinic. *American Journal of Orthopsychiatry* 19:517, 1949.

41. Riese, H. *Heal the Hurt Child.* Chicago: University of Chicago Press, 1962.

42. Sander, L. W. Adaptive Relationships in Early Mother-Child Interaction. *Journal of the American Academy of Child Psychiatry* 3:231, 1964.

43. Sander, L. W. Personal communication, in which he points out the similarity between this interactional process and that which needs to be established early in life between a mother and her infant. See Sander, L. W. Issues in Early Mother-Child Interaction. *Journal of the American Academy of Child Psychiatry* 1:141, 1962.

44. Stone, L., and Church, J. *Childhood and Adolescence.* New York: Random House, 1957.

45. Wann, K. D., Dorn, M. S., and Liddle, E. A. *Fostering Intellectual Development.* New York: Teachers' College, Columbia Univ., 1962.

46. Webster, T. G.   Problems of Emotional Development in Young Retarded Children. *American Journal of Psychiatry* 120:37, 1963.
47. Witmer, H. L.   Children and Poverty. *Children* 11:207, 1964.
48. Witmer, H. L., and Kotinsky, R.   *Personality in the Making.* New York: Harper & Row, 1962.
49. Wolffheim, N.   *Psychology in the Nursery School.* New York: Philosophical Library, 1953.

9

AREAS OF PROGRESS AND LIMITATION SHOWN BY THE CHILDREN IN NURSERY SCHOOL

Ilse Mattick

A s s e s s i n g the children's progress in nursery school required careful scrutiny of all records (see Chapter 4). This data analysis in depth provided us with dimensions of the children's functioning and of the learning process beyond the information obtained by standard tests. It helped to point up various aspects of the changes that had taken place and gave insights as well into the areas that proved resistant to change.

We found a *range* of developmental and behavioral change among the 21 children. Since our sample was small, the analysis of the progress made by individual children was primarily useful for the information it yielded about observable *trends* of change. Only 2 children remained in the nursery school for the full three years, 4 children attended for two years, 5 children were with us for one year and three or four months, while 8 children attended for one school year only and 2 children were in nursery school for no longer than two or three months. Thus, only 6 of the 21 children entered early enough and stayed long enough to have the benefits of a continuous two-year preschool experience.

Our findings could not be claimed to represent more than a beginning at understanding the behavior of young children from multiproblem families in a therapeutically oriented nursery school. For more precise verifications of our findings these will need to be correlated with many other investigations under similar as well as different conditions.

While the size of the sample was limiting it also was fortunate, as it allowed study in greater depth than is feasible with a large sample. It would be most difficult, if not impossible, to ascertain how much of the children's progress was due to our focused efforts and how much to their natural maturing process. While tests did reveal differences in mental age (M.A.), the kind and degree of developmental deviancy described in Chapter 4 seemed to differ little along the preschool-age continuum (that is, between 2½ and 6 years). It is therefore reasonable to assume that the program did have an impact on the children's development and that it provided an education—in the widest sense of the word—including nurturance not otherwise available to them. Those children attending our nursery school for the longest period also came to it at an early age; we have the impression that this combination of starting school at 2½ or 3 years of age and attending regularly for at least two years gave optimal opportunity for progress.

With widely differing variables such as the age of the children when admitted to school and overall length of attendance, it appeared most useful to trace each child's progress through the categories that we selected for evaluating the children's functioning soon after they came to school. These follow-up data served as a basis for establishing common features as well as variance within the total group.

OUTWARD APPEARANCE AND MOTOR ABILITIES

Most children developed a more favorable, attractive, sex-appropriate physical appearance. Age-appropriate fine motor coordination appeared in a number of children, in particular in those who had attended the school for longer than a year. It is our impression that most children tended to remain either small for their age, or somewhat thin and wiry. They gave, however, a healthy appearance. Increase in range of facial expressiveness was striking, particularly the expression of pleasure and enjoyment, which had been missing most conspicuously at the beginning of school. By and large suspicious and self-conscious glances, as well as fixed smiles, were much less frequent.

Improvements were noticeable in the enjoyment and skill of body use. Gross motor control became functionally excellent. While motor behavior remained a dominant avenue of tension release for some children, they no longer used their bodies in random discharge. The children had developed adequate spatial orientation: knew how to use play space both indoors and out, how to handle obstacles, how to find places and objects. Abuse of their bodies was, by the end of school attendance, at a minimum, occurring only under disorganizing crisis conditions. (Many occurrences in these children's lives were upsetting: a father out of work, an impending eviction, a mother drunk or with a hangover, relatives suddenly moving into already overcrowded quarters, a playmate being run over, suspension of a welfare check, comings and going of fathers and of mother's male friends, a furnace blowing up at 4 A.M., a midnight trip to the emergency ward of the hospital with a sore throat, a bloody street fight witnessed from the window, a drunk walking into the house and struggling with the mother, being at home alone for many hours or getting hurt and finding nobody at home . . . the list is endless. This represents just a random selection of recurring anxiety-producing experiences which we witnessed or confirmed.) The children differed widely in their growing ability to maintain a sense of self-confidence—as expressed by self-protection and self-direction—in the face of occurrences unsettling to any young child. While frequency of such situations naturally played a role, by far the most important factor was shown to be the degree to which a sense of self-worth had become established in the child *and* the degree to which the child had progressed in his ability to use avenues for dealing *actively* with his tensions. Thus, a child who could engage freely in dramatic play or use other creative materials expressively and who could communicate comfortably with the teacher was not apt to regress in motor ability when under stress.

The unfolding of the possibilities inherent in the children's considerable coordination resulted in competence, inventiveness, and sheer pleasure of mastery.

SELF-IMAGE

It is difficult to assess growth of self-esteem because it reveals itself in so many different ways, with preferred expressions of it varying for individual children. However, the prevalence of a very poor self-image as expressed in just about all areas of behavior when the children first came to school gave us a baseline against which to note improvements.

All the children showed substantial progress. At the very least they had developed a more positive self-image, and some of them demonstrated age-appropriate self-awareness with self-reliance and confidence in their own actions. Self-esteem was heightened considerably; the children showed pride in their accomplishments and valued themselves and their products. However, self-confidence needed to be bolstered by supportive action by the teacher to varying degrees. Nearly all children became, in fact, far more capable than they assumed themselves to be and continued to overdepend on approval, praise, and encouragement. Satisfaction experienced with specific achievements, repeated over a long time, led to greater self-confidence; those of the children, however, who spent just a year with us showed less marked improvement in this area.

It is widely assumed that the child's self-image will improve when he is taught to master tasks. We found that it is a back-and-forth process in which a better self-image leads to the ability and eagerness to confront and to solve problems and where, in turn, self-image builds on mastery. For some time the children did not believe in their own achievements and would belittle them. From all evidence it appears likely that an increasingly positive self-image was built up in the children through their experience of being valued for themselves (unconditional acceptance), of meeting repeatedly with success (instead of frustration), and of having their efforts valued and pronounced worth while (instead of being judged, compared, and so on).

Self-differentiation was accomplished by most of the children with the fluctuations one would expect in young children. In some cases identification and role confusion recurred. This was particularly so with the boys who had no stable male figure to identify with. Some perspective for future adult roles was shown by the most advanced children.

Most of them showed an improved body image. While some children expressed appropriate sexual curiosity and heightened interest in body functions, nearly all of them remained uneasy about sex differences and displayed a sense of shame when they had to change their clothes, urinate, or even when they played at undressing dolls. All children remained overly fearful of assault on their body integrity, with exaggerated reactions to minor sores or to medical examinations.

Improvements in affect expression consisted in a wider variety of responses, including crying and laughing at the appropriate times. On the whole, there was a prevalence of pleasurable affect, but also an increased freedom to show displeasure. Exaggerated expressions (such as shrieking, hysterical laughter) and marked impulsivity (sudden flare-ups, rages, screaming of curses) were evidence of some children's remaining difficulties with the management of their feelings, and the need for devices that would assist them in maintaining control.

COPING WITH DAILY LIVING

At the end of school daily routines were performed very well by almost all children, in a relaxed and pleasurable, age-appropriate manner. Most of the children were reasonably cooperative, but no longer blindly (and fearfully) obedient. The children found it possible to deal with reality demands with more flexibility, engaging in occasional negativism, as will most children in their efforts to assert themselves and to test out the response of the teacher. But the children remained prone to a certain amount of rigidity in adherence to definite routine structure, particularly the children attending briefly. All children were less tolerant of changes at times of stress in their lives. Most children continued to have difficulty in

changing from one activity to another when left to their own devices for too long.

Interest in the outside world was developed to varying degrees,
depending on their general feeling of safety or danger about their
surroundings. This correlated both with the current reality situation in their homes and with the attainment of a trusting relationship with the teacher. Optimal interest, curiosity, learning, and
good coping ability were seen when both of these were positive. A
close relationship to the teacher could at times serve to maintain
gains in adequate coping behavior even when stress at home was
severe.

A strong tendency toward danger orientation persisted, interfering intermittently with openness to new experiences. A tendency
to expect blame (and possibly also a strong fear of their own destructive urges) interfered with a more casual attitude toward
minor incidents of which they were not the cause. Compared with
others, these children remained somewhat suspicious and distrustful, even as they learned to sort out those aspects of the outside
world that they could respond to from those that frightened or distressed them. Prolonged attendance was necessary before spontaneous curiosity and exploration became operative in the children.

There was a shift from diffuse tension discharge—primarily
motoric—to a more focused mode of reacting to stress, which frequently included verbalizations. A significantly helpful coping device was the use of dramatic fantasy play for discharge and reassurance. It still remained very difficult for the children to cope with
their frequently recurring anxiety states. While all of them tended
to regress under stress, the range here was from temporarily greater
dependency on the teacher to more pervasive infantile behavior.

Hyperalertness, while becoming more selective, never really
ceased. It now more often triggered a positive orientation toward
self-motivated activity than the trouble-avoiding maneuvering
which depended on the intentions of others. The children were
much more alert and observant about child-appropriate aspects of
reality; they also asked for explicit directions and occasionally
questioned instructions, and they made known their expectations
of appreciation for jobs performed.

Along with better self-differentiation and greater self-awareness,
we saw a more age-appropriate reality-fantasy demarcation.

Expressions of unsatisfied needs, ranging from greediness for food to hunger for human contact, never disappeared, but they abated to varying degrees as the children experienced satisfaction in interpersonal relationships in school. Most children ceased battling over food at snacktime, but when, for instance, a visitor was present, a few of the children reverted to guarding their food or to making frantic demands for greater quantities. This was also true before or after school vacations. Even those of the children who appeared to have become sure of the teacher's availability kept checking visually with her, to assure themselves of continuous contact; when under stress, the possessiveness of nearly all of the children remained pronounced.

CAPACITY FOR RELATIONSHIP

Every one of the children began to show some improvement in his capacity to relate more meaningfully to the teacher. As their exposure to corrective interrelational experiences continued they showed gains progressively. *Improvement in other areas of a child's functioning can be seen to have been closely correlated with this progress in relationships.*

With adequate differentiation between people, the children showed a more trusting, warm, affectionate response, with some expectation on their part that the teacher was a consistently reliable person. Some of the children never quite moved beyond the testing-out stage (frequently shown by the kind of negativism one sees in 18-month- to 2½-year-olds) and a few of the others fell back on this when under stress.

There was a general shift from being overly demanding (of attention and of tangibles) to eagerly striving to gain approval for performance. Only when some of the children were particularly anxious did they regress temporarily to the former mode of behavior. The children often performed to please the adult; they seemed to enjoy their accomplishments in terms of reward or approval long before they showed evidence of gaining satisfaction from their own capacities. While the dependence-independence continuum became age-appropriate for many of the children, with a growing capacity shown for independent action with appropriate seeking of teacher guidance, this was true again only when stress in their lives was relatively manageable. Most of the children felt free to turn to the teacher for assistance or information, or to check their own understanding. Imitation of the teacher's as well as peers' actions became meaningful learning experiences.

Continuity of relationship, despite difficult periods in the children's lives, was generally maintained, even over summer vacations, but separations remained difficult for almost all of them. The children whose capacity for relationship showed significant qualitative gains were also the children who could talk freely about their worries concerning separation and loss. They could substitute verbalizations, dramatic play, and other representational activities for the "acting out" of the less advanced children.

A few of the children—only those with brief nursery school attendance or with particularly traumatic early experiences—remained basically need-oriented and distrustful, and a number of children continued to show a variety of signs of lingering distrust and insufficient capacity for mutuality in relationships. But all of those with whom we worked for an extended period of time came to accept and make use of the teacher's guidance, and they would approach her with warmth and pleasurable expectation. Importantly, they could maintain this positive response even when attention was not focused on them. It should be noted, however, that the boys showed particular difficulty in their ambivalent and often conflicted relationships with men.

The children's need to experience anew each person's trustworthiness constituted a characteristic limitation to relationships, regardless of how much they improved. When a new teacher came into the program, for instance, the children approached her with excessive distrust and demands they no longer made of their old teacher. They needed less time than previously to establish a new relationship, but far longer than children usually require. Nor could trust or positive anticipation be easily transferred by these children from familiar situations to new ones. Over and over again, the teachers, old and new, had to prove, or at least remind the children, that he or she would be helpful in each new instance as it came up. It is for this reason that we felt doubtful that these children actually internalized basic trust in people.

For most of the children who attended at least one year of nursery school, peer relationships developed up to a point of age-appropriate involvement. As they became better organized they began to identify with peers rather than with adults, choosing in particular the more capable and better-functioning children (including the more advanced children who were visitors to the nursery school) as models. Nearly all of the children learned to get along reasonably well in a group in nursery school and (as reported) in their day camps. At home, too, relationships among siblings improved and friendships were developed with neighborhood children.

Almost all of them learned to share and cooperate with each other. Most of them became very friendly and even generous. They became protective of each other, particularly of the younger children, and they showed interest in each other's activities and empathy with one another. Although the children remained somewhat rivalrous in their relationships, there was far less competitive spirit among them than one finds in many nursery schools. Even when a child bragged or "showed off" he rarely compared himself to others. Unlike our visiting children (from "upwardly mobile" families) who competed with others and occasionally showed envy or anger about another child's accomplishments, "our" children tended to be genuinely appreciative of each other's achievements. The only area where they showed little tolerance for one another was in uncontrolled impulsive behavior. Lack of control by a child would call forth strong reactions of disapproval, if not anger, by the others, giving evidence of their own shaky controls.

Most of the children continued to find it difficult to fight for their rights, and those who did had trouble modulating their often uncontrolled outbursts of anger. Both the aggressor and the aggressed-upon often required adult protection. The children remained more fearful than most other young children of showing, or of being the target of, aggression, feeling more comfortable with avoidance of conflict. They remained prone to using clever, devious manipulations, retreating when they met with opposition.

LANGUAGE AND
COGNITIVE DEVELOPMENT

Relative to the extremely poor use of language when the children first came to school, there was substantial improvement in all of them. For many children vocabularies increased significantly, beyond our expectations. Although some children's speech did not become very clear, most of them spoke distinctly and with good pronunciation. Communication became a natural component of their school life and frequently outside of school as well. Many children learned to express their thoughts, feelings, and experiences with an accuracy sufficient for communication. Many learned to look for information through focused exploration, through questions, and in books, to listen to descriptions, and to follow verbal directions.

However, compared with children of the same ages in a different setting (8), their language development remained deviant in important respects. For one thing, their vocabularies were smaller, consistent with their more restricted experience (1). For another, the language of even those children who conversed easily and with an adequate vocabulary was characterized by a production of peculiarly ungrammatical sentences.

Even more seriously, proneness to concrete thinking and a tendency toward inflexibility in the use of words remained sources of difficulties. While the children's stories were dramatic, they were also quite reality-bound, showing little ability for conceptualization. There was a dearth of playful use of language. Once a word had a certain meaning attached to it, the child refused to accept a possible second meaning, although he might understand that the context was different. (When sent "one flight up" to an office, a 6-year-old insisted that he was on an airplane "flight," although he knew the building he was in was a school.) All this led to many confusions and a constricted use of language, complicating the children's ability to learn and hampering seriously their growing intellectual functioning.

To describe the differences in the use of language as merely a "continuing lag in development" which could be alleviated by further exposure to accepted linguistic rules would be to misinterpret the qualitative differences that exist between the language used by these children and that typically heard in other nursery schools. (See Menyuk [9] for a comparison of normal and deviant language patterns.)

There is no question but that the children's cognitive development advanced significantly during their nursery school attendance. This has been shown throughout these outcome categories and will be described further under the heading "Capacity to Focus on Activity." The greatest gains were probably in the children's ability to seek out, order, and utilize a wide variety of new information. Its severest limitations lay in the relative inflexibility and concrete-bound aspects of the children's thinking and in the frequency of debilitating reaction to distress.

"The ability of problem solvers to use information correctively is known to vary as a function of their internal state. One state in which information is least useful is that of strong drive and anxiety." (2) While the viability of a relatively trustful relationship appeared to offset some of the anxiety engendered by the intermittent crises in the environment, the energy required for dealing with unpredictable occurrences and stresses was bound to diminish over-all learning capacity. Nonetheless the records abound with evidence of cognitive growth by the children, which appeared to be the result of cumulative learning experiences imbedded in the nursery school program.

CAPACITY TO FOCUS ON ACTIVITY

All the children began to enjoy playing after only brief nursery school attendance, and nearly all of them developed the capacity to become meaningfully involved in activities. They could increasingly take the initiative in selecting a task. While some children preferred, and did better, when the teacher initiated an activity (as in a preplanned, structured project), most of the children learned to plan for themselves and to make their own decisions about what to do and how to structure their own play. Many of the children performed their work with enthusiasm, sticking to their tasks with lively interest and bringing them to a successful conclusion.

Most children developed an adequate interest in problem solving and learned to see a problem through, even in the face of frustration. They all managed frustrations better (in varying degrees) and their attention span became adequate in most cases, and even very long for some children. Even those who could not always focus attention long enough to complete a project would at other times surprise us by their tenacity. Some children worked at tasks with remarkable perseverance, others had to make many brief, repeated attempts before achievement could be attained. On the other hand, the children had also become much freer about turning to a new activity when their interest in one type of play was waning. They no longer became stuck in repetitive stereotyped actions except occasionally on days when difficulties at home upset them.

Most children showed a willingness to experiment with a variety of materials, and were open to exploring new objects and new learning situations. Skills improved and in some cases, but not all, approached age-appropriateness. The ceiling to the children's ability to assimilate knowledge varied widely and appeared contingent on endowment, age, and length of time spent in our nursery school.

There were, however, definite limits beyond which we were not able to move these children in their engagement with activities.

One difficulty of considerable dimensions was the children's tendency toward inflexibility and rigidity. Just as in their speech, in activities too the children had difficulties in varying a once-learned procedure. They insisted on literal repetitions and showed a strong tendency to fight off suggestions for alternate methods or for combining procedures learned in different contexts. Elaboration of skills through spontaneous, imaginative application remained too rare to be meaningful adjuncts to learning experiences.

Altogether, the teacher had to provide more stimulation than should have been necessary for children as capable as these had become. A certain spontaneity, which one usually associates with the play of preschool children, remained missing here, or was seen only sporadically.

The children's continued need for support by the teacher also limited their independent involvement with constructive learning experiences. While general encouragement by the teacher was sufficient for some children, many others had to use the teacher to bolster their self-esteem. Thus, in order to function adequately the children continued to need a protective and reassuring environment.

There was also the children's tendency to approach objects only in terms of their own inner needs rather than to explore and learn as well about the object's properties and function. Watching the car being filled with gasoline, for example, caused several children to smack their lips or make sucking motions and declare they were hungry. When, subsequent to several visits to a service station, the teacher tried to promote a game of "gasoline station" the children participated enthusiastically as long as the teacher herself participated in the play; when she stepped aside the "cars" and "drivers" were "looking for their mommies," and the "pump" was used to dispense milk bottles! Similarly, a box of seashells, left on the table after a lively session about beaches and shells, was divided into "mommy shells" and "baby shells," with the usual dramatic sequence of the latter looking for the former. No matter how we tried to introduce variety into the play at the sandbox, it always ended up in filling dishes and in "feeding" games.

Such stimulus-bound approach to new experiences diminished, for some of the children considerably, for others barely, and for all of the children it reappeared when their anxiety was aroused.

Obviously then, any attempts to promote active learning had to go hand in hand with compensatory therapeutic efforts in order to be even moderately effective. Despite setbacks the children did become increasingly knowledgeable and, more importantly, showed increasing interest in investigating on their own and in searching out solutions. Their receptivity for age-appropriate stimuli increased apace with their heightened confidence in people and in themselves.

EPILOGUE

The next question in the reader's mind will undoubtedly be: What about the children's progress in grade school? Did they learn to read? Did they keep up with their classmates?

Since the project did not include a school follow-up study, we did not gather systematic data about the school adjustment and learning behavior of the children. We did gather some information informally, however, from a variety of reporters.

Nearly all the children eagerly looked forward to school and the initial adjustment proceeded with few difficulties. The teachers described most of them as friendly, eager, alert, interested. A few of the children were judged, by their teacher, to be of "more than average" maturity.

We do not have the children's grade school attendance records, but from their own accounts, from the parents' and the teachers' reports, it is my impression that attendance was regular at the beginning of the year, particularly for the children who went to school on their own, and more irregular for the children dependent on being escorted by their mothers. For many it became more irregular as the year progressed and as difficulties in school developed. An additional factor may have been that the school doors were locked as soon as school began. Any child arriving a few minutes late had the choice of either ringing a bell to be admitted and questioned or going home again (or roaming the streets).

Many of the children were placed in situations where more demands were made on them than they were mature enough to fulfill. At least five of them repeated one of the early grades.

It is our impression that as failures began to follow one another, the inevitable regression to more discouraged, impatient, frightened, passive behavior occurred. We observed this in our after-school play groups. These and intensive tutoring were helpful to some children, chiefly because of their interrelational satisfactions and focused attention and support. This enabled some children to maintain themselves in a setting not sufficiently responsive to their needs and interests. Other children were unable to handle pressures, such as the demands for filling pages in workbooks. As time went on, their newly found and still shaky self-esteem was lost again, the lively spark left their eyes, and their dealings with people again became guarded and manipulative. Teachers became "annoyed" or "disappointed," blaming the parents or accusing the children of "not trying hard enough." The children felt themselves disliked by teachers; some of them began to dread going to school, others expressed disappointment and anger.

We know that some children managed to slide by and that some did well. A few children again found an understanding, supportive adult and *as long as this person was available* they achieved remarkably well. Relative stability at home was an important factor. One child, for instance, started off very well for the first two grades but as pressures in her home life built up and there was no one to help her handle her distress, she rapidly went downhill and became less and less able to learn.

If our impressions reflect anything with consistency it is that:

1. All children entered school with highly positive expectations and most of them impressed the teachers as capable and well balanced.

2. While parents were eager for children to learn they were not always well enough organized to get them there on time and to help them with their work.

3. Regulations concerning placement in kindergarten and first grade at 4½ and 5½ respectively were particularly unfortunate for this group of children. (Few 5½-year-old middle-class children are expected to fulfill as many demands with as little individual help as was expected of these children.)

4. Most successful in school and most resourceful in coping with school demands were the children who had made the most substantial gains in nursery school and who were neither pushed into the grades too early nor subjected to very rigid demands. A warm, understanding teacher was of great importance.

It was our impression that even with good intentions on the part of the teacher, the children often did not receive the help they needed in order to progress adequately.

The recent voluminous literature dealing with the education of the slum child and the many conferences devoted to this subject abound with suggestions about teaching strategies. Despite incorporation of theoretical insights and technological advances, many of the soundest ideas seem solidly based on—or resemble those of— the best features of the progressive school movement of the thirties. It seems odd that we have just "discovered" once again that a child learns best "in his own way, at his own speed." The establishment of ungraded classes, at least for the primary grades, seems to follow logically if we seriously attempt to meet each child's needs and assist him in making maximal progress.

Yet, despite the familiar ring of many suggestions and the awesome realization that we actually have known far more for years than has been applied, particularly with working-class children (for example, a low teacher-child ratio diminishes teaching effectiveness, yet inner-city classes continue to be overcrowded), we are also cognizant of the limits of our present knowledge. This project has demonstrated how much we need to study and understand just what the children we try to teach are like. Only then can we evolve methods for helping them to learn. "The danger of attempting to prescribe materials and models at this stage of [our] knowledge," says Hunt (6) in reference to preschool education, ". . . is that the prescriptions may well fail to provide a proper match with what the child already has in his storage."

We know that in this country a fourth or fifth of the children do not learn well. We also know something about the deprivations that accrue from living in poverty and from interpersonal deficits. However, we do not know enough as yet about these children's adaptational systems and about the specifics of their cognitive functioning to modify educational strategies with any certainty of success. It seems only common sense that we learn to explore and experiment with more adequate curricula. This will take creativity, daring, and enthusiasm; luckily many teachers abound in these, if given an opportunity. "We must educate children who can contribute to our changing society in ways that we may not be able to anticipate today. This means we must broaden our definition of 'ability' or 'talent' to include behaviors based on values that, thus far, have not been prominent in middle-class culture" (7).

Whatever varieties of imaginative curricula we envision for preschool and primary grades they must encompass meaningful interactional experiences within the classroom setting, between each child and the teacher as well as among peers. Bruner reminds us that "It would not be unreasonable to guess that social contact provides a symbolic analogue or vicar for sensory intake" (3). Vygotsky (11) clearly states the importance of social interaction as a facilitator of language development, of internal speech and thought. Piaget (10) and Erikson (5) presume an "average expectable environment," with its meaningful relationships, as part and parcel of healthy development. The extent and particular dimensions of this "social contact" in the classroom may vary with the particular requirements of different children. Our findings would indicate that learning by children from disorganized lower-class families may hinge significantly on the quality of their relationship with their teacher.

Deutsch (4) is critical of the notion of "creating a supportive environment" which he equates with "protecting the child from stress." While it is true that some teachers may provide an overprotective and insufficiently challenging environment, the large body of early childhood educational theory emphasizes the importance of promoting maturation in all areas. Deutsch appears to be saying that an atmosphere which takes cognizance of the emotional needs of small children might not be conducive to fostering cognitive development. Our data suggest that the learning ability of these children is enhanced by the continued availability (long beyond that required by most other children) of encouragement and the kind of protectiveness that helps children cope with stress.

Perhaps the most frightening aspect of the inroads into education by modern technology is the complacency with which people speak of "replacing the teacher by more efficient methods of teaching." Individualized learning may well be facilitated by "plugging the child in" to a preprogrammed typewriter or some other teaching contraption, but it can be served far better by sound teaching methods geared to individual needs, without running the risk of divorcing the intellectual from its social context.

I am suggesting that we do not know as yet how to utilize technological innovations meaningfully; I am not asserting that such gadgets are "bad" or "useless." In fact, it has been proven that programmed instruction can meet with some success (for instance, by teaching normal bright middle-class preschool youngsters as well as some mentally ill children to type and to read). The question becomes one of intent and goals, perhaps one of giving priority to expediency versus helping children become more knowledgeable and thoughtful—that is, allowing them to develop the capacity to live and act as spontaneous and responsible social human beings.

REFERENCES

1. Bernstein, B. Social Class and Linguistic Development: A Theory of Social Learning. In Halsey, A. H., Floud, J., and Anderson, A. (Eds.), *Education, Economy and Society*. Glencoe, Ill.: Free Press, 1961.
2. Bruner, J. *Toward a Theory of Instruction*. Cambridge: Harvard University Press, 1966, p. 52.
3. Bruner, J. The Cognitive Consequences of Early Sensory Deprivation. In Solomon, P. (Ed.), *Sensory Deprivation*. Cambridge: Harvard University Press, 1961, p. 205.
4. Deutsch, M. Facilitating Development in the Pre-school Child. In Hechinger, F. (Ed.), *Pre-school Education Today*, New York: Doubleday, 1966, p. 92.
5. Erikson, E. H. Identity and the Life Cycle. *Psychological Issues*, Monograph 1. New York: International Universities Press, 1959.
6. Hunt, J. McVicker. The Psychological Basis for Using Pre-school Enrichment as an Antidote for Cultural Deprivation. In Hechinger, F. (Ed.), *Pre-school Education Today*. New York: Doubleday, 1966, p. 58.
7. Lesser, G. S., Fifer, G., and Clark, D. H. Mental Abilities of Children from Different Social-Class and Cultural Groups. *Society for Research in Child Development* Monograph 30:4, 1965.
8. Menyuk, P. Syntactic Structures in the Language of Children. *Child Development* 34:407, 1963.
9. Menyuk, P. Comparison of Grammar of Children with Functionally Deviant and Normal Speech. *Journal of Speech and Hearing Research* 7:109, 1964.
10. Piaget, J. *Play, Dreams and Imitation in Childhood*. New York: Norton, 1951.
11. Vygotsky, L. S. *Thought and Language* (1934). Cambridge: Massachusetts Institute of Technology Press, 1962.

III

THE FAMILIES

10

FAMILY FUNCTIONING: A PSYCHOSOCIAL PERSPECTIVE

Louise S. Bandler

Eᴠᴇʀʏ ᴄᴀsᴇᴡᴏʀᴋᴇʀ is familiar with the innumerable complex interrelated problems of disorganized multiproblem families described in this book. Few workers have approached these families with the psychological perspective that we brought to our work with them. This study also offers some leads for developing methods calculated to study the process of disorganization itself. At the present time, since there have been no developmental studies of family life, or of multiproblem family life, the nature of this process can only be reconstructed.

To approach the solution of the problems of these families requires the sustained mobilization of all our resources, all our combined efforts and talents. Few areas require more cooperation among disciplines, between public and private agencies, between governmental institutions and citizenry, and between therapists, clinicians, and social-action planners. And yet it is, by its nature and history, a problem area about which we reveal considerable division and isolation. Our knowledge and professional efforts have only recently been focused on this most needy group.

The project was begun in an effort to meet the challenge of disorganized families with preschool children, in order to explore service to and treatment of these previously unreached families, as an extension of family-centered child-guidance practice into the community. We have developed services to the families and know how to initiate and maintain their involvement, devised techniques for sustained work with the parents and for teaching the children in nursery school.

As a result of our work there is no question in our minds that the parents and children have changed for the better and "improved." However, if we ask ourselves, "Will this change make a significant difference in their future?" we are clearly uncertain. Raising such an issue is not a matter of self-doubt, but rather is based upon several considerations. We do not know how stable, lasting, and generalizable the changes are, partly because we do not know what impact the continuing and subsequent harmful environmental elements will have upon the families. The end results depend at least in part upon what happens subsequently in the community. We also do not know to what extent the parents will return to old patterns if they are put under substantial psychological stress.

In order to develop a methodology of working with these families and their children we had to define and identify the multi-problem-family group with which we wanted to work. As has been stated, we selected families with gross social and psychological pathology who had never worked constructively with a social agency. This included a spectrum from the most disorganized to those who were relatively organized within the framework of our definition. Consequently if one were to look from one extreme of the spectrum to the other extreme, the question could be raised as to whether the differences are not so great as to be almost qualitative. To complicate the problem further, we see many families in middle and upper classes who seem to have similar problems, similar family patterns and ways of coping. Are we then dealing with a different kind of stratification problem than we are normally accustomed to? For example, are our group of families in a different stratification system than one sees in sociological literature or do we fit them in some way into the typology that has been developed? That is, are we dealing with a group outside any customary typology, an across-the-board anomic kind of group, or are we dealing with a part of the lower class differentiated essentially in their family structure and their adaptation within the family and to the general social milieu?

Our own experience has been greatly enriched by data from a developmental study.* This study provided data about family life and parental behavior in another sector of the lower socioeconomic groups (8). From it we know that there is a vast difference in the functioning of these families from the psychosocial functioning of the multiproblem families. The stable families exhibited relatively consistent family patterns and child-rearing practices and were upwardly mobile.

In summary then, in the stable group, the parents assumed their expected roles and the children were mothered and trained in an organized home with regular routines. "Consequently maturation of the child's total development proceeded as an epigenetic process" ((8), p. 96). The children were the focus of the parents' feelings. The entire family unit interacted with each other and there was a clear separation of adult and child roles. Most of the children learned to trust others and developed age-appropriate autonomy. Although initiative and self-assertion were sometimes lacking, especially in the boys, by age six the children were ready to benefit from first-grade instruction and were able to become involved in the learning experience.

In contrast, the North Point families we worked with can be described as having completely different family structure and methods of coping and a different relationship to the larger social milieu. What is especially striking, however, is the fact that within this group there is a wide range of disorganization and pathology. In addition, within each family unit there is a range of disorganization and pathology over a period of time. Although the families have many similar psychosocial characteristics, they cannot be reduced to a type. This finding is similar to the findings of other researchers—Hylan Lewis (4), Ludwig Geismar (2), the St. Paul Group (1), the New York Group (7), and others. There is a wide spectrum of multiproblem families. The main type within this

* Longitudinal Study in Child Development, supported by N.I.M.H. Grants #M898 and #3325(1) and the National Association for Mental Health, 1959-1965. Awarded to the Division of Psychiatry, Boston University School of Medicine, Boston University Medical Center; chief investigators, Eleanor Pavenstedt, M.D., and Louis Sander, M.D.

hard-core group is the multiproblem asocial family. In our group of 13 families, 8 were considered asocial. These included four unmarried mothers and four interrelated families with the same parents where family organization was characterized primarily by deficiencies and inadequacy, leading to neglect.

Within our sample we also have the multiproblem psychotic family, Brown, the multiproblem psychotic-alcoholic family, Craven and Carolla, and the multiproblem antisocial family, Rossi and Leahy.

MAJOR ASSUMPTIONS AND CHARACTERISTICS

The Project's basic assumption (as formulated by Dr. Bernard Bandler) is "that there is a psychosocial continuum in which the characteristics of the slum Skid Row culture influence the growth and development of the children through the matrix of the family, particularly the mother, and that reciprocally, the children and their families by their behavior maintain the culture. The five basic characteristics of the community and its families are those of: (1) deprivation, (2) danger, (3) excesses, (4) inconsistency, and (5) passivity. These lead to deficiencies, defects, distortion and imbalance of development which in turn affect subsequent phases of development. Both the individual and the families compensate with specific adaptational and role-playing techniques which are perpetuated from one generation to another.

"By deprivation we mean unmet needs, whether psychological, educational, social, or cultural. By danger we mean the inner world of the impulses and the outer world of violent behavior. By excesses we mean the disorganized extremes of stimuli and of behavior. By inconsistency we mean the absence of sufficiently organized and patterned predictable behavior. This inconsistency has its psychological roots in the absence of inner character, in the internalization of ideals and controls, and its social bases in the absence in the culture of stabilized roles and value systems, and the presence of confusing, shifting patterns of behavior. By passivity we mean the atmosphere of lethargy and inconsistency in the community,

the absence of initiative in the families, and the receptive orientation of the children."

THE FAMILIES: SOME GENERAL CHARACTERISTICS

There was a wide variation in the kind of family units and the
kinds of family stability that existed in the 13 families, as will be
shown in the descriptions of the individual families. In all, there
were 45 children, two of whom died during the life of the project,
one of illness and one of an automobile accident. Ten babies were
born, two of them illegitimate. Only one of the unmarried mothers
had a baby. The other illegitimate baby was from the broken family with which we had no real involvement with either parent.

The families came from a variety of ethnic groups: Irish, Italian,
Syrian, Russian, Spanish, and American Indian. Conflicting cultural patterns within any one family unit were complicating factors in management and in child rearing. There was a range of
church affiliations from none to relatively regular attendance and a
range of other group affiliations from none to occasional settlement-
house contacts. The educational experience of the parents was limited, with one having only special-class education and several fin-
ishing high school. Four of the families were on Aid to Dependent
Children, one on Veterans' Disability, and one under the care of
the Division of Child Guardianship. Two families had irregular
incomes. It is of interest that five families where both parents were
in the home, except for periodic flights of the fathers, had relatively regular incomes.

All of our families resembled what Hylan Lewis describes as
"clinical families" (5). All of them were well along the continuum
of disorganization. In three families there were psychosis and alcoholism: the Carollas, the Browns, and the Cravens. In the Carolla
family both parents were alcoholic. In addition the father was involved in major criminal activity and one child was retarded. In
the Brown family both parents were diagnosed borderline psychotic and one child was mentally retarded. Mr. Craven had psychotic episodes and was alcoholic.

The Leahy family was the most pathological of the antisocial families. The father had a criminal record and the mother was a prostitute. The Rossi family was the second in our group described as antisocial. The father had a long record of delinquencies dating back to childhood. His father and brothers also had court records. Mrs. Rossi came from a family of extreme deprivation and alcoholism. Four families were fatherless and can be described as asocial.

The final four families can be described best as part of a small clan. In the family of origin there were parents and seven children. Of this family the mother and four married siblings with their husbands and fifteen children were known to our program. The patterns in this group of families, who can be called asocial, were those of deficiency and inadequacy leading to neglect (versus psychotic or antisocial delinquency patterns). However, there was juvenile delinquency during the adolescence of one sister. Marital discord, separation, divorce, and marked deficiencies in nurturing existed in all the families.

FAMILY STRUCTURE AND FAMILY LIFE STYLES

The families can be looked at from the point of view of family structure and family life styles. In attempting to understand the dynamics of family life we have employed the model of the developmental life process in which the mutual influences of psychological and social forces are given full consideration. Such a perspective includes a consideration of the families' values, roles, avenues and methods of communication, and ways of problem solving as well as their individual developmental histories and histories across generations.

From a study of the dynamics of family life it is clear, as stated earlier, that there is a range of disorganization among these families. There is also a range of personality types. Although the family units and parents have similar characteristics, there is no single family type or specific type of parent. Since we are dealing with processes both in the unfolding of family life and in the formation of personality, a search for specificity among problem families will probably be no more rewarding than it has been in studies of psychosomatic illness. Only developmental family studies can begin to untangle and identify the mutual influences of individual, family, and life situations on evolving family life.

The most striking characteristic of these families is that they are *families of children* and the parents have grown up without any clear normative system. Consequently they have failed to develop a patterning of consistent and meaningful interactions between children and adults. As a result they have failed to develop a consistent, durable role system. They show the kind of socialization that occurs when even minimal forms of cultural influence are missing from family life. This is socialization in a situation of extreme anomie. These parents have never consolidated their image of themselves and constantly shift their behavior and attitudes. The multiple, chaotic demands from reality reinforce the need for rapid shifts. Their ways of coping, however, interfere with personal growth and development and impede education, appropriate child-rearing practices, and cultural stability. These families have not had prior experience of learning competency in the handling of individual issues that arise in the course of growing up. Consequently they do not function in accordance with the demands of family life and the expectations of society.

Within the family unit *the needs of the parents take precedence over the needs of the children.* For this reason, among many others, the mothers cannot be adequate models for their children or provide the experiences necessary for growth and development. In giving priority to their own pressing needs, they are like their children. They have an advantage, however, over the children, because the children demand but do not receive.

The parents are in rivalry with their children and press for gratification in every direction because of their own early lives of deprivation. Their inability to provide adult models for their children springs from several sources. From the generational studies it is possible to reconstruct their childhood experiences. In their early experiences it is clear the parents have never had adequate models for growing up. In addition their educational experience, apart from the educational experience with their parents, has been deficient. Further, their personality deficits make child rearing difficult. Finally, deficits in the current environment restrict them.

The parents themselves had no stable, consistent parental figure with whom to identify. Their early lives were full of the same deprivation and dangers as we see in their children's lives. Their fathers, when they were present in the family unit, played no important role in the family's life and had little involvement with their children. Their mothers, like themselves, were the dominant figures in the household. Although there is little evidence that their relationship to their fathers was a tender, protective one, nevertheless the mothers presented "ideal affectionate fantasy images" of their fathers and recall stories of tender attention. While these recollections may in part be accounted for because of the passive relationship of the fathers to their daughters, they also represent an attempt to compensate for their harsh, depriving mothers. These mothers have no difficulty in verbalizing maternal deprivation.

The women in our study have a tremendous need for a maternal figure and they are constantly searching for one. Many of the women have found such figures in the environment with whom they share the care of their children. Unfortunately, for neurotic reasons they are likely to select women who are in the image of their mothers. In spite of their basic lack of trust they do trust these women in areas connected with their children. It is interesting that even in their current lives they turn to either mothers or old maternal figures as if they have not yet given up hope that the primary figure will in turn respond with love and care. This yearning for a tender, giving, maternal figure is a dominant and driving theme in their life. When nourished, it has proven to be the key to treatment and the avenue for enhancement of their capacity for mothering.

In their early pregnancies, the mothers appear to be acting out their relationship to their parents and particularly their yearning for a "ma" figure. In their adolescence they have sought a close relationship to a man, in part to realize their wishes for affection from a male image, but more particularly in a frantic attempt to get close to somebody. Often they attempt to do this via sex relationships.

Mrs. Barry stated that she went with her first boyfriend only because he was "kind and bought her food." These conceptions also represent a longing for fulfillment of the mother-child relationship which they fantasy having with their own child.

In the selection of their husbands and boyfriends, however, we see their failure to find a tender love object. Their husbands are replicas of their fathers. They are sporadic wage earners, have little to do with decision-making or problem-solving, and have shallow relationships to their children and primitive sexually aggressive relationships with their wives. One does not see much flexibility in the parents' behavior or the variety of patterns of adaptations which parents normally utilize in their adjustment to each other.

This profile of the husbands, however, is not a totally unrelieved picture. Mr. Leonard, for example, was the one who on occasion was the force in implementing tutoring and camp for the children. Mr. Rossi, although disappearing at the crucial moment, did make abortive attempts to carry through educational recommendations. Unfortunately his own conflict about education got in the way. Also Mr. Brown, in spite of his severe psychiatric disturbance, had a concept of the nature of family life and planned family recreation.

Because of their early experiences, the parents lack even minimal basic trust and their relationships are shallow and tenuous. These characteristics permeate every area in their life, from relationships to their own spouse and children and the extended family to relationships to every agent and institution of society. The relationships of the parents to each other are a mixture of the infantile, demanding behavior seen in their relationships to their children and sporadic attempts to deal with each other on a less need oriented basis. Their relations, however, do contain elements of partnership and they show some capacity to care for and give to each other. Their sexual relationships are characterized by primitive demands and there is minimal tenderness. The families are primarily matriarchies. This is particularly true of the Negro unmarried mothers, for whom the mother has been the dominant figure for generations.

Because of their lack of trust and poor object relations, these parents are extremely *low in self-esteem*. They have no clarity about their identity and have never consolidated any single image of themselves. In addition to an attempt to be close to anyone at all, their conceptions have represented an attempt to create some form of identity for themselves, a home, and a way of life, and particularly to experience feelings of belonging and having roots somewhere. Many of the mothers stated that children were the "first thing I have ever owned" and were the "first thing that belonged to me."

As one would expect from such pathology in their early lives and the deprivation in their current reality, these mothers have great *difficulty in child rearing*. In addition to the fact that they have had inadequate models for child rearing and hence have developed no consistent styles or patterns of behavior, their own personality deficits and the poverty of the environment create for their children a situation similar to the one in which they were brought up. That is, the parents not only perpetuate their early situation but recreate it again with their own children. Consequently their children's lives are filled with deprivation springing from unmet needs: psychological, educational, social, and cultural. The presence of the extended family in the intimate life of our families and the stereotyped, rigid responses the parents have developed in coping tend to make it especially difficult for them to shift their behavior and attitudes.

In their relationship to and nurturing of their children, their own needs are so pressing they are unable to distinguish them from the needs of their children, even when the latter are urgent. The developmental changes essential to learning of any kind, which are prerequisites of providing learning experiences for their children, are absent. The changes we have in mind are those associated with (1) impulse control, (2) modification of aggression, (3) postponement of gratification, (4) tolerance of frustration, (5) perseverance, and (6) initiative. These are developmental goals which are dependent on mature models. Since our parents could not learn or receive from their parents they could not teach or give to their children.

In the early *mother-child relationship around feeding,* parental needs and rivalry were rampant. Ability to feed a child was dependent on whether the mother had previously eaten herself. At family parties screaming babies would be ignored until the mothers partook of the refreshments. In the home where any real routine of family eating was absent, some children were given food on demand, others "snacked" all day like their mother. In the early care of the infant, holding a child was rare. The bottle was most often propped and rarely retrieved if the child lost it.

Their practices pertaining to *health needs* were minimal. This is reflected not only in their care of their children, but also in their care of themselves. For many reasons, during pregnancy and delivery the mothers seek almost no medical care for themselves.

The early mother-child relationship was characterized by very little interaction or stimulation or verbal communication. Often, when held, the children seemed more appendages of the mother than personalities in their own right. Frequently small children were placed in a room alone for the greater part of the day. Interest in a new baby was rare among the siblings. Recognition of needs was limited to two or three basic ones such as food, diaper changes, and sleep. Crying for anything beyond these needs was often considered willful and ignored.

The mother's relationship was to "children" not to an individual child. Except for gross patterns of identification such as "He is like his father" or "She is like me," few patterns of differentiation were verbalized by the parents or expressed through behavior.

The mothers' involvement in such activities as play with the children was absent. Unlike middle-class mothers, they seldom encouraged a child's activities and their self-care was minimal. There was little stimulation of curiosity and household objects which children often find fascinating, were scarce. Toys were either meager or absent. Frequently the mothers were physically or emotionally absent. They left their children alone and by themselves with no explanation. At other times, they were left with any available adult or adolescent or even child. The mothers were limited in their ability to give and could frustrate mercilessly. On the other hand they could overindulge and encourage infantile behavior.

These parents were *limited in language development* and in abstract thinking. Their thinking was concrete and their problem solving was action-oriented and impulsive. They rarely thought through a solution. Problem solving rarely included alternate solutions. Communication was primarily through action with paucity of verbal descriptions.

Communication was further handicapped by their limited capacity for introspection. They had little awareness or perception of feeling. Consequently they could not empathize with the underlying emotions in their children. Since they were unable to understand the needs of their children, they were limited in their capacity to respond to situations of stress experienced by them. This

failure to understand pain and unhappiness was further complicated by lack of more than minimal communication even when the
children were no longer infants.

The mothers often engaged in unpredictable, aggressive, violent
outbursts and impulsive acting out. This behavior itself was traumatic for the children but became increasingly traumatic because
of the mothers' undifferentiated relationship to their children. An
act of violence against one child could occur just because that child
was nearby when the real target of the aggression and the offender
was another child. Because they lacked the education and models
for control of impulses they had developed little control and
brought neglect, cruelty, and primitive sexual behavior into the
family life. These dangers, coupled with the aggressive sexual activity of the neighbors and brutality in the environment, were central in the failure of the children to develop impulse control. The
institutions in the community finally compounded the danger with
their punitive attitudes toward poor people as retaliation for consequences of uncontrolled drive behavior.

Their lack of social competence, because of the poverty of learning experiences in their early life, made it impossible for them to
achieve any goals they might have had. They did, however, share
the universal values of society in regard to health, education, good
housing, work, being a good mother, and keeping out of trouble.
There was a marked difference, however, between how they behaved and these values they held, which were not at first apparent
but which could be mobilized. Our families had not yet reached a
cutoff point in their implicit wish to achieve some of these things
for their children.

FAMILY ILLUSTRATIONS

We have selected the following families for presentation to illustrate the range of disorganization among the families and the diversity of the parents' behavior. Because of limitations of space
only a sampling of the families can be given and no attempt will be
made to give a systematic picture of any one family.

Families with Maximum Disorganization. The *Brown and Craven families* are two of the three families in the group which we consider had maximum disorganization. They were generally described as the multiproblem, psychotic, and psychotic-alcoholic families. The homes presented typical pictures of failure to create anything like a predictable environment for the children. Deprivations, danger, excesses, and inconsistencies permeated every area of family life and every relationship. Mrs. Brown dealt with every phase of child development in an impulsive, primitive, archaic fashion. Mrs. Craven had developed a kind of pseudosophistication with a more subtly unpredictable sadism.

Life in the Brown family was managed through a chaotic, unrelated set of behaviors. Responses, actions, decisions, and judgments were determined by contradictory values and violent, impulsive behavior. The children never knew at which point the mother would shower them with things and at which point their demands would be cut off with a violent blow. Neither type of response was predictable. Problem solving was on the most primitive level.

When the Browns first became known to us they presented such a chaotic household it was difficult to see where one could penetrate. The apartment was incredibly bare and filthy. There were no structured meals; food was given on demand. In fact, feeding the children was the mother's major activity. Pots of cooking food were always on the stove. Children's destroyed toys lay about. The children themselves were in evidence with or without clothing. Wishing to be a good mother, Mrs. Brown implemented medical care by frequent clinic visits. Health reports, however, were faked and medication was never given. Management of the children was handled by abuse and violent screaming. From this chaos the father retired evenings to a room he had to himself.

Although Mr. Brown did not interfere with his wife's way of life or methods of discipline he did have educational ambitions for his children and some concept of family recreation. In addition, although his work performance was limited, it was steady.

Mrs. Brown, aged 45, the mother of a boy and a girl, aged 5 and 3, had married a man with a schizoid personality. Of Mediterranean origin and married to a Central European, she defined her religious affiliations as "Protestant-Catholic." Mr. Brown, aged 50, was one of six children. Mr. Brown changed his name to dissociate himself from mental illness. He received little mothering because of his mother's mental illness. His early care was in the hands of his father and elder sister who was later permanently hospitalized for the same illness as that of her mother. One brother was mentally retarded. Mr. Brown was hospitalized twice as an adult with a ten-year interval. His diagnosis was a milder form of the same condition as that of his mother and sister. His marriage occurred shortly after his second hospitalization.

Mrs. Brown's early life is best described as a gypsy existence in a carnival setting, where routine and controls were at a minimum. A large, obese adolescent, she had little love from a mother who favored her brothers. Both siblings did considerably better than she. Mrs. Brown's mother died after an illness of five years. Mrs. Brown, who had one year of trade high school, had worked in a factory with her mother. She had been hired "only because they wanted my mother." She attended her mother during her illness and has many guilty feelings about her death. She described her father as indifferent to her because, after the mother's death, he expressed no need for her other than wanting her paycheck. As a consequence she moved to a roominghouse. About this time she met Mr. Brown in a free, casual setting when she was doing a great deal of sexual acting out.

She lived in her old family apartment where she had returned after marriage; her father had meanwhile moved out. The one room with adequate furniture was closed off. In it were stored her mother's furniture, dishes, and personal clothes. This room was a symbol of her aspirations.

When the worker entered this case, Mrs. Brown was in a state of confusion and close to nervous collapse. Education for her children, a primary goal, was closed to her. The public school authorities had refused to admit her 5-year-old boy into kindergarten. The boy's bizarre behavior and the questions concerning his intellectual capacity confirmed her image of herself. The experience with the school was a repetition of early relationships involving her mother and herself in which she had been the devalued one.

The Cravens, who likewise presented problems in every area of family life, did operate on a less primitive level than the Brown family.

The home consisted of maternal grandmother, parents, daughter Carla, 6 years old, and a baby sister aged 10 months. A second child had died at 9 months of a congenital defect when Carla was 3 years old. A third pregnancy had ended in a miscarriage when Carla was 4. Mrs. Craven, the oldest of three children, had experienced neglect, poverty, and constant rejection. Her mother, grandmother, and great grandmother had each been married twice to alcoholics. She is a cripple with a long history of medical illness. She married a veteran with borderline psychosis and with a family history of psychosis. After a life of gross neglect by both parents he had married an alcoholic before meeting Mrs. Craven. There was one child by this union.

Mrs. Craven's own mother neglected her and, as far as one can see, had a phobic relationship with her. At 6 years of age Mrs. Craven had rheumatic fever with double pneumonia and spinal meningitis. In spite of this history, she recalls that at 10 her mother took her around to bars, to "protect my mother." Mrs. Craven herself has great need to keep her daughter Carla close; she kept her particularly close after the death of her second child. Mrs. Craven had been separated from her mother twice in her adolescence because of her mother's alcoholism and promiscuity. When her parents were divorced in her adolescence, her dream of living with her father was shattered by his accidental death. Subsequently Mrs. Craven stayed close to her mother in what appears to be a phobia à deux. She says she was "forced to protect her mother from alcohol and men." She continued to be her mother's protector for three years after the mother again married an alcoholic. When we knew her she was involved with her mother and her own husband, who joined forces in alcoholic binges. The current triangle appeared to be a repetition of her involvement with her mother and father.

The Cravens experienced considerable economic insecurity in the early years of their marriage and lived in substandard housing. His work was irregular and on occasion their income was supplemented by his wife. Her most satisfying job was working in a jewelry store. Mrs. Craven had two years of high school, was bright and intensely ambitious.

Since she was dissatisfied with the first child, lost her second, and subsequently had a miscarriage, she had put great pressure on her husband for another child. Her husband's responses to her demands were complicated by his anxiety when she was pregnant. Any disturbance in Mrs. Craven's relationship to her mother tended to be accompanied by an increase in the alcoholism of Mr. Craven, massive symptomatology on the part of Mrs. Craven, or VA hospitalization of Mr. Craven. On two occasions during their marriage Mr. Craven was hospitalized, producing a rage in Mrs. Craven, who felt that he was having a holiday, with "all that care and all those parties." On each occasion she managed to get him to leave against advice. At times it appeared that they were competing to see who could have the most symptoms.

Early in her marriage, when she was pregnant with Carla, she was forced to move in with her mother because she and her husband were evicted from their home. Her relationship to her mother was reflected in her bitter comment that her cat was not permitted to accompany them because her mother's cat could not get along with hers. The pregnancy was a stormy one. A negative factor in Mrs. Craven's blood was a danger to the child and decreased respiratory reserve a danger to herself because of her deformity. She had three hospitalizations during this pregnancy, but finally delivered Carla who, although premature, was a normal baby.

In her early care Mrs. Craven held Carla very little and never during bottle feeding. She paid minute attention to food stains but neglected soiled diapers. Characteristically she did not allow her child to feed herself until she was 3 in order to avoid messes, and dressed her until she was 4, in spite of Carla's superior I.Q. Food and elimination were battlegrounds. Carla could either please or displease her mother by refusing to eat or eliminate. Threats of vomiting could also be implemented. Mrs. Craven's medical care of the child was unpredictable. She was as apt to keep her at home when she was well as she was to send her to school with a known temperature of 102 degrees. She kept away from doctors, as she feared they would detect a deformity in her child. She allowed her to be in danger by permitting wild adolescent boys to baby-sit and refusing to rescue her in fights. Instead she shouted through the window, "Fight or you will be killed!" She did errands leaving Carla on the streets for hours and then mobilized the environment and courts when Carla was snatched for a car ride.

As in all the families, the routines in respect to food were one index that reflected the degree of disorganization in the family life. Mrs. Craven never cooked meals. TV dinners were brought in. Food was served at irregular times and in irregular amounts. The family could get up and have a meal at midnight as well as earlier in the evening. When Mrs. Craven was reduced to lying on a couch because of her own symptoms, care of Carla was minimal. She would tell her to get the food she could reach or do without.

Her relationship to Carla was an ambivalent one. In spite of her normality, she called this child the dirty, deformed one. Her second daughter, who died at 9 months of a congenital condition, she called the lovely, feminine daughter. This split between the dirty and the lovely daughter probably represented the split in herself between femininity and masculinity, abnormality and normality.

Families with Severe Disorganization of a Different Order (Asocial Multiproblem Families). Members of the *Earley clan;* consisting of two generations of multiproblem families, were seen by one male caseworker who ultimately became an ideal father figure to all the families. The entire clan presented multiple patterns of deficiency, inadequacy, and neglect, with minor themes of antisocial and delinquent behavior. As stated earlier, the project worked with four interrelated couples, their fifteen children, and the children's grandmother. The major destructive element in this sociological unit was that no one took responsibility for any particular child. Responsibility was ineffectively shared by adults and finally shunted to the alcoholic grandmother. This grandmother, who had been rejected by all her daughters in their youth, became the dominating figure in their marriages. To her visits at the homes of her daughters and to the care of her grandchildren she brought every one of her destructive child-rearing practices. Unfortunately she functioned not as a grandmother but as a sibling and was even more in rivalry with her grandchildren than their own mothers were.

We shall describe just one family in the second generation, namely the *Leonard family.* Mrs. Leonard was the oldest of many siblings in her family of orientation.

The most striking characteristic of the Leonard family was the absence of initiative. A kind of lethargy permeated the entire family unit. There never appeared to be any motivation behind any piece of behavior. Life was undirected and timeless. The parents had little or no meaningful connection with society at large. They had little contact with neighbors and shared few, if any, community activities. The world that existed for them was the extended family, and the various households and figures of the clan provided a series of complicated networks through which the mother of the entire clan traveled from one household to another. Children and parents visited back and forth.

Like most of the families the Leonards confined themselves within a limited geographical area and did not use the resources of the working-class community. The family exemplified what all of the families showed to a greater or lesser degree, a mutual failure to relate and communicate in any constructive form with organized society. Mrs. Leonard and her family, along with her married brothers and sisters, were at least second generations of multiproblem families. In her family as well as those of her siblings there was a repetition of the maladaptive patterns seen in the household of her parents and grandparents.

Mrs. Leonard's family of orientation had been known to social agencies for many years by the time Mrs. Leonard was 6. The oldest of seven children, she had lived with her parents in a slum area in cramped quarters without any facilities. The family had deteriorated. Both parents drank heavily; the teenage children presented numerous difficulties; among them were stealing and precocious sexual acting out. The younger siblings were ill-fed and dirty. Discipline was absent. School attendance was irregular and medical care was nonexistent. Agency intervention and placement of the children brought about no shift in behavior. Later Mrs. Leonard appeared to be the only one who was able to do anything about the children and the marital difficulties. (It is interesting to note that she alone as the oldest child had not been placed.)

Poor housekeeping patterns, confused, inconsistent child-rearing practices, absence of medical care, marital discord, and unemployment permeated the Leonard household in much the same way as they did the home of her parents. Clothes were heaped in corners, remnants of garbage stalked the floors, beds were shared by three and four children. Periodically the children were left alone or to the irregularities of their grandmother, when Mrs. Leonard sought employment.

Mr. Leonard himself, although brought up in a lower-middle-class environment, had been involved in a number of delinquent episodes during his adolescence. Although he was the father of all seven children, he did not marry Mrs. Leonard until after the birth of their third child. The many shifts in their living arrangement reflected the status of their marital relationship. Mrs. Leonard only wanted to live in the area in which she was brought up. Mr. Leonard made abortive attempts to improve their situation by trying to live closer to his family. This conflict often was solved by each marital partner returning to his own family. Pressures from Mrs. Leonard were the most effective in keeping the family in slum areas.

Care of the children reflected Mrs. Leonard's inadequacies in the maternal sphere. Food was not only inadequately and irregularly given but was even harmful. At one point when affairs were at rock bottom, the baby, at 6 months, was admitted to the hospital with a failure-to-thrive syndrome. She recovered. The next child, however, when hospitalized at 3 months for the same syndrome, failed to recover. The pathological diagnosis was dehydration, duodenal ulceration, malnutrition, and terminal gastrointestinal hemorrhage. When Mrs. Leonard gave this account of illness and death to her worker, there was no expression of feeling and her story included no evidence of grief or depression. The striking thing about Mrs. Leonard, however, was that in spite of her disorganized behavior there was nothing vindictive or unkind in her relationship to the children. These relationships did appear to have elements of warmth and gentleness. Her lack of knowledge in homemaking skills and child care seemed to be closely related to the poverty of adequate models and experiences in her early life. The extent to which she was able to use her worker as a model, however, was striking. Calling him her "daytime husband" she did "whatever he told me to do."

When employed and not under maximum pressure, Mr. Leonard was able to contribute very positive elements in his relationship to the children. He was able to produce appropriate toys, especially for the only boy, who was a favorite of both parents. On rare occasions he even played Scrabble with this child. In contrast, his behavior was quite the opposite when under stress. At these times he was unable to mobilize sufficient strength within himself to give either his wife or children any support. During his wife's confinements, for example, he usually moved back to the home of his parents. At the birth of the sixth child, when he was unemployed, he withdrew even further, drank heavily, and found other women.

Multiproblem Families with Gross Pathology but Less Severe Disorganization.   The *Rossi family,* which we have characterized as a multiproblem antisocial family, represents a teenage marriage between two immature adolescents. The Rossi family was one of the two families known during the pilot phase of our program. (The Bailey family is the other.) Consequently they have been known since 1956. A family history going back two generations indicated that the Rossi parents had embarked on marriage with a poverty of learning experiences and meager equipment for family life and child rearing.

As in all the marriages in the group of families, there was no solid affection between the parents and no real base for the marriage. A series of gratuitous circumstances had brought the parents together to embark on a vicious circle echoing the past. Mrs. Rossi resented the fact that she had been caught from the age of 15 in a mesh of Mr. Rossi's delinquent activities because of a forced marriage. A braggart, boasting of being a Don Juan, Mr. Rossi had attracted his future wife's attention at a casual meeting. Shy and inhibited, with some phobic trends, she was easily influenced by his bravado and facile talk. Frightened when she discovered her pregnancy she yielded to his pressures that they marry. Later Mr. Rossi joked about "our honeymoon in the back yard, drinking a Pepsi-Cola." Mr. Rossi himself was looking for care and a home. At the time of the meeting he was again on parole from a training school. Adrift and unwilling to return to a much-hated father, he was full of fantasies about a home of his own.

Both of the Rossis had emerged out of dreary deprived households with little to look forward to and little encouragement from their respective families. Ludwig Geismar describes families who later develop disorganization as having similar background (2). Although Mrs. Rossi's Nordic background appears to have been somewhat better than her husband's, her life was colored by lack of love and opportunity. Her mother was a severe alcoholic who could never be depended upon. She gives an amazing history of having been on a bottle until she was 11. One wonders whether this was not a screen memory related to her mother's alcoholism. She also reported that from the age of 8 through her first pregnancy she slept in the parental bedroom. She appears to have been a middle child in a family with older sisters and younger brothers. Apparently whatever care she received was from an older sister who later told her about the facts of delivery and took care of her first child. Currently she is still extremely shy and inarticulate. This external behavior, however, masks an unexpected sturdiness and a subtle sense of humor. When speaking of her ambitions she stated, "No one ever heard me when I said I wanted an education to learn to be an artist."

Mr. Rossi was the fourth of eight children of Mediterranean background. His own early life was a replica of his father's early life in the old country. Both generations were beset by brutality toward women, neglect, alcoholism, and absence of education. This unrelieved picture was duplicated by his mother's background. His recollections of his mother was that "she did nothing but scream at me and drink." Nevertheless he stated he could "never stay away from her." His memories of his father were bitter ones. Food was rarely in the home. He hated his father because of alcoholism and brutal behavior toward his mother. "At eleven I ran away from home because I hated my father." At an early age Mr. Rossi with his brothers became involved in a series of delinquencies that have continued to the present. Even his hated father was often a partner in crime. His father's response to complaints of lack of money was "Rob a bank." Mr. Rossi's pattern of responding to any kind of pressure, internal or external, has been to flee. In adolescence he ran away from home. Later, falsifying his age, he joined the Army "to be cared for." During his marriage he had abandoned his family during his wife's pregnancies.

Problems centered on pregnancy have been the primary focus in the work with the Rossi family. When she was first seen, Mrs. Rossi was a frightened adolescent of 15 sleeping in her parents' bedroom in spite of the fact she was six months' pregnant. Her mother was running her life and an older sister planned to care for the baby. Her husband was living with his own parents and only on rare occasions stayed with Mrs. Rossi.

The following seven years were replete with seven pregnancies.
Mr. Rossi's irregular work, unpredictable behavior, and delinquencies and Mrs. Rossi's infantile behavior kept them each with their
respective families until after the birth of the third child. In all her
pregnancies Mrs. Rossi sought medical care only shortly before
term. After all her deliveries she hoped her alcoholic mother
would care for her family. Completely irresponsible, her mother
either left early or was not to be found. In identification with her
mother, who had all her babies at home, Mrs. Rossi left the hospital after delivery on the second or third day. It was not until the
fifth pregnancy that it was possible to keep Mr. Rossi at home with
his wife and family.

As has been stated, shortly after the birth of the third child the
Rossis were helped to establish a home. Without assistance Mrs.
Rossi would have been immobilized. Systematic work with Mr.
Rossi was initiated at this time. Irregularities in work, absences
from home, delinquencies, and lack of interest in the children almost led Mrs. Rossi to separate from her husband. However, at
the crucial moment the impending marriage of his male worker
seemed to consolidate some identification with the worker and
there was evidence of a more stable period of work and a beginning
interest in the children.

Mrs. Rossi's relationship with the children has been primarily
nonverbal. When they were very small she carried them about a
great deal as if they were part of herself, that is mere appendages.
Communication seemed to be through occasional patting, giving
of food, and half smiling. With the first baby, though frightened,
with help she was able to be loving and tender. With the advent of
the second child her interest shifted to the new baby. This pattern
was repeated with the third and fourth baby. It was as if each baby,
when small, was a part of herself and that this part of herself she
could love. When she established her own home it appeared as if
her reservoir of energy for the children began to diminish. With
three babies on bottles, she seemed only able to identify with the
needs of one baby, namely the youngest. Her greatest investment
has been in the fourth child, a boy with a congenital anomaly. This
baby, more than any other, became part of herself and there has
been a silent, strong tie between mother and child.

With the advent of the fifth child Mrs. Rossi's interest in her children seems to have reached a cutoff point. Although she has become increasingly skillful in the organization of her household and her capacity to cope with her husband, the last three children have been isolated from the family. It is interesting to note that what progress she has achieved in her care of the children has been via the dramatic use made by her worker of the illness and pregnancies of a pet cat. What she was unable to learn directly in relation to her children she learned through her empathy with the trials and tribulations of a mother cat. Much of this learning was later transferred to the care of her children—but without any insight on her part.

Multiproblem Asocial Families (Unmarried Mothers). Except for the Bailey family, this group of families presented less severe disorganization than those already mentioned.

The four unmarried mothers presented special problems in child rearing in addition to the ones already mentioned. The family unit was a unit of mother and children with the father or father figure not clearly identified and appearing and disappearing in an unpredictable fashion. Unexplained replacements of the male figure in the family and his anomalous status contributed to the uncertainties and dangers of the reality situation. The mothers all spoke of attempting to achieve some identity through bearing children. All of them spoke of having children as being their first experience of "owning something and really belonging to a family" Mrs. Barry (discussed in the next chapter) also clearly stated that the children constituted a defense against promiscuity and prostitution. "If I did not have children, I would be on the streets." Mrs. Zaylor, who had four illegitimate children, expressed her struggle to "feel like a mother" and take into account the needs of the children by saying, "I never liked children and if I did not have any of my own, I could not even begin to like or do for them."

The three Negro unmarried mothers, Barry, Zaylor, and Cook, however, had an especially powerful wish to be good mothers even though they were at a loss to implement their wish. The Bailey family is one where the degree of excesses and dangers compound great deprivation. This family demonstrates very clearly how the unmet reality and psychological needs of the mother infiltrate into every aspect of the family life.

For six years the *Bailey family,* consisting of mother and three children, had lived in a roominghouse run by Mrs. Bailey's alcoholic girl friend. The other lodgers were a group of transient or more permanent men. This intricate network of relationships formed the background of the family's social life. The natural father of the children was a married man to whom the children were shunted when their mother lost control and deposited them on his doorstep. Until the family was helped to leave the roominghouse setting he was prohibited from entering the family's life. Mother's girl friend refused to tolerate a "husband."

Mrs. Bailey had become an outcast from her family of orientation when she had her first illegitimate pregnancy. From an early age she had had a life of poverty with her family in a rural community. She recalls vividly a stubborn vindictive father and a weak, passive mother who was unable to protect herself from the brutality of her husband. She still blushes when she remembers the ridicule from other children because of ill-fitting clothes. After a promiscuous adolescence she left school at 16 and became enmeshed in a marriage that ended in desertion and divorce. Later she was accused by her mother of killing her father because she had interfered with a medical procedure. Her father's death seems to have propelled her soon afterward into a relationship with a married man. This relationship persisted and has been the setting for her illegitimate pregnancies.

Mrs. Bailey's management of her life and her children was characterized by inconsistencies and disorganized extremes of stimuli and behavior. The care of the children was not only chaotic but cruel. Mrs. Bailey's feelings of unworthiness and inadequacy influenced all her relationships and activities.

Her relationship to her first child was a hostile one from the beginning. This child was early identified with Mrs. Bailey's "bad" self and became the target for her feelings of insecurity and frustration. An enormous woman who "snacked" all day, she sat in her large chair eating while ignoring the baby's cries of hunger. When food was given it was irregular. As reported by the mother, vomiting and food fads emerged and were dealt with by sadistic forcing of food, cold bottles, or snatching away food.

From the time the second child, another girl, was 11 months old until six years later, Mrs. Bailey's whole life evolved around the care of this child, whose serious illness, followed by the loss of an important organ, necessitated eleven hospitalizations in six years. Mother's fears of death, separation, punishment, and suffering were all focused on this child, who represented a "visitation from heaven for all my bad behavior."

Mrs. Bailey's mismanagement of family life, particularly of health matters, was incredible. Care of this very ill child was unpredictable. Her denial was so powerful that she repeatedly failed to obtain medical care when there was an exacerbation of symptoms. When she did, she was unable to employ medical procedures at home. In rivalry with this child she developed massive symptomatology and haunted the medical and gynecological clinics. She became pregnant twice, aborted once, and fantasied the second pregnancy would end in a stillbirth. When this baby did die at one day of age she became depressed. Around this time the second girl was hospitalized and placed on the danger list. Mrs. Bailey responded by immediately making funeral plans. Her nights were filled with nightmares and her days with physical symptoms. The oldest child became the overt target for her aggression and irritability. Her compulsive, destructive impulses were so great we decided it would be wise to place both girls for a time. Although her subsequent pregnancy and delivery of a much-wanted boy softened her relationship to this third child, explosions of temper and continued threats to give the children away remained part of her daily behavior.

CONCLUSION

The parents have grown up with few of the learning experiences that foster maturity. They have had inadequate models for identification and marked learning deficits. They have had few, if any, experiences of a tender loving relationship with adults. They have known only inconsistencies in these relationships. They bring to their current family life, as if packaged from the past for distribution and perpetuation, all the same deprivations, dangers

springing from uncontrolled impulses, excesses leading to aggressive acts and asocial acting out, inconsistencies of every sort, and a
general passivity toward actively changing things.

It is clear that in our group we are dealing with families of children. When one examines the needs and patterns of adaptation of
the parents and the children, one is startled by the similarity of
their behavior and methods of coping. Except for differences in
size they could all be siblings. There is marked rivalry between
parents and children. Parents seek to satisfy their own needs even
when those of their children are pressing and urgent. Their management of child care is as unpredictable as their own impulsive
acting out. There are few routines. Food and sleep follow no pattern. Training is inconsistent and dependent on what adult is
around at a given moment. Development of the child proceeds or
fails to proceed with little recognition or knowledge by the mothers of age-appropriate response or behavior.

Love, which springs from understanding, and comfort, which
follows on the heels of perception of stress or pain, are minimal in
the parents' relationships to their children. Their responses, which
are sharply mobilized by their action orientation, contribute toward making family relationships inflexible, hostile, and unyielding.

And yet, when the responses and attitudes of the mothers are
examined more closely and over a period of time, it is clear that
their behavior is not as stereotyped and one-sided as it appears at
first. There are moments when their feelings about themselves are
softer and they are less filled with distrust and confusion about
themselves. At these times their motherliness, which has been
obscured by clouds, peeps out with momentary brightness and
warmth.

Psychologically it would appear that although the parents are so
infantile, primitive, and disorganized that they seem no more advanced than their children, they have achieved some islands of intact ego functioning covering every phase of development. The
mothers can give limited care to their children, their husband, and
their households. The real differences between them and their
children is that they have developed fragments of adulthood. That
is, they have what might be referred to as vestiges or tokens of
adult functioning. This is seen in their development of relation-

ships with the personnel of the program, their use of the program, and their shifts in their behavior to their children. (See next chapter.)

These parents do have certain ego functions. They can overcome their feelings of distrust sufficiently to form object relationships. In contrast to the narcissism described by Lidz in his discussion of schizophrenic mothers (6), the narcissism of multiproblem mothers is tied to their own imperative needs. In schizophrenic mothers the narcissism is fixated and repressed. In the case of our mothers, once some of their basic needs are taken care of, the developmental thrust can proceed without regressive trends toward more mature behavior.

In their relationship to their children they are highly competitive, like competing siblings. In their competition for need satisfaction they show marked aggression toward the children. However, unlike neurotic or psychotic disturbances where needs are not reality-determined, when the mothers arc able to obtain direct satisfaction, some of the aggression and competition toward the children tends to disappear.

Initially, the only form of love these parents are able to show is a narcissistic extension of their personality. However, because they are not schizophrenic they do have the capacity to proceed toward some altruism when they are no longer faced with need starvation. Actually, it is extraordinary to see how warm these women can be at times. In fact, they have flashes of warmth and object relations even when they are most competitive. This coexistence, as it were, of competitive, need-oriented drives and warm loving feelings is striking.

Our parents have also shown some capacity to sublimate. With the development of a relationship of trust with a family worker and the satisfaction of some of their reality needs, it has been possible for them to enjoy their children and their households. Within the framework of this relationship we have also seen a reduction of their aggression and competition. This development has been followed by involvement and satisfaction in the artificial culture of the project. Their capacity to obtain pleasure from their contacts with other families and the group activities, particularly the nursery school, has been very clear.

The mothers finally have shown a capacity to develop some social competence (3) and organization in their lives. They have been like people inundated by a volcano and unable to remove the debris. With assistance in sifting the earth from the stones they have been able to select problems out of the burdensome morass. With some realistic goals in sight they showed an unexpected capacity for initiative, competence, and organization.

We believe we have made some advances in our attempt to conceptualize the mutual influences of social and psychological forces. We have employed the same psychosocial perspective to understand family life and its natural history, the parents and the children through the process of growing up and through their entanglement and struggles with each other and their family of orientation, and finally the forces of social disorganization.

In this chapter we have attempted to highlight some of the ways family life becomes the focal point of and reflects the disharmonies between individual, family, and society. The complexities of human nature and family living are brought sharply to our attention through the inconsistencies and contradictions, in the ways in which the individual personality and family life unfold, in the process of adapting to and coping with the life situation in which the families find themselves.

We have found that full psychological understanding is needed to advance our knowledge of the mutual influences of personality, family, and society. Too often a microscopic view of the human dimension is omitted in our attempts to evaluate the reciprocal relationships of these forces and we obtain only a partial picture. Systematic longitudinal studies of children and families similar to the ones in our project are needed to validate or negate or modify our impressions and reconstructions.

REFERENCES

1. Family Centered Project, St. Paul, Minnesota:
   (a) What We Are Up To in St. Paul. Mimeographed paper presented at the Twin City Chapter of the American Association of Social Workers, April 18, 1955, by the staff, workers, and supervisors of the Family Centered Project of St. Paul.

(b) Staff of the Family Centered Project. Casework Notebook (mimeographed). St. Paul, July 1957.

(c) Families in Trouble (mimeographed). St. Paul, January 1958.

2. Geismar, Ludwig, and LaSorte, Michael A. *Understanding the Multi-Problem Family.* New York: Association Press, 1964.

3. Gladwin, Thomas. Social Competence and Clinical Practice. *Psychiatry* 30:30, 1967.

4. Lewis, Hylan. Child-rearing Practices among Low-Income Families. In *Casework Papers,* National Conference on Social Welfare. New York: Family Service Association of America, 1961.

5. Lewis, Hylan. Child-rearing Practices among Low-Income Families in the District of Columbia. Paper presented at the National Conference of Social Welfare, May 16, 1961.

6. Lidz, Theodore. *Schizophrenia and the Family.* New York: International Universities Press, 1965.

7. New York City Youth Board. A Study of Some of the Characteristics of 150 Multi-Problem Families (mimeographed). New York City Youth Board Research Department, January 1957.

8. Pavenstedt, Eleanor. A Comparison of the Child-rearing Environment of Upper-Lower and Very Low-Lower Class Families. *American Journal of Orthopsychiatry* 35:89, 1965.

NOTE

For a bibliography of material related to Chapter 10 and Chapter 11, see page 294.

CASEWORK—A PROCESS
OF SOCIALIZATION
GAINS, LIMITATIONS, CONCLUSIONS

Louise S. Bandler

I N T H E preceding chapter we attempted to give a detailed picture of the nature of family structure and family life styles of a small group of multiproblem families. In addition to a consideration of these families as social units caught up in the violence of an unpredictable environment, special attention was given to a detailed description of how the personality of the parents and their patterns of coping with each other and their children have affected their psychosocial functioning and competence in nurturing children. An understanding of the dynamics of family life must precede any discussion of methods of intervention and discussion of implications for social planning.

Historically, these families, which are the most needy, have been the least understood and consequently have been our greatest failures. They have captured the imagination of clinicians and social planners only during the last fifteen years and only recently have attracted the attention of the experts. Because of the complexity of their problems and lacunae in our knowledge, these families need the best efforts of social workers, clinicians, and social planners.

Until recent years little attempt has been made to gather systematic data about the nature of family organization and family life patterns among lower-class families, particularly those families which present the greatest social and psychological pathology. Consequently understanding and intervention have been based chiefly upon knowledge derived from other segments of society. We are still struggling to achieve sufficient flexibility and inventiveness in methodology to even begin to find ways of involving these families in problem solving. These facts, and the fact that these families tend to seek help only at times of social, economic, or health crises, make our task even more complicated. Since even at times of crises the families are not seeking treatment and lack any real, usable motivation, intervention has been transient and has not led to involvement or lasting gain. If we use public health concepts, intervention at a tertiary level is spotty and ineffectual and at a secondary level even less effective. Since we lack developmental studies of the natural history of the family life and the nature of the process of disorganization, there is at the present time no possibility of systematically working toward prevention. Consequently we need longitudinal studies of family life and new models for intervention if we are to identify basic needs, patterns of coping, and methods of communication between society and these families.

The work of this project represents four years of experience in working with a small group of families in an attempt to advance knowledge about them and at the same time develop new ways of thinking, adapt old methods of working, and devise new methods. The following discussion will describe and conceptualize one casework approach to working with multiproblem families. The casework perspective was one that was seen in the context of a multidiscipline approach to problems of intervention. The total effort represents the impact on family life and child-rearing practices when problems are dealt with by a variety of disciplines using multiple methods of intervention with families of preschool children.

All the disciplines have been involved, not only in the group activities designed to bring the families together, but also in the family life itself. The family work was carried on by two social workers, one public health nurse, and a casework supervisor. The public health nurse worked with families when either a major health problem or early postnatal care was central. In addition her services were made available to any family in the event of a medical crisis.

The work with the families proceeded on the basis of several assumptions: (1) The family workers would provide the bridge between the families and members of the other disciplines and all the group activities. (2) The establishment of a relationship to the parents was a prerequisite to family involvement and subsequent work directed toward problem solving focused on the interests of the children. (3) The families' understanding and perception of the allied disciplines would emerge out of the family work and become consolidated at whatever point actual involvement of the various disciplines took place. (4) The family workers and other project personnel would become an ideal extended family. (5) The milieu of the project's activities would provide an artificial but real community experience for the families.

Involvement of the family workers will be discussed in detail. Involvement with the nursery school teachers has already been described in previous chapters. The child psychiatrist, who headed the project, was identified early by the families as an expert with children and adults. The psychologist was identified as an educational consultant and an advisor in regard to age-appropriate activity. The social psychologist who made observations in the nursery school was viewed as someone familiar with this environment. The anthropologist was perceived as someone who was interested in the neighborhood and its improvement.

As we have already described, the families manifested a wide range of disorganization and pathology. Although the parents showed many of the same psychosocial characteristics and similar patterns of maladaptation, and lived in the same environment, there was no family type or parental type. Attempts at specificity seem to present problems rather than advance knowledge. Perhaps the most simple definition of multiproblem families is not that they are families that suffer from character disorders, but the negative one that they exemplify the mutual failure, both of themselves and of organized society, to relate and communicate in any stable and constructive form. There is mutual noninvolvement, except at times of social, economic, or health crisis. At such times involvement consists of being present physically during the time it takes to identify a concrete need and obtain a concrete solution. There is no engagement in a relationship, nor the establishment of trust directed toward problem solving and lasting gain.

The process which will be described represents one with a dual goal: (1) data gathering and (2) at the same time developing a methodology based, in part at least, on the unfolding of new information. We believe that accuracy of data and the possibility of a dynamic formulation depends largely on the degree and nature of the involvement that can be obtained with the families over a period of time. Interviews which are limited in number and spaced over a period of time cannot provide a continuous, consistent relationship with the interviewer. Data obtained intermittently tends to reveal extremes of behavior and personality characteristics. It fails to highlight the complexities and variety of patterns of adaptation which both parents and children show in their responses to life. Information of this order may then lead to misconceptions and inappropriate categorization. As much precise information as we can obtain in respect to the process of family life and family organization is crucial because of the limited knowledge presently available.

Many writers have examined problems of motivation in multi-problem families (1, 2, 5, 7, 8). Because of the difficulties in mobilizing motivation and achieving involvement directed toward problem solving and lasting gain, the concept of involvement and the casework techniques to secure involvement become of primary importance. What is meant by *involvement* with families who are unmotivated to seek it, who have little previous experience with it, who are suspicious, distrustful, and profoundly disorganized both socially and psychologically? Involvement is a complex concept and a complex process with many ramifications. It means in the early stages, among other things, the establishment of their trust in stable, consistent individuals and the arousal, stimulation, and sustenance of motivation. Involvement also means helping the families identify, clarify, and solve problems.

The *initial casework goal* was to get the family involved. This necessitated the establishment of a relationship of trust. The *second goal* was to help the families achieve some order in their lives. This was accomplished in part through aiding them to find a priority among the multitude of their clamorous, overwhelming problems. The *third goal* was to help the parents, particularly the mothers, to grow away from their narcissistic needs sufficiently to enable them to become altruistically concerned in child rearing and in their family life in such a way as to, at least at times, place their children's interest above their own. The *fourth goal* was to enable the parents to become, for the first time, part of a community, through their participation in the community of the project.

When the parents were ready for the children to enter nursery school they were introduced to the teachers, the psychiatrist, the nurse, the psychologist, and then other families whose children were in the group. In this phase the caseworker facilitated the transference of trust and positive feeling and self-confidence to this broad, artificial community which was the project. Later at family parties the sociologist and anthropologist became members of the extended family. The *final goal* was to help the families achieve a place in the real community through a greater use of values that had been mobilized in the course of the family work, which was a process of socialization.

The casework process followed in their socialization required considerable flexibility. Because of the criteria for selection, namely gross social and psychological pathology and inability to use existing institutions, the family workers were not hampered by rationalizations such as "unworkable, unmotivated." They assumed these facts and set out to overcome these handicaps and experiment with methodology. Such experimentation also meant a reexamination of old and tried methods to come to some conclusion as to the reason for past failures. A good deal of inventiveness and resourcefulness was necessary.

Because of the great deprivation of the parents and their intense rivalry with their children, the initial techniques were directed to the satisfaction of primitive dependent needs without the creation of insatiable infantile demands. The techniques also included considerable education of the parents by the worker in an attempt to fill in educational gaps and provide new models for accomplishing the tasks required in child rearing and family life. Although psychologically different from the parents of schizophrenics described by Dr. Theodore Lidz in his book *Schizophrenia and the Family* (6), parents in multiproblem families did lack both the experience and skills necessary to provide the gradual socialization of the child, because of inadequate models in their early life. The worker educated by imparting a great deal of information and by serving as a model by active demonstration, by precept, and by discussion.

When the caseworker was accepted, it was as a primary figure. In other words, the worker functioned more as a parental figure than as a transference figure as is true in other types of casework relationships. Kermit Wiltse's term *parenting role* (10), used to describe certain casework activities with public welfare clients, bears some kinship with our concept. The relationship was facilitated in part by the tremendous need these women have for a maternal figure and the fact that they are constantly searching for one.

INVOLVEMENT

The nature of the families' processes of communication, as we have stated, is extremely complicated and requires special attention in achieving involvement. Language is not a familiar vehicle for communication of feelings, or for identifying and categorizing, or conveying information. These families are action-oriented, concrete in their thinking, and not used to introspection or abstract thinking. They have little or no psychological insight into themselves or their behavior and little or no perception of conflict areas or psychological problems. Their solutions of economic, social, and psychological problems are impulsive and for immediate gain. The future is not taken into account. Consequently planning does not enter into their solutions. Problems in communication are compounded by their failure to trust anyone or any institution. Traditional casework methods, which are based on the assumption of trust and which are developed through ordinary avenues of communication are not adequate. Consequently certain adaptations of casework concepts and techniques were necessary to achieve the initial goal or involvement. Our families had not initiated help or even recognized that they needed it, so the classic setting of the agency was not possible. The primary setting of the home, and the worker's participation in the family-life activities as a primary figure—virtually a member of the family—were central to any real involvement. Interestingly enough, this led to none of the usual problems of relationship seen in work with other types of families. Few personal questions were asked except at times of interruptions in the relationship, such as vacations or transfer to another worker.

Like a member of one's own family, the family worker was treated as if she had always been a part of the life of the family and was someone who knew all the experiences the family had had. Concern arose only at points of separation.

The interpretation of both the referring agency and the project was, simply, that we were interested in families with very young children. In spite of their suspiciousness, these families do permit a period of testing before they turn their backs. Their sense of privacy begins at a different point from that of middle-class families, which begins at the portals of the home.

The initial interview took place in the home and was directed toward obtaining a foothold and establishing some reason for returning. Conversation was geared toward exploring with the family aspects of their current life in an attempt to identify some problem that was not too anxiety-provoking and that did not threaten their self-esteem. A basis was usually found in some immediate need of the parents. The worker moved toward a solution of the problem before identifying it. The bridge to the children came later. (The importance of this was clearly pointed out by the parents when the children were introduced too early to nursery school: they removed the children.) Because of their infantilism and intense rivalry with their children, the focus had to be on the parents' narcissistic needs even when problems of the children were pressing.

Although the worker was assisting the family by active involvement in the family life, by gratifying reality needs, she still needed full psychological understanding of the situation. This understanding would not be employed for a long time, if ever, through techniques such as clarification, interpretation, and insight-giving; it was used primarily to avoid ever-present dangers. These dangers are psychological land mines of neurotic dependency needs, acting out, and transference complications. The worker was not deterred from meeting needs because of fear that they would build up into insatiable demands. The reason was that these needs, apart from their psychological significance, are all realistic, emerging from the chaos of family functioning, whether in relation to the management of the household, the marital partner, or care of the children.

The establishment of trust was dependent, not only on the meeting of both psychological and reality needs, but especially upon the

behavior and attitude of the worker in responding to the long period of grueling, formidable testing on which these families embark. In such testing a parent might hang her head out of a window during the entire interview, or let the television set blare as
loudly as possible. (Frequently, reducing the volume of the television set, or finally turning it off, was a barometer of a family's acceptance of the worker.) Often the parents left the room during
the interview or even went out of doors, only to return later expecting to find the worker still there. On some occasions a mother
would surround herself with friends or relatives. On other occasions she would be rude, and take pleasure in the children's overt
aggression toward the worker.

The worker's response to this behavior was central to the establishment of trust. Standing up to the terrific ordeal of testing,
which sometimes lasted a year, and responding with flexibility,
consistency, constancy, and absence of retaliation, provided the
basic framework for the establishment of trust. This meant that the
parents accepted the worker as someone who was reliable, predictable, and consistent, and involved in the family activities, and that
the worker accepted herself in that role. A crucial stabilizing factor
was the scheduling of appointments, which the parents expected
the worker to keep even if they were out or had left a message that
she was not to come.

PRIORITY OF PROBLEMS

These families are in a state of chronic crisis. Various fragments
of their problems are reflected in their multiple contacts with various agencies. Their problems are so numerous and complex that
they have no way of ordering them. While establishing a relationship of primary trust, the worker was also striving toward the second goal, that of assisting the families to establish a priority of
problems, some order in their lives. The lives of these families are
unfocused and chaotic, and the parents, with a minimal capacity
for problem solving, attempt to deal with daily problems without
any planned, systematic approach. They live from day to day and
have a poor sense of time.

The worker gives priority and order to problems by her reactions and responses and accompanies her assistance with language —naming, identifying, categorizing, and explaining. She distinguishes between what issues are important and what issues are less important, what problems need immediate attention and what problems can be delayed for future solution. She provides reality testing in terms of what can be accomplished and what is not realizable. She conveys the concept of delayed gratification, taking into account the parents' own needs and their capacity for frustration. Giving is geared to real needs and crises, not to whim and demand. In this way the parents are assisted to discriminate legitimate needs from infantile demands, in themselves and in their children.

The sequence and ordering of problems are related to the degree of disorganization in the families and the specific developmental tasks with which the parent is struggling. Some examples may make this clear:

Mrs. Brown, American-born of Eastern Mediterranean parents, is a mother in a family of maximal disorganization. (See family study in previous chapter.) Her early, gypsylike existence was characterized by minimum routine and minimum controls. Her life was full of danger and shifting modes of parental behavior. Her husband, born of Central European parents, was brought up in a family with a psychotic mother and two psychotic siblings. He himself was diagnosed as a borderline psychotic. Mrs. Brown's management of her household and her two children, aged 2 and 5, was chaotic. Food was given to all members of the family on demand. The apartment was filthy. At the time of referral, Mrs. Brown was in a state of collapse because her boy was prohibited from attending school because of his bizarre behavior and retardation.

Mrs. Brown had problems of management in every area of life— food, housekeeping, money, children, school authorities, and husband. Mrs. Brown's self-esteem was low, and her need to be given to was almost insatiable. Her wish to be rescued, and her desire to have all problems resolved by magic, made it necessary for the worker to select a problem area which would not mobilize violent aggression and yet would be close to her own primitive needs. Her management of food was selected as an initial area of work that could eventually lead to some management of other phases of her household and of the children. Furthermore, this was related to Mrs. Brown's strong oral needs, and finally, it corresponded to one of the earliest developmental tasks, in which the mother assists the child to establish a routine and rhythm of eating.

Mrs. Craven, a cripple, was the mother of two children, a daughter aged 4 and one who died of a congenital disease at 9 months, just two months before referral. (See family study in previous chapter.) Mrs. Craven catalogued eight problems. She insisted that the worker stop her daughter's playing out the baby's death with dolls because she, the mother, "wanted to forget." She expressed fear that her stepdaughter, who was in foster placement, was in serious danger. She asked that her alcoholic mother and her husband stop drinking together. She complained about her daughter's feeding problem. She raved against the Welfare Department because their compensation check was not forthcoming. She cursed the housing authorities because she was to be evicted. She wanted assistance in having a telephone installed, saying that she needed one because she was crippled. Finally, she asked for money, although she knew the program had no funds.

Because of her guilty feelings about the death of her baby, Mrs. Craven's grief could not be dealt with. For the same reason, her daughter's behavior could not be dealt with directly. It was dealt with instead in terms of her anxiety about her step-daughter on whom a good deal of the anxiety had been displaced. Food was not dealt with because the worker did not wish to appeal to her orality; furthermore, her aggression was involved in handling food. The worker selected housing first, because it was an urgent problem and because it had special psychological significance for this mother. Her special feelings about herself and her deformity were dealt with through helping her to decorate her home and manage her housekeeping.

Joan Cook, an 18-year-old unmarried Negress on ADC, a mother of two illegitimate children, aged 1½ and 3, had left her mother's home with her two children to prevent the SPCC from taking her children because of her mother's alcoholism, and her mother's practice of permitting teenagers to use her home for illicit relations. Joan, up to this point, had been regarded by her children as a sibling and she had been in active competition with them for her mother's affection. There was also marked rivalry with her mother in her efforts to cope with her desire to grow up and care for her children. In setting up a household with her children and a boyfriend, her major problems were in succeeding in her housekeeping and in keeping her boyfriend. Except for having the children she had no capacity to deal with their care in any real measure. This was most clearly shown in her pattern of having them spend a good part of each week with her mother. Like two children playing at housekeeping, Joan and her boyfriend painted and decorated her apartment, danced to the phonograph, and gaily chased each other about.

In this instance the worker aligned herself with Joan's housekeeping efforts on all fronts, and finally gave her a frilly apron in recognition of her successful efforts. Feeling such beauty was not for her devalued self, she wept at first and was determined to frame it and hang it on the wall. At this time her efforts to make her boyfriend a part of the family were encouraged and only later was the worker able to deal with some of the realistic implications regarding her relationship with ADC so long as she continued this arrangement. Her needs were so pressing that even when nursery school was broached for the 3-year-old, it had to be dealt with through Joan's disappointment in the interruption of her own education when she became pregnant.

The casework process also necessitates considerable education of the families, with the worker serving as a model. These parents all have some competence in managing household matters, in caring for children and for the marital partner and in work. In her casework, the worker aligns herself with the parents' basic wish to do things for their children even if they do not know how to do them. The educational activities play an important role in the recognition, support, and consolidation of these constructive aims which we believe the parents already possess. These activities involve some synthesis of the self-image of the parents, particularly as parents.

The worker's educational activities, however, go far beyond her serving as a model for imitation and, to some degree, for identification. The families' difficulties are due not only to their psychosocial disorganization, but also to a significant degree to a genuine lack of knowledge. Their difficulties as parents appear to be related to their own educational deficiencies. Their hunger is not just for being cared for, but for real knowledge.

Mrs. Zaylor, for example, an unmarried Southern Negress with three illegitimate children, wanted her children to have an education and to keep away from the law. Her method of accomplishing this was by rigid controls and punishment, and suppression of any expression of feeling. This extreme was even carried over to the year-old baby whom she expected to learn to obey by not crying. Demonstrating that crying was not evidence of disobedience but of many other things, and showing Mrs. Zaylor how to identify and meet the infant's needs, reduced the crying. The worker also showed her that in the case of her other children, aged 3 and 5, emotional responses were indicative of the children's needs and not of their willfulness. All this led to Mrs. Zaylor's asking for further information to assist her in other aspects of the children's lives. It also led to an amelioration of her rigid disciplinary measures. The worker's recognition of her real wish to be a good mother, which Mrs. Zaylor doubted because of her illegitimate pregnancies and the fact that her boyfriend lived in the home, did much to soften her archaic superego and to develop her sense of self and some image of herself as a competent mother. Actually, this woman's capacity to care for her three children was remarkable.

In the case of *Mrs. Rossi,* her competence as a mother was made clear through the worker's interest in a pregnant cat. Mrs. Rossi, a mother of six children at 23, had never been able to take care of herself during pregnancy or to accept assistance from the worker. When her cat was sick during its pregnancy, the worker's care of the animal facilitated much talk about pregnancy and the care of the children. Mrs. Rossi, who had not been able to identify feelings in herself in respect to her children, could do so after experiencing her displaced feelings in relation to the cat.

The worker makes maximum use of derivative situations, relatively conflict-free situations, reality situations, and crises. She is not only demonstrating and giving information or making knowledge accessible through other channels, she is also teaching parents to recognize and to manage emotions, and teaching appropriate and less rigid responses. It is hoped that such a process may lead to more synthesis of self. The parents learn from the worker in much the way that small children do from their parents.

One of the most rewarding results of the whole process is the fact that these parents did respond when the way was opened to them. A long period of preparation and education, however, was necessary before the families were ready to identify feelings or utilize techniques that involve perception of feelings or analysis of relationships. They do, however, have a potential for progressive development and can move forward.

MOVEMENT TOWARD INCREASED SOCIALIZATION

The first bridge the families made to the total program was via the nursery school. Crucial to their development was their decision to let their children go. All attempts to introduce the nursery school failed until the family had achieved some trust, some involvement, and had known the worker for some months as a constant object. Secondly, some change in their self-esteem had to take place. They could not contemplate nursery school for their children until they were able to think of themselves as *good* mothers. Reduction of their fear that they were bad mothers also reduced their fear that nursery school might take away their children. Finally, the strong element of competition in their relationship to their children had to be moderated sufficiently to allow them to think of themselves as parents and act accordingly.

This gradual involvement with everything pertaining to the nursery school was the first step in providing a group experience which was a kind of culture and community for these parents. It was also our impression that the mothers, through their relationship to the worker, were able to overcome some of the phobic aspects of their relationship to their eldest daughter. Parents whose children had dropped out of other nursery schools and parents who had been unable to follow through with applications were able to visit the nursery school and subsequently complete the application interviews and forms. They became interested in evaluating the progress of their children.

The teachers also became models of education in the lives of these families, and the nursery school milieu became a medium for further socialization. The concept of birthday parties was one of many introduced. The parents attended and supplied the birthday cupcakes. Birthdays were carried over into the home, and children from other families were invited. Friendship was a new experience for these children.

Parties, including all project personnel, the families and their children, did a great deal in assisting the families to develop further a feeling of family identity. Parents were keen in noting the evolution of the relationship of their children to other children and the development of skills. Particularly striking was their capacity to identify and ponder various techniques used by the staff to assist the children in adapting to each other and the group situation. After three years together, many of the mothers were able to note the degree of group cohesiveness that existed instead of what they described as the "yelling, screaming" disorganized activity which was characteristic of the children initially.

INVOLVEMENT IN THE REAL COMMUNITY

Some of the families have been able to extend the process of socialization beyond the community of the project and have achieved the final goal of becoming clients of health, welfare, and group agencies. The details of these findings will be documented later when the nature and limitations of change in the families are discussed. Before examining these findings, however, let us turn to an analysis of the casework process with two of our families, the Cravens and the Barrys.

THE CASEWORK PROCESS

In working with the families an attempt was made to select a central theme in the life of the mothers to give some direction and focus to the treatment process. In the Craven family, which has been described in some detail in the previous chapter, problems related to pregnancy were a major area of interest.

The Craven Family. As stated, Mrs. Craven catalogued eight problems which were dealt with initially in terms of the developmental tasks with which she was struggling and in terms of reality pressures. An extensive period of testing accompanied her demands. During the initial visits Mrs. Craven kept her head well out of the window; on occasion she left the house to find her child; on another occasion she bought Carla and herself a popsicle and announced to the worker on her return that she had eaten it downstairs so she would not "have to share it." Once she accused the worker of not wanting her "dirty brew," referring to coffee, and another time when the worker requested a spoon she replied, "Do I have to dirty a spoon for you?"

When Mrs. Craven's demands began to level off the worker raised the question of nursery school. Mrs. Craven's response was to tell the worker what a failure Carla's attendance at a neighborhood nursery school had been. Carla had been unable to separate from her mother. After remaining with her in nursery school for ten days, mother terminated Carla's attendance. Mrs. Craven did manage to move toward the project's nursery school to the extent of bringing Carla in for a visit and having an application interview. She failed, however, to complete the medical forms and talked about how difficult she knew separation could be for Carla. In her ambivalence she permitted Carla to attend one session at school but at the same time began testing the worker with increased demands and began acting out her rivalry with Carla. Her demands were in respect to more information about Mr. Craven's daughter. Her rivalry with Carla was reflected in her hostility toward nursery school teachers and toward the worker if any attention was paid to Carla. When her cat jumped into the worker's lap, Mrs. Craven beat it severely. The worker clarified again the stepdaughter's situation and scheduled visits now only when Carla was in nursery school.

Mrs. Craven's struggle to work through her separation from Carla, when the latter went to nursery school, was complicated by her third pregnancy. Her own physical needs took precedence over her attempts to complete the medical forms for the nursery school. The worker dealt with this conflict by stepping in promptly and taking both Mrs. Craven and Carla, at the same time, to the pediatric and gynecological clinics. By seating Mrs. Craven next to her in the car, the worker symbolically gave Mrs. Craven's need priority.

When it was established that Mrs. Craven was pregnant for the third time her hostility extended to her entire household and her care of her household became completely chaotic. Her chief target was her mother, who had completely abandoned her by announcing that the pregnancy would really kill Mrs. Craven. Her mother had also attacked Mr. Craven and berated him for his part in the "tragedy." Mrs. Craven refused to feed her family at all. Previously she had not planned meals and had been dependent on such things as TV dinners. Now she sent Carla to neighbors for food or had her help herself and let her husband fend for himself. Neither he nor her mother responded to this crisis by giving assistance. When she did pour coffee for the worker, it was with a "damned if you do or damned if you don't" attitude.

At this time the worker increased the number of her visits and attempted to step into the role Mrs. Craven's mother should have occupied in organizing household tasks and reassuring both Mr. and Mrs. Craven. Recognizing that Mrs. Craven was attempting to resolve her conflicts over the second child's death via this pregnancy, the worker tried to stem the tide of Mrs. Craven's masochistic orgy on all fronts. She had Mrs. Craven go over conversations with her mother to correct misinformation and gave her facts from the medical record. She tried to reestablish Mr. Craven's relationship with the Veterans Administration to take care of his anxiety.

Unfortunately, this was not enough. At three months Mrs. Craven miscarried. When the worker visited the day she had miscarried she learned that preceding this miscarriage Mrs. Craven had

washed and waxed floors and had carried a large bundle of groceries upstairs, and that the miscarriage had taken place in the
presence of Carla. Mrs. Craven was rushed to the hospital.

During the period of Mrs. Craven's hospitalization and for a
time after her return home, the family worker, the nursery school
teacher, and the psychologist had maximum involvement. The
family worker had long interviews with Mrs. Craven's mother to
alleviate her guilty feelings and reduce her pressures on Mr. Craven, whom she held responsible. She helped the husband with his
guilt enough to enable him to turn to a psychiatrist. Mr. Craven
had remained out of work, saying he was as ill as Mrs. Craven.
After Mrs. Craven's return to the home she had so many physical
complaints the worker sent in a Home Medical doctor and provided for a homemaker to care for the family's needs and to permit
Mrs. Craven to be as inactive as she chose.

The nursery school teacher and the psychologist dealt with Carla's needs. Mrs. Craven had demonstrated her aggression toward
Carla by drawing her close in what appeared to be an affectionate
gesture, but what the worker heard was: "What I need is to get her
out of my sight." Carla was kept all day in nursery school instead of
the usual half day. The teacher picked her up at home and spent
twenty minutes with her alone in school before the other children
came. The psychologist took her out of nursery school twice a week
for forty minutes to give her further individual attention from an
adult. Both the teacher and the psychologist helped Carla with her
fears that she, as well as her father, was responsible for her mother's
illness.

The next period of work was directed toward supporting Mrs.
Craven in her wish to move to a better environment. Mrs. Craven's
mother did everything she could to prevent this move, as she did
not want to leave the neighborhood in which she had been
brought up. The move to what Mrs. Craven called "middle-class
housing in the country" marked a major shift in the relationship of
Mr. and Mrs. Craven. Mr. Craven obtained the first steady job he
had had, earning $95.00 a week. To buy his wife extra furniture he
also took on a second job. Mrs. Craven supported him now in his
efforts to obtain regular psychiatric appointments, and the work
with the family was synchronized with Mr. Craven's treatment at
the VA.

The family's response was quite different when Mrs. Craven became pregnant for the fourth time. Mr. Craven was very protective and helpful instead of competing with symptoms. Mrs. Craven's mother held her peace. Mrs. Craven herself stated she "could wait until her *husband* waxed the floors." Before she was able to speak about prenatal appointments she talked about her pregnancy in other ways. She talked about her mother's and her husband's reaction to pregnancies; she spoke of the babies of her friends. She gathered medical information from encyclopedias, and later used this information to follow the course of the development of the fetus. She and the worker discussed current styles in maternity clothes, and Mrs. Craven later told the details of her effort to find her favorite maternity dress. In the past she had always made her maternity clothes. Demonstrating her capacity to give to Carla, she finally told of her plan to buy her a complete Easter outfit.

During her pregnancy the worker took Mrs. Craven to prenatal appointments and helped her understand her medical condition. After one appointment when she was about five months pregnant, she collapsed on the hospital steps because she felt that the doctors would take her baby before they saved it. This confusion was clarified by returning with her to the doctor.

It was around this time that material emerged about Mrs. Craven's childhood and early hospitalizations, and some tender memories of her father. For the first time she spoke of her mother's neglect, and the fact that her mother had cautioned her in her adolescence that she could never marry or have children. Mrs. Craven was supported in her desire to have private care, and was taken to the maternity ward and introduced to the nurses.

After Mrs. Craven gave birth to a normal girl, the worker was active in every phase of the infant's development. The psychologist also visited to discuss age-appropriate activity. Mrs. Craven made many references to her early poor handling of Carla. This was followed by better handling of food with Carla and a diminution of her aggression toward her, in contrast to her response to Carla just after her daughter was born, when she completely ignored her. Although her major satisfaction from Carla is still narcissistic, it is less aggressive and she does get real satisfaction from her child's attractive appearance and her accomplishments at school. Recently she bought Carla a talking doll, and made a very elaborate and beautiful wardrobe for her.

The setting of the worker's visits currently is remarkably different from the one three years ago. Mrs. Craven's mother has moved out. Mrs. Craven does all her jobs before the worker arrives so they can "relax and have a cup of coffee together." She not only pours the coffee and offers it to the worker in new china, but accompanies it with something she has just baked. Visits have a new intimacy. She tests with the worker all kinds of theories of her own regarding marriage, household management, and child care. She usually does this in terms of "You may have experienced . . ." or "I know a lot of mothers find . . .", or "Have you noticed . . . ?" Often these theories, presented as her own, are matters previously discussed with the worker. She and her husband visit Mr. Craven's girl regularly. They attend Alcoholics Anonymous together for social hours. Mrs. Craven involved her husband in the church through their minister, who is active in AA. Mrs. Craven has started to organize her household, and for the first time prepares meals regularly, and the family sit down together.

DISCUSSION.   The most impressive feature in this case is its relatively favorable outcome. The psychosocial pathology was so extensive that any prediction that might have been made in respect to successful intervention would have appeared foolhardy. One is led to the conclusion that in spite of the extensive pathology repeated through a succession of generations, there are islands of intact functioning and natural capacities that can be developed.

The phases of the casework process seem relatively clear. First came the period of intense testing with the gratification by the worker of dependency needs, and her involvement in the family as a primary figure and constant object, resulting in the establishment of trust. Then followed the worker's activity in establishing priority of problems and bringing order out of chaos. The gradual synthesis of the self-image of Mrs. Craven as a good mother emerged almost plastically before our eyes. The worker's skill in developing this self-image and the reduction of Mrs. Craven's tremendous sense of guilt was exercised in the setting of the home in the presence of Mrs. Craven's mother, her husband, and sometimes her stepfather. The worker became actually the good mother with whom the client could identify so that she finally became a good mother herself.

Progress was not steadily forward. There were periods of regression and renewed testing, particularly when Carla first went to nursery school and Mrs. Craven and the worker were confronted with the full storm of Mrs. Craven's sibling rivalry. Mrs. Craven's pregnancy, which culminated in the birth of her daughter, involved most intensive casework with a client who was now fully motivated. During this time important changes were taking place in her marriage. It is interesting to speculate that the worker's noncompetitive relationship to Mrs. Craven and helpful, nonseductive relationship to Mr. Craven permitted a reliving of the oedipal triangle with a more normal resolution. One might say that dynamically this was a corrective family experience. At the present time Mrs. Craven is able to live in a better neighborhood and be a better mother to Carla, as well as a good mother to her other daughter, and for the first time to be a homemaker for her husband. She now relates to the worker more like a daughter to a mother who has overcome her ambivalence after the birth of her first child. The worker's educative activity throughout the casework process is so obvious it requires no elaboration.

The Barry Family.   When Mrs. Barry was first known, she was involved with four different social agencies and had been known to several others. An unmarried mother with two children and pregnant with a third, she saw little possibility of finding love or casting off her feelings of self-devaluation. She had been struggling for a long time to control her impulses and establish some kind of identity through the matrix of the family. Except for some screen memories, she recalls little of the first seven years of her life. She was the fourth illegitimate child of a mixed racial union. The only fact she knows about her mother is that after Mrs. Barry's birth her mother became a nun. Her siblings were reported to have been adopted and Mrs. Barry feels currently that she was not adopted primarily because she "was the darkest." Her first seven years were spent in a series of adoptive homes and she recalls no lasting relationship to any woman during that period. In fact she has no memory of close attachments to any female figure.

She believes that all her placements were short-lived until she was placed with Mrs. Smith at the age of 11. In this home she was one of a group of girls ranging from 11 to late adolescence. Her memories of this home, where she remained until she became illegitimately pregnant at 18, are all unhappy ones. She characterizes the home as one which was neat and clean, where the children were well fed but one that was dominated by a woman who was strict, cold, and full of admonitions about boys and sexuality. When information about menses or other adolescent problems was sought from the foster mother, the answer was, "You live in the streets and should know everything." In moments of great despair currently Mrs. Barry states with infinite pathos that she had to learn the worst about life.

She describes herself as having been a tomboy in adolescence. With women she feels awkward and clumsy, and as a result has always felt more kinship with men. Nevertheless, she can name no male figure who has played a crucial part in her life until currently. She recalls no foster father and has many fantasies about the crudeness and brutality of her father as contrasted to fantasies of a blond-haired, gentle mother. The only positive experience she identifies in her adolescence is her relationship to a Negro group-work agency. This she states "was the only mother I had."

At 18, still in high school, Mrs. Barry became illegitimately pregnant by a Negro six years older than herself. Overwhelmed with a desire to be loved, she "went out with him because he was good and bought me food." She expressed no interest in him and lost track of him after impregnation. Her foster mother regarded her as one of her failures and rejected her.

Mrs. Barry's pregnancies have occurred at a time when all her basic conflicts have been mobilized to plague her. Her self-esteem has been virtually nonexistent, her conflicts about her parents have been heightened, and she has struggled between her yearning to be cared for and her wish to be a mother. Her attempts to love and care for her first child failed. He became the target of her aggression and a symbol of male brutality. Rejecting him as she had been rejected he was placed in a foster home for several years. She believes currently that her powerful feelings of alienation and aggression toward him are due to their long separation. This feeling that he cannot be her child is an echo of her feeling that she cannot be the daughter of a blond woman.

In an attempt to effect a reconciliation and establish a home for her son, she later married. Feeling only contempt for her husband she divorced him after a brief period. With her aggression focused now on her son, life alone with him became intolerable. She could not bear what she described as "foolish, dependent, and affectionate behavior."

Unable to love her son and filled with great loneliness, she became pregnant once more. During this pregnancy her hostile impulses toward her son mounted so dangerously that she became confused and depressed. A stormy pregnancy terminated in the birth of a daughter. As with all our mothers, her search for a maternal figure ended in part with the birth of her first daughter. She named the girl after "the Blessed Mother, Ursula Anne." Her early care of the baby was relatively conflict-free and she was able to hold her during feedings and treat her lovingly and tenderly. The satisfaction she derived from this child seemed to make it possible for her to tolerate her son at home.

At the time she was first known to the project Mrs. Barry was again pregnant. Once more her pregnancy had become the focus for her conflicts. Caught in her ambivalence, she struggled to cast her other children aside. Her aggression toward her son Benjamin became intolerable and she placed him in a foster home. Sending him away, however, filled her with unbearable guilty feelings. Identifying Ursula with her bad self, all her tender feelings vanished and she made frantic demands on Ursula to "grow up." The child's activity and what she called "impetuous" behavior threw her into a rage. At the same time she seemed to be trying to recapture their earlier closeness. She insisted on having Ursula share her room and shop with her and refused to permit her to go to nursery school.

Mrs. Barry's initial response to the project worker, a nurse, was a negative one. Because of a similar name, she had identified her with a social worker she had known in the past who had "recommended she give up Ursula." Her rage toward women mounted as she told the worker she had moved opposite her foster mother to prove to her she could be a "good housekeeper." Soon she stated more importantly that she had established her home to flaunt a series of illegitimate children before her foster mother's eyes.

In an effort to test the worker's response she made countless demands. She insisted that the worker tell her what to do about Benjamin. She wanted help in making Ursula take care of herself. She expected the hospital would be critical during her delivery. She worried about what her ADC worker would think about this pregnancy. Expecting rejection from the project worker, she tested her further by never being at home at the time of appointments. She invariably shopped or visited friends at the scheduled hours and depended on the worker's ingenuity in tracking her down. When she was located, she was always prepared to return home and talk.

The overriding issue for Mrs. Barry seemed to be her relationship to the current pregnancy. How she experienced this pregnancy would inevitably be reflected in all her relationships.

The initial goal was directed toward assisting Mrs. Barry to recapture some self-esteem. Attempting to quickly dissociate herself from female figures who had been rejecting, and identify herself with one of the few positive experiences she had had, the worker emphasized the fact she was a nurse. She made no attempt to deal directly with Mrs. Barry's negative feelings about the children. Instead she adopted the behavior and attitude of a loving mother. She supported her placement of Benjamin to reduce the daily impact of Mrs. Barry's aggression on him and on her unborn child. She encouraged her to talk about every aspect of the pregnancy so that she could experience this pregnancy as a time when she and the baby were valued. They discussed ways of making best use of the limited space in the apartment. They spoke of baby diets and discussed menus. Knowing that her early feelings toward Ursula had been positive, the worker assisted her to revive these memories in the setting of the relationship.

This active involvement in Mrs. Barry's daily life and all her concerns soon mobilized fantasies about her mother. She wondered if her mother had really been fair. She recalled an incident of being held very tenderly by a blond, fair woman when she was very young and some happy memories of a nurse who was good to her when she was hospitalized as a young child. (Mrs. Barry's project worker was fair.)

The worker gave her further assistance in enhancing her self-esteem by letting her discuss some of the social issues in the neighborhood. Mrs. Barry spoke contemptuously about Negro women who went out with inferior whites and about southern Negroes who were destructive and did not know how to dress or care for their children. In this context she expressed her own fear of her impulses and criticized women who neglected their children and who dressed up to attract men. She revealed her own defensive measures when she spoke of always buying nice clothes for the children but only drab, secondhand ones for herself.

The worker increased her visits to Mrs. Barry just before delivery and brought her a present after her baby boy was born. As if to please the worker, Mrs. Barry announced she was giving up men and planned to devote her life to her children. After all she "had had her children to be a 'good' woman" and "to keep off of the streets." (This is an interesting expression of her conflict of motherliness versus sexuality and her defensive maneuvers against promiscuity.) She also felt having a family would give her a "feeling of belonging to someone." After a long absence from church she announced she was going to have the new baby baptized. In this act she appeared to be turning to the church in identification with her mother. This pattern of rejecting sexuality after the birth of a child was repeated again later after her fourth pregnancy.

With the satisfaction of her own needs and the enhancement of her self-esteem, Mrs. Barry showed a new face to the world. Her guilty feelings toward Benjamin were lessened, her demands on Ursula were reduced, and her relationship to the new baby was marked with great tenderness. She seemed ready to deal directly with some of her children's needs.

The worker and Mrs. Barry together began to watch for every new development in the baby's responses. Mrs. Barry became intrigued in eliciting smiles and gurgles. She confided in the worker that instead of using a book for directions as she had done with Ursula, she seemed "to *know* what to do with the new baby." None of the aggression apparent in her relationship to her first boy was evident in her responses to this one. About this time she brought up the subject of nursery school for Ursula and permitted her to go.

Mrs. Barry became one of the mothers who participated most actively in every aspect of nursery school. She was quick to imitate the nursery school teacher's behavior and gradually introduced certain school experiences into the home. She discussed with the worker appropriate toys and wrote for recommended books. She welcomed testing for all three children and looked forward to her discussions with the psychologist about age-appropriate behavior. When Ursula responded to Luke's arrival with whining and later with bed-wetting, Mrs. Barry accepted this as expected regressive behavior. She brought handsome birthday cakes to school parties. In contrast to some mothers who carefully gathered up what was left to take home, she grandly offered it to the staff. Instead of complaining about Ursula's "activity" she now took pride in her skills and accomplishments and in her "lively" behavior.

Her group experiences with the program mobilized memories of earlier contacts with a group-work agency. Taking advantage of Mrs. Barry's enjoyment of her contacts with the project personnel and other families, her worker effected a rapprochement with the settlement house which had rejected her in her teens following her second pregnancy.

Along with these developments Mrs. Barry was also attempting to work through her relationship to Luke's father. He had been the first male to play a meaningful role in her life. In spite of her attachment to him, however, she refused him when he asked her to marry him. Steady employment and the fact that he wanted to marry her made no difference. She was unable to make a permanent alliance. She told the worker that even though he was the first man she had ever really cared for, "the children were the ones she loved." He responded by marrying someone else.

Unfortunately in the subsequent months Mrs. Barry had to deal with a change of workers. In spite of careful preparation she could not work through her feelings of abandonment and loss. In desperation she turned to Luke's father and involved him in her life and once more became pregnant. She had become again the woman predicted by her foster mother.

The combination of the worker's departure, her boyfriend's marriage, and her pregnancy led to marked regressive behavior. The first months with the new worker were difficult ones. All the old patterns of coping reappeared. Testing resumed. She had to be sought out at the time of appointments. When she was home, the TV was on loudly. She pressed Luke to "grow up." She rejected the idea of sending him to nursery school although she had earlier expressed a wish to do so. She spoke negatively of the nursery school teacher, saying she was "too attached to Ursula" and that nursery school teachers "let children run wild." She had difficulty letting Ursula leave and kept her at her side instead of permitting her to go to day camp as planned. Finally, under pressure of guilty feelings, she talked of bringing Benjamin home.

In spite of the fact that it looked as if the edifice that had been erected had really crumbled, Mrs. Barry was able to deal with her feelings of loss through work with her new worker. She was encouraged to talk about her longing for the previous worker. She spoke of how "more often than not they talked of things they were not supposed to," that is, "certain things about myself instead of about my children." She was able to speak directly of her ambivalence toward her pregnancy. She spoke of her fear of losing the baby.

The worker dealt with her fears symptomatically and realistically. She rigged up a system of bells to call her girl friend at night and gave Mrs. Barry her own telephone number. When Mrs. Barry spoke of her fear that the hospital would not welcome her, she was taken to the maternity ward and introduced to all the personnel. When she talked of her anxiety that she would deliver at Christmas and be alone without presents, as had been the case during her very first pregnancy, the worker helped her write to the local Santa and plan for a Christmas for herself and the children.

As Mrs. Barry approached term, her ambivalence toward the children diminished. Because she was relating so well to Luke, the worker supported her wish to bring Benjamin home. When he returned Mrs. Barry showed no evidence of her previous aggression. She entered him in school and arranged for him to join a group at the settlement house. In spite of her cramped quarters she rearranged her household to meet the needs of *all* the children. When she arrived home with the new baby she handled her like an expert.

With the termination of the project, Mrs. Barry handled the transfer to her ADC worker with none of the problems of separation or regressive patterns shown earlier. The ADC worker, with Mrs. Barry's consent, had been part of all the final planning.

Two years later her ADC worker reported the family had moved to larger quarters in the same neighborhood. Benjamin was doing well in school and had continued with his group and had also become a member of the Boys' Club. Ursula was doing well in grade two. Luke was performing nicely in kindergarten and the baby was well. Mrs. Barry herself had been editor of the settlement-house paper.

DISCUSSION.   The extent to which Mrs. Barry was able to modify her image of herself and devote herself to her children is remarkable. Initially, she regarded herself as an outcast, someone who deserved the respect of no one. This belief was supported by reality, because of her behavior on the one hand, and because of the way the community regarded her on the other hand. Through her relationship with the worker, who treated her at all times as she would have liked to think of herself, she gradually began to perceive herself as a good mother. This was experienced initially at the time of the worker's support of her plan to place Benjamin and later during her participation in every detail of her pregnancy. To everyone except the worker her rejection of her son again and her repeated illegitimate pregnancy were further confirmation of her inability to mother adequately.

In addition to creating a relationship of trust in which feelings of self-esteem could emerge and develop, the worker assisted Mrs. Barry with her ambivalence toward her pregnancy. As a consequence, as her guilty feelings diminished, she was able to obtain careful medical care of herself, plan for her delivery, and reorder her household. This growing awareness of tenderness in herself and the realization that she could mother modified her aggressive behavior. The attitude of the worker and her educative activities enabled Mrs. Barry to experience, for the first time, a pregnancy free of condemnation and loss of love.

The reality aspects of the relationship were of special significance in fostering Mrs. Barry's new perception of herself. These aspects were, first, the reality of the person of the worker—that is, that she was a nurse—and secondly, the activities she shared with Mrs. Barry, in which the nurse provided a series of new problem-solving models in the capacity of a primary figure. These activities are clear and need no elaboration. The particular nature of the nurse-mother relationship, however, does need clarification.

The built-in features of a nurse had a particularly powerful impact on the development of Mrs. Barry's self-esteem and her increasing capacity to mother. The acceptance of the nurse's nurturing role provided a conflict-free bridge to the development of a positive relationship and facilitated the modification of Mrs. Barry's image of early maternal deprivation. Furthermore, the fact that a nurse is thoroughly at home with the body and all bodily processes made sharing these aspects of her life easier. The non-erotic earthiness of the nurse's attitude toward Mrs. Barry's pregnancy and delivery provided a setting in which her motherliness could blossom and develop.

Mrs. Barry's new perception of herself was advanced further during her participation in the community of the project. Experiencing approval and liking from the total project personnel and the other families who respected her opinions increased her self-esteem considerably. Gradually she was able to recapture the image of her mother and believe herself loved once more.

Unfortunately at this point the structure which had been so carefully erected was threatened by the loss of her worker and her boyfriend. Mrs. Barry experienced the impact of regressive forces. Once again she felt she was an outcast. This belief she confirmed by becoming pregnant a fourth time.

It is striking, however, that in spite of her overwhelming feelings of loss and abandonment which led to a reappearance of old patterns, Mrs. Barry was able to overcome her ambivalent feelings toward her new worker in a relatively brief time. Acceptance of Mrs. Barry's aggression by the worker and immediate involvement in her daily problems in spite of severe testing led to a new relationship of trust. The forward momentum already begun with the first worker was now able to proceed and continue its positive development.

The experience of being accepted as a Negro by both her workers and the rest of the project personnel made it possible for her to accept herself as being a Negro. The removal of this determinant of her self-devaluation contributed to further enhancement of her self-esteem. This development was reflected in her improved care of the children and her beginning interest in the advancement of Negroes.

Mrs. Barry's experiences with the artificial community of the project not only consolidated the advances made with her workers but provided some of the essential ingredients for the ease with which she finally related to the real community. Her relationship to the other families in the project, who were in fact elements of the real community already present, finally provided the bridge to the community. Consequently, when the scaffolding of the project was removed there was possibility of moving out to the community easily because she was already related to it.

We have examined in detail the work with two of the families and have documented some of the shifts in relationships, attitudes, and behavior. It is now appropriate to summarize the findings of the entire group of families.

NATURE AND LIMITATIONS OF CHANGE IN THE FAMILIES

Other studies (3, 4, 9) have shown and we have found that families show a wide range in their capacity to become involved and advance along the problem-solving continuum. At one end of the continuum were the families where the involvement with the worker led to total participation in the community of the project and attempts to deal with problems in most areas of family life. At the other extreme were the families who were able to engage in a relationship, but so far as one could see, it was not a relationship that led to problem solving. There was a clear correlation between the kind of relationship that developed with the worker, the extent of participation in the project, and the degree of problem solving.

The following discussion of the degree of involvement and gains made has been based on a view of the entire four years' work. Looking at any one segment of time or any one piece of behavior can lead either to extreme optimism or extreme pessimism. The following descriptions of the gains made in the families must be regarded as general trends. The process of change is never steadily forward. Gains in certain areas are often matched with losses in others. Only long-time follow-up will demonstrate to what extent the gains we have seen have been consolidated and to what extent they have been modified by regressive forces in the family and environmental stress.

Gains will be discussed under the general heading of nature of involvement and problem solving. Three areas of family life will receive particular attention: (1) nurturing, (2) family organization, particularly family relationships, and (3) patterns of socialization. Because of the focus of this book, the gains directly related to the children will be dealt with in greater detail than those which are clearly gains for the parents. We are assuming, however, that whatever improvement has been achieved with the parents will ultimately affect the mental health of the total family group.

The most striking change in the parents was the blossoming of their self-esteem and the shift in their image of themselves as parents. Their greatest advances in their relationship to their children was their increasing pleasure in their children and their interest and activity in areas of health and education. Increased social functioning outside the home was reflected in their increasing capacity to make good use of community resources. The degree of involvment with the project did not seem to depend upon whether or not a father was in the home. The mother was the dominant figure and central force in the family life.

Families with Maximum Involvement and Maximum Problem Solving: Zaylor, Bailey, Barry, Cook, Craven, and Rossi. In all six of these families, gains were clearly reflected in improved *family relationships* and *child-rearing practices*. The gains made by the four unmarried mothers have been striking.

Among the unmarried mothers, the Zaylor family was by far the most organized. Mrs. Zaylor was able to move her home and establish herself without the complications that the pressure of her psychotic mother had previously presented. For Mrs. Zaylor this meant freedom from supervision by the extended family and autonomy in her care of the children. She became very involved in theories of child care and age-appropriate activity and her care of the two babies reflected her increasing knowledge about feeding, training, and communication. Her major difficulty had been in the area of discipline. Although her relationship to the oldest boy is still problematic and her disciplinary demands are great, she has modified much of her rigid pressure on all the children and is able to identify needs. The displaced pressures she placed on the children because of her fear of pregnancy were eliminated when she was successfully assisted to use birth-control measures. Success in this area also consolidated her relationship with the one boyfriend she had had over four years.

In the Bailey family, as has been documented earlier, Mrs. Bailey's powerful aggression toward her three children shifted as she was assisted in dealing with the illnesses of the second child. Murderous wishes in a 250-pound mother were diluted and converted into positive activities for the health and welfare of all three children. Her great strides in obtaining medical care led to her being able to manage illness at home and in real emergencies to adequately prepare her daughter for hospitalization and medical procedures. In the area of discipline, she made great gains in becoming increasingly consistent and maintaining self-control. Likewise Mrs. Bailey was able to free herself from a powerful attachment to an alcoholic woman. There also seemed to be some softening in her attitude toward the children's father.

Mrs. Barry, like all the mothers who had babies during the life of the program, was able to use what she had learned in respect to feeding, physical contact, and stimulation in the care of the new baby. Mrs. Barry was able to make maximum use of knowledge and was an avid reader of books on child care, using Spock as her "bible." (Much of this has been described earlier in the discussion of the casework process.)

The most striking shift in her relationships to her children was in her relationship to her oldest boy. Whereas she had been obliged previously to send him away because of abuse and neglect, she had him at home for the last two years of the project with no ill effects. She had a strong investment in his welfare and took particular care of his health needs and education. Her relationship to her second child became increasingly more tolerant and she had some understanding of the child's ambivalence toward her siblings. She has been very stimulated by her wish to be "a good mother" and her care of the new baby has been excellent.

Mrs. Barry also achieved a real rapprochement with her foster mother. Her relationship to her boyfriend remained ambivalent.

Joan Cook, the fourth unmarried mother, gradually assumed parental responsibility for her children in contrast to her earlier sibling relationship to them. She was sufficiently free from ambivalence to arrange good medical care for her mother. She was the only mother in the program who wished to have a career and was able to plan for and begin to implement her desire to become a beautician. In identification with her worker, who married, Joan discarded several boyfriends and turned to the father of her second child. This relationship was maintained until the end of the project and Joan described this man as "the only man she had ever wanted to marry."

The details of progress in the Craven family have already been documented. In spite of maximum pathology this family, as described, has made great strides in problem solving.

The final family in this group, the Rossi family, is in some ways the most complicated to evaluate because of the fluctuations in the father's behavior, which constantly upsets the family equilibrium. (See case summary in the previous chapter.) Mrs. Rossi, however, has moved from a frightened adolescent dependent on total assistance in child care and the management of her home to a woman who, in spite of the fact that she has seven children at twenty-five, has demonstrated an extraordinary capacity to accomplish her daily tasks and take into account the major needs of the children. She has been able to evolve a regular routine in respect to feeding, naps, school, plans for vacations, and tutoring. The three oldest children have been given increasing age-appropriate responsibility and have been developing an interest in age-appropriate activities.

The most recent family crisis reflects the degree of organization Mrs. Rossi has been able to maintain in spite of her husband's most recent delinquency of breaking and entering. In the face of possible eviction and a two-year jail sentence for her husband, she was able to keep the children in nursery school and public school. She was able to accept temporary public welfare although this family has been self-supporting. She carried through camp plans and plans for tutoring for the three oldest children. In the area of medical care, where she has her greatest difficulty, she was able to follow through with eye surgery for one of her daughters. She showed some beginning capacity to face the intellectual limitations of her fifth child. With assistance from her worker she visited her husband in jail to give him some support. Finally, she was able to bring all seven children to the final picnic for the families and discuss plans for the future.

All six families have advanced in the process of socialization as they have participated in the activities of the program and related to the entire staff. They have responded to every phase of nursery school and attended family parties. Mrs. Zaylor has been the one exception to regular attendance at parties. Her suspiciousness and tendency to isolate herself kept her from many of these activities, although she always sent the children.

Participation in the nursery school program served as a bridge to a relationship to the public school system. All the parents developed a major interest in education for their children. They visited school regularly. Mrs. Bailey became a devotee of meetings of the Parent-Teachers Association and three of the families were able to accept tutoring programs. Their investment was great in spite of the fact that they were unable to accept certain sophisticated recommendations such as a year's delay in entering grade one because of immaturity.

Except for the Cravens, who are on their own, the other five families are making good use of welfare and group work agencies.

Families with Good Involvement and Fair Progress in Problem Solving: Brown and Leonard. The progress in these two families has been of a different order than in the case of the above six families. There is no doubt that the equilibrium in the Brown family is precarious and that the interrelationships are extremely complicated. (See summary in preceding chapter.) This family has a long road to travel before it achieves any real stability. Nevertheless, when the degree of pathology within the family is taken into account, the changes that have occurred are rather extraordinary. With some enhancement of her self-image as a good mother and the assuagement of her needs by a trusted worker, Mrs. Brown has been able to experience some satisfaction from her mothering. She has also been able to accept some frustration of her own primitive needs. Her homekeeping has improved and the appearance of her home is tidier. She summed up her strivings by saying, "Now it looks the way it did when my mother was living."

An adjustment to the demands of growing boys has put a heavy burden on this mother, whose whole patterning has been to infantilize. In her relationship to the boys there have been improvements in several major areas. Massive feeding has ceased. She has struggled and succeeded in permitting more responsibility. She does not insist on dressing them herself and no longer permits them about with inadequate clothing when strangers are present. She has attempted to establish some privacy in sleeping arrangements. She has also permitted them leeway and they can be outdoors on their own and have more friends. This is in marked contrast to their earlier confinement to the home. The boys are also permitted now to make choices. While advances of this nature may seem limited for boys of their age, for boys of Mrs. Brown they represent major gains.

The most noteworthy gains, however, have been in regard to the boys' education. Education is a major goal in the Brown family. Although the behavior of both boys was too disrupting for regular attendance in our nursery school, with extended family work both boys have been able to enter public school and remain in school. The bizarre behavior of Charles and the violent aggressive behavior of Fred had made school originally a real impossibility. Over a period of time Mrs. Brown has been able to draw heavily on the family worker for advice and for models in dealing with school. As a result both boys have been in school for two years. Fred is doing well in grade one. He is not a behavior problem and will be promoted. Charles has remained in special class and although his mother questioned his placement there she has been able to accept special class. Her constant interference in school affairs has been moderated and channeled into more constructive actions, such as planned visits and PTA meetings. She has changed from an explosive figure in the school situation to a woman who is able to exert some constraint and reduce her constant visiting.

A reduction of her fear of school personnel has played a part in her decision to let the boys go to camp and join other groups. Permitting this amount of sharing in her boys' lives is phenomenal for this woman.

In her relationship to her husband Mrs. Brown has been able to encourage and support psychiatric care and tolerate her husband's long psychiatric illness. In spite of her husband's severe illness she has been able to run her household with some financial assistance from relatives. Her support of psychiatric care is in contrast to her chaotic relationship to good medical care for the children.

The Leonard family has been the only family unit of the "Earley clan" who has been able to make good use of the program and show unquestioned progress. Initially it had seemed that no one and no kind of intervention could arouse this family from its crippling state of apathy.

Mrs. Leonard, however, showed an unexpected response to her male worker whom she described to a friend as "my daytime husband." In making use of this image the focus of the work has been the care of the children. Almost overcome by what she described as "Mr. Smith's kindness," she was able to develop a real interest in her children and shift her methods of caring for them from patterns of gross neglect to those of moderately good care. Earlier her neglect had led to the death of one of her children. (For details, see family summary in previous chapter.) Perceiving her worker as a tender, protective, interested figure, the first male figure in her life who had ever behaved this way, Mrs. Leonard wanted to be the "good mother Mr. Smith asked me to be." Under the impact of this relationship she paid close attention to every suggestion and recommendation. While not always successful, she tried hard to carry out these suggestions.

Because of this burning wish to "please" her worker she was able to accept nursery school relatively quickly. Previously she had regarded education as one of the burdensome routines in life; very quickly it became an experience with value. It was impressive to see her get the children dressed and off to nursery school. (Mr. Leonard probably had more feeling about the importance of early training in school. It was he who ultimately put the stamp of approval on nursery school.) Her wish to please also led her to improve her housekeeping.

In the same fashion in which she obediently responded to nursery school, Mrs. Leonard never missed a family party. She dressed her children carefully and viewed them with pride. At the parties she was like a small child viewing the wonders of refreshment and games. It was clear that parties were a new experience for her and she participated like one of the children. Mrs. Leonard, more clearly than any of the mothers, demonstrated the therapeutic advantages of taking care of the needs of the mother at the very moment that identical needs in the children were being satisfied.

Mrs. Leonard has been able to make the transition from nursery school to public school and has seen that the children attend regularly. This is in marked contrast to her own mother's behavior. She has, however, found it difficult to feel as safe at public school as she had at nursery school and has done very little visiting. She has been able to send the three oldest children to camp "because Mr. Smith wanted me to." Finally she has developed an ongoing relationship with her public health nurse. This community relationship is the most crucial one because of the family's long history of neglect. Perhaps it is too much to hope that Mrs. Leonard will bring issues not only to the public health nurse but to her husband as she used to do with her worker.

Families with Some Involvement but Minimum Gains: Carolla and Arrows.　Although the Carolla Family was the most disorganized and pathological of all the families, it was possible to establish a relationship and deal with some of their problems at times of severest crises. The relationship to the worker, however, presented many complicated issues because of the mother's alcoholism and the father's psychotic behavior. Every advance made in this family was tenuous and followed by regressive behavior. Separation of the parents and children finally took place.

The Arrows family presented the greatest enigma of the entire group. To the community this family presented a relatively "well-adjusted front" and the parents were not able to identify any problem areas in child rearing. There was enough of a relationship to the worker, however, to enable both parents to use help at times of severe marital crisis. Because of massive denial and patterns of coping through malingering and environmental manipulation, all efforts to mobilize concern in the parents for their children failed.

Work with the remaining three families was of a different order. Because of death of the child in one case and divorce of the parents in another, contact was minimal. Work with the final family was in collaboration with a protective agency who finally took total responsibility.

Throughout the entire project but especially during the last year, the project personnel worked very closely with community agencies. The final year's work was directed toward detailed sharing of our knowledge and experience with the families, in the process of transferring the families to community agencies.

As one would expect, the extent to which the families were able to use existing community agencies depended on the quality of their relationship to the project and the advances they had been able to make. An additional crucial factor was the problems of separation these families presented. (This is an area, however, that needs a special chapter devoted to its complexities.) The work in the last year of the project paid particular attention to separation issues. Those families where problems of separation were resolved sufficiently were able to make the best bridge to the community. Only follow-up, however, can determine precisely how regressive forces operated after the termination of the project.

CONCLUSION

Psychologically it would appear that although these mothers are so infantile, primitive, and disorganized that they seem no more advanced than their children, they have achieved some fragments of intact ego functioning, covering nearly every phase of development. There is evidence that some natural capacities can be developed and that these parents can move forward. It is possible to assist the mothers to realize some of their maternal aspirations. Their child-rearing practices can be modified. The universal wish to be a better mother does exist in these women in spite of the fact that it is not always apparent at first. The children's behavior can be modified in nursery school. The families can be helped to move toward greater socialization. Such a process of socialization requires active participation by the worker as a primary figure. The families do not need initial motivation for treatment, and intervention is possible without a crisis being present and without money being offered. Mutual involvement and the gradual establishment of trust in the worker are achieved through the worker's gratification of dependency needs, which need not lead to insatiable demands. During the period of testing the social worker gradually emerges as a constant object and a figure who establishes some order, and a priority of problems, in their chaotic lives. Through such a relationship there appears to develop some enhancement of self-esteem and some improvement in the management of household and children. The sequence of goals in the casework process can lead the parents to increasing involvement and more effective striving for a better life for themselves and their children.

Although in her work the worker assisted the family by active involvement in family life, she still needed full psychological understanding of the situation. For a long time this understanding was not employed through techniques such as clarification, interpretation, or insight but used primarily to avoid ever-present dangers. These dangers are psychological land mines of neurotic dependent needs of acting out and transference complications. The casework process did include further considerable education of the families, with the worker serving as a model by active demonstration, by precept, by discussion, and by imparting real knowledge. This educational role of the caseworker plays a more crucial part in the casework process with these families than with more highly motivated agency clients.

The involvement in a relationship to the worker was crucial in extending the process of socialization. The relationship became the bridge to the acceptance of other personnel and acceptance and involvement in the community of the project. The experience with the community of the project finally provided some of the essential ingredients for the families to reach the real community. The perception of and experience with the project personnel as an ideal extended family and the relationship to other families who were in fact elements of the community made this step possible.

This experience has been just one small attempt to deal with one segment of the impoverished population. There are still many gaps in our knowledge and there are many areas still requiring social work research. Continued research could give form and direction to social action. A number of questions merit more extensive study:

1. What likelihood is there that such families will maintain their improved functioning through present organized community channels once the worker and the project personnel are withdrawn?

2. What happens when families are assisted to move forward and discover that there has been little expansion of opportunity? Will we then have created a new category of problems?

3. How can the findings of this project and other recent investigations be used for planning new approaches and dealing with those areas of development that have responded most to this process?

4. Can the families' response to the project as a transitional

community be utilized to extend the socialization and education of these families to other group experiences?

5. What types of groups can provide avenues of enrichment for these families personally, educationally, and socially, and could such enrichment promote increased perception of themselves and their children as well as increased family communication?

6. How can the casework process and the techniques formulated in the experience of this project be refined and focused to achieve earlier involvement and problem solving with other multiproblem families, and with other families not necessarily identified as multiproblem but who are the target population of large-scaled programs? In brief, to what extent is the experience of this project generalizable?

7. If it is true that full psychological understanding and experience is necessary in working with these families, how can we reconcile this with the reality of a shortage of trained manpower and the pressing needs of great numbers of families? Are there ways, perhaps, of using consultation and supervision in a more imaginative and flexible fashion? And are there groups of untrained people who can be trained for specific tasks?

REFERENCES

1. Brandeis University Papers in Social Welfare No. 9: Education for Social Work with "Unmotivated" Clients. Institute Proceedings 1965, sponsored by the Florence Heller Graduate School for Advanced Studies in Social Welfare, Brandeis University, Waltham, Mass., and the Children's Bureau, Welfare Administration, U. S. Department of Health, Education, and Welfare.

2. Fantl, Bertha. Integrating Social and Psychological Theories in Social Work Practice. In Roger Miller (Ed.), *The Work of Bertha Fantl*. Smith College Studies in Social Work, June 1964.

3. Geismar, Ludwig, and Ayers, Beverly. *Measuring Family Functioning*. St. Paul, Minn. Family Centered Project, 1960.

4. Geismar, Ludwig, Ayers, Beverly, and Tinker, Katherine. *Patterns of Change in Problem Families*. St. Paul, Minn. Family Centered Project, 1959.

5. Henry, Charlotte S. Motivation in Non-Voluntary Clients. *Social Casework* 39:2, 1958.
6. Lidz, Theodore. *Schizophrenia and the Family*. New York: International Universities Press, 1966.
7. New York City Youth Board:
(a) Reaching the Un-reached. Fundamental Aspects of the Program of the New York City Youth Board, ed. by Sylvan S. Furman, 1952.
(b) Mrs. Mary Diamond, Director of Child Welfare. Reaching Out to Deprived Families, 1957.
8. Tinker, Katherine. *Patterns of Family Centered Treatment*. St. Paul, Family Centered Project, 1959.
9. Tinker, Katherine. *Let's Look at Our Failures*. St. Paul, Family Centered Project, 1957.
10. Wiltse, Kermit T. The "Hopeless" Family. *Journal of Social Work* 3:12, 1958.

BIBLIOGRAPHY

Related Material for
Chapters 10 and 11

Ackerman, Nathan W. *Psychodynamics of Family Life*. New York: Basic Books, 1958.

Ackerman, Nathan W., Beatman, Frances, and Sherman, Sanford (Eds.), Explaining the Base for Family Therapy. In *Papers from the M. Robert Gomberg Memorial Conference*. New York: Family Service Association of America, 1961.

Brim, Orville G., Jr. *Education for Child Rearing*. New York: Russell Sage Foundation, 1959.

Buell, Bradley, Beisser, Paul T., and Wedemeyer, John M. Reorganizing to Prevent and Control Disordered Behavior. *Mental Hygiene* 42:155-194, 1958.

Buell, Bradley, and Associates. *Community Planning for Human Services*. New York: Columbia University Press, 1952.

Erikson, Erik. Identity and the Life Cycle. *Psychological Issues,* Monograph 1. New York: International Universities Press, 1959.

Family Casework in the Interest of Children. *Social Casework* 34: Nos. 2, 3, 1958.

Gans, Herbert. *The Urban Villagers.* Glencoe, Ill.: Free Press, 1962.

Geismar, Ludwig L., and LaSorte, Michael A. *Understanding the Multi-Problem Family.* New York: Association Press, 1964.

Geismar, Ludwig, and Ayers, Beverly. *Families in Trouble* (mimeographed). St. Paul, Minn. Family Centered Project, 1958.

Hill, Reuben. *Families Under Stress.* New York: Harper, 1949.

Hollingshead, Augustus B., and Redlich, Frederick G. *Social Class and Mental Illness.* New York: Wiley, 1958.

Hunt, J. McVicker, and Kogan, Leonard S. *Measuring Results in Social Casework* (mimeographed). New York: Family Welfare Association of America, 1952.

Hurwitz, Jacob, Idelson, Roberta, Stone, Edward, and Zilback, Joan. *The Place in Darkness.* Unpublished ms. Boston: United Community Services, 1962, vol. 3, p. 621.

Kaufman, Irving M. S. Understanding the Dynamics of Parents with Character Disorders. *Casework Papers.* New York: National Conference of Social Welfare, Family Service Association of America, 1960, pp. 5-16.

Kaufman, Irving M. S., and Reiner, Beatrice. *Character Disorders in Parents of Delinquents.* New York: Family Service Association of America, 1959.

Keller, Suzanne. The Social World of the Urban Slum Child: Some Preliminary Findings. *American Journal of Orthopsychiatry* 33:823-832, 1963.

Kluckhohn, Florence. Variations in the Basic Values of Family Systems. *Social Casework* 39:63-72, 1958.

Kluckhohn, Florence, and Spiegel, John. *Integration and Conflict in Family Behavior.* Publication of Group for Advancement of Psychiatry. Bound volume report no. 27, August 1954.

Koos, Earl L. *Families in Trouble.* New York: King's Crown Press, 1942.

Lagen, Joseph C., and Ayers, Beverly. *Community Treatment Programs for Multi-Problem Families* (mimeographed paper). Vancouver Community Chest and Councils of the Greater Vancouver Area, December 1962.

Leitcher, Hope J. Kinship Values and Casework Intervention. *Casework Papers.* New York: National Conference on Social Welfare, Family Service Association of America, 1961, pp. 58-79.

Lindenberg, Ruth Ellen. Hard to Reach: Client or Casework Agency? *Journal of Social Work* 3:23-30, 1958.

Litz, Theodore. *The Family and Human Adaptation.* New York: International Universities Press, 1963, p. 113.

Overton, Alice. Serving Families Who Don't Want Help. *Social Casework* 34:304-309, 1953.

Overton, Alice, and Tinker, Katherine. *Casework Notebook* (mimeographed). St. Paul, Minn. Family Centered Project, 1957, p. 174.

Parsons, Talcott, and Bales, Robert. *Family Socialization and Interaction Process*. Glencoe, Ill.: Free Press, 1955.

Scherz, Francis H. Strengthening the Parental Role of Adults with Character Disorders. *Casework Papers*. New York: National Conference of Social Welfare, Family Service Association of America, 1960, pp. 16-31.

Scherz, Francis H. An Appraisal of Treatment Objectives in Casework Practice. *Casework Papers*. New York: National Conference of Social Welfare, Family Service Association of America, 1962, pp. 158-173.

Schlesinger, Benjamin. *The Multi-Problem Family: A Review and Annotated Bibliography*. Toronto: University of Toronto Press, 1963.

Willie, Charles V. *The Structure and Composition of "Problem" and "Stable" Families in Lower Income Population* (mimeographed paper). Youth Development Center, Syracuse University, 1962.

Wiltse, Kermit T. New Approaches to the Administration of A.D.C. Programs. *Casework Papers*. New York: National Conference on Social Welfare, Family Service Association of America, 1959, pp. 20-31.

Wiltse, Kermit T. Orthopsychiatric Programs for Socially Deprived Groups. *American Journal of Orthopsychiatry* 33:806-813, 1963.

IV

THE ENVIRONMENT

SOCIOCULTURAL PERSPECTIVES
ON THE NEIGHBORHOOD AND THE
FAMILIES

Maurice R. Stein

THE NORTH POINT AS NEIGHBORHOOD AND AS ASYLUM

Nᴏʀᴛʜ ᴘᴏɪɴᴛ is a neighborhood composed of quite distinct kinds of people who coexist in a fashion that has yet to be fully studied. The most visible group in the neighborhood are the bums, partly because their activities take place so frequently in doorways and on the street. The institutional complex which services the bums, and to a lesser degree the roominghouse dwellers, consists of the familiar arrangement of bars, liquor stores, pawn shops, missions, flophouses, old-clothes stores, whorehouses, and the like. The visibility of this complex is enhanced by the failure of the city to clean up its debris, so the broken bottles, Sterno cans, and other vestiges of widespread heavy drinking are all over the streets, doorways, and vacant spots between the apartment houses. The skid row where anyone can make out or eke out a minimum level of existence is an essential urban place. North Point has been the main area serving this purpose in this city for at least fifty years.

Urban renewers have already begun to attack the skid row and, in the process, the whole neighborhood is being changed. One wonders at the effects on the bums of the loss of their familiar territory, at the effects on them of having to move into a new territory probably somewhat further west and somewhat further south, and at the effects on the neighborhoods which receive them. Our study has to be confined to the effects on the life of a few families within a neighborhood that is both an area of ethnic lower-class settlement and also a skid row.

The total population of North Point was 34,133 in 1960, of which 20,095 persons were white, and most of the rest were Negro. The Casey Square area housed 2,167 persons and showed markedly higher indices of deterioration than most other parts of the neighborhood. While the streets which provide the boundaries of North Point for census purposes can be identified, field work in the neighborhood suggests that people living within it are quite vague about where it begins and where it ends. Kevin Lynch's excellent study *The Image of the City* (6) shows that non-North Pointers are as vague as residents of the neighborhood with respect to its boundaries, and indeed with respect to where the North Point is located in relation to the rest of the city. Though only a short distance from a wealthy business and residential area, the North Point remains peculiarly isolated and peculiarly indistinct.

This contrasts sharply with the Italian section, which has a profound sense of neighborhood identity, and which is generally clearly recognized as such by nonresidents. It also contrasts sharply with the kind of neighborhood feeling which the old West End used to manifest, if one can believe informants who lived there before an unfortunate urban-renewal program destroyed it. Though the West End did, and the Italian quarter still does, house people from ethnic backgrounds with relatively low incomes, neither has possessed the large visible settlement that has marked the North Point at least since 1890. Any effort at a comparative analysis of these neighborhoods would have to start with this differentiating feature of the North Point, the fact that it has provided asylum for unattached older men and for alcoholics.

The Italian quarter has been studied with great skill by William Foote Whyte, whose *Street Corner Society* (10), written in the early forties, provided the working conceptions of slum social organization for an entire generation of sociologists. Jane Jacobs in her *The Life and Death of the Great American Cities* (5), turned to this area as an illustrative contrast showing the vitality of an old ethnic "slum" compared with the homogenized housing developments erected by city planners and by urban renewers. The West

End was studied by Herbert Gans, whose book *The Urban Villages* (4) showed the existence of a working-class peer-group society with standards that stressed ongoing ties along familial and generational lines at the expense of upward mobility and competitive acquisition of commodities.

There is an important study of North Point written in 1898 by Robert Woods and associates, called *The City Wilderness* (11), which shows that the neighborhood was at that time already sheltering a large skid-row population. Woods, too, compared North Point with the Italian section: ". . . however cosmopolitan [North Point] may be, it is not so strikingly foreign in its population as the [Italian section] is. [North Point] people have, to some extent at least, become toned down and adapted to their environment through the influence of a longer residence in this country or a closer contact with American institutions." In the Italian section the immigrant has remained foreign because isolation is possible there. His associates are his own countrymen, his neighbors are immigrants from other countries, he does not become American for the simple reason that this area is not American. In the North Point the process of assimilation has advanced a step. *Although there still is a tendency for the nationalities to group themselves, extended isolation is no longer possible.* There is a more permanent tone to the life, the older immigrants have settled down in their American homes and their children know no other. *The sifting of the competent from the incompetent is still taking place, but future progress for the most part must be made by the children.* While the newly arrived immigrant manifests a certain amount of energy, *the chief ambition in a district like this is merely to keep from falling in the social scale; and the exertion put forth is often all too small to accomplish it.* The problem in the Italian section is "the problem of immigration to be solved at the ports of the United States. The problem at [North Point] is the internal social problem" (11).

It is no small testimony both to the analytic powers of the authors and to the stability of the neighborhoods that their general comments remain applicable to both Italian and North Point areas some sixty years later. The Italian section remains an integral ethnic neighborhood with special institutions and lifeways of its own, while the North Point remains an unintegrated combination of people who have more or less failed to establish their own lifeways or make peace with American lifeways. The chief ambition for most North Point residents remains to keep from falling further, though some are clearly at the bottom. In fact, the North Point is an asylum for people who no longer have any energy either to keep from falling or to rise. Where the racketeering in the Italian quarter has more or less been absorbed into the political and economic life of the community, in the North Point it seems to do very little for local residents other than relieve them of badly needed funds.

Coming to the neighborhood sixty years after Woods' study (11), we find it far less ethnically integrated and far more skid row dominated than he did. The Italian, Irish, and Jewish ghettos that he described have long since given way, and their more viable members have filtered upward and outward, leaving only the least capable behind in an atmosphere of failure. The Negroes who have moved in unfortunately exist in more economically and socially deprived conditions than the immigrants of earlier decades, and the fit between the lower-class Negro subculture and the skid-row system is too close for comfort. This entire situation, then, renders the hope that future progress can be made by the children even less promising than it may have been sixty years ago. But that is the premise upon which our study of multiproblem families has been based.

The North Point today is still a very complicated network of groups and social types in various states of existence. Our multiproblem families are almost by definition the people least capable of managing their own affairs or of utilizing those facilities that the neighborhood has to offer. Many of the adult white members of these families are children of people who failed to extricate themselves from this or similar neighborhoods in earlier decades. When we watch these multiproblem parents with their children, we perceive the myriad failures of mothering which prevent the children from developing the qualities of autonomy, identity, and self-control in which the parents are themselves deficient. These failures are reinforced in both parents and children by the general atmosphere of the neighborhood.

When Woods (11) studied the North Point, the skid row was definitely part of the environment. The neighborhood had changed from a prosperous residential area to a respectable rooming-house area and finally to a combination skid row and ethnic settlement by 1898. However, at that time, the ethnic settlements were recruiting ambitious Italians, Irish, and Jews as they came off the boats by offering them cheap rents, congenial neighbors, and accessible employment, as well as the social amenities of their traditional cultures. The tone of the neighborhood was set both by the bums and the ethnic settlements. Indeed, one gets the sense from Woods, as well as from Nels Anderson's book *Hobo* (1), written in the twenties, that American hobo culture has taken a sharp turn for the worse with the loss of its itinerant occupations and its mobility through the decline of rail travel. It is hard to imagine men that we have been interviewing in the North Point ever participating in a trade-union movement like the Wobblies or ever thinking of themselves as "knights of the road"; being on the skids in an affluent America in the sixties involves being in a subculture far less self-respecting than Woods and other sources suggest it was in earlier periods of American history. Hobo culture seems to have gone the way of other traditional ethnic or class subcultures in the face of the overwhelming power of the acquisitive ethic.

The atmosphere, as described by Woods, of a vital though sometimes deplorable neighborhood seems to have been maintained through the late thirties or early forties, if the memories of older residents and social workers can be trusted. During the Depression, being poor and being an immigrant were handicaps, but they were handicaps shared by many others. Even the neighborhood which provided asylum for the victims, the skid row, could participate in the general amnesty provided by the failure of the system. However, the trend over the last twenty years seems to have been one in which the immigrants who could get out did so, leaving behind only a hard core of tag-end families who could not get out. The bums became increasingly dominant, to the point where the main motifs in the neighborhood—empty bottles, men sleeping in doorways or staggering down the street, bars, liquor stores, pawn shops, flophouses, missions, whorehouses, and the like—overwhelm the signs of ethnic residence almost completely, except where the lower-class Negro institutions shade off into the institutions of skid row.

By 1960, when our project started, the North Point had lost

most of the glamour that neighborhoods like this sometimes retain. Though there are traces of a North Point mythology, including a Golden Age and mythological heroes who have gone on to do great things in politics, nobody except a few old-timers and a few settlement-house workers seem to take much of this very seriously. Even the ethnic groups which have stubbornly clung to the North Point as their areas of first settlement, like the Greeks and the Syrians, now regard the neighborhood as having always been pretty much of a skid row.

Of the North Point groups that I was able to gather information about, the Greeks approximated most closely the conditions of first-settlement ethnic living. The older Greeks consider the North Point and especially its border area with downtown as their neighborhood of origin. Several older Greeks have remained here despite the removal of their children to areas of second settlement in suburban areas. North Point Greeks are tied to friends and relatives in the suburbs very closely with much mutual visiting. One can find among them many of the familiar conflicts between the generations that characterize other first areas of settlement. I suspect that the Syrians have, in general, been less economically successful but that they are much like the Greeks in general social characteristics.

We know about another group of families who lived in the North Point from the files of the child-development study (7). These families were sufficiently organized both to pay a fee for medical care and to get their children to the hospitals for appointments, achievements which seem small in themselves, but which remain considerably beyond the range of our multiproblem families. It is interesting to notice that 70 percent of this group of families selected only a few years ago has now moved itself out of the North Point into the suburbs.

In the summer of 1961 a research assistant studied a few "better-adjusted" families in the neighborhood to provide background for viewing the multiproblem families. He selected families who were regarded as exceptional by the director of a local housing project. They were, with one exception, not as exceptional as the child-development study families, if ability to move out of the neighborhood is the measure. I will paraphrase some comments on these families which compare them with multiproblem families as a way of introducing the latter. This will also introduce my interpretive framework, which depends heavily on tracing analogies between skid row patterns and multiproblem family patterns.

We noticed that the "adjusted" families differed from the multiproblem families in that they were able to organize their lives along lines quite familiar to middle-class people. For example, the mothers in these families had a time sense which permitted them to arrange household duties in an orderly fashion, while the fathers had a time sense that involved plans for ongoing work as well as realizable plans for future job betterment. In addition, both parents and the growing children all talked about and thought about the futures open to the children in pleasurable and realistic terms. Even though these families did not necessarily plan to leave the North Point immediately, or indeed at any time, this possibility was one they considered. Both parents and children moved in a wide orbit in the neighborhood, drawing distinctions between regions dominated by bums and respectable regions, though they felt free to move through both when necessary. In addition, they moved around the city quite freely, having frequent contacts elsewhere with relatives and with friends.

Our multiproblem families tended to stay within limited orbits in the neighborhood. They rarely, if ever, traveled to the city or the suburbs and then only with considerable discomfort. The rhythms of housekeeping among our families were marked by haphazard activity, tasks being accomplished, when they were accomplished at all, almost whenever they were noticed. This included child care, often to the great detriment of the children. The multiproblem families showed a minimal ability to plan ahead, living very largely in an uncomfortable present, against the background of a shifting but profoundly denigrated past and in the light of a dark future which could contain, at best, simply more of the same.

In these several respects the multiproblem families seem more like the skid-row dwellers than like either North Point model families or families from working, lower or middle-class America. The rhythm of life on skid row arranges itself haphazardly around the central activity of obtaining, consuming, and sleeping off the effects of wine and whiskey. The panhandling and petty thievery or the occasional odd jobs through which money is obtained are utterly irregular and the bum takes his chances as they come.

There is little planning either of the day's activity or of any larger time span. One sleeps pretty much where one falls as long as it is fairly safe and one cares for one's self when urgent needs press, but none of this activity is aimed at changing one's social position or one's social presentation.

The integration between skid-row activities and the activities of our multiproblem families is accomplished through the bars where they meet, as well as on the streets and in the tenements they share. Almost every one of the families, except the Negroes, have backgrounds of heavy drinking.

The model families carefully distinguish their social position from that of the bums, and teach their children to do so. Our multiproblem families tend to shade off into the circle constituted by the bums and draw only minimally effective boundary lines. Even among the unmarried mothers, attitudes differ. A white mother, Mrs. B., has a complex typology allowing her to relate to bums in a friendly or a hostile way, depending upon their demands upon her, the stage of their alcoholism, and several other factors. A Negro mother, Mrs. Barry, refers to the Negroes living closer than she does to the center of skid row as being poor unfortunates because they have to contend with the bums whereas she has to deal only with dope pushers and prostitutes. But neither unmarried mother views herself as standing entirely apart from the community of the bums, despite their varying degrees of contempt and their slight effort at maintaining distance. Somehow the bums and the multiproblem families share a sense of being themselves together at the bottom of the society.

Any effort at investigating alcohol addiction must take in the stylization of drinking along age, sex, class, and ethnic lines. There are also several distinct drinking subcultures, ranging from the cocktail set to skid row. Research seems to show that skid-row drinkers are often men who suffer from severely unresolved dependency needs which they try to resolve or dissolve through alcoholism, which allows them to avoid independent economic or familial roles while focusing their dependency on the bottle as a substitute object and on their drinking companions if they are social drinkers. Skid-row bums often yearn for primary relationships and indeed sentimentalize the marriages which create so much tension for them. They find beyond their capacities the sustained performance demands and organized self-presentations which economic roles and other secondary relationships require. They share this latter problem with multiproblem fathers.

The themes which Ralph Conner identified in his article "The Self Concepts of Alcoholics," which appears in the useful symposium volume *Society, Culture and Drinking Patterns* (3), confirm my impressions. He reports two such themes:

The first . . . is the primary relationship aspect, the pronounced emphasis the alcoholic places on primary relationship terms when he undertakes to describe himself. . . . The second major theme . . . is . . . a generalized lack of organization and integration of the self which is manifested by, and includes, the other three aspects of the alcoholics' self-description we have discussed—the lack of homogeneity and extensiveness, the absence of secondary relationship terms, and the use of terms characteristic of neurosis.

This analysis proceeds:

. . . justification for the alcoholic's emphasis on primary-relationship qualities must reside in the alcoholic's felt need for such relationships, in the sense of isolation from their warmth and gratification. We should expect this since the early impact of excessive drinking will be almost completely in the area of primary relationships and will consist of the alienation or deterioration of primary group satisfaction and support from essential sources. In the absence of such support for the self there can be no question but that the individual will experience greater difficulty in the management of remote, formalized and demanding secondary relationships which embody so much of the apprehension and stress of our culture. This difficulty produces greater stress, and correspondingly greater need for primary group supports.

My own observations of alcoholics in the North Point support Conner's observations about the profound lack of self-organization and differentiation among them. Their difficulties in relationships where distance must be maintained and self-presentations organized leads them to retreat into an impulsive search for oral gratification through alcohol, with the concomitant release of guilt and release from demands for further formal or differentiated interaction which the company of alcoholics proffers. I did, however, discover during several periods of observation and interviewing in

North Point a series of loosely connected self-constellations or role patterns among the alcoholics. These constellations and patterns also appear among our multiproblem families.

This phenomenon came to my attention when I found the same informant telling me two or more contradictory stories of his life, each told with the same degree of conviction and all told within a short period of time. After this happened several times with alcoholics and a few times with members of multiproblem families, I began to try to conceptualize the alternatives. Among alcoholics, the possible images run from that of the Total Failure, through that of the Temporary Victim coupled with that of the Prospective Reformee, and finally to that of the Militant Bum.

The Total Failure image-constellation is marked by self-pity and pleas for sympathy from the listener. It is useful for panhandling and centers around themes of opportunity missed due to weakness, of friends betrayed, and of families abandoned. The present is dismal and the future even worse. The Temporary Victim-Prospective Reformee constellation is more active in tone than the Total Failure and less self-pitying, with greater blame placed on others, on bad luck, or on the society. This constellation is probably useful for encouraging mission workers or welfare workers who need to feel that their efforts are not in vain. The themes here stress temporary residence on skid row due to unfortunate circumstances which can easily be reversed by a little encouragement, good luck, and effort. The person is simply biding his time until he kicks the habit and leaves the North Point forever, to go onward and upward to assume the social position that he rightfully deserves. Finally, there is the Militant Bum image-constellation. This is hard to elicit and seems more likely to appear when bums talk with each other than when they talk with an outsider. It looks like a vestige of the old Knights of the Road routine without the full-blown self-acceptance that this seems to have involved. This image affirms the skid-row world as the center of genuineness and friendliness, denigrates middle-class phoniness and coldness, and affirms the North Point as a place to be. Outsiders are assumed to be "squares," "suckers," and "crooks." On the other hand, big-time crooks like the Brinks robbers are local heroes, at least until they are caught.

These three image-constellations, the Total Failure, the Temporary Victim-Prospective Reformee, and the Militant Bum, constitute a gamut of rationales which serve the purpose of motivating activity within skid row. I am certain that other images could be identified, but I am more interested in their multiplicity and their mode of coexisting within the self-conception than I am in the substantive details. In formal terms the three represent rather different stances toward the larger society. The first accepts the norms of larger society, concedes one's degradation in terms of them, and offers no promise of reform; the second accepts the norms of the larger society, concedes one's misfortune in terms of them, and offers a promise of reform; while the third attacks the norms of the larger society, proclaims one's failure to conform to them, and denies any intention of change. One can easily see how they might conform to various moods in which an alcoholic could find himself and they probably have some sort of cyclic interrelationship. My impression is, however, that they are three ways of responding to the stigma of being an alcoholic, and they can be evoked by moods or by circumstances. They have obvious adaptive relationships to the several social systems with which the alcoholic has dealings. Thus middle-class contacts like welfare workers might prefer the Temporary Victim-Prospective Reformee routine, criminal contacts might prefer the Militant Bum presentation, and family or friends might let one off easier as a Total Failure.

The oscillation between these images or identities constitutes the social-psychological orbit of the bums. Self-esteem is maintained, though precariously, by refusing to commit oneself to any one of the three identities, leaving oneself open to shift to an alternative when a given image is threatened. To the outside observer there is a terrible hopelessness about these identity games. They all involve a moral career in which the acceptance of stigmatized activities and the avoidance of socially valued activities remains central. Once a person has begun to oscillate within an orbit of alcoholic identities, his capacity to control his presentations diminishes. Physical deterioration, due as much to the exigencies of skid-row living, eating, and sleeping as to the physiological effects of alcohol, takes its toll. The circle is indeed vicious, as the victim cannot get out. Only Alcoholics Anonymous seems to have much success breaking into it. Insofar as our families may be caught in analogous vicious circles, we might explore AA techniques for leads.

Another group in the neighborhood which contributes its share to the general atmosphere of futility and failure is the group of older roomers who remain in the North Point because it offers cheap rooms, privacy, and undemanding companionship. I know very little about the roomers; many appear, however, to be poor and aging. Being unemployed and unwanted seems as likely to deteriorate faculties as does alcohol. Again, there are older people like the Greek patriarchs who do not meet this description. Even within the rooming-house complex, arrangements like the semi-respectable Old Men's Tavern undoubtedly occur more often than can easily be detected. Still, older people in this neighborhood are not likely to be overjoyed with their situation and they do tend to contribute to the atmosphere of hopeless waiting which the bums generate. Their conversation, even among the more privileged as in the Tavern, consists largely of symbolic acknowledgement of each other's existence and one cannot escape the impression that this ritualized talk reflects relatively low degrees of individuation.

MULTIPROBLEM FAMILIES WITHIN THE NEIGHBORHOOD AND WITHIN THE ASYLUM

The first portion of this chapter shows the coexistence within the North Point of two general categories of people. The first would include all of the "respectable" elements, including the Greeks and Syrians who remain ethnically integrated, of whose upwardly mobile families the child development study's subjects (7) were a sample, the older roomers who use the Old Men's Tavern, the model families, a group of upper-middle-class Negroes clustering around Circle Park, and many other persons not covered by my survey. All these people live within the context of an ethnic, a working-class, a lower-class, or a middle-class set of traditions. They all establish minimally respectable styles of life, extending from their ability to hold jobs, through the ways in which they raise their children, to their knowledge about and calculated distance from the "nonrespectables" who predominate in the North Point. These people might be said to live in the North Point as people ordinarily live in a disadvantaged neighborhood. They make the best of the facilities available, they make plans to leave when possible, and they certainly try to raise their children in such a way as to allow some hope that the next generation will have greater opportunities than they did.

The second category in the North Point are the people who live in it as one lives in an asylum, and, in fact, as one lives in an asylum from which there is no release. My objective in the first part of this chapter was to establish the terms on which the most deprived inmates, the alcoholics, set the tone for other inmates. In this section, I will try to show how the multiproblem families respond to this tone and adapt their affairs to life within the asylum that is the North Point.

Our multiproblem families are distinguished by the fact that they are all unable to establish working relationships with ordinary agencies in the neighborhood. Indeed, we selected them because they had run into serious difficulties and because they appeared to be "unreachable." In addition, of course, they all had children under 5 years of age. Ordinary agencies are set up to work with a broad spectrum of families. They seem most effective with upwardly mobile working- or lower-class clients simply because such clients can understand and appreciate the value of the services offered, even if the services and the people offering them come from an alien class. Our families lacked the minimum elements of internal organization and motivation to allow them to enter into ordinary client roles with standard agencies. They could not make arrangements to take their children to nursery school, they were not able to separate themselves from the children or vice versa to the degree necessary to make attendance at nursery school possible, and the children were either too impulsive or too passive to participate with reasonably well-socialized children in nursery school activities.

On looking further into these families, we discover several other shared social characteristics. None of the adult males, in those families that have an adult male regularly present, are working at jobs with any promise of upward mobility. Only a few have anything like a consistent work record. The unmarried mothers are not likely ever to become married mothers simply because there are no unmarried fathers in the appropriate category who can earn anything like the amount of money these mothers need to support themselves and their children. The families, for the most part, have no plans to leave the neighborhood, nor could they sustain the demands for organized living which a better neighborhood would necessarily impose. They have all received considerable public assistance in various forms, as did their parents before them, and as will their children after them unless the vicious circle is somehow broken.

But these are all rather obvious characteristics almost implicit in the term *multiproblem family*. The primary social-psychological characteristic that appeared during the course of our study is the enormous confusion in each family about the differences between adults and children. This can be documented ad infinitum from the record and undoubtedly will be in the psychological reports. All of our adults show persisting failure to exercise self-restraint or self-discipline at crucial points when their own anxieties are aroused while dealing with their children. In fact, none of them seem capable of consistently recognizing any specific set of childish capacities or needs to which they must respond.

To the nonsociologist, the last observation may not seem as shocking as it actually appears to be to anyone trained in the study of comparative cultures. The literature on multiproblem families keeps trying to force these families within lower-class culture or working-class culture, or one or another ethnic culture, not to mention a bizarre recent invention called "the culture of poverty." This is the major sociological interpretive strategy adopted in *The Multi-Problem Family*, edited by Schlesinger and others (8). The alternative to locating these families within a substantive subculture is to call them "retreatists" and therefore give them credit for being in flight from the dominant culture.

My own experience with the project families has been one of finding myself regularly forced to concede the irrelevance of the cultural background in patterning significant behavior around crucial issues. It characteristically makes little difference whether the families are Irish, Italian, Negro, or mixed in origin where child rearing is concerned. The distinguishing feature in each instance is the absence of a pattern which might intrude between parental impulses or fantasies and parental behavior to govern the actions that the parent takes toward the child. Rather than a culture of poverty, we seem to have here an acute poverty of culture.

And this seems to hold in all areas, especially those which involve impulse control or delayed gratification.

My first impression, recorded in my first progress report, was that we were watching "families of children" in action. You could hardly distinguish the adults from the children except for the fact that the former were taller. Parents seemed to lack sufficient self-definition and role-playing ability to keep in mind the fact that children are undifferentiated, impulsive beings who have to be nursed and coerced into differentiated growth. This latter capacity is the bare irreducible minimum for child rearing in any culture, regardless of how widely definitions of adult responsibilities and childish faculties might vary. One has the feeling that these parents were never allowed to be children by their own parents, and that they in turn cannot afford to allow or acknowledge, not to mention appreciate, childishness in their children.

The multiproblem families display the same kinds of oscillating identity themes as do the alcoholics. Though both groups quickly are identified by the world at large according to their respective objective categories, both groups resist this identifying process by operating in terms of a set of mutually contradictory identity themes among which they oscillate. It is as if they somehow escape awareness of their objective situation by refusing to develop sufficient self-coherence to be able to recognize it for very long. The several self-constellations or subidentities with which these people operate must remain disconnected from each other or their capacity to facilitate evasion of responsibility and commitment would be diminished.

The multiproblem adults actually struggle with at least two of the same image-constellations as do the alcoholics. They certainly have the tendency to see themselves as Total Failures at various points, and they have the tendency to see themselves as Temporary Victims and Prospective Reformees at others. They present and feel the former when they want sympathy, while they present the latter when they want to convince agency workers that they are doing their best. But far more central to the multiproblem adults is their repertory of familial subidentities.

If we turn to our Negro unmarried mothers, I think we can begin to trace the disparate self-constellations in each mother. Maternal self-conceptions can differ with different children, which suggests the concrete component as against the component of cultural patterning.

Mrs. Barry is a woman whose impulsive aggression toward her oldest son took such violent form that the neighbors finally intervened and forced her to give the child up. Yet she retained an identity as a considerate mother, despite her occasional violent hostility to her younger children. She has pretty much given up any serious effort at maintaining a middle-class façade either through the furnishings or the orderliness of her household. During a single sociological interview, she manifested various subidentities, including the Abused Wife, the Vengeful Wife, the Good Pick-up, the Tough Pick-up, the Good Mother, the Tough Mother, the Good Negress, and the Bad Negress.

She probably treats the children differently in all these roles and shifts from one to the other with what must be confusing rapidity for the children. In her world picture, she appears to have made her way through a jungle. She is very much involved in the war between women and men. She fought her husband so hard that she drove him completely out of the house and out of her life. Her recent reconciliation with her daughter and apparent improvement in rearing a young male child seem susceptible to reversal. Her inclination is to seek total control over others by force, as she must have herself felt totally controlled and totally victimized in the past.

Mrs. Cook is another story but with related themes. She has experienced good mothering and also severe deprivation as well as loss. She is caught, too, with a split between an Adult-Parental self and an Adolescent self. This latter, in light of her age, seems somehow appropriate in the abstract if not in the concrete. Her capacity to find men is not quite as distorted by aggression as is Mrs. Barry's. She does, however, react inappropriately to the demands of her children, however much justification there might be. She is torn about her Negro identity because she is lighter and could pass. The case work record lends itself to an interpretation which sees her as having a split between a White Good self and a Black Bad self. I would expect that the gamut of identities, from Total Failure to Total Victim and Prospective Reformee to Militant Bum, appear in her presentations.

Since this report cannot attempt an inventory of all the families, or even of any one, I will skip over the detailed issues raised by Mrs. Barry and Mrs. Cook and will also abstain from introducing either Mrs. Zaylor or Mrs. Barry's friend T., both of whom raise very interesting questions about the varieties of adaptation open to Negro mothers. Mrs. Zaylor's recent arrival and her immersion in an extended kin group distinguish her, while T.'s marriage and her membership in an old North Point family make her peculiarly interesting. These unmarried mothers (and T.) constitute our most homogeneous grouping.

Returning to the analysis of identity among our families, let me state another version of the same hypothesis. For many converging reasons, members of multiproblem families are people who have never been able to or have never been allowed to develop a consistent sense of self or identity and have developed instead a plurality of inconsistent identities which adapt them to differing elements and differing social systems within the skid-row complex. However, it would be a mistake to assume that they really adapt; instead the shifting identity structure allows them to adapt to being maladapted. If it weren't too much of a paradox, I would say our families are addicted to multiple problems, or even that they are addicted to parenthood almost the way alcoholics are addicted to alcohol. The alcoholics who cannot sustain secondary relationships, and who are ambivalent about primary ties to the point where they can't form families, achieve ultimately self-defeating substitutes in the bottle group and the bottle. Our adults are only slightly more capable of managing secondary relationships and slightly more able to sustain primary ties. They are able to bear children physically, but they cannot bear the emotional responsibilities that being parents to children presupposes. Yet once they bear children, they become addicted to them, and, like any addict, spend their lives hating and craving the objects to which they have become compulsively attached. I do not refer here only to the fact that parenthood makes them more like the middle-class world, though this is indeed involved. After all, they may not have husbands, but they do have children, which makes them significantly more like middle-class people than unmarried women who have neither husbands nor children, or than bums who have nobody.

However, the crux of the matter lies elsewhere. Limits on the extent to which one can act out a series of internal psychodramas with other adults are imposed by the capacity of the adults to withdraw. Thus, Mrs. Barry's husband obviously could not take the punishment, but Ursula and now Luke and Betty have much less choice for the moment. Mrs. Bailey was able to project her good and bad selves onto her daughters with occasional rotation and can act out on her son, again without much interference, her ambivalence toward her father, toward Lem, and toward men in general. Or take Mr. Rossi, who has seven characters with whom to work out his fantasies. Poor Mrs. Rossi can't do much of this, because she is kept too busy getting through the day, but I suppose she can console herself that her day is somehow better spent than the day of her alcoholic mother or her unmarried but childbearing friends.

What being in a neighborhood means in terms of identity differs from ethnic group to ethnic group, and I am certain there is variation within each group. The point to be understood, however, is that there is a necessity for coping with the collective sense of inferiority which the larger community imposes on the North Point and which the residents react to in various ways. My impression is that more integrated families acknowledge the undesirability of the neighborhood and remain on their own terms or plan to leave.

How can we differentiate the multiproblem families from other types of disturbed families in modern society? The most simple answer in my terms would simply be that any family that can't distinguish between children and adult falls into our category. But Seeley's study reminds us that his suburban mothers are exploitative, and his evidence must be dealt with (9). In addition, I am certain that the Greek mothers, and most mothers for that matter, are exploitative in some ways.

The difference obviously doesn't lie in any verbal capacity to distinguish between children and adults. Under pressure, even Mrs. Cook can present herself as a good middle-class mother. There are flaws, of course, in the verbal presentation and in the accompanying behavior, but I am certain a careful observer in a typically neurotic suburban household would pick up similar disparities between verbal statements and actual behavior.

At one point I suggested that our adults and the children too can be viewed as existing in relatively undifferentiated plural self-other transactional fields; in this case a whole set of such fields often consolidated at quite different times in their lives. This is one meaning of the impression that they are families of children. Each adult still carried with him or her a set of childish selves which can attach themselves utterly inappropriately to human objects in their immediate vicinity. Thus Mr. Rossi can become a sibling to his son, a lover to his daughter, and even, I suspect, a son to his daughter under certain circumstances. After all, she does bring home the milk from the store.

Those of us with a minimum of psychoanalytic sophistication know that this happens in ordinary families, but the point is that it remains largely on the plane of suppressed fantasy with only a minimum of behavioral expression. Among our families, I think that the balance between suppression and expression is reversed more often than not. In the middle-class family where fantasies of this sort are suppressed or repressed, the child responds unconsciously perhaps, but is able to make sufficient progress in ego development to defend himself against the fantasies, to suppress his own counter fantasies, and finally to accomplish the tasks of autonomy and individuation. If anything, this would seem likely to drive him to neurotic overindividuation, which is, I think, the characteristic condition of most middle-class Americans. The reciprocal trait of underdifferentiation is obviously also present, so that what we really have in middle-class life is the existence of pseudoindividualists who understand neither how they are connected with others nor how they are distinct from them at deeper levels, but who manage to control their role playing to maintain the impression of individuality.

This whole question of autonomy and individuality highlights the difference between our families and suburban families. I think that we can safely acknowledge that, despite all the focus on status, the failure to permit real identity struggles due to the enforced split between the idealized values and the operative values, and the resulting manipulative orientations uncovered in suburbia, the compensations there are greater than the compensations in North Point. The middle-class normal-neurotic is haunted by unresolved childish emotions, but he is able to hold these ghosts in place or discharge them vicariously through entertainment through a double life, or perhaps through psychoanalysis. Despite reservations about the quality of the adjustment which is typically achieved, it probably makes possible more real satisfactions than the plural self-constellations which the alcoholic or the multiproblem adult require to keep going in their situations. At least the suburbanite has the illusion and even occasionally the real experience of partially shaping his own destiny. He may live in a hypocritical world which is moved by forces outside his control and beyond his understanding, but he can still detach himself and reattach himself within the range of alternative subworlds available, in order to experience some autonomy and perhaps achieve some individuality.

To understand the plural self-constellations of the alcoholics and of the North Pointers which I outlined at the beginning, as well as their use of this psychic pluralism to avoid psychic destruction in crises, a helpful analogy is found in the concentration camp. Bettelheim, in *The Informed Heart* (2) provides us with a detailed case where the strategy of plural selves was adopted deliberately to permit continued existence in an impossible situation. He describes the way in which he undertook, within the concentration camp, to construct a new self-image, congruent with his pre-Nazi occupational experience as a psychoanalytic sociologist. He consciously created an observing-and-recording self which got real satisfaction from learning about and anticipating concentration camp structures and brutalities in order to prevent his victim-self, which was being objectively degraded, from being swept away into oblivion. He was fighting for physical and psychic existence in a setting that was inconceivably destructive to both.

Now the North Point is hardly a concentration camp, nor are our families sophisticated intellectuals like Bruno Bettelheim. But our families do manifest a form of self-splitting which parallels Bettelheim in certain respects just as it parallels the suburban self-split in others. The issue for us is to try to understand the different strategies of self-maintenance appearing in the various families as well as the strategies that they share. My aim in this chapter has been to seek a general descriptive picture of the plural self-system of the alcoholics and of the parallel plural self-system of our families.

The multiproblem families, then, are not simply families with a few more problems than ordinary families, nor, if this interpretation is correct, are they simply dwellers within lower-class culture or within a culture of poverty. Instead, they appear to be persons who have had forced upon them extreme dissociations reaching into the depths of their personalities and reinforced by the haphazard skid-row social system of which they are a part. One might speculate that similarities between children in our families and institutionally reared children arise because our mothers are no more able to create a reassuring and reactive maternal matrix than are the attendants in institutions. And, for families like ours, the North Point remains a sort of asylum in which the effects of inadequate mothering in the form of failures in psychic development are rendered less devastating by the dissociated functioning characterizing adult roles and identities.

The social patterns seem so ingrained that at times one wonders whether any sort of psychiatric or social work effort has ever or will ever significantly alter the modes of cultural and social functioning manifested by families who have been "victimized" by their society in the fashion described earlier. It is more likely that the "therapeutic" agents will themselves simply be absorbed within the plural self-systems.

REFERENCES

1. Anderson, Nels. *Hobo: The Sociology of the Homeless Man* (1923). Chicago: University of Chicago Press, 1961.
2. Bettelheim, Bruno. *The Informed Heart.* Glencoe, Ill.: Free Press, 1960.
3. Conner, Ralph. The Self-Concepts of Alcoholics. In Pitman, David J., and Snyder, Charles R., *Society, Culture and Drinking Patterns.* New York: Wiley, 1962.
4. Gans, Herbert. *The Urban Villagers.* Glencoe, Ill.: Free Press, 1962.
5. Jacobs, Jane. *The Life and Death of the Great American Cities.* New York: Random House, 1961.
6. Lynch, Kevin. *The Image of the City.* Cambridge: Massachusetts Institute of Technology and Harvard University Press, 1960.
7. Pavenstedt, Eleanor. A Comparison of the Child-rearing Environment of Upper-Lower and Very Low-Lower Class Families. *American Journal of Orthopsychiatry* 35:89, 1965.
8. Schlesinger, Benjamin (Ed.). *The Multi-Problem Family.* Toronto: University of Toronto Press, 1963.

9. Seeley, John, *et al.*   *Crestwood Heights.* New York: Basic Books, 1956.
10. Whyte, William Foote.   *Street Corner Society.* Chicago: University of Chicago Press, 1943.
11. Woods, Robert.   *The City Wilderness.* Boston: Houghton Mifflin, 1898.

V

THE PROBLEM OF ASSESSMENT OF CHANGE

REVIEW OF FINDINGS AND RECOMMENDATIONS

Eleanor Pavenstedt

OUR REASONS FOR UNDERTAKING THE NORTH POINT PROJECT

THE NORTH POINT PROJECT was undertaken as an attempt to break into the repetitive cycle of disorganization, deprivation, and alienation involving successive generations of hard-core families, by bringing certain new experiences, considered essential for normal development, to bear upon their very young children. In order to reach the children and to reduce or modify the differences between the milieu of the project nursery school and that of their homes, it was deemed necessary to bring into their homes thoughtfully conceived casework, adapted to the special characteristics and requirements of these crisis-ridden families.

The project was based on the concept of action-research. In order to meet the specific needs of these families and their children we had to explore their personality structures, their developmental retardations, deviancies, and precocities, their patterns of dealing with people, the degree of their intrafamilial communication, their values, their inconsistencies. The family structure and functioning, particularly as a child-rearing environment, were under constant scrutiny. Pure research would not have been tolerated by this group. The skill of diligent observation, acquired by most of the staff in the course of clinical training or in previous collaboration with clinicians, was focused on all of the above-mentioned areas. Their reports were assessed and analyzed by the staff as a whole or in supervisory or consultative sessions. Considerable time was devoted to seeing more clearly, to reaching tentative formulations, and to confirming their accuracy in the home or nursery school. Programming of the work with the families and with the children was based, at each step, on the conceptualizations arrived at. The keenness of the observations and the implementation of the concepts were, to a considerable extent, of course, dependent on the empathy and inventiveness of the individual staff workers.

The preceding chapters have given full recognition to all these areas: observations; theoretical formulations, sometimes daring but always based on meticulous, thoughtful probing; and the actual work with the children and the families. Progress and limits to advancement have been set forth as each writer perceived them. Did we succeed in the overall goal of the project? Did we break into the repetitive cycle? Will the children who attended our nursery school—at least those who attended regularly for two years—make a more self-respecting, satisfying place for themselves, *within* our society?

At the present time these questions must remain unanswered. Despite our intensive involvement with the entire family, the children continued to be overwhelmed by the slightest threat to their security or competence. This basic instability was sufficient evidence that more fundamental environmental changes were required. Even after the parents had been helped to recognize their parental obligation, they were still at times prey to their own impulses and at such moments prone to uncontrolled, inconsistent, and unfocused behavior. Although more aware of their children's requirements, they were still struggling to have their most basic needs met. Despite a recent change to greater flexibility in the dispensation of welfare funds, these are far from adequate. The attitude of the population at large is still one of moral opprobrium toward recipients of relief. The truly nurturing climate in which children flourish can hardly be provided for them under the present impoverished living conditions in our urban slums.

The schools for which the children left us at the tender age of 5 had as yet made few adaptations to their specific inadequacies of which the educators were only becoming aware. Even if the children have been able to manage the first grade or two, their "rigidly concrete psycho-cognitive styles" (3) may curtail their later career at school. We do not know whether they will reach the stage of conceptualization and abstraction required—so we are told—for jobs in modern industry. They may have to compete for manual jobs with the educable mentally retarded, who progress through the lower grades. However, the bold statements, made as recently as one year ago, that these jobs would employ only 10 percent of the population, are being questioned (6).

It is possible that the 3- and 4-year-olds in the project experienced a sufficient degree of comfort from being accepted, protected, and supported to have stored it away in their memory as something that exists and is available somewhere and it is possible that they will seek it out. Sufficient curiosity and initiative may have been freed so that it can be revived in situations that are not too fraught with anxiety. Having had, during such an important moment of their lives, constructively active people to imitate, these imitative identifications may remain with them and be stimulated afresh in an auspicious setting. The urge to reexperience pleasure may serve as an incentive to action as well. Above all, their familiarity with a relationship to another human being, even though they remained the dependent partner, may add a vital dimension to their lives.

The project reported in this book was exploratory and should be followed up with testing of our theoretical propositions and clinical findings. The multiple-problem group presents multiple problems to researchers as well. The difficulty in gaining their collaboration leads to failures in adhering to schedules—it was impossible to impose a nursery school schedule according to which the children would begin at the same age, attend regularly and for the same length of time. This eliminated the possibility of making comparative assessments of change, except for each child individually. The same was true for psychological testing where absences or resistance made retests impossible, and anxiety and the need to manipulate the tester, when a child did come, interfered with the procedure. Future researchers, forewarned of the problems they may encounter, may be able to overcome them.

To attempt to even guess at outcome, where so many unknown

variables are involved, is fruitless. Let us rather turn now to a discussion of the important findings that have implications for immediate action.

OUR FINDINGS AND THEIR IMPLICATIONS

In Terms of the Children.   Throughout this book mention has been made, at various points, of a longitudinal study of development, from birth to age 6, of first-born children of stable working-class families.* It was fortuitous that our interests led us to undertake this study simultaneously with the North Point Project, because it permitted a comparison of the two categories of child-rearing environments and of the children's development at 3, 4, and 5 (4). In the course of both projects staff members with identical disciplinary backgrounds made repeated house visits, so that observations of the home environments are eminently comparable. (Three staff members worked with both groups of families and children.) The fact that many of the young working-class families lived in or adjacent to the North Point skid-row area has already been reported.

The contrast between (1) the child-rearing environments of these two groups, (2) the developmental levels of the children between 3 and 6, (3) the adjustment of both groups to school, and (4) the adaptation of both groups of parents to employment reveals extremes in each of these dimensions. Of great interest is a dissimilarity between the developmental levels of children living in the same neighborhood. Whereas the children in the stable working-class study by and large fell within the expected norms, the North Point Project children showed striking retardations and deviancies. There is an equally striking disparity in the two groups as regards child rearing.

Since the children from the upper end of the poverty group do well in first grade without any intervention, and many children at the lower end do not do well in school even with enrichment, clearer distinguishing of these two divergent groups has critical

* Supported by N.I.M.H. grant #M898, 1955-1960, and N.A.M.H. grant #5-925-00-561, 1961-1966.

importance for programming for the low socioeconomic group of children. Furthermore the continuum between the two extremes contains many unknowns. *Most programs of special preschool education or enrichment for "poor" children do not specify where on this continuum their subjects are. Therefore the evaluation of the results of these programs remains in doubt.*

Educational and preventive programs will lack specificity unless their subjects are diagnosed as belonging at one or the other end of this range or to some group in between. Educational programs and techniques are in danger of being discarded prematurely, without adequate reason, because they fail with children coming from a stratum on the low economic continuum where therapeutically oriented work must accompany any form of special educational help. Other programs and techniques may be considered successful when the children would have done well in any case.

We need an exhaustive study of the entire poverty group to ascertain whether the children are on a continuum from the normal developmental patterns of the stable working-class group to the retarded and deviant development of the disorganized family group; or whether there exist between these two poles subgroups, each with its own constellation of retardations, fixations, and deviancies, its own areas of normal and precocious development. Such distinctions would provide leads for the timing, the character, and the duration of intervention strategies. Where precocious organization interferes with reorganization, as seen in many of the project children, we may have to find ways of adapting them to our society rather than attempting to remedy their rigidly fixed modes of operation.

An effort is being made with schools, through Operation Counterpoise, to meet the educational needs of the poor by lowering the teacher-child ratio—a little—by providing the school with team leaders, a tester, and a counselor, and when necessary by doubling the child's stay in a class by inserting an intermediary grade (pre-first grade, pre-second grade, and so on). We cannot emphasize enough that the standard intelligence tests, while they are predictive of the children's functioning in school, fail to identify the component difficulties we have identified, namely, the energy diverted from learning to self-protection, the defensive not hearing, not seeing, not knowing, their self-devaluation, their inexperience in ver-

bal communication, their failure to generalize from one situation
to another, the rigidity of their thought process, their passivity,
their failure to assimilate experiences which leads to an unreliable
memory, their anxiety, and their extreme sensitivity to failure.
These traits will make them seem more retarded than their potential intelligence warrants. It is certainly just as important to do
research on teaching methods for these environment-determined
mental retardates as for those who are handicapped constitution-
ally or by birth traumas. The proportion of children from disorganized families or their cousins on the poverty continuum who
are assigned to special classes in the schools is probably very high.
Their educational problems deserve special attention. "Poor" children are certainly receiving this but, we repeat, without any attempt to differentiate the subgroups. (We have consciously
avoided the term *cultural retardation* because our subjects did not
belong to any particular race nor were they limited to any particular culture.)

   In Terms of the Work with the Families.   The methods described in Chapter 11 brought about observable changes in the
families. Calling attention to the adults' initial resistance and testing out, as a transference phenomenon, supported the worker's
optimistic perseverance. The thoughtful selection from among the
family's many demands of one that was realistically open to change
and unencumbered by emotional conflicts led to an initial resolution. As it was followed by others, it taught the adults to discriminate constructively among their many wants. The workers' respect
for their struggle, awareness of a parent's often unformulated aspirations, and appreciation of any and every small gain built the
foundations for a relationship. This was strengthened by shared
trips to a clinic or to visit a child. However, the relationship was
constantly under scrutiny; awareness of how a parent was using her
or his worker, what role or what association from the past the
worker was temporarily being fitted into, prevented pitfalls and
sudden impulsive rejections. The reliability of the relationship—
as in the child-teacher transactions—and the worker's willingness
to share her own experiences with children, household matters, or
family concerns eventually gave the client a sense of being an
equal. This paved the way for a process of imitative identifications

upon which some growth in long-delayed development could occur.

Because of the research aspect of the project, the worker's case load was limited to four or five families. Now that the technique has been demonstrated, this drastic reduction is no longer required. However, for the sake of morale, the usual case load could be more diversified and plenty of opportunity be made available for an exchange of experiences and ideas and professional stimulation. Only people with genuine optimism can fill this role, which requires a kind of control that does not block spontaneity, empathy, humor, and endless patient perseverance.

The methodology described Mrs. Bandler in Chapter 11 has immediate application to the widespread work now being carried on by social work and public health nursing agencies. Trained indigenous personnel will readily appreciate the almost superhuman demands on the mother of a poor family with six to eight children. They will more readily be accepted as equals but they will need a great deal of consistent help to overcome their own critical and devaluating attitudes toward disorganized families whose conduct is so often out of line with society's demands.

The Anthropological Findings. The question as to whether there is a "culture of poverty" is still in considerable dispute. Whether the North Point Project families belong to this culture is another question. Dr. Stein prefers to think of them as a proto-culture which gives emphasis to their rootlessness.

His documented impression that the adults, like chronic alcoholics, have "many faces" deserves the attention of all of those who are concerned with hard-core families. For one very important thing, it means that questionnaires yield no reliable information, since the answers will be representative of the "face" presented to data gatherers. It also means that progress cannot be based on reports but only on repeated observation. The same is true of historical information, which tends to vary from one meeting to the next and is sometimes elaborated. If Dr. Stein is correct, most workers engaged in a program see only one aspect of the personality, usually the drab devalued side which may well be compensated for by a much more colorful and gregarious self. Middle-class workers probably seldom catch a glimpse of these other "faces." In Chapter

2, mention was made of Dr. Stein's valuable consideration that the project may have been experienced by the families as a small community—the first stable grouping, possibly, that any of them had ever related to and become involved with. We had from the beginning attempted to connect the individual family to the total project by introducing multiple workers to the family, whenever the situation warranted it, and by arranging various gatherings and parties involving all the families and the entire staff. Although we would have welcomed learning from someone unrelated to our project what the families thought of it and how they spoke about us when wearing their other "faces," no such opportunity ever materialized.

SUGGESTIONS AND RECOMMENDATIONS

Overall Programs. Every member of the North Point Project staff concurs in the conviction that far-reaching social and economic change must take place in order to fundamentally alter the lives of the families described in this book. Alvin L. Schorr (6) has recently reviewed various income-maintenance programs which would benefit children. His final recommendation is for "preschool allowance payments" which he concurs "may be in such amounts as to encourage poor families to *take off*"; that is, "a payment large enough *to assure poor families surplus income at a critical point in the family-income cycle*" (our italics). He thinks "public services delivered through schools and community centers" may take over from age six. "Take-off for poor families requires *surplus money for investment in self-improvement* (italics ours), as well as the skill and drive more usually asked of them." Of the two periods in the family-income cycle, when dependable income "might be particularly useful," the first is of special importance to preschool children: "the half-dozen years around the time a family starts out." He shows us by means of statistics that the timing and circumstances of first marriage or childbearing have a decisive impact on family stability and income, with *early* marriage and childbearing leading to a high percentage of family breakdown and later to "income squeeze."

Schorr is concerned with the vast numbers of poor children in our country who would be benefited by allowance payments. The program he proposes would in most instances not suffice to salvage the children of disorganized families, although it would clearly reduce the stress. Whereas the staff is convinced that more money must somehow be made available to disorganized families, they do not believe that this alone would meet their needs. Programs of the nature of the North Point Project need to be instituted. They will be more effective when dire want has been alleviated.

Dr. Malone is of the opinion that the results and effects of our work as a community are prejudiced by our separatist and rivalrous positions. We are regularly involved in professional status and role problems; we are easily drawn into arguments over who is to have "responsibility" and in such arguments we barter over responsibility in an irresponsible manner. We act as though the life of an individual child does not have biological, social, and psychological continuity. Thus his fetal or prebirth care is assigned to one service, his infant care to another, his preschool needs to yet another. School programs divorce themselves from the child's preschool and extraschool life. Our work with families similarly appears to be predicated on assumptions of nonunity and noncontinuity over time. Thus we divide up their care into compartments —welfare here, health somewhere else, social services at still another place. This is further complicated by vagueness, as well as confusion, in our broad or specific plans concerning the functions and goals of agencies and/or clinics in the various compartments. The whole gamut of educational assistance in matters of family and child health, welfare, and mental health is, for the most part, neglected in our traditional format of services.

In our discouragement about planning and carrying out comprehensive services for disorganized families, we may abandon hope, deny what we know, and launch out on panacea programs to counteract poverty, delinquency, alcoholism, school failure, or unemployment. We often do this in two- to three-year programs when we know that any real and lasting effects will be at best partial, and at that would take five or ten years, or perhaps even longer.

Mrs. Bandler has already made a plea for the close collaboration of educators, welfare workers, city planners, recreation workers, and politicians with the medical and paramedical professions.

Multiservice Centers. There seems to be general agreement on the value of multiservice centers in the heart of low-income neighborhoods. Some exist already, many are in the planning phase. In some places the services will be given in a health center, in others they will be grouped around social agencies. In these centers the social work, health and mental health, nursing and day-care services will concentrate on comprehensive family and child care. Head Start classes are one such effort. We believe that the principles, the understanding of the children, the educational procedures and techniques, and the therapeutic ingredients evolved by the North Point Project and described in this book will be of great assistance to the staffs working in such comprehensive family-child service units.

We wish to make a special plea that services to children begin with pregnancy, with attention to the mother's many concerns and realistic problems as well as to her routine prenatal care. A relationship thus established, and carried on through infancy and early childhood, can be of great value in supporting the necessary mothering care during infancy and in assisting good child-rearing interaction during early childhood. It might permit some harassed mothers to entrust their toddlers to be cared for for a few hours a day away from home. Experienced and informed care could serve to further development in the toddler and to teach the mothers more constructive management, particularly in the area of discipline. It would also relieve a mother for a few hours from the clinging and demanding behavior of her 1-year-old, which is bound to follow increased attention and stimulation during the first year.

These comprehensive centers will require a restructuring of existing health, social, welfare, and educational services in poverty areas. The necessary procedures to attract disorganized families and their children to these centers have been explicitly stated in Chapter 8.

The training and employment of nonprofessional residents of the area served, or from adjoining neighborhoods, will succeed in relation to the validity of the selection procedure and also in relation to the respect of the professional staff for these assistants. It can provide an essential link between the children's home environment and the outside care. When the nonprofessional staff is met with respect, they can more easily accord the same respect to the children's parents. This will require close supervision. It is to be hoped that these children will move on to ungraded classes, where the anxiety-provoking experience of failure can be held at a minimum. The comprehensive center personnel would do well to assist the children in this transition and to acquaint kindergarten and first grade teachers with their characteristic concerns, deficiencies, and precocities.

Research and Preventive Programs.   An enormous amount of research is needed and some is already underway. We will mention here only a few studies that particularly intrigue the contributors to this volume.

Mrs. Mattick is interested in pursuing a careful study of the language patterns of these children. Although Bernstein's findings (1), as well as some of those of other recent investigators, closely resemble her observations, she became aware of specific linguistic features characteristic of this group which have not been explored as yet. As Chomsky (2) suggests, for any meaningful study of children's grammar, such research would need to provide "a variety of evidence," far beyond formal testing, "to determine what in fact is [these children's] underlying linguistic competence at each stage of development." This calls for "rather devious kinds of observations of [their] performance, abilities, comprehension in many different kinds of circumstance." Mrs. Mattick feels strongly that this information is essential for determining interventive measures that may mitigate the presently debilitating language deviance of these children.

Dr. Malone calls for a developmental study of children of disorganized families. His proposals were boldly conceived and require verification. Given the nature of multiproblem families, this research will be fraught with complications. Even observations of mother-child interaction must be tempered with objectivity, since researchers will be exposed to only one of the mother's "faces."

Mrs. Bandler advocates a naturalistic study of families in various stages of disorganization to learn at which point intervention would be the most effective. A study of the families' values and change of values, as disorganization accumulates, would yield important information.

This author has begun a study of the range of child-rearing environments and their relationship to developmental profiles in the first 2½ years in a large bleak integrated public housing project. Her acquaintance with the North Point Project children through staff reports and a limited amount of observation, as well as Dr. Malone's analysis of Mrs. Mattick's observations, led her to a specific question. Do environmental pressures upon the children induce them to accentuate their efforts at accommodation while neglecting—to some extent at least—the important work of assimilation? Space does not permit here an exposition of the reasoning behind this question. If this actually happens it would interfere with their internalizing ideas and experiences and integrating new thoughts with previous ones to organize their thinking. This would result in a failure on the part of the children to build up an internalized hierarchical structure of experiences and information which Piaget (5) considers essential for later learning.

Dr. Malone has emphasized the children's arrest in the process of identification, an arrest that impedes the development of the body image, of the limits between self and outside world, of a sense of self.

Both of these failures—in assimilation and identification—contribute to the characteristic drifting quality, so striking in these children, and to their effort to adapt by imitating more adequate children and adults, and to learn only by rote within rigid boundaries.

Intervention to avoid this trend in the children must begin very early. The writer suggests and plans to try out inducing mothers who are found to have such older children to engage in playful interaction with their infants. If the mothers could be helped to become engaged in mutually responsive play they would be extremely gratified by the intimate relationship that would ensue. A deep and abiding longing for a close dependent relationship to their own mother is a common characteristic of these women. They could be led to fulfill their own needs by fulfilling the baby's. Smiling interchange would lead to mirror-image play and the identification process would be off to a sound start. There would be at least a beginning of a mother-child relationship. It seems unlikely that a mother could, after some months of this, fail to individualize her child. It is to be expected that children who had been engaged in such a relationship and playful interaction would later spontaneously play by themselves. Piaget (5) sees play as pure assimilation, so that the process of internalizing experiences would also follow. With mental representation, language will be less imitative, more integrated. Even limited experiences of having been the object of mother's love might counteract the self-devaluation so pervasive in the family and the neighborhood.

It is our hope that others will explore our findings to confirm or to refute them, and will be spurred on by the many fascinating problems to undertake research, intervention, and educational programs. The vast numbers of the poor are in themselves a cause for deep concern and a stimulus to action. We have set before you the findings of a small project with families representing only a fraction of the poverty population. It is a segment, however, that demands more carefully conceived intervention than the group as a whole, and which will not be taken care of by broad programs alone.

REFERENCES

1. Bernstein, Basil. Social Class and Linguistic Development: A Theory of Social Learning. In Halsey, A. H., Floud, J., and Anderson, A. (Eds.), *Education, Economy and Society.* Glencoe, Ill.: Free Press, 1963.
2. Chomsky, Noam. Formal Discussion of "The Development of Grammar in Child Language" by W. Miller and S. Ervin. *Society for Research in Child Development* Monograph 29:35, 1964.
3. Fowler, William. Concept Learning in Early Childhood. In *Teaching the Disadvantaged Child.* National Association of Young Children, publication No. 112. New York: Mental Health Materials Center, 1966.
4. Pavenstedt, Eleanor. A Comparison of the Child-rearing Environment of Upper-Lower and Very Low-Lower Class Families. *American Journal of Orthopsychiatry* 35:89, 1965.
5. Piaget, Jean. *Play, Dreams and Imitation in Childhood.* New York: Norton, 1951.
6. Schorr, Alvin L. *Poor Kids: A Report of Children in Poverty.* New York: Basic Books, 1966.

INDEX

Accommodation process, 131, 133
Adaptation, psychosocial, 12, 43, 86-88
ADC families, 9
"Adjusted" families, 304-305
Aggression, 98
  parental, 135-136
  and project children, 69, 119, 136, 181-182
Aggressor, identification with, 121, 135-137
Alcoholics, skid-row, 45-48, 306-309
  image constellations, 308-309
Allowance payments, preschool, 330-331
Anxiety, 11, 40, 115
  in children, 37, 42-43, 78, 210-211, 215, 218
Appalachia, 8
Asocial multiproblem families, 241-244, 247-249
Assimilation, 139, 335
Autonomy, 317-318. See also Child development
  pseudo-. See Project children, pseudoautonomy

Baltimore public school project, 26
Books in nursery school, 195-196
Boston School Department project, 25-26

Bowlby, J., 109-110
Buell, Bradley, 4
Bums, self-identities of, 308-309

Case histories of project families, 236-249, 263-266, 269-291
Casework
  concept, adaptations of, 260
  goals in, 258-259
  process, 259-260, 265
    bolstering self-esteem in, 267
    education in, 265
    examples of, 269-283
    identification of feelings in, 266
    involvement with initial goal of, 260
    moderation of rivalry with children, 267
    ordering of problems in, examples, 262-267
    participation in, active, 261
    psychological understanding in, 261
    relationship in, 35, 251, 283
  techniques, 259-260
Caseworkers, 7, 241, 243, 246, 256-257
  parental figure, functioning as, 260
  testing of, by families, 262
Child development, 34, 86-102, 234-235, 250

337